Journal of Comparative Poetics
No. 40, 2020

Mapping New Directions
in the Humanities

Editors in Chief: Ferial J. Ghazoul, Walid El Hamamsy
Associate Editor: Mohamed Birairi
Managing Editor: Ramy Amin
Editorial Assistants: Bushra Hashem, Hossam Nayel, Menna Taher

Editorial Board (alphabetically by last name):

Omaima Abou Bakr (Cairo University)
Saad Albazei (King Saud University)
Gaber Asfour (Cairo University)
Mohammed Berrada (University of Mohamed V)
Ira Dworkin (Texas A&M University)
Ziad Elmarsafy (King's College London)
Sabry Hafez (SOAS, University of London)
Richard Jacquemond (Aix Marseille University)
Céza Kassem-Draz (AUC and Cairo University)
As'ad Khairallah (American University of Beirut)
Andrew N. Rubin (University of Texas at Dallas)
Randa Sabry (Cairo University)
Doris Enright-Clark Shoukri (AUC)
Hoda Wasfi (Ain Shams University)

People who participated in the preparation of this issue:

Naeema Abdel Gawad, Tahia Abdel Nasser, Hassan Abdelrahman, Randa Aboubakr, Roger Allen, Saeed Alwakil, Amani Badawy, Mona Baker, Jehan El-Bayoumi, Michael Beard, Nabil Boulos, Mohamed Amine Brahimi, Charles Butterworth, Elliott Colla, Molly Courtney, Vincent Crapanzano, Sayyed Daifallah, Souleymane Bachir Diagne, Doaa Embabi, Ali Hadi, Hala Halim, Ahmad Khan, Christina Lee, Margaret Litvin, Megan MacDonald, Layla Al-Maleh, Khaled Mattawa, Gretchen McCullough, Hasna Reda Mikdashi, Anwar Moghith, Ghassan Mourad, Khozeima Moutanabbir, Stephen Nimis, Kamran Rastegar, Christopher Rundle, Maha El Said, Kathleen Saville, Daniel Selden, Bachir El Siba'i, Susan Stephens, John Swanson, Zeinab Taha, May Telmissany, Michael Wood.

Cover image: *Hands in Box* by Huda Lutfi, mixed media on wood, 40 x 40 cm, 2018. Courtesy of the artist.

© 2020 Department of English and Comparative Literature, AUC. Distributed by AUC Press.
Dar el Kutub No. 6188/20
ISSN 1110-8673
ISBN 9781617979668

Earlier issues of *Alif* include (available at prices listed):
Alif 1: Philosophy and Stylistics
Alif 2: Criticism and the Avant-Garde
Alif 3: The Self and the Other
Alif 4: Intertextuality
Alif 5: The Mystical Dimension in Literature
Alif 6: Poetics of Place
Alif 7: The Third World: Literature and Consciousness
Alif 8: Interpretation and Hermeneutics
Alif 9: The Question of Time
Alif 10: Marxism and the Critical Discourse
Alif 11: Poetic Experimentation in Egypt since the Seventies
Alif 12: Metaphor and Allegory in the Middle Ages
Alif 13: Human Rights and Peoples' Rights in the Humanities
Alif 14: Madness and Civilization
Alif 15: Arab Cinematics: Toward the New and the Alternative
Alif 16: Averroës and the Rational Legacy in the East and the West
Alif 17: Literature and Anthropology in Africa
Alif 18: Post-Colonial Discourse in South Asia
Alif 19: Gender and Knowledge
Alif 20: The Hybrid Literary Text
Alif 21: The Lyrical Phenomenon
Alif 22: The Language of the Self: Autobiographies and Testimonies
Alif 23: Literature and the Sacred
Alif 24: Archeology of Literature: Tracing the Old in the New
Alif 25: Edward Said and Critical Decolonization
Alif 26: Wanderlust: Travel Literature of Egypt and the Middle East
Alif 27: Childhood: Creativity and Representation
Alif 28: Artistic Adaptations: Approaches and Positions

Alif 29: The University and Its Discontents: Egyptian and Global Perspectives
Alif 30: Trauma and Memory
Alif 31: The Other Americas
Alif 32: The Imaginary and the Documentary: Cultural Studies in Literature, History, and the Arts
Alif 33: The Desert: Human Geography and Symbolic Economy
Alif 34: World Literature: Perspectives and Debates
Alif 35: New Paradigms in the Study of Middle Eastern Literatures
Alif 36: Friendship: Representations and Cultural Variations
Alif 37: Literature and Journalism
Alif 38: Translation and the Production of Knowledge(s)
Alif 39: Transnational Drama: Theater and Performance

Price per issue:
    Egypt: LE 60
    Other Countries: Individuals: $ 60
                          Institutions: $ 120

Electronic version: issues 1-39 available at http://www.jstor.org

Correspondence and subscriptions:

Alif: Journal of Comparative Poetics
Department of English and Comparative Literature
The American University in Cairo
PO Box 2511
Cairo 11511
Egypt

Telephone: 2-02-27975107
E-mail: alifecl@aucegypt.edu
Website: https://huss.aucegypt.edu/alif

Contents

English Section

Editorial..8

David Konstan: Mapping Diversity in Classical Studies...........9

Claire Gallien: A Decolonial Turn in the Humanities................28

Antonio Pacifico: The Cultural Turn in the Study of Arabic Literature..59

Youssef Yacoubi: Redirecting Postcolonial Theory: Arab-Islamic Reason, Deconstructionism, and the Possibility of Multiple Critique...85

Levi Thompson: Re-Orienting Modernism: Mapping East-East Exchanges between Arabic and Persian Poetry......115

Brian James Baer: From Cultural Translation to Untranslatability: Theorizing Translation outside Translation Studies...139

Nadia Hashish: Towards Holistic Medical Humanities..........164

Yasmine Sweed: New Directions in Disability Narratives: Cyborgs and Redefining Disability in Young Adult Literature...186

English Abstracts of Articles...212

English Notes on Contributors..219

Arabic Section

Editorial..8

Abdesslam Benabdelali: Modern Paths in Philosophical Studies..9

Shereen Abouelnaga: Arab Feminism: Positions and Practices..32

Hala Kamal: From Autobiography to Life-Writing: Trajectories and Intersections across the Humanities and Social Sciences..65

Samia Al Hodathy: Postcolonialism and Arabic Literature: Rerouting or Re-Rooting?...104

Tamer Amin: Educational Linguistics and the Problem of Language: Science and Mathematics Education in the Arab World..142

Hassan Hilmy: "Contemporary" American Poetry: Reflections..168

Hossam Nayel: Arabic Literature and Digital Technology: An Exploration..215

Naglaa Saad Hassan: Game Theory and Literary Analysis: Horizons and Limitations..247

Arabic Abstracts of Articles..266

Arabic Notes on Contributors...273

As the political ascendancy of neo-liberalism has come to infuse public policy and the public sphere itself with a kind of overarching commercial mentality, universities have lost much of their autonomy and the "academic freedom" that used to go with it. What was once a place where colleagues could share their knowledge with one another and pass on what they knew to the younger generation in a spirit of community has become a place for doing business. And as a result, the humanities, or the human sciences, have become an endangered species. . . . It is a multidimensional hybridization process that is called for, a vast project of socio-cultural learning. We in the social and human sciences need to combine forces with scientists and engineers to develop educational and research programs so that our fellow citizens can make more beneficial use of our technical achievements and scientific discoveries—and not simply be given more gadgets to play with, at the expense, we now know, of the planet's capacity to sustain life.

Andrew Jamison, "To Foster a Hybrid Imagination," *N.T.M.* 16 (2008): 119; 122.

Mapping New Directions in the Humanities

This volume of *Alif* is dedicated to redefining and reorienting the Humanities in the light of global institutional and intellectual realities. The word "mapping" in this title can be construed in several ways: the literal meaning of geographical "reorientation" indicative of efforts to redefine the relationship between global North and South, or between Western and non-Western intellectual traditions. It can also refer to the remapping of the modern university by interdisciplinary and multidisciplinary work in the Humanities, work that brings the Humanities to new shores in Science and the Social Sciences. Mapping often means searching for clues to new directions in such literary genres as the Novel, Poetry, and Life-Writing, since the seeds of academic branching out are often detected in artistic movements. The articles in this volume highlight how different disciplines and genres are exploring new directions, including the Classics, Philosophy, Literary Theory, Linguistics, Translation Studies, etc. It is important to note that the Humanities is not an island apart; it is impacted by developments in other fields—Mathematics, Medicine, Digital Culture, Disability Studies, and Gender—a fact that contributions in this volume demonstrate.

Alif is a peer-reviewed, interdisciplinary journal, published annually in the spring, which includes critical scholarship in Arabic, English, and French. *Alif* welcomes original submissions from the various disciplines of the Humanities, including—though not limited to—Literature and Cultural Studies.

The next issues will center on the following themes:
Alif 41: Literature, History, and Historiography
Alif 42: Literature Confronting Mortality
Alif 43: Brotherly/Sisterly Relations in Literature and the Arts

Mapping Diversity in Classical Studies

David Konstan

Let me begin with an anecdote. In the spring of 2018, the Classics Department in my institution, New York University, was seeking authorization to make a new hire, and a discussion arose in one of our regular department meetings as to the profile we should propose to the Dean of the Faculty, in relation to departmental needs (in the end, authorization was granted to hire a Latinist). The following summary of the discussion was recorded in the departmental minutes (March 27, 2018):

> We ought to make the case for a junior hire that also meets the University's wider mission for expanding diversity. Specialties discussed included an archaeology at the "margins" of the Roman Empire; Late Antiquity/Byzantine world; or Homeric/lyric poetry. It was finally agreed that a competence in cultural history, with an ability "to thread material and texts together" and a "theoretical self-consciousness," would be a capacious enough framing, again with an eye towards attracting a diversity hire.

What is notable, in the first instance, about this admittedly vague and very preliminary job description is how it seems to embrace two different matters under the heading of "diversity." In the United States, "diversity" in hiring normally refers to efforts to secure a desirable balance in gender, ethnicity, religious affiliation, and other socially acknowledged identities. In the Classics in particular, considerable progress has been made over the past half century to remedy unequal representation of men and women, although even now, at the highest ranks, there remain some disparities (see "CSWMG Report"). Ethnic balance has proved more elusive, and there is no doubt that blacks and Latinos, for example, are drastically underrepresented in the profession in proportion to their numbers in the society at large (see Blouin). In the meantime, gender too has become more complex, as sexual orientation together with the deconstruction of binary gender categories have given rise to an awareness of other types of exclusion.[1]

In addition to the praiseworthy desire to increase diversity in this sense, the discussion also recognized a need to diversify the field of Classics itself. Traditionally, the "Classics" has been understood to mean the study of the cultures of ancient Greece and Rome, concentrating principally on the great works of literature produced in classical Greek and Latin and the political history of Greece and Rome, with a special focus on the great age of the Greek city-states, above all Athens, and the late Republic and early Imperial periods in Rome. Its methods, moreover, were narrowly circumscribed, holding at bay the wider world and interaction with other disciplines.[2] But over the past half century or so, the discipline has burst its boundaries and now extends far more widely in space, time, and variety of approaches. The minutes mention, for example, "archaeology at the 'margins' of the Roman Empire." The Roman Empire included within its frontiers parts of what are today Great Britain, France and the Low Countries, North Africa, Syria, Iraq, and more. But much else might be regarded as pertaining to the margins of the Empire, areas that came within Rome's sphere of influence or were engaged in trade, military hostilities, or other relations with Rome. Today, there are penetrating studies of the classical world in relation to areas that lie within the borders of modern-day Iran, Afghanistan, Russia, India, and even China (see, for example, Haubold; Seaford). But it is not just a matter of geographical extension, but also of method. As the excerpt from the minutes indicates, the Classics now takes archaeology under its broad wing, and not just the excavation of famous sites like the Roman forum or the Athenian agora. Rather, it embraces far-flung regions, no longer limiting itself to texts but taking account of all the evidence, physical as well as literary, that might illuminate not just the narrow territory we think of as classical Greece and Rome but pretty much the entire ancient world.[3] This grand reach may sound like disciplinary imperialism with a vengeance, but, in fact, classicists these days do not simply seek signs of Greek or Roman influence in these remote lands. There is rather a powerful awareness of the two-way nature of such interchanges, as the influence of other cultures on Greece and Rome is increasingly recognized: Whether or not

Athena was originally black, to use the title of Martin Bernal's famous three-volume challenge to Greek exclusivism, the debt of Greece and Rome to the sophisticated societies at their periphery was massive (for more recent and less polemical studies of the interrelationship between Greece and the surrounding civilizations, see West; Stephens; Collins et al.; Moyer; Rutherford). As Tim Whitmarsh writes in the "Prelude" to his recent book on the origins of the ancient novel, "the dominant scholarly construction of Greek literary history . . . places far too much emphasis upon the idea of Greek cultural identity as continuous and hermetically sealed (a 'tradition'), and not enough on its openness to new admixtures from other cultures" (xii).

Comparative studies of ancient civilizations are illuminating even when–sometimes especially when–there is no evidence of cross-influence, since they may reveal transhistorical constants in the development of political institutions, values, or psychological categories.[4] To take an event in which I myself participated, in 2015 a workshop comparing emotion terminology in ancient Greek and classical Arabic took place at NYU's campus in Abu Dhabi. Whereas classicists have for some time now treated emotions as at least in part socially constructed and hence subject to historical analysis, this was a novelty in Arabic studies. Differences in emphasis between the two cultures came to light; Arabic sources, for example, highlighted distress and sadness as emotions (one paper bore the title "Sadness in Classical Islam: Between Stoicism and Neo-Platonism"), whereas Greek texts concentrated more on shame and wonder (see "Emotions"). To be sure, there was considerable interaction between Greek and Arabic during the latter part of the first millennium, and the two cultures certainly did not evolve in isolation from one another. This is not the case, however, with classical Greek and Chinese, and a follow-up workshop comparing emotion terms in these societies is planned for the autumn of 2019, to be held in Shanghai (among many recent examples of such cross cultural studies, see Mutschler).

The expansion of classical horizons is not just spatial. There is also a vast amplification of the temporal dimension, which is reflected in the suggestion in the NYU Classics Department minutes that diversity might be achieved also by taking account of "Late Antiquity" and the "Byzantine world." The inclusion of these periods is not simply a matter of adding later texts to the traditional classical repertoire. The profound transformation that took place in both the Eastern and Western parts of the Roman Empire with the conversion to Christianity, and the subsequent encounter with rising Islamic civilization, require a new set of analytic tools on the part of classicists, not to mention the impact of other nations that impinged on the Empire down to its final fall in 1453 at the hands of the Ottoman Turks. But if it is beginning to look as though the Classics is seeking to embrace all of pre-modern history and culture, there is still more. One of the most dynamic fields in the Classics today is reception studies, which tracks the relationship between classical antiquity and its descendants down to our own time. In contrast to what had previously been known as "the classical tradition," which identified echoes of classical works in subsequent literature and art, reception takes into account the way we necessarily construct meaning in dialogue with a work, situating it within our own horizon of expectations (see, for example, Martindale; Broder). Reception thus requires a deep knowledge of the recipient culture, which itself varies from one continent or country to another, and recent studies have taken account of local differences, in which no region is privileged as having the exclusive key to interpreting the past. To take but one example, the new edition of the venerable German multi-volume encyclopedia of the Classics commonly known as Pauly-Wissowa (the names of the early editors), which is still the premier reference work of classical antiquity, has recently been completely updated and made available in English as well as German, under the title *Brill's New Pauly*. Unlike its predecessor, this edition devotes five of its twenty-two volumes to reception in societies all over the world: Asia, Africa, and South America are very well represented in the collection (see Cancik et al.; several supplemental volumes also treat reception). I may add that ancient Greece and Rome themselves were heir to earlier traditions, and so classical reception reaches back to prehistoric epochs as well (see, e.g., Currie on self-conscious allusion in archaic Greek poetry to near-eastern models; West).

One of the desirable qualities in candidates mentioned in the NYU minutes is "theoretical self-consciousness," and basic to it is an awareness of the various ways in which classical antiquity has been viewed in different times and places. Reception is one way of reflecting on our own historically embedded position, or rather positions, in relation to the ancient world, but the Classics over the past half century or so has been thoroughly transformed by its openness to new methods and theories, with regard to both literature and history. In the United States, the first manifestation of a theoretically inspired approach to texts came in the form of the New Criticism, which encouraged close attention to symbols and paradoxes that inform literary works, especially lyric poetry. This was a welcome departure from the kind of biographical and moral criticism that flourished in the Victorian era and beyond, but it was also resolutely opposed to situating literature in its social context or identifying the political conditions of its production. But more systematic and socially aware theories were taking shape in France, with the structuralism associated with Claude Lévi-Strauss and then various post-structuralist approaches conceived by Jacques Derrida, Michel Foucault, the enigmatic and provocative Jacques Lacan, Pierre Macherey, and others, along with developments in semiotics (especially in Italy), reader response theory (here Germany and Switzerland made important contributions), and more, and these so-called continental methodologies were gradually making headway against inveterate Anglo-Saxon common-sense pragmatism even in so conservative a discipline as the Classics (see, e.g., Schmitz). Indeed, it is fair to say that classical scholars in the United States, Great Britain, and other predominantly English-speaking countries are now leading the way in the political and social interpretation of literature. Today, historical inquiry is no longer limited to documenting wars and the achievements or rivalries of aristocratic men; the focus is more on the roles of women, slaves, foreigners, and other dispossessed groups which, thanks to refined methods including demography, network theory, economics, comparative politics and anthropology, and more socially informed attention to sources such as inscriptions, papyri, pictorial and architectural remains, and even coins, have moved in from the margins of classical historiography to the very center of research (examples are legion; for one recent work, see Richlin, with ample bibliography). Greek and Roman culture is no longer perceived as the bearer of timeless truths and perfection, but as the product of deeply flawed societies which, just for this reason, have much to teach us about our own world.[5]

But these new approaches would never have taken root in classical philology in the United States, at least, and certainly not so deeply, if it had not been for the emergence of feminism within the profession, which opened the way to an unprecedented receptiveness to anthropological approaches and an awareness of the time-bound nature of classical values.

Let me indicate just a couple of landmark events in this development. In the 1960s, the Women's Classical Caucus was formed within the professional society of classicists, then called the American Philological Association or APA, but since renamed the Society for Classical Studies (SCS). A brilliant and courageous group of feminist scholars, chiefly but not exclusively women, undertook to address the status of women in antiquity in a critical way; not content simply to describe the ways in which women were constrained, they sought to understand how such limitations were ideologically legitimated. In 1972, a panel on "Marxism and the Classics" was sponsored by the APA (I was one of the co-organizers), a first in the discipline, which led to a special issue of the journal *Arethusa* (1975), itself established as a vehicle for new approaches. It was now acceptable, or at least permissible, to speak of class struggle in relation to ancient societies. But this openness to so radical an approach as Marxism, less than two decades after the experience of McCarthyism in the United States, would not have been possible, I am certain, had it not been for the active role of the women who broke through the ingrained resistance to the discussion of such issues. Still other activists entered the fray, bringing to the fore issues such as sexuality, which achieved institutional status in the APA with the formation of the Lambda Classical Caucus: A Coalition of Queer Classicists and Allies, founded in 1989 under the name Lesbian and Gay Classical Caucus. A similar desire to broaden the horizons of the profession is evidenced in the awarding of a Minority Scholarship in Classics and Classical Archaeology, which was introduced in the APA in 1994.

Changes in the class composition of the profession also had an impact on the Classics as in other disciplines. The main impulse to this transformation in the United States was a government policy known as the "G. I. Bill." The *Wikipedia* article under that title summarizes it as follows:

> The Servicemen's Readjustment Act of 1944, also known as the G. I. Bill, was a law that provided a range of benefits for returning World War II veterans (commonly referred to as G. I.s). . . . Benefits included cash payments of tuition and living expenses to attend high school, college or vocational/technical school, low-cost mortgages, low-interest loans to start a business, as well as one year of unemployment compensation. . . . By 1956, roughly 2.2 million veterans had used the G. I. Bill education ben-

efits in order to attend colleges or universities, and an additional 5.6 million used these benefits for some kind of training program. (n. pag.)

In 1965–four years after I completed my college education and was about to enter graduate school–there were slightly fewer than 6 million students in American universities. In 1951, it was probably around half that number, and before the war, much fewer. A report published by the US Department of Education notes:

> By the end of the 1940s, college enrollment was surging. Large numbers of World War II veterans entered colleges assisted by such programs as the Servicemen's Readjustment Act which provided education benefits. In fall 1949, about 2.4 million students enrolled in colleges, or about 15 per 100 18- to 24-year-olds. (qtd. in Snyder 65)

The increase in the student population also had what might be regarded as a negative side. As the report shows, "In 1943–44, about half of the students in colleges were women." After the war, however, "The proportion of women on campus dropped to 30 percent" (qtd. in Snyder 65). But imagine the overall impact on university life. Rather than privileged youngsters, classrooms were now full of older students with substantial life experience, indeed experience of war, who were eager to learn. To reach this population, classicists had to create new ways of communicating the value of their subject to not-so-young men and women who had no previous exposure to Latin or to Greek. The solution was the so-called humanities courses, in which the great works of classical antiquity were taught in English versions rather than the original. This kind of instruction lent itself to broader styles of interpretation and, at the same time, gave rise to an entire new industry of translation, in which scholars sought to produce versions as close to the original text as possible. The translation that to this day remains the standard of such an ambition is Richmond Lattimore's *Iliad*, first published in 1951 (Pelliccia 42). As Peter Green has remarked, "The occasion that produced such an English *Iliad* was, of course, the huge expansion of American university education in the humanities, largely fostered by the G. I. Bill in the years immediately following World War

II" (n. pag.). Richmond Lattimore himself was a lieutenant in the Navy in World War II and worked as a cryptanalyst, and he first published passages from his translation of the *Iliad* in the 1945 anthology *War and the Poet*. I recall hearing from one of his a fellow officers that Lattimore was observed in his leisure hours translating Pindar's *Odes* into English–from memory. In this same period, scholars such as Moses Finley brought a new sophistication to the analysis of the ancient economy, and elucidated the class structure of classical societies.

What emerges from this rapid survey of the history of the field of the Classics in the latter part of the twentieth century is that diversity in methodologies and subject matter went hand in hand with diversity in what we may call social identity: Women, gay people, working class men and some women, people of color, as students and as teachers, made their concerns felt; they assumed a political role in the profession and its institutions, with the result that attention began to be paid to marginal groups inside and outside the classical state. The Classics was now relevant to them and the world they lived in. The apparent slippage from the disciplinary to the labor force sense of diversity in the NYU job description reflects the interconnectedness of the two domains in real life.

After all this ferment, the Classics has reached what I consider to be a moment of self-reflection, taking stock of what has been achieved and what paths remain to be explored. This explains, I believe, the plethora of handbooks, companions, and manuals that have been published in recent years. They cover all aspects of the field, and often several, issued by different editors and publishers, address the same topic, whether an author like Plato or Virgil, or a broader concept such as intertextuality or slavery or the ancient novel. Indeed, their range is impressive in itself. What is more, these companions are remarkable in that the contributors include the leading specialists in the field as well as some of the finest younger scholars, and their quality is almost invariably exceptionally high. The several chapters in these handbooks regularly sum up the state of research on the question in a clear and critical way, and suggest new and interesting directions for future investigation. They are thus invaluable both for novices and advanced professionals, and are by no means to be dismissed as mere compilations of received views and approaches. They are a sign that the discipline is at a pivotal moment, in which scholars are simultaneously taking stock of the state of current knowledge, which is a function of the methods and assumptions at work, and feeling their way to new ways of seeing and understanding the past. In one sense, they mark the end of the period of grand theorizing: Structuralism, deconstruction, reader response, queer theory, psychoanalytic criticism, have all done their job and the results are in. They can and should still be deployed, of course, but scholars are now paying attention to details and not just to the big picture: Micro-histories involving careful demographic calculations, along with an interest in local chronicles, fragmentary works, genres hitherto regarded as minor or subliterary, are at the center of attention. Cumulatively, these investigations will ultimately alter the larger perspective.[6]

Of the approaches now in vogue, we may mention material culture, which looks beyond texts to artefacts of every sort, and attempts to see how they speak to each other and modify what the elite literary tradition alone may indicate. To take an example, whereas on the basis of surviving Latin poetry and prose one would necessarily conclude that men and women did not normally refer to members of the opposite sex as "friends"–it was prostitutes who called men their friends, a euphemism for lover or client–inscriptions tell a very different story, as Craig Williams has demonstrated: In these, men and women refer freely to friends of both sexes, without the least suggestion of an illicit relationship (see Williams). Another approach that is currently transforming our perception of Greek and Roman works is performance criticism, which seeks to recover the conditions of production of ancient literature, beyond the textual notations that are the primary evidence of classical works but offer only a limited, and sometimes misleading, image of their effect and meaning. I say "literature" rather than drama, because Greeks and Romans recited works aloud, from the lyric poems sung in symposia to courtroom speeches, epic poems, philosophical treatises, and the rhetorical exercises that were the staple of Roman declamation. Gestures, tone of voice, and the living interaction with a not always civil audience were part and parcel of such renditions, and setting written texts in their performative context has enriched our sense of the dynamics of oral interaction. Even props and scenery have a role in the enactment of texts, and recent studies have explored the emotional attachment that objects can inspire (a theoretical development sometimes called the new materialism or object studies; see, for example, Bennett; Boscagli). Analysis of the modern staging of ancient plays suggests new perspectives on how the originals themselves may have been presented. There has been in recent years a systematic effort to collect information on all known productions of classical theatrical works, undertaken under the auspices of the Archive of Performances of Greek and Roman Drama, based at Oxford University, which conducts "research into performances of Greek and Roman drama worldwide, from antiquity to the present, on stage, screen and radio, in opera and dance" ("Archive" n. pag.) The multiple forms of communication implied in performance criticism, moreover, have inspired an engagement with the cognitive and affective sciences (see, for example, Meineck, *Theatrocracy*; Meineck et al.; Budelmann and Sluiter). Nor is this a one-way street, where classicists appropriate a theory developed in other disciplines and apply it to their own object of study. Experimental psychologists and neuro-scientists are increasingly coming to realize that what one authority on comparative linguistics has described as a tendency to "absolutize the English folk-taxonomy of the emotions" (Wierzbicka 171)–and, we may add, of the human cognitive apparatus generally–can lead to serious misrepresentations of the way the brain works. If, for example, what we call "anger" or "shame" has no precise correlate in languages other than English, what reason is there to suppose that these other ostensibly equivalent terms (for instance, ὀργή [orgê] ancient Greek, or غضب [ghaḍab] in classical Arabic), and the sentiments or ideas they may represent, will all have an identical physical manifestation in the brain? This was precisely the focus of the workshops on comparative emotion terms mentioned above, and it is worth noting that recent meetings of the International Society for Research on Emotion have emphatically welcomed contributions on the history of the passions. The Classics has contributed as well to disestablishing the Cartesian notion that thinking itself is located exclusively in the brain, and has taken part in theoretical developments such as "distributed cognition," which posits that cognition is a function of the entire body and indeed, under certain circumstances, extends to objects that may assist in problem solving and even to groups (see Anderson et al.).

Performances of ancient Greek plays, whether of comedy or tragedy, are not of academic or even aesthetic interest only. One of the surprising discoveries of recent years is that they can also be therapeutic, achieving something like the catharsis that Aristotle spoke of, rather mysteriously, in his *Poetics*. One of the contexts in which performances of Greek tragedy have been especially salutary is with war veterans, and more particularly in connection with post-traumatic stress disorder or PTSD (see Meineck "These are men"; Doerries). The experience of veterans watching and also acting in performances of Greek tragedy inspired a re-examination of PSTD in classical antiquity itself: Did the continual warfare, the hand-to-hand combat, the enormous numbers of casualties result in something like a shell-shocked sub-population in Greece and Rome? Or did exposure to violence, combined with a celebration of military valor, succeed in somehow protecting soldiers and civilians against at least some of the psychological consequences of war? Both views have been defended, but the very fact that the question has been posed is a result of the increasing sense that ancient literature, despite—and sometimes precisely because of—its distance from modern values and habits of thought, may strike new chords in modern audiences (see Shay; Meineck and Konstan). This connection between the Classics and the aftermath of war replays in a different key the new directions in classical studies that followed upon the G. I. Bill, when former soldiers swelled the traditional population of the academy.

Another novel area of investigation in the Classics is disability studies, here again reflecting a new awareness in the society at large of the rights and dignity of the disabled (see, for example, Garland; Penrose Jr.; Laes). Research on classical antiquity has marched in step with efforts to eliminate discrimination within the profession and the society at large in this domain too, just as in the scholarly attention to questions of race, gender, and sexuality. In recent years, sensitivity to others has leaped across the boundary between species, resulting in a wave of activism in support of animal rights. The Classics has not ignored this movement either, as witnessed by a great number of studies not only on animals in antiquity as such but on ancient attitudes toward animals, which exhibited, not unexpectedly, a great variety but which, at one extreme, saw animals as kin to human beings, capable of reason and morality (see, e.g., Sorabji; Newmyer; Li Causi). Beyond living beings, there is evidence of an ancient concern with nature as a whole, and here again we can see a reflex of the modern preoccupation with ecology and the condition of the material world (see Salmon and Shipley; Thommen; Hughes; McInerney and Sluiter).

Variety of social identity and moral commitment among practitioners of the Classics continues to enrich the field, introducing new concepts and augmenting the range of topics that are investigated. Again, the rough outline of a job description proposed by the NYU Classics Department was not wrong to combine both kinds of diversity. Of course, there is no necessary or natural connection between identity and professional interest; hence the slippage between the two aspects of diversity, since social roles are not essentialist and do not determine individual values, although they are not without influence. What is more, disciplines have their own structures and instabilities, and generate new problems intrinsically according to a logic of their own. New techniques, such as magnetic resonance imaging, for example, have enabled scholars to decipher papyri and palimpsests that were hitherto illegible, and so have stimulated renewed interest in topics such as ancient Epicureanism (thanks to the papyri that were scorched when Vesuvius erupted in 79 AD), simply because relevant materials are newly available. The Internet, along with the digitization of sources from inscriptions to papyri, the production of so-called hypertexts, and more has made possible whole new methods of research (one can track the uses of a word over millions of pages of text in seconds). The Classics has been in the lead in developing these approaches, as evidenced by the *Thesaurus Linguae Graecae*, the Perseus Project, and more (for an overview, see Romano, and for more on the the uses of the Internet in the Classics, see "Digital Humanities" [Society for Classical Studies]; "Digital Humanities" [Harvard University]; "Digital Classics"). Individual insights or theories too open up new perspectives. Nevertheless, in addressing the question of future directions in the Classics, it is useful to think what kinds of public concerns are likely to emerge in the decade or so to come and what kind of impact they may have on the shape of the field.

So permit me to gaze into the crystal ball, even if it is a blurry one, and indulge in some hazardous prognostication. It seems to me that the radical polarization of politics that has emerged in the past few years, which has enabled and been encouraged by the rise of populist movements (as they are called: more precision is of course required), will sharpen tensions within the humanities but also invite closer attention to political behavior in the past, not least in classical Greece and Rome, which have so often been treated as the fountainhead of modern democratic republics. These modern political movements are a response, no doubt, to events on the world stage that seem threatening or difficult to manage, such as the globalization of trade and attendant economic crises, extensive migration, and new forms of ideologically motivated war and terrorism, along with anxieties arising from electronic surveillance and the loss of privacy, new conceptions of sexuality, an aging world population and the provision of health care, and the contested nature of citizenship. How will these changes be reflected in the Classics, on the level of both scholars themselves and research focus? It is worth noting that the Classics has always been an international enterprise, and has become still more so in the past few decades. Whereas French and German, along with English, were the primary languages of scholarship in the field for most of the past two centuries, Spanish and Italian are now recognized as essential, and Modern Greek and Russian are not far behind. Beyond Europe, the Classics is now experiencing a surge in interest in Japan, China, Korea, Latin America, and much of Africa, even if often under difficult conditions. The presidential panel at the SCS conference in January 2019 was devoted to the future of the Classics in the global 21st century, and scholars from India, China, Egypt, Zimbabwe, and Mexico delivered stimulating talks on the state of the Classics in their region (see Cancela, Correa, Konstan "The Classics," and Pozzi for papers that arose out of the presidential panel at the [then] APA in 1999; see also Ponce Hernández and Rojas Álvarez). There will be backlashes, without a doubt, and the work of overcoming various degrees of prejudice within the field is far from over. At the same SCS conference, Dan-el Padilla Peralta delivered a brief but momentous talk titled "Racial Equity and the Production of Knowledge" at a panel on "The Future of Classics," in which he demonstrated "the systematic marginalization of people of color in the credentialed and publicly recognized knowledge production of the discipline," above all in the flagship journals in the field.[7]

Nevertheless, I am hopeful that the Classics will no longer be the province of a European culture that defines itself by contrast to the rest of the world, and that post-colonial theory, rich as it has been as a means of challenging Europe's self-appointed cultural hegemony, will give way, perhaps, to more global approaches, reflecting the interpenetration of cultures round the world. The artificiality of the distinction between West (the marked term) and East in Classics has always been suspect: The Middle East, after all, was the primary transmission belt between ancient Greek thought and the Latin Middle Ages. Nor did Persia or India evolve separately, in isolation from Egypt or Greece or points further west.

To be sure, the Classics is a highly specialized discipline, and depends on a thorough command of remote languages and skills such as epigraphy, numismatics, papyrology, codicology, linguistics, art and architecture, philosophy, the many branches of archaeology, and more. Experts in the Classics communicate in an idiom of their own, which may be opaque to outsiders; in this respect, they form a single intellectual community, a small state in the great Republic of Letters. But these technical requirements need not be construed as a barrier, or a sign of the elite nature of the field. With the entry into the discipline of scholars from around the world, bringing their experience of the reception of classical antiquity in multiple cultures, the interpretation of ancient Greek and Roman societies will be a zone of contestation in new ways; diversity in the profession will again, I expect, be accompanied by diverse approaches to the classical past. Perhaps, too, we will see the emergence of common understandings that may even offer novel perspectives on current areas of conflict.

Notes

[1] Note, for example, the call for papers for a panel at the Society of Classical Studies, under the title "[Tr]an[s]tiquity: Theorizing Gender Diversity in Ancient Contexts," for the 2017 annual conference (see "[Tr]an[s]tiquity"). At the 2019 annual meeting, The Lambda Classical Caucus of the SCS also hosted the panel "Turning Queer: Queerness and the Trope."

[2] In my article "*Arethusa*," I list some of the papers published in *Classical Quarterly*, perhaps the leading English-language journal in the Classics, in 1968, the momentous year when the journal *Arethusa* was founded. Titles included "Trimalchio's Zodiac Dish. (Petronius, *Sat*. 35.1-5)," "A Note on *Odyssey* 10.86," "A Problem in Aeschylus' *Septem*," "Some Problems of Text and Interpretation in the *Hippolytus*," "On the Use of the Vocative in Alexandrian Epic," "The Text of Parmenides, fr. 1.3," "Meges and Otus of Cyllene," "Split resolution in Greek Dramatic Lyric," "Two Friends of Clodius in Cicero's Letters," and "Molon's Influence on Cicero." There were some titles of wider scope, most conspicuously "Redistribution of Land and Houses in Syracuse in 356 B.C. and its Ideological Aspects." But the preponderant character of the contributions is clear. Some twenty years later, a new editorial board of the *American Journal of Philology*, the oldest and most prestigious Classics journal in the United States, published

an editorial discouraging submissions that reflected fashionable innovations: "While *AJP* will always have an interest in certain kinds of literary and philosophical interpretation, the emphasis is still on rigorous scholarly methods.... The Editors ... will not settle for the fashionable and *outré*, because it is likely to be the ephemeral." The editors recommended two types of investigation endorsed by the founder of the journal, Basil Gildersleeve, namely "lexicographical and syntactical studies," which, they lamented, "do not receive the attention they deserve in our day and age" ("*AJP* Today" vii-ix). This spirited response was short-lived: The editorial board was again altered the following year, and *AJP* proclaimed its hospitality to new approaches to the Classics. At the annual breakfast meeting of *AJP*'s editorial board which took place at the conference of the Society of Classical Studies in January 2019, there was a productive discussion of Gildersleeve's active role in defending slavery and racial segregation and a call to examine its implications at a future conference.

3 Classical archaeology, like other areas in the Classics, benefitted mightily from interactions with neighboring disciplines, such as the archaeology of the New World, which had long exploited advanced scientific methods. Surface surveys, for example, may reveal the size and location of latifundia or large rural estates, thereby contributing to the understanding of the ancient economy in ways that complement the results of trench digs. Such attention to large-scale social phenomena contrasts with an earlier focus on famous names and places, such as the quest for Agamemnon's tomb that motivated Schliemann's excavations at Mycenae, an approach that my colleague Stephen Dyson once characterized as "the search for Socrates' toilet seat."

4 Of course, there are dangers, too; as Geoffrey Lloyd, a specialist in Chinese and Greek philosophy, observes, "Comparing can be anything but fruitful.... In principle it is possible to compare anything with anything else. In practice many comparative studies seem to engage in an arbitrary juxtaposition of widely different objects without any concern for context or for what may validate the exercise" (1). See also the stimulating analysis in Detienne.

5 For a spirited defense of an idealized view of classical antiquity, together with an attack on those who would expose its limitations (including the author of the present article), see Heath and Hanson; needless to say, there have been numerous replies to this polemical book.

6 I note, by way of illustration, some chapter headings in the *Companion to Catullus* by Skinner: "The Contemporary Political Context"; "The Intel-

lectual Climate"; "Gender and Masculinity"; "Catullus and Elite Republican Social Discourse"; "Catullus in the Secondary School Curriculum"; "Catullus in the College Classroom." These chapters sit comfortably side by side with "History and Transmission of the Text" and close examinations of style and intertextual relations with other poets. *A Companion to Roman Imperialism* by Hoyos is remarkable for its topic, with chapters on "Co-opting the Conqueror" and "The Provincialisation of Rome."

[7] A member of the audience called into question Padilla Peralta's scholarly credentials, leading to considerable online discussion of racial discrimination and its causes in the Classics (see Padilla Peralta, "Some Thoughts" for his response).

Works Cited

"*AJP* Today." *American Journal of Philology* 108.3 (Autumn 1987): vii-x.

Anderson, Miranda, Douglas Cairns, and Mark Sprevak, eds. *Distributed Cognition in Classical Antiquity*. Edinburgh: Edinburgh UP, 2019.

"Archive of Performances of Greek and Roman Drama (APGRD)." *Faculty of Classics, University of Oxford*. <https://www.classics.ox.ac.uk/archive-performances-greek-and-roman-drama-apgrd>.

Bennett, Jane. *Vibrant Matter: A Political Ecology of Things*. Durham, NC: Duke UP, 2010.

Bernal, Martin. *Black Athena: The Afroasiatic Roots of Classical Civilization*. 3 vols. New Brunswick, NJ: Rutgers UP, 1987-1991.

Blouin, Katherine. "Classical Studies' Glass Ceiling is White." *Everyday Orientalism*. January 10, 2017. <https://everydayorientalism.wordpress.com/2017/01/10/classical-studies-glass-ceiling-is-white>.

Boscagli, Maurizia. *Stuff Theory: Everyday Objects, Radical Materialism*. NY: Bloomsbury P, 2010.

Broder, Michael. "Tradition vs. Reception as Models for Studying the Great Books." *Classical World* 106.3 (Spring 2013) 505-15.

Budelmann, Felix and Ineke Sluiter, eds. *Minds on Stage: Cognitive Approaches to Greek Tragedy*. Oxford: Oxford UP, 2018.

Cancela, Elina Miranda. "Classical Studies in Cuba." *Classical Bulletin* 77.2 (2001): 240-44.

Cancik, Hubert, Helmuth Schneider, and Manfred Landfester, eds. *Brill's New Pauly*. English edition edited by Christine F. Salazar and Francis G. Gentry. Leiden: E. J. Brill, 2002-2015.

Collins, Billie Jean, Mary R. Bachvarova, and Ian Rutherford, eds. *Anatolian Interfaces: Hittites, Greeks and Their Neighbours*. Oxford: Oxbow Books, 2008.

Correa, Paula Da Cunha. "Classics Studies in Brazil." *Classical Bulletin* 77.2 (2001): 216-39.

"CSWMG Report Comparing 2003-2004 and 2013-2014 Departmental Surveys." *Society for Classical Studies*. <https://classicalstudies.org/about/cswmg-report-comparing-2003-2004-and-2013-2014-departmental-surveys>.

Currie, Bruno. *Homer's Allusive Art*. Oxford: Oxford UP, 2016.

Detienne, Marcel. *Comparer l'incomparable*. Paris : Le Seuil, 2009.

"Digital Classics." *Wikipedia*. November 21, 2017. <https://en.wikipedia.org/wiki/Digital_classics>.

"Digital Humanities." *Department of the Classics, Harvard University*. <https://classics.fas.harvard.edu/type/digital-humanities>.

"Digital Humanities." *Society for Classical Studies*. <https://classicalstudies.org/blogs/digital-humanities?page=1>.

Doerries, Bryan. *The Theater of War: What Ancient Greek Tragedies can Teach us Today*. NY: Knopf, 2015.

"Emotions Across Cultures Working Papers: Proceedings of a Workshop Held in February 2015 at NYU AD." NYU Faculty Digital Archive. <https://archive.nyu.edu/handle/2451/33966>.

Garland, Robert. *The Eye of the Beholder: Deformity and Disability in the Graeco-Roman World*. London: Bristol Classical P, 2010.

"G. I. Bill." *Wikipedia*. February 13, 2019. <https://en.wikipedia.org/wiki/G.I._Bill>.

Green, Peter. "Homer Now." *The New Republic*. June 7, 2012. <https://newrepublic.com/article/103920/homer-the-iliad-translations>.

Haubold, Johannes. *Greece and Mesopotamia: Dialogues in Literature*. Cambridge: Cambridge UP, 2013.

Heath, John and Victor Davis Hanson. *Who Killed Homer? The Demise of Classical Education and the Recovery of Greek Wisdom*. NY: Encounter Books, 2001.

Hoyos, Dexter, ed. *A Companion to Roman Imperialism*. Leiden: Brill, 2012.

Hughes, J. Donald. *Environmental Problems of the Greeks and Romans: Ecology in the Ancient Mediterranean*. Baltimore: Johns Hopkins UP, 2014.

Konstan, David. "*Arethusa* and the Politics of Criticism." *Contextualizing Classics: Ideology, Performance, Dialogue*. Eds. Thomas Falkner, Nancy Felson, and David Konstan. Lanham, MD: Rowman and Littlefield, 1999. 335-46.

---. "The Classics in the Americas." *Classical Bulletin* 77.2 (2001): 209.

Laes, Christian. *Disabilities and the Disabled in the Roman World: A Social and Cultural History*. Cambridge: Cambridge UP, 2018.

Li Causi, Pietro. *Gli animali nel mondo antico*. Bologna: Il Mulino, 2018.

Lloyd, G. E. R. "Introduction: Methods and Problems." *Ancient Greece and China Compared*. Eds. G. E. R. Lloyd and Jingyi Jenny Zhao, in collaboration with Qiaosheng Dong. Cambridge: Cambridge UP, 2018. 1-29.

Martindale, Charles. "Introduction: Thinking Through Reception." *Classics and the Uses of Reception*. Eds. Charles Martindale and Richard F. Thomas. Oxford: Blackwell, 2006. 1-13.

McInerney, Jeremy and Ineke Sluiter, eds. *Valuing Landscape in Classical Antiquity: Natural Environment and Cultural Imagination*. Leiden: Brill, 2016.

Meineck, Peter. *Theatrocracy: Greek Drama, Cognition and the Imperative for Theatre*. London: Routledge, 2017.

---. "These Are Men whose Minds the Dead have Ravished': Theater of War/The Philoctetes Project." *Arion* 17.1 (Spring/Summer 2009): 173-91.

--- and David Konstan, eds. *Combat Trauma and the Ancient Greeks*. NY: Palgrave Macmillan, 2014.

---, William Michael Short, and Jennifer Devereaux, eds. *The Routledge Handbook of Classics and Cognitive Theory*. London: Routledge, 2019.

Moyer, Ian S. *Egypt and the Limits of Hellenism*. Cambridge: Cambridge UP, 2011.

Mutschler, Fritz-Heiner, ed. *The Homeric Epics and the Chinese Book of Songs: Foundational Texts Compared*. Cambridge: Cambridge Scholars Publishing, 2018.

Newmyer, Stephen Thomas. *Animals in Greek and Roman Thought: A Sourcebook*. London: Routledge, 2010.

---. *Animals, Rights, and Reason in Plutarch and Modern Ethics*. London: Routledge, 2006.

Padilla Peralta, Dan-el. "Racial Equality and the Production of Knowledge." January 5, 2019. <goo.gl/56Akpw>.

---. "Some Thoughts on AIA-SCS 2019." <https://medium.com/@danelpadillaperalta/some-thoughts-on-aia-scs-2019-d6a480a1812a>.

Pelliccia, Hayden. "The Art of Wrath." *The New York Review of Books* October 12, 2017. 42-43. [Review of Peter Green's translation of *The Iliad* and Barry B. Powell's *The Iliad by Homer*].

Penrose Jr., Walter D. "The Discourse of Disability in Ancient Greece." *Classical World* 108.4 (Summer 2015): 499-523.

Ponce Hernández, Carolina and Lourdes Rojas Álvarez, eds. *Estudios clásicos en América en el tercer milenio*. Mexico City: Universidad Nacional Autónoma de México, 2006.

Pozzi, Dora Carlisky. "Classics in Argentina." *Classical Bulletin* 77.2 (2001): 210-15.

Richlin, Amy. *Slave Theater in the Roman Republic*. Cambridge: Cambridge UP, 2017.

Romano, Allen J. "Classics and Digital Humanities." *Expositions* 5.2 (2011): 142-46. <https://fsu.digital.flvc.org/islandora/object/fsu:205230/datastream/PDF/view>.

Rutherford, Ian, ed. *Greco-Egyptian Interactions: Literature, Translation and Culture, 500 BC-AD 300*. Oxford: Oxford UP, 2016.

Salmon, John and Graham Shipley, eds. *Human Landscapes in Classical Antiquity: Environment and Culture*. London: Routledge, 1996.

Schmitz, Thomas. *Modern Literary Theory and Ancient Texts: An Introduction*. Malden, MA: Wiley-Blackwell, 2007.

Seaford, Richard. *Universe and Inner Self in Early Indian and Early Greek Thought*. Edinburgh: Edinburgh UP, 2016.

Shay, Jonathan. *Achilles in Vietnam: Combat Trauma and the Undoing of Character*. NY: Atheneum, 1994.

Skinner, Marilyn, ed. *A Companion to Catullus*. London: Blackwell, 2007.

Snyder, Thomas D., ed. *120 Years of American Education: A Statistical Portrait*. Washington, DC: US Department of Education, 1993.

Sorabji, Richard. *Animal Minds and Human Morals: The Origins of the Western Debate*. Ithaca, NY: Cornell UP, 1993.

Stephens, Susan. *Seeing Double: Intercultural Poetics in Ptolemaic Alexandria*. Berkeley: U of California P, 2003.

Thommen, Lukas. *An Environmental History of Ancient Greece and Rome*. Cambridge: Cambridge UP, 2012.

"[Tr]an[s]tiquity: Theorizing Gender Diversity in Ancient Contexts." *Society for Classical Studies*. <https://classicalstudies.org/annual-meeting/2017/148/transtiquity-theorizing-gender-diversity-ancient-contexts-afg-2017>.

West, Martin L. *The East Face of Helicon: West Asiatic Elements in Greek Poetry and* Myth. Oxford: Clarendon P, 1997.

Whitmarsh, Tim. *Dirty Love: The Genealogy of the Ancient Greek Novel*. Oxford: Oxford UP, 2018.

Wierzbicka, Anna. *Emotions across Languages and Cultures: Diversity and Universals*. Cambridge: Cambridge UP, 1999.

Williams, Craig. *Reading Roman Friendship*. Cambridge: Cambridge UP, 2012.

A Decolonial Turn in the Humanities

Claire Gallien

This article presents a critical survey that maps out the development and reception of the decolonial turn in Western and French academia. It traces its genealogical foundations, its points of overlap with and departure from postcolonial studies; illustrates the theoretical contributions of its founding figures; and discusses its limitations in relation to its own conceptual blind spots and the neo-liberal context and contemporary regime of coloniality which restrict its development.

The article examines key decolonial concepts—such as "epistemicide," the "hubris of the point zero," "coloniality," the "zone of non-being," "delinking," "pluriversality"—and how they constitute new venues for critical thinking in the West, especially regarding the question of what counts as "knowledge" and what does not. The article argues that the decolonial turn is not about augmenting and elevating Western episteme with new content. Rather, responding to Dipesh Chakrabarty's call to "provincialize" Europe, it clears a space for other epistemologies and cosmovisions to circulate in Western academia.

The decolonial approach does not restrict itself to a critique of the colonial episteme and world order. It entails a recognition of one's own positionality as scholar, critic, and speaker, recognizes the necessity to decenter and pluralize knowledge formations, and finally offers alternative ways to conceptualize and experience the world. Thus, decoloniality is best described as a gesture that de-normalizes the normative, problematizes default positions, debunks the a-perspectival, destabilizes the structure, and as a program to rehabilitate epistemic formations that continue to be repressed under coloniality.

The article also explores critical zones insufficiently addressed by decolonial thinkers, namely, the field's reliance on a homogenized version of "the" West and of "modernity," its controversial relation to, and participation in, the system itself, and finally the problematic interactions of various epistemic formations under pluriversality. How is the common good created and sustained under conditions of pluriversality, if the languages, concepts, methodologies are all different, and if the starting point is the recognition that what counts as beneficial to one may very well be detrimental to the other? In other words, how does one relate in the pluriverse?

After mapping out the genealogies and interventions of the field, the article offers case studies of its reception in the Republic of South Africa, the UK, and particularly France, where it was first introduced by racialized activist groups. A decolonial literature has emerged in French thanks to academic journals such as *Cahiers des Amériques Latines*, *Mouvements*, *Multitudes,* and *Tumultes*, and to the publishing house La Découverte. Despite its circulation in English and in translation, the field has met much resistance both inside and outside universities. For instance, Its presence continues to depend on the commitment of specific individuals organizing seminars and workshops, but not on any official program. In this article, I argue that the non-reception of decolonial studies, ranging from careless dismissal to violent rejection amongst conservatives and secularists alike, should be understood in the context of systemic racism and Islamophobia in France, and should also be related to the precedent of postcolonial studies, which have met with a strong opposition, especially in the social sciences.

Postcolonial and Decolonial Turns: Overlaps and Departures

Since the 1990s, the postcolonial turn has had a profound impact on a large number of disciplines, including literary criticism, history, and translation studies. Decolonial studies emerged as a university field a decade later, largely under the impulse of predominantly male scholars from Latin and South America now working for US and European universities and research centers.[1] In the US in particular, the migrant or minority communities are distributed across distinct fields of study—a higher proportion of scholars from the Caribbean and South Asia do postcolonial studies, while Native scholars are often allocated positions in ethnic studies, Black in Black-American studies, and those from Latin and South America have taken to decolonial studies, because of their roots on the other side of the imperial border and their connections with indigenous knowledges.

Both postcolonial and decolonial studies engage with global structures, experiences, and discourses of colonial domination. This is evident, for instance, in Postcolonial critics' emphasis on writing "post" and "colonial" without the hyphen to indicate that the field does not consider the colonial moment as something of the past but as an ongoing one in the present. Both fields focus on marginalized people, whose experiences, imaginations, and knowledge of the world count less, or simply do not count at all. Those identified by Franz Fanon in *Black Skin, White Masks* (originally published in French as *Peau noires, masques blancs* in 1952) as belonging to the "zone of non-being" (*Black Skin* 2) are the ones living today on what Ghassan Hage calls the wrong side of the "global apartheid" (38-39), those whom Arundhati Roy refers to in her latest novel *The Ministry of Utmost Happiness* as the "surplus people" (95), and whom the current regime of coloniality considers as "disposable" people. Building on the Fanonian concept of the "zone of non-being," decolonial thinker Boaventura de Sousa Santos describes Western modernity as a form of "abyssal thinking" that creates a radical line of distinction between the social realms of visibility and invisibility: "What most fundamentally characterizes abyssal thinking is thus the impossibility of the copresence of the two sides of the line. . . . Beyond it there is only nonexistence, invisibility, nondialectical absence" ("Beyond" 45-46). This process of invisibilization is what Nelson Maldonado-Torres calls the "metaphysical catastrophe" because

> [l]iving in the zone of being human means finding oneself, others, and the institutions of one's society affirming one's status as a full human being. . . . Living in the zone of sub-humanity means, not only that one is not meant to have easy access to basic means of existence, but also that it is normal for everything and everyone, including oneself, to question one's humanity. ("Outline" 13)

Decolonialism shares with postcolonial theory this space of the margin; but perhaps, in addition to what postcolonialism has already done in analyzing processes of disenfranchisement and oppression, decolonialism uncovers the alternative epistemologies and thereby alternative cosmovisions these marginal spaces contain. The marginalized groups it focuses on are no longer considered as waiting at the border of Western modernity but are "extra-moderns" (see Skafish).

It also shares with postcolonialism a suspicion towards identity politics (nativism) and any homogeneous understanding of identity. Decoloniality does not propose a nostalgic and ethnocentric return to traditions, but an engagement in the present with forms of knowledge that have been discarded by colonial modernity (see Mignolo, *Local*). Ramón Grosfoguel insists that the key function of decolonial critique is to go beyond both hegemonic and marginal, Eurocentric and Third World, fundamentalisms ("Decolonizing" n. pag.). He maintains that being socially located on the oppressed side of power does not automatically imply that one is thinking decolonially: "Precisely, the success of the modern/colonial world system consists in making subjects that are socially located in the oppressed side of the colonial difference, to think epistemically like the ones on the dominant positions" ("Decolonizing" n. pag.). For Maldonado-Torres, decoloniality implies "giving oneself to and joining the struggles with the *damnés*" and such action transforms individuals "beyond recognition" ("Outline" 30).

The implications of this are two-fold: first, that "armchair" decolonialism constitutes an aberration and, second, that decoloniality transforms those engaged with it. Therefore, the decolonial community is never a given but one that configures and reconfigures itself through action. It is important to underline this point in a context where the detractors of decolonial studies, wittingly or unwittingly, misread the field's intentions and suggest that it essentializes and re-Orientalizes the native (Chibber 293). The risk is there and it is up to decolonial critics to make sure they explain the difference between asserting the existence and the need for alternative epistemologies (to the modern/colonial system) and repeating an Orientalist gesture that would turn what should register as alternatives for all humanity to inscrutable, exotic, and essentialist versions of the Other.

In *Borderlands/La Frontera*, Chicana writer Gloria Anzaldúa, one of the founding figures of decolonialism, compellingly articulates a theory of identity as formation and as struggle, where essentialist representations and default positions are called into question. Drawing from Aztec mythology, she reveals how identity emerges while the individual situates him/herself in the *nepantla*, which is this "uncertain terrain one crosses when moving from one place to another, when changing from one class, race, or sexual position to another, when traveling from the present identity into a new identity" (180). *Nepantla* marks a violent moment when one is confronted with danger and instability, hence Anzaldúa's characterization of it as a state of crisis. It is also a space where the de-centering of the self occurs, where cultures become de-essentialized, where one can move from a-perspectivism to the multiplicity of perspectives gathered in this space in-between.

Nepantla is also a space for re-membering the self and re-suturing it with others, for building "(un)natural bridges" ("Preface" 1-5) that are fragile, susceptible to change, and must be taken care of to build communities. Precisely in so far as experiencing the self in decolonial terms may lead to a common ground held together with "un-natural" bridges, a place of articulation for the *nos/otras* (a play on the feminine form of the Spanish first-person plural pronoun, *nosotras*, to indicate the multiple and split identities that constitute the self), decolonial life can never be the reformulation of a nativist agenda: "Bridging is the work of opening the gate to the stranger, within and without. To step across the threshold is to be stripped of the illusion of safety because it moves us into unfamiliar territory and does not grant safe passage. To bridge is to attempt community, . . . to risk being wounded" ("Preface" 3).

Decolonial and postcolonial studies also share a common intellectual history rooted in independence struggles and the Bandung era. Fanon obviously comes to mind and with him many thinkers from the colonial margins, such as Aimé Césaire, Amilcar Cabral, and C. L. R. James, who challenged not only colonial rule (colonization) but also colonial thinking and ideology (coloniality). Another important shared legacy may be found in the Indian subaltern movement in historiography. For instance, in *Routine Violence*, Gyanendra Pandey, one of the founding members of the Subaltern history group, emphasizes their commitment to history written from below, against grand narratives, and in defense of the fragment. Pandey's work underlines the presence of a rural (as opposed to the Marxist urban and industrial) proletariat and resistance, and thereby disrupts the universalist pretention of Western epistemology whose formulae are posited as valid for decoding situations in all places and times. Immanuel Wallerstein's *European Universalism: The Rhetoric of Power* came out a year later and similarly exposes how a Western discourse of "progress" and "development" has from the Enlightenment to the present day justified not only colonial expansion but also the pretention to know what the colonized Other wants, should want, thinks, and how he/she should think.

Despite the common ground, postcolonialism and decolonial thinking do not share the same objectives and methodologies. While postcolonialism has sought to excavate and critique the legacy of colonialism by borrowing from Western poststructuralist theory—a move which Mignolo bluntly equates with a new form of academic colonialism (see "Colonial"), decolonialism relinquishes Western epistemology and aligns itself with other modes of thinking belonging to groups which have been undermined, repressed, discriminated against, or massacred under colonial, imperial, neo-liberal, patriarchal, and/or secular rule. Decolonial thinking proposes to re-experience, re-imagine, and re-think the world based on different epistemic foundations and ontologies. In other words, if postcolonial critique produced studies *about* the systemic subjugation of subalternized people, decolonial studies focus on the production of alternative discourses *with* and *from* a subaltern perspective.

A relevant illustration of this difference may be found in the case of "border thinking" which is a key concept in decolonial theory that Walter Mignolo and Madina Vladimirovna Tlostanova borrow, and transform, from Gloria Anzaldúa. It refers to a mode of thinking (and living) emanating from what European colonial modernity constituted as its exterior. Mignolo and Tlostanova defined border-thinking as "the epistemology of the exteriority; that is, of the outside created from the inside" ("Theorizing" 206). The notion can easily be misread as an equivalent to postcolonial "interstice" or "Third Space." Homi Bhabha coined the term "Third Space" to refer to the space and time of enunciation, where utterance displaces the meaning of a statement and reappropriates it in view of liberation:

> It is only when we understand that all cultural statements and systems are constructed in this contradictory and ambivalent space of enunciation, that we begin to understand why hierarchical claims to the inherent originality or "purity" of cultures are untenable, even before we resort to empirical historical instances that demonstrate their hybridity. . . . It is that Third Space, though unrepresentable in itself, which constitutes the discursive conditions of enunciation that ensure that the meaning and symbols of culture have no primordial unity or fixity; that even the same signs can be appropriated, translated, rehistoricised and read anew. (37)

By taking into account the existence of the "Third Space," a re-evaluation of the ability of colonized people to appropriate and disrupt the colonizer's discourse was possible. Thus, the difference between "border-thinking" and "Third Space" encapsulates the difference between the two fields themselves. While notions of "interstice" and "Third Space" refer to spaces of contestation, border thinking means recovering knowledge traditions and languages discarded by colonial modernity.

Furthermore, their disciplinary involvements do not entirely overlap. Both find resonance in the Humanities at large, yet while postcolonialism has thus far been prevalent in anthropology, history, and literary criticism, decolonialism has found a stronger echo in philosophy, due to its focus on epistemologies.

The "postcolonial turn" in anthropology from the 1970s onwards was translated into a recognition of the discipline's participation in colonization and colonialism, which in turn transformed the relation of ethnographers to their theory and practice (see Devisch and Nyamnjoh). Postcolonial revisionism in anthropology has entailed a departure from Western projections of exotic alterity and mistrust towards pretension to universal truth. It further implies a turn towards modes of knowing from elsewhere, otherwise, and *with* the Other, as opposed to *about* the Other. Anthropologists are no longer engaged in processes of explaining other worlds with exogenous tools and languages familiar to readers and peers back home, but are rather engaged in alternative ways of understanding and experiencing worlds.

James Clifford is one example of a prominent ethnographer who has theorized about this turn over the course of his career from *The Predicament of Culture* (1988), *Routes* (1997), *On the Edges of Anthropology* (2003), to *Returns* (2013). Clifford refers to an embarrassed recognition of "the liberal privilege of 'making space' for marginal perspective" (3). Disentangling oneself from the anthropological predicament would mean engaging with the privileged position of the liberal white Western male anthropologist. Thus, the recognition of one's own positionality must have an impact on practices as well, including the willingness to make room for alternative ontologies and to modify one's mode of writing in order to accommodate them. For instance, the concepts of "indigenous becoming" and cultural identity as "return" or re-configuration imply a form of anthropological writing as "collage," assembled, disassembled, modular, a collage that mixes genres and can be envisaged as "academic novella" (10).

Clifford is not a unique case. Many anthropologists have felt the need to decolonize their theories and practices so as to stay emically connected with the people whose lives and cosmovisions they study. In his 1984 essay entitled "The Writer as an Outsider," Epeli Hau'ofa proposes to write ethnography in the form of fiction so as to remain as close as possible to the type of knowledge produced in the oral cultures he studied (106-08). Steven Feld, in turn, resorts to drone imagery to film the paths and river lines in the rainforest that are imaginatively depicted in Bosavi songs (see *Voices of the Rainforest*). Placing multiple microphones in the near environment of the poet-singer allows him to record the various and intermingling soundtracks of birds, rain, river flow that interplay with their voices (see *Bosavi*). These sounds are included not to represent exotic backgrounds but as the very elements from which the singers draw their inspiration and rhythm, and with which they modify the pronunciation of words. In all these cases, the ethnographer's method adapts itself to the environment he/she studies and not the other way round.

It would be a task of epic proportion to list the various ways in which ethnographers decolonize their practices: Steven Feld's presence with the Bosavi people in Papua New-Guinea and his development in acoustemology; Barbara Glowczewski's remapping in Central and Western Australia of Warlpiri, Djugun, and Yawuru territories erased under colonial maps but preserved in traditional songs, stories, and paintings (also called "songlines" or "dreaming tracks"); Keith Basso's study of the place-names of the Western Apaches in Arizona in "Speaking with Names" and *Wisdom Sits in Places*; Viveiros de Castro's question in *Cannibal Metaphysics* concerning what anthropologists owe, conceptually, to the people they study and his exposition of how Arawaté perspectivism enacts a complete reversal of Western ontology have in fact moved their discipline onto decolonial grounds. The shift is threefold and achieved by modifying their methods of enquiry and adapting them to epistemologies belonging to the groups they study, by overturning knowledge hierarchies, and, finally, for some at least, by reconnecting research with activism.

Because epistemic violence is always connected with other forms of violence, be they economic, social, or ecological, scholarly commitment is more often than not connected with activist life. As Maldonado-Torres states: "Decoloniality is the dynamic activity of giving oneself to and joining the struggles with the damnés. . . . If coloniality emerges as part of the 'downturn' of demographic and metaphysical catastrophe, decoloniality is rooted in practical and metaphysical revolt" ("Outline" 30). For some decolonial thinkers, theory follows activism and not the other way round. This is the case of Arturo Escobar whose theory, including the elaboration of concepts such as "post-development" initiative, "sentipensar" and "relational ontology," as well as "pluriversal" (as opposed to universal) co-existence, is inspired by his fieldwork with Afro-descendants in Columbia and the Proceso de Comunidades Negras's (PCN) resistance against racial injustices (see Escobar).

In other words, one could argue that what Maldonado-Torres conceptualized as the "decolonial turn" (coming after other turns such as the linguistic and the pragmatic ones) in philosophy (see "Thinking") constitutes an equivalent of what came to be called the "postcolonial turn" in anthropology. Indeed, decolonial theory condemns "epistemicide" (see Scholte; Santos, *Epistemologies*), i.e., the ranking and elimination of epistemic systems that do not correspond to Western modernity, and instead advocates "delinking" (see Mignolo) from Western colonial modernity so that other epistemic formations may be acknowledged, reckoned with, and considered as alternatives to capitalism and colonialism.[2] In the current distribution of intellectual labor, it is still the case that the "rest" of the world cannot dismiss knowledge produced in the North or in European languages, while the North may, if generous, agree to recognize the existence of other epistemes but it does not have to take them, or the languages in which they are couched, into account. No putting on par between the West and the "rest" has truly happened yet, and the "abyssal line" that says that on the other side "there is no real knowledge; there are beliefs, opinions, intuitive or subjective understandings, which at the most may become objects or raw materials for scientific enquiry" (Santos, "Beyond" 47) still needs to be overcome. Two directions are possible: 1- universities in the Global South overturn the epistemic hegemony of the North and reclaim knowledge traditions crushed under modern capitalism and colonialism; 2- universities in the Global North recognize what epistemic privilege means and decolonize their own curricula by re-reading the classics in view of their collaborations with epistemic oppression. Of course, this capacity to decolonize from the interior of the border (I have in mind here Mignolo's notion of "border thinking") already constitutes a privilege.

Conceptual Tools Towards a Decolonization of Knowledge

The first step towards decolonizing Humanities in the North is to overcome the myth of non-situatedness, or what Castro-Gómez calls *Zero-Point Hubris* and Grosfoguel refers to as "the myth of a non-situated Ego" ("Decolonizing," n. pag.), which in reality conceals epistemic, ideological, political, and economic locations. For Grosfoguel, the issue is not that scholars lack partiality but that geo-political and body-political "loc[i] of enunciation" are insufficiently theorized and recognized. This is all the more relevant since, after the demise of Third-World movements and the collapse of the Communist Block, only the liberal secular worldview holds center stage. Thus, decolonizing the mind starts with a recognition of the privilege of writing and speaking from the interior of the border and of the fact that borders are created and sustained by the center and for its benefit.

Hegemonic epistemologies create the conditions for epistemicides, and the decolonial literature today aims at acknowledging this condition as a fact, analyzing the processes of occlusion, and subverting the colonial cartography through the re-introduction of other modes of knowing and being, in other words, through promoting what Santos called "ecologies of knowledges" ("Beyond" 45). This is the reason why the decolonial option questions Humanities at large and not just anthropology or philosophy and confronts all academics, including literary critics. It demands clarifications about the default positions held, the language spoken, and the types of selection endorsed in research and pedagogy; in other words, it entails learning to unlearn (see Tlostanova and Mignolo, *Learning*).

The global decolonial turn in the Humanities is composed of two intersecting strands—the historiographical strand based on the study of the genealogies of coloniality and modernity and the critique of epistemicides, and a second strand that is rooted in minorized knowledges with leanings towards activism and the reform of pedagogy. These distinctions highlight the diversity of approaches that are gathered under the umbrella term of decoloniality and the fact that they are not exclusive but rather complementary. For instance, decolonial Islam is used in social activism as a form of liberation theology (see Esack), in feminist struggles (see Ali; Karimi; Lamrabet), and reclaimed also to combat Islamophobia (see Hage; Martin-Muñoz et al); it is also used as epistemological category to question secularism (see Asad; Mahmood) and to critique a teleological and hegemonic reading of Western "democracy" as ultimate and universal political model (see Sayyid).

Decolonizing Humanities in the West means engaging in praxi-theory; in other words, having a theory that is always connected with action. For instance, Mignolo's concepts of "delinking," "border-thinking," and the "pluriverse," may serve as tools to decolonize curricula and reverse systemic racism and sexism (see Mignolo, "Delinking," "Re-emerging," *The Darker Side of the Renaissance*, *The Darker Side of Western Modernity*; Tlostanova and Mignolo, *Learning*; Mignolo and Walsh). Mignolo proposes delinking (from the Western episteme and canon) as precondition for the decolonization of the mind and for the emergence of pluriversality, i.e., the recognition and re-emergence on the global map of systems of knowledge produced outside the Global North (see "Re-Emerging"). Once delinking is in place, a re-emergence of knowledge systems, previously disposed of in the zone of non-being by the global center, is possible. Using his formation in linguistics, Mignolo suggests that decoloniality is not a change of the enunciated (the content) but of the "principles managed at the level of the enunciation" ("The Conceptual" 149). He writes:

> As long as controversies and interpretations remain within the same rules of the game (the same terms of the conversation), the control of knowledge itself is never called into question. And in order to call the modern/colonial foundation of the control of knowledge into question, it is necessary to focus on the knower rather than on the known. ("The Conceptual" 149-50)

The task of the decolonial critique is to render visible the structuring force of Western enunciation and re-connect with what has been so far discarded. In other words, as Mignolo explains, it is not enough to dissent from within the Eurocentric structure ("The Conceptual" 151); one must develop a "non-Eurocentric critique of Eurocentrism," also viewed as "decoloniality in its planetary diversity of local histories that have been disrupted by North Atlantic global expansions" ("The Conceptual" 151).

Delinking is the necessary step towards pluriversality, which is the third key concept in decolonial thinking. This concept occurs in several of Mignolo's works, especially in *The Darker Side of Western Modernity*. Tlostanova and Mignolo endorse a "pluriversal hermeneutics" against the "monotopic hermeneutics growing out of Western reason" ("On Pluri-Topic Hermeneutics" 15) and beyond Raimundo Panikkar's "diatopic hermeneutics." Panikkar defines diatopic hermeneutics as the art of crossing spaces or traditions (dia-topoi), which do not have a grammar in common. It is therefore premised on the acknowledgment of the existence of other ways of understanding the world and positioning oneself in it, and undermines Western universalism:

> To cross the boundaries of one's own culture without realizing that another culture may have a radically different approach to reality is today no longer admissible. . . . Diatopical hermeneutics stands for the thematic consideration of understanding the other without assuming that the other has the same basic self-understanding. (9)

Monotopic hermeneutics is premised on intelligibility, while diatopical hermeneutics starts from unintelligibility and aims to bringing into contact different human horizons, in order to create the conditions of possibility of a dialogue without negating cultural differences. The issue here, as with pluriversality, is that it remains unclear how the bridges and connections are designed when what is at stake is the bringing together of (potentially radically) different worldviews, for instance, neo-liberalism with the *zones-à-défendre* (zones to defend) in France, which are areas occupied by militants attempting to block destructive development projects. Is there a common ground? Should we seek one? Furthermore, the issue of power relations within the pluriverse remains undertheorized. Are worldviews put on par, and how? Or is domination bound to resurface only in a different place and under a different guise?

Finally, while acknowledging the importance of this shift from the mono-topos to diatopic and pluriversal hermeneutics, the terms employed are problematic if premised on a conception of cultures as separated and cohesive units. The publications of Naoki Sakai and Jon Solomon in translation studies underline the problematic nature of diatopic and pluritopic structures, which return to a monolingual conception of language and identity (see Sakai; Sakai and Hanawa; Sakai and Solomon). Comparative literature and inter-cultural dialogue have become suspect precisely insofar as they imply the conception of a plurality of demarcated identities that are made to discuss across a border. According to them, identities, languages, and literatures may be viewed otherwise, as points of intersection, always in flux, and made of what traverses them at a moment in time.

In *Local Histories/Global Designs* and in "De-Colonial Cosmopolitanism and Dialogues among Civilizations," Mignolo adumbrates answers to these pressing queries. He makes a number of important distinctions—first between a multi-polar world (or a world made of a multiplicity of centers competing with one another) and the pluriverse (where we have recognition of difference without competition); then between global linear thinking (which is an expression he actually borrows from Carl Schmidt to designate a new nomos of the earth, after Tordesillas, in the form of bordered territories) and essential entanglements (where global interdependence is not only recognized but becomes the premise from which all decisions are made).

A crucial point that Mignolo underlines is that de-Westernization is not enough to create the pluriverse, because de-Westernization does not rule out linear thinking and power differentials. The pluriverse cannot be comprehended as long as we remain within a system of capitalist exploitation and extractivism and thus think of the world as essentially divided into territories and zones of influence and power. But another imagination of the world, another nomos is possible, and it would be truly decolonial this time. The reservations we might have had concerning the interactions of worlds and entities within the pluriverse only obtain within a nomos of the world *à la Schmidt*, i.e., in a world designed along partitions. However, decolonial thinking offers new formulas to rethink relations between diverse cosmovisions and, within these cosmovisions, between individuals, humans and non-humans, who inhabit the earth. Decolonial thinking designs a new pluri-trans-versal nomos of the earth or what Mignolo calls a new decolonial cosmopolitanism, where the world is not only multiplied into worlds but also imagined in terms of transversality as a space of entangled co-existence.

Resistant Humanities

> Infiltrated by students' unions, by "indigenous" groupuscules, paralized by the cowardice of the university hierarchy, departments and some elite higher education institutes have been turned into ideological battlegrounds.

Pressures and threats are frequent and no holds are barred. (Waintraub n. pag.; my translation)

To infiltrate, verb. a) Transitive. Sb infiltrates sth. [The predicate designates a collective]. To introduce clandestinely isolated elements with the goal to disorganise, change the course of action, and possibly take control. ("Noyauter" n. pag.; my translation)

Decolonial thinkers habitually describe their interventions as forms of praxi-theory, that is theory leading to action and vice versa. Contrary to the belief in a-perspectival and universal truth in scientific discourse, decoloniality presupposes that knowledge is always the result of an embodiment and commitment. The impact of decolonial theory in the Humanities has been three-fold—the foundation of popular and indigenous universities especially in Latin America, the organization of numerous decolonial summer schools generating communal transnational thinking, and the call for the decolonization of the curriculum.[3] If we take the call to de-colonize to also mean de-modernize, de-nationalize, and de-patriarchize, then the movement can be said to have crossed all disciplines in the Humanities, with particular emphasis on anthropology and philosophy, but also on history, language and translation studies, and literature.

These attempts to rethink knowledge production are premised on Paulo Freire's *Pedagogy of the Oppressed* (1970), bell hooks's *Teaching to Transgress* (1994) which gives a feminist impetus to reforming pedagogical methods, and Linda Tuhiwai Smith's *Decolonizing Methodologies* (1999) which focuses on indigenous education (see Gran et al.; Emeagwali; Emeagwali and Dei; Diversi and Moreira; Tlostanova and Mignolo, *Learning*; Ndlovu-Gatsheni and Zondi; Fataar; Bhambra et al.; Wane and Todd). What Smith writes about from New Zealand, other First Nation scholars, such as Shirley Ida Williams, Edna Manitowabi, and Leanne Simpson, advocate also in the Canadian context. For instance, Williams, who describes herself as a survivor of residential school in Canada, has spent her academic career explaining how indigenous people have been robbed of their languages and cultures through colonization, and how the modern liberal state, along with its reconciliation narrative and educational programs, constitutes a schizophrenic and colonial threat to Canadian First Nations. She has been an advocate of the return of indigenous studies and languages at the university level, and has published a dictionary of Ojibway and Odawa words entitled *Gdi-nweninaa* (see Williams; "Gdi-nweninaa").

This form of knowledge production is from the ground up, and has local and political relevance. First Nation writer and academic Leanne Simpson exposes the urgency of learning native languages in order to decolonize knowledge, because concepts, teachings, and ways of connecting with the world(s), both in body and mind, never entirely translate. As she points out: "We listen to the sound of our voice with our full bodies: our hearts, our minds and our physicality" (61). This recalls an earlier appeal from African writers and academics, such as Taban lo Liyong from Sudan in "Language and Literature Studies at University College Nairobi" and Ngũgĩ wa Thiong'o from Kenya in "On the Abolition of the English Department" and *Decolonising the Mind*, to abolish separate English Departments in African universities and press forward for the creation of African languages and literatures departments instead.

In this globalized neo-liberal day and age, and with the shrinking of state funding in (higher) education, Humanities are usually the most strongly hit. Even if one can argue that all disciplines are ultimately called to serve the system, including the ones one would categorize as most dissident, precisely because they can always be recuperated as signs of freedom of thought and of speech in Western liberal democracies, direct actions towards what Mignolo proposes as "epistemic disobedience" have created beneficial trouble on campuses. Calling for a genuine decolonization of curricula and teaching methods, I focus here on three cases in the Republic of South Africa, the UK, and France, to analyze the specific dynamics and impediments each has been confronted with and also highlight in all three cases the persistence of latent systemic forms of racism.

The colonial South African background—with the official end of apartheid in 1994 only—resurfaced in 2015 when students from the University of Cape Town demanded the removal of the controversial statue of Cecil Rhodes from the campus. This call led to the formation of a wider Rhodes Must Fall movement across the Republic of South Africa and beyond, advocating a decolonization of curricula, which, in turn, brought to the fore long overdue debates over who determines curricula, what models, templates, and agendas they follow, who they serve, and how they can be changed so as to bring real emancipation and social/racial/sexual justice.[4] South African universities, including the University of Cape Town, of Stellenbosch, and of Johannesburg, have had their faculties of arts and social sciences, economy and management, education, law, medicine, agriculture, and theology affected by the campaign to decolonize the canon. Aslam Fataar explains what decolonizing education means for the university engaged in the process, namely, the undermining of "knowledge parochialism" and "the inclusion of all knowledge forms bequeathed to humanity including African, indigenous, Arab-Islamic, Chinese, Hindu, Indo-American, Asiatic, and Western knowledge forms" (vii). In a series of recent publications, African scholars have written a decolonial blueprint that includes re-reading Western classics with a decolonial lens, relinking body and mind in pedagogical practices and redefining knowledge from embodied positions, making knowledge locally relevant and participatory, examining the politics of defining what counts as knowledge, the dynamics of inclusion and exclusion, and calling for the pluralization of languages of study (see Emeagwali; Emeagwali and Dei; Botha; Council on Higher Education; Fataar and Subreenduth; Mbembe; Bozalek and Zembylas; Le Grange; Ndlovu-Gatsheni and Zondi; Muswede; Ndoferipi).

The movement has resonated worldwide, including at Oxford University where a Rhodes Must Fall campaign was launched (see "#RHODESMUSTFALL"), and a number of events and seminar series dedicated to the question of decolonizing the canon and racism at the university were organized (see, for instance, "Decolonising the Curriculum"). These events are organized and attended mainly by non-whites, and have a strong representation of the student body. Demands focus on the reform of curricula, which are considered too narrow and too Eurocentric, and reviewing hiring practices in order to have more female and academics of color in permanent academic positions. A report published in 2018 by the University and College Union states that black female professors in the UK face systemic racism, bullying, and discrimination, with just 25 black women recorded as working as professors compared to 14,000 white men for the academic year 2016-2017 (see " Black Female"; "The Experience").

#RhodesMustFall and #FeesMustFall campaigns have raised awareness and confronted important taboos in the West concerning the persistence of colonialism and racism in society and its repercussions at the university level. Yet, their success has remained limited. The campaigns have been met with much hostility from those at the top, precisely because they act as a force of contestation and disruption of the system as it stands. In the South African context (and the same applies to higher education in Latin and South America, for instance), universities function according to neo-liberal rules, and curricula are still largely modeled on the West. However, these decolonial experiences also call into question our evaluation of what counts as success or failure. Students and academics involved in the campaigns did not necessarily envisage that they would, then and there, revolutionize institutions. However, they were able to generate difficult but necessary debates about institutionalized racism, white privilege, neo-liberal, sexual, and colonial hierarchies and aggression. This capacity to redirect the terms of the debate and to make visible the violence of economic, social, racial, and epistemic hegemony does count as decolonial success.

In France, the first decolonial movement was not carried out at the university level by student movements but by activists and thinkers outside French universities, most often with family ties in the French former colonies (Sadri Khiari, Houria Bouteldja, and Françoise Vergès are cases in point), fighting against institutionalized racism and Islamophobia in France. This, coupled with a hint of bad faith and ignorance of the academic literature, accounts for Gilles Clavreul declaring he can provide a "radiography" of decolonialism in France while in reality restricting his analysis to the political positions of the militant group Les Indigènes de la République, formed in the wake of the 2005 révolte des banlieues, and which later became the PIR (Parti des Indigènes de la République) (see Clavreul). This "suspicious" origin in activism and the focus on issues that are taboo in France, including institutionalized racism and Islamophobia, has contributed to the delegitimization of the field. The opposition to decolonial studies is clearly ideological, and decolonialism is perceived as an intellectual scandal threatening the integrity of the French Republic and French *laïcité*.

One must also highlight the fact that decolonial thinking comes after the already charged history of the reception of postcolonial studies in France, discredited as an "academic carnival" (see Jean-François Bayart) that has colonized all social sciences. While in the US and British contexts postcolonial studies started in English and Comparative Literature departments, it was redistributed in France across political theory, sociology, and anthropology; meanwhile, French literature departments are, by and large, still considered as having less political impact.

Riven by controversies, the PIR has been used by its enemies to discredit decolonial thinking at large. False accusations of anti-Semitism and of reverse or anti-white racism were used to undermine their confrontations of taboos triggered by institutional racism and the colonial unconscious in France. The collective has responded to these accusations in a number of interviews and articles published on their website and collected in the volume *Nous sommes les indigènes de la République* (see Boutledja et al.). For instance, in "Le 'racisme anti-blanc' des Indigènes de la République," Houria Bouteldja writes:

> Social races exist and the evidence for this is their struggles. In France, the *indigènes* have taken up the weapon of race in order fight against a formidable narrative, namely universalism. And more specifically, white universalism, which masks and negates the structural hierarchies that constitute the French Republic.
>
> In the struggle we wage, we risk through the use of categories such as "White" and "*Indigènes*" what we call with Gayatri Chakravorty Spivak "strategic essentialism." Of course, we know that white people and the *indigènes* are not to be reduced to that status, that they are infinitely more complex.... But for us, "strategic essentialism" is a tool, including in the construction of a collective identity and of political awareness. Furthermore, these concepts resonate with the intuitive perception of a racial divide, and consequently they are efficient. How does one understand the conditions of the proletariat if one does not understand the concept of class, how does one understand the conditions of women if one does not understand the concept of gender, and how then are we to understand the conditions of the *indigènes* if one does not understand social race? ... I do not believe that it is—in itself or in the absolute—problematic to essentialize a group. What is required however is for one to be able to identify the author of the essentialization and most importantly his/her position with regards to power. (378-80; my translation)

In the post 9/11 context and with France's military interventions, as well as political and economic interference, in the Middle-East and Africa, the colonized threatening Other, embodied in the figures of migrants, refugees, and Muslims, has moved from the periphery to the center of media attention, reactivating and trivializing latent and manifest racism in France. The Muslim question in French academia is a no-go zone, and Muslim discourse must either be domesticated in the form of "moderate" Islam, which in fact amounts to a re-Orientalization of the religion, or be silenced and rendered illegible. If French anthropology for instance is open to the fact that American or Oceanian societies have produced other cosmovisions and ecological models of relation, it is absolutely inconceivable to assume that an Islamic episteme may play the same role as alternative model to the secular liberal modernity. Islam is never considered as a force of proposition to be reckoned with, but always as an intractable issue and persistent trouble.

In other words, it appears that when decolonial options are offered by distant societies, the system finds room for accommodation, while when the Other is not distant but very near—Muslims, racialized displaced persons, women—then he/she becomes threatening. The rhetoric of invasion and fear is deployed *ab-nauseam* in the French press and media from right to left, with a gallery of celebrity intellectuals and experts used as crucial relays in the witch-hunt. The opinion column in *Le Point* magazine of November 28, 2018, undersigned by 80 French intellectuals, scholars, and writers, is a perfect model of its type. The socio-professional profile of the signatories reveals that, in their overwhelming majority, they belong to an older generation of academics and writers, hold high position in academia (professorship and higher), and are mostly male. They are all well known for their conservative and Republican biases, their defense of liberal feminism and of the French *laïcité*. In the column, they present themselves as the target of decolonial attackers "ostracizing" them—reviving colonial anxieties where those in positions of domination present themselves as victims—and of "lacking scientificity," a reactivation of the colonial idea that only the scientific system underpinning Western modernity may act as bearer of the truth. Additionally, they portray themselves as the true defenders of the (French) state and its universal values, writing as if state violence did not exist, as if logics of exclusion and precariousness were not permanently at play in the very institutions they are serving. Finally, the signatories call upon the state and the judicial system to act and prevent decolonial "gangs" from further interventions. I translate from the column:

> Yet, while posing as progressive people (antiracists, decolonizers, feminists …), these movements are in reality engaged in the diversion of struggles for individual emancipation and liberty, to the benefit of objectives which are their very opposites and constitute frontal attacks of Republican universalism, namely racialism, differentialism, segregationalism (based on skin color, sex, and religious practice). They go as far as to invoke feminism in order to legitimate the veil, *laïcité* in order to vindicate their religious rights, and universalism in order to support communitarianism. Finally, they denounce, against all odds, a clamp down of "state racism" in France—the very same state from which they demand, and from which they incidentally receive, benevolence and financial support through social security. ("Le 'décolonialisme'" n. pag.)

Republican universalism is here paired with the habitual anti-poor and anti-immigrant discourse of stealing jobs and benefiting from state pensions in order once again not to engage with the critical interventions of decolonial scholars. In *Le Figaro* of May 10, 2019, journalist Judith Waintraub uses the term *noyautage* (meaning "infiltration") to describe the work of scholars involved in decolonial, Islamic, and gender studies. Calling them indigenous "gangs," accusing them of collusion with radical student unions and of infiltrating the university, her article constitutes a frightening instance of the campaign of disparagement and discredit launched against decolonial studies in French mainstream media in order to prevent proper intellectual debates from taking place. The "decolonials" are considered politically subversive, as enemies of the interior, and are never engaged with on theoretical terms. The fact that Waintraub uses the context of student and staff protests against the discriminatory rise in the university fees of foreigners to lambast the decolonial field constitutes a crude indication of where these journalists position themselves on the political spectrum. The French mainstream Left and its media outlet (*Le Monde*, *L'Obs*) does not do any better to dispel the confusion, especially when it comes to decolonizing Islam. In what he presents as a "formal investigation" and assessment dated November 38, 2018, Matthieu Aron fails to address decoloniality as an academic field and persistently describes it as a "dogmatic" movement, reducing its scope to the all-too-politicized debate over the veil and terrorism (see Aron). For a French reader with no prior knowledge on the state of the arts, decolonial scholars become supporters in disguise of bearded terrorists.

Fortunately, there has been an attempt to clear a space, albeit limited and fragile, for proper debate over decolonial matters in France, via publications and French translations of American writers in Spanish and in English.[5] The independent news website *Mediapart*[6] and scientific journals such as *Cahiers des Amériques Latines*, *Mouvements*, *Multitudes*, and *Tumultes*[7] are redressing the balance and providing a clearer picture and much more scientifically relevant debate over the function of the decolonial turn in the resistant Humanities. Furthermore, workshops, summer schools—such as the one funded by an Erasmus Mundus grant at the philosophy department of the University of Toulouse in August 2016 and entitled "Philosophies européennes et décolonisation de la pensée"—as well as publications and conferences[8] are crucial tools to push against a French culture of hysteria, which eludes the real issues of race, Islam, and colonial history, by resorting to disparagement, lambast, and intellectual dishonesty towards decolonial thinking.

Conclusion

This article positions itself as a critical survey of the "decolonial turn" in the Humanities at large (not just in philosophy) and how it has productively affected the conception of knowledge in the West, by averring that a traditional understanding of the Humanities has led to epistemicides, and that a decolonial approach to the Humanities as pluriversal is possible.

In literature, for instance, a decolonial approach would include what we identify as postcolonial preoccupations, such as taking issue with the ways in which canons were/are conceived, with the ways in which literatures are made to operate along national borders, with inequalities of accessing books and e-prints, with the outsourcing of proof-editing jobs to countries of the global South (Malaysia and India, for instance), with lower-paid workers to accrue benefits for the big publishing groups based in the global North. The decolonial option entails this postcolonial critique along with an articulation of alternatives to dominant conceptions of knowledge and culture. Thus, a decolonial conception of literature would provide critics with the tools to study scribal literatures for instance, or forms of "writing without words" (see Boone and Mignolo). It would look at places where the modern/colonial dichotomy between oral and written spheres of literary expressions is not the norm but the exception, all the while reminding Western readers of the current colonial forces at play to invisibilize other canons and other ways to do literature.

The decolonial approach combines a postcolonial critique of the current world order as reflected in the distinction between dominant and dominated epistemic formations along with a recognition of the necessity to decenter and pluralize knowledge, and to conceptualize and experience the world otherwise. That said, the article takes issue with some of the criticism that decolonial literature made against postcolonial studies. While recognizing the Western theoretical framework of postcolonialism, it also highlights parallels between the postcolonial turn in anthropology and the decolonial turn in philosophy and sheds light on overlapping concerns with regards to the continuity of colonial structures of power under globalization today. It is crucial not to reduce postcolonialism to what conservative opponents have made of it, namely, a plot engineered by Black and Asian Americans to colonize the social sciences with a program of unwanted reforms, or to undermine it as yet another avatar of Western theoretical domination and make it say what it never claimed, namely, that we live in a "post-colonial" age.

However, by exposing the genealogy of the field and its main conceptual tools, I aimed to highlight the points of departure between the two fields (for instance in my analysis of the difference between postcolonial Third Space and decolonial border-thinking) and between a postcolonial and contestatory or dissident use of Western theory directed against power and a decolonial adoption of other-than-Western theoretical frameworks.

In mapping contentious, and sometimes violent, receptions of the field in the South African, British, and French academic contexts, the article explained how this needs to be related to a concatenation of various forces, including capitalism, secular liberalism, racism, and colonialism.

While urging for a better understanding of the critical force of decoloniality in academia, the article has also raised important questions regarding what it believes to be still under-theorized zones of the field, namely, the question of the interactions of various (when not adversarial) epistemic formations under pluriversality and its reliance on a monolithic version of "the" West and of "modernity." For instance, Bruno Latour argues in *Nous n'avons jamais été modernes* that the early-modern separation—what he calls "purification"—between experimental and political sciences, between objects and humans, between nature and culture, on which Western modernity was built has hidden and even actually fostered the production of hybrids (See Latour). The more experimental science constitutes itself as objective and a-political, the more social it becomes. While, in theory, the "modern Constitution" claims a separation of the spheres, in reality it facilitates and accelerates the deployment of collectives, the only trouble being that it has invisibilized this production and no longer has the means to conceptualize it.

The point I am emphasizing here is that while the decolonial critique is correct in analyzing the political force of Western modern ideology as it globalized and colonized the rest of the world, it is putting itself in the somewhat ambiguous position of restating/reinforcing the myth it combats. The article does not call into question the reality of the modern/colonial system and the effects, direct and indirect, it has had on conceptualizing the dominant nomos of the earth since the discovery of the Americas by European powers, and on structuring relations among humans, and between humans and non-humans. Nevertheless, it outlines the need for a more finely grained description of categories it resorts to, such as "the" West and "modernity," and advanced engagement with the power relations that infallibly must also animate the other epistemological orders and cosmovisions it brings to light.

Notes

[1] Such scholars include Enrique Dussel, Argentinian and Mexican academic who has held various positions in Mexico and the US; Boaventura de Sousa Santos, Professor at the School of Economics, the University of Coimbra, Portugal, and distinguished scholar at the University of Wisconsin Law School and the University of Warwick; Arturo Escobar, Colombian-American anthropologist and Professor of anthropology at the University of North Carolina at Chapel Hill, USA; Santiago Castro-Gómez, Colombian philosopher, Professor at the Pontificia Universidad Javeriana, and the di-

rector of the Pensar Institute in Bogotá; Ramón Grosfoguel, Puerto-Rican sociologist and now Associate Professor at the University of California, Berkeley; Aníbal Quijano (d. 2018), Peruvian sociologist; Walter D. Mignolo, Argentinian semiotician, educated at the École des Hautes Études in Paris, and professor at Duke University; Catherine Walsh, who describes herself as an intellectual-militant for social/racial justice active in the US and, over the past 25 years, in Ecuador and Latin America.

[2] The link among capitalism, colonialism, and modernity is foundational to what decolonial thinkers name the Western episteme. The interactions are exposed in several studies, and I refer readers specifically to Mignolo's *The Darker Side of the Renaissance* and Grosfoguel's "Colonial Difference."

[3] One example, for instance, is the MA Euro-Philosophie at the universities Toulouse 2 Jean Jaurès in France and Louvain in Belgium, financed by the ERASMUS+ program of the European Union, and which has organized a seminar series and a summer school. Another example is the Critical Muslim Studies network which organizes an annual summer school entitled "Decolonial Struggles and Liberation Theologies" usually in Granada, Spain, and in 2020 at the University of Johannesburg.

[4] For further details on the movement within the South African context of social inequality and racial violence post-colonization and post-apartheid, see Nyamnjoh.

[5] RED or Réseau d'Études Décoloniales, for instance, plays a major role in publishing online translations of decolonial thinkers in Spanish and Portuguese with free access (see *Réseau*).

[6] See, for instance, the article *Mediapart* published by Olivier Le Cour Grandmaison, a specialist in French colonization of Algeria. Le Cour Grandmaison equates the current panic about the decolonial movement in French universities with previous collective hysteria about the "Red threat" and Marxism (see Le Cour Grandmaison).

[7] *Cahiers des Amériques Latines* (n°62/2009) published various articles in French related to decolonial studies, including one by Capucine Boidin entitled "Études décoloniales et postcoloniales dans les débats français" and another by Walter Mignolo entitled "La fin de l'université telle que nous la connaissons," in a special issue of the journal. In *Mouvements* (n°72/2012), see Seloua Luste Boulbina et al.'s "Décoloniser les savoirs." *Multitudes* had a special issue (n°59/Summer 2015) on "Décoloniser la laïcité" edited by Amer Meziane Mohamed. And, finally, I must mention two recent publications: Zahra Ali and Sonia Dayan-Herzbrun's "Pluriversalisme décolonial" and Françoise Vergès's *Un féminisme décolonial*.

[8] See, for instance, the first decolonial convention in France in 2018 entitled "Bandung du Nord: Vers une internationale décoloniale." The filiation between the decolonization moment and the decolonial turn is clearly flagged in the choice of title for the conference. Obviously, the fact that it took place at the Bourse du Travail (trade union center) in St Denis, a *banlieue* north of Paris, is not incidental. Panels tackled issues of inter-community racism, strategic alliances, police state and state repression in the North, intersections between oppressed feminine and masculine identities, overcoming the modernity paradigm, and left-wing political alliances (see "Bandung").

Works Cited

"#RHODESMUSTFALL." *RMF Oxford*. <https://rmfoxford.wordpress.com/>.

Ali, Zahra, ed. *Féminismes islamiques*. Paris : La Fabrique éditions, 2015.

Ali, Zahra and Sonia Dayan-Herzbrun, eds. *Pluriversalisme décolonial* [Special issue of *Tumultes* n°48]. Paris : Éditions Kimé, 2017.

Anzaldúa, Gloria. *Borderlands/La Frontera: The New Mestiza*. San Francisco: Aunt Lute, 1987.

---. "Preface: (Un)natural Bridges, (Un)safe Spaces." *This Bridge We Call Home: Radical Visions for Transformation*. Eds. Gloria Anzaldúa and Analouise Keating. NY: Routledge, 2002. 1-5.

Aron, Matthieu. "Les 'décoloniaux' à l'assaut des universités." *L'Obs*. 30 Novembre, 2018. <https://www.nouvelobs.com/societe/20181130.OBS6347/les-decoloniaux-a-l-assaut-des-universites.html>.

Asad, Talal. *Formations of the Secular: Christianity, Islam, Modernity*. Stanford, CA: Stanford UP, 2003.

"Bandung du Nord: Vers une internationale décoloniale." <http://bandungdunord.webflow.io>.

Basso, Keith. *Wisdom Sits in Places: Landscape and Language Among the Western Apache*. Abulquerque: U of New Mexico P, 1996.

Bayart, Jean-François. *Les études postcoloniales, un carnaval académique*. Paris : Éditions Karthala, 2010.

Bhabha, Homi. *The Location of Culture*. London: Routledge, 1994.

Bhambra, Gurminder K. et al., eds. *Decolonising the University*. London: Pluto P, 2018.

"Black Female Professors Must Deal with Bullying to Win Promotion, Report Finds." *The Guradian*. February 4, 2019. <https://www.theguardian.com/education/2019/feb/04/black-female-professors-report>.

Boidin, Capucine. "Études décoloniales et postcoloniales dans les débats français." *Cahiers des Amériques Latines* 62 (2009). 129-40. <https://journals.openedition.org/cal/1620>.

Boone, Elizabeth Hill and Walter Mignolo, eds. *Writing Without Words: Alternative Literacies in Mesoamerica and the Andes*. Durham: Duke UP, 1994.

Botha, M. M. "Africanising the Curriculum: An Exploratory Study." *South African Journal of Higher Education* 21.2 (2007): 202-16.

Boulbina, Seloua Luste et al. "Décoloniser les savoirs: Internationalisation des débats et des luttes." *Mouvements* 72.4 (2012) : 7-10. <https://www.cairn.info/revue-mouvements-2012-4-page-7.htm#>.

Boutledja, Houria. "Le 'racisme anti-blanc' des Indigènes de la République." *Nous sommes les indigènes de la Républiques*. Eds. Houria Boutledja et al. Paris : Éditions Amsterdam, 2012. 378-80.

--- et al. *Nous sommes les indigènes de la Républiques*. Paris : Éditions Amsterdam, 2012.

Bozalek, V. and M. Zembylas. "Critical Posthumanism, New Materialisms and the Affective Turn for Socially Just Pedagogies in Higher Education." *South African Journal of Higher Education* 30. 3 (2016): 193-200.

Castro-Gómez, Santiago. *Zero-Point Hubris: Science, Race, and Enlightenment in New Granada (1750-1816)*. Trans. George Ciccariello-Maher and Don T. Deere. Lanham, MD: Rowman & Littlefield International, forthcoming [2020].

Chakrabarty, Dipesh. *Provincializing Europe: Postcolonial Thought and Historical Difference*. Princeton, NJ: Princeton UP, 2000.

Chibber, Vivek. *Postcolonial Theory and the Specter of Capital*. London: Verso, 2013.

Clavreul, Gilles. "Radiographie de la mouvance décoloniale : Entre influence culturelle et tentations politiques." *Fondation Jean Jaurès/Penser pour agir*. December 22, 2017. <shorturl.at/mCLSX>.

Clifford, James. *Returns: Becoming Indigenous in the Twenty-First Century*. Cambridge, MA: Harvard UP, 2013.

Council on Higher Education (CHE). *A Proposal for Undergraduate Curriculum Reform*. Pretoria: CHE, 2013.

"Le 'décolonialisme', une stratégie hégémonique : l'appel de 80 intellectuels." *Le Point*. 28 Novembre, 2018. <shorturl.at/yGNT8>.

"Decolonising the Curriculum: Towards a Manifesto." *TORCH: The Oxford Research Centre in the Humanities*. <https://www.torch.ox.ac.uk/event/decolonising-the-curriculum-towards-a-manifesto>.

Devisch, René and Francis Nyamnjoh, eds. *Postcolonial Turn: Re-Imagining Anthropology and Africa*. Bamenda: Langaa Research and Publishing CIG; Leiden: African Studies Centre, 2011.

Diversi, Marcelo and Claudio Moreira. *Betweener Talk: Decolonizing Knowledge Production, Pedagogy, and Praxis*. Walnut Creek, CA: Left Coast P Inc., 2009.

Emeagwali, Gloria. *Africa and the Academy: Challenging Hegemonic Discourses on Africa*. Trenton, NJ: Africa World P, 2006.

--- and George J. Sefa Dei. *African Indigenous Knowledge and the Disciplines*. Rotterdam: Sense Publishers, 2014.

Esack, Farid. *Qur'an, Liberation and Pluralism*. Oxford: Oneworld, 1997.

Escobar, Arturo. *Encountering Development: The Making and Unmaking of the Third World*. Princeton, NJ: Princeton UP, 1996.

---. *Designs for the Pluriverse*. Durham, NC: Duke UP, 2018.

---. *Feel-thinking with the Earth*. Medellin, Colombia: Ediciones Unaula, 2014.

"The Experiences of Black and Minority Ethnic Staff in Further and Higher Education." *UCU: University and College Union*. February 2016. <shorturl.at/exLV8>.

Fanon, Franz. *Black Skin, White Masks*. Trans. Charles L. Markmann. NY: Grove P, 1967.

---. *Peau Noires, masques blancs*. Paris : Éditions du Seuil, 1952.

Fataar, Aslam. "Decolonising Education in South Africa: Perspectives and Debates." *Educational Research for Social Change (ERSC)* 7 (June 2018): vi-ix.

--- and S. Subreenduth. "The Search For Ecologies of knowledge in the Encounter with African Epistemicide in South African Education." *South African Journal of Higher Education* 29.2 (2015): 106-21.

Feld, Steven. *Bosavi: Rainforest Music from Papua New Guinea*. Washington DC: Smithsonian Folkways, 2001.

---, dir. *Voices of the Rainforest, A Day in the Life of Bosavi Demo*. 2019. <https://vimeo.com/264683557>.

Freire, Paulo. *Pedagogy of the Oppressed*. Trans. Myra Bergman Ramos. NY: Seabury P, 1970.

"Gdi-nweninaa (Our Voice—Our Sound)." *The Revitalization of the Nishnaabemwin Language Project*. <http://www.trentu.ca/faculty/rnl/lexicon.html>.

Glowczewski, Barbara. *Les Rêveurs du désert. Peuple Warlpiri d'Australie*. Paris : Actes Sud, 1996.

---. "Standing with the Earth: From Cosmopolitical Exhaustion to Indigenous Solidarities." *Inflexions* 10 (October 2017): 1-24. <http://www.senselab.ca/inflexions/exhaustion/main.html#n2>.

Gran, Peter et al., eds. *History after the Three Worlds: Post-Eurocentric Historiographies*. Lanham, MA: Rowman & Littlefield, 2000.

le Grange, L. "Decolonising the University Curriculum." *South African Journal of Higher Education* 30.2 (2016): 1-12.

Grosfoguel, Ramón. "Colonial Difference, Geopolitics of Knowledge, and Global Coloniality in the Modern/Colonial Capitalist World-System." *Review* 25.3 (2002): 203-24.

---. "Decolonizing Post-Colonial Studies and Paradigms of Political-Economy: Transmodernity, Decolonial Thinking, and Global Coloniality." *Transmodernity* 1.1 (2011). <https://escholarship.org/content/qt21k6t3fq/qt21k6t3fq.pdf>.

Hage, Ghassan. *Is Racism an Environmental Threat?* Cambridge: Polity P, 2017.

Hau'ofa, Epeli. "The Writer as an Outsider." *We are the Ocean: Selected Works*. Honolulu: U of Hawai'i P, 2008. 97-109.

hooks, bell. *Learning to Transgress: Education as the Practice of Freedom*. NY: Routledge, 1994.

Karimi, Hanane. "Assignation à l'altérité radicale et chemins d'émancipation : étude de l'agency de femmes musulmanes françaises." Diss. Université de Strasbourg, 2018.

Lamrabet, Asma. *Women in The Qur'an: An Emancipatory Reading*. Markfield: Kube Publishing, 2016.

Latour, Bruno. *Nous n'avons jamais été modernes : Essai d'anthropologie symétrique*. Paris : Éditions La Découverte, 1991.

Le Cour Grandmaison, Olivier. "Universités : La 'dictature des identités' et des minorités 'indigénistes'?" *Mediapart*. 23 Avril, 2019. <https://blogs.mediapart.fr/olivier-le-cour-grandmaison/blog/230419/universites-la-dictature-des-identites-et-des-minorites-indigenistes>.

lo Liyong, Taban. "Language and Literature Studies at University College Nairobi." *Research in African Literatures* 2.2 (Autumn 1971): 168-76.

Mahmood, Saba. *The Politics of Piety: The Islamic Revival and the Feminist Subject*. Princeton: Princeton UP, 2005.

Maldonado-Torres, Nelson. "Outline of Ten Theses on Coloniality and Decoloniality." *Frantz Fanon Foundation*. 2016. <shorturl.at/achjr>.

---. "Thinking through the Decolonial Turn: Post-continental Interventions in Theory, Philosophy, and Critique–An Introduction." *Transmodernity:*

Journal of Peripheral Cultural Production of the Luso-Hispanic World 1.2 (Fall 2011): 1-15.

Martin-Muñoz, Gema, et al. *Islamophobie dans le monde moderne*. Paris : Institut International de la Pensée Islamique, 2008.

Mbembe, Achille. "Decolonizing Knowledge and the Question of the Archive." <shorturl.at/fvKY2>.

---. "Decolonizing the University: New directions." *Arts and Humanities in Higher Education* 15.1 (2016): 29-45.

Mohamed, Amer Meziane, ed. *Multitudes* 59 (Summer 2015). [Special issue on "Décoloniser la laïcité?"].

Mignolo, Walter. "Colonial and Postcolonial Discourse: Cultural Critique or Academic Colonialism?" *Latin American Research Review* 28.3 (1993): 120–34.

---. "The Conceptual Triad: Modernity/Coloniality/Decoloniality." Walter Mignolo and Catherine Walsh. *On Decoloniality: Concepts, Analytics, Praxis*. Durham: Duke UP, 2018. 135-52.

---. *The Darker Side of the Renaissance: Literacy, Territoriality, and Colonization*. Ann Arbor, MI: Michigan UP, 1995.

---. *The Darker Side of Western Modernity: Global Futures, Decolonial Options*. Durham: Duke UP, 2011.

---. "De-Colonial Cosmopolitanism and Dialogues among Civilizations." *Routledge Handbook of Cosmopolitan Studies*. Ed. Gerard Delanty. NY: Routledge, 2012.

---. "Delinking: The Rhetoric of Modernity, the Logic of Coloniality and the Grammar of De-Coloniality." *Cultural Studies* 21.2-3 (2007): 449–514.

---. "Epistemic Disobedience, Independent Thought, and De-Colonial Freedom." *Theory, Culture, and Society* 26.7-8 (2009): 159-81.

---. "La fin de l'université telle que nous la connaissons." *Cahiers des Amériques Latines* 62 (2009). 97-109. <https://journals.openedition.org/cal/1608>.

---. *Local Histories/Global Designs: Coloniality, Subaltern Knowledges, and Border Thinking*. Princeton, NJ: Princeton UP, 2000.

---. "Re-emerging, Decentering and Delinking. Shifting the Geographies of Sensing, Believing and Knowing." *IBRAAZ*. May 8, 2013. <http://www.ibraaz.org/essays/59>.

--- and Madina Vladimirovna Tlostanova. "Theorizing from the Borders: Shifting to Geo- and Body-Politics of Knowledge." *European Journal of Social Theory* 9.2 (2006): 205–21.

--- and Catherine Walsh. *On Decoloniality: Concepts, Analytics, Praxis*. Durham: Duke UP, 2018.

Muswede, T. "Colonial Legacies and the Decolonisation Discourse in Post-Apartheid South Africa." *African Journal of Public Affairs* 9.5 (2017): 200-10.

Ndoferipi, A. "African Universities on a Global Ranking Scale: Legitimation of Knowledge Hierarchies?" *South African Journal of Higher Education* 31.1 (2017): 155-74.

Ndlovu-Gatsheni, Sabelo J. and Siphamandla Zondi. *Decolonizing the University, Knowledge Systems and Disciplines in Africa*. Durham: Carolina Academic P, 2016.

Ngũgĩ wa Thiong'o. *Decolonizing the Mind: The Politics of Language in African Literature*. Suffolk: Boydell and Brewer Ltd., 1981.

---. "On the Abolition of the English Department." *The Post-colonial Studies Reader*. Eds. Bill Ashcroft et al. Routledge: London, 1995. 438-42.

"Noyauter." *CNTRL*. <https://www.cnrtl.fr/definition/noyauter>.

Nyamnjoh, Francis B. *#RhodesMustFall: Nibbling at Resilient Colonialism in South Africa*. Mankon: Langaa Research and Publishing Common Initiative Group, 2016.

Pandey, Gyanendra. *Routine Violence: Nations, Fragments, Histories*. Redwood City, CA: Stanford UP, 2005.

Panikkar, Raimundo. *Myth, Faith, and Hermeneutics*. NY: Paulist, 1979.

Réseau d'Études Décoloniales. <http://reseaudecolonial.org>.

Roy, Arundhati. *The Ministry of Utmost Happiness*. London: Hamish Hamilton, 2017.

Sakai, Naoki. *Translation and Subjectivity: On Japan and Cultural Nationalism*. Minneapolis: U of Minnesota P, 1997.

---. and Jon Solomon, eds. *Translation, Biopolitics, Colonial Difference*. Hong-Kong: Hong-Kong UP, 2006.

--- and Yukiko Hanawa, eds. *Specters of the West and the Politics of Translation*. Ithaca: Cornell UP, 2001.

Santos, Boaventura de Sousa. "Beyond Abyssal Thinking: From Global Lines to Ecologies of Knowledges." *Review* 30.1 (2007): 45-89.

---. *Epistemologies of the South: Justice against Epistemicide*. Boulder: Paradigm Publishers, 2014.

Sayyid, Salman. *Recalling the Caliphate: Decolonisation and World Order*. London: Hurst and Company, 2014.

Scholte, Bob. "Reason and Culture: The Universal and the Particular Revisited." *American Anthropologist* 86.4 (1984): 960–65.

Simpson, Leanne Betasamosake. *Dancing on Our Turtle's Back*. Winnipeg: Arbeiter Ring Publishing, 2011.

Skafish, Peter. "The Metaphysics of Extra-Moderns: On the Decolonization of Thought—A Conversation with Eduardo Viveiros de Castro." *Common Knowledge* 22.3 (2016): 393-414.

Smith, Linda Tuhiwai. *Decolonizing Methodologies: Research and Indigenous Peoples*. NY and London: Zed Books, 1999.

Tlostanova, Madina Vladimirovna and Walter Mignolo. *Learning to Unlearn: Decolonial Reflections from Eurasia and the Americas*. Columbus, OH: Ohio State UP, 2012.

---. "On Pluri-topic Hermeneutics, Trans-modern Thinking, and Decolonial Philosophy." *Encounters* 1.1 (Fall 2009): 11-27.

Vergès, Françoise. *Un féminisme décolonial*. Paris : La Fabrique Éditions, 2019.

Viveiros de Castro, Eduardo. *Cannibal Metaphysics*. Trans. and ed. Peter Skafish. Minneapolis, MN: Univocal, 2014.

Waintraub, Judith. "Islamo-gauchisme, décolonialisme, théorie du genre… Le grand noyautage des universités." May 10, 2019. <shorturl.at/DMOSV>.

Wallerstein, Immanuel Maurice. *European Universalism: The Rhetoric of Power*. NY: New P, 2006.

Wane, Njoki Nathani and Kimberley L. Todd, eds. *Decolonial Pedagogies: Examining Sites of Resistance, Resurgence, and Renewal*. NY: Palgrave, 2018.

Williams, Shirley Ida. *Gdi-Nweninaa: Our Sound, Our Voice*. Peterborough, Ontario: Neganigwane Company, 2002.

The Cultural Turn in the Study of Arabic Literature

Antonio Pacifico

In his keynote speech at the 11th EURAMAL (European Association for Modern Arabic Literature) conference held in Madrid, May 7-10, 2014, Roger Allen points out that the field is "considerably more variegated and elaborate than it was during its earliest phases in the mid-20th century" ("Transforming" 22). He additionally notes that nowadays "scholars in modern Arabic literature studies conduct their research within the framework of a set of theoretical principles that are shared with similar specialists in other world literary traditions" (22). The field, according to him, is experiencing a "pleasing and ongoing expansion in the parameters" employed for the analysis of this heterogeneous literary production (24). Allen was probably not the only scholar at that conference to think that way. In fact, during the past few decades, the fields of study on modern Arabic literature(s) as well as on classical and post-classical Arab periods have witnessed a number of unprecedented developments. This is evident, for instance, in the significant increase in scholarly publications available on such prominent databases as Index Islamicus which records all published material in European languages on matters related to Islam and the Muslim world (Snir ix).[1] This is even more apparent in the large variety of new approaches that, together with new multi-perspectival insights and methods, have helped (re)shape our understanding of this massive and thriving body of symbolic goods. In this regard, one may note that after World War II the field opened itself to various contributions coming from neighboring disciplines, and that it was then that its areas of research came to include contemporary productions of the Arab world(s). If before that time the range of inquiry was dominated only by texts written in classical Arabic, since then and up to the present day, modern Arabic has also received increased attention. In a similar way, colloquial materials have become more frequent subjects of research, as have writings dealing with politically or socially marginalized groups: women, ethnic and/or religious minorities, etc.

Nonetheless, over the course of this long phase from the aftermath of World War II to the current moment, the field of Arabic literary studies has been confronted with multiple dramatic events that have forced its actors, on many occasions, to modify their theoretical frameworks vis-à-vis the literary texts of Arab writers and "scribes" (see Jacquemond, *Entre scribes*). These events, of course, encompass the Palestinian exodus of 1948, best known as the *nakba*, the peak of Arab nationalism and Pan-Arabism during the 1950s, and the disillusionment that followed the Six-day war in 1967.[2] Yet they also include some more recent phenomena, like the constant process of Islamization that has spread in many Arab countries from the 1970s onwards.[3] All the dramatic and radical changes mentioned above have certainly had an impact that expanded far beyond the field of study of modern and contemporary literature(s) to affect even the analysis of older and medieval literary productions. However, while some of the main turning points of Arab cultural history have already been investigated by scholars working in this field, its cultural turn that has recently taken place, especially in the West, still needs to be scrutinized in more detail. This requires looking at the literary texts of the Arab world mainly as cultural practices, avoiding a process of analysis that focuses solely on their textual dimension. Adopting the main assumptions of Cultural Studies, using concepts from other disciplines in the Humanities and the Social Sciences, scholars who follow this latter approach have also carried out a specific type of literary investigation where issues such as social agency, ideology, or authority gain prominence. Moreover, they have also contributed to demystifying the literary terrain, rendering often excluded and marginalized practices more important.

After all, as Allen puts it, "Literary Histories also have their own History" ("Literary History" 205) and this process is not without vulnerabilities and problematic aspects that must be addressed in greater depth, too. Suffice it to say that some of the elements that are intimately related to the birth and the development of this epistemological turn in the study of Arabic literature, such as the methods and concepts of the field of Cultural Studies, are still struggling to find their way in the Middle East and North Africa (see El Hamamsy and Soliman). Or that this approach, also in the West, has been applied in a different and uneven manner, depending on specific cultural histories, especially given the cross-disciplinary sensibility that this cultural approach requires. From this point of view, the academic fields of English-speaking countries seem to be less compartmentalized precisely because of their deeply-rooted tradition in the area of Cultural Studies that has enabled many scholars to escape the "hegemony of the text" and, at the same time, has facilitated the circulation of different frameworks and research methods within the Humanities, as well as across the Humanities and the Social Sciences in a broader sense.[4] Conversely, despite the use of post-structuralist, feminist theories or other research tools, such as for instance those elaborated in the field of psychoanalysis, the academic fields of other European countries are a long way from achieving the same level of interdisciplinarity and dialogue between different disciplines; not to mention that this condition gets even worse when it comes to the field of Arabic studies (Jacquemond, "Un mai" 134-35).

In light of the above, and without any claim to offering an exhaustive and comprehensive account of all the efforts made in this area over the past years, the present article aims to (re)map not only the main trends of the cultural turn existing today in the field of Arabic literary studies, but also its multiple histories and distinct practices. Far from a normative perspective that would focus on dating beginnings and, maybe, even locating a precise place of birth for such a phenomenon, it will also deploy a diachronic approach in order to reflect on both the causes underlying the most striking uncertainties as well as the future directions of these trends. Therefore, some of the radical changes that Arab civil societies have been involved in, recently, will be connected even more directly to several paradigms of their respective "fields of cultural production" (see Bourdieu). By way of illustration, one may look at the rapid growth and proliferation of sophisticated forms of media, particularly Internet-related technologies, that have opened up new possibilities for literary experimentation, such as blogging, techno-writing, and interactive literature (see Pepe).[5] But the Information Technology Revolution still represents only one element in a whole variety of unprecedented and unexpected developments that had a bearing on the cultural practices produced in contemporary Arab context(s). As noted by Jacquemond, numerous studies have shown that the transformations that occurred in the Arabic cultural fields before and after the uprisings of 2011-2012 led to a larger individualization of the mechanisms of production and consumption of the symbolic goods, along with a greater level of their commodification and the emergence of a wide range of artistic forms that blur the boundaries between what is often called "high culture," on the one hand, and what we usually name in a less prejudiced way "popular culture," on the other ("Un mai 143). In the same vein, other eminent scholars, such as Stephan Guth, Barbara Winckler, and Tarek El-Ariss have come to similar conclusions for the more specific literary subfields (see Guth, "Programs"; Winckler; El-Ariss, *Trials*).[6] Hence, an accurate investigation of the main principles and the potential of what has been termed here the cultural turn in the study of Arabic Literature may prove to be crucial even for a better engagement of this portion of Literary studies with extra-academic pressures coming from the subject(s) of their analyses.

Interdisciplinary Perspectives and Genesis of the Cultural Turn

The main trends of the cultural turn that the present article seeks to map out have not materialized out of thin air. As indicated above, some of the revolutionary elements inherent in its innovative approach have resulted from the pooling of knowledge and practices between the Humanities and other academic fields, primarily the Social Sciences. This intense exchange of elements amongst different scholarly frameworks, also known as interdisciplinarity, has entailed for several scholars working in the field of Arabic literature the familiarity with components of two or more neighboring disciplines as well as overcoming thematic and methodological boundaries.[7] That said, the interdisciplinary turn, that seems to have started during the 1980s following a preliminary phase throughout the 1970s, is not to be understood as a well-defined chronological stage that clearly precedes the one referred to in the previous section. It should rather be seen as an element that, together with other elements like those mentioned above, has played a crucial role in the birth and development of this cultural shift in Arabic literary studies.[8] In 1987, even a scholar working on classical Arabic poetry like Renate Jacobi overtly welcomed the opening up toward new concepts and methods as a positive, promising, and fertile trend. In her concise survey, "Allgemeine Charakteristik der arabischen Dichtung," she connected interdisciplinarity to another critical issue, namely, the move of Arabic poetry out of its exotic corner. Obviously, Jacobi wanted her subject of research to be accessible to comparative literatures and comparative studies in general, and it is with this in mind that she emphasizes the role of interdisciplinarity in replacing static ideas with more dynamic notions and strategies. In doing so, Jacobi demonstrates that this radical innovation had an impact well beyond the specific field of contemporary Arabic literary studies, with implications for the relationship between Western and non-Western intellectual histories.

During the same year, Fedwa Malti-Douglas made similar observations about the growing interdisciplinarity that characterized the field. Noting how this epistemological perspective led to the creation of "two bridges, that between Eastern and Western scholars of Arabic, and that between Arabic and Western literary studies" (274), she concludes that the research on Arabic literary texts has "progressed from the intellectual foundation provided by Anglo-American 'new criticism' through the current concern for the reintegration of the *hors-texte*, in a process of continual refinement and exploration of the implications of discourse and textuality" (275). According to Malti-Douglas, it is precisely by means of a cross-disciplinary approach that one could (re)incorporate all the extra-textual elements linked to the texts within the process of literary analysis. Yet, as she notes, all this was not free of risks, especially for the field of Arab studies. Malti-Douglas, in fact, cautions her reader by arguing that "Traditional Orientalism (and, in this sense, it has been taken over by area studies) was an interdisciplinary approach" and that "its practitioners skipped happily back and forth among linguistics, philosophy, history, and other academic specialties" (272). However, in contrast to cross-disciplinary investigations, the intellectual system of traditional Orientalism has too often "restricted Arabic literary studies to the twin areas of philology and a Lansonian literary history, one almost obsessively concerned with bio-bibliographical data and historical influences" (272).

Traces of a certain shift toward the breaking down of thematic and methodological boundaries may also be found in other initiatives by researchers in the field of Arabic literary studies. One of the most significant advances, in this respect, took place at both the 26th and the 27th congress of the German Oriental Society (Deutsche Morgenländische Gesellschaft) held in Leipzig in 1995 and in Bonn in 1998. In the course of these two conferences, a workshop entirely devoted to questions of method—and, more specifically, to interdisciplinarity—was convened (see Kilpatrick). The second conference, besides, was also followed by proceedings in which the authors—all working on texts of different Near Eastern literatures at the time—approached their subjects from a cross-disciplinary perspective. The book edited by Beatrice Gruendler and Verena Klemm titled *Understanding Near Eastern Literatures: A Spectrum of Interdisciplinary Approaches* is deeply engaged in the ongoing dialogue with literary theory by presenting nineteen different readings of Arabic, Persian, and Turkish works of classical and modern times. It is worth noting that the common ground amongst them was the shared belief that "interdisciplinarity begins for each of us individually as a confrontation with an unfamiliar approach and the question of the transferability of its categories and concepts," as the editors write in their introduction (4). Furthermore, each scholar was "required to examine to what extent externally developed concepts can suit his or her Near Eastern sources" (4-5). In other words, the main idea of this contribution was that the concrete implementation of interdisciplinarity should not be separated from the context of production of the literary texts and, more importantly, that in this specific case, interdisciplinarity may be practiced only by taking into account the relation between Arabic literature(s) and other intellectual traditions of the Middle East.

On the same subject, one may also consider another project undertaken by a group of noteworthy scholars during the 1990s. In 1999, Abdallah Cheikh-Moussa, Heidi Toelle, and Katia Zakharia decided to dedicate a special edition of *Arabica*—the French periodical founded by Evariste Lévy-Provençal—to questions of method and epistemological strategies. Their particular issue, given the title "Vers de Nouvelles Lectures de la Littérature Arabe" (Towards New Approaches to Arabic Literature), covered a wide variety of methodological aspects. All essays in the volume shared a belief in the possibilities and the potential of cross-disciplinary analyses. The three editors' position with regard to the topic of interdisciplinarity is made explicitly manifest. They strongly denounce a certain lack of dialogue between Arabic literary studies and other disciplines in the Humanities and the Social Sciences:

> On constate, en effet, une coupure presque complète entre les études littéraires arabes et les interrogations et les acquis dans les autres "sciences de l'homme et de la société." (Cheikh-Moussa et al 524)

> [We find, in fact, that there is an almost complete incommunicability between Arab Literary studies and the concerns and the achievements of other Humanities and the Social Sciences.][9]

But, far beyond that, Cheikh-Moussa, Toelle, and Zakharia firmly asserted the relevance of a cross-disciplinary perspective also with the purpose of seizing the highest number of elements that shape the literary texts, and not merely their textual components:

> Aussi, un même texte gagne-t-il à être abordé par différents chercheurs ayant chacun une seconde specialité, afin que l'éclairage pluridiscipinaire permette de mieux le lire. Il ne s'agit pas de prôner le travail d'équipe, dont l'utilité est manifeste, comme la seule approche salutaire des textes, mais au moins d'inciter les chercheurs à considérer que des perspectives différentes ne sont pas antithétiques; bien au contraire elles peuvent être utilement complémentaires. L'échange interdisciplinaire est donc une nécessité pour toute analyse des textes anciens ou modernes. (524-25)

> [Also, it would be appropriate for a text to be analyzed by different scholars each having a second specialization, since a multidisciplinary approach allows us to better read it. It is not a question of advocating teamwork, the usefulness of which is already obvious, as the only helpful approach to texts, but also to encourage researchers to consider that different perspectives are not antithetical. On the contrary, they may be usefully complementary. Interdisciplinary exchange is therefore a necessity for any analysis of ancient and modern texts.]

To all these initiatives, one should add a whole set of workshops, roundtables, and panels in conferences that have also promoted an interdisciplinary perspective of Arabic literary productions over the past few years. A recent example of this tendency is the call for a panel launched by some Arab academics, namely Marie Thérèse

Abdelmessih, Said Allouche, Lobna Ismail, and Fatiha Taib, in the context of the XXII ICLA (International Comparative Literary Association) congress, Macau, July 27-August 2, 2019. (see "Panel CFP").[10] The panel, called "Interdisciplinarity in Comparative Literature: Recent Prospects in Arabic Studies" encourages reflection on the cross-disciplinary dimension of comparative analyses in the field of Arabic studies by linking the issue of interdisciplinarity to the relation existing between Arabic literary history and other traditions.

Some recent school programs have been of great importance, too. They have supported, for instance, a certain (re)appropriation of the knowledge generated by the tireless work of renowned intellectuals of the past century like that of Edward Said. While Said's critique and its further development by Postcolonial studies belong today to the theoretical and methodological canon(s) of Arabic studies, his considerations have found their way into actual teaching and research practice also through the mediation of several educational activities, such as the one implemented by the Arabische Philologien im Blickwechsel.[11] Since 2013, this international bilingual school program has promoted a broad interdisciplinary approach to the literary texts of the Arab world, depending on the work of a large number of young researchers from both shores of the Mediterranean sea. It is not surprising, then, that some of the most significant contributions that have led to the genesis of the above-mentioned cultural turn could be found in initiatives such as the latter. Here, more than elsewhere, a certain epistemological openness and fluidity resulted in unexpected consequences.

The Cultural Turn in Arabic Literary Studies: Major Trends and Research Topics

Doubtless, not all efforts in the direction of a higher level of interdisciplinarity in the field of Arabic literary studies have directly translated into constitutive elements of what we referred to as their cultural turn. This radical breakthrough that has led a significant number of scholars to envisage the literary texts mainly as cultural practices has taken different forms, depending on the context and the quality of its actors' cross-disciplinary activity. Additionally, this phenomenon has emerged in several academic fields more than in others, and its main representatives, within its broad scope, have given rise to diverse and variegated trends. It has already been highlighted that the dissemination of the concepts and methods of Cultural Studies in a particular context may have played a major role in building a "cultural sensibility" towards Arabic literary production to a greater or lesser extent. But that has not been the only factor which has affected the growth and the development of this epistemological perspective.

Amongst the major trends related to this theoretical framework, a certain part of the work done in the French academic field and, more specifically, the excellent analyses conducted by such distinguished scholars and professors like Yves Gonzalez-Quijano or Richard Jacquemond are of particular interest. Despite the lack of dialogue between the Humanities and Social Sciences in the French field of Arabic studies, the latter have contributed more significantly by carrying out a variety of research projects.[12] At the same time, they have also contributed very actively to the epistemological debate surrounding the literary texts by providing alternative strategies and approaches. Examining the major contributions of this trend, one has to consider primarily the monograph by Yves Gonzalez-Quijano, *Les gens du livre: Édition et champ intellectuel dans l'Égypte républicaine*. In the book, Gonzalez-Quijano traces the mechanisms of production and consumption of texts produced in the Egyptian literary field, connecting them with political, religious, and social influences. He points out the relevance of many extra-textual elements, including laws regulating the processes of distribution or elements governing the economic market linked to the sale and the purchase of books. Likewise, he bequeaths to future generations of researchers at least two or three critical insights that cannot be ignored in the present survey. Referring to the long-standing tradition of French sociological studies on literature and art, Gonzalez-Quijano concludes that the production and distribution of of symbolic goods always occurs in a specific context with its own operating rules:

> En effet, la production et la diffusion des biens symboliques s'effectuent au sein d'un espace qui possède ses propres lois de fonctionnement, lesquelles tiennent à la spécificité de son produit. (*Les gens* 10)

> [Indeed, the production and the dissemination of symbolic goods takes place within a space which has its own operating rules that are related to the specificity of its product.]

His second insight concerns the relation between the texts and the social space in which they are produced, and may be seen as a consequence of the first. Indeed, according to Gonzalez-Quijano, one cannot avoid taking into account the symbolic norms that regulate a specific social space, except if one wants to end up exactly where one started:

> Car à ne pas se poser la question de la définition sociale de la culture et à faire l'impasse sur le rôle structurant de l'espace de production qui détermine, en fonction de combinaisons multiples, les différentes positions possibles au sein de l'espace de production, ou encore à mettre en relation directe, comme on l'a fait trop souvent, fait culturels et événements politiques censés s'éclairer mutuellement, on encourt très certainement le risque de ne retrouver, en fin de compte, que les présupposés de la recherche. (10)

> [Because if we don't reflect on the question of the social definition of culture and ignore the structuring role of the space of production that determines, through multiple combinations, different possible positions within the space of production, or if we establish a direct link, as has been done too often, between *faits culturels* and political events that are supposed to enlighten each other, we certainly incur the risk of finding, in the end, only the preliminary assumptions of our research.]

As for his third insight, it has to do with the sources that are usually employed by researchers in the field. In that regard, the author proposes to adopt a perspective that does not privilege the main actors of a cultural context, one that (re)integrates those elements that are usually considered of minor importance:

> On peut ainsi observer, à côté des premiers rôles en définitive assez bien connus (l'élite de l'élite intellectuelle ou encore la haute intelligentsia selon la formule de Régis Debray), tout un monde d'acteurs de second rang, intermédiaires et entrepreneurs culturels, consommateurs privilégiés, etc. (20)

> [We can thus observe, beyond the first actors that are in the end quite well-known (the elite of the intellectual elite or the high intelligentsia according to Régis Debray), a whole world of second-tier players, intermediaries and cultural entrepreneurs, privileged consumers, etc.][13]

Hence, he points to the elitism that has dominated the works of conventional Orientalism for so long.

Similar ideas, are proposed in another text by the same scholar: "Littérature arabe et société : Une problématique à renouveler. Le cas de la *nahḍa*". In this article, Gonzalez-Quijano draws on all the theoretical insights formulated in his former research in order to demonstrate that such an approach may prove crucial also to solve some of the most serious problems raised in the field, such as the severe lack of communication between scholars focusing on medieval literary texts and those working on modern and contemporary literature(s), or the dominance of the former over the latter. Here, deploying Bourdieusian terminology, the word "literature" is replaced by expressions like "fait littéraire" that allow the author to demystify the very notion of literary text as something that resembles much more a symbolic monument than a product of a certain epoch and society.

Jacquemond's writings are equally relevant in this regard, too. One could, for instance, look at his multiple works dedicated to the role of translation and the status of satiric literature and other popular genres. His pioneering research on the Egyptian literary field, "Le champ littéraire égyptien depuis 1967," has shown the importance of the Bourdieusian notion of "field of cultural production" with respect to the literary production of the contemporary Arab world:

> Le recours à la notion de champ ainsi définie permet donc d'analyser les débats sur la définition de la littérature et de l'écrivain, dans une perspective non plus théorique, mais sociologique, autrement dit, de prendre ces définitions pour qu'elles sont en réalité : des prises de positions par lesquels leurs auteurs se situent au sein de cet espace social spécifique qu'est le champ littéraire—et souvent, du même coup, au sein de l'espace global. (14)

[The application of the notion of field defined in this way allows us to analyze the debate on the definition of literature and the writer from a perspective that is no longer theoretical, but sociological. In other words, this allows us to take these definitions for what they really are, i.e., positions taken by their authors in order to situate themselves within this specific social space that is the literary field—and often, at the same time, within the global space.]

Yet this last notion could only be applied to the Arab context after several adjustments:

Cela dit, l'application au contexte égyptien contemporain d'un modèle théorique élaboré essentiellement à partir du cas du XIX siècle français ne va pas sans difficultés et impose certains aménagements. (15)

[That said, the application of a theoretical model developed essentially from the case of French nineteenth century to the contemporary Egyptian context is not without difficulties, and requires certain adjustments.]

Similar meaningful reflections can also be traced in one of his most recent articles—also based on Bourdieusian theory—titled "Un mai 68 arabe ? La révolution égyptienne au prisme du culturel." More broadly, one could note that while Gonzalez-Quijano proposes an epistemological strategy capable of shedding light on the whole set of elements that form a text, Jacquemond has been much more engaged in identifying the forces that shape a given field of literary production. However, Jacquemond has also argued for an epistemological approach that consists, first of all, of embracing an interdisciplinary perspective and, secondly, investigating the context of consumption of the literary texts, along with the mechanisms of their production:

Cette approche par le culturel peut être comprise–et pratiquée–de deux manières : la plus courante–et la plus aisée–est celle qui consiste à analyser les productions culturelles, en elles-mêmes (lectures internes) ou dans leur contexte (lectures externes) ou, mieux, les deux à la fois ; plus rare et plus difficile, l'approche par les pratiques culturelles, autrement dit, la sociologie de la réception, de la consommation des biens culturels. ("Un mai" 133-34)

[This cultural approach may be understood—and practiced—in two different ways: the most common—and the easiest—is that which consists in analyzing the cultural productions themselves (internal readings) or through their context (external readings) or, better, through both at the same time. The cultural practice approach, i.e. the sociology of reception or the sociology of consumption of the cultural goods, is rather more rare and more difficult.]

An approach "par le culturel" is not simply desirable, but also necessary to address the political dynamics of contemporary cultures, their historical foundations, defining traits, conflicts, and contingencies. This is especially pertinent if one thinks of the unprecedented developments experienced in recent times by the cultural fields of many Arab countries, where Jacquemond notes the decline of a certain elitism that had previously characterized the production of symbolic goods since the *nahḍa*:

En ce sens, la nouveauté radicale des révolutions arabes résiderait justement dans le dépassement de ce "paradigme nahdawi" : dans le fait que pour la première fois dans l'histoire moderne de ces pays, les dynamiques de changement ne sont plus contrôlées par ces élites, mais par des couches sociales bien plus larges—dans une sorte de version inversée de l' *Utopia* d'Ahmed Khaled Towfiq . . . les acteurs décisifs des révolutions sont justement des "classes moyennes" entendues dans un sens large. ("Un mai" 144)

[In this sense, the radical novelty of the Arab revolutions lies precisely in the overcoming of this "nahdawi paradigm." It lies in the fact that for the first time in the modern history of these countries, the dynamics of change are no longer controlled by these elites, but by much wider social strata—in a kind of reverse version of . . . *Utopia* of Ahmad Khaled Towfiq, the decisive actors in the revolutions are precisely from the "middle classes" understood in a broader sense.]

To put this differently, under the influence of several ideas coming from the research area of Sociology, the efforts of these scholars have focused mostly on the material conditions underlying the literary texts, besides questions like that of elitism which connected to the the cultural field involved in my investigation. But how do we approach other scholarly contributions relating to the cultural turn mentioned above?

Samia Mehrez's work—for which Bordieusian theory has also provided a good basis—is noteworthy. Mehrez's writings have extensively dealt with the representation of national history in contemporary Egyptian literature, as in the case of her monograph *Egyptian Writers between History and Fiction: Essays on Naguib Mahfouz, Sonallah Ibrahim, and Gamal al-Ghitani*. Yet she has also been the editor of several anthologies, such as *A Literary Atlas of Cairo* and *The Literary Life of Cairo*, besides overseeing a collective project conducted by students of the American University in Cairo (AUC) on Egypt's ongoing revolution, *Translating Egypt's Revolution: The Language of Tahrir*. It should be noted that, beyond her Bourdieusian sensibility, Mehrez has also drawn on the main conceptual tools of other disciplines, such as Cultural Studies, Translation Studies, and Gender Studies, and has offered a systematic analysis of the often neglected subject of cultural politics and battles for representation in present-day Egypt. More particularly, in her *Egypt's Culture Wars*, Mehrez provides an insider view and an accurate study of the activities of government institutions and their impact on creative production. By not restricting her analysis to the textual dimensions of literature, she has been able to make broader connections between culture and politics, and also between different cultural sub-fields, such as media, cinema, the visual arts, and the academy. All this has allowed her to deconstruct some of the main (mis)representations circulating about Egypt and its contemporary culture, along with the widely spread idea that censorship, in Arab countries, may only be the result of political and top-down processes:

> By exploring the strategies of contestation and resistance that cultural players have used in their cultural wars in

> Egypt these case studies also unsettle the dominant representation of the binary relationship in which an authoritarian state is pitted against a dominated cultural field. . . . At another level, these case studies reveal that the rules of the game of censorship no longer lie solely with the political field but that the autonomy of the cultural field is under threat of contamination by extrinsic religious, aesthetic, and social values and mores that have come to dominate Egyptian society at large during the past quarter of a century. (*Egypt's Culture Wars* 11)

From a perspective much more rooted in the field of Cultural Studies, Walid El Hamamsy and Mounira Soliman have carried out a project similar to Mehrez's work, yet with some differences. These scholars have engaged deeply in questions of representation, digital media, and the production of marginalized groups. They have also been the editors of a collection of essays: *Popular Culture in the Middle East and North Africa: A Postcolonial Outlook*, where literature has been addressed alongside a wide range of cultural productions that range from music to dance, and from comics to TV programs. The most notable contribution of their work lies in the fact that they have been able to include in their analysis many elements of "popular culture" that, particularly in the Middle East and North Africa, has been viewed for a considerable time as consumerist, superficial, and lacking substance. Indeed, as previously noted in the introduction of the present article, the main theories and methods that allow scholars of different backgrounds to look at this neglected portion of the cultural field have taken root mostly in Western countries, while studies on "popular culture" are practiced in a very discontinuous way in the Middle East and North Africa, since the distinction in the Arab Academy "between what is high and what is low, what is worthy of academic study and what is not, is much more rigid than in the West" (El Hamamsy and Soliman 4). Thus, in order to achieve this objective, El Hamamsy and Soliman adopt a theoretical framework that clearly refers to the thought and the concepts of one of the founders of the modern field of Cultural Studies, Stuart Hall. By relying on his idea of the relationship between the popular and power structures as one of "containment" and "resistance," they state that "containment—the foil of resistance in that dialectic relationship—in particular, depends to a great extent on a process of indoctrination and manipulation wherein mainstream/dominant culture tries to 'neutralize' popular culture" (3). They argue for an approach to the study of culture at large—and, by extension, literature—"that has at its core a conception of cultural production as a *fluid* process":

> Rather than a view of the mainstream and popular culture that sees both and the relations between them as fixed, this is an outlook that perceives these forms of cultural production as more malleable and flexible. It is this malleability and flexibility that the different factors—economic, political, historical, etc.—capitalize on in designating certain forms of cultural productions as "elitist," others as less so. Consequently, and because of that fluidity, cultural production is in a state of ongoing flux, border crossing occurring and recurring all the time and constantly reinventing itself. (3)

Nonetheless, it cannot be denied that another portion of the cultural turn discussed here has been much more concerned with detecting possible links between Arabic literary texts and further intellectual traditions than analyzing a specific symbolic context. Stephan Guth is an example of a scholar who has adopted such an approach. This, of course, does not mean that he has devoted his entire work to this project, or that he has not investigated other important issues, such as those addressed by Jacquemond and Gonzalez-Quijano.[14] However, a great part of his contributions has been consecrated to this particular focus. One may refer to some of his renowned initiatives launched in the past few years. Unsurprisingly, exploring the numerous volumes edited by him—together with other Arabic literary studies scholars—demonstrates that the issue of boundaries is well present in a number of them: both theoretical oppositions as well as boundaries unduly established between national literatures by the professionals of Literary studies at large. Thus, one of the most recurring questions raised in his *Borders and Beyond: Crossings and Transitions in Modern Arabic Literature* (co-edited with Kerstin Eksell) is "whether modern Arab literature has its own Arab 'specificity', or whether it should be viewed as part of world literature" (Eksell 11).[15] And this question appears both in the general approach adopted by the editors of the book as well as in the individual essays within it. Tetz Rooke for example, in his "Arabic World Literature: New Names, Old games?," challenges the opinion of other preeminent scholars, such as Sabry Hafez and Magda Al-Nowaihi, to conclude that Arabic literature should be placed within the broader frame of global literature. Yet Guth himself, in "From Water-Carrying Camels to Modern Story-Tellers," leans towards the hypothesis corroborated by Rooke, despite implementing a lexical and semantic investigation in which the context is particularly relevant. As a matter of fact, his study clearly points to the importance of avoiding more traditional nation-based approaches to the history of Arabic literary genres, in addition "to the desirability of comparing the development of the novel in Egypt with the previous development of the genre in Europe" (13). This is a difficult task that he also carries out in another research project titled "The History of Middle Eastern Literatures Revisited." By opposing traditional readings of modern Middle Eastern literatures as "national literatures," Guth also compares two or more of them with each other, and/or with simultaneous developments in European literatures.[16] Against this background, he highlights the traits which these literatures have in common, demonstrating the inconsistency of the notorious narrative of "lagging behind" with regard to the theme of modernity in the contemporary Arab world. Furthermore, he argues for an epistemological approach, by taking into consideration the specificities of the context of production of the literary texts as well as its similarities with other symbolic spaces, an appoach that is based on the idea of the "multilingualism" of modernism, as evidenced by the short quote by Schulze added at the end of the description of his project: "modernism is at the same time both specific and universal" ("The History" n. pag.).

This last topic has also been a crucial issue for another group of scholars who have significantly contributed to the birth and the development of the cultural turn in Arabic literary studies. Researchers like Christian Junge, Stephan Milich, Barbara Winckler, and Tarek El-Ariss are only a few examples. As with other scholars mentioned earlier, they have explored multiple epistemological matters, but they have also attempted to integrate the knowledge produced by the so-called Affect theory within their field of research (see Massumi; Gregg and Seigworth). Aside from their remarkable scholarly production, Christian Junge and Barbara Winckler for instance have put in place—in the framework of the educational activities of the Arabische Philologien im Blickwechsel, and in association with other scholars such as Bilal Orfali and Fatiha Taïb—a summer school fully dedicated to the applicability of this "emotional/affective perspective" in the study of both classical and modern Arabic texts.[17] The school was held at the University Mohammed V in Rabat, Morocco, Nov. 1-3, 2018, under the title of "Emotions that Matter: Interdisciplinary Approaches to Feeling, Affect, and Body in Arabic Literature, Arts, and Culture." It centered on questions like the history of individual and social emotions; practices of the body in relation to feeling, e.g. watching movies, sports activities, or political protests; forums and functions of affects, as experienced in moments of break down, euphoria, or vulnerability; and theories and representation of emotion, affect, and the body in literature, in addition to other arts and fields (see "Emotions that Matter").

Milich, for his part, has applied these same theoretical strategies to other fundamental topics of the contemporary Arab world, notably the issues of national trauma and nostalgia for the motherland (see Milich). In his essays, he examines the literary texts, especially poetry, of different Iraqi authors, adopting an approach that does not restrict itself to the narrow model of representation. Through this method, he confronts the intimate perceptions of their authors as well as the feelings of many other ordinary individuals whose lives have been destroyed by the horrific events that have overwhelmed the Middle East in recent times.

One scholar who has been engaged more than anyone else in the debate around modernity by means of an epistemological approach that directly refers to Affect theory is Tarek El-Ariss. In his *Trials of Arab Modernity: Literary Affects and the New Political*, he offers a close reading of the simultaneous performances and contestations of modernity that one may find in works by authors such as Rifāʿa al-Ṭahṭāwī, Aḥmad Fāris al-Shidyāq, al-Ṭayyib Ṣāliḥ, Ḥanān al-Shaykh, Ḥamdī Abū Gulayyil, and Aḥmad al-ʿĀydī. By resisting its prevalent conceptualizations, "both those that treat it as a Western ideological project imposed by colonialism, and others that understand it as a universal narrative of progress and innovation" (pos. 105), El-Ariss shows that "the trials of Arab modernity are activated at a variety of sensorial levels embodied in the texts" (pos. 186). The main theoretical foundations of this work come from the contributions of Affect theorists like Brian Massumi, the essays of other intellectuals such as

Walter Benjamin and Michel Foucault, and the studies on performativity by scholars like John Austin and Judith Butler, along with other fundamental concepts of the deconstructive approach. Thanks to these theoretical instruments, El-Ariss is able to challenge not merely the studies of many eminent scholars that examine the literary productions of Arab countries "through the binaries of tradition and modernity, Islam and the West, and trace works to the intentions of their authors by situating them within uncomplicated historical and cultural contexts" (pos. 243), but also "to break with dialectal engagement with texts and ideas, and, as Massumi argues, with the figurative framework of literary criticism and its emphasis on representation" (pos. 189). It goes without saying that his academic activity has not stopped at questions like that of modernity. In another of his pioneering books, *Leaks, Hacks, and Scandals: Arab Culture in the Digital Age*, he focuses on a new generation of activists and authors from Egypt and the Arabian Peninsula, connecting together literary and non-literary phenomena: *Wikileaks* with *The Arabian Nights*, *Twitter* with mystical revelations, cyberattacks with pre-Islamic tribal raids, digital activism with affective scene-making of Arab "popular culture."

Conclusion

This short overview of the major trends and research themes of the cultural turn under discussion cannot be regarded as an exhaustive treatment of the subject. A single article alone is not sufficient to map out all the efforts implemented during the past decades in this area; if for no other reason, then because the trends of this specific turn cover a variety of topics. However, some of the elements contained in the present survey could still help us to elaborate several preliminary remarks on the potential of this approach as well as on some of its most flagrant vulnerabilities. First of all, as indicated above, it can be argued that this epistemological approach to the literary productions of the Arab world has been useful in many respects and has served a significant number of purposes. To research that has taken into account questions like symbolic elitism strictly connected with the forces that shape a particular literary field and its complex relation with the wider international field of cultural production, one should add the studies conducted on other thorny issues that have to do with censorship, the impact of government institutions on creative production, and "popular culture." Moreover, one may consider the analyses implemented on the literary practices of many politically and socially marginalized groups, or other matters such as affect, emotions, and the body, along with more generic questions, like gender or sexuality. This cultural approach has proven itself to be versatile, flexible, and multifaceted. One wonders if this framework should not be deemed one of the most appropriate to address some of the phenomena that have recently come to the fore in the Arab cultural scene, such as techno-writing and all other literary forms mentioned in the introduction to this article in which the boundaries between different fields of knowledge and the processes of production and consumption are increasingly blurred.

With respect to the main uncertainties of this approach, it should be clear by now that they mostly concern those elements that, together with an interdisciplinary background, have contributed to its birth and development. If indeed within the Arab academic fields interdisciplinarity remains a chimera and all theories generally relating to Cultural Studies are perceived to have gained some ground mainly in Western countries, the reception of other theories that have played a major role in shaping some of the main trends illustrated above is not one of full success. The debate surrounding the concept of Affect seems not to have taken root at all, or barely, in the Middle East and North Africa, and a notion such as that of *adab al-būb* or "pop literature" is almost or completely absent in Arab literary criticism (see Konerding 293). The same situation, furthermore, also applies to the sociological theories of renowned sociologists like Pierre Bourdieu. In one of his recent articles, Jacquemond shows that the general economy of the translations of his main works into Arabic is characterized as selective, didactic, and militant, while a foreignizing—and at times literalist—translation norm dominates their poetics (see Jacquemond, "Les traductions"). Meanwhile, the field of study of comparative literature which could help create a larger debate around the possible links of the Arabic literary texts with other intellectual traditions is still limited, within the Arab region, to foreign language departments and "the discipline is likely to remain sidelined, especially as long as departments of Arabic—the national language—continue to show their disinterest" (Ghazoul 122). For these same reasons, one cannot avoid thinking that all this may affect or may have already affected both the quantity and the quality of the analyses implemented through a "cultural" approach in the Arab academic fields. Still, one cannot overlook the fact that over the past few years, there clearly have been some positive signs which bode well for the future. Neither can we disregard the fact that some of these signs have come precisely from the same cross-disciplinary fluidity that has favored the rise of the cultural turn in the West, as can be seen from the case of Arab scholars Walid El Hamamsy and Mounira Soliman who both teach at Cairo University and are the editors of one of the best works we have on the subject of popular culture in the Arab region.[18] All this points to other potentially interesting questions that are closely related to the main topic of this article. In view of the above, one might ask whether this particular intellectual "turn" is not itself the product of essentially Western intellectual trends. Moreover, one might go on to wonder about the implications of this apparent inter-cultural academic disconnect in the near and long-term future of the field of Arabic literary studies. Sufficiently answering such questions would require more space and time, in addition to a longer historical perspective, that, maybe, it is not yet possible to fully address them now.

Notes

[1] Presently, Index islamicus contains over 590,000 records. For further information on this database, see "Index Islamicus."

[2] On the impact of these events on contemporary Arab cultures, see Kassab.

[3] One of the best examples of the impact of this phenomenon on the Arab literary field is the well-known case of religious censorship against Naguib Mahfuz's *Awlād Hāratinā* (*Children of the Alley*). On this particular case, but also on the much wider problem of the so-called "street-censorship" existing in Arab countries, see Jacquemond, *Entre scribes*.

[4] For a survey of the history and the development of Cultural Studies in the contemporary Arab context(s), see Sabry.

[5] On the specific features of the literary forms implemented through the Internet, see Ciccoricco.

[6] The studies conducted on this topic have been numerous. Here, I only mention those implemented in the same perspective as the cultural turn under discussion.

[7] In this and the next sections of this article, I discuss the main texts that have marked, first, the transition towards a larger interdisciplinarity within the

field of Arabic literary studies and, then, the shift in the direction of its cultural turn. I focus specifically on those contributions that have engaged more directly the theoretical debate relating to the analysis of the literary texts.

[8] It is interesting to note that some of the scholars mentioned later in the article with regard to the interdisciplinary turn have also implemented, in their individual scholarly work, a great number of studies that go in the direction of the cultural turn. For instance, scholars like Beatrice Gruendler and Verena Klemm have been the editors for a very long time of a famous peer-reviewed book series named Literaturen Im Kontext, precisely devoted to the study of Near Eastern and North African literatures in both their local/regional and global context.

[9] All translations from French are mine.

[10] There is a much longer history of interdisciplinarity within the Arab world that has not been traced here. For several examples of Arabic scholarly contributions produced in this area, one may consider the crucial work throughout the past few decades by *Alif: Journal of Comparative Poetics,* published by the American University in Cairo. On this topic, see also al-Baḥrāwī.

[11] On the legacy of Said's scholarship and the reception of his main works within the intellectual circles of the Arab world, see Hafez.

[12] Within the French field of Arabic studies, the lack of dialogue between the disciplines belonging to the Humanities and those considered as Social Sciences is still huge. On this phenomenon, see *Livre blanc* 43.

[13] On the question of the consumers of literary texts, see also al-Bahrawi.

[14] However, both Richard Jacquemond and Yves Gonzalez-Quijano take into account the relationship between a specific cultural context and the literary practices of other contexts, as well as the influence of the wider International field of cultural production on the cultural practices produced in the Arab world. The distinction between these two approaches, hence, is much more blurred than one may think.

[15] Over the last decades, there has been a heated debate on the meaning of the expression "World Literature." For more information on this topic, see Damrosch; Prendergast; D'haen et al. On the question of "World Literature" with regard to the literary productions of the Arab world and Middle East in a wider sense, see also *Alif: Journal of Comparative Poetics*.

[16] Undoubtedly, this research project by Stephan Guth shares a number of similarities with other projects implemented over the past years in this field of study. By way of illustration, one may also look at the initiative carried out by Beatrice Gruendler and Verena Klemm referred to in relation to the Interdisciplinary turn.

[17] As for the notions and methods of Affect theory, to our best knowledge, they seem to have been appropriated nowadays only by few Arab scholars and researchers. Additionally, amongst them, many reside in the West.

[18] Even though the cultural turn is more prominent in writings on Arabic literature in English and French, as this article has demonstrated, I would like to note a similar turn in scholarship written in Arabic. This is evidenced, for example, by the Egyptian periodical *Fossoul*, published by the General Egyptian Book Organization, especially under the Editorship of critic Mohammed Badawi (issues 80-96, Winter 2012-Winter 2016). The Editor highlights this turn explicitly in his Editorial to issue 80 (see Badawi), and several of the scholars mentioned in this article contributed to *Fossoul* during this period, including Walid El Hamamsy and Richard Jacquemond, among others.

Works Cited

Alif: Journal of Comparative Poetics 34 (2014). Special issue on "World Literature: Perspectives and Debates."

Allen, Roger. "Literary History and the Arabic Novel." *World Literature Today* 75.2 (Spring 2001): 205-13.

---. "Transforming the Arabic Literary Canon." *New Geographies: Texts and Contexts in Modern Arabic Literature*. Eds. Roger Allen, Gonzalo Fernández, Francisco M. Rodriguez Sierra, and Tetz Rooke. Madrid: UAM Ediciones, 2018. 15-24.

El-Ariss, Tarek. *Leaks, Hacks, and Scandals: Arab Culture in the Digital Age*. Princeton, NJ: Princeton UP, 2018.

---. *Trials of Arab Modernity: Literary Affects and the New Political*. NY: Fordham UP, 2013. Kindle.

Badawi, Mohammed. "'Amma qabl" [Editorial]. *Fossoul* 80 (Winter 2012): 9-10.

al-Baḥrāwī, Sayyid. *Al-baḥth 'an al-manhaj fī-l-naqd al-'arabī al-ḥadīth*. al-Qāhirah: Dār Sharqiyyāt li-l-Nashr wa-l-Tawzī', 2003.

al-Bahrawi, Sayyed. "Le public de la littérature, un domaine à étudier." *Bulletin du CEDEJ* 25 (1989) : 177-89.

Bourdieu, Pierre. *The Rules of Art: Genesis and Structure of the Literary Field*. Trans. Susan Emanuel. Stanford, CA: Stanford UP, 1996.

Cheikh-Moussa, Abdallah, Heidi Toelle, et Katia Zakharia. "Pour une re-lecture des textes littéraires arabes : Éléments de reflexion." *Arabica* 46.3 (1999) : 523-40.

Ciccoricco, David. "Digital Fiction: Networked Narratives." *The Routledge Companion to Experimental Literature*. Eds. Joe Bray, Alison Gibbons, and Brian McHale. London and NY: Routledge, 2012. 469-82.

Damrosch, David. *What is World Literature?* Princeton and Oxford: Princeton UP, 2003.

D'haen, Theo, David Damrosch, and Djelal Kadir, eds. *The Routledge Companion to World Literature*. London and NY: Routledge, 2012.

Eksell, Kerstin. Introduction. *Borders and Beyond: Crossings and Transitions in Modern Arabic Literature*. Eds. Kerstin Eksell and Stephan Guth. Wiesbaden: Harassowitz, 2011. 7-13.

--- and Stephan Guth, eds. *Borders and Beyond: Crossings and Transitions in Modern Arabic Literature*. Wiesbaden: Harassowitz, 2011.

"Emotions that Matter: Interdisciplinary Approaches to Feeling, Affect, and Body in Arabic Literature, Arts, and Culture." *Arabic Philologies*. <http://arabic-philologies.de/en/rabat2018.html>.

Ghazoul, Ferial J. "Comparative Literature in the Arab World." *Comparative Critical Studies* 3.1-2 (2006): 113-24.

Gonzalez-Quijano, Yves. *Les gens du livre. Édition et champ intellectuel dans l'Égypte républicaine*. Paris : Éditions du CNRS, 1998.

---. "Littérature arabe et société : Une problématique à renouveler. Le cas de la *nahḍa*." *Arabica* 46.3 (1999) : 435-53.

Gregg, Melissa and Gregory J. Seigworth, eds. *The Affect Theory Reader*. Durham and London: Duke UP, 2010.

Gruendler, Beatrice and Verena Klemm, eds. *Understanding Near Eastern Literatures: A Spectrum of Interdisciplinary Approaches*. Wiesbaden: Reichert, 2000.

Guth, Stephan. "From Water-Carrying Camels to Modern Story-Tellers, or How "riwāya" Came to Mean [NOVEL]: A History of an Encounter of Concepts." *Borders and Beyond: Crossings and Transitions in Modern Arabic Literature*. Eds. Kirsten Eksell and Stephan Guth. Wiesbaden: Harassowitz, 2011. 147-80.

---. "The History of Middle Eastern Literatures Revisited." <https://www.hf.uio.no/ikos/english/people/aca/middle-east-studies/tenured/guthst/the-history-of-middle-eastern-literatures-revisited.pdf>.

---. "Programs of Renewal: Towards an 'adab al-bawḥ wa-l-ṣidq wa-l-karāma? An Analytical and Comparative glance at the Forewords of Some Recent (Literary?) Publications." *New Geographies: Texts and Contexts in Modern Arabic Literature*. Eds. Roger Allen, Gonzalo Fernández, Francisco M. Rodriguez Sierra, and Tetz Rooke. Madrid: UAM Ediciones, 2018. 65-80.

Hafez, Sabry. "Edward Said's Legacy in the Arab World." *Journal of Palestine Studies* 33.3 (Spring 2004): 76-90.

El Hamamsy, Walid and Mounira Soliman. "Introduction: Popular Culture—A Site of Resistance." *Popular Culture in the Middle East and North Africa: A Postcolonial Outlook*. Eds. Walid El Hamamsy and Mounira Soliman. NY and London: Routledge, 2013. 1-15.

"Index Islamicus." Eds. C. H. Bleaney, S. Sinclair, P. García Suárez, and G. Schwarb. *Brill*. 2019. <https://urlzs.com/fxbgE>.

Jacobi, Renate. "Allgemeine Charakteristik der arabischen Dichtung." *Grundriß der arabischen Philologie*. Ed. Helmut Gätje. Wiesbaden: Literaturwissenschaft, 1987. 7-19.

Jacquemond, Richard. "Le champ littéraire égyptien depuis 1967." Diss. Université d'Aix-Marseille, 1997.

---. *Entre scribes et écrivains : Le champ littéraire dans l'Egypte contemporaine*. Paris : Sindbad, 2003.

---. "Un mai 68 arabe ? La révolution égyptienne au prisme du culturel." *Revue des mondes musulmans et de la Méditérranée* 138 (décembre 2015) : 131-45.

---. "Les traductions arabes de Pierre Bourdieu." *Arabica* 57.5-6 (2010) : 559-88.

Kassab, Elizabeth Suzanne. *Contemporary Arab Thought: Cultural Critique in Comparative Perspective*. NY: Columbia UP, 2009.

Kilpatrick, Hilary. "Deutscher Orientalistentag, Leipzig, September 1995: Theoretical Approaches to Arabic Literature–New Perspectives and Projects." *Arabic and Middle Eastern Literatures* 1.1 (1998): 113-16.

Konerding, Peter. "Adab al-Būb wa-l-riwāya al-'arabiyya". *New Geographies: Texts and Contexts in Modern Arabic Literature*. Eds. Roger Allen, Gonzalo Fernández, Francisco M. Rodriguez Sierra, and Tetz Rooke. Madrid: UAM Ediciones, 2018. 293-96.

Livre blanc des études françaises sur le Moyen-Orient et le monde musulman. Paris : GIS Moyen-Orient et mondes musulmans, 2014. <https://urlzs.com/y7Kgt>.

Malti-Douglas, Fedwa. "The Revolution in Arabic Literary Studies." *Al-'Arabiyya* 20.1-2 (1987): 271-75.

Massumi, Brian. *Parables for the Virtual: Movement, Affect, Sensation*. Durham, NC: Duke UP, 2002.

Mehrez, Samia. *Egypt's Culture Wars*. London/ and NY: Routledge, 2008.

---. *Egyptian Writers between History and Fiction: Essays on Naguib Mah-*

fouz, Sonallah Ibrahim, and Gamal al-Ghitani. Cairo and NY: American U in Cairo P, 1994.

---, ed. *The Literary Atlas of Cairo: One Hundred Years on the Streets of the City*. Cairo and NY: American U in Cairo P, 2010.

---, ed. *The Literary Life of Cairo: One Hundred Years on the Streets of the City*. Cairo and NY: American U in Cairo P, 2011.

---, ed. *Translating Egypt's Revolution: The Language of Tahrir*. Cairo and NY: American U in Cairo P, 2012.

Milich, Stephan. "From Nostalgia to Nightmares: Enactments of Trauma and Travel in Contemporary Iraqi Poetry." *Tropics of Travel 4. Homes*. Ed. Frédéric Bauden. Louvain, Paris, and Walpole: Peeters, 2015. 69-80.

---. "Narrating, Metaphorizing, and Performing the Unforgettable? The Politics of Trauma in Contemporary Arabic Literature." *Commitment and Beyond: Reflections on/of the Political in Arabic Literature since the 1940s*. Eds. Friederike Pannewick, Georges Khalil, and Yvonne Albers. Wiesbaden: Reichert, 2015. 285-302.

"Panel CFP: Interdisciplinarity in Comparative Literature: Recent Prospects in Arabic Studies." *Humanities and Social Sciences Online*. December 4, 2018. <https://urlzs.com/oYSxi>.

Pepe, Teresa. *Blogging from Egypt: Digital Literature, 2005-2016*. Edinburgh: Edinburgh UP, 2019.

Prendergast, Christopher, ed. *Debating World Literature*. London and NY: Verso, 2004.

Rooke, Tetz. "Arabic World Literature: New Names, Old Games?" *Borders and Beyond: Crossings and Transitions in Modern Arabic Literature*. Eds. Kirsten Eksell and Stephan Guth. Wiesbaden: Harassowitz, 2011. 127-47.

Sabry, Tarik, ed. *Arab Cultural Studies: Mapping The Field*. London and NY: I. B. Tauris, 2012.

Snir, Reuven. *Modern Arabic Literature: A Theoretical Framework*. Edinburgh: Edinburgh UP, 2018.

Winckler, Barbara. "'New Media' and the Transformation of the Public Sphere in the Nahḍa Period and Today: How the Advent of the Periodical Press and the Internet Have Affected the Arab/ic Literary Field – Analogies and Differences." *New Geographies: Texts and Contexts in Modern Arabic Literature*. Eds. Roger Allen, Gonzalo Fernández, Francisco M. Rodriguez Sierra, and Tetz Rooke. Madrid: UAM Ediciones, 2018. 27-64.

Redirecting Postcolonial Theory: Arab-Islamic Reason, Deconstructionism, and the Possibility of Multiple Critique

Youssef Yacoubi

Intramural Calling

In this article, I start by considering a brief meditation on this issue's collocation, "Mapping New Directions in the Humanities." I will deal with what I consider ubiquitous theoretical intimations. Perhaps the redirection inferred in the title implies a swerving from the creative, speculative, and critical essence of what the Humanities is, or has been thus far over the centuries. Alternatively, the swaying itself may come out of a need to abandon an obsolete direction dislodged by epistemic shifts, paradigmatic transitions, or historic exigencies. For direction inevitably involves a self-regulating process that leads to a destination. Thinking a new direction is then explicitly veering towards uncharted locations and, therefore, fresh maps and realities. I want to suggest from the very outset—as I look at the interdisciplinary landscapes between postcolonial studies and contemporary Arab thought—that in the idea of outlining a new direction, there is an *in-built* interruption of direction's "original" drive for teleology. Redirection, then, suspends finality/finitude (or its appearance as such) and opens up the possibilities for change, hesitation, and suspicion. To imagine new directions for the Humanities is to continue to unsettle the restrictions imposed by the telos and the logos. The latter grapple with disquietude *only* in their process of becoming and self-questioning and, thus, opening a plenitude of meanings and connections between disciplines. Hence, "mapping," in both its materialization as a fresh road to be taken and a new destination to be targeted, describes that uncompromising judgment of constant dirigibility internal to humanistic disciplines. Mapping is "innate" to the Humanities' secular and secularizing formations. These aim to theorize and narrate culture, society, and subjectivity, and, in turn, foster the possibilities for such theories and concepts to subvert and reshape cultural, social norms and perceptions. To redirect the Humanities with all of its foundational or emerging disciplines and sub-disciplines in philosophy, theology, philology, language, literature, history, the arts, anthropology, linguistics, religion, criticism, law, the social sciences, and many more is to recognize the fact that culture and society are irrepressibly reinvigorated, reimagined, and reconstructed. In other words, every direction rooted in its temporality and historic specificity may demand its own mobility in order to preserve its own duration/durability, political or pedagogical impact and presence. The speedy evolution of technological modes of expression, design, and analysis, for example, has shifted our classic sense of the Humanities into the new concept of "Digital Humanities." Of course, the relationship between the two is not necessarily exclusionary or regressive in quality or even purpose, but the "digital" *in* and *next to* the term "humanities" (now becoming a phraseme) is what marks that moment of neoteric agility. By loosening the tracks of the Humanities, we may ultimately operate some strategic deviation, which comes out of an intramural calling or out of that movement of *différance* inside what Derrida calls tradition's "auto-immunity" (*Acts* 82), which allows re-direction itself to proceed with self-assurance. Mapping new directions is inescapably multi-directional and political.

One of my major concerns in this article is to attempt to test this possibility of measured realignment of interdisciplinarity in relation to the limits of postcolonial theory. Postcolonial theory—deeply grounded in the humanistic enterprise and sensibility of European enlightenment and its *homo europeus*—arrives in the midst of a decolonizing pursuit of resistance to structures of imperial power, and takes on the emergency of "writing back." Early anti-colonialist intellectuals, leaders, or civil rights activists like Léopold Sédar Senghor, Franz Fanon, Amílcar Cabral, Eqbal Ahmad, Mehdi Ben Barka, Nelson Mandela, 'Abd al-Karīm al-Khattābī, W. E. B. Du Bois, and many others had grounded ideological and conceptual parameters of a postcolonialist consciousness always on the move.

To answer the question, then, of a fresh trajectory for postcolonial theory in relation to contemporary Arab thought, I will be making three central claims. First, I shall investigate to what extent the critical revisions done on pre-colonial Arabic and Islamic—mainly classical Humanities—by Mohamed al-Jābirī (1935-2010) and Mohamed Arkoun (1928-2010) may respond to this process of re-envisioning non-Western Humanities as part of the pedagogical and political concerns of postcolonial theory. I read their intellectual schemes together operating with the assumption that they exhibit blindness and insight. This selection depends more on my own anxiety to carve out a counter-chronological, "self-deconstructionist" terrain of interpretation that brings nuanced, fluid, and problematizing methods of humanistic analysis mostly excluded in postcolonial debates. I have chosen al-Jābirī and Arkoun because their critical judgments of "double critique"—to use Abdelkebir Khatibi's terms (11)—unveil two constructively conflicting redirections of Arab-Islamic reason itself. Furthermore, the epistemic "decolonizing" drive of their work, in what they respectively called "Critique of Arab Reason" and "Critique of Islamic Reason" through "Applied Islamology," underscores a revealing paradox. On the one hand, their hermeneutic recalibration of Arab-Islamic reason has had an extensive impact in the Arab and Islamic worlds for over 30 years, yet, on the other hand, their decolonizing effort had gone almost unnoticed by postcolonial scholars.

As I move into Arkoun's hermeneutic act of shattering the traditional boundaries of revelation and the divine, my second line of argumentation reinserts deconstructionism. I consider the latter a nexus in interdisciplinary discourse between postcolonial theory and Arabic-Islamic critique. For Arkoun, the mobility of reason alone disassembles the telos and the logos of orthodoxy. Third, I move to conclude that reorienting an alternative notional framework for a sub-field across these two disengaged disciplines must compel a move towards "multiple critique." The latter meshes the study of the Islamicate worlds and the analysis of their interconnected western lineages by augmenting inquiries inside, outside, and across medieval, classical knowledges—always sustaining a theoretical resistance to Western systems of ethnocentric Orientalism.

I. Postcolonial Disciplinary Borderlines

The term "postcolonial" and its other compounded labels, "postcolonial theory," "postcolonial studies," "postcolonial critique," have all been probed from the start (see Ashcroft et al.; McClintock et al.; Ahmad; Dirlik; etc.). John McLeod has recently pointed out that the field of postcolonial studies has been characterized by a history of conceptual quarrels. Since the emergence of Said's *Orientalism*, the discipline has been "persistently quarreling inwardly with its conceptual and political character, its shortcomings and elisions, and the precarious position of the postcolonial intellectual." (McLeod 98). Postcolonial theory is entrenched in the variety of philosophical-conceptual lineages, enunciations, deliberations, negotiations, and appellations associated with the Humanities since at least its residual rise out of medieval and Renaissance Europe. Far less then, postcolonial theory has barely dared to recover humanistic impulses coming from the Islamic east. Equally, it has paid less attention to the Humanities of the Easternized Christian West through Islamic Spain and the Mediterranean Sea. The contribution of the medieval translation movement of the House of Wisdom, or the role of Abbāsid Baghdād at the turn of the eighth century in disseminating Greek sciences and philosophy may amount at times to no more than name dropping of a vanished past, or a declaration of an "inconvenient truth" to be brushed away *ad libitum*.

This epistemic and methodological conundrum raises several questions. What axioms of (un)intelligibility do we detect as postcolonial theory effectively engages, or fails to engage, with fields and disciplines that examine the Islamicate world and its reasons? Why is it that postcolonial theory has locked the domain of Islam to political and religious discourses? Why has it consistently ignored fundamental questions about "post colonialist" movements of critique and "double-critique" operating outside the periodizing boundaries of European Enlightenment? What is it that isolates a critically sovereign knowledge of the Islamic Arab world from sculpting new pathways in the postcolonial debates about the Humanities? What happens when the beckoning to map a redirection for postcolonial theory has to do less with content, thematization, information, annals and more with form and questions of approaches and pedagogical attitudes and decisions? Should postcolonial theory incorporate those pre-colonial archives and their internal contemporary zoetic revisions?

Several readings have emerged in the last twenty years grappling with questions of limits, theoretical predicaments, and outstanding promises for postcolonial studies to keep a theoretical grip on rising dynamics of real oppression and discursive obscurantism. Postcolonial studies continues to expand its "Siamese" fields such as Subaltern studies, Diasporic studies, Trans-national studies, the least critical colonial and postcolonial cases (see Boehmer and De Mul; Forsdick and Murphy). Other corrective gestures pertain to crossing over to hyphenated subfields such as Medieval (see Lampert-Weissig), Biblical studies (see West), Theology (see Moore and Rivera), Renaissance (see Raman), eighteenth-century British literature (see Kaul), Romantic literature (see Bohls), Victorian literature (see Brantlinger), Modernist literature (see Patke), postwar British literature (see MacPhee). Postcolonial perspectives have permeated multiple disciplines by now, and, in the process, every discipline begins to interrogate potentially its defunct methodical and didactic assumptions. Interdisciplinarity of this type usually generates new rhetorics of conceptual up-to-datedness.

Some of the most recent and critical voices include demands on postcolonial theory to deliver its promises on the ground. Rumina Sethi reallocates postcolonialism (by distinguishing between postcolonial studies and postcolonial theory) less in academia and more in practices of activism and revolutionary resistance based on a more sustained critique of globalization (111-12). Lisa Lampert-Weissig, like several others, has noted postcolonial theory's parochial tendencies to focus more on the Anglophone tradition (1). She demands that postcolonial theory find for itself a new prism through which it can understand "ideologies of colonialism" through medieval literature and culture. From her perspective, the fields of postcolonial and medieval studies are well established and "have interrelated genealogies" (20).

Robert Young affirms that postcolonial theory is still relevant in our era, dominated by the rhetorics and politics of far-right racism, terror, terrorism, and the return of religious fundamentalisms. Young sees that postcolonial theory vacillates between "the politics of invisibility and of unreadability" (22) which must include excluded groups and domains such as indigenous struggles, illegal migrants, and "political Islam" (22). Young argues "the postcolonial remains" are always "operating in a dialectic of invisibility and visibility" (23). In their response to Robert Young and Dipesh Chakrabarty's essays, Robert Stam and Ella Shohat have stressed the need for "a decentered, multidirectional narrative for the circulation of ideas in order to better chart the past itineraries and future possibilities of the postcolonial" (371). These issues persist because of unfolding configurations of postcolonial realities and dynamics of struggle and survival of the new wretched, deracinated, and undocumented *aliens*. This cognitive and epistemic shuttle in postcolonial theory between "visibility and invisibility"—unearthing the realities of subjugation—locks it in the predominant structures that ascertain that these *floating* bodies and identities (regardless of their status as victims) must not be seen but instrumentalized as objects of global economy. Iain Chambers speaks of the "legal framing" of the migrant that enables Europe to continue to define its borders: "the 'illegal' immigrant lies beyond the law and is fundamentally without rights. The nation state, far from withering away, here reasserts its authority" (4). Such "remaining" is perhaps most conspicuous in US imperialistic adventures, its obstinate military presence (with 750 bases in 130 countries), its interventionist policies in the Middle East, and its unilateral economic sanctions against the Islamic Republic of Iran and several other nation states.

Young and Lampert-Weissig concede that the postcolonial must return to pre-colonial articulations of cross-cultural difference. The case of Islamic Spain in contrast to the violence of the Reconquista is a site open for unexplored inquiry. Young proposes to take *dhimma* (the status of non-Muslims under Islamic rule) as an organizing theological and political principle regulating cultural harmony. It allows the postcolonial critic to think again about the relevance of the cosmopolitan manners by which al-Andalus had managed its humanism and ethics of tolerance. As Young laments, "The tolerant society of al-Andalus remains Europe's most sustained and successful experiment in communal living in a pluralistic society; yet, because it occurred under Muslim rule, it merits little discussion among analysts of multiculturalism or toleration today" (31). Al-Bagdadi makes a similar remark on the concept of *adab* (paideia) which has received "no comprehensive history" primarily because "of its enormous flexibility and complexity, which prevents it from being captured as one single, clearly identifiable subject in some kind of stable form" (440). These borders of the disciplines are surveyed in order to secure the moral, legal, and scientific legitimacy of the modern nation state.

These examples may easily be extended to racial mixing, miscegenation, translation, *'ilm al-kalām* (theology) that gave a common lexicon to Muslim, Christian, and Jewish philosophers in the medieval world.[1] These philosophers recast in particular Aristotle's systems of thought in analyzing and interpreting Abrahamic scriptures. This science allowed the Muslim Abū al-Walīd Muḥammad Ibn Aḥmad Ibn Rushd (Averroes, 1126-1198) and the Jewish Moses Maimonides (1135-1204) to bring religion and philosophy into an interdisciplinary arbitration driven—as Ibn Rushd tells us—by those "decisive" connections of divine law itself prone to conceptual speculation. Interdisciplinary conversation brought the operations of metaphor/allegory, syllogism, and demonstrative reasoning into the grind of the hermeneutic exercise. In his elaboration of negative theology, Maimonides concedes that shuttling between the two fields requires in addition to reason an attention to "homonyms, metaphorical, or hybrid expressions" (93). With such interwoven bonds of both reason and metaphor, one wonders: Who speaks the Arab epistemic point of view? Can the "subaltern" Arabs and Muslims speak their manifest tongue in the post-*Nakba* (catastrophe) of 1948, the post-*Naksa* (setback) of 1967, the post-Rushdie Affair of 1989 and the post-9/11 tag of terrorism? Can the Arab intellectual enunciate the narrative and structure of Arab reason in its complex totality and aporia so that the current cycles of the "Arab Springs" may begin to make *other* senses?

Young himself has fallen short of taking the long view of history even back to an earlier period that had fashioned the Islamic case of Enlightenment in Spain from 711 to 1492. A central premise of my argument will be that any reconsideration of the past by postcolonial theorists has to begin much earlier: at the formative periods of Islamic thought and cultural sensibility, or more precisely with the translation and archiving movement in Baghdād that may organically trace its beginnings to *jahiliyya* (the pre-Islamic period). The palimpsest of pre-colonial archives may relapse *ad infinitum*. Of greater significance, the moment of revelation and its transmissions may have something to do with forming an archeology of reason, faith, and their inscrutable intersections. We must begin with theology and philosophy emerging in a decidedly Eastern geography. We must begin by reading patiently the critical and contradictory findings of "indigenous" scholars who attempted to enmesh the trauma of postcoloniality with all trans-historical conditions and epistemologies of repression. Can we push time back at least into fifteen centuries of epistemic and political production of reason?

Those postcolonial scholars who engaged with medieval studies have questioned Europe's grounding of its cultural legacy in the epistemic and cultural *modus operandi* of the medieval period. They have inevitably uncovered some of the ideological constructions of colonial periodization whose aim is to freeze other cultures outside the central temporality of European modernity. The dialogical exchange between medievalists and critical theorists has revealed important flaws in postcolonial perspectives. Geraldine Heng, for example, makes a strong case that race should "be understood differently from its definition by canonical twentieth-century race theories" (21). Heng questions the reliability of the modern idea in the Scientific Revolution, or in discoveries of race or formation of Nations. She questions the fact that the Middle Ages is irrelevant in interrupting the symbolic self-definition of modernity (21). She explains:

> Religion—the paramount source of authority in the medieval period—could function both socioculturally and biopolitically: subjecting peoples of a detested faith, for instance, to a political theology that could biologize, define, and essentialize an entire community as fundamentally and absolutely different in an interknotted cluster of ways. Nature/Biology and the sociocultural should not thus be seen as bifurcated spheres in medieval race formation: they often crisscrossed in the practices, institutions, fictions, and laws of a political—and a *bio*political—theology operationalized on the bodies of individuals and groups. (3)

The case of Islam—Muslims and "their" Prophet, for example—was framed within how the Crusades were a "crucible of race-making and political theology, as a racializing system of knowledge: blood-races are theorized; as the enemy is dehumanized into an abstraction, or evil incarnate, or comestibles; as *gens Christiana* emerges as the name of Latin Christendom racial form in the first Crusade" (Heng 7). European modernity anchors much of its cultural vision of exceptionalism and cultural superiority in medieval and renaissance constructions of Christendom menaced by the bio-racialized "Saracen" conquest.

What Heng argues for is an elaboration of the concept of race outside foundationalist generalities such as *otherness* or *difference* locked by the postcolonial lexis in a fixated temporality. The construction of race in medieval literature and culture discloses its institutional, ideological, and legal operations that map alternative categories of more specificity and ambiguity, and whose emergence from the twelfth century defines much of what we refer to as the "West" (Heng 5). The example of race in the medieval imaginary that Heng scrutinizes more closely demonstrates that every move of recasting a new understanding across the boundaries of history, culture, and religious traditions elicits an appreciation of the value of a patient epistemic inquiry over the imperative of ideological expediency. Chambers suggests we should not be limited by "the teleology of progress," and instead be willing "to embrace an ethics of limits" (8). To confront the specters of the pre-colonial "colonial" past, the trauma of history, it is time we understood secularism and religion differently in contexts and societies inappropriately and unfairly constructed as non-secular and therefore pre-modern—irrelevant to discussions within "our" Humanities. The latter must remain global, faithful to its senses of *humanitas* and *adab*, international and inclusive, or as Stam and Shohat contend: postcolonial theory must stay attentive to "transnational interlocutions" (380).

II. Arab-Islamic Reason: Trans-Colonial and Double Critique

Interlocution occurs when interlocutors can participate in an interdisciplinary mediation. An interlocutor is not an interloper but a logical partner in commingling renewed strategies, methods, and attitudes that continue to interpellate "the state of the postcolonial union." Al-Jābirī who writes exclusively in the Arabic language does so not because he cannot write in French, but because he believes Arabic ideas can be expressed more properly through the national and native tongues of its peoples. Most significantly, it was through Arabic that much of pre-Western cultural norms and attitudes came to shape European Renaissance and later Enlightenment. Robert Phillipson's *Linguistic Imperialism* (1992) describes this as *linguicism* which benefits from a *deodorized* image of a dominant language, usually attributed to values of inclusion and serious scholarship as opposed to other non-dominant languages attributed to acts and expressions of exclusion (55). Linguicism gives English and European languages their "scientific" and "rational" aura. Other languages, for example Arabic in the case of al-Jābirī, are usually portrayed as "dangerous," "emotional," "poetic," "esoteric," or "irrational." Postcolonial Arabs and Muslims have ceased to ask the question "Why have Arabs and Muslims turned away from Arabic philosophical and theological inquiry to enrich other languages and traditions, and to turn the post-colonizing crises of *al-Nakba*, *al-Naksa*, and 9/11 into an autopsy about the epistemic Self?" Al-Jābirī's work eludes the limits of earlier readings on the crisis of philosophical inquiry in Arabic by investigating colonial and postcolonial Arab realities of depersonalization and trauma through the prism of a *contrapuntal* history of ideas.[2]

It is through a highly stratified Arabic that al-Jābirī subordinates the exercise of critique of Arab reason to the scholar's imperative to be sensitive to the specificity of Arab realities and epistemologies over the centuries. The explicit relationship between language and reason in Arab culture helps us grasp the multilayered nature of the postcolonial condition in the Arab-Islamic world. One of the merits of Said's *Orientalism* is to have exposed the Orientalist's tendencies to collapse subtle distinctions into abstract generalities. Al-Jābirī insists that there is always a cultural peculiarity shaped by not only geography, history, and social norms but by trans-historical imaginings, statements, opinions, belief systems, epistemological structures, and manners of reasoning and rationalism that may all themselves bear their own specificity (al-Jābirī, *Takwīn* 13). No wonder al-Jābirī excludes the works of Orientalists in any systematic reconstruction of Arab reason.

Al-Jābirī spent most of his formative years (late 1950s-1970s) in the midst of nationalistic anti-colonialist and anti-authoritarian politics. This experience equipped him to envisage a groundbreaking project of radical critique tracing an archeology of Arab reason. In fact, there is no way of making sense of his contrapuntal postcolonial reading without understanding the interference between his autobiography and ideological maturity.[3] Al-Jābirī's critique assumes a fundamental correlation between critical revisionism and Arab Renaissance, *Nahḍa*. In other words, the Arab world may not attain its proper modernity unless it operates its own internal interrogation that traces the epistemic structures of its multiple ruptures. Such critique involves a total assessment of the old, of conceptual frameworks and cultural postulations. It recasts a new modernity that may be capable of countering European ethnocentrism. This is a political act of *provincializing* Europe to use Chakrabarty's term. Al-Jābirī's critique must include, among other things, "the understanding that this equating of a certain version of Europe with 'modernity' is not the work of Europeans alone; third world nationalisms, as modernizing ideologies par excellence, have been equal partners in the process" (Chakrabarty 21).

In 1958, al-Jābirī departed towards Damascus, a center of pan-Arab nationalism, to begin his studies. He arrived a few months after the unfolding Syrian Crisis of 1957, which was a period of severe diplomatic confrontations with Turkey during the Cold War. In Damascus, al-Jābirī was not only a student, but also a free-lance journalist writing for the first Moroccan newspaper *al-'Alam* of the Independence Party. At a very young age, al-Jābirī was involved in the national anti-imperialist movement for independence, working with 'Allāl al-Fāsi, and Mehdi Ben Barka. Discerning his bilingual proficiency, Ben Barka immediately recruited him as a translator from French into Arabic for the newspaper. This carved out his later role in becoming the ideological architect of the Union Nationale des Forces Populaires (UNFP) opposition socialist party between 1959 and 1981. He was directly immersed in political activism, collaborating with the major players in the anti-imperialist politics of resistance, especially the secretary of the tricontinental conference Mehdi Ben Barka. He also worked closely with Abderraḥmān El Youssoufi who became the Prime minister of the first left-center government (1998-2002) and Fqīh Basri. Al-Jābirī became known as a visionary theorist for the idea of a transnational Historic Block of Resistance. His prolific work runs like a chronological testament of his development as a public organic intellectual in the Gramscian sense. There is a clear symbiotic interface between his anti-colonialist perspective as a socialist activist and his commitment to decolonizing any totalizing reason.[4] In 1981, he resigned from political life and devoted himself to intellectual activism.

All of this political acumen grounded al-Jābirī's methodically critical revisionism of Arab-Islamic reason. The four volumes he produced for this purpose were comprehensive and encyclopedic. Their concern for a "double critique" was a nationalist and pan-Arabist preoccupation to liberate the Arab scholar from essentialist readings coming from both the European and the Arab-Islamic traditions of interpretation. As al-Jābirī explains, "We have embarked on a journey inside the galleries of Arab culture in order to study its foundations and pillars critically and to avoid paying attention to its exhibits" (*Takwīn* 6). What determines Arab reason according to him is the thinking process—always circumscribed by the constraints of both the specificity and divergences of any culture. Arabic culture carries the history of Arab civilization and represents its reality. It expresses its future aspirations, and reveals the causes and reasons behind the current state of decline; its consistent continuities among Arabs and Muslims (*Takwīn* 13-14).

His fourplex study *Naqd al-'aql al-'arabi* is organized according to the order of a focused appraisal of specific epistemic genealogies of reason/reasoning and rationalism in Arab-Islamic context since its inception in the early Abbāsid period (750–1258). *Takwīn al-'aql al-'arabi* (1984), *Binyat al-'aql al-'arabi* (1986), *Al-'aql al-siyāsī al-'arabi* (1990), and *Al-'aql al-akhlāqī al-'arabi* (2001) constitute al-Jābirī's archeological re-mapping of rationalism being only characteristic of three major civilizations: the Greek, the Arab-Islamic, and the European. Al-Jābirī still wants to demarcate Arab reason from Greek and European reasons despite their unalterable interpenetrations. Al-Jābirī distinguishes between philosophical, rational, or juridical knowledge and allusive, figurative narratives like the story and the legend (*Takwīn* 17). For al-Jābirī, what he calls "the constitutive reason means a set of principles and procedures that Arab culture supplies to its members as a foundation for epistemological acquisition or adaptation, *al-naql*" (*Takwīn* 16). He goes on to explain that constitutive reason "relates to that specificity that distinguishes man from animal, which is the 'speaking authority' to use the vocabulary of the ancients" (*Takwīn* 16). Al-Jābirī insists that what characterizes Arab reason is the fact that rational relationships center around three cornerstones: God, Man, and Nature that continue their reverberations in the colonial and postcolonial zones of confrontation with Western late capitalist cultures and structures of thought (*Takwīn* 29).

Therefore, al-Jābirī uses the term "deconstructionism" (*tafkīk*) when he describes his method in *Takwīn al-'aql al-'arabi* (5) to imply more the process of archeological excavation which involves the unearthing of the very instruments by which epistemology is formed and deformed. In Arabic, the term has more of a sense of dismantling a unit and breaking it into its constitutive parts, then reassembling it in another procedure of reconstruction. Al-Jābirī belongs to a generation of archeologists of thought like Michel Foucault and Jacques Derrida interrogating and reassembling the very epistemic and discursive foundations of philosophy and history. Al-Jābirī's use of *tafkīk* is closer to Foucault's method in *The Order of Things: An Archaeology of the Human Sciences* (1966). Derrida's textual concept in *Of Grammatology* (1967) relates more to Arkoun's application of deconstructionism as will become clear later in the article. Al-Jābirī's method of critique remains structuralist, formalist, multidimensional, shuttling from Cartesian schemes of analysis into "modern" classical philosophical Arab-Islamic criticism as he reclaims two foundational medieval philosophers: Ibn Khaldūn, born in Tunis, and Ibn Rushd, born in Islamic Córdoba.

In addition to his highly hierarchical and methodical deployment of *tafkīk*, al-Jābirī activates a variety of conceptual frameworks of the social sciences (i.e., the totality of the social phenomenon in non-capitalist societies, the unity of infrastructure and the superstructure, the importance of religion and kinship, the economic factor, etc.). Yet, what seems strategically postcolonial about al-Jābirī's scheme is the way he insists on the total historic independence of the Arab experience. Doubtless, this is not to deny its internal plurality or to ignore the splinters and wounds of its modern experience. Al-Jābirī rather stresses that the Islamic East has no straightforward relation either with its past Enlightenment or with its present modernity, carved out mainly through colonial violences. Al-Jābirī entertains these social and political theories because they bring the scholar closer to the Arabic structure and allow him to return to Ibn Khaldūn, in the case of the sociology of ideas, and Ibn Rushd, in the case of the philosophy of history. From a historical perspective, al-Jābirī divides Islamic philosophy into two camps. The first was established during the Abbasid Dynasty in Baghdād, and was typified by a dual interest in Gnosticism, Eastern religions of Persia, and Greek metaphysics. The second was developed in al-Andalus and North Africa, and was distinguished by a dominant scientific mathematical and liberating tradition. It is liberating not only because of Ibn Rushd's meticulously critical assessment of Aristotle's philosophy, but also because of the fact that "demonstrative reasoning" for him must be transcultural and trans-historical. Ibn Rushd urged the religious thinker in particular to study logic and philosophy and to learn this craft "from the ancient masters, regardless of the fact that they were not Muslims," and to learn philosophy "from our predecessors" since the Law itself urges believers to study ontology and to always seek truth regardless of its origin (Averroes 114). Ibn Rushd grappled with the theological factor through the demands compelled by philosophical reasoning. Thus, he settled the crisis of hermeneutics in his context by claiming that "Demonstrative truth and scriptural truth cannot conflict . . . if the apparent meaning of Scripture conflicts with demonstrative conclusions it must be interpreted allegorically, i.e., metaphorically (115). Al-Jābirī argues that Ibn Rushd was, thus, more innovative and insightful in his commentary on Aristotle than Avicenna—who, of course, was operating within the polemical theological climate of the Abbasid period. Ibn Rushd maneuvers what al-Jābirī calls a corrective method of analysis (*taṣḥīḥ*,) including his scientific verification of Aristotle's system of metaphysics distinguishing between Aristotle's own ideas and Aristotelianism (al-Jābirī, *Ibn Rushd* 153-66).

Through re-reading Ibn Khaldūn, al-Jābirī aims ultimately not to discover the value and significance of the ideas of this universal classical thinker. Neither does he want to weigh them according to the Western standards of scientific procedures as many have done already (see, for example, Alatas; Khatibi 25-71). Al-Jābirī's pedagogical objective is to recuperate medieval sociology because it exposes contemporary socio-political reality. Such reality breathes and generates similar determinations that Ibn Khaldūn explicated, analyzed, and then constituted as a self-sufficient sociological theory which he called "the science of human architecture" (al-Jābirī, *Al-'aql al-siyāsī* 12). Ibn Khaldūn tells us that group feeling (*'aṣabiyya*) is one of its fundamental structures, which "gives protection and makes possible mutual defense . . . and every other kind of social activity" and is usually bestowed to one person who must "have superiority over the others. . . . Such superiority is royal authority. . . . Royal authority means superiority and the power to rule by force" (*The Muqaddimah* 106). Al-Jābirī justifies his excavation of Ibn Khaldūn by his wish to find non-Western categories of disentombing the bones and traces of sectarianism, tribalism, and fundamentalism. Khatibi teases out at least three scientific models (Khaldūnian, Marxist, Segmentary) that may be mobilized together (despite their inevitable limitations) to understand the status of social and political structures, dynamics, and mutations in contemporary Maghrebi societies in Ibn Khaldūn's analysis (70-71).

Al-Jābirī sees these conditions and trends as "keys" mobilized by Ibn Khaldūn himself as he was theorizing the past of his own time. Al-Jābirī's retrieval of Ibn Khaldūn's conceptual framework demonstrates the integrity of Ibn Khaldūn's theory as he scrutinizes the establishment of the state as the very manifestation of the movement of history. Ibn Khaldūn maps out the evolution of the state in terms of psychology (man's natural impulse for hostility), sociology (the structure of the tribe and religion), and economics (the state's royalty system). Ibn Khaldūn manages to eschew the trappings of metaphysics of his own time in constructing a philosophy of history (al-Jābirī, *Fikr Ibn Khaldūn* 243-45). Thus, he is the most relevant theorist to comprehend contemporary postcolonial realities. The architecture system he used remaps Arab political reason in terms of the pre-Islamic period of *jāhiliyya*, which determined the supremacy of the tribe and war spoils. Second, the prophetic period shaped the centrality of doctrine and belief. Third, the Caliphate and conquest (*futūḥāt*) periods characterized the establishment of sectarianism and tribalism with the reign of the Umayyads (661–750) and Abbasids (750–1258). If the first volume of *Naqd al-'aql al-'arabi* examines the foundations of what al-Jābirī calls "the epistemic act" (*Takwīn* 16), the third volume dismantles more precisely the workings of what he calls the "reason of Arab reality" (*Al-'aql al-siyāsī* 5) across the medieval and modern contexts.

Ibn Khaldūn's *The Muqaddimah* (Prolegomenon), then, is not limited only to the notion of group feeling/kinship or religious "proselytization" (*da'wa*) as "keys" to Arab-Islamic historiography and postcoloniality. Al-Jābirī contends that there is "a third key" which was always present in Ibn Khaldūn's thinking even though he did not name it. The economic factor was not prominent enough in a pre-capitalist society. It was less self-encompassing by comparison to kinship but still had a deterministic role to play. Through Ibn Khaldūn's concept of kinship, al-Jābirī re-reads the political structure of Arab-Islamic society today as a form of economic production (integral to global capitalism) based mainly on the extraction of the surplus of production by force, the power of the prince, the tribe, and state. This is what he terms the "royalty-based economy" (*Al-'aql al-siyāsī* 13). The archaic term "Spoils" mediates the role of the economic factor in structuring political hierarchies of control. Al-Jābirī calls it a royalty-based economy because it is usually limited to a distribution of wealth involving in the first place state representatives and their clan. Oligarchy, thenceforth, is a form of power structure limited to discursive and ideological constructions of nobility, wealth, and family ties handed down from one generation to the next. Royalty-based economy, kingship structure, and religious zealotry are regulatory frames that unlock the contemporary Arab present. These keys were exactly what Ibn Khaldūn deployed to scrutinize the past of his own political culture. Therefore, al-Jābirī suggests that Arab-Islamic political reason should be better understood through the lenses of these three overlapping components: Tribe, Spoils, and Creed/

Doctrine. Adding the colonial and neo-colonial experience, it is the multifaceted interpenetration across these systems of economic, social, and political managements that explains much of the structures of authoritarianism and Machiavellian behavior in several Arab regimes and their unruffled cohabitation with imperialism and ethnocentrism. In his analysis of the tribe, for example, Ibn Khaldūn insists that "royal authority" dismantles itself from the inside through its pursuit of luxury, dynastic wealth, and the submergence of the "tribe" in a life of prosperity (106). Interestingly, this particular obstacle applies to several oil-based plutocratic states today, for, as Ibn Khaldūn concludes: "When a group feeling is destroyed, the tribe is no longer able to protect itself, let alone press any claims. It will be swallowed up by other nations" (106). Al-Jābirī further explains that in capitalist societies, these components are present but have come to reside more in the political unconscious (*Al-'aql al-siyāsī* 11). In less organically capitalist societies—such as agricultural, rural societies—or in those oligarchies, these tend to take center stage, at the heart of consciousness itself.

Creed, an issue that Arkoun takes up more seriously, has less to do with theology for al-Jābirī. Creed is the realm of revelation and pertains more to the structure of *engineering* belief and partisanship or, in Gramsci's term, consent. Belief/faith always depends on non-rational properties such as symbolism, metaphor, and analogy. Al-Jābirī concludes that both belief and ideology in the Arab-Islamic context function rhetorically and not rationally. This is why al-Jābirī arranges political Arab reason according to the following tripartite categories: rhetorical, epistemic, and evidentiary.

One major conclusion in al-Jābirī's critique is the fact that the epistemic interfaces with the political in an organic manner even though the political does not necessarily submit to the epistemic. The epistemic usually tries to structurate political life by imposing its process of decision-making. Political reason, then—unlike epistemic reason—is neither rhetorical, epistemic, nor evidentiary, but it instrumentalizes statements—mechanisms of diverse epistemic structures—to serve its interests and ends. Politics, especially since the Caliphate dispensation, has depended primarily on an oratorical and structurally emotive efficiency in order to maximize the very pragmatic and centralized exercise of arbitrary power. Political reason, as a practice and as an ideology, remains a social phenomenon grounded in the social imaginary where both colonial and "local" structures of repression may operate their rhetorical mechanisms. According to al-Jābirī, this "ontological cover" accompanies political discourse (*Al-'aql al-siyāsī* 9-10).

Therefore, the "remaining" that Young speaks about is contingent upon encountering other specters of what is more unmapped and unthought of in postcolonial and other medieval studies. Al-Jābirī's thesis has received so much criticism, and many have pointed out his several "scientific," "pedagogical," and "historiographical" inaccuracies and misrepresentations. Doubtless, al-Jābirī's critique proceeds with several limitations, but the approach itself has so much to offer postcolonial discussions about the so-called "political Islam" (see Eyadat et al.).[5] My aim has been not to evaluate the literature of reception of al-Jābirī's work, since this is indeed another argument all together. Instead, I want to highlight to what extent al-Jābirī's revisionist project has elevated the quality of critical and interdisciplinary discourse on Arab-Islamic tradition of critique. By sustaining a double-critique, al-Jābirī democratizes the academic practice of commentary on the Islamicate world. A conversation across the disciplinary boundaries of these two fields inevitably opens up a critique running both ways. Around an interdisciplinary "ocean," everyone "wins"—most of the time. Such similar moves in philosophy, theology, and religion would chart Arab-Islamic criticism within the borderlines of postcolonial theory's fundamental anxiety to dismantle texts of discursive ambiguity or systems of political coercion. It would give rise to multiple and polyphonic "epistemologies of liberation." As Derrida notes:

> the surge <déferlement> of "Islam" will be neither understood nor answered as long as the exterior and interior of this borderline place have not been called into question; as long as one settles for an internal explanation (interior to the history of faith, of religion, of languages or cultures as such), as long as one does not define the passageway between this interior and all the apparently exterior dimensions (techno scientific, tele-biotechnological, which is to say also political and socioeconomic, etc.). (*Acts* 58)

This approach would unravel the epistemic and empirical peripheries of periodization limited by the demands to theorize the nation state and nationalism as the essential signifier of the modern globalizing project. An inquiry into the philosophy of religion, medieval and classical Islamic Humanities may incite a new breakthrough in the way the interior and exterior boundaries of the Islamic East intersect, sharpening postcolonial conjectural procedures, and creating zones-of-disciplinary contact.

III. Applied Islamology, Deconstructionism

Whilst al-Jābirī schematized an archaeology of Arab-Islamic knowledge, Arkoun focused on navigating a new approach of analysis called "Applied Islamology." This method emphasizes the amalgamation of several specialisms in the Humanities and social sciences that would aim at normalizing those zones of contact between experts. Of greater significance, this approach insists on the pertinence of other Humanities in subverting European Enlightenment thought. Arkoun's point of departure is theology, not philosophy. In essence, Arkoun is inspired by the hermeneutic gains of nineteenth-century Biblical criticism in rediscovering fresh conceptual mappings in the work of scholars such as Paul Ricoeur, André Neher, Jean Daniélou, Karl Barth, Rudolf Bultmann, among others. Islam—as a cultural and religious category—will only be understood properly if specialists graciously participate in critical debates taking place in other disciplines. Arkoun suggests that one major conceptual breakthrough needed in the study of Islam (*le fait islamique*) is to begin to think of it within the constrictions of history and the demands of theory. Arkoun's systematic project of critique begins with an anxiety of applying interdisciplinary methods. They should generate a critical examination of the totality of formative classical texts of theology written by al-Bukhārī, Muslim, al-Rāzi, al-Tabarī, and Ibn Taymiyyah, among others. The aim of an interdisciplinary critique is to dismantle a number of hermeneutical boundaries imposed by classical commentators, and particularly their practice of exegesis (*tafsīr*) that has remained an exercise in repetitive apologetics over the centuries. Arkoun's tactic goes further by excavating debates, metanarratives, heresies already raised by peripheral figures of the classical period. In this sense, like al-Jābirī, he is operating from within the epistemic and ideological confines of tradition.

Mohammad Arkoun was educated in Algeria and France, and taught at the University of Sorbonne for over seventeen years. Even though his work is more known in France and the Maghreb, the Arabic translations of almost all of his writings have attracted wide interest in the Arab world. Only a handful of his essays have been translated into English, namely, a collection of answers to specific questions related to Muslim theology and culture in *Re-thinking Islam* (1993), and a collection of his most significant essays in *The Unthought in Contemporary Islamic Thought* (2002). No doubt, Arkoun's originality stems from his privileged and double intellectual background. He is primarily a byproduct of the French tradition of philology. However, as he rebelled against old assumptions of traditional French Orientalism, he became increasingly interested in the relevance of contemporary critical theories and social sciences to the study of Islamic reason. This dual and conscious allegiance makes Arkoun stand out as one of the most audacious thinkers on Islamic theology. In his own deconstructionist mode, he provides a contrapuntal re-reading of tradition.

"Applied Islamology" suggests that the major question which scholars should really tackle is the relationship that exists between language and truth. Arkoun conducts close readings of classical texts based on a tripartite concept he calls the thinkable, the unthinkable, and the unthought (*le pensable*, *l'impensable* et *l'impensé* (*Lectures* viii). This tool of excavating structures of epistemic modes reveals, for example, that the thinkable is limited to those norms constructed by a linguistic community within a specific period. The unthinkable encompasses epistemic norms that the community decides to ignore or undermine because of self-censorship, political exigencies, or the unavailability of cognitive readiness. The unthought is related to the unthinkable in the sense that the community deploys social and cognitive devices that make particular boundaries of thought outside denunciation. By focusing on what he calls "les questions demeurées impensables et l'étendue de l'impensé [the questions that have remained unthinkable and the thread of what is unthought]" (*Lectures* vi). Arkoun insists that one must explore the relationship of interdependency that associates literature with philosophical thinking. Arkoun and al-Jābirī may agree on the importance of unravelling epistemological structures but it seems that al-Jābirī's rigid structuralist remapping of Arab-Islamic reason categorically disregards the interconnectedness between the philosophical and the literary in Islamic culture. In other words, the transition of what Arkoun designates as Book/book (referring to all Abrahamic scriptures) from their primordial orality into the artifice and craft of writing tells us more about the complexity of commentary and interpretation.

Unlike al-Jābirī, Arkoun recognizes the importance of those "irrational" properties and, thus, his insight unsettles the aporetic moment in al-Jābirī's critique. His "Applied Islamology" claims new grounds of critique *unsighted* by al-Jābirī. In fact, Arkoun's work facilitates a redirection happening inside the grand postcolonial debates of the 1960s and 1970s on Arab-Islamic reason driven by nationalist and Pan-Arabist political preoccupations. Arkoun contends that there is a need for a systematic inquiry into the collision, gaps, and fragments of the literary/imaginary and the rational/scientific. Arkoun demands: "We must abandon the dualist framework of knowledge that pits reason against imagination, history against myth, true against false, good against evil, and reason against faith" (*Rethinking* 36).

Binaries and constructed dualisms usually constitute the foundations of ethnocentrism and logocentrism. Arkoun's 1972 essay "Logocentrisme et vérité religieuse dans la pensée islamique" has transformed the analysis of religious discourse through an uncompromising argument that Islamic theology is deeply implicated in historical problems of political agency, hermeneutic limitations in rethinking subjectivity, culture, and the state. The essay was published a few years after Derrida's publication of *De la grammatologie* and *L'écriture et la différence* in 1967.

What interests Arkoun is not the biographical information that we find in the Quran, or the major texts of Islamic commentary and sciences, but "the implicit information contained in any discourse" (*The Unthought* 170). He has chosen, for example, to analyze *Kitāb al-i'lām bi-manāqib al-islām* by Abu Ḥasan al-'Āmirī (d. 992) where he finds the activation of the Islamic logos. The word that refers to reason in Arabic is *nuṭq*, which means an articulated utterance: "This link between word and reason is conformed in *manṭiq*: logic or domain of reasoned discourse; and in *nāṭiq*: speaking and rational being" (171). Therefore, Arkoun locates the crisis of hermeneutics in the concept of logos/*nuṭq* as he tries to retrace it through Aristotle's formation of the logos as dialectically discursive:

> If we want to make use of a document dealing with the history of ideas, we have to resurrect the relationship between writing/text/reading in all its complexity. Any text, once written, escapes from its author and takes on a life of its own. . . . It becomes the setting for an intense dialectic between reader and author. . . . All these movements,

> exchanges and interactions help determine the life of the *logos*, in other words the mind embodying itself in a language and giving birth to many languages. (172)

These intersections (*croisements*) operate inside what Arkoun calls the logocentric enclosure (*la clôture logocentrique*): "this expression designates the inability of reason to manifest itself to either itself or to another without the intermediary of language in an internal, external or written word." (173). In other words, there is an arbitrary relationship between the signified and the signifier—and as we read sacred scripture or classical texts and commentaries of jurisprudence or other religious sciences, we must understand how the reality "portrayed' is always transfigured rhetorically. Arkoun, like Derrida, suggests that deconstructionism here would mean to free figurative and rhetorical structures out of their enclosure. Structure recasts itself in terms of an exigency for *différance* as a point of departure for any inquiry into truth. Thus, the movement of restructuring is also a "rejection of the explicit and implicit repetition of the values and intellectual procedures born, amplified and perpetuated in a given cultural tradition" (*The Unthought* 174). In *Of Grammatology*, Derrida traces the contours of European logocentrism through a close analysis of the discursive privileging of speech over writing in the Western metaphysical tradition. On this account, deconstructionism inescapably and always conducts a postcolonial critique.

Arkoun outlines six characteristics of Arab-Islamic logocentrism, which tend to center around the idea that reason remains teleological. It aims to operationalize the finality of the Supreme Being, but, most significantly, reason—operating within the confines of a constructed dogma—implicates religion, culture, and the state within its logocentric boundaries in order to reduce or eliminate movements and traditions of dissent, difference, and subversion (*The Unthought* 176-77). Hence, as he locates those gaps in al-'Āmirī's *Kitāb al-i'lām*, he concludes that it is not a work of art "but a text aimed at making a coherent formulation of representations and convictions broadly shared by a vast community. Al-'Āmirī's text looks like 'an act of historic solidarity'" (179). It draws on "vocabulary and cultural models already constituted, assimilated and collected in manuals which provide clear evidence of its degree of expansion" (180). The work of many formative theologians and jurists shows consistency of collective and not individualized intellectual writing, since, for example, they conform to the lexicon, cultural and criterialogical assumptions, circumscribed by the same mental procedures of Arab-Islamic reason: "The status and operating conditions of the religious sciences are defined using the schematic Platonic and Aristotelian features of philosophical learning. Reason thus asserts a methodological supremacy, but only to subject it to the service of a creed" (203). *Tafsīr*—that exercise of repetitive and apologetic commentary—fails when it turns the worldly singularities of history and human anthropology into structures of "origin" (*aṣl*). This mode of rationalism used in the religious sciences and appropriated by using Aristotle's models tend to operate exclusively within the vicious circle of imitation/repetition/reproduction (*taqlīd*). It is therefore more mythic, circular, and clichéd.

However, Arkoun's *Pour une critique de la raison islamique* (1984) recognizes that a systematic philosophical rationalism of the first three centuries was instrumental in mobilizing the metaphoric sense of writing, "the system of signified truth" (229). In *Contribution à l'étude de l'humanisme arabe* (1970), he goes further by reading closely the major writings of Abū Ḥayyān al-Tawḥīdī (923–1023) and Ibn Miskawayeh (932–1030), tracing in a deconstructionist mode what he calls a humanist streak that was repressed later and must be revived to grapple with postcolonial erosions of Arab-Islamic latent vulnerability to rationalism and auto-critique. Ibn Miskawayeh, al-Tawḥīdī, al-Jāḥiẓ (776-868/9), and other classical humanists are modern in the epistemological sense of the word because they asked *proper* critical questions about their tradition. Of greater significance, they were consistently swerving towards a redirection of Islamic Humanities of their own time exploring paronomasia, aphorisms, apophthegm, ellipsis, etc., facilitating a certain fidelity and movement between reason and metaphor, philosophy and literature (*adab*). By applying methods in social sciences as well as deconstructionism, Arkoun updates the findings of important contributions on humanism in classical Islam, specifically of Joel L. Kraemer, Everett K. Rowsen, George Makdisi, and Josef van Ess.

The Possibility of Multiple Critique

As established and practiced in the Anglo-American academy, postcolonial theory has largely inhabited political as well as academic comfort zones. Despite the "gains" of the postcolonial turn, the postcolonial approach of analysis seems to impose a form of provincial epistemology of an "Orient" irreducible by its themes, contents, methodology, and intellectual achievements that may not participate in unnerving the ethnocentric premises of Western Humanities. For al-Jābirī, a radically fresh postcolonial re-orientation of approach is to move from ideological inquiry and analysis into an epistemic inquiry. In his deconstructionist move, Arkoun resuscitates the significance of peripheral narrative strategies in literature since allusions, allegories, and secret codes represent an open hermeneutical paradigm in the figural life of the Book/book. Whilst postcolonial theory has taken the critique in Said's *Orientalism* seriously, it has overlooked Said's own hermeneutic borderlines where we may discern the relevance of an internal critique of Arab-Islamic reason (see Yacoubi). Such a comparative crisscrossing of multiple and global Humanities represents an alternative epistemology of liberation that pushes for a more global, democratic production and circulation of knowledge about the Islamicate world.

It is time postcolonial theory inserted the Islamicate world using a different manner of representation by exploring new attitudes that complexify the presence of the Islamicate phenomenon in postcolonial critique as internally worldly, trans-historically secular, and self-reflexive. To operate beyond the conceptual limits of postcolonial theory, we may need to borrow and absorb concepts of other spaces and times/temporalities. One would be able to revive what al-Jābirī has called "the Averroist Spirit," which really means that "it must be made present in our thought, in our esteem and in our aspirations in the same way the Cartesian spirit is present in French thought or that the spirit of empiricism, inaugurated by Locke and by Hume, is present in England" (*Arab-Islamic Philosophy* 128). By moving away from an ideologically based inquiry into an epistemic inquest, al-Jābirī conducts a radically decolonizing and internal re-orientation of approach. This is by no means to valorize one over the other, but to investigate the blind spots in overlooking what ties and unties them.

Arkoun's "Applied Islamology" calls for a multiplicity of modernities (all of them *unfinished*), and not the supremacy of one over the other. Modernities are transhistoric events, ruptures, and passages-of-thought, and, therefore, equipped to resist erasure, amnesia, and dormancy. Classical Muslim littérateurs and philosophers produced original, critical, and of course aporetic perspectives on Being, structure, and difference; yet because of that, their work remains relevant to current postcolonial emergencies for corrections through returns.

Humanities—being a shifter—has constantly exhibited gaps, openings, and hidden spaces. An attention to the medieval and classical Islamicate world, from within and outside itself and from a postcolonial perspective, would create new interdisciplinary altercations. Most significantly, this would allow more pedagogical efficacity since dialogue is driven by theoretical partnership, giving more visibility to the interconnections between the work of Arab and Muslim intellectuals on contemporary Islamic philosophy and theology, and on the work of several postcolonial scholars. They all engage unevenly and unequivocally with Cartesian methodology, Sartrean phenomenology, Lacanian psychoanalysis, Marxisms, post-modernism, and deconstructionism. Postcolonial theory and Arab-Islamic theory should by now have "interrelated genealogies." In Said's understanding of beginnings, this is something a postcolonial critic ought to do and ought to think about because a "beginning is basically an activity which ultimately implies return and repetition" (*Beginnings* xxiii). Above all, to begin to return to Arab-Islamic Humanities is an "intention" of "making or producing difference" that combines "the already-familiar with the fertile novelty of human work in language" (xxiii).

Al-Jābirī's and Arkoun's systematic re-evaluation of an entire humanistic tradition with an arsenal of deconstructive devices signals that certain perceptual elements of Western Humanities have radically changed, or are always pervasively changing. Such reciprocal inter-readability confirms that the alleged methodical incompatibility between the two fields (internally fragmented) is grounded in ideology. The tendency of Anglo-centric critics, for example, to exclude scholarship written in other languages outside the main languages of international scholarship (English, and, to a lesser extent, French and German) circumvents how other analytical movements of the postcolonial have fostered alternative understandings and theoretical frameworks that are imbued with heterogeneous, political, and humanistic visions.

The work of these humanists stresses the compulsion to bring these conversations and methodologies of "radical" and decolonizing critique together. Therefore, to mediate such ungraspable complexity is to undertake multiple critique. This is to say that if double critique—as Khatibi postulates—operates across two epistemologies, multiple critique would include all movements internal to the many within one. For double is not just limited to two; the doubling itself means twice as much, or many. Doubling is necessarily a *double-back*, which is taking a new direction opposite to the previous one even while integral to it. Furthermore, it is a matter of a certain multiple bind since the Humanities in its Western genealogy of *humanitas* and its Arab-Islamic genealogy of *adab* binds all structures of authority to "nuclear" and persistent critique. On this account, multiple critique involves genealogies of traditions of critique within the European heritage in conversation with the equally robust critical traditions of the Arab-Islamic heritage since the pre-medieval and medieval periods up to contemporary post-Enlightenment revisions and returns. Cultural critique of this kind appreciates the internal procedures of these genealogies by virtue of their historic specificity as well as their overlapping collusions through epistemic processes, historic experiences, and measures of colonizing cultural contact.

By now, postcolonial theory is a polygonal and lingering field of inquiry still on the move and in business. Charting a new direction means one more interruption of direction's "original" drive for teleology and an appeal for redirection to make its political and contrapuntal *beginnings*. The counterpoint would be to sustain these two lines of investigation together. The main ontological limitation of the practice of all criticism remains that not all issues may be sighted or properly excavated at once and by every scholar. The enterprise of writing criticism or theory is always circumscribed by the pressures of selectivity, authorial and institutional positioning, and, of course, by conscious or subconscious ideological postulations, or, as Simon Critchely has once put it, "betrayal is the fate of all commentary" (60). There is always "the ethical and political necessity" to continue to interrogate the pedagogical and ideological assumptions of the postcolonial because by "interrogating the modes through which the world is seen and rendered legible, sparks the beginnings of a fertile (self-)critical quarrel, not its short-circuiting" (McLeod 110). What Robert Young calls "the necessary mode of perpetual auto critique" (22) is the only safeguard against intellectual complacency, and the only prism through which multiple critique may disperse and reflect new lights of understanding.

Notes

[1] The tradition was founded by Wāṣil b. ʿAṭāʾ (d. 748) who established the practice of *kalām*. Its scholars were mainly influenced by Hellenic thought. In the ninth century, Ḥunayn Ibn Isḥāq (d. 873) founded a school of the best translators of the literature of India and Persia.

[2] Earlier deliberations on the question of modernity and tradition (*turāth*) and related issues include the earlier works of Mohammad ʿAbdū, al-Tahtāwī and al-Afrānī, and the later divergent readings by Taha Hussain, Qāsim Amīn, Ahmad Amīn, Mustafa ʿAbd al-Razāq, ʿAli Sami al-Nashar, Ibrahīm Madkūr, Tayyib Tizinī, Ḥussain Muruwwa, ʿAbd al-Raḥmān Badawī, Salāma Mūsā, Khālid Muḥammad Khālid, among others. However, these were in the style of reflections, contestations, and forethoughts. Despite—and at times because of—the criticisms leveled at al-Jābirī's studies on the Arab and Islamic world, his archeological work remains the first most systematic and methodical examination of Arab-Islamic reason using the tools of structuralism, formalism, "deconstructionism," and classical methods of rational philosophy.

[3] Al-Jābirī has published over 30 books. For the sake of clarity, I divide al-Jābirī's work into phases. The earlier phase in the 1970s saw his work on the political thought of Ibn Khadūn, *Fikr Ibn Khldūn: Al-ʿaṣabiyya wa-l-dawla* (Ibn Khaldūn's Thought: Tribalism and the State, 1971). During the same period, he also wrote on issues related to postcolonial educational strategies and the importance of promoting the teaching of philosophy in Moroccan schools and universities. His book, *Nahnu wa-l-turāth* (Tradition and Us, 1980) paved the way for the second phase of his four-part study *Naqd al-ʿaql al-ʿarabi* (Critique of Arab Reason). In the 1990s and in addition to several books on culture, the role of public intellectuals, Islam and the West, human rights, and most importantly his work on Ibn Rushd, he returns to finish his sequel. Then, he finally turns to a subject matter he may have avoided earlier—the issue of Quranic exegesis—by publishing *Madkhal ila-l-Qurʾan* (Introduction to the Quran) and *Fahm al-Qurʾan al-ḥakīm* (Understanding the Quran).

[4] Al-Jābirī's detailed political autobiography is published in three volumes as *Fī ghimār al-siyāsa fikran wa-mumārasa*. These are based on a monthly series of booklets called *Mawāqif* [Positions] written between 1959 and 2002. His memoir was published in 1997 as *Ḥafriyāt fi-l-dhākira min baʿīd*.

[5] Al-Jābirī's Critique of Arab Reason received a wide and sustained contestation among several critics such as Hussain al-Idrīsī, Adunīs, Taha Abda-

raḥmān, Joseph Massad, among others. Yet, the harshest remains George Tarābīshī's, *Naqd naqd al-'aql al-'arabi*. Tarābīshī dismisses al-Jābirī's fundamental distinction between Eastern and Maghrebi epistemologies, the first being carved out by mysticism/hermiticism and the second by rationalism. Tarābīshī indignantly accuses al-Jābirī of performing his own "xenophobic" *'aṣabiyya* in order to concoct an epistemic rupture between the Islamic East and the Maghreb. His response to al-Jābirī's thesis attempts to dismantle this "epistemic geographical mapping" by arguing a counter case for the epistemic and historic unity of Arab-Islamic reason.

Works Cited

Al-'Āmirī, Abu Ḥasan. *Kitāb al-i'lām bi-manāqib al-islām*. Riyadh: Mu'assasat al-'Aṣāla l-il-Thaqāfa wal-l-Nashr wa-l-i'lām, 1988.

Ahmad, Aijaz. *In Theory*. London; NY: Verso, 1994.

Alatas, Farid. *Applying Ibn Khaldūn: The Recovery of a Lost Tradition in Sociology*. NY: Routledge, 2014.

Arkoun, Mohammad. *Contribution à l'étude de l'humanisme arabe au IVe/ Xe siècle: Miskawayh, philosophe et historien*. Paris : J. Vrin, 1970.

---. *Lectures du Coran*. Paris : G.-P. Maisonneuve et Larose, 1982.

---. "Logocentrisme et vérité religieuse dans la pensée islamique." *Studia Islamica* 35 (1972) : 5-51.

---. *Pour une critique de la raison islamique*. Paris : Maisonneuve et Larose, 1984.

---. *Re-thinking Islam*. Trans. Robert D. Lee. Oxford: Westview P, 1993.

---. *The Unthought in Contemporary Islamic Thought*. London: Saqi Books in Association with The Institute of Ismaili Studies, 2002.

Ashcroft, Bill et al., eds. *The Empire Writes Back: Theory and Practice in Postcolonial Literatures*. London; NY: Routledge, 1989.

Averroes. "The Decisive Treatise Determining the Nature of the Connection between Religion and Philosophy." *On the Harmony of Religion and Philosophy*. Trans. G. F. Hourani. London: Luzac & Co., Ltd., 1961. 44-53.

Al-Bagdadi, Nadia. "Registers of Arabic Literary History." *New Literary History* 39.3 (Summer 2008): 437-61.

Boehmer, Elleke and Sarah De Mul. "Towards a Neerlandophone Postcolonial Studies." *Journal of Diversity and Gender Studies* 1.1 (2014): 61-72.

Bohls, Elizabeth. *Romantic Literature and Postcolonial Studies*. Edinburgh: Edinburgh UP, 2013.

Brantlinger, Patrick. *Victorian Literature and Postcolonial Studies*. Edinburgh: Edinburgh UP, 2009.

Chakrabarty, Dipesh. *Provincializing Europe: Postcolonial Thought and Historical Difference*. Princeton, NJ: Princeton UP, 2009.

Chambers, Iain. *Mediterranean Crossings: The Politics of an Interrupted Modernity*. Durham, NC and London: Duke UP, 2008.

Critchley, Simon. *The Ethics of Deconstruction: Derrida and Levinas*. Indiana: Purdue UP, 1999.

Derrida, Jacques. *Acts of Religion*. Ed. Gil Anidjar. NY: Routledge, 2002.

---. *De la grammatologie*. Paris : Minuit, 1967.

---. *L'écriture et la différence*. Paris : Seuil, 1967.

---. *Of Grammatology*. Trans. G. Spivak. Baltimore, MD: Johns Hopkins UP, 1976.

Dirlik Arif. *The Postcolonial Aura: Third World Criticism in the Age of Global Capitalism*. Boulder: Westview P, 1998.

Eyadat, Zaid et al., eds. *Islam, State and Modernity: Mohammed Abed al-Jābirī and the Future of the Arab World*. NY: Palgrave Macmillan, 2018.

van Ess, Josef. *Theology and Society in the Second and Third Centuries of the Hijra: A History of Religious Thought in Early Islam*. Trans. John O'Kane and Gwendolin Goldbloom. 4 vols. Leiden: Brill, 2016-2018.

Forsdick, Charles and David Murphy, eds. *Postcolonial Thought in the French Speaking World*. Liverpool: Liverpool UP, 2009.

Foucault, Michel. *The Order of Things: An Archaeology of the Human Sciences*. NY: Pantheon Books, 1970.

Heng, Geraldine. *The Invention of Race in the European Middle Ages*. Cambridge: Cambridge UP, 2018.

Ibn Khaldūn. *The Muqaddimah: An Introduction to History*. Trans. Franz Rosenthal. Princeton: Princeton UP, 1987.

Al-Jābirī, Mohammad. *Al-'aql al-akhlāqī al-'arabi* [Ethical Arab Reason]. Casablanca: al-Markaz al-Thaqāfī al-'Arabi, 2001.

---. *Al-'aql al-siyāsī al-'arabi* [Political Arab Reason]. Casablanca: al-Markaz al-Thaqāfī al-'Arabi, 2003.

---. *Arab-Islamic Philosophy*. Trans. Aziz Abbassi. Austin: Center for Middle Eastern Studies, University of Texas at Austin, 1999.

---. *Binyat al-'aql al-'arabi* [Structure of Arab Reason]. Casablanca: Al-Markaz al-Thaqāfī al-'Arabi, 1986.

---. *Fahm al-Qur'an al-ḥakīm*. Casablanca: Dar al-Nashr al-Maghribiyya, 2009.

---. *Fī ghimār al-siyāsa fikran wa-mumārasa* [Inside the Deluge of Politics: Theory and Practice]. Beirut: Al-Shabaka al-'Arabiyya li-l-Abḥāth wa-l-Nashr, 2009-2010.

---. *Ḥafriyāt fi-l-dhākira min ba'īd* [Excavating Memory from Afar]. Beirut: Markaz Dirāsāt al-Wiḥda al-'Arabiyya, 1997.

---. *Fikr Ibn Khaldūn: Al-'aṣabiyya wa-l-dawla*. Beirut: Markaz Dirāsāt al-Wiḥda al-'Arabiyya, 2014.

---. *Ibn Rushd: Sīra wa fikr, dirāsa wa nuṣūṣ* [Ibn Rushd: Biography and Thought, Study and Texts]. Beirut: Markaz Dirāsāt al-Wiḥda al-'Arabiyya, 2015.

---. *Madkhal ila-l-Qur'an*. Beirut: Markaz Dirāsāt al-Wiḥda al-'Arabiyya, 2006.

---. *Nahnu wa-l-turāth: Qira'āt mu'āṣira fi turāthina al-falsafi*. Beirut: al-Markaz al-Thaqāfī al-'Arabi, 1993.

---. *Takwīn al-'aql al-'arabi* [Formation of Arab Reason]. Casablanca: Dar al-Nashr al-Maghribiyya, 2000.

Kaul, Suvir. *Eighteenth-Century British Literature and Postcolonial Studies*. Edinburgh: Edinburgh UP, 2009.

Khatibi, Abdelkebir. *Plural Maghreb*. Trans. Burcu Yalim. NY: Bloomsbury Academic, 2019.

Kraemer, Joel L. *Philosophy in the Renaissance of Islam: Abu Sulayman al-Sijistani and his Circle*. Leiden: Brill, 1986.

Lampert-Weissig, Lisa. *Medieval Literature and Postcolonial Studies*. Edinburgh: Edinburgh UP, 2010.

MacPhee, Graham. *Postwar British Literature and Postcolonial Studies*. Edinburgh: Edinburgh UP, 2011.

Maimonides, Moses. *Guide for the Perplexed*. Trans. Shlomo Pines. Vol II. Chicago: U of Chicago P, 1963.

Makdisi, George. *The Role of Humanism in Classical Islam and the Christian West*. Edinburgh: Edinburgh UP, 1990.

McClintock, et al. *Dangerous Liaisons: Gender, Nation, and Postcolonial Perspectives*. Minneapolis: U of Minnesota P, 1997.

McLeod, John. "Postcolonial Studies and the Ethics of the Quarrel." *Paragraph* 40.1 (March 2017): 97-113.

Moore, Stephen and Mayra Rivera. *Planetary Loves: Spivak, Postcoloniality, and Theology*. NY: Fordham UP, 2011.

Patke, Rajeev. *Modernist Literature and Postcolonial Studies*. Edinburgh: Edinburgh UP, 2013.

Phillipson, Robert. *Linguistic Imperialism*. NY: Oxford UP, 1992.

Raman, Shankar. *Renaissance Literature and Postcolonial Studies*. Edinburgh: Edinburgh UP, 2011.

Rowsen, Everett K. *A Muslim Philosopher on the Soul and its Fate: Al-'Āmiri's kitāb al-amad 'ala l-abad*. New Haven: American Oriental Society, 1988.

Said, Edward. *Beginnings*. London: Granta Books, 1985.

---. *Orientalism*. NY: Pantheon Books, 1978.

Sethi, Rumina. *The Politics of Postcolonialism: Empire, Nation and Resistance*. NY: Pluto P, 2011.

Stam, Robert and Ella Shohat. "Whence and Whither Postcolonial Theory?" *New Literary History* 43.2 (Spring 2012): 371-90.

Tarābīshī, George. *Naqd naqd al-'aql al-'arabi* [Critique of the Critique of Arab Reason]. London: Dar al-Saqi, 2002.

West, Gerald. "Doing Postcolonial Biblical Interpretation @Home: Ten Years of (South) African Ambivalence." *Neotestamentica* 42.1 (2008): 147-64.

Yacoubi, Youssef. "Thinking a Critical Theory of Postcolonial Islam." *Difference in Philosophy of Religion*. Ed. Philip Goodchild. London: Ashgate, 2003. 135-54.

Young, Robert J. C. "Postcolonial Remains." *New Literary History* 43.1 (Winter 2012): 19-42.

Re-Orienting Modernism: Mapping East-East Exchanges between Arabic and Persian Poetry

Levi Thompson

In 1922, just a few years after the shocks of the Great War, a new literary movement emerged from the ashes. The man who announced the birth of this new movement, which came to be called modernism and would eventually find its way into all corners of the globe, had studied foreign language in high school and later expanded his investigations of his own language in the interests of his craft to include a thorough examination of the tradition that preceded him. Critics initially rejected his innovations because, despite their roots stretching back into canonical works of the premodern period, they challenged current literary standards as well as what topics were fit for proper literature. As his modernist style developed over the years, his younger followers took up his innovative approaches to earlier literary forms along with the revolutionary integration of ancient mythic themes into his work to directly address the contemporary moment in both his own society and the broader world. Thoroughly steeped in the tradition of the culture that produced him, this man—Nīmā Yūshīj—became the voice of a generation, and his work came to set the standard for the modernists that followed

In 1922, independently of the modernist rumblings that quickly turned into a roar in Europe during the interwar years,[1] the Iranian poet Nīmā Yūshīj (pen name of ʿAlī Isfandiyārī; d. 1960) laid the groundwork for modernist poetry in Iran with his revolutionary long poem *Afsānah*, or *Myth*. Like T. S. Eliot (d. 1965), whose *The Waste Land* first appeared in 1922, Nīmā found inspiration both in the mythic past and from the work of foundational figures of French modernism such as Charles Baudelaire (d. 1867) and Stéphane Mallarmé (d. 1898). Like Ezra Pound (d. 1972), whose edits shaped the final version of *The Waste Land*, Nīmā directed his call for poetic innovation to the coming generation of poets, declaiming "*Āy shāʿir-i javān!*" ("O Young Poet!") in the introduction to *Afsānah* before laying out his new conception of what poetry could be (Yūshīj 37). Like James Joyce (d. 1941), whose *Ulysses* was first published in its entirety in 1922, Nīmā pushed the boundaries of language due to his status as an outsider to the Iranian literary establishment in Tehran. And like Marcel Proust (d. 1922), whose first volume in English translation of *In Search of Lost Time* came out in 1922, Nīmā explored the central role of memory and experience in creating a literature appropriate to the modern age. However, unlike these Western modernists, Nīmā also built his modernist project on a foundation anchored in a local—Near Eastern tradition that Western modernism only drew on superficially. While Eliot's *The Waste Land* could not have existed without the death-and-rebirth myth of the ancient Mesopotamian deity Tammūz or the "Shantih shantih shantih" mantra of the *Upanishads*, the poem remains in many ways a specific response to a certain moment in British history after the War, a strange mix of local and global, particular and universal. In the same way, Nīmā's *shiʻr-i naw* ("new poetry"—as modernist poetry came to be called in Persian) developed out of the interplay of the global movement of modernism and more local, regional developments that lay outside the bounds of European influence.

Several scholars working in Iran have recently taken notice of these parallels and begun to address the similarities of themes across Arabic and Persian modernist poetry. A number of studies by Iranian researchers address Iraqi modernist ʻAbd al-Wahhāb al-Bayātī's (d. 1999) engagement of the Persian tradition (see Fawzī; Fawzī, Amjad, and Rawshanfikr; Muḥsinī'niyā and Māsūlah; Mutaqqā'zādah and Bashīrī; Nuhayrāt; and Rawshanfikr and Ismāʻīlī). The renowned Iranian literary critic Muḥammad Riżā Shafīʻī Kadkanī has also translated selections of Bayātī's poetry into Persian under his penname M. Sirishk. Iranian academics have likewise worked to put the pioneering Iraqi modernist Badr Shākir al-Sayyāb's poetry into conversation with modernist Persian poetry (see Aṣgharī and Ganjī; Jāsim; Nāẓimiyyān and Khayrātī; Rajabī; and Riżāʼī and Āramāt), compared the role of night in the foundational poetry of the Iraqi Nāzik al-Malāʼikah (d. 2007) and Nīmā's poems (see Salīmī and Mir'ātī), and addressed parallels between the work of the Iranian Aḥmad Shāmlū (d. 2000) and the Syrian Muḥammad Māghūṭ (d. 2006) (see Qādirī and Zaynī) as well as between Shāmlū's and the Syro-Lebanese Adūnīs's (1930-) poetry (see Qudūsī and Ṣidqī). Yet other Iranian critics have taken a wider perspective to comparatively address the similarities in formal poetic developments between Arabic and Persian modernist poetry (see Khāqānī and Maṭlabī; Mumtaḥan and Hājī Zādeh). Other than al-Malā'ikah's brief treatment of the possible influence of Persian form on Arabic poetry in Iraq with what she calls the "*band*" (a term found in the Persian *tarjī'band* and *tarkīb'band* poetic forms, but not in Arabic) in *Qaḍāyā al-shi'r al-mu'āṣir* (Issues in Contemporary Poetry; 169-81), we find very little critical work comparing these poetries in Arabic. In Western languages, there exists neither a comprehensive comparative study of Arabic and Persian modernist poetries nor even brief treatments of the shared cultural transactions that shaped the two in the modern period.

In this article, I argue for the necessity of this sort of comparative work in order to re-orient modernism. By this I mean that we ought to re-map the networks of literary exchange that produced modernist poetry in the Arab world and Iran. In the interests of space, I address just two prominent features of Middle Eastern modernism that remained beyond the reach of Western modernist influence: the retention of elements of traditional Arabic prosody (the *'arūḍ*) and intertextual references to premodern Arabic and Persian poetry, including the use of mythic figures particular to the ancient Near East and the Islamic tradition. After an explanation of the theoretical foundations of my comparative approach, I begin my analysis with Nīmā's intricate and nuanced retention of Arabic prosodic form in his early modernist poem, "*Quqnūs*" ("The Phoenix"). I briefly move through Nīmā's pairing of prosodic innovation in this poem with his subtle intertextual engagement of the story of Sufi mystic al-Ḥusayn ibn Manṣūr al-Ḥallāj's martyrdom as recounted by Farīd al-Dīn al-'Aṭṭār (d. 1221). I then follow Ḥallāj's spirit from Nīmā's poem to Bayātī's poetry in Iraq to show how Middle Eastern modernists from different generations and different traditions integrated the same poetic content into their work. Bayātī's intertextual references to Ḥallāj and other premodern Near Eastern figures further exemplify how East-East literary exchanges often went on between Arabic and Persian without the mediation of Western modernism—though these poets were thoroughly familiar with the changes going on in Western poetry at the time. In my conclusion, I contend that we ought to seek out more of these regional exchanges that may have been more important for modernist poetic developments in the Middle East than the obvious influences that came from the West, particularly when considered in light of Western colonial history in the region.

A Theory for Mapping East-East Exchanges

Nīmā's poetic innovations as well as those of his followers in Iran and their contemporaries from the Arab world call us to consider a new direction in comparative literary studies. By working against a Eurocentric model of poetic change and analyzing close formal and thematic links between Arabic and Persian modernist poetry, I not only re-map the history of modernist poetic development between two Eastern traditions but also argue for a re-orientation of modernist studies more broadly. I take a "planetary" approach to the growth of modernism inspired by Susan Stanford Friedman's *Planetary Modernisms* as well as Aamir Mufti's *Forget English!* While we must of course account for the role Western modernism played in the changes Arab and Persian poets introduced to their respective projects, I here highlight foundational modernist innovations that occurred outside of explicit Western influence. These innovations include the retention of several elements of premodern poetic form based in the Arabic prosodic tradition, such as the continued presence of the Arabic metrical foot (*tafʿīlah*) in both Arabic and Persian modernist poetry during the early decades of their growth. I argue that these metrical connections, along with references to Near Eastern mythic and religious traditions in both Arabic and Persian modernist poetries, constitute a significant instance of unity among literary traditions in the Global South—connections with political stakes extending to other marginalized literary traditions across the planet that I explore in my conclusion.

This article thus seriously considers the implications for studying Middle Eastern literatures of "the planetary turn" that Friedman highlights in her book. "[S]tudies of non-Western modernisms in the late nineteenth and early twentieth centuries," she argues, "have provided in-depth examinations of how these modernisms wrestle with and maintain considerable independence from Euro/American modernisms" (6). Regrettably, many critical approaches to Arabic and Persian modernisms often situate these movements in relation to European poetic developments but not in relation to other regional developments. To work against this trend, I draw on Mufti's recent work in which he argues that world literature as it is currently conceived emerges out of practices informed by European Orientalism (19). I therefore propose looking to East-East literary exchanges, such as those we find between Arabic and Persian, as one way we might forget English.

But how exactly are we supposed to forget about English, and what sort of "planetary" model could we use to address the exchanges that go on in East-East literary networks lying beyond the reach and beneath the radar of Western modernist metropoles? It is not enough to simply notice the similar changes in Persian and Arabic modernism because we could easily just look to Europe, trace the contrails of influence moving from West to East, and be done with it. We could also chalk the resemblance of these Eastern modernisms up to parallel engagements with European modernism and style them merely the result of trends in top-down globalization. Alternatively, we have Lionnet and Shih's model of "transnationalism-from-below,"[2] but the systemic workings of this approach remain undertheorized, at least within the context of Cold War cultures. One way to bolster our theoretical framework of analysis for East-East literary exchanges is to understand literature(s) as part of a set of systems, a dynamic grouping Itamar Even-Zohar (1939-) calls a polysystem. "The idea that semiotic phenomena," Even Zohar explains,

> i.e. sign-governed human patterns of communication (such as culture, language, literature, society), could more adequately be understood and studied if regarded as systems rather than conglomerates of disparate elements has become one of the leading ideas of our time in most sciences of man. Thus, the positivistic collection of data . . . has been replaced by a functional approach based on the science of *relations*. Viewing them as systems made it possible to hypothesize how the various semiotic aggregates operate. The way was subsequently opened for the achievement of what has been regarded throughout the development of modern science as a supreme goal: the detection of the laws governing the diversity and complexity of phenomena rather than the registration and classification of these phenomena. (9)

The re-orienting I am arguing for here aims at just such a goal: to delineate the hows and whys (i. e., the "laws") behind the profound interconnection of Arabic and Persian modernist poetry, both of which have mainly been "registered and classified" within the context of national literary productions defined either by or against European imperialism and colonization. By considering Arabic and Persian modernist poetry transnationally, I suggest a move beyond previous studies based on cataloging instances of European influence and local response. This re-orientation thus draws on polysystem theory, which provides us tools to account for multiple nodes of connection and disconnection among various literary systems. Even-Zohar points out how students of literature, when confronted with a reality in which two literary systems exist among one community, generally limit themselves to one out of convenience, though "how inadequate the results are cannot be overstated" (12). (The problem is particularly acute in modern studies of Arabic and Persian literatures, and in academic approaches to the Global South more generally, to say nothing of an unfortunate focus on Anglophone literature [whether original or in translation] in the field of postcolonial studies.)

I do not mean to say we ought to collapse Arab and Iranian poets into a single literary community juxtaposed against Europe. Instead, I suggest that we consider the planetary movement of modernist poetry to be a systemic whole made up of smaller systems (English, French, Arabic, Persian, etc.) that continually transact with each other—while also, of course, accounting for the power dynamic of the colonial relationship. Even-Zohar explains that "with a polysystem one must not think in terms of *one* center and *one* periphery, since several such positions are hypothesized" (14). The polysystem allows us to create a model of literary study that challenges the notions of center and periphery engendered by colonial relationships and opens up the possibility of dynamic engagement between a group of unstable, changing systems that can, and often do, operate in concert beyond or even against colonial states in spite of the unequal power relations at work.

Travel Forms: Arabic Prosody
and the Beginnings of Persian Modernist Poetry

I begin with Nīmā Yūshīj's project of poetic modernism.[3] As I mentioned earlier, Nīmā began to lay the foundations of his modernist edifice in 1922, just after Riżā Shāh Pahlavī's 1921 coup and the subsequent creation of the *Anjuman-i āsār-i millī* (The Society for the National Heritage of Iran [SNH]), also in 1921—their founding bylaws were composed in 1922. Talinn Grigor has amply demonstrated in her work how the SNH immediately set about "effectively and shrewdly co-opt[ing] the visual and the spatial into the mainstream of Pahlavi ideology and program" (18) with their plans for a series of archeological and architectural projects, including the "invention of patrimony" (25) by way of constructing a number of mausoleums for important figures from the Persian literary past: Firdawsī (d. 1020), Ḥāfiẓ (d. 1390), 'Umar Khayyām (d. 1131), and others. In elaborating their plans for these projects, Grigor argues, the SNH's "techniques of cultivating and naturalizing the new parameters of modernity persistently intersected with their anxiety over collective memory, public space, and the cultivation of cultural taste—*all of which were formulated along western lines*" (18; italics added). Nīmā's more open engagement of Persian, but also Arab and Islamic, cultural patrimony contrasts with the SNH's invention of a glorious Iranian past—and particularly the pre-Islamic Iranian past. This is not to say that Nīmā's modernism offered nothing new, but instead to highlight how different his modernist project was from the SNH's due to its transnational engagement of both Western poetic influences along with Arabic poetic form. In this section, I demonstrate how Nīmā's modernist poetry comes to be by way of sublating Arabic prosody and Iran's Islamic past into an Iranian modernism at odds with the SNH's myopic view of the past's role in the present.

Nīmā's sublating (in the multiple senses of the German *Aufhebung*: "abolishing," but also "transcending" and "preserving"), rather than co-opting or refashioning, of Iran's cultural past first emerges in his 1922 *Afsānah*. Unlike the SNH, which sought to establish a particular version of the Iranian past and its historical and mythic figures in the interests of the new Pahlavi regime, Nīmā challenges a static notion of the past in his poem. In one of its oft-quoted passages, '*Āshiq* (Lover) shouts at *Afsānah* (Myth), with whom he is carrying out a dialogue:

> *Ḥāfiẓā! Īn chih kayd u durūgh-īst*
> *ka-z zabān-i may u jām u sāqī-st*
> *nālī ar tā abad bāvaram nīst*
> *kih bar ān 'ishq'bāzī kih bāqī-st*
>   *man bar ān 'āshiqam kih ravandah-st.*

(Yūshīj 55)

> [O Ḥāfiẓ, what sort of trick and lie is this
> that comes in the language of wine, goblet, and cup-bearer?
> Despite your moaning on into eternity, I do not believe
> in falling in love with things that remain
> > I am in love with things that are ephemeral!][4]

While Nīmā's Lover here takes the famed premodern Persian poet Ḥāfiẓ to task (in a nod to the neo-classical *bāzgasht* movement in vogue in Persian letters during the early twentieth century), *Afsānah* remains grounded in the Arabo-Persian prosodic tradition. In fact, the above lines are in the *mutadārik* (continuous) meter, a perfectly acceptable premodern meter (Philsooph 103). Lover's demands for new poetic content that goes beyond tradition and deals with the ephemeral (*ravandah*) are thus tempered by the retention of the old poetic form as something eternal, permanent, remaining (*bāqī*) (Philsooph 102-03). The retention of premodern form restrains Lover's outburst that we find in the content, thereby limning the central point of Nīmā's modernist project: the demand for a modernity that sublates (transcends and preserves) elements of the past rather than only abolishes it.

Consider how this sublation of premodern metrics into a modern form works in Nīmā's 1938 poem "*Quqnūs*" ("The Phoenix").[5] The poem opens,

> *Quqnūs, murgh-i khushkhvān, āvāzah-yī jahān,*
> *āvārah māndah az vazish-i bād-hā-yi sard,*
> *bar shākh-i khayzurān,*
> *binshastah ast fard.*
> *Bar gird-i ū bih har sar-i shākhī parandigān.*
> *Ū nālah-hā-yi gumshudah tarkīb mīkunad,*
> *az rishtah-hā-yi pārah-yi ṣad-hā ṣidā-yi dūr,*
> *dar abr-hā-yi misl-i khaṭ-ī tīrah rū-yi kūh,*
> *dīvār-i yak banā-yi khayālī*
> *mīsāzad.* (Yūshīj 222)

> [The Phoenix, sweet-singing bird, known across the world
> made homeless by gusts of cold wind
> sits, alone, on
> a stalk of bamboo.

The other birds gather around it on every branch.
It composes lost laments
from the tattered shreds of a thousand distant voices,
in clouds like a dark line on the mountain,
the wall of an imaginary edifice, it
builds.]

These opening lines present us with several key features of Middle Eastern modernist poetry. First and most obviously, the poem depends on the ancient Near Eastern myth of the Phoenix and the cycle of death and rebirth, central to the planetary modernist movement. Second and not immediately evident is Nīmā's intertextual reference to *The Conference of the Birds* by Farīd al-Dīn 'Aṭṭār (d. 1220?). We find this extremely subtle reference to 'Aṭṭār in the rhymes of the first line (*khushkhvān*; *jahān*), the "*ān*'s" of which send us back across the centuries to 'Aṭṭār's own first line about the Phoenix: "*hast quqnūs ṭurfah murghī dilsatān/ mawża'-ī īn murgh dar Hindūstān*" (The Phoenix is a peerless bird, heart-enrapturing/This bird's abode is Hindustan) ('Aṭṭār, *Manṭiq* 153).[6] Nīmā's "The Phoenix" can thus be read as a contrafaction or an *imitatio*, what's called in Arabic a *mu'āraḍah*, although Nīmā noticeably does not employ the same meter as 'Aṭṭār like we would expect in a traditional *mu'āraḍah*.[7] By engaging the premodern tradition in such a way, Nīmā thus invites us to consider his new poem in terms of its relationship with the poetry that came before it while also pushing the boundaries of the very same tradition. Including such a complex reference to 'Aṭṭār's original in the first line of the poem emphasizes the sublation of the old into the new. This sublation extends to the poem's innovative metrics. "The Phoenix" simply does not look like premodern Persian or Arabic poetries, which follow strict rules of prosody requiring the same number of feet in regular patterns in each and every line.

In order to bring the old into the new, Nīmā does not fully break away from these rules. Instead, he sublates the premodern into the modern by retaining the premodern poetic foot (or, in this case, pairs of feet) as the basis of his metrics. The poem's meter is a version of *al-baḥr al-muḍāri'* (the similar meter) according to the descriptive system for Arabic meter al-Khalīl ibn Aḥmad (d. between 777 and 786) developed. This system, called the *'arūḍ* in Arabic or *'arūż* in Persian, organizes poetry according to the sequences of long and short syllables that make up the set numbers of poetic feet (*tafʿīlāt* in Arabic; *arkān* in Persian) in the various Arabic poetic meters, feet that came to be represented by *ad hoc* words created from the three-letter Arabic root *fāʾ - ʿayn - lām*. Persian poets adopted the Arabic *ʿarūḍ* system following the Islamic conquests of the Sasanian Empire in the seventh century. With this in mind, here is how a prosodist can represent the meter of "The Phoenix" using both the Khalīlian system and traditional Western scansion (with " ˗ " indicating a long syllable, " ˘ " a short, and " / " a separation between poetic feet). (The strike-throughs indicate missing feet. I leave those feet out of the Western scansion.)

mafʿūlu fāʿilātu mafāʿīlu fāʿilun	˗ ˗ ˘ / ˗ ˘ ˗ ˘/ ˘ ˗ ˗ ˘ / ˗ ˘ ˗
mafʿūlu fāʿilātu mafāʿīlu fāʿilun	˗ ˗ ˘ / ˗ ˘ ˗ ˘/ ˘ ˗ ˗ ˘ / ˗ ˘ ˗
mafʿūlu fāʿilātu ~~mafāʿīlu fāʿilun~~	˗ ˗ ˘ / ˗ ˘ ˗ ˘
mafʿūlu fāʿilātu ~~mafāʿīlu fāʿilun~~	˗ ˗ ˘ / ˗ ˘ ˗ ˘
mafʿūlu fāʿilātu mafāʿīlu fāʿilun	˗ ˗ ˘ / ˗ ˘ ˗ ˘/ ˘ ˗ ˗ ˘ / ˗ ˘ ˗
mafʿūlu fāʿilātu mafāʿīlu fāʿilun	˗ ˗ ˘ / ˗ ˘ ˗ ˘/ ˘ ˗ ˗ ˘ / ˗ ˘ ˗
mafʿūlu fāʿilātu mafāʿīlu fāʿilun	˗ ˗ ˘ / ˗ ˘ ˗ ˘/ ˘ ˗ ˗ ˘ / ˗ ˘ ˗
mafʿūlu fāʿilātu mafāʿīlu fāʿilun	˗ ˗ ˘ / ˗ ˘ ˗ ˘/ ˘ ˗ ˗ ˘ / ˗ ˘ ˗
mafʿūlu fāʿilātu ~~mafāʿīlu fāʿilun~~	˗ ˗ ˘ / ˗ ˘ ˗ ˘/ ˘ ˗ ˗
mafʿūlu fā~~ʿilātu mafāʿīlu fāʿilun~~	˗ ˗ ˗

Nīmā's third and fourth lines stop midway through, but the first two usual poetic feet remain unaffected. While this is out of the ordinary, it only hints at the metrical experimentation to come. In line ten, Nīmā ingeniously pushes the meter's limits with the plodding succession of syllables in *mīsāzad*, which means "builds." The meaning in combination with the meter encapsulates Nīmā's conception of poetic modernism in a single word—and we might even say this represents the project of modernism across the planet: At the same moment the poet creates something new, he also shakes its foundations. Metrics and content stand at odds with one another, and their dissonance sounds out the inner workings of Nīmā's modernist project, which builds as it breaks away and thereby sublates the old into the new.

Furthermore, the "wall of an imaginary edifice" from line nine is *dīvār-i yak banā-yi khayālī*. *Banā*, from the Arabic *bināʾ*, means building or structure. I translate it as edifice here because of the dual meanings of this word in English: either a large, stately building or a figurative reference to a system of belief. Nīmā's Phoenix simultaneously tears down and rebuilds the system of Persian prosody, just as the mythical Phoenix is only reborn by destroying itself. The Phoenix thus represents the process behind Nīmā's composition of modernist poetry, which continues the older tradition in a new form born out of its ashes. The meter, therefore, constitutes the *banā* of these lines which provide the edifice upon which Nīmā's modernist imagination (*khayāl*) is firmly based.

Nīmā's modernist imagination only begins to take shape for us when we consider the interrelationship of form and content in the poem. In addition to the foundational elements of traditional Arabic prosody at the core of "The Phoenix," the poem's content remains closely linked to the pre-modern Persian poetic tradition through its intertextual *muʿāraḍah* reference to ʿAṭṭār. This reference reaches back into the mystical tradition of Islam, giving new life to the Sufi martyr put to death for his unorthodox practices by the Abbasid Caliphate in 922, al-Ḥusayn ibn Manṣūr al-Ḥallāj, whose traces we find across modernist poetry in the Middle East and North Africa as well.

As I have already suggested, we cannot limit our considerations of modernist developments to the ones that led to the rise of modernism in the European literary scene in 1922. That same year was not only when we find Nīmā beginning to explore the possibilities of modernism in *Afsānah*, but it was also the one-thousand-year anniversary of Ḥallāj's execution. Ḥallāj's reemergence in Persian and Arabic modernist poetry corresponds with an increased interest in him in the West, best represented in the French Orientalist Louis Massignon's *La passion de Husayn Ibn Mansûr Hallâj : Martyr mystique de l'Islam* (*The Passion of al-Ḥallāj: Mystic and Martyr of Islam*), which also came out in 1922. However, Arab and Iranian modernists like Bayātī, Adūnīs, the Egyptian Ṣalāḥ ʿAbd al-Ṣabūr (d. 1981), and Nīmā used Ḥallāj's story to develop a locally-specific modernist myth to their own ends.

Nīmā's Phoenix thus emerges at a significant node within a transnational Middle Eastern network of exchange that retained elements of the Islamic past by sublating them, in stark contrast to the modernization project of the Pahlavi state. Ḥallāj's ghost haunts "The Phoenix" by way of the poem's immediate intertextual reference to ʿAṭṭār, who "included a relatively long biography of [Ḥallāj] at pride of place, the very climax, of his *Taḏkerat al-awliā'* [Biographies of the Saints]" (Mojaddedi n. pag.). Moreover, Nīmā's retelling of the

Phoenix myth and the bird's immolation on a pyre surrounded by acolytes at the end of the poem parallels 'Aṭṭār's account of Ḥallāj's execution, which "contains motifs that would become associated closely with Ḥallāj in Persian poetry, such as fearless self-sacrifice, eagerness to ascend the gibbet and die in order to return to God, and celebration at his own bleeding and the approach of death" (Mojaddedi n. pag.).[8] Such intertextual engagements of premodern Near Eastern figures like Ḥallāj also shaped the modernist movement in the Arab world and contributed to a network of transnational transaction that existed beyond the bounds of European modernism.

Modernist Spirits: The Past in the Present of Middle Eastern Modernism

Like Nīmā, the leftist Iraqi poet Bayātī drew heavily on Ḥallāj's martyrdom in elaborating his modernist poetics. In this section, I take up Bayātī's incorporation of Ḥallāj's life and work along with that of other premodern Near Eastern poets and philosophers into his poetry by way of *taḍmīn*, or poetic quoting (van Gelder n. pag.). Like Nīmā's intertextual references to 'Aṭṭār's work, Bayātī's use of *taḍmīn* serves to sublate elements of premodern poetic and religious tradition into a poetry dealing directly with the contemporary moment.

Before turning to Bayātī's innovative method of bringing Ḥallāj's voice into modernist poetry, I offer two examples of *taḍmīn* quoting from elsewhere in Bayātī's *oeuvre* to set the stage for how these sorts of intertexts work and as a direct parallel to Nīmā's modernist technique in "The Phoenix." As with Nīmā and many other Middle Eastern modernist poets, Bayātī relied on myths of death and rebirth in his work. In his 1968 collection *al-Mawt fī al-ḥayāh* (Death in Life), the second poem is titled "*al-'Anqā*'" ("The Phoenix"). Bayātī here employs a *taḍmīn* from the noted Arab poet and skeptic Abū al-'Alā' al-Ma'arrī (d. 1057), including—word for word—part of one of his verses at the end of the poem. "And [Abū al-'Alā'] told me, 'Take heed, for the Phoenix/is too big to hunt/So go back to the graves,/the yellowed books, and the inkwells/Keep moving from one country to another'" (al-Bayātī, *al-A'māl*, II: 132). By borrowing from Ma'arrī's line ("I understand that the Phoenix is too big to hunt, so be headstrong in taking on what you can"),[9] the poem spurs its speaker onward to keep him writing despite the impossibility of sparking the Marxist revolution he hopes for, a challenge it equates to hunting the elusive Phoenix. Like Nīmā's near-*muʿāraḍah* of ʿAṭṭār's *The Conference of the Birds*, Bayātī's use of *taḍmīn* sublates the premodern Near Eastern poetic and mythic past into a new poetry speaking directly to contemporary times.

In a second example, from Bayātī's breakthrough collection *Abārīq muhashshamah* (Broken Pitchers, 1954), the poet plays with the formal limits of *al-shiʿr al-ḥurr* (lit. "free verse" in Arabic, though it retains the premodern poetic foot of the *ʿarūḍ* as its metrical base) by including a *taḍmīn* from the famous poet al-Mutanabbī (d. 965). In the collection's title poem, Bayātī fully integrates the quoted line, which is from a poem in a different meter. He pushes the boundaries of *taḍmīn* quoting yet further by splitting one of the poetic feet across two lines in his new poem, in the fourth and fifth lines here:

> Allāhu, wa-l-ufqu[10] 'l-munawwaru, wa-l-ʿabīd
> yataḥassasūna quyūdahum:
> "shayyid madāʾinaka 'l-ghadāh
> bi-l-qurbi min burkāni Fīzūfin, wa-lā taqnaʿ
> bi-mā dūna 'n-nujūm
> wa-li-yuḍrama 'l-ḥubbu 'l-ʿanīf
> fī qalbika 'n-nīrāna wa-l-faraḥa 'l-ʿamīq."
>
> (al-Bayātī, *al-Aʿmāl* I: 113).

Though it is difficult to reflect the use of *taḍmīn* and the innovative enjambment of the foot between lines 4 and 5, I offer this translation to show how the quoted line fits seamlessly into the poem's meaning:

> God, the glowing horizon, and the slaves
> feel the weight of their chains:
> "Build your cities in the morning
> beside the volcano, Vesuvius, and do not be content
> with anything less than the stars.
> Let violent love light
> fires and boundless joy in your heart."

Bayātī uses a novel method of enjambment in these lines. In the following, the "/" indicates separations between poetic feet. The poem is in the *kāmil* (perfect) meter (Wright 362-63), a favorite of Bayātī and the other pioneers of Arabic modernist poetry. It generally consists of four repetitions of the foot *mutafāʿilun* (˘˘ˉˉ) or a variant *mutfāʿilun* (ˉˉ˘ˉ). Bayātī includes both in this poem, as follows:

ˉˉ˘ˉ / ˉˉ˘ˉ / ˘˘ˉ˘ˉ
˘˘ˉ˘ˉ / ˘˘ˉ˘ˉ
ˉˉ˘ˉ / ˘˘ˉ˘ˉ
ˉˉ˘ˉ / ˉˉ˘ˉ / ˉˉ˘ˉ / ˉˉ
˘ˉ / ˉˉ˘ˉ
ˉˉ˘ˉ / ˉˉ˘ˉ
ˉˉ˘ˉ / ˉˉ˘ˉ / ˘˘ˉ˘ˉ -11

He splits the first two syllables of the fourth foot of line 4 from the second two, which begin line 5, thus calling the reader's attention to the lines (though someone listening to the poem would neither experience the lines in the same way nor notice the splitting of the foot). Even if one were not familiar with the reference to Mutanabbī, the enjambment of the poetic foot signals to the reader that something noteworthy is happening in these lines. The line quoted from here is "*idhā ghāmarta fī sharafin marūm//fa-lā taqnaʿ bi-mā dūna 'n-nujūm*," with " // " indicating the caesura. The line translates, "Should you go to great lengths in search of a desired honor//do not be content with anything less than the stars."[12] Surprisingly, Mutanabbī's poem is not in the *kāmil*, but rather in the *wāfir* (exuberant) meter (Wright 363). The *wāfir* has a variant as well (either ˘ˉˉˉ or ˘ˉˉ˘ˉ), but its feet do not ever exactly match either of the variants found in the *kāmil* (ˉˉ˘ˉ or ˘˘ˉ˘ˉ). Mutanabbī's line scans: ˘ˉˉˉ / ˘ˉˉ˘ˉ / ˘ˉˉ // ˉˉˉˉ / ˘ˉˉˉ / ˘ˉˉ. In splitting the first foot of the second half of Mutanabbī's line, Bayātī's ingenious *taḍmīn* allows him to incorporate the quotation without breaking from the meter of the new poem. Invoking Mutanabbī's line about striving for one's goals and never giving up even in the face of great odds strengthens the wish of the persona in *Abārīq muhashshamah* with the force of Mutanabbī's original imperative. Moreover, the quotation marks—denoting another speaker internal to the poem—do not demarcate the *taḍmīn* but instead surround a longer demand, from whom we cannot be sure. The poet takes on Mutanabbī's voice and adds the speaker's to it, following the traditional requirements of *taḍmīn* while also bringing premodern Arabic poetry into the avant-garde of the new modernist poetic movement.

Although Bayātī draws on the Arabic poetic past, his use of the premodern Near Eastern tradition often extended beyond Arabic to include poets and thinkers from the Persian-speaking world. He wrote poems about 'Aṭṭār, al-Suhrawardī (d. 1191), and Ḥāfiẓ, among many other luminaries of the Persian philosophical and poetic past, as well as Iranian cities such as Shiraz, Isfahan, Tehran, and Nishapur. He also carried out an extended poetic and dramatic engagement with the works and biography of 'Umar Khayyām (see Thompson, "A Transnational"). For our purposes here, I draw attention to Bayātī's engagement of Ḥallāj's story as a direct parallel to Nīmā's references to him, though there are many other instances we might turn to, such as the centrality of the Phoenix in Middle Eastern modernist poetry that we have already seen.

"In the Arab lands," Reuven Snir tells us, "in which [Ḥallāj] was less renowned than in those areas influenced by the Persian mystical tradition, he has recently gained fame and recognition, especially among poets who tend to highlight his social message" (247). Many Middle Eastern modernists looked to Ḥallāj's ministry and martyrdom for inspiration. For instance, Ḥallāj's suggestion that believers forego the *hajj* pilgrimage to Mecca, instead build a Kaaba in their own homes, and then donate the money saved to the poor appealed to their sensibility for social justice, however anachronistic applying the concept to Ḥallāj's life and work might be. In his translation of Ḥallāj's poetry, Carl Ernst writes that it was in fact Ḥallāj's above suggestion that led to his death sentence under the Abbasid Caliphate, though "the legend of Hallaj has obscured both his life and his death" (Ḥallāj 5). Ernst goes on to explain that 'Aṭṭār's narration of Ḥallāj's life popularized the story of "his public utterance of the daring statement 'I am the Truth' (*ana al-haqq*), a brazen claim to divinity," which supposedly riled political and religious authorities and resulted in his execution (5). In any case, Ḥallāj serves as a symbol of revolt against state-sponsored violence across modernist Persian and Arabic poetries. The Abbasid state intended its inscription of violence onto Ḥallāj's body to serve as a warning by making him and his ideas taboo. Legends about him include gruesome recountings of how the Caliphate tortured and dismembered his body: flogging, amputating limbs, crucifying, beheading, and finally burning his corpse to ashes. In the end, however, their plan backfired because memories of Ḥallāj have persisted until today.

Ḥallāj figures prominently as the title character of Bayātī's 1964 "'*Adhāb al-Ḥallāj*" ("The Passion of Ḥallāj"). In it, Bayātī's poetic persona puts on a Ḥallāj mask as he poetically reconstructs 'Aṭṭār's narrative of Ḥallāj's ministry and execution. In so doing, Bayātī also extends the possibilities of *taḍmīn* quoting to their furthest ends in inverting the poetic device by not actually quoting but instead obliquely referring to Ḥallāj's famous statement, "*anā al-ḥaqq*." As with Nīmā's "The Phoenix," the mythic past of the Near East haunts Bayātī's poem, calling us to consider it in a different light.[13]

To briefly address the poem's content, it moves through six sections mirroring Ḥallāj's biography. It starts with "*al-Murīd*" ("The Novice"), then "*Riḥlah ḥawla al-kalimāt*" ("A Journey Through Words"), "*Fusayfisāʾ*" ("A Mosaic"), "*al-Muḥākamah*" ("The Trial"), "*al-Ṣalb*" ("The Crucifixion"), and finally "*Ramād fī al-rīḥ*" ("Ashes in the Wind").[14] Of most interest to us here is the fourth section, "The Trial," which begins with Ḥallāj railing against a political leader and Bayātī's inversion of the *taḍmīn* device.

Bayātī's Ḥallāj persona starts the section, "*Buḥtu bi-kalimatayn li's-sulṭān/qultu lahu: jabān*" ("With two words I let the Sultan know the secret/'Coward!' I said to him") (al-Bayātī, *al-Aʿmāl* II: 15). Instead of quoting Ḥallāj's famous two-word proclamation, "*anā al-ḥaqq*," Bayātī puts a single new word in Ḥallāj's mouth, "*jabān*," or coward. Other than the fact that *jabān* rhymes with *sulṭān*, there are at least two more possible interpretations of Bayātī's choice to not quote Ḥallāj here. First, we could read Bayātī's replacement of the "two words" he alludes to in the first line with "coward" as a specifically political choice that transforms Ḥallāj from a Sufi seeker into a political revolutionary whose socially-just religious practices set him at odds with the state. In this interpretation, by not including the *taḍmīn* the poem takes on an explicit political function by calling out the (unnamed) Sultan for his cowardice. Second, and in a diametrically opposite reading of these same lines, we might regard the missing "*anā al-ḥaqq*" as a sign of Bayātī's reticence to repeat Ḥallāj's ultimate "sin" once more, whether we want to consider it in relation to the poetic persona or perhaps even the poet himself. This second interpretation would then cast a pall of political ambivalence over the poem as a whole, as the poet's neglect to actually say Ḥallāj's famous phrase might be read as a subtle indication of his will to distance himself from its revolutionary power, *anā al-ḥaqq*'s direct disavowal of worldly political authority.

In either case, "The Trial" section of the poem only makes sense when understood in relation to the traditional Ḥallāj myth. By having his Ḥallāj declare the Sultan a "coward" instead of using a *taḍmīn* of "*anā al-ḥaqq*," Bayātī challenges the reader's expectations and draws our attention to the interplay between Ḥallāj's myth and the present moment. Even though we do not find the expected quotation of Ḥallāj's famous dictum, a reader familiar with the Ḥallāj legend would recall it anyway. Thus, Bayātī's mere suggestion of a *taḍmīn* (but lack of any actual quoting) cleverly sublates the content of the Ḥallāj myth into the present moment. This example takes us to the very limits of modernist experimentation in the Middle East: techniques that draw not just on Western modernist developments but rather depend on shared local poetic, historical, and religious traditions.

Conclusion: Re-Orienting Modernism

In the limited scope of this article, I have addressed two facets of an interconnected modernist network that links Arabic and Persian modernist poetries: the initial retention of premodern Arabic metrics (*'arūḍ*) and the frequent use of intertextual references to the Near Eastern past (here, we looked at *mu'āraḍah*, contrafaction, and *taḍmīn*, quoting). There are of course many more instances of literary exchange that tie these two poetries together, including but not limited to shared experiences of Western colonialism and imperialism, regional religious affiliations, a common science of rhetoric grounded in the Arabic tradition, and—as we have seen some aspects of—a mutual trove of pre-Islamic, Near Eastern myths.

We would do well to remember that Western modernists drew on these same myths, though they did so at a cultural remove from their Eastern sources. This article therefore addresses modernism as a planetary movement with the assistance of polysystem theory, which provides us with the theoretical apparatus to approach multiple—sometimes converging, sometimes diverging—nodes of modernist innovation. As we have seen, Arab and Persian modernists were not beholden to the Western reception of death-and-rebirth myths. While they certainly expressed interest in, for instance, Eliot's *The Waste Land*, the Islamic and ancient Near Eastern past offered entirely different possibilities for engaging with the same themes and addressing them to the contemporary moment in the Middle East.

The transnational approach for re-orienting modernism I use here focuses on the dynamism of the polysystem and develops out of modernist thought itself. Adūnīs, the most prominent of the Arab modernists, argues convincingly for us to consider modernism as a dynamic response to a static past, and the parallels between his thought and Even-Zohar's theory of the polysystem are striking. Adūnīs's monumental study of Arab culture, *al-Thābit wa-l-mutaḥawwil: baḥth fī al-ibdāʿ wa-l-ittibāʿ ʿinda al-ʿarab* (The Static and the Dynamic: A Study of Innovation and Imitation among the Arabs) explores the relationship between two distinct systems in Arabic literature, one static and linked to religious orthodoxy (the past) and the other dynamic and directed toward new possibilities (the future). Though polemical, Adūnīs's conception of the relationship between the static and the dynamic within Arabic literary history parallels Even-Zohar's usage of the same categories in his theory of the polysystem, which also favors dynamic, diachronic approaches to how literary systems function and interact.

In engaging with the texts I read in this article as dynamic parts of a literary polysystem, I show how modernist poetry grounded in a shared reserve of Near Eastern myth and symbol brought the Arabic and Persian literary traditions together at a time when political vicissitudes worked to define the boundaries of imagined communities in distinct nation-states.[15] Moreover, there are also implicit transnational links between the Arab and Iranian modernists, whom I approach as members of one of the "minor-to-minor networks that circumvent the major altogether" (Lionnet and Shih 8). I thus posit that a transnational unconscious, an "attitude of modernity"[16] brought on by similar experiences of Western colonial intervention in the Middle East, developed concurrently within Arab and Iranian modernist poetry. Because there were rarely any direct contacts between the leading figures in Arab and Iranian poetic modernisms, we are left to address the formation of this transnational unconscious by looking at the features shared within their poetry.

In many notable instances of these transnational connections, we often find Middle Eastern modernists using poetry to political ends, whether directed against the consolidation of power in the modern nation state (as we found in Nīmā's "The Phoenix") or more generally against the neo-imperial machinations of the West that stretched across the twentieth century (a critique that Bayātī's work puts forth). The techniques modernist poets writing in Arabic and Persian used, like *muʿāraḍah* and *taḍmīn*, take on political meaning when understood in terms of their sublating function. By mining the past for poetic content and retaining certain formal elements of ʿarūḍ prosody, Arab and Iranian modernist poets reinvigorated local cultural patrimony at the very moment it was being otherwise challenged on two separate fronts: the creation out of whole cloth of national/nationalist pasts in the service of nation states, on the one hand, and the undeniably powerful forces of cultural globalization driven by capitalist market forces (or, in some instances, Soviet cultural and political programs), on the other.

By re-orienting modernism and looking to how minor modernist poetries interact with each other, we might further provincialize or even subvert modernist centers in the West. The project outlined here not only considers the political function of modernist poetry in Arabic and Persian but also proposes a politically-motivated analysis intended to redress the imbalances that have followed in the wake of globalizing Western culture. In light of Arabic and Persian modernist poetries' growth in concert with one another, as well as out of their interactions with European modernist poetry, we can now ask: Where does modernism really begin? Arabic and Persian modernist poetries are neither wholly the results of Western influence, nor is Western modernism a *sui generis* product of Western literary developments. The poems I analyze in this article help us to tell a more complete story of the planetary movement of modernism, re-orienting our focus to modernist sources located in the Middle East. Notwithstanding the newfound interest of many academics in innovative approaches to minor literatures under the rubric of world literature, there remains a troubling lack of attention to Middle Eastern modernisms and their interactions with each other. This article constitutes a starting point for further investigation of the largely-unstudied connections of, and transactions between, Arabic and Persian modernist poetries, an invitation to re-orient our attention to the edges of modernism where we might find new beginnings.

Notes

[1] Kevin Jackson lays out in excruciating detail the case for marking 1922 as the advent of (European) modernism in *Constellation of Genius*.

[2] As opposed to "transnationalism from above," which is concomitant with the processes of globalizing capital. "Transnationalism from below," on the other hand, "is the sum of the counterhegemonic operations of the

non-elite who refuse assimilation to one given nation-state" (Mahler qtd. in Lionnet and Shih 5-6).

[3] For a thorough introduction to Nīmā's life and work, see Karimi-Hakkak.

[4] My translation. Cf. Papan-Matin (178) and Yūshīj (40). Also see Hushang Philsooph's comments on Papan-Matin and Arthur Lane's translation (102-03).

[5] Majid Naficy addresses the symbolism of the Phoenix figure in this poem and notes the "new metric" Nīmā employs within it (49-51 and 93), but he does not provide any details about Nīmā's prosodic innovations. For readers of French, Amr Taher Ahmed gives the entire metrical breakdown of the poem along with a translation (423-27).

[6] My translation, for which I have consulted both 'Aṭṭār (208) and Darbandi and Davis (n. pag.).

[7] For a concise definition of *mu'āraḍah*, see Schippers.

[8] For 'Aṭṭār's entry on Ḥallāj, see his *Tadhkiratu 'l-awliya* (135-45).

[9] See al-Ma'arrī (35) for the original Arabic.

[10] Bayātī uses an accepted variant of the word, normally *ufuq*, due to the meter.

[11] Ru'ūbīn Sanīr gives a full metrical analysis of the poem in his comprehensive study of Bayātī's work (Sanīr 27).

[12] For the rest of the poem and its explanation, see *Sharḥ dīwān al-Mutanabbī* (391-92).

[13] It should be no surprise that Shafī'ī Kadkanī included this poem in his collection of Bayātī's poems translated into Persian (84-95).

[14] For the original, see al-Bayātī, *al-A'māl* (II: 9-20). You can find an English translation in Semaan (65-69).

[15] On the role of shared language in creating the modern nation-state, see Anderson.

[16] I borrow this conception from Foucault, who "wonder[s] whether we may not envisage modernity rather as an attitude than as a period of history" (39). For more on how Foucault's "attitude of modernity" might apply in our readings of modern Arabic literature, see Thompson, "Strange" (267-68).

Works Cited

Adūnīs ['Alī Aḥmad Sa'īd Isbar]. 1974. *Al-Thābit wa-l-mutaḥawwil: baḥth fī al-ibdā' wa-l-ittibā' 'inda al-'arab*. Bayrūt: Dār al-Sāqī, 2011.

Ahmed, Amr Taher. *La «Révolution littéraire» : Étude de l'influence de la poésie française sur la modernisation des formes poétiques persanes au début de XXe siècle*. Wien [Vienna]: Verlag der Österreichischen Akademie der Wissenschaften, 2012.

Anderson, Benedict. *Imagined Communities: Reflections on the Origin and Spread of Nationalism*. NY: Verso, 2006.

Asgharī, Muḥammad Jaʿfar and Nargis Ganjī. "Tajalliyyāt al-intiẓār fī qaṣīdatay ʿUnshūdat al-maṭar' wa 'Dārūg' li-Badr Shākir al-Sayyāb wa Nīmā Yūshīj (dirāsah muqāranah)." *Faṣliyyat al-lisān al-mubīn (buḥūth fī al-adab al-ʿArabī)* 4.10 (1391 [2012/2013]): 21-37.

ʿAṭṭār, Farīd al-Dīn. *Manṭiq al-ṭayr*. Bi-taṣḥīḥ va ihtimām-i Muḥammad Javād Mashkūr, bā muqaddamah va taʿlīqāt. Tihrān: Kitābfurūshī-ʾi Tihrān, 1341 [1962].

---. *The Speech of the Birds: Manṭiq't-Tair*. Presented by Peter Avery. Cambridge, UK: The Islamic Texts Society, 2001.

---. *Tadhkiratu 'l-awliya ("Memoirs of the Saints") of Muḥammad ibn Ibrahim Faridu'd-Din ʿAṭṭar*. Ed. Reynold A. Nicholson. Part II. Persian Historical Texts. Vol. V. London: Luzac & Co., 1907.

al-Bayātī, ʿAbd al-Wahhāb. *Al-Aʿmāl al-shiʿriyyah*. 2 vols. Bayrūt: al-Muʾassasah al-ʿArabiyyah li-l-Dirāsāt wa-l-Nashr, 1995.

---. *Avāz-hā-yi Sindibād*. Tarjamahʾi M. Sirishk [Muḥammad Riżā Shafīʿī Kadkanī]. [Tihrān]: Intishārāt-i Nīl, 2536 [1976/1977].

Darbandi, Afkham and Dick Davis. "From Ashes: In Search of the Phoenix." *Lapham's Quarterly*. 1984. <http://www.laphamsquarterly.org/magic-shows/ashes>.

Even-Zohar, Itamar. "Polysystem Theory." *Polysystem Studies* [= *Poetics Today* 11.1] (1990): 9-26.

Fawzī, Nāhidah. *ʿAbd al-Wahhāb al-Bayātī ḥayātuh wa-shiʿruh (dirāsah naqdiyyah)*. Tihrān: Intishārāt-i S̱ār Allāh, 1383 [2004/2005].

---. "Hājis al-ightirāb wa-l-tirḥāl ʿinda ʿAbd al-Wahhāb al-Bayātī." *Majallat Markaz Dirāsāt al-Kūfah* 1.21 (2011): 25–44.

---, Maryam Amjad, and Kubrā Rawshanfikr. "Barʾrasī-ʾi shiʿr-i Muḥammad Riżā Shafīʿī Kadkanī va ʿAbd al-Wahhāb al-Bayātī az manẓar-i adabiyyāt-i taṭbīqī." *Pazhūhash-hā-yi adabiyyāt-i taṭbīqī* 2.1–3 (1393 [2014]): 79–97.

Foucault, Michel. "What is Enlightenment?" Trans. Catherine Porter. *The Foucault Reader*. Ed. Paul Rabinow. NY: Pantheon Books, 1984. 32-50.

Friedman, Susan Stanford. *Planetary Modernisms: Provocations on Modernity Across Time*. Modernist Latitudes. Eds. Jessica Berman and Paul Saint-Amour. NY: Columbia UP, 2015.

van Gelder, G. J. H. "*Taḍmīn*." *Encyclopaedia of Islam*. Eds. P. Bearman et al. <http://dx.doi.org/10.1163/1573-3912_islam_SIM_7284>.

Grigor, Talinn. "Recultivating 'Good Taste': The Early Pahlavi Modernists and Their Society for National Heritage." *Iranian Studies* 37.1 (2004): 17-45.

Ḥallāj, al-Ḥusayn ibn Manṣūr. *Hallaj: Poems of a Sufi Martyr*. Trans. Carl W. Ernst. Evanston, IL: Northwestern UP, 2018.

Jackson, Kevin. *Constellation of Genius: 1922: Modernism Year One*. NY: Farrar, Straus and Giroux, 2012.

Jāsim, Muḥammad. *Ramz va usṭūrah dar shiʻr-i muʻāṣir-i Īrān va ʻArab: bar'rasī-'i taṭbīqī-'i ramz'girāyī dar shiʻr-i Badr Shākir al-Sayyāb va Mahdī Akhavān S̱āliṯ*. Tihrān: Intishārāt-i Nigāh, 1394 [2015/2016].

Karimi-Hakkak, Ahmad. "Nima Yushij: A Life." *Essays on Nima Yushij: Animating Modernism in Persian Poetry*. Eds. Ahmad Karimi-Hakkak and Kamran Talattof. Leiden: E. J. Brill, 2004. 11-68.

Khāqānī, Muḥammad and Rūḥallāh Maṭlabī. "Buḥūr qaṣīdat al-tafʻīlah fī al-adabayn al-ʻarabī wa-l-fārisī." *Buḥūth fī al-lughah al-ʻarabiyyah wa-ādābihā, niṣf sanawiyyah li-qism al-ʻarabiyyah wa-ādābihā bi-jāmiʻat Iṣfahān* 1 (1388 [2009/2010]): 51-61.

Lionnet, Françoise and Shu-mei Shih, eds. *Minor Transnationalism*. Durham, NC: Duke UP, 2005.

al-Maʻarrī, Abū al-ʻAlāʼ. *Dīwān Abī al-ʻAlāʼ al-Maʻarrī al-mashhūr bi-saqṭ al-zand*. Ed. Shākir Shuqayr. Bayrūt: al-Maktabah al-Waṭaniyyah, 1884.

a-Malāʼikah, Nāzik. *Qaḍāyā al-shiʻr al-muʻāṣir*. Baghdād: Maktabat al-Nahḍah, 1967.

Massignon, Louis. *La passion de Husayn ibn Mansûr Hallâj : Martyr mystique de l'Islam*. [Paris]: Gallimard, 1975.

---. *The Passion of al-Hallāj: Mystic and Martyr of Islam*. Foreword and trans. Herbert Mason. 4 vols. Princeton, NJ: Princeton UP, 1982.

Mojaddedi, Jawid. "Ḥallāj, Abuʼl-Moḡīt̲ Ḥosayn." *Encyclopædia Iranica*. 2003. <http://www.iranicaonline.org/articles/hallaj-1>.

Mufti, Aamir R. *Forget English! Orientalisms and World Literatures*. Cambridge, MA: Harvard UP, 2016.

Muḥsinī'niyā, Nāṣir and Sipīdah Akhavān Māsūlah. "Bāztāb-i farhang va adab-i Īrān dar shiʻr-i ʻAbd al-Wahhāb al-Bayātī." *Kāvish-nāmah-'i adabiyyāt-i taṭbīqī (muṭālaʻāt-i taṭbīqī-'i ʻarabī —fārsī)* 3.12 (1392 [2014]): 95-119.

Mumtaḥan, Mahdī and Mihīn Ḥājī Zādah. "Bar'rasī-'i sayr-i taḥavvul-i shiʻr-i naw dar zabān-i ʻarabī va fārsī." *Muṭāliʻāt-i adabiyyāt-i taṭbīqī* 5.16 (1389 [2010/2011]): 153-180.

Mutaqqā'zādah, 'Īsā and 'Alī Bashīrī. "Al-Athr al-fārisī fī shi'r 'Abd al-Wahhāb al-Bayātī." *Iḍā'āt naqdiyyah* 2.6 (1391 [2012]): 129–50.

Naficy, Majid. *Modernism and Ideology in Persian Literature: A Return to Nature in the Poetry of Nimâ Yushij*. Lanham, MD: UP of America, Inc., 1997.

Nāẓimiyyān, Riżā and Fāṭimah Khayrātī. "Al-Rumūz wa-l-tiqniyyāt al-mushtarakah 'inda Nīmā wa-l-Sayyāb: 'Kār-i shab pā' ('Mihnat khafīr al-layl') wa 'al-Mūmis al-'amyā'' namūdhajan." *Idā'āt naqdiyyah* 3.9 (1392 [2013]): 171-89.

Nuhayrāt, Aḥmad. "Shakhṣiyyāt Īrāniyyah fī dīwān 'Abd al-Wahhāb al-Bayātī." *Majallat al-jam'iyyah al-'ilmiyyah al-Īrāniyyah li-l-lughah al-'arabiyyah wa-ādābihā* 9.26 (1392 [2013]): 1–28.

Papan-Matin, Firoozeh. "Love: Nima's Dialogue with Hafez." *Essays on Nima Yushij: Animating Modernism in Persian Poetry*. Eds. Ahmad Karimi-Hakkak and Kamran Talattof. Leiden: E. J. Brill, 2004. 173-92.

Philsooph, Hushang. "Book Review: *Essays on Nima Yushij: Animating Modernism in Persian Poetry*." *Middle Eastern Literatures* 12.1 (2009): 100-05.

Qādirī, Fāṭimah and Muhrī Zaynī. "Zamīnah-'i ijtimā'ī-'i ash'ār-i Shāmlū va Māghūṭ." *Adabiyyāt-i taṭbīqī ('ilmī – pazhūhashī) Dānishkadah-'i Adabiyyāt va 'Ulūm-i Insānī – Dānishgāh-'i Shahīd Bāhunar Kirmān* 1.1 (1388 [2009]): 109-31.

Qudūsī, Kāmrān and Ḥāmid Ṣidqī. "Kārkard-i miḥvarī-'i niqāb-i dīnī dar shi'r-i Shāmlū va Adūnīs." *Dūfaṣlnāmah-'i 'ilmī – pazhūhashī-'i pazhūhash-hā-yi adabiyyāt-i taṭbīqī* 2.2–3 (1393 [2014]): 1-26.

Rajabī, Farhād. "Marg-i zindagī-bakhsh dar shi'r-i Badr Shākir al-Sayyāb va Nīmā Yūshīj." *Adab-i 'Arabī* 3.2 (1390 [2011]): 185-206.

Rawshanfikr, Kubrā and Sajjād Ismā'īlī. "Bar'rasī-'i taṭbīqī-'i nūstālzhī dar shi'r-i 'Abd al-Wahhāb al-Bayātī va Shafī'ī Kadkanī." *Dūfaṣlnāmah-'i 'ilmī – pazhūhashī-'i pazhūhash-hā-yi adabiyyāt-i taṭbīqī* 2.2–3 (1393 [2014]): 27-55.

Riżā'ī, 'Alīriżā Muḥammad and Sumayyah Āramāt. "Bar'rasī-'i taṭbīqī-'i ash'ār-i Badr Shākir va Nīmā Yūshīj." *Adabiyyāt-i taṭbīqī* 6 (1387 [2008]): 161-73.

Salīmī, 'Alī and Mahdī Mir'ātī. "Muṭāla'ah-'i taṭbīqī-'i vājah-'i shab dar shi'r-i Nīmā Yūshīj va Nāzik al-Malā'ikah." *Adabiyyāt-i taṭbīqī ('ilmī – pazhūhashī) Dānishkadah-'i Adabiyyāt va 'Ulūm-i Insānī – Dānishgāh-'i Shahīd Bāhunar Kirmān* 2.3 (1389 [2010/2011]): 157-78.

Sanīr, Ru'ūbīn. *Rak'atān fī al-'ishq: dirāsah fī shi'r 'Abd al-Wahhāb al-Bayātī*. Bayrūt: Dār al-Sāqī, 2002.

Schippers, A. "*Mu'āraḍa*." *Encyclopaedia of Islam*. Eds. P. Bearman et al. <http://dx.doi.org/10.1163/1573-3912_islam_SIM_5276>.

Semaan, Khalil I. "'Al-Ḥallāj': A Poem by 'Abd al-Wahhāb al-Bayātī." *Journal of Arabic Literature* 10 (1979): 65-69.

Sharḥ dīwān al-Mutanabbī. Waḍa'ahu 'Abd al-Raḥmān al-Barqūqī. Rāja'ahu wa-fahrasahu Dr. Yūsuf al-Shaykh Muḥammad al-Buqā'ī. 4 vols. Bayrūt: Dār al-Kātib al-'Arabī, 2010.

Snir, Reuven. "A Study of 'Elegy for al-Ḥallāj' by Adūnīs." *Journal of Arabic Literature* 25.3 (1994): 245-56.

Thompson, Levi. "Strange Bedfellows: The Crisis of Modernity in Najīb Maḥfūẓ's *Al-Qāhira al-jadīda*." *Middle Eastern Literatures* 18.3 (2015): 264-82. <https://doi.org/10.1080/1475262X.2016.1199094>.

---. "A Transnational Approach to 'Abd al-Wahhāb al-Bayātī's 'Umar Khayyām." *Transnational Literature* 11.1 (2018): 1-14. <https://dspace.flinders.edu.au/xmlui/bitstream/handle/2328/38761/Thompson%20_A_Transnational_Approach.pdf>.

Wright, W. *A Grammar of the Arabic Language*. Revised by W. Robertson Smith and M. J. De Goeje. 2 vols. New Delhi: Munshiram Manoharlal Publishers, Pvt. Ltd., 2004.

Yūshīj, Nīmā. *The Bird of Sadness (Selected Poems)*. Trans. Munibar Rahman. Aligarh: Aligarh Muslim U, Institute of Persian Research, 2010.

---. *Majmū'ah-'i kāmil-i ash'ār-i Nimā Yushij: Fārsī va Ṭabarī*. Tihrān: Intishārāt-i Nigāh, 1370 [1991].

From Cultural Translation to Untranslatability: Theorizing Translation outside Translation Studies

Brian James Baer

Since the 1990s, the concept of translation has assumed an increasingly central place in disciplines across the humanities and social sciences, a phenomenon commonly referred to as the "translational turn." This turn has often been accompanied by rather grandiose claims for translation's capacity to revolutionize the study of language and culture in ways perhaps no less profound than Saussurian linguistics. As Elizabeth Lowe puts it, "Translation theory is reformulating the parameters of cultural studies, post-colonial studies, and the field of comparative literature—in short, reframing the very notion of the humanities" ("Premises" 19). Lowe's use of translation theory in the singular is notable to the extent that it implies a discrete body of knowledge that can be simply mined or borrowed by those working in adjacent fields. Borrowing, however, as Dipesh Chakrabarty demonstrates so convincingly in *Provincializing Europe*, is never a simple act of transfer; it always involves the grafting of new terms and concepts onto existing bodies of knowledge, transforming both.[1] Not surprisingly then, the interest in translation theory in disciplines outside Translation Studies has led to a proliferation of "translation theories," or new and competing conceptualizations of translation. In what follows, I will examine two of the most popular and influential of these conceptualizations: "cultural translation," which arose in the early 1990s in the context of postcolonial studies, and "untranslatabilty," which became popular in comparative literature circles in the 2010s.

Although I am by no means the first to critique the way translation is construed in the concepts of "cultural translation" (the various criticisms are laid out clearly in Maitland [18-27])[2] or "untranslatability" (see Venuti, "Hijacking Translation"), I seek to contribute to the scholarly debate by connecting the two conceptualizations, which, at first glance, appear to be quite different, with cultural translation representing through the metaphorization of "translation" a radical broadening of the concept and untranslatability representing a radical limiting of the concept of untranslatability to a discrete set of terms. That being said, they share a fundamental characteristic, namely, a deep ambivalence toward what I will call, following Coldiron and Emmerich, the fact of translation, or, in Chakrabarty's formulation, "the everyday process of translation (xiv)—by which they refer to the actual rendering of a text or utterance from one natural language or idiom into another. The nature of that ambivalence, I will argue, is expressed in the first instance by eliding or mystifying the fact of translation, and in the second by impoverishing it by focusing on a discrete set of "untranslatables," defined as words that "one keeps on (not) translating" (Cassin xvii).[3]

Insofar as the situatedness of theory—glossed by Walter D. Mignolo as, "I am where I think" (xvi)—is central to my analysis of these conceptualizations, I should acknowledge at the very outset that my political critique of this ambivalence is deeply informed by recent events, specifically, the rise of ethno-nationalist movements across Europe and the United States, which have deliberately targeted translation and interpreting services. More generally, this essay speaks to the pressing need to promote translation literacy; as schools and universities move to "globalize" their curricula by incorporating an increasing number of translated texts from an ever wider variety of languages and cultural traditions, it is no longer acceptable to pretend that the translated text is the original or to treat it as a necessary evil. This is not to say that instructors are not aware that a translation is not an original, but they are left without the pedagogical tools to raise the question in a productive way, that is, without defaulting to a Romantic discourse of loss and distortion, which often leaves students frustrated and dissatisfied. In order to better understand the circulation of cultural texts across linguistic and cultural borders, we need, as David Damrosch has argued, "more a phenomenology than an ontology of the work of art" (6). Against that historical backdrop, I hope to highlight precisely what is at stake when we allow the fact of translation to be elided or impoverished.

Cultural Translation, or Mystifying the Fact of Translation

The use of translation as metaphor was inaugurated in the context of postcolonial studies in the early 1990s by such influential post-colonial scholars and writers as Homi Bhabha, Stuart Hall, and Salman Rushdie to refer specifically to the experience of migrants. This was elaborated in Bhabha's chapter "How Newness Enters the World: Postmodern Space, Postcolonial Times and the Trials of Cultural Translation" in *The Location of Culture*, various writings by Hall, and many of Rushdie's fictional works concerned with what he famously called "translated men." There is no denying the productivity of the metaphor, and in fact all of these thinkers understand translation outside a Romantic framework stressing loss and distortion, focusing instead on "translation" as generative and productive. Indeed, Bhabha opens his chapter with a quotation from Walter Benjamin's essay "On Language as Such and the Language of Man": "Translation passes through continua of transformation, not abstract ideas of identity and sincerity" (qtd. in Bhabha 212).

Stuart Hall is arguably the most liberal in his use of translation as metaphor to refer to everything from cognition to representation, as evident in the following passages:

> To capture this sense of difference which is not pure "otherness," we need to deploy the play on words of a theorist like Jacques Derrida. Derrida uses the anomalous "a" in his way of writing "difference"—différance—as a marker which sets up a disturbance in our settled understanding or *translation* of the word/concept. It sets the word in motion to new meanings without erasing the trace of its other meanings. ("Cultural Identity" 229; italics added)

Elsewhere, Hall uses translation to refer to a post-structuralist understanding of representation that is divorced from traditional notions of mimesis and reproduction:

> We should perhaps learn to think of meaning less in terms of "accuracy" and "truth" and more in terms of effective exchange—a process of *translation*, which facilitates cultural communication while always recognizing the per-

> sistence of difference and power between different "speakers" within the same cultural circuit. (Introduction 111)

Where Hall does refer to a "literal" understanding of translation, it is not clear he is referring to interlingual translation at all:

> How, then, to describe this play of "difference" within identity? The common history—transportation, slavery, colonization—has been profoundly formative. For all these societies, unifying us across our differences. But it does not constitute a common origin, since it was, *metaphorically as well as literally, a translation*. ("Cultural Identity" 228; italics added)

By "literally" it seems that Hall is referring not to interlingual translation at all but to translation as "carrying over," an interpretation implied by his emphasis on displacement ("transportation, slavery, colonization").

In Bhabha, on the other hand, the use of translation seems to teeter on the edge of metaphor without ever collapsing into it, as in this now famous passage:

> Translation is the performative nature of cultural communication. It is language *in actu* (enunciation, positionality) rather than language *in situ* (*énoncé*, or propositionality). And the sign of translation continually tells, or "tolls" the different times and spaces between cultural authority and its performative practices. The "time" of translation consists in that movement of meaning, the principle and practice of a communication that, in the words of de Man "puts the original in motion to decanonise it, giving it the movement of fragmentation, a wandering of errance, a kind of permanent exile." (228)

While one might argue that Bhabha's abstract notion of cultural translation does not *exclude* the fact of translation, he does elide it in a number of ways in the analysis that follows. On the level of subject matter, that elision is accomplished by the fact that Bhabha discusses only migrant authors who write in English: Joseph Conrad, Salman Rushdie, and Derek Walcott. That elision is further reinforced on a metanarrative plane by the fact that the theorists promoting translation as metaphor, Bhabha, Hall, and Rushdie, also all write in English. One must ask whether the fact of translation and translation as metaphor are interchangeable in these formulations, or was the metaphorical translation of these authors into international Anglophone culture so successful precisely because they did not depend on the fact of translation? In other words, translation as metaphor glosses over or mystifies, in the Marxian sense of the word, the class implications of fluency in English.

As Peter Ives and Rocco Lacorte argue, the proliferation of translation as a metaphor threatens to weaken its political import:

> Translation has ... become a key metaphor, often unexamined, in such a wide variety of discussions of "globalization" in all the different ways the term is used. Advocates of cosmopolitanism, multiculturalism, identity politics and global governance are quick to grasp at "translation" as a metaphor but rarely offer much theoretical underpinning for it. All too often, the concept of translation (not unlike language) is *stripped of its political content* and used to cast a vaguely positive glow of acceptance, accessibility, and interest in things "other." (10-11; italics added)

Specifically, translation as metaphor, that is, translation untethered from the fact of translation, may mystify the distinction between the experience of migrancy of these Anglophone writers and scholars and that of migrants without similar access to the cultural capital of English, migrants who might be better described as "non-translated men and women." For such migrants, the question of language access in legal and health-care settings is a matter of life and death. Consider P. Wells's heartrending description of an immigrant with limited English dying of AIDS in a US hospital: "to be ill in a foreign country was simply to experience in advance the reality of all illness, which is to be homeless. It was to be in a permanent foreign land—one where the language used is barely comprehensible, or at least where words seem to match, only clumsily, what they represent" (qtd. in Binnie 112). But there is no need to resort to fiction. Take the case of Deisy Garcia, a Spanish-speaking New Yorker who filed a domestic violence complaint in Spanish at the local police department. Garcia was murdered by her husband before the complaint was ever translated into English. As CNN reported, "New York Police Department officials say they can't explain why a fearful woman's domestic-abuse report—written in the woman's native language of Spanish—was never translated into English for review, and for possible action" (Boyette and Santana n. pag.). Or consider the fact that enrollment in the Affordable Care Act by Spanish-speakers in the US was lower than average due, some have suggested, to the poor quality of the Spanish translation of the website (Corley n. pag.).

This point is especially relevant today as ethno-nationalist movements have specifically targeted translation and interpreting services. In fact, one of the first moves of the Trump administration was to remove all Spanish-language content from the White House website, while in Great Britain Communities and Local Government secretary Eric Pickles has launched an all-out war on translation services for non-English speakers. Pickles argues that translation and interpreting services are the result of "a misinterpretation of equality or human rights legislation" that have the unintended consequences of disincentivizing the study of English (n. pag.)—although there is no research to support this claim. Such politicization of translation and interpreting services further underscores the necessity of keeping the fact of translation front and center in any discussion of migrancy.

The other risk posed by eliding the fact of translation is that the concept of translation is allowed to circulate unmoored from the whole question of language proficiency that is a pre-requisite for translation. Indeed, the growing popularity of translation as metaphor in the 1990s stands in an inverse relationship to enrollment trends in foreign language courses, as documented in the MLA reports. It also tracks with disturbing trends in the publishing industry. Elliot Weinberger, the English translator of Octavio Paz, comments on the decrease in English translations of Latin American literature following the short-lived boom in the 1990s, attributing it to multiculturalism, "which he says has led not to internationalism but to a new form of nationalism. Instead of promoting foreign writers, the publishing industry promotes 'hyphenated' American writers, foreign-born or of foreign parents" (Lowe and Fitz xv). As Weinberger comments, "I think publishers feel, 'Oh well. We have this Latino writer, you know, what do we want a young Mexican or Peruvian writer for?'" (qtd. in Lowe and Fitz xv). To the extent that translation as metaphor allows translation to circulate untethered from any notion of language proficiency, one might argue that it risks inadvertently supporting the hegemony of English—Who needs foreign languages when everyone speaks English?—thereby mystifying the role of translation and translators in the circulation of texts and ideas. As Anthony Pym notes, "Bhabha is remarkably uninterested in the translators of the *Satanic Verses*, even those they were the ones who bore the brunt of the fatwa or Islamic condemnation of the novel" (145).

In addition, the popularity of translation as metaphor has real implications for our understanding of the contemporary "geopolitics of knowledge," to use Wallerstein's term, which encourages scholars to publish in English-language journals and views translation, if at all, as a necessary evil. Consider, for example, a recent study by the sociologists Erynn Masi de Casanova and Tamara Mose of fifty book-length ethnographies of Latin Americans published in English. They found that fewer than 25% mentioned the fact of translation, although such ethnographic work is impossible without it. As the authors note, "Examining recent English-language ethnographies of Latin America, we find little evidence of what we call linguistic reflexivity: recognition of linguistic boundaries and language-based identities in fieldwork" (3). How can we hope to foster the kind of linguistic reflexivity imagined by de Casanova and Mose when translation is allowed to circulate as metaphor wholly divorced from the fact of translation? Without such reflexivity, we allow an instrumentalist approach to translation to reign, thereby "preempt[ing] . . . a more productive understanding of translation as an interpretive act that inevitably varies the source text according to intelligibilities and interests in the receiving culture" (Venuti, "Hijacking Translation [abstract]" n. pag.).

Untranslatability, or Impoverishing the Fact of Translation

The recent interest in "untranslatability"—made popular with the publication of Barbara Cassin's *Dictionnaire des intraduisibles*, later published in English under the title *Dictionary of Untranslatables*, and Emily Apter's *Against World Literature: On The Politics of Untranslatability*—has been met with a frosty if not hostile reaction from scholars in Translation Studies, with Lawrence Venuti going so far as to accuse Apter and others in the field of Comparative Literature of "hijacking" translation ("Hijacking Translation" 179). At first glance, Venuti's hostility may seem a little surprising given the fact that both he and Apter aim to challenge and resist the appropriation of other cultures by a hegemonic Anglophone West. However, the way they conceptualize translation's role within that project is almost diametrically opposed, with Venuti placing the power to "foreignize" in the hands of the translator and Apter situating untranslatability in a discrete set of words.

Whereas the use of translation as metaphor described in part one represents an abstraction that elides or mystifies the fact of translation, the recent promotion of "untranslatability" in the field of Comparative Literature impoverishes the fact of translation, at least in Apter's influential formulation. Our understanding of translation is impoverished by Apter's locating untranslatability in a discrete set of words or semantic units "that cannot easily be rendered from one language to another, an 'intransigent' nub of meaning that triggers endless translating in response to its resistant singularity" (*Against* 235). Positing an intransigent semantic nub has the whiff of essentialism, implying that all other words—that is, those that do not contain this resistant nub—are unproblematically transposable. In this, Apter is less nuanced than Cassin who acknowledges that incommensurability runs across languages and so defines untranslatables not as unique instances of untranslatability but as "symptoms of difference" (Cassin xvii), which inspire repeated attempts at translation. Indeed, Apter regularly conflates untranslatability and incommensurability, as in the following: "The result has been a practice that accounts insufficiently for *incommensurability or the untranslatable* within literary heuristics" ("Doing Things" n. pag.). By implication, translation proper is then conflated with commensurability, or all that is transposable. This conflation is becoming increasingly evident as scholars outside Translation Studies use translation as a lens through which to study cross-cultural communication. Héctor Domínguez-Ruvalcaba, for example, claims that "the irreconcilability of the mestizo binary gender system and the Zapotec third-sex conception *hinders the possibility of a full cultural translation*" (36). So, then everything else about Zapotec culture could be given a full cultural translation? In other words, the problem with untranslatability from a Translation Studies perspective is not that it posits something as absolutely incommensurable and so incapable of being translated—Cassin does not claim that, in fact arguing that untranslatables inspire repeated translation—but that it implies the easy commensurability of everything that is not an untranslatable. This is why I prefer Cassin's description of the untranslatable as a symptom of widespread incommensurability rather than Apter's positing of a resistant "semantic nub."

The more common view in Translation Studies is to see linguistic asymmetries or incommensurabilities as distributed across languages, not only in discrete words but also in syntax, deixis, thematic progression, textual cohesion, and so on, as mapped by Mona Baker in her textbook *In Other Words*. In that sense, almost nothing is simply transposable—hence Ricoeur's paradox, that languages are diverse but that "people have always translated" (13). This is also what Chakrabarty was getting at when he stated that a "defiance of translation" is an integral part of the translation process itself (xiv). Moreover, even the most common objects, which would seem to be the easiest to translate, that is, the most transposable, may reference quite different prototypes in the minds of target readers. This is a point Susan Bassnett drives home in regard to the translation of the English word *butter* into Italian:

> When translating butter into Italian there is a straightforward word-for-word substitution: butter—burro. Both butter and burro describe the product made from milk and marketed as a creamy coloured slab of edible grease for human consumption. And yet within their separate cultural contexts butter and burro cannot be considered as signifying the same. In Italy, burro, normally light coloured and unsalted, is used primarily for cooking, and carries no associations of high status, whilst in Britain butter, most often bright yellow and salted, is used for spreading on bread and less frequently in cooking. Because of the high status of butter, the phrase bread and butter is the accepted usage even where the product used is actually margarine. So there is a distinction both between the objects signified by butter and burro and between the function and value of those objects in their cultural context. The problem of equivalence here involves the utilization and perception of the object in a given context. (27-28)

Walter Benjamin makes a similar point regarding *Brot*, or bread (18).

Therefore, even in instances where transposability appears possible, the thing referenced is not the "same," making incommensurability not the exception inevitably undermining the translator's task but the enabling condition of that task. Not surprisingly then, what scholars outside Translation Studies have described as "untranslatables" or "non translations" are viewed within the field of Translation Studies as legitimate translation techniques. Indeed, "borrowing" comes first in Vinay and Darbelnet's well-known list of translation strategies (46-55). Borrowings are not situated outside translation proper nor do they mark a failure of translation, although they are often used to index culture specificity. Moreover, even borrowing is not a simple act; translators must decide whether to highlight the borrowing through formatting (bolding, italicization, etc.), to add an in-text definition or a note, and, when working with languages using different scripts, how to render the borrowing, in the original language's script or in a transliteration, of which there are often more than one option. On top of that, my own study of borrowings in English translations of Mikhail Lermontov's *A Hero of Our Time* revealed that there was no consensus among the translators over what should be borrowed (see Baer, "Translating"). Therefore, when we gloss incommensurability as untranslatability, we necessarily restrict our understanding of the translator's task.

When certain words are designated as *essentially* untranslatable, then untranslatability risks becoming a largely ahistorical linguistic or philosophical problem, thus foreclosing the far more interesting political question: *Cui bono?* Who benefits from claims of untranslatability? When we reject the idea of untranslatability as a feature of certain words endowed with a resistant semantic nub, then we can turn our attention to the various political, philosophical, and even theological investments that lie behind claims of untranslatability in specific historical and cultural contexts. Naomi Seidman, for example, unpacks the different theological investments in the question of (un)translatability in her book *Faithful Renderings: Jewish-Christian Difference and the Politics of Translation*, where she argues that the Jewish tradition is marked by monism, as reflected in a distinct resistance to the translation of its most sacred texts, while the Christian tradition is marked by universalism, as reflected in the imperative to preach the Gospel to all peoples (11-30). In the modern world, it is often nationalists who assert untranslatability as proof of a unique national genius. As Alexandra

Jaffe puts it in her study of Corsican translators, "When [Corsican] translators talk about the untranslatable, they often reinforce the notion that each language has its own 'genius', an essence that 'naturally' sets it apart from all other languages and reflects something of the 'soul' of its culture or people" (271).[4]

This traditional association of untranslatability with claims of national specificity is why Soviet translation scholars considered untranslatability to be a bourgeois fallacy closely tied to capitalist conceptions of private property. Consider, for example, Andrei Fedorov's 1941 argument that untranslatability reveals "a lack of faith in the ultimate tasks of translation, a lack of faith in the possibility of knowing an original with the help of a translation" (11). He then goes on to argue that this "idealist worldview" is informed by a radical understanding of subjectivity, according to which "everything outside ourselves cannot be objectively apprehended; the only thing that is real is our subjective perception" (11), thus tying untranslatability to the construction of the bourgeois liberal subject.

Fedorov provides a more detailed argument in his 1953 *Introduction to Translation Theory*, focusing his attention on the rhetoric of untranslatability, which I will quote in its entirety, as it is central to my argument:

> What is important to note here is that this pessimistic view of translation in Western European literature, one that completely rejects or severely limits the possibility of translation, is extremely widespread and actively supported. This can be explained by the legitimate difficulties of translation stemming from the national specificity of the two languages in question as well as the ease with which one can prove this position through primitive empirical means. In fact, nothing could be simpler than proving the specificity of this or that language by pointing to, for example, the presence of aspectual verb forms in Russian or the presence of articles and complex forms of the past tense in German, French and English. One could also prove this by pointing out the absence of formal equivalents in another language and concluding from that the untranslatability of the concept described by that formal element (although the thought could be transferred by

> other means, for example, by a collection of words). One should also stress here that the theory of untranslatability is widespread in bourgeois philology as confirmation that the cultural values created in politically dominant cultures cannot become the property of other peoples. (32)[5]

Here Fedorov unpacks untranslatability as a philosophical fallacy supported by a rhetorical device that conflates the specificity of natural languages, or their incommensurability, with the impossibility of translation, or untranslatability. In quoting Fedorov, I am not asserting that he is "right" or that his position is somehow "correct." Rather, I am pointing out how different his leftist, Marxist-informed view of untranslatability is from Apter's, underscoring again the situatedness of theory.

Apter's designation of certain terms or concepts as "untranslatables" finds an echo Haun Saussy's monograph *Translation as Citation*, winner of the 2017 ACLA book award.[6] As Saussy explains in the introduction, he will focus not on translation (proper) but on what he labels "non-translation":

> Certainly translation takes up a great deal of space in the world of words today—but not all the space, for like everything, it has an edge and an *Other*. It is this other thing, non-translation, that I would like to investigate. . . . The Other I have in mind I have in mind is vanishingly close to translation, so much so that it is often mistaken for translation, as it happens usually at close quarters to it and achieves, more or less, the same ends. To see this Other, we have to examine translation, but to look askance, to look away from the specific operations that translation, in the classic formulations of that term, performs. (2; *italics added*)

Carving out a space for what Saussy terms *non-translation* requires first setting up translation proper as a proverbial straw man, which he does in the following paragraph by defining interlingual translation as follows: "the *creation* of an expression *in language B* that will be the *equivalent* of a *pre-existing* expression in language A." (2). This is Saussy's own rewriting of Jakobson's famous definition of interlingual translation "or *translation proper* [as] an interpretation of verbal signs by means of some other language" (Jakobson 114). So, by adding both "equivalent," which Jakobson avoids in favor of "interpretation," and "pre-existing," which Jakobson does not mention as a necessary pre-condition for translation proper, Saussy asserts the existence of non-translation, which, like Apter's untranslatables, is something that supposedly lies outside translation or marks the failure of translation.[7]

This rhetoric is also manifested on a meta-disciplinary level in claims that the field of Translation Studies is itself invested in, or defined by, the promotion of this impoverished understanding of translation as total transposability. In other words, Translation Studies is presented as deeply invested in and understanding of translation as total transposability. Fiona J. Doloughan makes this point in her *English as a Literature in Translation*, arguing that the field of Translation Studies has for too long fostered a very restrictive notion of what constitutes translation, one that is only today being broadened under pressure from neighboring disciplines, such as Comparative Literature:

> What has been established to date is the fact that within the discipline or interdiscipline of Translation Studies, both from the UK and from the US perspective, there is evidence to suggest that conceptions of translation and translational activities have broadened, not randomly or idiosyncratically, but in response to a succession of changes, both environmental and intellectual. (11)

The comparatist Brian Lennon lends a historical dimension to the argument by claiming that Translation Studies sold out its capacity for radical critique in favor of the bureaucratic benefits of being a full-fledged discipline:

> In transforming translation from a secondary (re)writing practice into a primary scholarly discipline, Translation Studies erased precisely the theoretical advantage of that practice: its deixis with respect to theories of literary theory itself as something other than (or in addition to, or more than) descriptive science. This doubling down on discipline is a mode of bureaucratic leverage with benefits, and costs, that are plain. (6-7)

In both cases, Translation Studies is associated with a narrow, indeed impoverished, understanding of translation, which then leaves translation open to being co-opted by the forces of international capital in the form of international publishing conglomerates. The rhetoric of untranslatability, therefore, does double duty by impoverishing our understanding of what constitutes both the fact of translation and the field of Translation Studies.

Naoki Sakai, too, paints the discipline of Translation Studies as promoting a notion of translation predicated on the transposability of content, that is, of a message divorced from the code in which it was originally formulated. As he explains:

> Translation studies, a scholarly discipline established in an increasing number of universities in the world today, for the most part conceives of translation premised on the model of communication, thus trusting in the possibility of a principled distinction between message (content) and code (rule). When content is translated from one language (to adopt the vocabulary of translation studies, the "source language") to another (the "target language"), this content contains elements that, like a proper noun, do not necessarily follow the rules of a particular language. It is generally accepted that a proper noun is *not translated*, nor is there any need to do so strictly following the code of the target language. Aside from such an exception, translation is expected to be an all-encompassing transformation of rules (code). When content (message) in the source language is translated into content in the target language, the rules of the source language should presumably be completely erased from the content expressed in the target language. Translation conveys content to us, but does not teach us the grammar of a different language. (n. pag.)

Sakai's rather reductive characterization of the entire discipline of Translation Studies is especially surprising given his concern with the politics of "bordering." Nevertheless, what is more interesting for our purposes here is his rhetoric; Sakai's claim that "translation is expected to be an all-encompassing transformation of rules (code)" is a dubious one, as scholars in the field of Translation Studies have repeatedly demonstrated that, despite societal norms of readability, translated texts inevitably manifest features of source-text patterning and lexis, described by Baker and others as translation universals (see Blum-Kulka and Levenston; Blum-Kulka; Baker, "Corpus" ; and Mauranen and Kujamäki), and by others as constituting the essentially hybrid nature of translated texts (see Hermans; Schiavi; Schäffner and Adab, among others).

Poor but Not Impoverished

The challenge facing translation theory is, therefore, dual: to resist the elision of translation, on the one hand, and its impoverishment, on the other. The solution is, likewise, dual: to promote a translation theory that is poor but not impoverished. In using the adjective "poor," I am alluding to Ngugi wa Thiong'o's concept of "poor theory," which he introduces in his Rene Wellek lectures, which were subsequently published in book form under the title *Globalectics*. In the introduction, entitled "The Riches of Poor Theory," wa Thiong'o critiques theory that is "weighed down by ornaments" (2). As he goes on to explain: "*Poor*, no matter the context of its use, implies the barest. . . . Poor theory and its practice imply maximizing the possibilities inherent in the minimum" (2). One of the major benefits of poor theory, wa Thiong'o argues, is to

> provide an antidote to the tendency of theory becoming like a kite that, having lost its mooring, remains floating in space with no possibility of returning to earth; or an even more needed critique of the tendency in the writing of theory to substitute density of words for that of thought, a kind of modern scholasticism. (2)

He then cites E. P. Thompson's critique of Althusserism, where "theory is forever collapsing into ulterior theory," so that, "in disallowing empirical inquiry, the mind is confined forever within the compound of the mind" (Thompson 167). At the same time, the threat of such theoretical insularity should not lead us to reject abstraction altogether, as Spivak argues in her Wellek lectures, published under the provocative title *Death of a Discipline*. There Spivak writes:

> We cannot and should not reject the impulse toward generalization [which she elsewhere refers to as global commensurability] which has something like a relationship with globalization. If we do—and some have the ignorance and/or luxury to do so—we will throw away every good of every international initiative. (46)

Read in this light, translation theory becomes poor when translation as metaphor is not separated or untethered from the fact of translation. The productivity of poor translation was illustrated by Chakrabarty in *Provincializing Europe*, where he shows how the universal pretensions of Western theory can be challenged, or provincialized, by paying "critical and unrelenting attention to the very process of translation" (17). Paul Ricouer makes a similar point when he writes, "We need to get beyond these theoretical alternatives, translatable *versus* untranslatable, and to replace them with new practical alternatives, stemming from the very exercise of translation" (14). Ives and Lacorte offer an example of poor translation theory in action in their volume on Gramsci, which was inspired by Gramsci himself, who "is concerned about the actual politics of translation but also uses the linguistic concept to its full metaphorically analytical power" (9). And so, the various chapters examine translation and translatability as conceptualized by Gramsci alongside studies of Gramsci's own translations (he translated stories of the Brothers Grimm, among other things) as well as studies examining the challenges of translating Gramsci's work into other languages. Their volume demonstrates that the metaphor is in fact more powerful and illustrative when combined with facts of translation, that is, when translation is considered as at once "a metaphor, process and act" (Wilper 216).

A poor theory of translation as represented by the work discussed above is, however, predicated on a refusal to impoverish translation by conflating incommensurability with untranslatability and, by extension, translation proper with transposability. As Chakrabarty states so succinctly, "no human society is a *tabula rasa*. The universal concepts of political modernity encounter pre-existing concepts, categories, institutions, and practices through which they get translated and configured differently. (xii). This calls for a more sophisticated understanding of the challenge of translation, rooted in the asymmetry of natural languages and their divergent histories.

That being said, scholars in the field of Translation Studies have themselves been seduced by the rhetoric of untranslatability, as evident in one of the founding texts of the field, Roman Jakobson's 1959 essay "On Linguistic Aspects of Translation." While in the first part of the essay, Jakobson clearly distinguishes total translatability from transposability when he states that "languages differ essentially in what they *must* convey and not in what they *may* convey" (116), in the second half, he addresses the specific challenges posed by poetry and paramasia, in which form and content are inseparably connected, declaring such works to require not translation but "creative transposition" (118). More important from a rhetorical point of view, however, is not Jakobson's use of the term transposition but his use of the modifier "creative," suggesting that the kind of translation described earlier in the essay is somehow uncreative, mechanical. By making creative transposition into the exception, Jakobson implies a notion of translation proper as mechanical substitution, despite the fact that the examples discussed in part one, such as how to render the feminine Russian word for worker *rabotnitsa* into English, involve if not a high degree of creativity, then certainly some level of decision-making; they are not automatic. And so, if we define creativity broadly as involving decision-making, then it is difficult to sustain any *essential* distinction between the kind of translation described in the first part of the essay and the kind described in the second; the difference appears more quantitative (a question of degree) rather than qualitative (a question of essence). It is interesting in that regard that when Jakobson ends the essay by invoking the Italian proverb *traduttore-tradittore*, he provides a deliberately "bad" translation: "the translator is a betrayer" (118), that is, one that fails to capture the assonance or rhythm of the original. It is, paradoxically, that "creative rendering"—he might have offered "translator-traitor"—that he bases his claim of untranslatability on.

This rhetoric of impoverishment continues to be peddled by translators and even translation scholars when they resort to the tired trope of translation as treason. Ossified in the Italian proverb *traduttore—tradittore*, with which Jakobson ends his essay, the trope continues to circulate, as in the title of Gregory Rabassa's autobiography *If This Be Treason: Translation and Its Dyscontents* (2005), and more recently in Polizzotti's *Sympathy for the Traitor* (2018). The trope of translation as treason, which implies that a faithful translation is characterized by total transposability, lives on even in Translation Studies in such concepts as *manipulation*, coined by the influential Manipulation School, and *subversion*, as in Suzanne Jill Levine's *The Subversive Scribe*. If we consider that pre-modern scribes in fact introduced countless interpretive and other changes into manuscripts, then we see that the scribe, like translation proper, functions for Levine as a straw man; the image of a perfectly faithful copyist must be put forward so that the translator can then be cast as his subversive doppelganger.[8]

An especially striking manifestation of the trope is offered by Ilan Stavans:

> In its colonial enterprise, Portuguese, too, rebuilt itself as a sequence of *forgeries*. Elizabeth Lowe and Earl E. Fitz, in *Translation and the Rise of Inter-American Literature*, delve into these intricacies in suitable fashion, from the outside in.... Their protagonists are the English-language inheritors of Benengeli and Melquíades (Gregory Rabassa, Helen Lane, Margaret Sayers Peden, Edith Grossman, et al.), *falsifiers* whose task it is to make authentic the inauthentic. Reading their pages, it becomes clear that only through translation, which is nothing but the art of embellished *falsification*, are the Hispanic and Portuguese Americas best appreciated, as an echoing landscape where imitation becomes truth. (xii; italics added)

These provocative conceptualizations of translation, while lending a certain element of bravado to the traditional image of the slavishly obedient translator, nonetheless work to obscure the true nature of the translator's task insofar as the decision-making necessitated by the asymmetry of natural languages and their divergent histories makes total transposability impossible. The "creative" operations this necessitates, therefore, should not be cast as treason, manipulation, subversion or falsification, for there is nothing *improper* about them; indeed, they constitute translation proper. Chakrabarty makes this clear, when he writes:

> Yet nothing concrete and particular could ever be the universal itself, for intertwined with the sound-value of a word like 'right' or 'democracy' were concept-images

> that, while (roughly) translatable from one place to another, also contained elements that defied translation. *Such defiance of translation was, of course, part of the everyday process of translation.* (xiv; italics added)

Here untransposablity or incommensurability are not cast as untranslatability, that is, as somehow outside the scope of translation or as a failure of translation, but rather as integral to it—indeed its very condition.

Nevertheless, it should be noted, that even scholars like Sandra Bermann, who acknowledge that "language is not a simple nomenclature for pre-established and universally recognized 'meanings,' as most contemporary language philosophers agree" (5), find it difficult to avoid a Romantic rhetoric of loss and distortion: "translation can *never be a complete or transparent transferal* of semantic content" (5). Later she writes: "yet even in its *imperfect*, or *simply creative* negotiations of difference, translation provides a necessary linguistic *supplement*" (5; italics added). If total transposability is impossible, then why should translations be cast as always already imperfect and the decision-making they require, as "simply creative"? Such discourse seems haunted by an impossible desire for sameness, something that was brilliantly parodied by Borges in his short story "Pierre Menard, Author of the Quixote." So, it is important not only to dismiss the reductive model of translation as transposability but also the Romantic rhetoric of loss and distortion that often accompanies the recognition—at least among many Western scholars—that translation cannot ever achieve perfect transposability.

Finally, let me say that this advocacy for a translation theory that is poor but not impoverished is not a merely academic argument. There is much at stake, I would argue, in the mystifying and impoverishing of the fact of translation. First, both are equally detrimental to the cause of promoting translation literacy, which has become a concern no less pressing in our increasingly digitized and globalized world than information and digital literacy. Second, both reduce the capacity of translations to "counter the framing terms of our standard critical practice and . . . serve as important sites of critical inquiry" (Coldiron 339). When the concept of translation is elided and impoverished, not only is translation weakened as a critical practice, it is also left open to the charge of collusion with the forces of globalization, making translation "easily conflated with globalization [perceived] as the play of free or autonomous, nonsocial or inhuman market forces" (Lennon 7). Only when we refuse to abstract or impoverish translation can we move definitively past Romantic concepts of ineffability and loss in favor of an understanding of translation as a complex generative site of negotiation and world-making, the very place at which "newness enters the world."

Notes

[1] As Chakrabarty explains in his preface to the 2000 re-edition of *Provincializing Europe*, "To provincialize Europe was then to know how universalistic thought was always and already modified by particular histories, whether or not we could excavate such pasts fully" (xiv).

[2] Among the various critiques of cultural translation from within the field of Translation Studies, Trivedi is one of the most cogent.

[3] My use of the fact of translation is similar to Dilek Dizdar's use of "translation proper" but avoids any confusion related to the use of translation proper to distinguish interlingual translation from intralingual and intersemiotic translation (see Jakobson). The "fact" of translation, on the other hand, is meant to contrast the actual translation of texts or utterances between natural languages to translation as an abstract concept denoting processes of cultural transfer and exchange.

[4] If we see untranslatability as an ahistorical feature of certain words, we will be unable to see the connection between untranslatability and the current state of literary studies and, more broadly, the humanities in the Global North. A study conducted of reviews of translated books in the *New York Times* in 1900, 1950, and 2000, for example, revealed the nature of the translation criticism in the three years under investigation to be markedly different, with the 2000 corpus being uniquely characterized by assertions of untranslatability, or the impossibility of translation (see Baer, "Translation"). Compare that with the optimism of the 1950 corpus, with W. H. Auden declaring in his review of a translation of ancient Greek poetry that "Every translator is an international agent of good-will" (qtd. in Baer, "Translation" 16). The historical specificity of "untranslatability," therefore, may reflect a broader pessimism in the Global North related to the very possibility of knowing and representing difference.

[5] All translations from the Russian are mine unless otherwise indicated.

[6] Venuti notes contradictions in Saussy's 2004 report to the American Comparative Literature Association, *Comparative Literature in an Age of Glo-*

balization. The report, Venuti argues, reflects an uncertainty about what translation is and does by arguing first that "A translation always brings across most successfully aspects of a work for which its audience is already prepared" but then asserts the implicitly contradictory view that "A translator always perturbs the settled economy of two linguistic systems" ("Hijacking Translation" 182).

[7] Similarly, one could argue that Bhabha's "cultural translation" rhetorically implies that translation proper is somehow not cultural, but exclusively linguistic, as if language and culture could be separated.

[8] As Reynolds and Wilson note, "It is to be noted that the difficulties facing the reader of an ancient book were equally troublesome to the man who wished to transcribe his own copy. The risk of misinterpretation and consequent corruption of the text in this period [Antiquity] is not to be underestimated. It is certain that a high proportion of the most serious corruptions in classical texts go back to this period and were already widely current in the books that eventually entered the library of the Museum at Alexandria" (5).

Works Cited

Apter, Emily. "Doing Things with Untranslatables: The Problem of Translation and Untranslatability in the Comparative Humanities." Transdisciplinarity and the Humanities: Methods, Histories, Concepts, Center for Research in Modern European Philosophy, Kingston University, 25 January 2015. Workshop Talk. <https://backdoorbroadcasting.net/2012/01/emily-apter-doing-things-with-untranslatables-the-problem-of-translation-and-untranslatability-in-the-comparative-humanities/>.

---. *Against World Literature: On the Politics of Untranslatability*. London and NY: Verso, 2013.

Baer, Brian James. "Translating Foreign Words in Imperial Russian Literature: The Experience of the Foreign and the Sociology of Language." *International Journal of the Sociology of Language* 207 (February 2011): 127-51.

---. "Translation Criticism in Newspaper Reviews: The Rise of Readability." *Authorizing Translation*. Ed. Michelle Woods. NY and London: Routledge, 2016. 12-31.

Baker, Mona. "Corpus Linguistics and Translation Studies—Implications and Applications." *Text and Technology: In Honour of John Sinclair*. Eds.

M. Baker, G. Francis, and E. Tognini-Bonelli. Amsterdam: John Benjamins, 1993. 233–50.

---. *In Other Words: A Coursebook on Translation*. London and NY: Routledge, 1994.

Bassnett, Susan. *Translation Studies*. NY and London: Routledge, 2002.

Benjamin, Walter. "The Task of the Translator: An Introduction to the Translation of Baudelaire's *Tableaux Parisiens*." *The Translation Studies Reader*. Ed. Lawrence Venuti. NY and London: Routledge, 2000. 15-23.

Bermann, Sandra. Introduction. *Nation, Language, and the Ethics of Translation*. Eds. Sandra Bermann and Michael Wood. Princeton: Princeton UP, 2005. 1-10.

Bhabha, Homi K. *The Location of Culture*. London and NY: Routledge, 1994.

Binnie, Jon. *The Globalization of Sexuality*. London, Thousand Oaks, New Delhi: Sage Publications, 2004.

Blum-Kulka, Shoshana. "Shifts of Cohesion and Coherence in Translation." *Interlingual and Intercultural Communication: Discourse and Cognition in Translation and Second Language Acquisition Studies*. Eds. J. House and S. Blum-Kulka. Tübingen: Gunter Narr, 1986. 17–35.

--- and Eddie A. Levenston. "Universals of Lexical Simplification." *Strategies in Interlanguage Communication*. Eds. C. Faerch and G. Kasper. London and NY: Longman, 1983. 119–39.

Borges, Jorge Luis. "Pierre Menard, Author of the *Quixote*." *Collected Fictions*. Trans. Andrew Hurley. London and NY: Penguin, 1998. 88-95.

Boyette, Chris and Maria Santana. "A Woman's Plea in Her Native Language Goes Untranslated, Three Lives Are Lost." *CNN*. February 20, 2014. <https://edition.cnn.com/2014/02/19/us/new-york-domestic-killing-warnings/index.html>.

de Casanova, Erynn Masi and Tamara R. Mose. "Translation in Ethnography: Representing Latin American Studies in English." *Translation and Interpreting Studies* 12.1 (2017):1-23.

Cassin, Barbara. Introduction. *Dictionary of Untranslatables: A Philosophical Lexicon*. Ed. B. Cassin. Princeton and Oxford: Princeton UP, 2014. xvii-xx.

Chakrabarty, Dipesh. *Provincializing Europe: Postcolonial Thought and Historical Difference*. Princeton: Princeton UP, 2000.

Coldiron, A. E. B. "Translation's Challenge to Critical Categories: Verses from the French in the Early English Renaissance." *Critical Readings in Translation Studies*. Ed. Mona Baker. London and NY: Routledge, 2003. 337-58.

Corley, Cheryl. "Language Remains a Barrier in Latino Healthcare Enrollment." *NPR*. January 20, 2014. <https://www.npr.org/2014/01/20/263361444/language-remains-a-barrier-in-latino-health-care-enrollment>.

Damrosch, David. *What Is World Literature?* Princeton and Oxford: Princeton UP, 2003.

Dizdar, Dilek. "Translational Transitions: 'Translation Proper' and Translation Studies in the Humanities." *Translation Studies* 2.1 (2009): 89-102.

Doloughan, Fiona J. *English as a Literature in Translation*. NY and London: Bloomsbury Academic, 2016.

Domínguez-Ruvalcaba, Héctor. *Translating the Queer: Body Politics and Transnational Conversations*. London: Zed Books, 2016.

Emmerich, Karen. *Literary Translation and the Making of Originals*. NY and London: Bloomsbury Academic, 2017.

Fedorov, Andrei V. *O khudozhestvennom perevode* [On Literary Translation]. Leningrad: Khudozhestvennaia Literatura, 1941.

---. *Vvedenie v teoriiu khudozhestvennogo perevoda* [Introduction to the Theory of Translation]. Moscow and Leningrad: Literatura na inostrannykh iazykakh, 1953.

Hall, Stuart. "Cultural Identity and Diaspora." *Colonial Discourse and Post-Colonial Theory: A Reader*. Eds. Patrick Williams and Laura Chrisman. NY: Columbia UP, 1994. 222-37.

---. Introduction. *Representation: Cultural Representations and Signifying Practices*. Ed. Stuart Hall. London, Thousand Oaks, New Delhi: Sage Publications, 1997. 1-11.

Hermans, Theo. "The Translator's Voice in Translated Narrative." *Target* 8.1 (1996): 23-48.

Ives, Peter and Rocco Lacorte. "Introduction: Translating Gramsci on Language, Translation and Politics." *Gramsci, Language, and Translation*. Eds. Peter Ives and Rocco Lacorte. Lanham: Lexington Books, 2010. 1-15.

Jaffe, Alexandra. "Locating Power: Corsican Translators and Their Critics." *Critical Readings in Translation Studies*. Ed. Mona Baker. NY and London, Routledge, 2010. 265-83.

Jakobson, Roman. "On Linguistic Aspects of Translation." *The Translation Studies Reader*. Ed. Lawrence Venuti. NY and London: Routledge, 2000. 113-18.

Lennon, Brian. *After Babel: Multilingual Literatures, Monolingual States*. Minneapolis: U of Minnesota P, 2010.

Levine, Suzanne Jill. *The Subversive Scribe: Translating Latin American Fiction*. Champaign, IL and London: Dalkey Archive P, 2009.

Lowe, Elizabeth. "Premises of a New Translation Pedagogy: Changing the Paradigm of Cultural Studies." *Context* 22 (2008): 19–21.

--- and Earl E. Fitz. *Translation and the Rise of Inter-American Literature*. Gainesville: UP of Florida, 2007.

Maitland, Sarah. *What Is Cultural Translation?* London, Oxford, NY, New Delhi, Sydney: Bloomsbury, 2017.

Mauranen, Anna and Pekka Kujamäki, eds. *Translation Universals: Do They Exist?* Amsterdam and Philadelphia: Routledge, 2004.

Mignolo, Walter D. *Local Histories/Global Designs: Coloniality, Subaltern Knowledges, and Border Thinking*. Princeton and Oxford: Princeton UP, 2000.

Pickles, Eric. "Communities and Local Government: Translation into Foreign Languages." [UK Parliament Written Ministerial Statements.] March 12, 2013. <https://publications.parliament.uk/pa/cm201213/cmhansrd/cm130312/wmstext/130312m0001.htm#13031234000003>.

Polizzotti, Mark. *Sympathy for the Traitor: A Translation Manifesto*. Cambridge, MA, and London: MIT P, 2018.

Pym, Anthony. *Exploring Translation Theories*. London and NY: Routledge, 2010.

Rabassa, Gregory. *If This Be Treason: Translation and Its Dyscontents: A Memoir*. NY: New Directions Books, 2005.

Reynolds and Wilson. *Scribes and Scholars: A Guide to the Transmission of Greek and Latin Literature*. London: Oxford UP, 1991.

Ricoeur, Paul. *On Translation*. Trans. Eileen Brennan. London and NY: Routledge, 2006.

Sakai, Naoki. "Translation and the Schematism of Bordering." Gesellschaft übersetzen: Eine Kommentatorenkonferenz, University of Konstanz, October 29-31, 2009. Conference Paper. <http://www.translating-society.de/conference/papers/2/>.

Saussy, Huan. *Translation as Citation: Zhuangzi Inside Out*. Oxford: Oxford UP, 2017.

Schäffner, Christina and Beverly Adab. "The Idea of the Hybrid Text and Translation: Contact as Conflict." *Across Languages and Cultures* 2.2 (September 2001): 167-80.

---. "The Idea of the Hybrid Text and Translation Revisited." *Across Languages and Cultures* 2.2 (September 2001): 277-302.

Schiavi, Giuliana. "There Is Always a Teller in a Tale." *Target* 8.1 (1996): 1-21.

Seidman, Naomi. *Faithful Renderings: Jewish-Christian Difference and the Politics of Translation*. Chicago: Chicago UP, 2006.

Spivak, Gayatri. *Death of a Discipline*. NY and London: Columbia UP, 2003.

Stavans, Ilan. "Foreword." Elizabeth Lowe and Earl E. Fitz. *Translation and the Rise of Inter-American Literature*. Gainesville: UP of Florida, 2007. xi-xii.

wa Thiong'o, Ngugi. *Globalectics: Theory and the Politics of Knowing*. NY: Columbia UP, 2014.

Thompson, Edward P. *The Poverty of Theory and Other Essays*. NY: Monthly Review P, 1978.

Trivedi, Harish. "Translating Culture vs. Cultural Translation." *Translation: Reflections, Refractions, Transformations*. Eds. P. St.-Pierre and P. S. Kar. Amsterdam and Philadelphia: John Benjamins, 2007. 277-87.

Venuti, Lawrence. "Hijacking Translation [abstract]." *b2o*. February 19, 2015. <http://www.boundary2.org/2015/02/hijacking-translation/>.

---. "Hijacking Translation." *boundary 2* 43.2 (2016): 179-204.

Vinay, Jean-Paul and Jean Darbelnet. *Stylistique comparée du français et de l'anglais*. Paris, Bruxelles, Montreal : Didier, 1969.

Wilper, James. "Translation and the Construction of a 'Uranian' Identity: Edward Prime-Stevenson's [Xavier Mayne's] *The Intersexes* (1908)". *Sexology and Translation: Cultural and Scientific Encounters across the Modern World*. Ed. Heike Bauer. Philadelphia: Temple U P, 2015. 216-32.

Towards Holistic Medical Humanities

Nadia Hashish

This article aims to explore the dire need to include humanities into the medical field and to highlight the vital role played by female healers in women's health care in early twentieth-century Western world. Although this period marked the beginning of the modern age with its evolving scientific progress and technological achievements, it led to a conflict between modernity and folk traditions in the medical field. This conflict manifested itself in two attitudes: the first advocates reductionism, an approach which explains human illnesses through biological concepts, while the second advocates holism, an approach which explains human illnesses through incorporating other factors—social, cultural, personal, and political—into medical theory.[1] Though services offered by science and technology to medicine are undeniable, including humanities into medicine remains highly desirable. In childbirthing, for example, reductionism prioritizes the role of science and technology and pathologizes this medical experience by regarding the birthing mother as a patient who is under the full control of a professional obstetrician and his administration of biomedicine, or anesthesia. Holism, on the other hand, views childbirthing as a life event that addresses other crucial issues like the birthing mother's emotional and physical health, in addition to her right to a share in decision-making concerning her uniquely personal experience as to where she would like to deliver her baby—at home or at a hospital, for instance—or to whether she would choose to be anaesthetized or not. Her medical state should also be indiscriminately assessed regardless of any social, economic, or ethnic differences and treated according to structural Social Determinants of Health (SDOH), such as her dietary history and economic constraints, which may impact her and her baby's welfare. Thus, in favor of this holistic, humanistic approach in medicine which is more respectful to women's health and gender, this article examines two early twentieth-century medical issues, namely, the conflict between reductionism and holism in medicine and the issue of patriarchal authority versus women's relative lack of agency in women's health care, as they were explored in fiction.

Reductionism vs. Holism

The development of science and technology in the early twentieth century has highly influenced the medical field, in general, and childbirthing as a medical practice, in particular. Whereas in medicine the scientific development in biology is remarkable, in medical practice, biological developments alone fail to address certain human illnesses that physicians encounter in their everyday clinical work. This leads to the rise of a new major critical debate between reductionism and holism in medical theory. A reductionist approach is adopted to magnify the benefits of using technological progress in medical tools and drugs. Childbirthing is a medical experience which is drastically affected by this modern technological leap and the supremacy of science above all other disciplines, including the human sciences. Professionally educated medical obstetricians rise in prominence and are contrasted with wisdom-educated midwives, a fact which highlights a real conflict between modernity and folk traditions in the medical field. Female midwifery, which has always been a cultural norm up to the modern period, is at stake when professional male obstetricians enforce themselves into the birthing room, fight to strip female midwives off their usual duties, and seek to transform childbirthing practice into a professional business.[2] Alongside their business-oriented motives and profit-targeted plans, they are backed by a Western materialistic Health Care System, and their enterprise is further facilitated by the introduction of maternity homes that advocate modern hospital birthing to replace traditional home birthing. A holistic approach to medicine reveals the drawbacks of reductionism and gradually leads to the emergence of Medical Humanities as a new genre in literary criticism. Medical Humanities attempts to bridge the gap between biologically based medical theory and reality-based human/patient experience.

The shift from the reductionist approach of modern medicine towards the holistic approach of traditional folk remedies is reflected in Ami McKay's debut novel *The Birth House*. The article shows how the novel manifests this shift from modern medical obstetrics to traditional midwifery practice. It also shows how the author uses holistic childbirthing as a tool to portray how women painstakingly struggle to have agency, gain control over their own bodies, and make decisions about specifically female issues such as childbirthing, lactation, birth control, and termination of unwanted pregnancies. The novel is unique in presenting full details of the childbirthing process.

The novel falls into three parts and describes life in the small, isolated, pre-electricity seaside community of Scots Bay in the early twentieth century. Seventeen-year-old Dora Rare becomes Miss Babineau, the local midwife's apprentice and assists her in difficult childbirthing, stillbirths, breech deliveries, undesired pregnancies, and unfulfilling marriages. The arrival of Dr. Gilbert Thomas, a trained physician with promises of "a pain-free birth" (132) and "the latest methods of obstetrics—chloroform, ether, chloral, opium, morphine, the use of forceps . . . Twilight Sleep" (132-33), makes women of the Bay question Miss Babineau's traditional "Home remedies" (132).

In part one, Dora helps Miss Babineau with Experience Hope's thirteenth childbirth. Brady Ketch, her abusive, drunken husband forces her to "milk the goat, . . . muck the stalls" (8), and cook. When she collapses, he "shoves her down to the floor" (8) which results in her early delivery and stillbirth as the baby soon dies. Part Two starts as Miss Babineau disappears from the Bay leaving the childbirthing business to Dr. Thomas. Dora also stops midwifing after marrying Archer, though she preserves Miss Babineau's handed down folk traditions. In Part Three, Experience Hope's secret visit to Dora to terminate her fourteenth pregnancy starts a sequence of unexpected events. At her desperate pleading, Dora prepares her a mixture. Shortly afterwards, she dies and Mr. Ketch denounces Dora who then flees to her brother at Boston.

There, she witnesses social and political upheavals like the Feminist movement, suffragist meetings, and women's right-to-vote callings. Months later, she returns to the Bay when the truth is revealed about Experience Hope's real murderer. According to her children, Mr. Ketch "brutally beat their mother and then pushed her down the stairs" (335). Meanwhile, women organize a march "in support of rural midwives" (361) and women's rights "of saying where they're going to have their babies" (361). Dr. Thomas leaves the town and his hospital is closed. Dora establishes her own birth house, one that dictates that "No woman or child shall be turned away. No payment shall be required" (363).

Reductionism in Theory and Representation

Reductionist thinking was first introduced by biologists, and acts as the basis for many of the well-developed branches of modern sciences such as physics, chemistry, and biology. It was pioneered by Daniel Clement Dennett, Richard Dawkins, and John Polinghome, and views the human experience as a system reduced into parts which can be subjected to detailed analysis without consideration of the interaction among these parts. It has recently been applied to the medical field, since this analytical approach is one of the essential premises that governs prevailing modern medical care. Richard Looijen points out that:

> Reductionism, in its extreme or radical form, is the claim that it is possible, if not in practice then in principle, to reduce all the concepts, laws and theories that have been developed for a certain higher level of organization to concepts or theories that have been developed for (a) lower level(s) of organization. . . . According to the reduction thesis, the specific concepts, laws and theories of the higher sciences can eventually all be reduced, step by step, to the fundamental theories of physics. (29)

Looijin's definition sounds logical since, in science, reductionism implies that certain fields of study deal with areas that examine small-scale organizational units. Reductionist thinking, with its reliance on analytical processes, may fit well with medicine, an area which is based on experimentation in, and analysis of, small-scale units. However, as Rick J. Carlson mentions:

> To Smuts and others, the reductionist perspective resulted in an unrelenting analysis of the parts of systems without consideration of how those parts interacted in larger systems and without consideration, or even acknowledgment of phenomena which represented more than the sum of any set of parts. (467)

Thus, this thinking is questionable when applied to the human sciences.

In *The Birth House*, Dr. Thomas tends to analyze Dora's psychological state—an area that is beyond, and irrelevant to, his medical education—in terms of the medical terminology that he knows. In his attempt to pathologize her subjective experience of abusive marriage, he diagnoses Dora "as having neurasthenia, 'a female disorder that presents itself through hysterical tendencies.' He said it is not uncommon among the young women of today and that 'the condition is treatable, but not always curable'" (194). Dr. Thomas is not aware of the fact that his pathological, medically oriented diagnosis is not compatible with cultural, psychologically oriented illness. He claims that the treatment he administers to Dora, which is actually no more than a massaging machine, "prepares the womb, leaving it ripe and waiting for a dear little soul" (195). Speaking to Dora, he assures her that the treatment is "sending blood rushing to your congested parts, releasing inner stress, relieving you of your suffering. . . . Fast laboured breathing is what I like to see. It excites the nervous system, clears away disease" (196-97).

Dora's illness, however, is not cured, despite feeling instantaneous improvement. Dr. Thomas diagnoses Dora's yearning for pregnancy by her unfaithful husband, Archer—whom she often sees courting another woman, Grace Hutner, in public and in front of her eyes—as hysteria. Unconvinced of his treatment, Dora shuns Dr. Thomas and decides to rely on her own wisdom and exhibit agency by buying a "White Cross Home Vibrator" (200) and administering it herself. At the same time, she is adamant about following Miss Babineau's traditional folk remedies and astrological beliefs so that she might have a baby when Archer returns:

> I am strict with my daily ritual: a good dose of Miss B.'s Moon Elixir four (or more) times a day—breakfast, lunch, tea, supper, and then a double dose along with a vibratory treatment before bed. I sleep on my back only, with a firm pillow under my hips, keeping my womb properly "tipped" until morning. Miss B.'s recommended moon-bath was a cold and unsettling affair. I chose to lie in the cross where Three Brooks road and the old logging road back to Miss B.'s meet. (203-04)

In *The Birth House*, the reductionist Dr. Thomas underestimates Miss Babineau's holistic attitudes in childbirthing.[3] In Part I, he suspects that Miss Babineau caused the death of Experience Hope's newborn baby boy. He tries to convince Miss Babineau of avoiding her traditional way in childbirthing: "You are a brave woman, Miss Babineau, taking on this responsibility all these years. Everyone I talk to has said how skilled you are, how blessed, but with new obstetrical techniques available, women can rely on more than faith to see them through the grave dangers of childbirth" (31-32).

Miss Babineau, however, knows more than the professionally educated Dr. Thomas, and can evaluate the situation of the women of the Bay from many angles: social, cultural, and psychological; hence employing a holistic approach to folk medicine that he never believes in.[4] Not only does the midwife relate Mrs. Ketch's poor health, pain, and struggle back to her giving birth for the thirteenth time to a weak boy who shortly dies in a stillbirth, but also to her drunken husband's abusive treatment of her. She tells Dr. Thomas that "If his wife's in trouble it's 'cause he can't keep his hands from her one way or another. If he's not puttin' a bun in her oven, he's slapping her black and blue. If I've ever given Experience Ketch a thing, it's been to tell her she's workin' herself to death" (33).

Holism in Theory and Representation

Holistic thinking was first introduced by Jan Christian Smuts who believes that the whole is more than the sum of its parts. According to Smuts, "a whole is a synthesis or unity of parts, so close that it affects the activities and interactions of those parts, impresses on them a special character. . . . It is a new structure of those parts, with the altered activities and functions which flow from this structure" (qtd. in Lefkaditou and Stamou 317). Holistic thinking as Carlson asserts "has come to be applied to almost every aspect of human behavior" (467), particularly in the medical field. It views a human being as a whole entity with dynamically interacting versatile dimensions: physiological, emotional, and intellectual. It also acknowledges the direct influence of other factors: social, cultural, and political. Defining the holistic approach, Looijen notes that:

> Holists, at the other side, maintain that it is impossible, in principle, to reduce theories about higher levels of organization in biology to theories about lower, physi-

co-chemical levels.... Consequently, they maintain that it is impossible to reduce biology as a whole to physico-chemistry. It is particularly in this respect that holists are anti-reductionists. (29)

McKay contrasts Dr. Thomas's materialistic reductionism with Miss Babineau's thoughtful holism as she shows how Miss Babineau is considerate of the social and cultural background of the Bay and its inhabitants. For instance, she never charges women money for her midwifery services and lives on charitable, appreciative gestures. Women are thankful to her and "leave coffee tins, heavy with coins that have been collected after Sunday service. In season, families bring baskets of potatoes, carrots, cabbage and anything else she might need to get by. They hide them in the milk box by the side door, with folded notes of blessings and thanks" (27).

Pro-Holistic Medical Humanities

Medical Humanities is directly related to this debate on reductionism and holism. Ron Miller notes that "holism has become a powerful theoretical perspective in . . . medicine" (6). According to him, a person should not be judged "in terms of analytical or judgmental categories . . . or merely in terms of social role-'patient'. . . . To be a person is to be a complex whole which is greater than the sum of its parts or roles" (6). Thus, a patient's case should be considered with respect to larger humanistic concepts that give meaning to his life and medical experience such as his/her culture, beliefs, social status, family, and community.

The Birth House reveals McKay's preference for a holistic attitude to medicine to a reductionist one. In tackling the subject of childbirthing to its minutest details, she is presenting two types of childbirthing: home-based childbirthing attended by Miss Babineau, a kind, honest, and understanding local midwife, vs. hospital-based childbirthing monitored by Dr. Thomas, a greedy, materialistic, and unthoughtful town obstetrician. However, Dora is not deceived by his being "impeccable with his manners and polite at every turn" (59). She easily perceives that "Dr. Thomas was less concerned with a woman's circumstances and more concerned with selling his services" (59). She recalls Miss Babineau who refuses to attend Dr. Thomas's lecture as she realizes early on his greediness, telling him: "You ain't tellin', you sellin'" (29).

This brings us to the issue of the need to maximize the importance of humanities in medicine. According to Ronald A. Carson et al, the word "humanities" is derived from the Latin word "*humanitas*" and

> *humanitas*—in English 'humanity'—meant humane feeling, which today could be known variously as sympathy, empathy, compassion, pity, concern, or caring. . . . *Humanities* in this sense was similar to the Greek term *philanthropia*, that generous spirit towards others that ideally results from education in the liberal arts. (2)

Critical Medical Humanities, as a fairly new trend in literary theory, is, indeed, in need of mapping, its theoretical rules require charting and its critical conventions call for clear definition. Anne Whitehead and Angela Woods present a critical framework to Medical Humanities by distinguishing between two phases of this area: first-wave, or mainstream, Medical Humanities, which is the earlier traditional trend of Medical Humanities, and second-wave, critical, Medical Humanities, which is the later trend recently developed. They describe first-wave mainstream Medical Humanities as a fluid phase because of its constant shifting and developing within the incessantly changing contexts of health care, culture, and politics. As for second-wave critical Medical Humanities, they point out that: "We ask what, precisely, is 'critical' about the critical Medical Humanities, examining how the field mobilises the notion and practice of critique, as well as how it orients itself in relation to other 'critical' turns" (1).

Since any medical experience involves two crucial participants: medicine and patient, Whitehead and Woods are particularly interested in the space occupied by humanities within this medical experience. They observe that "humanities act, or are positioned, as a kind of third party to it: the humanities are looking at medicine looking at the patient" (2). Dissatisfied with this third-party role of the humanities in the medical scene, they argue that it will, then, be the preoccupation of critical Medical Humanities to question such role and to try to change the posture of humanities so that it moves to the forefront; looking at the patient first and considering his/her status with respect to medicine and not vice versa. They pose more critical questions about the way medical experience has been addressed by traditional Medical Humanities.

An Interdisciplinary Biopsychosocial Model

Cathy N. Davidson and David Theo Goldberg refer to the leap of humanities from its traditional position into modern boundaries of "new interdisciplinary paradigms" (2), including scientific ones like medicine. They emphasize the vital role played by humanities in the global society and stress its interactions with almost all the intellectual fields (2). They explain that for any policy to be implemented, whether in the medical, global health, or any other field, it should be preceded by deep consideration of "the social hierarchies, cultural practices, belief systems, histories and relations among subgroups (ethnic, religious, racial, sexual, etc.). . . . Without deep knowledge of culture, language, and history, public policy is doomed to fail. No social policy ought to be conceived, let alone enacted, without humanities infusion." (4)

Jehan El-Bayoumi similarly points out the deficiency of the approach of the Health Care System. She advocates "creating a biopsychosocial model . . . for all members of the group—male and female" (193). Since women usually care for others, but "they always delay seeking out medical care for themselves" (191), El-Bayoumi asserts that if the society really cares for the health of its women, many factors should be taken into account: "Attention should be given to their individual, family, gender, culture, socioeconomic, age, physical and emotional needs, no matter who they are" (192). In other words, women's health care depends on the SDOH.

Davidson and Goldberg believe that it is only through humanities that both of the social and scientific worlds can be integrated. Humanities offer the social and cultural contexts needed for any scientific experience to be implemented. They also provide various ways to understand the value of scientific and technological inventions, especially in medicine, in the social and cultural milieux surrounding the medical experience to which they are applied.[5] The authors assert that "A world without the humanities would be one in which science and technology knew no point of social reference, had lost their cultural compass and moral scope. It would be a world narrowly limited and limitlessly narrow" (5).

Understanding the Current Health Care System

For Medical Humanities to be an efficient critical tool, understanding the current Health Care System is crucial. The scientific progress in medicine at the beginning of the twentieth century and the consequent commercialization of health care in general led to "dehumanizing tendencies . . . not enough time to see patients; technology that shifts attention to machines rather than patients; growing incentives to put profits above patients; a biomedical reductionalism that attends to pain but not suffering and to disease but not illness" (Carson et al 1). Medical Humanities started as a movement in the 1960s to address these dehumanizing tendencies in health care, in general, and the reductionist attitude of the rapid development in science towards medicine, in particular. Advocates of Medical Humanities worry about the dehumanization of medicine, such as "excessive specialization, reductionist thinking, commercialism, and moral drift" (Carson et al 4).

The aim of Medical Humanities is to improve the students' medical education and revive the relations between medical physicians and their patients in an attempt to regain lost values such as trust, compassion, empathy, and humanity, which should be intrinsic features of medical physicians in general. Courses of humanities have recently been incorporated into medical studies. The current requirements to get into medical schools de-emphasize pure science majors and include humanities studies such as anthropology, psychology, and sociology.

Rather than concentrating on the problems caused by this dehumanizing role of medical practices, or looking for radical solutions to them, Medical Humanities tends to explore what is termed "medical ethics," also known as "bioethics," focusing on specific traits of the whole experience of medicine such as its cultural and social contexts, its historical background and its literary representations. Robert Arnott et al define Medical Humanities as an academic field of teaching and research:

> The Medical Humanities is, in the United Kingdom, a relatively new term for a sustained interdisciplinary inquiry into aspects of medical practice, education and research expressly concerned with the human side of medicine. These are, most especially, the nature, importance

and role of human experience on the part of patients and practitioners alike, including their experience of the patient-practitioner relationship.

Historically, the first and most obvious feature of this inquiry was the modern exploration of medical ethics. "The medical humanities" is the name of a more inclusive inquiry, though one that embraces ethics. (104-05)

They note that Medical Humanities is "concerned with the human experiences of health, disease, illness, medicine and health care" (105). Arnott et al refer to this interdisciplinary feature of Medical Humanities:

The medical humanities should be viewed as integral to medicine (i.e. as constitutive of our understanding of medicine's nature and goals, alongside the medical sciences) rather than as a series of optional extras to an essentially scientific conception of medicine.

The medical humanities are therefore interdisciplinary. . . . This means that the contradictory disciplines attempt to understand and share one another's perspectives and metaphors—and, ultimately, that humanities and sciences also attempt this with regard to each others' [sic] conceptions of medicine. (105)

This idea of the interdisciplinarity of Medical Humanities also advocates a holistic attitude towards medicine by stressing the importance of incorporating humanities into medicine. At the same time, the authors are implicitly challenging the ideology of reductionism in science, in general, and medicine, in particular, which has been embedded in Western thought since the eighteenth century, a time that witnessed an unprecedented leap into science and technology.

Western thought, according to Jacques Derrida, is one "whose destiny is to extend its domains while the boundaries of the West are drawn back" (4). One of the values that Western thought cherishes is the superiority of reason over all other values which renders its view of reality in light of irreconcilable binary oppositions that act as rigid, unchanging structures such as reason/emotion, modern/ancient, new/old, and science/tradition.

Understanding Reductionism Through Structuralism

Reductionism, like Structuralism, in a way, idolizes a supreme value, that of scientific progress, at the expense of any other humanistic value. Science is thought to be the center that governs the structure of Western thought that Derrida especially examines. In his disruption, or deconstruction, of this idea of the center, he speculates that:

> [I]t has always been thought that the center, which is by definition unique, constituted that very thing within a structure which while governing the structure, escapes structurality. This is why classical thought concerning structure could say that the center is, paradoxically, *within* the structure and *outside* it. (279)

Being relevant to the debate of reductionism and holism, Derrida's theory of Deconstruction can best be understood in relation to its predecessor: Structuralism. Like reductionism in medicine, Structuralism propagates the concept of a fixed center. Medicine is thus reduced to mere analysis of components which conform to a structure governed by science which occupies its center.

LaQuandra S. Nesbitt refers to "the nine key drivers" of opportunities for health: "education, employment, income, housing, transportation, food environment, medical care, outdoor environment, and community safety" (n. pag.). These are the structural SDOH that though set by modern states to guarantee and measure the rate of health care permitted to their individuals, they "reflect a larger historical context going back many decades—even centuries" (Nesbitt n. pag.).

In *The Birth House*, Dr. Thomas totally disregards the SDOH and preoccupies himself with belittling midwifery, attacking Miss Babineau and accusing Dora of causing the death of her patient. Talking to Miss Babineau, he tells her that: "You, as well as other generous women in communities throughout Kings County and across the dominion have had to serve in place of science for too long" (29).

While Derrida's Deconstruction resists the idea of the existence of one single, accepted truth to explain life and language, the text of the novel also resists this falsified truth. It deconstructs a seemingly universal truth about science as the only service provider and caregiver of humanity. The novel shows that science is flawed and may harm the mother and the child. For Miss Babineau, the maternity home Dr. Thomas is building is nothing more than "[o]ne of those butcher shops they calls a hospital" (30). Dr. Thomas tries to convince Miss Babineau of the "benefits that modern medicine can offer women who are in a compromised condition . . . a sterile environment, surgical procedures, timely intervention and pain-free births. The suffering that women have endured in childbirth can be a thing of the past" (29). However, she is quick to discern his dishonesty and his financially driven motive. She tells him: "It's best you leave the women of the Bay to me" (34). She would always let nature take its course.[6] Miss Babineau could figure out by her wisdom that Dr. Thomas is a man of the materialistic Health Care System and that his hospital is an emblem of the structural inequality of the SDOH.

Patriarchal Authority vs. Women's Agency

The second issue I would like to explore is that of patriarchal authority versus women's agency in health care. McKay shows how during World War I, women's concerns were of no public interest and their problems were not seriously tended to. The women's suffrage movement was lightly considered and the press was more interested in news like "Margaret Sanger had been arrested, yet again, for distributing information about family planning" (McKay 383) than in topics that constituted priorities for women such as "fertility awareness, birth control and the science of obstetrics" (383). Women's focus was more on gaining their political right to vote than on calling for personal rights. McKay notes that:

> A woman's struggle to gain the right to choose what happened to her body was a silent issue, recorded in personal journals or through letters, one woman to another. Traditions, information and ideas about childbirth, as well as women's health and happiness, were shared in the sisterhood of knitting circles and around the kitchen table. In small, isolated communities, the keeper of this wisdom was the midwife. (383)[7]

In this world, Dora decides to be more than a witness by taking part in its activities, acting out of a deep sense of her own agency. She is enthralled by, and envious of, Boston women's incessant struggle for their rights. In her letter to Bertine, her friend and a member of the Knitting circles, she describes how Maxine, Charlie's lover, is engaged in holding suffragist meetings and sending postcards to senators to convince them of women's right to vote. At the same time, she develops a great sense of responsibility towards the women of the Bay. She expresses her sense of lack of agency to Bertine:

> Why is it that I have often thought to myself how unfair life has been for women . . . but have never been strong or bold enough to protest? Women have been imprisoned, have died for these rights, while I was complacent, happy enough to sit at home and knit. Even with children in our arms, there is always more we can do. (322)

The novel also lends itself to analysis in light of the recent association between Feminism and Affect Theory, which emerged at the beginning of the third millennium. Carolyn Pedwell and Anne Whitehead point out the recent inclination in Affect Theory towards consideration of an individual's emotions, passions, and feelings, causing remarkable changes on many levels: social, political, or theoretical. Affect Theory challenges the reductionist approach of science with its reliance on reason and objectivity at the expense of feelings and subjectivity. Dora's feelings, in turn, reveal that her power and her work as a midwife are employed to achieve a political end: having agency through the women's knitting circles.

Affect Theory seeks re-centering of the individual body as opposed to mind. Affect goes beyond analyzing emotions only in a fixed text or discourse. It provides a potential for multiple functions. In opposition to reductionism, "[a]ffect thus cannot be reduced to either 'discourse,' or 'emotion,' but rather exceeds these categories" (Pedwell and Whitehead 116). Pedwell and Whitehead point out how the power of language and "social ethics" have contributed to excluding women from certain circles occupied by men:

> Feminist theories have long been concerned with the relationships between affect, knowledge and power. Fundamental in this regard have been their efforts to interrogate the gendered nature of the reason/emotion binary.

> Throughout the history of Western thought, language and ethics, this dualism has functioned to exclude women . . . outside the white, masculine mainstream. (119)

In the novel, Dr. Thomas, for instance, employs powerful words with implicit threats to belittle Miss Babineau's midwifery practice and force her out of it. He tells her: "I think you should be made aware that the Criminal Code of 1892 states: 'Failing to obtain reasonable assistance during childbirth is a crime'" (34). By ignoring his words and asking him to leave her house, Miss Babineau is resisting his power and showing that she also has her own power.

Dr. Thomas, failing to convince Dora of leaving the childbirthing business to himself, blackmails her by implicitly threatening to inform her husband about her psychological state. She "proceeded to empty a 2-gallon jug of 'Sure Sweet Molasses'" (234) on his head only to find herself described the following day in the newspaper *The Canning Register* as a hysterical woman who has attacked the local doctor. Dora's resistance might not have caused a change at that moment, but it acts as a necessary step in a chain of many others that follow until the women of the Bay drive Dr. Thomas out of town and close his maternity home forever. Dora is furious at Dr. Thomas's justification of his greediness by telling her that "A man's business is no one's business" (233). She immediately responds that "the secrets a woman chooses to keep between her sheets are not your business" (233).

Jackson explains how ancient medical practice was determined by social and cultural values which rated male physicians higher in the social and economic hierarchy than female midwives:

> For the most part, elite physicians were men but there were some women practitioners who provided treatment to other women, particularly in the management of childbirth. . . . Although the social and professional boundaries between the various categories of medical practitioners were not always clear-cut, male physicians were assumed to possess superior moral character, higher educational qualifications and more extensive professional experience, and they certainly enjoyed greater official recognition from civic authorities than other practitioners. (19)

The novel's hegemonic view of women in early twentieth century as too delicate to decide on their own issues leads Judith Mintz to state that "men decided what was best for women, rather than women having agency over their own lives and birthing experiences" (109). Gabrielle Levesque similarly notes that "a key factor that maintains women in a state of inferiority is the discrepancy between the female gendered self associated with the ethic of care that is 'produced' under patriarchy and the values that are rewarded under the same system" (5). This system allocates the task of caring for others to women, not to men, while at the same time undervaluing women's role as care-givers

Dr. Thomas, in McKay's novel misuses his power by following his materialistic ends and providing thoughtless care for pregnant women's serious conditions. As a result, he is earlier hated by Miss Babineau, later on by Dora, and finally fails to maintain any good relationship with the women of the Bay. What really exposes his methods in front of the women of the Bay is his negligence of Ginny's swelling symptoms. Laird Jessup, Ginny's husband, who once believed in Dr. Thomas's modern obstetric theory, now, seeing the deteriorating condition of his wife, could not help but resort to Dora's traditional childbirthing technique.

It is Dora who senses the seriousness of Ginny's case as she notices that "She's swollen all over, suffering from crippling headaches and nearly blind each time she starts to stand up. . . . Her face is puffed up, features gone coarse" (340). Dora's diagnosis of Ginny's case proves to be correct. She thinks "it's what Miss B. called *visage d'etranger*, the stranger's face. When you don't know the woman no more by lookin' at her, then she got the mask of death come on her. . . . her symptoms should have been attended to weeks ago" (341). Dora decides to help Ginny give birth earlier than her due time. She keeps Ginny at her house, believing that "If I can bring Ginny's swelling down and keep her strength up for the next couple of days, then I should be able to bring the baby along without any trouble. (Albeit three, possibly four weeks early.) We cannot afford to wait" (341). Dr. Thomas's early diagnosis of Ginny's case as neurosis does not do her any good. He tells her "like you, the majority of women are neurotic" (342) and "that if the swelling in her ankles and hands didn't go down he'd have to perform a bloodletting" (342). His diagnosis is senseless exactly like his advice to her of "[m]ore exercise, less meat" (342) which actually weakens her blood.

Dora checks Miss Babineau's Willow Book journal for a similar case:

> *Stranger's Face*: I see it in a woman over Blomidon way. By the time I got to her she was gone out of her mind with convulsions. I had to cut the baby out, losing the mother to save the child. The baby dies anyways. Was too early to have enough strength to survive.
>
> Miss B's sprawling script wanders across the pages of the Willow Book. . . .
>
> Skullcap tincture—good for any variety of anxiety. Potato skins and beets will put her back on her feet. Raspberries and nettle, sweet as can be, perfect for a Mother's tea. . . .
>
> Homeopathy: Apis, phosphorous, sulphur, colchicum" (341-43).

When Ginny feels better, Dora decides to start the birthing process supported by traditional superstitious beliefs. She knows "it will be a slow, gradual birthing. The moon's on my side. It's the Harvest moon tonight, perigee tide too. Clouds moving in from the northwest. A thunderstorm certainly wouldn't hurt. I'll put my laundry on the line, to invite the rain" (343).

In *The Birth House*, the role of science as contrasted with that of folk tradition is challenged. The novel deconstructs a seemingly universal truth about the absolute power and benefit of science by offering the example of Dr. Thomas who totally believes in the role of science and technology in medicine, and refuses any belief in Miss Babineau's traditional folk remedies. He denies two important facts about the origin of medicine. The first fact is that it began in folk remedies before the invention of modern drugs.[8] The second fact is that it is mainly a woman's business, as women are the ones usually assigned the duty of caring for others. Jackson states that:

> Health care has been dispensed not in specialist institutions, including hospitals, workhouses, monasteries and hospices, but also regularly in the community, on the battlefield and at home. Within these diverse environments, advice and treatment were delivered by a range of practi-

> tioners often trained in quite different ways and possessing different, although usually complementary, skills and knowledge. In sickness and health, patients sought the services of shamans, diviners, priests, midwives, nurses, physicians, charlatans and quacks. (xiv)

What is important about the above is how it shows that health and healing have not historically been restricted to male practitioners. This directly contests the view that male obstetricians are superior to female midwives.

One of the reasons why the *daya*, Arabic for midwife, is denigrated and why her popularity is undermined—associating her tools with sorcery, superstition, and magic potions—is because she is judged according to the European standards of the early twentieth-century Western Health Care System which relied on documented scientific knowledge and not on orally transmitted midwives' tales. Elise G. Young states that "European trained male physicians disqualified midwives because the knowledge of midwives remained oral and experiential at a time when modern science and medicine authorized knowledge through documentation" (23) This issue may not resolve the early twentieth-century conflict between male obstetricians and female midwives, yet it might at least offer an insight into the issue of patriarchal authority versus women's lack of agency in women's health care.

Midwifery has been a strong resisting force to the medicalization of childbearing in the early twentieth century. Diana C. Parry suggests that midwifery has been used as a tool by women to assert their agency and power in self-attainment and decision-making. She believes that "with its focus on shared decision making, midwifery offers women an alternative choice to medicalized pregnancy and childbirth" (790). Unlike medical obstetrics, midwifery permits a lengthy relationship between the childbearing woman and the midwife which includes prenatal and postnatal care, a shared decision-making process concerning the woman's health care, and continuous support of her choice of her delivery setting. For an early twentieth-century woman, taking a decision about childbirthing was just the beginning of an ensuing struggle for other rights on many levels—social, political, and economic.

Before the spread of hospitals in the early twentieth century as well as in recent years, women believed that choosing their birthing setting themselves was mostly a sign of "control and empowerment"

(Zielinski et al 373). This choice gave women the opportunity to maintain control over their own bodies without any exterior "obstetric interventions such as epidural anesthesia, forceps, vacuum, augmentation of labor, or episiotomy" (Zielinski et al 373). By gaining this kind of control, women felt that they had a share in the decision-making process, choosing their birthing method on their own terms, which led to a sense of empowerment and agency.

Though a woman should be at the center of the motherhood experience, women were decentered on purpose for the benefit of the Western male-oriented patriarchal Health Care System at the beginning of the twentieth century. In insisting on her right to decide on her own maternal issues, the early twentieth-century woman was thus struggling to have a voice within the patriarchal society.

Conclusion

This article examined two early twentieth-century issues: the reductionism/holism debate and patriarchal authority vs. women's agency in women's health care with special reference to their demonstration in a literary work. McKay's *The Birth House* was analyzed from a Medical Humanities perspective. Examining this novel which tackles the medical issue of childbirthing, the article delineated the conflict between modern medical obstetrics, as a reductionist approach, and traditional midwifery, as a holistic approach. It also explored women's painstaking struggle for their own agency and body control while preserving traditional folk remedies that are threatened by technological advances in modern medicine and the commercialization of health care. McKay's novel—set about a century ago—is aware of such issues and presents them in a fictional genre, reflecting on contemporary debates.

Notes

[1] It is important to note here that I am referring to the particular context of the early twentieth century. While the conflict between science and folk traditions was prominent during WWI, herbal and homeopathic treatments have since been integrated in some medical practices, and such traditions are now becoming part of the "system." This demonstrates a modified at-

titude toward the use of herbal/natural cures, which was not the case at the particular period I am referring to.

[2] Here, I would like to emphasize that despite the rising number of women obstetricians currently practicing, the norms still tend to be shaped by masculine and scientific reductionism.

[3] Mark Jackson explores how medicine in pre-twentieth-century culture was expansive in its contours that surpassed the physical dimensions into psychological and religious ones. He states that "medicine has embraced religion, magic, alchemy and astrology, as well as the application of herbal remedies, the use of healing rituals, sacrifices and offerings to the gods, and the relief of poverty" (xiv-xv). In this sense, traditional medicine is anti-reductionist as it is folk-oriented and does not rely on analysis of its parts, but on the synthesis of many factors together, such as traditional remedies, folk wisdom, personal experience, and faith.

[4] R. Puustinen, M. Leiman, and A. M. Viljanen point out that for professionally educated medical doctors, the person is no more than "a body, a case, a patient . . . the effects of the person's individual experience and his cultural context are dispelled" (77).

[5] Carson et al similarly admit that "Existential questions—questions about the meaning of life and death—are essential to medicine" (1). They contend that these questions concerning the personal and emotional states of patients are of utmost importance in the experience of medicine.

[6] In a review of the novel, Jen Lawrence writes that "*The Birth House* is a powerful illustration about a dark period in our history when men and commerce tried to wrestle even the birthing process away from women" (n. pag.).

[7] In a review of *The Birth House*, Ange'lique describes the novel as "a beautiful window opened to Eastern Canada at the very beginning of the twentieth century. It's a time of drastic changes: the industrial revolution is challenging traditions and the First World War opens the most recluse communities to a much bigger, frightening world. It's also the beginning of feminism" (n. pag.).

[8] Ryan Abbott notes that: "Traditional medicine (TM) describes a group of health care practices and products with a long history of use. It frequently refers to medical knowledge developed by indigenous cultures that incorporates plant, animal and mineral-based medicines, spiritual therapies and manual techniques designed to treat illness or maintain wellbeing. TM tends to be practiced outside of allopathic medicine (also known as biomedicine, conventional or Western medicine), which is the dominant system of medicine in the developed world" (3).

Works Cited

Abbott, Ryan. *Documenting Traditional Medical Knowledge*. N. p.: World Intellectual Property Organization, 2014.

Ange'lique. "Review: *The Birth House* by Ami McKay". *Maple Books*. August 24, 2015. <www.maplebooks.ca/review-the-birth-house-by-ami-mckay>.

Arnott, Robert, Gillie Bolton, Martyn Evans, Ilora Finlay, Jane Macnaughton, and Richard Meakin. "Proposal for an Academic Association for Medical Humanities". *Medical Humanities* 27.2 (December 2001): 104-05.

El-Bayoumi, Jehan. "Women and Health Here and There: A Medical Testimony." *Alif: Journal of Comparative Poetics* 19 (1999): 185-93.

Carlson, Rick J. "Holism and Reductionism as Perspectives in Medicine and Patient Care." *The Western Journal of Medicine* 131.6 (December 1979): 466-70.

Carson, Ronald A., Thomas R. Cole and Nathan S. Carlin. *Medical Humanities: An Introduction*. NY: Cambridge UP, 2014.

Davidson, Cathy N. and David Theo Goldberg. "A Manifesto for the Humanities in a Technological Age". *The Chronicle Review*. February 13, 2004. 1-6. <http://sect.uchri.org/archives/3/pdfs/Manifesto_Humanities.pdf>.

Derrida, Jacques. *Writing and Difference*. Trans. Alan Bass. Chicago: The U of Chicago P, 1978.

Jackson, Mark. *The History of Medicine: A Beginner's Guide*. London: Oneworld Publications, 2014.

Lawrence, Jen. "Midwifery and Magic: A Review of *The Birth House*". *Literary Mama*. October 2006. <http://www.literarymama.com/reviews/archives/2006/10/midwifery-and-magic.html>.

Lefkaditou, Ageliki and George P. Stamou. "Holism and Reductionism in Ecology: A Trivial Dichotomy and Levins' Non-Trivial Account". *History and Philosophy of the Life Sciences* 28.3 (January 2006): 313-36.

Levesque, Gabrielle. "Care, Gender Inequality and Resistance: A Foucauldian Reading of Carol Gilligan's Ethic of Care." Diss. University of British Columbia, 2013.

Looijen, Richard. "Holism and Reductionism in Biology and Ecology." Diss. University of Groningen, 1998. <https://www.rug.nl/research/portal/publications/holism-and-reductionism-in-biology-and-ecology(c02f6194-6102-4135-9cef-dbe6f51d92b3).html>.

McKay, Ami. *The Birth House*. Toronto: Vintage Canada, 2006.

Miller, Ron. "Introducing Holistic Education: The Historical and Pedagogical Context of the 1990 Chicago Statement." *Teacher Education Quarterly* 19.1 (Winter 1992): 5-13.

Mintz, Judith. "Pushing Boundaries and Exploring Limits: Ami McKay's *The Birth House* as (Hys)torical Fiction." *Pivot* 2.1 (2013): 107-32.

Nesbitt, LaQuandra S. *Health Equity Report: District of Columbia 2018*. Office of Health Equity, District of Columbia, Department of Health. 2019. <https://app.box.com/s/yspij8v81cxqyebl7gj3uifjumb7ufsw>.

Parry, Diana C. "We Wanted a Birth Experience, Not a Medical Experience: Exploring Canadian Women's Use of Midwifery." *Health Care for Women International* 20.8-9 (September 2008): 784-806.

Pedwell, Carolyn and Anne Whitehead. "Affecting Feminism: Questions of Feeling in Feminist theory". *Feminist Theory* 13.2 (August 2012): 115-29.

Puustinen, R., M. Leiman, and A. M. Viljanen. "Medicine and the Humanities — Theoretical and Methodological Issues." *Journal of Medical Ethics: Medical Humanities* 29.2 (December 2003): 77-80.

Whitehead, Anne and Angela Woods. Introduction. *Edinburgh Companion to the Critical Medical Humanities*. Eds. Anne Whitehead and Angela Woods. Edinburgh: Edinburgh UP, 2016. 1-31.

Young, Elise G. "Between *Daya* and Doctor: a History of the Impact of Modern Nation-State Building on Health East and West of the Jordan River." Diss. University of Massachusetts Amherst, 1997.

Zielinski, Ruth, Kelly Ackerson, and Lisa Kane Low. "Planned Home Birth: Benefits, Risks, and Opportunities". *International Journal of Women's Health* 7 (2015): 361-77.

New Directions in Disability Narratives: Cyborgs and Redefining Disability in Young Adult Literature

Yasmine Sweed

Disability studies is an interdisciplinary field that examines the nature, representation, and implications of disability across a broad range of disciplines including medical and political sciences, sociology, cultural studies, history, and the arts (Goodley xi). In spite of the fact that disability has always been a constant component in human experience, disability studies as a field that involves theory, research, practice, and activism started to gain momentum in the 1970s in the UK and the 1990s in the US (Shakespeare 215). Attempting to find a global definition of disability that encompasses its complicated multidimensional nature can be quite problematic because the meaning of the term varies greatly across time, cultures, and disciplines. David L. Braddock and Susan L. Parish maintain that "throughout Western history, disability has existed at the intersection between the particular demands of a given impairment, society's interpretation of that impairment, and the larger political and economic context of disability" (56).

The difference between disability and impairment resulted in an ongoing debate between an older disability paradigm, the medical model, which dominated the nineteenth and the first half of the twentieth centuries, and a newer and more popular social model, which started to gain prominence in the 1970s. The medical paradigm posits that disability arises from impairment and is, consequently, an individual problem that needs to be fixed through medical or technological intervention. The social model, on the other hand, maintains that disability arises only when an impaired body functions in an unwelcoming environment that is not prepared to accommodate how it works and is shaped by a strict notion of how "normal" bodies should operate.

Michel Foucault, in his book *The Birth of the Clinic: An Archaeology of Medical Perception*, contends that the rise of the medical model can be traced back to the Enlightenment era with its emphasis on science and empirical knowledge, which changed people's perception about God, Nature and Man. Disability was regarded as "a form of biological deficit that has to be cured or contained" (Shakespeare 214). This challenged the medieval view of disability, which was believed to have demonological or supernatural causes and was interpreted in terms of divine punishment for moral failing (Braddock and Parish 17). Foucault refers to this shift as a "recasting at the level of epistemic knowledge (savoir) itself" (169). The prevalent scientific discourse at that time could be seen as the new episteme or metanarrative that dominated the eighteenth and nineteenth centuries. The increasing ascendency of science and the decline of the religious view of disability made physicians and caretakers believe in their capability of perfecting or fixing what had been previously perceived as an unchangeable God-ordained condition. Foucault highlights the relation between what he calls the "medical gaze" of the doctor and the politics involved in the construction of "normalcy" and "deviance" in Europe. He maintains that the medical gaze was not the gaze of "any observer, but that of a doctor supported and justified by an institution, that of a doctor endowed with the power of decision and intervention. Moreover, it was a gaze . . . that could and should grasp colours, variations, tiny anomalies, always receptive to the deviant" (110).

This gaze resulted in the development of complex diagnostic methods and classifications of disability, as well as the proliferation of schools and medical institutions across Europe and North America during the nineteenth and twentieth centuries. Consequently, this led to the establishment of "scientifically structured discourse about an individual" (Foucault xvi), and a new alliance was forged between "words and things, enabling one to see and to say" (Foucault xiv). Foucault's words are important because they highlight the power of the medical gaze to define, control, and create knowledge about the body. The prevalent medical discourse shaped how people viewed and defined themselves against the categories of "normal" and "abnormal." Rosemarie Garland-Thomson maintains that "the medical model assumes that any somatic trait that falls short of the idealized norm must be corrected or eliminated" (79). This medical discourse, together with Darwin's evolutionary ideas, led to the rise of the Eugenics Movement, which used the metaphor of the body to depict "unfit" individuals as a threat to the nation and national fitness. This resulted in marriage restrictions on, and sterilization of, large numbers of people with impairments and their segregation in mostly dilapidated special institutions away from those who were dubbed "normal" or "ordinary." This dismal condition continued well into the twentieth century with more than 47,000 recorded cases of sterilization of people with mental impairments in the United States between 1907 and 1949 (Braddock and Parish 38–39).

In spite of the fact that the segregation of people with impairments had an extremely negative psychological and social impact, it helped them to gradually construct group identities, which eventually made the rise of political activism in the second half of the twentieth century possible (Braddock and Parish 11). With the rise of the civil rights movement in the US and progressive identity politics in the UK in the 1960s and 1970s, they started to self-organize in a politically and socially significant manner and began forming organizations that were for the first time led by people with impairments. This shift in perspective is significant because it gave them voice and agency to represent themselves and express their own challenges after years of silencing and marginalization. Not only did they challenge the existing medical discourse of disability, but they also called for a revolutionary social approach that radically redefined disability by highlighting the distinction between impairment and disability.

Unlike the medical model that defines disability as an individual deficit and thus focuses on remedying the impairment, the social paradigm views it as a socially and culturally constructed category and thus emphasizes the importance of removing social, cultural, and economic barriers. According to Tom Shakespeare, the social model emerged from the political and intellectual debates of the Union of Physically Impaired Against Segregation (UPIAS), which came into prominence in 1975 in the UK, the term itself coined by Mike Oliver in 1983 (215). According to the UPIAS, disability is "now defined, not in functional terms, but as the disadvantage or restriction of activity caused by a contemporary social organization which takes little or no account of people who have physical impairments and thus excludes them from participation in the mainstream of social activities" (qtd. in Shakespeare 215). The social paradigm maintains that people with impairments find themselves oppressed and disabled by inadequate housing, unsuitable public and private transportation, and inflexible work conditions in offices and factories. That is why, the UPIAS, alongside other organizations, offers community support and development for people with impairments by lobbying for anti-discrimination laws and running projects that advocate equality and inclusion. It advocates the right of people with impairment to live independently, be a fully active part of society, and assume agency.

The social model has continued to dominate the landscape of disability well into the twenty-first century. However, recent studies in the field started to pinpoint some of the drawbacks of this paradigm. The article draws on recent work by renowned critic Tom Shakespeare, who expounds the pitfalls of strict adherence to the social paradigm in spite of being one of its early proponents. In his important article "The Social Model of Disability: An Outdated Ideology?," Shakespeare questions the main premise of the social model and contends that the physical aspect of impairment cannot be ignored, and that people with impairments are disabled by both exclusionary society and their biological conditions. Similarly, Michael Bury argues that it is unrealistic to imagine that "a severe loss of mobility or dexterity, or sensory impairments, would not be 'disabling' in the sense of restricting activity to some degree. The reduction of barriers to participation does not amount to abolishing disability as a whole" (137).

Shakespeare adds that one of the weaknesses of the social model is that it "so strongly disowns individual and medical approaches, that it risks implying that impairment is not a problem" (217). This can make some people feel stigmatized or ashamed of seeking medical cure or rehabilitation of impairment. He contends that some physical conditions such as fatigue, chronic pain, and degenerative impairments cannot be merely solved by social activism and that the role of medical sciences in alleviating pain and enhancing the quality of life of disabled people cannot be overlooked. That is why he argues that the social model "has now become a barrier to further progress. . . . Politically, the social model has generated a form of identity politics which has become inward looking and separatist" (220). Moreover, it can be argued that in practice, it becomes quite problematic to distinguish between the impact of social and cultural barriers and that of the impairment itself, since both interact together to shape how an individual experiences disability. This article argues that this model by itself does not fully capture the complexity and the multifaceted nature of disability that requires a broad range of paradigms to address it.

In the literary field, artistic expressions of disability usually affect, and are affected by, dominant social and cultural attitudes towards impairment and take part in the ongoing debate between the medical and the social paradigms.[1] In narratives that reflect a medical paradigm, disability is usually synonymous with abnormality, and characters with disability "often aroused pity, voyeuristic prurience or horror" (Kramar 3). Hence, a large number of these texts usually celebrate man/machine couplings and depict cyborg characters that resort to medicine and technology to rectify their "abnormality," overcome their disability, and return to the realm of the "normal." While there is nothing wrong with the depiction of characters that choose to resort to medical intervention to address impairments, the creation of a binary of normality and abnormality that degrades characters with impairment and forces them to conform to socially and culturally constructed expectations is quite oppressive.

However, with the prevalence of the social model, David T. Mitchell and Sharon L. Snyder maintain that disability narratives witnessed a radical shift in perspective as they attempt to capture the complex "political reality of disabled characters, from architecture to attitudes. Realistic depictions . . . offer familiarity with an experience that has been understood as thoroughly alien" (199). Irving Zola, who conducted a survey on popular detective novels that feature disabled investigators, pinpoints the gap between artistic representations of disability and lived reality of people with impairments by highlighting the fact that none of the wheelchair using characters ever said "God dammit, how I hate stairs" (qtd. in Mitchell and Snyder 199). That is why texts that propagate the agenda of the social paradigm strive to correct social and cultural misconceptions and create a more inclusive society rather than mainly focus on cyborg characters which might feel pressured to seek medical intervention to be "normalized."

This article argues that the past decade has witnessed the rise of a new trend of disability narratives that redefine the meaning of disability and represent the next step in the ongoing debate between the social and medical paradigms. The article maintains that this trend goes beyond the existing dichotomy by adopting a hybrid approach that is sensitive to the pitfalls of a medical model that can overlook diversity and reproduce stereotypical notions about disability, but is not totally dismissive of it. At the same time, it does not blindly favor an extreme form of the social model, which focuses on social and cultural representation of disability, but can sometimes disregard the real physical problems that impaired people suffer from. The article explores the complex relationship between disability and technology in three award-winning young adult texts that transport the figure of the cyborg from the realm of science fiction to that of lived experience to depict new ways of being that redefine the meaning of "disability" and "normalcy."[2] The new trend of texts depicts an uneasy grappling with the protagonists' cyborg identities and closely examines the cultural, social, and psychological implications of being a cyborg. The article argues that the hybrid figure of the cyborg — that is neither fully impaired nor fully abled from a traditional perspective — offers a measure of resistance to the existing order as it problematizes society's notions about disability.

The term cyborg was first coined by Nathan S. Kline and Manfred E. Clynes in 1960 to refer to an "enhanced human" that can survive unusual circumstances in outer space (Reeve, "Cyborgs" 92).[3] However, the term has quickly evolved and become associated with man/machine couplings in different contexts. Donna Haraway is one of the first critics to touch upon the connection between cyborgs and disability in her essay "Cyborg Manifesto": "Perhaps paraplegics and other severely handicapped people can (and sometimes do) have the most intense experiences of complex hybridization with other communication devices" (qtd. in Reeve, "Cyborgs" 93). However, she does not dwell on the implication of this connection on the lived experience of people with impairments or on the politics of identity construction.[4] John Cromby and Penny Standen maintain that the term refers to both "the physical augmentation of the bodies of people with and without disabilities" and "the transformation of subjectivity by the array of communication technologies currently available" (97). Both usages are particularly relevant to the lived experience of people with impairments that depend on pacemakers, cochlear implants, prosthetic limbs, or communication aids and can, consequently, identify as cyborgs. The fact that the cyborg is "never an either-or but always both" (Gane 153) blurs the boundaries between human/machine, as well as ability/disability. By destabilizing the discourse of otherness and the hierarchies within the dichotomies that legitimate the domination of ableist assumptions, the figure of the cyborg can be seen as a potent form of resistance and a new mode of being that can redefine the meaning of disability. It is important to note that while the texts draw on Haraway's vision of the cyborg as a subversive figure, the article argues that they offer a more balanced and realistic view of life as a cyborg since each character does not merely seek "a pleasurable survival as a border-crosser in the ironic political myth of a cyborgean materiality" (Erevelles 97). They do not readily accept the cyborg aspect of their identity like Haraway's cyborgs do and the writers carefully highlight both the challenges and benefits of cyborg fusions.

By offering three different responses to their protagonists' cyborg identity, Antony John's *Five Flavors of Dumb* (2010), Wendelin Van Draanen's *The Running Dream* (2011), and Cammie Mcgovern's *Say What You Will* (2014) examine their characters' complex relation with their cyborg status and how it blurs or deconstructs the divide between abled and disabled.[5] The texts transport the figure of the cyborg from the world of science fiction to that of young adult literature, which, according to Jen Scott Curwood, has witnessed a dramatic increase in the tendency to depict characters with impairments in the last ten years (17). This tendency, in the words of Janine J. Darragh, has a positive impact on the emotional well-being and the self-image of young adult people with impairments, who find characters that they can identify with in literature. Moreover, it helps readers who are not impaired to understand the challenges of impairment, which can translate into a more positive and inclusive social attitude (5-6). Both *Five Flavors of Dumb* and *The Running Dream* have received the Schneider Family Book Award, which is annually offered by the American Library Association to works that offer complex and realistic portrayal of characters with disabilities. The three novels depict the varied coming-of-age stories of their adolescent female protagonists that challenge stereotypical representations of characters with impairments and destabilize the dichotomy of the medical and social paradigms.

By employing a first-person narrative point of view, the three writers give voice and agency to their protagonists to offer realistic accounts of their experiences with impairment. The readers become privy to how Jessica in *The Running Dream*, Amy in *Say What You Will*, and Piper in *Five Flavors of Dumb* grapple with their own understanding of their impairment and the cyborg aspect of their identity. Jessica is a sixteen-year-old high school student whose dreams to become a professional runner are destroyed after a truck dashes into her track team bus, killing one of her colleagues and causing her to lose one of her legs. The novel depicts her struggles to adapt to the rapid changes in her life and traces how she negotiates the different components of her identity as a runner, a person with impairment, and a cyborg. Unlike Jessica, who has developed an impairment at a later stage in her life, Amy, a senior high school student, is born with cerebral palsy, which forces her to use a walking aid and a computerized speech device. She forms a friendship with one of her classmates who suffers from obsessive-compulsive disorder, and their friendship enables them to face the ongoing struggles caused by their impairment and the society's exclusionary attitude. Piper, on the other hand, occupies a liminal space between disability and ability because her hearing loss can be partially remedied by the use of hearing aids that she can use at will. The novel depicts Deaf Culture and attempts to challenge stereotypical social perspectives regarding the abilities of deaf people by depicting her struggles as a manager of a music band and her attempts to raise enough money to join a world-class art school for people with impairments.

As has been previously mentioned, a new trend of disability narratives attempts to go beyond the dichotomy between the medical and the social paradigms by adopting a hybrid stance that is arguably better suited to address the complex experience of disability. The three texts portray the physical struggles of their protagonists to illustrate that disability is not merely a social construct. Jessica finds it difficult to become accustomed to living with persistent phantom pain that constantly reminds her of her loss while also battling painkiller dependency: "They're unpredictable. And always different. Sometimes the missing part of my leg burns. Sometimes it stabs. Sometimes it feels twisted. Sometimes it's a combination. The nerves are cut, but they're still connected to my brain" (Draanen 29).

Her persistent physical pain and her feelings of helplessness because of her limited mobility and loss of identity as a runner drive her to envy her teammate that died in the crash: "I know it's selfish, but I can't help thinking Lucy is the lucky one. For Lucy there's no pain, no rehab, no learning to live disabled. There's no anger or self-revulsion. For Lucy there's just resting in peace" (35). Listing all the challenges that she has to face as a result of leaving the sphere of "normality" reminds the readers that the lived reality of impairment is far too complicated to be addressed solely with one paradigm or the other. The physical realities of her experience cannot merely be remedied by removing environmental barriers and changing social and cultural perceptions of disability.

Similarly, Amy lists the physical realities of her impairment, and while pain is not an element of her experience like Jessica, limited mobility, lack of muscle control, and uncoordinated movements greatly affect her: "Typing was slow. She'd try for a joke that came out five comments too late to be funny. She was too clumsy to play at recess, too messy to eat lunch with, too slow to keep up" (McGovern 22-23). Piper, on the other hand, due to the nature of her impairment, does not suffer from pain or lack of muscle control. Her challenges are mainly social and emotional in nature. The depiction of unique and varied physical realities for each type of impairment adds to the realism and the individuality of the characters and removes them from the sphere of stereotypes. However, this does not mean that the novel is shunning the great impact of the social paradigm in lobbying for laws that ensure equality and inclusion. In fact, the impact proves very beneficial in Amy's case since the school has provisions for disabled students and is paying for professional aides to help her in several aspects of her school life: "The law mandated every child with a disability have equal access to the same education all children had, meaning that—to some extent anyway—an aide had to do whatever Amy needed" (McGovern 24).

However, McGovern cleverly shows that while the aid that the school offers can solve some of her physical challenges, this happens at the expense of her privacy, independence, and quality of her social interactions. The novel illustrates that the laws can be a partial solution to ensure equality, but it avoids the simplistic assumption that inclusive policies and barrier removal can by themselves address all of her needs. Amy does not realize that she does not have true friends until one of her schoolmates pinpoints this fact to her" "Being with you means being with a teacher" (23). Donna Reeves rightly maintains that people with certain impairments that require constant monitoring might feel that they are under surveillance because safety usually overrides other factors such as intimacy and privacy ("Cyborgs" 98). However, Amy decides to stop using the adult aides that the school has provided for her because she feels that this impedes her social interaction with her peers and decides to enlist the help of her schoolmates. When the readers become aware of the hard choices that Amy has to make, she becomes more humanized and relatable.

In addition to portraying real and varied physical difficulties that the protagonists confront, the three texts depict the challenges involved in the process of self-definition. Sometimes their view of themselves mirrors how society sees them, while at other instances they challenge these perceptions. This comes in line with the postmodern view of identity as an ongoing process rather than a fixed and stable essence. Initially, Jessica believes that her identity as an accomplished runner is destroyed: "For me, running was like eating and breathing—it was something I had always done, and without it I felt miserable" (Draanen 20). She now describes her new self in terms of her impairment: "I'm not sick. I'm crippled. Disabled. A gimp" (15). Jessica's image of herself reflects how she believes society sees her. Her words erase all the other aspects of her identity as she believes that she is nothing more than her impairment. Her initial perception of her new identity is greatly defined by what Garland-Thomson calls "the single stigmatic trait" (11). Garland-Thomson refers to the situation where a person's identity is reduced to his/her impairment. Consequently, Jessica detests her "legless" body and feels repulsed by her ugly useless stump" (Draanen 40). Now, she faces huge obstacles just to climb the stairs, use the bathroom, or take a shower. Her hatred of her new identity and her inability to accept it make her refer to her leg as an object that she is forced to endure: "I have to learn to clean it. Learn to dress and protect it. Learn to massage it and desensitize it. Learn not to vomit at the sight of it" (24).

Her identity crisis exacerbates on her first school day after the accident as she has to fathom her public image as a disabled person. Some of the students behave awkwardly because they do not know how to properly respond to her changed identity. Some stare too much and others pretend she is invisible. She starts to revise her own attitude towards people with impairment when her teacher asks her if she prefers to sit in a wheelchair-accessible table at the back of the class with Rosa who has cerebral palsy. Jessica is shocked: "Do people think I'm special needs now? Is that how they see me?" (103). This realization makes her feel like a "freak" (103). This even leads to another perspective-shifting realization: "I've never stared at her, but I have ... overlooked her. No—the truth is, I've totally acted like she isn't there. It's been easier. Less uncomfortable. For me" (103). Jessica's acknowledgment of her own participation in the exclusionary practices that render people with impairment invisible invites readers to reconsider their own outlook and stresses the importance of changing discriminatory social attitudes towards disability. Her newly gained awareness of her responsibility to cultivate a more informed and inclusive attitude is evident when a friend asks her about Rosa and she describes her in terms of her achievements as a friend and a student rather than in terms of her impairment: "She's my friend, and a math genius" (231).

Jessica starts to heal and begins a new challenge as she has to grapple with her cyborg identity when she gets fitted for a prosthesis. It can be argued that the text depicts the long process of creating and making modifications to Jessica's prosthetic leg to raise readers' awareness and familiarize them with an experience that can be outside the usual range of their everyday realities, making it less alienating. However, it offers a realistic representation of a cyborg's lived experience that does not smooth over difficulties in favor of an unproblematic and unrealistic portrayal of disability and power. The medical paradigm can help her function physically, but she still has to come to terms with her cyborg identity. The first time Jessica tries out her prosthetic leg, she experiences the awkward feeling of being "some sort of doll where the parts snap on and off" (179), indicating that she still has no secure sense of self. The fact that she calls her prosthetist Dr. Hank "Hankenstein" (115) demonstrates that she does not feel as a unified whole, and that the different aspects of her identity are still disparate.

The novel illustrates the importance of integrating both the medical and social paradigms to help Jessica construct a positive sense of self. Knowing how much her identity as a runner means to her, her coach shows her videos of different runners, including South African Olympic champion Oscar Pistorius, competing against non-disabled runners with their prosthetic blades. By subverting the stereotypical view of the capabilities of people with impairment, the readers are challenged to reconsider their outlook on disability. Jessica's response is that these runners "'look like cyborgs!" and asks herself, "Is running worth becoming a cyborg?" And decides that the answer is "Yes!"' (140). The realization that she can integrate her impairment and her running dream, seemingly disparate parts of her identity, helps her accept her cyborg identity and have a renewed sense of purpose. However, the extremely high cost of the running blade that might impede her from becoming who she wants to be brings home the problem that not all people have equal access to medical aid. Donna Reeve rightly maintains that "people with impairments do not have automatic 'rights' to become the cyborg body they want because these 'rights' are economically determined" ("Cyborgs" 95). The text highlights the positive impact of community participation and social responsibility in addressing this problem. The fact that her adolescent teammates offer psychological and financial support by setting up a public fundraising campaign to pay for her $20,000 running blade raises the awareness of the readers of the importance of subjectivism which, according to Maria Bakardjieva, involves:

> small-scale, often individual decisions and actions that have either a political or ethical frame of reference (or both) and remain submerged in everyday life. . . . It is not about political power in the strict sense, but about personal empowerment seen as the power of the subject to be the person that they want to. (95)

When Jessica finally receives her long-awaited running blade, her initial reaction indicates that she does not fully feel at ease with her cyborg body: "It's a strange contraption. Stilty, and almost scary" (275). However, her identity as a runner makes her capable of accepting her cyborg status. That is why when she actually starts to run with the blade, she realizes: "This isn't a walking leg, or even a jogging leg. It's a running leg. And when I finally really push for the first time, something inside me clicks" (275). The "click" signifies the successful integration of the disparate aspects of her identity, which culminates in an "electrifying feeling" (275) of wholesomeness, ability, and agency.

Jessica's newly acquired feeling of agency, her revised attitude towards disability, and her friends' acts of subactivism inspire her to engage in a symbolic act of social activism. She decides to fulfill Rosa's ultimate desire: "That people would see me, not my condition" (244) by participating in a ten-mile race while pushing her friend in a wheelchair. Again, the text invites the readers to consider how their simple everyday acts contribute to cultural and social construction of disability. Her success in completing the race and making Rosa feel visible and important marks her development and growth as a result of all the challenges that she has faced in her journey. It can be argued that Jessica's newly constructed cyborg identity makes her a more inclusive and a better-informed human being.

Similar to Jessica, who developed an impairment at a later stage in her life, Piper in *Five Flavors of Dumb* started to lose her hearing at the age of six. However, her hearing impairment is depicted as a single aspect of her multifaceted character. It certainly affects how she interacts with the world and how her family and friends see her, but she is not defined entirely by it as a character. The first chapter depicts a vivid description of a concert in Piper's school from her point of view. It is only at the end of the chapter that she tells the readers that she is deaf and they realize that all that she has described is only visual: "I think that's what everyone was talking about. But in the interests of accuracy, I should admit that it's kind of hard for me to tell because, well, you know. I'm deaf" (John 5). This opening gives the readers the impression that the book is not about Piper as a deaf character, but is about Piper as a character who happens to be deaf. In spite of the fact that the book depicts the challenges that she faces as she tries to succeed as manager of Dumb, her high school music band, in order to raise enough money to join university, John makes sure she is not defined by a single stigmatic trait.

Unlike Jessica, Piper does not view her impairment as a tragic disabling condition. She is used to Deaf Culture because her maternal grandparents were deaf. Her abilities to interact through the use of hearing aids, lip reading, and sign language allow her to occupy an ambivalent liminal space that blurs the boundaries between ability and disability. Her ambivalent position is manifest in the contradiction between her desire to attend Gallaudet University—one of "the finest liberal arts colleges in the world for deaf and hard-of-hearing students—a place where I'd automatically fit in, instead of standing out in all the wrong ways" (15)—and her acceptance of the position of a manager of Dumb without questioning her ability to succeed in her rather atypical position. Her confident response to her friend Marissa, who is skeptical of the intensions of the band members, illustrates her own feelings of agency:

> MARI55A: ur sure they're not setting u up?
> P1P3R: YES
> MARI55A: then why would they want a deaf manager?
> P1P3R: why wouldn't they?
> MARI55A: r u serious?
> P1P3R: I can do this. I can help. (John 57)

Accepting the offer and having faith in her skills destabilize stereotypical notions about the capabilities of people with hearing impairments. Piper takes the challenge seriously and starts researching the history of popular rock bands. She enhances the band's online presence and films better video clips of their songs. She recruits new members and makes sure that all of them are working harmoniously as a team. She manages to get them a paid performance on a radio show and schedules a professional recording session for them. Both Draanen and John delineate a broad range of challenges that people with impairments face due to the unique nature of each disability. Jessica is battling pain and physical limitations, but she enjoys the support of her family, trainer, and teammates. Piper, on the other hand, is battling psycho-emotional disablism, which, according to Donna Reeve, is any behavior that restricts who people can be through hurtful remarks and underestimating or stigmatizing the actions of others, which can have a negative impact on their sense of self and psycho-emotional wellbeing ("Psycho-emotional" 99). Piper suffers from the condescending attitude of her parents, who believe that she should be applying for scholarships intended for people with impairments rather than wasting her time with the band:

> "You're deaf, Piper, okay? That may be painful, but it's a fact."
> "You're wrong. You're so wrong it's practically a joke. One of these days you're going to work out there's nothing *painful* about being deaf. But I find it pretty significant that you keep using that word. Is that why you spend every waking minute cooing over Grace instead of talking to me? Does it make you feel better to know that at least you were able to cure one of us?" (197-98)

In spite of her success with the band, Piper's family finds it difficult to support her choice and wants her to fall in to a more typical behavior. The conversation between Piper and her father echoes the ongoing debate between the medical and the social models of disability. Piper's embittered words endorse the premise of the social paradigm that disability arises from a disabling environment and confining stereotypical attitudes and not from impairment itself. She is not affected by her impairment as much as she is affected by how her family sees it as a tragic condition: "Could it really be that after eighteen years Dad saw me that way—a poor girl struggling to be understood, who achieved self-sufficiency only by virtue of others' help?" (16). Piper's belief that there is nothing painful about being deaf echoes that of many deaf people, who do not believe that deafness is an impairment and, consequently, do not accept ableist assumption that they are "disabled" (Davis, *Enforcing* 19).

Piper's interaction with her family sheds light on important concepts in Deaf Culture that can be unfamiliar to many readers. She is even more embittered by her family's decision to use her own college fund money, set up by her deaf maternal grandparents, to finance her sister's cochlear implants surgery: "My father wasn't indifferent to my deafness; he was mortified by it. For him, Grace's total loss of hearing was an insurmountable disability, something that had needed to be remedied at the earliest opportunity through major surgery" (16). The family's decision reproduces the medical paradigm's premise that disability arises from impairment that must be fixed or cured even if it happens at the expense of Piper's choice to join a program for deaf people, where, she believes, she would easily fit in. Her parents' decision to cure her sister makes her feel isolated and rejected: "Angry and frustrated, yes, but it was more than that. I felt like I'd been judged and found to be inadequate, a problem beyond remedy." But that wasn't even the worst thing. "Alone. It makes me feel alone'" (45). These repeated arguments between Piper and her family over how they perceive her and how she perceives herself indicate that the process of identity construction is an ongoing one that does not have a simple definitive ending. Moreover, they highlight the politics involved in the process of identity formation as many deaf people construct cultural identities based on the belief that they belong to a linguistic subgroup: "Their culture, language and community constitute them as a totally adequate, self-enclosed, and self-defining subnationality within the larger structure of the audist state" (Davis, *Enforcing* xiv). In fact, the family's decision to "cure" her sister makes her the only person with impairment in her family, which adds to her sense of isolation and exclusion.

Her relation with her family is further complicated by her ambivalent stance towards her cyborg identity. Piper feels pressured to succumb to "society's bias toward oral communication" (John 16), in spite of the fact that her old hearing aids work well only in the limited occasions when she is talking to one person at a quiet place. She resents the fact that the only reason everyone "assumes my hearing aids work fine is because I can lip-read with Olympic precision, and the combination of the two helps me get by. But it's still hard work" (8). Similar to *The Running Dream*, *Five Flavors of Dumb* highlights the economic factors that prevent people with impairments from equal access to sophisticated assistive aids. Piper is unable to use her old hearing aids at school because they cause annoying distortions and she cannot afford to buy a newer model that enables her to hear her computer and cell phone because her dad lost his job. The novel adopts an integrative model that does not reject the cyborg fusion of man and machine, but illustrates that it is not readily available to all who need it. Moreover, it calls for changing exclusionary cultural and social practices that promote the social isolation of those who do not wish to conform to society's ableist assumptions.

The novel highlights the psychological and social oppression involved in forcing people with impairments to embrace a cyborg identity that they are not totally comfortable with. Piper confronts her father who has never fully accepted her impairment and does not exert adequate effort to learn sign language: "It's not fair you never bothered to learn more than fifteen signs, even though you know it's how I prefer to communicate ... You don't know a single sign to express an emotion ... happiness, sadness ... nothing! Signing with you is like talking to a computer" (98). Piper's words are significant because they reject narratives of overcoming. Her preference of sign language challenges an ableist assumption that a cyborg fusion of technology and the impaired body is always preferred over an organic experience. John highlights the importance of choice and agency in the process of identity construction. People with impairments have the right to choose whether they wish to become cyborgs or not. This article maintains that Amy's attitude towards the cyborg component of her identity contradicts with Haraway's cyborgs, who, according to T. Siebers, are "spunky, irreverent, and sexy; they accept with glee the ability to transgress old boundaries" (63). It can be argued that the new trend of disability narratives depicts cyborg fusions in a more realistic manner that portrays both the potentials and the problems they entail. They are not depicted solely as a source of power and resistance as Haraway has originally envisioned them.

However, the text does not present a simplistic rejection of Piper's cyborg status. In fact, she does not altogether reject the role of technology in her life. She can be seen as a cyborg through her use of communication technologies that extend her subjectivity. For example, Piper and her close friend Marissa prefer to use ooVoo, a video chatting application that is specifically tailored to users of sign language, over instant messaging because it allows them to communicate via sign language, which is their favorite mode of communication: "She couldn't smile on IM, or laugh that ridiculous laugh, or rescue me with a pretend hug before I'd even had a chance to say what was wrong" (31–32). Piper's selective use of the communication technologies that she sees fit for her life choices allows her to construct her cyborg identity on her own terms, an act that reflects a sense of agency and empowerment. Moreover, her preference of sign language over writing mirrors Lennard Davis's argument that sign language as a system of signification leads to a more immanent form of communication because it is linked to the performative, which does not create a difficulty in indicating or pointing like writing (*Enforcing* 20). Piper's preferred mode of communication debunks ableist assumptions regarding the superiority of oral and written communication over other systems of signification.

Towards the end of the novel, Piper succeeds in managing the band members, securing a paid performance for them, and making profit. However, her greatest achievement is how she stands up for herself against attempts of psycho-emotional disableism that usually ended with her desire to cry in earlier parts of the novel. The writer cleverly highlights the fact that abuse and stigmatization will not stop; it is Piper's increased ability to confront abusers and demand respect that makes all the difference: "Everyone knows I'm deaf, Josh. They know I'm reading your lips ... So stop trying to humiliate me. I'm not disabled, Josh, and trying to make out that I am just makes you look like an even bigger jerk than usual" (298).

Similar to Piper, Amy challenges the stereotypical ableist view of impairment as a tragedy. Both face specific challenges pertinent to their impairments, but what they truly suffer from the most is the psycho-emotional disabling attitude of their society that makes them feel isolated and pitied. In fact, Amy, who is a talented writer, believes that she is "lucky" and "blessed" because her impairment frees her from traditional social expectations and worries that plague her abled peers:

> I don't wish I was fine. I don't pine for working legs or a cooperative tongue. It would be nice not to drool and warp the best pages of my favorite books, but I'm old enough to know a little drool isn't going to ruin anyone's life. I don't know what it would feel like to be beautiful, but I can guess that it makes demands on your time. . . . It introduces fears I will never experience. (Mcgovern 16)

Unlike *The Running Dream* or *Five Flavors of Dumb*, which mainly depict the challenges of characters with impairments, *Say What You Will* highlights the idea that both abled and impaired individuals suffer from different manifestations of the same problem. Both feel confined by the judgments of others and social and cultural expectations that can affect their self-image, an idea that blurs the boundaries between ability and disability. However, Mcgovern maintains a careful balance between offering a subversive non-defeatist perspective on disability and a realistic portrayal of the difficulties that it entails. A recurrent theme that appears in the three texts is the trope of invisibility and isolation. As a high school student, Amy contemplates the fact that for eleven years, none of her colleagues ever tried to call her, in spite of the fact that her number is listed in the school directory. All the mothers of her friends give different excuses to her mum when she tries to set up play dates with their kids, and her classmates refuse to let her touch shared science projects because of her lack of muscle control.

Amy's invisibility persists with her in college. She receives a short-lived media attention after succeeding in her application to six elite colleges including Stanford. By depicting other aspects of Amy's life and showing her capabilities, Mcgovern avoids defining her in terms of her impairment. In school, her colleagues start to smile and wave to her instead of the usual staring and awkward silence. However, her moment in the limelight quickly subsides and she becomes invisible and suffers from awkwardness and isolation again when she attends Stanford because her colleagues and professors tend to avoid her. As a result of her lack of integration, she transfers to UC Berkeley, not only because of its accessible campus and specialized programs for people with disability, but because "IT'S GOOD. IT'S WHERE I BELONG" (317). Amy's words are significant because they highlight the fact that accessible buildings and specialized programs do not compensate for the lack of fulfilling social interaction experienced by students with impairments: "Around them, with all their many eccentricities, she didn't feel disabled so much" (333). Amy's words indicate that disability is not an obstacle that one can overcome and leave behind, but is rather a sequence of challenges that people with impairments have to experience throughout their lives. The text also highlights the reasons that might drive high-achievement students like Amy to drop out of their schools, limiting their potentials. This highlights the need for a hybrid paradigm that addresses the multifaceted aspects of impairment.

Similar to *The Running Dream* and *Five Flavors of Dumb*, *Say What You Will* subverts the stereotype of the helpless protagonist with impairment by depicting characters that play an effective role in other people's lives, whether they are impaired or not. They depict a model of interdependence as expounded by Lennard Davis who posits that the categories of abled and disabled, which are derived from an Enlightenment notion of an autonomous independent self, are a socially constructed metanarrative. He maintains that "impairment is the rule, and normalcy is the fantasy," and contends that all human beings are disabled and need "the social and the technological to arrive at functionality" ("The End" 241). He proposes a model of interdependence where people come to terms with the fact that they depend on, and are depended upon, by other people, thus subverting the categories of abled and disabled.

This is evident in the positive and mutually beneficial relationship of solidarity between Amy and Mathew, who suffers from anxiety and OCD: "The truth is I have problems like you do, only mine don't show" (Mcgovern 52). The text challenges the traditional hierarchy of disability, which views OCD as a less challenging form of impairment. Amy and Mathew form a special bond based on their similar experiences. Both understand the feelings of vulnerability associated with impairments that render them invisible and isolated in their community. Both long for meaningful communication and fulfilling interactions that do not solely focus on their impairments. In order to help Mathew, Amy does extensive research to expand her knowledge of his condition to help him manage his symptoms and slowly grow out of his comfort zone; she supports his decision to seek psychiatric therapy and medication. On the other hand, he helps her feel visible and appreciated for aspects other than her impairment like her talent as a writer and quality as a friend.

Similar to Jessica, whose cyborg status helps her gain a renewed sense of self, Amy's use of her electronic speech device can be seen as an extension of her subjectivity. There is a seamless fusion between her and her device that "remembered her favorite expressions, learned the rhythm of her sentences, and anticipated responses with amazing accuracy" (Mcgovern 35). The novel highlights the great importance of medical and technological intervention. Amy's embrace of her cyborg identity is evident in the fact that she has learned two coding languages by the time she has reached fourth grade. However, Mcgovern still maintains a realistic depiction of her cyborg status in other aspects of her life. It can be argued that her cyborg identity contributes to her alienation from her peers. She resents the fact that she has to use devices that lack "an honest-to-God human-sounding voice. For years she'd never understood why these devices could include wireless capability, Bluetooth connection, 3G internet access, and still make a girl sound like Stephen Hawking" (35). Her comment illustrates that assistive technology is effective in functional terms, but it can be construed as a marker of difference that makes her stand out rather than fit in. Her feelings of alienation make her choose to surround herself with people who accept her cyborg identity. At the end of the novel, she chooses to join a university where she can fit in and professes her love to Mathew, a person whom she feels at ease with.

In conclusion, the three novels can be read in the light of the ongoing debate between the medical and the social paradigms of disability. They depict their protagonists' complex relationship with their cyborg status and its impact on their physical, social, and psychological well-being. The article argues that these texts fall under a new trend of disability narratives that represents the next step in the debate as they depict new ways of being that redefine the meaning of disability. This trend postulates that neither model is capable in and of itself of addressing the multifaceted nature of impairment. That is why it goes beyond this prevalent dichotomy by adopting a hybrid or an integrative paradigm that attempts to avoid the drawbacks of the previous models.

The article maintains that this new trend of disability narratives tends to offer more realistic depictions of physical struggles such as pain, limited mobility, and uncoordinated movements to illustrate the ongoing challenges of their protagonists. The portrayal of unique physical challenges for each type of disability adds to the individuality of the characters and removes them from the sphere of stereotypes. The protagonists of the three texts do not shy away from resorting to assistive medical technology to address their conditions, but at the same time, the novels are not structured as traditional narratives of overcoming that depict impairment as a deficit that must be fixed or cured by the end of the story. Moreover, unlike earlier texts in which characters were pressured to embrace cyborg fusions, the new trend depicts an uneasy grappling with the protagonists' cyborg status and allows the characters to construct their cyborg identities on their own terms, an act that reflects a sense of agency and empowerment.

On the other hand, the novels highlight the indispensable role of the social model in lobbying for laws that promote inclusion and equality, removing barriers, and creating group identity. However, they maintain that political and social activism is more successful in changing laws than in changing exclusionary ableist cultural attitudes. That is why the texts attempt to raise readers' awareness of different forms of psycho-emotional disabling behaviors that people with impairments suffer from such as avoidance, exclusion, and being defined by a single stigmatic trait. By depicting the negative impact of these biased practices on their protagonists' self-image and emotional well-being, the texts help the readers who are not impaired to understand the challenges of impairment, which can translate into more positive and inclusive social attitudes. Moreover, the writers challenge the stereotype of a helpless impaired character by portraying strong-willed, capable female protagonists who help both impaired and abled characters. This echoes Davis's model of interdependence that rejects the categories of ability and disability by postulating that all people are disabled and are in need of both technological and social aid to function properly.

Finally, the article contends that the three texts depict different responses to their protagonists' cyborg status to highlight the individuality of human experience and the fact that there is not one simple approach that can address the multifaceted complex nature of disability. The hybrid figure of the cyborg can be viewed as an effective mode of resistance that subverts the discourse of otherness that legitimates ableist attitudes and redefines the meaning of disability. The article argues that by succeeding to avoid stereotypical representations of the impaired body through depicting real people with diverse personalities, struggles, and lifestyles, this new trend of novels can possibly help in mapping new directions for disability narratives in the twenty-first century.

Notes

[1] David T. Mitchell and Sharon L. Snyder maintain that there is a "measurable gap" between the reality of the lived experience of people with impairments and the depiction of their lives in literature and film (215). Citing Shakespeare's hunchbacked evil king, Richard III; Brontë's madwoman in the attic; Frankenstein's deformed monster; Melville's one-legged obsessive Captain Ahab and Dickens's innocent hobbling boy Tiny Tim, they maintain that throughout history, many authors resorted to a restrictive mode of characterization that usually sacrificed the humanity of characters with impairments. They usually offered dehumanizing stereotypical representations that lack complexity and realism (i.e., monster, suffering innocent, madman, freak, and beggar) (196). Moreover, Barbara H. Baskin and Karin H. Harris maintain that one of the prevalent trends in the representation of disability was the use of characters with impairments as a vehicle for social criticism, which allowed writers to express their ideas and concerns about the human condition at the expense of offering a credible portrayal of impairment. For example, a mute character can stand for the isolation of human beings and their inability to share feelings and ideas with one another. A mad person can voice insightful statements about the world. A mad Lear is even more perceptive than his old sane self (23). Disability, in earlier texts, is usually treated as a metaphor rather than a complex lived reality.

[2] Unlike many recent narratives that strive to offer a more realistic depiction of adolescents with impairments, many texts that were written between 1940 and 1975, according to Baskin and Harris, tended to offer "outrageously endowed, blessed or heroic" characters (34). Although this representation was meant to enhance their social and cultural inclusion, it came at the expense of their credibility and depth. One can also argue that earlier representations of disability in young adult literature were more didactic than recent ones. Baskin and Harris explain that examples of innate goodness such as generosity and courage were in many cases rewarded with a complete recovery from disability. This unrealistic portrayal of impairment could propagate the belief that perhaps those who were not miraculously "cured" are less deserving (31). This can have a negative impact on the ability of young readers with impairment to identify with these characters and find adequate self-representation. In the second half of the twentieth century, texts started to become less sentimental and less didactic with the advent of a new realistic streak in young adult literature.

Lois Keith maintains that topics like death, racism, bullying, and disability, which were once viewed as emotionally distressing or too sophisticated, were now deemed appropriate for young readers (206). She maintains that although many writers attempted to offer more credible portrayals of the challenges of everyday life of their characters, the lack of research and adequate understanding of the realities of impairment led to some inaccuracies in a number of these texts. For example, characters that lost a leg were able to walk independently within only one week and others that could use wheelchairs to race around the streets would rely on colleagues to help them move from one classroom to the other (197). Moreover, unlike recent trends of disability narratives, which depict young people with impairments as the main protagonists and give them voice to narrate their own stories, many of the earlier texts, according to Keith, resorted to second-hand narration, where able-bodied protagonists reflect on the lives of characters with impairments (208). He adds that although the figure of the outsider, who is depicted as the center of the story and with whom readers could identify, was a prevalent trope in the second half of the twentieth century, the disabled adolescent is usually portrayed as a marginal outsider who aids the main protagonist in his/her journey of development (208-09). This marginalization makes it difficult for adolescents with impairments to find characters that they can identify with and reinforces feelings of isolation and exclusion.

[3] Although the term was coined in the 1960s as a result of the scientific breakthrough at that time, the figure of the cyborg in literature can be found in American texts that date back to the nineteenth century. It can be argued that in many of these works, the trope of the cyborg was used as a metaphor or a vehicle that reflects political, social, and philosophical anxieties of the age. For example, Edgar Allan Poe in his short story "The Man that was Used Up" (1839) uses the figure of the cyborg to question male military identity by depicting an outwardly magnificent soldier who hides the fact that he consists almost entirely of prosthetics after being injured by Native Indians in battles. Similarly, Perley Poore Sheehan and Robert H. Davis's Play *Blood and Iron* (1917) reflects people's anxiety regarding soldiers who returned from World War I with several impairments by portraying half-man/half-machine super soldiers. Bernard Wolfe's novel *Limbo* (1952), which depicts a dystopic world that is dominated by cyborgs, was written at the backdrop of the tensions between the US and the Soviet Union (Stableford and Langford n. pag.). However, unlike the texts

examined in the present article, these works rarely touched upon the implications of the cyborg fusion on the identity of people with impairments, particularly in a realistic setting.

[4] Zoe Jaques maintains that unlike Haraway's conceptualization of the cyborg as a subversive figure that destabilizes essentialist binaries of being, man and machine, nature and civilization, and male and female, early accounts of the cyborg like that of Kline and Clynes are not originally intended to destabilize boundaries as they delight "not in the possibilities of evolving beyond the human, but of making the human even more magnificent . . . to reinforce what they locate as uniquely human capacities for exploration, creation and feeling" (4). On the other hand, there is another strand of texts that does not share this optimistic view of cyborg fusions and expounds their negative and possibly irreversible consequences on human identity, consciousness, and existence. This is evident, according to William S. Haney, in William Gibson's *Neuromancer* (1984), Haruki Murakami's *Hard-Boiled Wonderland and the End of the World* (1985), and Neal Stephenson's *Snow Crash* (1992), which express anxiety towards the destabilized boundaries between man and machine (ix).

[5] It is worth mentioning that while the texts reflect the unique individual experiences of the protagonists who grapple with their cyborg identity, what is common among all of them is the fact that the main characters live in the US and have access to assistive technology even if they face financial problems that can limit their access to it. More studies can be conducted on the experiences of the individuals who live in places where access to assistive technology is extremely limited or non-existent and the implications of this on their identity. While the selected texts reflect a distinctive American experience of disability, they invite readers everywhere to question their own attitudes towards people with impairment and raise their awareness regarding issues that they may not be familiar with, which can eventually lead to a more informed social attitude towards people with impairment.

Works Cited

Bakardjieva, Maria. "Subactivism: Lifeworld and Politics in the Age of the Internet." *The Information Society* 25. 2 (March 2009): 91-104.

Baskin, Barbara H. and Karen H. Harris. *Notes from a Different Drummer: A Guide to Juvenile Fiction Portraying the Handicapped*. NY: R. R. Bowker, 1977.

Braddock, David L. and Susan L. Parish. "An Institutional History of Disability." *Handbook of Disability Studies*. Eds. Gary L. Albrecht et al. London: Sage, 2003. 11-68.

Bury, Michael. *Health and Illness in a Changing Society*. London: Routledge, 1997.

Cromby, John and Penny Standen. "Cyborgs and Stigma: Technology, Disability, Subjectivity." *Cyberpsychology*. Eds. Á. J. Gordo-López and I. Parker. London: Palgrave Macmillan, 1999. 95-112.

Curwood, Jen S. "Redefining Normal: A Critical Analysis of (Dis)ability in Young Adult Literature." *Children's Literature in Education* 44.1 (March 2013): 15-28.

Darragh, Janine J. "Exploring the Effects of Reading Young Adult Literature that Portrays People with Disabilities in the Inclusion Classroom." *Journal for Inclusive Education* 3.4 (Summer/Fall 2015): 1-48

Davis, Lennard J. "The End of Identity Politics and the Beginning of Dismodernism: On Disability as an Unstable Category." *The Disabilities Studies Reader*. Ed. Lennard J. Davis. NY and London: Routledge, 2006. 231-42.

---. *Enforcing Normalcy: Disability, Deafness, and the Body*. London and NY: Verso, 1995.

van Draanen, Wendelin. *The Running Dream*. NY: Random House, 2011.

Erevelles, Nirmala. *Embodied Rhetorics: Disability in Language and Culture*. Eds. James C. Wilson and Cynthia Lewiecki-Wilson. Carbondale: Southern Illinois UP, 2001.

Foucault, Michel. *The Birth of the Clinic: An Archaeology of Medical Perception*. Trans. A. M. Sheridan Smith. NY: Vintage Books, 1973.

Gane, N. "When We Have Never Been Human, What Is To Be Done? Interview with Donna Haraway." *Theory, Culture & Society* 23.7-8 (December 2006): 135–58.

Garland-Thomson, Rosemarie. *Extraordinary Bodies: Figuring Physical Disability in American Culture and Literature*. NY: Columbia UP, 1997.

Goodley, Dan. *Disability Studies: An Interdisciplinary Introduction*. London: Sage, 2010.

Haney, William S. *Cyberculture, Cyborgs and Science Fiction: Consciousness and the Posthuman*. Amsterdam and NY: Rodopi, 2006.

Jaques, Zoe. *Children's Literature and the Posthuman: Animal, Environment, Cyborg*. NY and London: Routledge, 2018.

John, Antony. *Five Flavors of Dumb*. NY: Dial Books, 2010.

Keith, Lois. *Take Up Thy Bed and Walk: Death, Disability and Cure in Classic Fiction for Girls*. London: The Women's P, 2001.

Kramar, Margaret R. "Plotting Life Writing through various Disability Models." Diss. University of Kansas, 2012.

McGovern, Cammie. *Say What You Will*. NY: Harper Collins, 2014.

Mitchell, David T. and Sharon L. Snyder. *Narrative Prosthesis: Disability and the Dependencies of Discourse*. Ann Arbor: U of Michigan P, 2000.

Reeve, Donna. "Cyborgs, Cripples and iCrip: Reflections on the Contribution of Haraway to Disability Studies." *Disability and Social Theory*. Eds. D. Goodley et al. London: Palgrave Macmillan, 2012. 91-111.

---. "Psycho-emotional Disablism in the Lives of People Experiencing Mental Distress." *Madness, Distress and the Politics of Disablement*. Eds. J. Anderson, B. Sapey and H. Spandler. Illinois: U Chicago P, 2015. 99-114.

Shakespeare, Tom. "The Social Model of Disability: An Outdated Ideology?" *The Disability Studies Reader*. Ed. Lennard J. Davis. NY and London: Routledge, 2006. 214-21.

Siebers, T. *Disability Theory*. Ann Arbor: U of Michigan P, 2011.

Stableford, Brian M. and David Langford. "Cyborgs." *The Encyclopedia of Science Fiction*. August 11, 2018. <http://www.sf-encyclopedia.com/entry/cyborgs>.

Abstracts of Articles
(Alphabetically by last name)

Arab Feminism: Positions and Practices

Shereen Abouelnaga

This article traces the epistemological research directions and intersections on which feminism in the Arab world has been founded, especially in the humanities. It delineates the main ideas and visions that have guided and interacted with feminism, resulting in the formulation of an experience that corresponds to a changing socio-political reality; hence, revealing un-trodden areas worthy of research. In its attempt to highlight the main intellectual trajectories that resulted from remarkable mobility in the public sphere in different contexts, the article focuses on the academic manifestations of feminism without delving into the field of development.

Educational Linguistics and the Problem of Language: Science and Mathematics Education in the Arab World

Tamer Amin

Many obstacles to improving the quality of teaching science and mathematics pose themselves in the Arab world, including language-related challenges. As a tool for communication and thinking, language must be used effectively by teachers and students. However, challenges of teaching in multilingual settings arise due to either the use of foreign languages in instruction or diglossia, when Arabic is used. Given the limited research in the Arab region addressing such issues, this article outlines a research program that draws attention to the role of Educational Linguistics as an approach to the study of language in education that can help fill this gap.

From Cultural Translation to Untranslatability: Theorizing Translation outside Translation Studies

Brian James Baer

This article discusses two recent influential conceptualizations of translation that arose outside Translation Studies: cultural translation and untranslatability. It addresses the ambivalence in both conceptualizations toward interlingual translation, or translation proper. As a metaphor, cultural translation tends to elide or mystify interlingual translation, while untranslatability impoverishes our understanding of interlingual translation by focusing on a discrete set of words, implying that everything but those words is easily transposable. The author advocates for a poor translation theory, one that refuses to let translation as abstraction become untethered from interlingual translation, while recognizing incommensurabilty to be distributed across natural languages.

Modern Paths in Philosophical Studies

Abdesslam Benabdelali

Instead of discussing philosophy through movements and schools of thought, this article weaves intellectual networks that encompass different thinkers expressing similar thoughts in diverse areas. The article articulates such networks through key-terms that modern philosophy revolves around, including structure, difference, tradition, and ideology. The author concludes that such terms were employed to reconsider the history of philosophy, shook the logical foundations on which it was based, and ultimately re-conceptualized the notion of historical time itself. As a result, other concepts like dialectics, truth, genesis, and subjectivity were also reassessed.

A Decolonial Turn in the Humanities

Claire Gallien

This article presents a critical survey that maps out the development and reception of the "decolonial turn" in Western Humanities.

It traces its genealogical foundations, its points of overlap with and departure from postcolonial studies; illustrates its theoretical contributions; and discusses its controversial reception in the Republic of South Africa, Britain, and in particular France. The article also highlights critical zones insufficiently addressed by the field, such as its reliance on a homogenized version of "the" West and of "modernity," its participation in the modern/colonial system itself, and the possibility of interactions without domination under pluriversality.

Towards Holistic Medical Humanities

Nadia Hashish

This article explores Medical Humanities, a relatively new field in literary theory which stresses the need to include the humanities into medical studies. Early twentieth-century scientific development gave rise to a conflict in medicine between a reductionist approach which explains human illnesses through biological concepts and a holistic approach which explains them through social and cultural factors. The article analyzes Ami McKay's *The Birth House*, a novel about childbirthing, as an example that reflects the shift from reductionist modern obstetrics to holistic traditional midwifery, showing how midwives use childbirthing to advocate holism for female agency and body control.

Game Theory and Literary Analysis: Horizons and Limitations

Naglaa Saad Hassan

This article deals with the challenges of using Game Theory in literary analysis, given the theory's focus on mental strategies as means of conflict resolution and interest maximization. Tracing its historical background, the article shows how the theory, initially born in the field of economy, gradually inched towards the Humanities in general and literature in particular. The article surveys a number of studies which both advocate and criticize Game Theory as a critical framework of literary interpretation. Primary among its limitations are the mechanization of literary analysis, disregard for the spontaneity of literary production, and the theory's incompatibility with other critical schools.

"Contemporary" American Poetry: Reflections

Hassan Hilmy

The article presents an introductory overview of contemporary American poetry to the Arab reader, with the intention of offering a contextualized account of new significant developments in both its theory and praxis. It explores the theoretical foundations of some of the most prominent currents that seem to be most influential in determining the evolution of the major contemporaneous American poetic trends. The article surveys representative samples of poetic work by such poets as Susan Howe, Charles Bernstein, Linda Bierds, Robert Kelley, Fanny Howe, and Joshua Clover, with the purpose of illustrating the diversity of their poetries and situating their work in its relevant socio-historical background.

Postcolonialism and Arabic Literature: Rerouting or Re-Rooting?

Samia Al Hodathy

As many voices within Postcolonialism call for bridging the gap between theory and praxis, questions about literary representation and cultural hegemony are being replaced with more materialist issues like territorial conflicts and environmental exploitation. This article argues that Arabic literature from Palestine and Gulf States can illustrate this Postcolonial material turn. Palestinian literature can pave the way for more fluid and inclusive definitions of material concepts like nationalism, nation-states, and borderlands. Gulf Literature, on the other hand, draws attention to the encounter between international oil companies and the natives, and the subsequent destruction of ecological systems.

From Autobiography to Life-Writing: Trajectories and Intersections across the Humanities and Social Sciences

Hala Kamal

This article charts an epistemological map of Autobiography as an interdisciplinary literary genre between the Humanities and Social Sciences. It traces its trajectories, in processes that have led to the emergence of new trends and directions across generic boundaries, offering new forms of self-expression. Structured around three main points, the article deals comparatively with different aspects of Autobiography. Firstly, Writing the Self and the Rise of Autobiography; secondly, Comparative Theoretical and Critical Concepts; and thirdly, New Directions in Self-Writing. The author concludes that the interdisciplinary position of Autobiography has made it possible for it to cross the borderlines between the Humanities and Social Sciences.

Mapping Diversity in Classical Studies

David Konstan

"Diversity" in the Classics has diverse senses. On the one hand, it refers to the desired balance in the profession with respect to gender, ethnicity, religious affiliation, and other socially acknowledged identities, which is still far from being achieved. On the other hand, there is the diversification of the discipline of the Classics itself, from its traditional focus on the intellectual achievements and political history of ancient Greece and Rome to a wider concern with what we may call the margins of the classical world. This article explores the necessary and fruitful interaction between these two aspects of diversity in the Classics.

Arabic Literature and Digital Technology: An Exploration

Hossam Nayel

This article explores the Arab controversy on literature and technology exemplified by the 1973 conference in Tunisia on "Arab Literature and the Technological Revolution," the writings of Hossam El Khatib (1996), and what Mohammed Aslim calls "the theory of digital realism" by Mohammed Sanajleh (2007). The article examines the implications of Sanajleh's "digital realism" for perceptions of the human, society, and the world, in an attempt to explore his theory's political, economic, and ontological potentials. In discussing these aspects, the article draws on theoretical writings by Hannah Arendt, Niall Ferguson, and Martin Heidegger.

The Cultural Turn in the Study of Arabic Literature

Antonio Pacifico

During the past few decades, the field of Arabic literary studies has witnessed an impressive growth and a phase of deep renewal that has involved both the objects of analysis and the methods used to examine them. Thus, by mapping the work done by several distinguished scholars, the present article sheds light not only on the main trends of the cultural turn existing today in the field, but also on its multiple histories and distinct practices. The article does not offer a normative perspective; rather, it deploys a diachronic approach in order to reflect on the most striking vulnerabilities and future directions in the field.

New Directions in Disability Narratives: Cyborgs and Redefining Disability in Young Adult Literature

Yasmine Sweed

This article explores the relationship between disability and technology in three young adult novels that redefine the dichotomy between the terms "disabled" and "normal." The novels represent the next stage in the ongoing debate between the medical and social paradigms of disability, by adopting a hybrid approach that is sensitive to the pitfalls of both models. The article argues that the trend of new writings—which avoids stereotypical representations of the impaired body and instead portrays real people with diverse personalities, struggles, and lifestyles—can contribute to mapping new directions for disability narratives in the twenty-first century.

Re-Orienting Modernism: Mapping East-East Exchanges between Arabic and Persian Poetry

Levi Thompson

This article argues for a new direction in comparative literary studies by analyzing close formal and thematic links between Arabic and Persian modernist poetry. It re-maps the history of modernist poetic development between the two Eastern traditions and advocates for a broader re-orientation of modernist studies. The article highlights foundational modernist innovations that occurred beyond the reach of Western influence, including the retention of several elements of premodern poetic forms based in the Arabic prosodic tradition. This includes the continued presence of the Arabic metrical foot (*tafʿīlah*) in both Arabic and Persian modernist poetry during the early decades of their growth.

Redirecting Postcolonial Theory: Arab-Islamic Reason, Deconstructionism and the Possibility of Multiple Critique

Youssef Yacoubi

This article makes three central claims. First, it explores the extent to which critical revisions done on pre-colonial Arabic and Islamic Humanities by Mohamed al-Jābirī and Mohamed Arkoun may respond to a process of re-envisioning non-Western Humanities as part of the pedagogical and political concerns of postcolonial theory. Moving into Arkoun's hermeneutic act of shattering the traditional boundaries of revelation, the second line of argumentation reinserts deconstructionism, seen as a nexus in interdisciplinary discourse between postcolonial theory and Arab-Islamic critique. The article concludes that reorienting an alternative notional framework for a sub-field across these two disengaged disciplines must compel a move towards "multiple critique." The latter meshes the study of the Islamicate worlds and the analysis of their interconnected Western lineages by augmenting inquiries concerning medieval classical knowledges, while sustaining a theoretical resistance to Western ethnocentric Orientalism.

Notes on Contributors
(Alphabetically by last name)

Shereen Abouelnaga is Professor of English and Comparative Literature at Cairo University, and a literary critic. She has published critical articles that focus on gender studies from a socialist feminist perspective. Her published books include *The Passion for Difference* in Arabic and *Women in Revolutionary Egypt* in English.

Tamer Amin is Associate Professor of Science Education and Chair of the Department of Education at the American University of Beirut. His research and publications address the development of scientific understanding and reasoning, with a particular focus on the roles of language in teaching and learning.

Brian James Baer is Professor of Russian and Translation Studies at Kent State University and Leading Research Fellow at the Higher School of Economics in Moscow. He is author of *Translation and the Making of Modern Russian Literature* (2016) and founding editor of the journal *Translation and Interpreting Studies*.

Abdesslam Benabdelali is Professor of Philosophy at Mohammed V University in Morocco. His published works in Arabic include: *Conversation with French Thought* and *Welcoming the Stranger*. His translations into Arabic include: Pierre Bourdieu's *Leçon sur la leçon*, Roland Barthes's *Leçon et autres textes*, and Amina Achour's *Kilito en questions*.

Claire Gallien is Associate Professor of English at the University Paul Valéry Montpellier 3 and member of the CNRS in France. Her research focuses on early-modern Orientalism; postcolonial, World, and comparative literatures; as well as on translation and decolonial studies. Her latest co-edited book is entitled *Eastern Resonances in Early Modern England*.

Nadia Hashish is Assistant Professor in the Department of English, Faculty of Arts, Ain Shams University. Her recent publications include "Revisiting Slavery in Selected Works by Joyce Hansen and Sharon Draper: An Afrocentric Perspective" and "Postmodern Conceptualization of Focalization, Temporality and Spatiality as Three Narrative Aspects in Darren Greer's *Just Beneath My Skin*."

Naglaa Saad Hassan is Associate Professor of English at Fayoum University. Her research interests revolve around critical theory, Anglophone literature, and English poetry. She has published articles in *Alif*, *Dictionary of Literary Biography*, and *The Encyclopedia of Postcolonial Studies*, in addition to a number of studies on contemporary Arabic poetry.

Hassan Hilmy is Professor of English at Hassan II University, Morocco. Among his publications are translations into Arabic of works by Blake, Hölderlin, Yeats, Rilke, Pound, Valéry, and an anthology of contemporary American poetry. He has also published a book on Pound as well as translations into English of some Arab poets.

Samia Al Hodathy is a PhD candidate at the Université Paris Nanterre. She is writing a dissertation on resistance in contemporary Palestinian-American poetry. Her research interests include Ecocriticism, Feminism, and Postcolonialism.

Hala Kamal is Professor of English and Gender Studies at the Faculty of Arts, Cairo University. Her latest publications include the following: "'Women's Writing on Women's Writing': Mayy Ziyada's Literary Biographies as Egyptian Feminist History" (2018) and "'Travelling Concepts' in Translation: Feminism and Gender in the Egyptian Context" (2018).

David Konstan is Professor of Classics at New York University. His research focuses on Greek and Latin literature and philosophy, with books on friendship, pity, emotions, forgiveness, and beauty. He has held visiting appointments in Australia, Brazil, Argentina, South Africa, and Egypt. He is former President of the American Philological Association.

Hossam Nayel teaches literary criticism at the Higher Institute of Artistic Criticism, the Academy of Arts, Cairo. He translated a number of books into Arabic on Deconstruction, socio-political sciences, philosophical thinking and cultural analysis, network theory, and literary theory. He is the author of *Lessons from Deconstruction: Man and Nihilism in Contemporary Literature* in Arabic.

Antonio Pacifico received his MA in Comparative Literature from the University of Napoli "L'Orientale" and completed a research internship in Arabic historiography with the "Escuela de Estudios Arabes," affiliated with the Spanish National Research Council (CSIC). His research interests include contemporary Iraqi literature and the relationship between literary and historical narratives.

Yasmine Sweed is Assistant Professor at the Faculty of Languages, MSA University, Cairo. She received her MA and PhD from Ain Shams University. Her PhD focused on Gothic literature, and her MA on literary adaptation studies. Her interests lie in the areas of digital humanities, literary theory, and transnational literature.

Levi Thompson is Assistant Professor of Arabic in the Department of Asian Languages and Civilizations at the University of Colorado Boulder. He teaches courses on modern Middle Eastern literatures and cultures and conducts research on the development of modernist poetry in Arabic and Persian during the twentieth century.

Youssef Yacoubi is Assistant Professor of Languages, Literatures, and Cultures and Co-director of Middle Eastern and North African Studies at Seton Hall University. His research focuses on literary, theological, and cultural intersections among Mediterranean, Islamic, Arab, British, and North American traditions. He is the author of *The Play of Reasons: The Sacred and the Profane in Salman Rushdie's Fiction*.

ياسمين سويد مدرّسة بكلية اللغات بجامعة أكتوبر للعلوم الحديثة والآداب. حصلت على الدكتوراه في الأدب القوطي المقارن والماجستير في دراسات الاقتباس الفني من جامعة عين شمس. تشمل اهتماماتها البحثية الإنسانيات الرقمية والنظرية الأدبية والأدب العابر للقوميات.

هالة كمال أستاذة الأدب الإنجليزي ودراسات الجندر بكلية الآداب، جامعة القاهرة. تركز كتاباتها على الأدب والنقد النسوي وتقاطعات دراسات الترجمة مع النظرية النسوية. ومن أحدث دراساتها المنشورة بالإنجليزية: «"كتابة النساء عن كتابة النساء": مي زيادة وكتابة السير الأدبية بوصفها تاريخاً نسوياً مصرياً»، و«"ارتحال المفاهيم" عبر الترجمة: النسوية والجندر في السياق المصري».

ديفيد كونستان أستاذ الكلاسيكيات في جامعة نيويورك. تركز أبحاثه على الأدب اليوناني واللاتيني والفلسفة. صدرت له عدة كتب تتناول مواضيع الصداقة والمشاعر والمغفرة والجمال. عمل أستاذاً زائراً في كل من أستراليا والبرازيل والأرجنتين وجنوب أفريقيا ومصر. شغل منصب رئيس الجمعية الأمريكية للفيلولوجيا سابقاً، وهو الآن زميل الجمعية الأمريكية للفنون والعلوم.

حسام نايل مدرِّس النقد الأدبي بالمعهد العالي للنقد الفني بأكاديمية الفنون بالقاهرة. ترجم العديد من الكتب إلى العربية في مجالات: دراسات التفكيك؛ العلوم الاجتماعية والسياسية؛ التأمل الفلسفي والتحليل الثقافي؛ تطبيق نظرية الشبكات؛ نظرية الأدب. له كتاب منشور بعنوان **دروس التفكيك: الإنسان والعدمية في الأدب المعاصر**.

يوسف اليعقوبي أستاذ مساعد اللغات والآداب والثقافات ومدير مشارك لبرنامج دراسات الشرق الأوسط وشمال أفريقيا بجامعة سيتون هول بالولايات المتحدة. تركز أبحاثه على التقاطعات الأدبية واللاهوتية والثقافية في الفكر النقدي للثقافات العربية والإسلامية والمتوسطية والإنجليزية والأمريكية. وهو مؤلف كتاب **تقاطع العقلانيات: المقدَّس والمدنَّس في كتابات سلمان رشدي بالإنجليزية**.

ليڤاي تومسون مدرّس اللغة العربية بقسم اللغات والحضارات الآسيوية في جامعة كولورادو بولدر بالولايات المتحدة. يتخصص في دراسة آداب الشرق الأوسط الحديث وثقافاته، كما تركز أبحاثه على تطور الشعر الحديث في اللغتين العربية والفارسية في القرن العشرين.

كلير جاليان أستاذة مشاركة في الأدب الإنجليزي بجامعة بول ڤاليري مونبلييه ٣ وعضوة المركز القومي للبحث العلمي بفرنسا. تركز دراساتها على الاستشراق في بدايات العصر الحديث، وأدب ما بعد الاستعمار، وأدب العالم، والأدب المقارن، كما تهتم بدراسات الترجمة ودراسات تقويض الاستعمار. شاركت في تحرير كتاب **أصداء شرقيةٍ في بدايات العصر الحديث في إنجلترا بالإنجليزية**، كما تعمل حاليا على كتاب حول أدب العالم في الإسلام.

سامية الحديثي طالبة دكتوراه في جامعة نانتير بباريس. تتناول أطروحتها مفهوم المقاومة في الشعر الفلسطيني الأنجلوفوني المعاصر. تركز اهتماماتها البحثية حول النقد البيئي والنسوي وما بعد الكولونيالي.

نجلاء سعد حسن أستاذة مشاركة بقسم اللغة الإنجليزية بكلية الآداب، جامعة الفيوم. تدور اهتماماتها البحثية حول النقد الأدبي والأدب الأنجلوفوني والشعر الإنجليزي. لها مقالات منشورة بالإنجليزية في **ألف وقاموس السيرة الأدبية وموسوعة دراسات ما بعد الكولونيالية**، بالإضافة الي دراسات متعددة حول الشعر العربي المعاصر.

نادية حشيش تدرّس الأدب الإنجليزي بقسم اللغة الإنجليزية، كلية الآداب، جامعة عين شمس. من دراساتها المنشورة «عودٌ على الرق في أعمال مختارة لجويس هانسين وشارون دريبر من منظور أفريقي» و«مفهوم ما بعد حداثي للتبئير والزمانية والمكانية باعتبارها ثلاثة عناصر سردية في رواية دارين جرير **يكاد يكون تحت جلدي**».

حسن حلمي أستاذ الأدب الإنجليزي بجامعة الحسن الثاني بالمغرب. صدرت له ترجمات أعمال شعرية لكل من وليام بتلر ييتس، خورخي لويس بورخيس، وليام بليك، راينر ماريا ريلكه، فريدريش هلدرلين، إزرا باوند، وبول ڤاليري، بالإضافة إلى أنطولوجيا للشعر الأمريكي المعاصر، ومختارات من قصص ڤرجينيا وولف. كما نشرت له ترجمات إلى الإنجليزية لبعض الأعمال الأدبية العربية.

تعريف بكتّاب العدد
(أبجدياً بالاسم الأخير)

شيرين أبو النجا أستاذة الأدب الإنجليزي والمقارن بجامعة القاهرة. من كتبها المنشورة **عاطفة الاختلاف بالعربية والنساء في مصر الثورة** بالإنجليزية. تدور اهتماماتها البحثية في مجال دراسات الجندر من الناحية الأدبية والنقدية والثقافية. تنطلق في رؤيتها من النسوية الاشتراكية وتضع نصب عينيها موقعها بوصفها نسوية في العالم الثالث.

تامر أمين أستاذ مشارك متخصص في تعليم العلوم ورئيس دائرة التربية في الجامعة الأميركية ببيروت. تتناول اهتماماته البحثية وأبحاثه المنشورة بالإنجليزية تنمية التفكير العلمي واستيعاب المفاهيم العلمية، مع التركيز بشكل خاص على أدوار اللغة في التعليم والتعلم.

أنطونيو پاتشيفيكو حاصل على الماجستير في الأدب المقارن من جامعة لورينتال في نابولي. أكمل تدريبا في مجال البحوث التاريخية العربية في مدرسة الدراسات العربية التابعة للمجلس الوطني الإسباني للبحوث. تتضمن اهتماماته البحثية الأدب العراقي المعاصر، والعلاقة بين النصوص الأدبية والنصوص التاريخية.

براين جيمس باير أستاذ الروسية ودراسات الترجمة في جامعة ولاية كينت بالولايات المتحدة وزميل باحث بكلية الاقتصاد العليا في موسكو. صدر له كتاب بعنوان **الترجمة وتأسيس الأدب الروسي الحديث بالإنجليزية** في عام ٢٠١٦، وهو رئيس تحرير ومؤسس مجلة دراسات الترجمة والترجمة الفورية.

عبد السلام بنعبد العالي أستاذ الفلسفة بكلية الآداب في جامعة محمد الخامس بالمغرب. من أعماله: **أسس الفكر الفلسفي المعاصر، حوار مع الفكر الفرنسي، في الترجمة، وضيافة الغريب**. ومن ترجماته عن الفرنسية: **أتكلم جميع اللغات، لكن بالعربية** لعبد الفتاح كيليطو، **درس السيميولوجيا** لرولان بارت، **الرمز والسلطة** لبيير بورديو، **وكيليطو موضع أسئلة** لأمينة عاشور.

الأدب العربي والتكنولوجيا الرقمية : محاولة استكشافية

حسام نايل

تستكشف المقالة الجدل العربي حول الأدب والتكنولوجيا بدءاً بمؤتمر تونس حول «الأدب العربي والثورة التكنولوجية» في ١٩٧٣ ، مروراً بكتابات حسام الخطيب في ١٩٩٦ ، وانتهاءً بما أطلق عليه محمد أسليم «نظرية الواقعية الرقمية» عند محمد سناجلة في أوائل القرن الحالي . ثم تفحص المقالة ما تنطوي عليه «الواقعية الرقمية» عند سناجلة من تصورات للإنسان والمجتمع والعالم ؛ في محاولة لاستكشاف مآل «النظرية» سياسياً ، واقتصادياً ، وأنطولوجياً . تعتمد المقالة في مناقشتها لهذه الجوانب الثلاثة على الآراء النظرية لحنة أرندت ونيل فرجسن ومارتن هيدجر .

إعادة توجيه نظرية ما بعد الكولونيالية : الفكر العربي-الإسلامي والمنهج التفكيكي وإمكان التعددية النقدية

يوسف اليعقوبي

تقدم المقالة ثلاث أطروحات مركزية . فهي تناقش أولاً مدى استجابة مراجعات محمد الجابري ومحمد أركون النقدية للدراسات الإنسانية العربية-الإسلامية التي أجريت قبل الاستعمار إلى عملية إعادة تصور العلوم الإنسانية غير الغربية بوصفها جزءا من الاهتمامات التربوية والسياسية لنظرية ما بعد الاستعمار . وبالانتقال إلى عمل أركون المفصلي المتمثل في تحطيم الحدود التقليدية للوحي ، تضمِّن المقالة المنهج التفكيكي باعتباره حلقة وصل بينية تجمع نظرية ما بعد الاستعمار بنقد العقل العربي-الإسلامي . وتخلص المقالة إلى أن إعادة توجيه إطار عمل نظري بديل لحقل فرعي عبر هذين التخصصين المنفصلين يجبرنا على الميل نحو «التعددية النقدية» . تدمج تلك الأخيرة دراسة العوالم الإسلامية بتحليل سلالاتها الغربية المتداخلة من خلال تعزيز الدراسات حول المعارف الكلاسيكية في العصور الوسطى مع الحفاظ على مقاومة المركزية العرقية التي تخيِّم على الاستشراق الغربي .

خلال سرد يبرز التجربة الحياتية لدى السايبورج (شخص يستخدم عضواً اصطناعياً تعويضياً). ترى المقالة أن هذه النصوص تمثل المرحلة القادمة في النقاش الدائر بين النموذج الطبي والنموذج الاجتماعي في دراسات الإعاقة من خلال تبني نهج هجين يسعى إلى تجنب سلبيات كلا النموذجين. ومن ثم، توضح المقالة أن هذا النمط الجديد من النصوص يمكن أن يساعد في فتح آفاق جديدة لروايات الإعاقة في القرن الحادي والعشرين من خلال تصوير أناس حقيقيين ذوي شخصيات متنوعة وصراعات وأنماط حياتية مختلفة.

من «السيرة الذاتية» إلى «كتابة الحياة»: مسارات وتقاطعات عبر العلوم الإنسانية والاجتماعية

هالة كمال

تسعى هذه المقالة إلى صياغة خريطة معرفية للسيرة الذاتية بوصفها نوعاً أدبياً يحتل مساحة بينية داخل العلوم الإنسانية والاجتماعية، وما شهدته من تطورات في مساراتها، وما صاحب ذلك من ظهور تيارات واتجاهات جديدةٍ تتجاوز حدود الأنواع الأدبية التقليدية وتزعزع منهجياتها المستقرة وتطرح أشكالاً جديدة من التعبير عن الذات. تأتي المقالة في ثلاثة محاور أساسية تتناول جوانب من كتابة الذات من منظور مقارن. أولاً، «كتابة الذات ونشأة السيرة الذاتية». ثانياً، «مفاهيم نظرية ونقدية مقارنة». ثالثاً، «اتجاهات جديدة في كتابة الذات». وتخلص إلى أن موقع السيرة الذاتية البيني داخل الإنسانيات هو الذي أتاح لها لاحقاً تجاوز الحدود الفاصلة بين الإنسانيات والعلوم الاجتماعية.

معالم التنوع في الكلاسيكيات

ديفيد كونستان

لكلمة «التنوع» في مجال الدراسات الكلاسيكية دلالات متعددة. فمن جهة، تشير الكلمة الى التوازن المبتغى – الذي لا يزال بعيد المنال – فيما يتعلق بالجنوسة والعرق والانتماءات الدينية وغيرها من هويات معترف بها اجتماعياً. ومن جهة أخرى، فهناك تنوع تخصص الكلاسيكيات نفسه، وخروجه من تركيزه التقليدي على الإنجازات الفكرية والتاريخ السياسي اليوناني واللاتيني القديم إلى اهتمام أوسع بما يمكننا أن نسميه هوامش العالم الكلاسيكي. تتناول هذه المقالة التفاعل الضروري والمثمر بين هذين الجانبين من التنوع في مجال الكلاسيكيات.

نحو شمولية الإنسانيات الطبية

نادية حشيش

تتناول المقالة الإنسانيات الطبية باعتبارها مجالاً جديداً نوعاً ما في النظرية الأدبية يحث على إدراج العلوم الإنسانية في الدراسات الطبية. لقد أدى التطور العلمي في أوائل القرن العشرين في مجال الطب إلى ظهور صراع بين اتجاه اختزالي يفسر المرض من خلال مفاهيم حيوية بحتة و اتجاه آخر شمولي يفسره بالنظر إلى عوامل اجتماعيةٍ وثقافية. تتناول المقالة رواية **بيت الولادة** للكاتبة إيمي ماكاي بوصفها نموذجا يعكس التحول من النظرة الاختزالية لطبيب التوليد الحديث إلى النظرة الشمولية التي تتمتع بها القابلة التقليدية. توضح الرواية كون عملية الولادة التقليدية مجالاً تمارس فيه المرأة أحقيتها في إبداء الرأي والتحكم فيما يخص جسدها.

إطلالة على الشعر الأمريكي «المعاصر» : تأملات

حسن حلمي

تقدم هذه المقالة إلى قارئ العربية لمحة موجزة عن الشعر الأمريكي المعاصر وعرضاً للسياقات المرتبطة بالتطورات المهمة في النظرية والممارسة الشعرية، وذلك بتناول المنطلقات النظرية لبعض التيارات الفاعلة التي حددت مسارات الممارسة الشعرية في أمريكا. تعرض المقالة بإيجاز نماذج تمثيلية تعكس التنوع في مجال الراهن الشعري في الولايات المتحدة، كما تمثله تجارب عدد محدودٍ من الأصوات الشعرية المهمة التي أسهمت في تشكيل المشهدِ الشعري، خصوصاً في فترة نهاية القرن العشرين وبداية هذا القرن. تثير المقالة أيضاً بعض القضايا المتعلقة بالتحقيب والتصنيف والتجريب، وربط النماذج المعروضة بخلفياتها التاريخية والاجتماعية.

نحو آفاق جديدة في أدب الإعاقة :
السايبورج وإعادة تعريف الإعاقة في أدب الشباب

ياسمين سويد

تناقش المقالة العلاقة بين مفهوم الإعاقة والتكنولوجيا في ثلاث روايات تنتمي إلى أدب الشباب. ترسم هذه النصوص صورة مغايرة للتمثيل النمطي للأشخاص ذوي الإعاقة، وتعيد تعريف مصطلحي «الإعاقة» و«القدرة» من

عنها ، كما تحدد إسهاماته النظرية وتناقش استقباله المثير للجدل في جنوب أفريقيا ، وبريطانيا ، وعلى وجه التحديد في فرنسا . تبرز المقالة أيضاً نقائص هذا المجال النظري التي لم يتم تناولها بشكل كافٍ ، مثل اعتماده على الصيغة التقليدية المهيمنة لمفاهيم «الغرب» و«الحدَاثة» ، وكونه جزءاً من النظام الحداثي/الاستعماري الذي يبتغي تقويضه ، كما تطرح المقالة إمكان التفاعل دون هيمنة في ظل التعددية .

الدراسات ما بعد الكولونيالية والأدب العربي: بحثٌ عن الجذور أم تغيير للمسار؟

سامية الحديثي

تكاد الأصوات المتفائلة بمستقبل أفضل للدراسات ما بعد الكولونيالية تتفق على أهمية الأدب العربي المعاصر والدور الذي سيلعبه في دراسة إشكاليات النقد في الألفية الثالثة . تثير هذه المقالة التساؤل حول محورين في الأدب العربي قد يسهمان بشكل كبير في تغيير مسار الدراسات ما بعد الكولونيالية ، وهما الطوباوية في الأدب الفلسطيني ولحظة اللقاء بالنفط في أدب دول الخليج العربي . وهذان المحوران يتوافقان مع النزعة المادية والتأثير الماركسيّ المتزايد للنقاد المعاصرين . فدراسة الأدب الفلسطيني والأدب الخليجي تحتّم على الباحث النظر في الظروف المادية التي كُتب فيها النص ، مثل المشهد السياسي والخريطة الجغرافية وآليات الإنتاج وتوزيع الثروة .

نظرية الألعاب والتحليل الأدبي : الآفاق والتحديات

نجلاء سعد حسن

تهدف هذه المقالة إلى عرض وتحليل إمكانات تطبيق نظرية الألعاب على النصوص الأدبية والتحديات التي قد تقف حيال ذلك . وتوضح كيف أن النظرية التي ولدت في مجال الرياضيات والاقتصاد قد بدأت تشق طريقها إلى الإنسانيات بشكل عام والأدب بشكل خاص ، الأمر الذي جعل النظرية وتطبيقها علي الأدب محل نقد ودراسة ما بين مؤيد ومعارض . تتناول المقالة إيجابيات تطبيق النظرية على النص الأدبي - مثل التفسير العقلاني للسلوك البشري والنظر إلى الأمور الحياتية بطريقة ممنهجة مسبقاً - كما تلقي الضوء على العقبات التي تعترض الباحثين حال تطبيق النظرية ، مثل صعوبة منهجة العمل الأدبي وإغفال العوامل العاطفية والسيكولوجية ، والتعارض مع المدارس النقدية الأخرى .

المسارات الحديثة في الدراسات الفلسفية

عبد السلام بنعبد العالي

عوضاً عن تناول هذه المقالة لموضوعها من خلال بلورته في اتجاهات ومذاهب وتيارات، تحاول المقالة أن تنسج شبكات فكرية تضمّ مفكرين يقولون الشيء ذاته بأنحاء مختلفة، وأن تشخصن تلك الشبكات في مفهومات-مفاتيح تعتقد أن الحداثة الفلسفية تدور حولها. ومن ضمن هذه المفهومات، البنية والاختلاف والتراث والإيديولوجيا. يخلص كاتب المقالة إلى أن هذه المفهوماتِ وظفت لإعادة النظر في تاريخ الفلسفة، فانتهت إلى خلخلة المنطق الذي تحكم فيه، بل أعادت النظر في مفهوم الزمان التاريخي ذاته، مع ما ترتب عن ذلك من مراجعة لمفهومات الجدل والحقيقة والهوية والأصل والذات الفاعلة.

إعادة توجيه الحداثة: مسارات التبادل
بين الشعر العربي والفارسي

ليڤاي تومسون

تتناول هذه المقالة اتجاهاً جديداً في دراسات الأدب المقارن من خلال تحليل الروابط الشكلية والموضوعية المشتركة في الشعر الحديث المكتوب باللغتين العربية والفارسية. تعيد المقالة رسم خريطة التطور التاريخي المشترك بين كلا التراثين الشعريين، كما تحث على إعادة توجيه دراسات الحداثة الأدبية نحو الشرق. تسلط المقالة الضوء على محاولات حداثية تأسيسية في التجديد نشأت خارج مجال التأثير الأدبي الغربي، ومنها الاحتفاظ ببعض العناصر الشكلية النابعة من أنساق الشعر العربي المكتوب ما قبل الحداثة، مثل استمرار المحدثين في استخدام التفعيلة العروضية في الشعر العربي والفارسي الحديث خلال عقوده الأولى.

المنعطف المقوِّض للاستعمار في الإنسانيات

كلير جاليان

تقدم هذه المقالة رؤية نقدية لتطور واستقبال المنعطف «المقوِّض للاستعمار» في الدراسات الإنسانية الغربية. تعرض المقالة التسلسل الذي أسس لهذا المنعطف ونقاط التقائه بدراسات ما بعد الكولونيالية وانصرافه

برنامجاً بحثياً يسلط الضوء على الدور الخاص للغويات التربوية بوصفه مقاربة لدراسة اللغة والتعليم تساعد على سد هذه الفجوة .

المنحى الثقافي في دراسة الأدب العربي

أنطونيو باتشيفيكو

شهد مجال الدراسات الأدبية في العالم العربي خلال العقود الأخيرة نمواً هائلاً وعدداً من التغييرات الجذرية ، فيما يتعلق بكل من المواضيع المطروقة وأساليب تحليلها . لذا ، من خلال تحليل أعمال بعض الأكاديميين البارزين ، تهدف هذه المقالة إلى تسليط الضوء على الاتجاهات الرئيسية للمنحى الثقافي الذي أثر في دراسة الأدب العربي في الوقت الراهن ، بالإضافة إلى تحليل تاريخه وممارساته المتعددة . وبعيداً عن أي منظور تقييدي ، تقوم المقالة باتباع منهج تاريخي تعاقبي للتأمل في أوجه ضعفها وتوجهاتها المستقبلية .

من الترجمة الثقافية إلى استحالة الترجمة :
تنظير الترجمة خارج مجال دراسات الترجمة

براين جيمس باير

تناقش هذه المقالة مفهومين مؤثرين للترجمة ظهرا حديثاً خارج مجال دراسات الترجمة ، وهما الترجمة الثقافية (النقل من ثقافة إلى أخرى مع تعديلات مصاحبة) واستحالة الترجمة (عدم إمكان نقل بعض المسميات من لغة إلى أخرى) . تتناول المقالة تضارب كلا المفهومين مع مفهوم الترجمة البينية (الترجمة بين اللغات) . فمجازياً ، تميل الترجمة الثقافية إلى تقويض مفهوم الترجمة البينية وطمسه ، بينما تحدّ نظرية استحالة الترجمة من فهمنا للترجمة البينية بتركيزها على مجموعة منفصلة من الكلمات وإلماحها إلى أن كل شيء إلا تلك الكلمات يمكن نقله بسهولة . يدعو الكاتب إلى نظرية متواضعة في الترجمة لا تقصي تعريف الترجمة عن ممارسة الترجمة البينية ، في الوقت الذي تدرك فيه أن اللامشترك ملمح موجود في كل اللغات البشرية .

ملخصات المقالات
(أبجدياً بالاسم الأخير)

النسوية العربية: مواقف وممارسات

شيرين أبو النجا

تهدف هذه المقالة إلى تناول التوجهات والتقاطعات البحثية التي أنتجت رؤى معرفية ارتكزت عليها النسوية في مجال العلوم الإنسانية في العالم العربي، وهو تناول يحاول رصد وتتبع الأفكار الرئيسية التي وجهت المسار الفكري النسوي وتفاعلت معه بشكل أدى إلى تراكم خبرة معرفية ساندته في الاستجابة لمتغيرات الواقع السياسي والاجتماعي، ومن ثم، إلى الكشف عن مناطق معتمة جديرة بالبحث. وعليه، لا تسعى المقالة إلى جمع معلومات أو رصد أحداث مطلقاً. ففي سعيها إلى محاولة الإمساك بالمحطات الفكرية التي كانت نتاجاً للحراك اللافت في المجال العام والسياقات الاجتماعية والسياسية، تركز المقالة على المسار البحثي الأكاديمي ولا تنخرط في طرح الجانب التنموي النسوي.

اللغويات التربوية ومشكلة اللغة في تعليم العلوم والرياضيات في العالم العربي

تامر أمين

تواجه الدول العربية العديد من العقبات أمام تحسين جودة تعليم العلوم والرياضيات وغيرها من المواد، من بينها تحديات مرتبطة باللغة. فاللغة أداة تواصل وتفكير، وعلى المعلم والمتعلم إتقان استخدامها في التعليم والتعلم. بالإضافة إلى ذلك، يتم التعليم في سياقات ذات تعدد لغوي عندما تدرس هذه المواد بلغة أجنبية، وحتى عندما يتم التدريس باللغة العربية بسبب ظاهرة ثنائية اللغة العربية: ديجلوسيا. تخلق هذه السياقات اللغوية تحديات تربوية متعددة يصعب تخطيها بسبب قلة الأبحاث في هذا الموضوع. توجز هذه المقالة

Hall, Stuart. "Encoding, Decoding" *The Cultural Studies Reader*. Ed. Simons During. London and NY: Routledge, 1993.

Heims, Steve J. *Jon von Neumann and Norbert Wiener: From Mathematics to the Technogies of Life and Death*. Cambridge: MIT P, 1980.

Hutchinson, Peter. *Games Authors Play*. London: Methuen, 1983.

Leonard, Robert. *Von Neumann, Morgenstern, and the Creation of Game Theory: From Chess to Social Science, 1900-1960*. Cambridge: Cambridge UP, 2012.

Morgenstern, Oskar. *Wirtschaftsprognose: Eine Untersuchung ihrer Voraussetzungen und Möglichkeiten* [Economic Forecasting: An Investigation of its Presuppositions and Possibilities]. Vienna: Julius Springer, 1928.

Nash, John F. Jr. "Biographical." *The Nobel Prize*. 1994. <https://www.nobelprize.org/prizes/economic-sciences/1994/nash/biographical/>.

---. "Equilibrium Points in N-Person Games." *Proceedings of the National Academy of Sciences of the United States of America* 36.1 (January 1950): 48-49.

von Neumann, John and Oskar Morgenstern. *Theory of Games and Economic Behavior*. Princeton and Oxford: Princeton UP, 2007.

Poore, Benjamin. "The Game is Afoot: Hunting and Playing in Sherlockian Theatre." *Sherlock Holmes from Screen to Stage*. London: Palgrave Macmillan, 2017. 69-101.

Rapoport, Anatol . *Two-Person Game Theory: The Essential Ideas*. Ann Arbor: U of Michigan P, 1966.

---. "The Use and Misuse of Game Theory." *Scientific American* 207.6 (December 1962): 108-18.

Reeb, Tyler. "Playing Games and 'Making' a Novel: Mark Twain and Game Theory in *Adventures of Huckleberry Finn*." *The Mark Twain Annual* 7.1 (2009): 97-116.

Snow, C. P. *The Two Cultures*. Calbridge: Cambridge UP, 2008.

Swirski, Peter. *Of Literature and Knowledge: Explorations in Narrative Thought Experiments, Evolution, and Game Theory*. London and NY: Routledge, 2007.

المراجع العربية

ألف ليلة وليلة . القاهرة : مطبعة بولاق ، ١٢٥٢ هـ .
محفوظ ، نجيب . بداية ونهاية . القاهرة : دار الشروق ، ١٩٤٩ .
--- . زقاق المدق . القاهرة : مكتبة مصر ، ١٩٤٧ .
المعموري ، محسن حسن . مبادئ علم الاقتصاد . عمّان : دار اليازوري ، ٢٠١٨ .

المراجع الأجنبية

Binmore, Ken. *Game Theory: A Very Short Introduction*. Oxford: Oxford UP, 2007.

Bodi, Russell J. *Philological Applications of Play and Game Theories*. Ann Arbor: The U of Toledo, 1997.

Brams, Steven J. *Game Theory and the Humanities: Bridging Two Worlds*. Cambridge, Mass.: MIT P, 2011.

Bruss, Elizabeth, W. "The Game of Literature and Some Literary Games." *New Literary History* 9.1 (Autumn 1977): 153-72.

Cagle, Jeremey. "Elegant Complexity: The Presence of Cold War Game Theory in Postmodern American Fiction." Diss. University of South Carolina, 2010.

Charles, Aurelie. "Book Review of *Jane Austen, Game Theorist* by Michael Suk-Young Chwe." *Eastern Economic Journal* 40.4 (September 2014): 611-12.

Chwe, Michael Suk-Young. *Jane Austen, Game Theorist*. Princeton and Oxford: Princeton UP, 2013.

Deresiewicz, William. "No, Jane Austen Was Not a Game Theorist." *The New Republic*. January 19, 2014. <https://newrepublic.com/article/116170/jane-austen-game-theorist-michael-suk-young-chwe-joke>.

Edwards, Brian. *Theories of Play and Postmodern Fiction*. NY: Routledge, 1998.

Eisenhower, Dwight D. "Citation Accompanying Medal of Freedom Presented to Dr. John von Neumann." *The American Presidency Project*. February 15, 1956. <https://www.presidency.ucsb.edu/documents/citation-accompanying-medal-freedom-presented-dr-john-von-neumann>.

Ghazoul, Ferial. *Nocturnal Poetics: The Arabian Nights in a Comparative Context*. Cairo: The American U in Cairo P, 1996.

الاقتصادية والعسكرية، أو كما يقول سويرسكي: «لا يوجد نظام رياضي غيَّر من دراسة علم الاقتصاد والعلوم الاجتماعية والبيولوجية مثلما فعلت نظرية الألعاب» (Swirski 125)؛ إذ نجحت النظرية في تفسير كل الصراعات الحقيقية و«الوهمية» من خلال المعادلات الرياضية، كما قدمت بدائل للتفاوض وحل المعضلات المختلفة في شتى فروع المعرفة. إلا أن إقحامها في المجال الأدبي بكل فروعه يبقى أمراً شائكًا لا يخلو من سلبيات. فهناك خياران، أولهما أن نفترض أن الكاتب على دراية بالنظرية، ومن ثم يقوم بنسج صراعات القصة وحلولها من خلال معادلاتها، وهو أمر يصعب تصديقه، لأنه يخنق حقيقة الخلق الإبداعي وجوهره، فيتحول الكاتب إلى آلة ميكانيكية مهمتها رسم الشخصيات وصراعاتها وفق مبادئ النظرية. أما الخيار الثاني فهو أن نقول إن القصة بوصفها منتجاً أدبياً تخضع - على سبيل الصدفة - لقواعد نظرية المباراة، وتصير مهمة الناقد في هذه الحالة تتبع الاختيارات والتفضيلات والآليات التي يُحل بها الصراع. وبينما قد تنجح بعض القصص في الالتزام بقواعد اللعبة الرياضية - وبخاصة في الأدب البوليسي - قد يحيد النص في معظم الأحيان عن السبيل الرياضي، مثلما هو الحال في عدد غير قليل من الدراسات التي طبقت نظرية الألعاب في مجال الرواية، وأثبتت في نهاية الأمر فشل الشخصيات في المفاوضة أو الاختيار، رغم عقلانيتها المزعومة. ومن ثم تصبح جدوى تطبيق النظرية محل استفهام.

تفرض العقلانية، كما يقول ناش، قيوداً على علاقة المرء بالكون، وبالمثل تفرض العقلانية في المجال الأدبي - سواء في الخلق أو التفسير - قيوداً على النص لا يحتاج إليها الكاتب أو القارئ، بل قد تهدد كينونة النص ذاته ووجوده، بإلغاء بعض جمالياته التي تكمن في الغموض واللانهائية. ورغم ذلك، يبقى حق تطبيق النظرية - مثلها مثل بقية النظريات الأخرى، بدءاً من مدرسة النقد الجديد، ومروراً بالنسوية، وانتهاءً بالتفكيكية وما بعد الحداثة، على سبيل المثال لا الحصر- في الأوساط النقدية المختلفة، سواء على المستوى العربي أو الغربي، اختياراً فردياً متاحاً أمام الكاتب والقارئ على حد سواء.

وبالمثل ، لا ينكر بيتر سويرسكي أن نظرية الألعاب قد تعد حقلاً خصباً للتطبيق على الأدب ، حيث يرى أنها تساعد في تحليل المحتوى والشخصيات وتفسير تصرفاتهم ودوافعهم والعواقب المترتبة عليها تفسيراً عقلانياً ، وأنها قد تفيد في توضيح الاختيارات الإستراتيجية بفحص العلاقة بين تحركات الأشخاص وبنيه الحبكة . ويذهب أيضا إلى أن الدراسات الأدبية المعتمدة علي نظرية الألعاب قد تكون مفيدة لعلماء الاجتماع ، من حيث تمدهم بمعلومات ثرية حول السلوك الإنساني الذي تقدمه الروايات (Swirski 126) . إلا أنه يرى بعض الصعوبات التي ربما تقف دون الوصول إلى درجة الكمال من حيث فائدة التجربة . فكما يقول ، ستقف النظرية عاجزةً أمام عدم التعيين النصي ، أو ما يسميه عدم الموثوقية التي تعد جزءاً أصيلاً من ماهية الأدب السردي بكل أنواعه ، وبخاصة إذا كان السرد باختيار ضمير محدد . بالإضافة إلى ذلك ، هناك الذاتية واللاموضوعية اللتان تميزان الإستراتيجات التي تتبعها شخصيات الرواية – على تعددها – في تعاملها مع الصراعات المختلفة ، وهو ما قد لا يلقى إجماعاً بالقبول أو الرفض من القراء (128) .

وربما تثير نظرية الألعاب باعتمادها على نموذج رياضي ممنهج يقوم بتحليل الاختيارات المختلفة للشخصيات من منظور عقلاني بحت – قد يؤكد على دور العقلانية في السلوك البشري – حفيظة بعض أنصار المدارس الأدبية الأخرى ، كالرومانسية بتأكيدها العاطفة عاملاً رئيسياً في الخلق والتفسير الأدبي ، ومدرسة التحليل النفسي بتأكيدها دور العوامل النفسية والفسيولوجية في القرارات الإنسانية ، وكذا نظرية المشاعر Affect Theory التي توضح كيف أن مشاعر الإنسان ترتبط بمظاهر فسيولوجية بعينها ، وأنها تؤثر في قراراته المختلفة .

خاتمة

تفرض العقلانية قيوداً على مفهوم الشخص عن علاقته بالكون . (Nash, "Biliographical" n. pag)

فيما بين التأييد والمعارضة ، تتضح لنا المعضلة الوجودية التي تواجهها نظرية الألعاب في دخولها معترك التحليل والنقد الأدبي . فمما لا شك فيه أن النظرية حققت نجاحات غير مسبوقة في المجالات

يجعلهم يتحدّون قوانين اللعبة ، أو يقلبونها رأساً على عقب ، أو يعيدون هيكلتها . وهنا ، تجدر بنا الإشارة إلى نظريات أدبية ركزت في مجملها على دور القارئ ، مثل مدرسة استجابة القارئ Reader Response التي قدمت مفهوم «القارئ الحقيقي» الذي يملي على النص ما يمتلكه من إرث إيديولوجي وفلسفي ولغوي وسياسي – تلك الخلفية التي تساعد في تفسير النص . وكذا نظرية السيموطيقيا Semiotics التفسيرية عند ستيوارت هول ، الذي قدم مفهوم الترميز والتشفير ومنهجية قراءة النص التي قسمها إلى إستراتيجيات ثلاث : القراءة السيادية التي يفسر فيها القارئ النص من المنظور الذي انتواه الكاتب ؛ والقراءة المضادة التي ينتهج فيها القارئ منهجاً تفسيرياً مضاداً لما انتواه الكاتب عند خلقه النص ؛ والقراءة التفاوضية التي تسمح بقبول بعض رسالة الكاتب وتفسير بعض أجزاء أخرى من منظور القارئ (انظر Hall) .

وهناك مجموعة من النقاد وقفت موقفاً وسطاً تجاه تطبيق النظرية ، وكانت الحيرة هي السمة السائدة لديها . فعلى سبيل المثال ، ترى إليزابيث براس Elizabeth Bruss أن تطبيق نظرية الألعاب على النص الأدبي من شأنه إضفاء بعد جمالي جديد على العمل الأدبي ، وهو ما تطلق عليه دراسة «جمال الإستراتيجية» من خلال مجموعة عوامل مشروطة تطرحها نظرية الألعاب (12) . غير أن حقيقة ما إذا كان النص الأدبي سيلتزم بهذا أم لا ، وما إذا كانت هذه القوانين ملائمة أم لا لمختلف نوايا الشخصيات المتباينة ، مع الأخذ في الاعتبار سمة التعقيد والتركيب التي يتميز بها الأدب ، فتظل موضع شك (170) . وتذهب براس إلى أبعد من ذلك ، فتقول إن نظرية الألعاب ، بكل قوانينها التي توضح صفات العقل والدافع ، وكذا السلوك الفردي ، تتسم بالبدائية مقارنة بالطرق الأعقد التي يعالج بها الأدب هذه الصراعات ، حتى إن فكرة اللعبة ذاتها تبدو محدودة وضعيفة حين تطرح مجموعة قواعد محددة نهائية ، ومساحة محددة المعالم للعب ، ومجموعة تفضيلات واضحة وحسابات معينة واعية (170) . ويرى براين إدواردز أن فائدة النظرية أو عدمها يرجع إلى الطريقة التي يتناول بها الناقد النص الأدبي مستعملاً إياها ، ولكن الآراء النظرية لا تعد حلولاً للنصوصِ الأدبية بطبيعتها المعقدة . وإذا توقعنا أن النظرية ستفعل ذلك بوصفه نوعاً من التبرير لصالحها وفائدتها ، فذلك يعني أننا نفرض على الأدب شروطاً يجب في الحقيقة أن يبرأ منها (Edwards 16) .

عملية حسابية تغفل تماماً عامل التلقائية والتأثير البيئي والثقافي والنفسي الذي يجعل الكاتب يطوع شخصياته وفقاً لمتطلباتها . فإذا كان من الممكن تقبل أن كاتباً بعينه يصوغ حبكة رواياته وفق منهج رياضي معين ، أو أنه يجعل اختيارات شخصياته خاضعة لتوازن ناش – أو غيرها من المعادلات الرياضية – في حالة الأدب البوليسي والتراجيديا التي تسير على منهج أرسطو مثلاً ، فإن ذلك يصير صعباً في بقية أصناف الأدب . ويتضح هذا من النتائج التي استخلصها معظم النقاد الذين طبقوا النظرية على نصوص أدبية لا تقع في هذين المجالين . فذهب البعض في استنتاجاتهم إلى أنه رغم وضوح بعض تفضيلات الشخصيات واعتمادها على العقلانية إلى حد كبير في نهجها ، فإن بعضها يعاني الفشل والخسارة في صراعاته الحياتية .

وقد ذهب البعض إلى أن نظرية الألعاب تصلح للتطبيق على العلاقة بين القارئ والكاتب في تناولهما النص الأدبي . وفي هذه الحالة، يتمحور الصراع حول تفسير النص الأدبي وفك رموزه التي تتأرجح بين عقائدية الكاتب والقارئ . فعلى سبيل المثال ، يرى إدواردز أنه بينما نجد أن نموذج اللعب بين شخصين قد يكون مفيداً في تفسير هذه العلاقة ، يتميز النص الأدبي بكونه أكثر «لعباً» في قدرته على تخطي قواعده وتقاليده ذاتها ، وذلك من خلال العديد من التقنيات ، كالمحاكاة الساخرة والسخرية الناقدة والتجريب ذاته (Edwards 14) . وبينما تحدد نظرية الألعاب مجموعة اختيارات ونتائج جلية غير مبهمة ، فالحقيقة – كما يدعي إدواردز – أن الغموض صفة أصيلة في الأدب (14) . ويمكننا الإضافة هنا أن الغموض كان محور ارتكاز بعض نظريات التفسير الأدبي ، كما هو الحال في مدرسة النقد الجديد New Criticism التي ركزت على الغموض في الشعر بوصفه ميزة أصيلة في كينونته . كما لا يفوتنا أن نذكر أيضاً أن الغموض واللانهائية ميزتان أفسحتا الطريق لإبراز دور القارئ في تفسير النص الأدبي . فكما يقول إدواردز، بمقدور الكاتب أن يخلق اللعبة (النص) ، ويضع القواعد الموجهة لفهم قوانينها ، إلا أنه توجد حقيقة واضحة ، هي أن القارئ يؤثر في النص مثلما يؤثر النص في القارئ ، ومن ثم يصعب القول بأن القارئ سينصاع لقانون اللعبة . ويضيف أن تفسير عمل أدبي من خلال قوانين لعبة معينة يتطلب تقسيم رمزية العمل الأدبي تقسيماً صريحاً (14) . ويبقى مع ذلك أنه بينما قد يتقيد بعض القراء بقوانين اللعبة كما وضعها الكاتب ، تملك أغلبية القراء الآخرين من الحرية – بوصفهم لاعبين – ما

في كل الروايات الأخرى التي تندرج تحت مدرسة بعينها ، كالواقعية على سبيل المثال . فالأدب هو من خلق الكاتب ، والقرارات التي يمليها على شخصياته لا تخضع لنظام رياضي ، وإنما تنبثق من وجهة نظر الكاتب التي تتلون بدورها بلون خبرته ومعتقداته . ورغم أنه يمكن تناول شخصيات روائي معين ، كما هو الحال مع جين أوستن ، لتوضيح المنهجية المنتظمة التي سلكتها الشخصيات في اتخاذ القرارات الحياتية المختلفة ، فلا يعني ذلك أن الشخصيات تمتلك خطة إستراتيجية تقف وراء تلك الاختيارات . وبالمثل ، يمكن القول إن تطبيق نظرية الألعاب على أعمال نجيب محفوظ قد يفيد في تفسير بعض اختيارات الأفراد أطراف الصراع ، ويلقي الضوء على أهمية إعمال العقلانية في تطورات الحبكة الروائية وصولاً إلى العقدة ثم الحل ، إلا أن الناقد لا يمكنه الجزم بأن نجيب محفوظ مثلا قد عول على نظرية الألعاب إبان نسجه للرواية ، أو أن هناك إستراتيجيات محددة تنتهجها الشخصيات في تعاملاتها الحياتية وفق ترتيب عقلاني يتحكم فيه الروائي .

وتؤتي النظريات الرياضية للألعاب ثمارها في تفسير إستراتيجيات الفكر الإنساني التي تقف وراء تصرف بعينه عندما تتلاشى جميع الحواجز التي من شأنها التمييز بين البشر ، كالعنصرية والاستعمار . يقول المبدأ العام للنظرية إن المشاركين في اللعبة من المفترض أن يكونوا على درجة من المساواة والتكافؤ في القوة ، وهنا تكمن حقيقة المنافسة على الفوز ، وعندما ينعدم هذا المبدأ تصبح قوانين اللعبة عارية من الصحة . ولا يفوتنا أن نذكر هنا أن أول تطبيق لنظرية الألعاب كان في المجال السياسي بين القوتين العظميين في العالم إبان الحرب العالمية الباردة ، ولم يكن مثلا بين قوة مهيمنة إمبريالية وأخرى ترزح تحت وطأة الاستعمار . هنا ، يتضح أن التساوي في القوة بوصفه شرطاً لدخول اللعبة يغفل مبدأ التنوع والتباين بين أطراف اللعبة في النص الأدبي ، الذي هو سمة أصيلة تميز شخصيات العمل الأدبي ، ويغفل أيضاً العوامل التاريخية والاجتماعية التي قد تدفع طرفا في لعبة معينة إلى اختيار تفضيل معين من أجل ظروف معينة . فالعقلانية وحدها لا تحكم اختيارات المرء في الواقع أو في العالم الخيالي للأدب .

تحوّل إستراتيجيات التفكير التي تقع في صميم نظرية الألعاب المؤلف إلى كاتب آلي ؛ هذا إذا اعتبرنا أن الكاتب على دراية بنظرية الألعاب ، كما هو الحال في جين أوستن التي يدعي أنها كانت على دراية تامة بمبادئ النظرية قبل أن تظهر إلى النور (Chwe 7) . ومن ثم ، يصير التأليف الأدبي

للإنسانيات ، فإن تطبيقها على الأعمال الأدبية قد يلقى رفضاً من عدد غير قليل من النقاد . يرى براين إدواردز Brian Edwards ، مثلاً ، أن تلك الخصائص التي جعلت نظرية الألعاب تؤتي ثمارها في مجال الاقتصاد والعلوم السياسية والتخطيط العسكري - وهي اهتمامها الأقصى بقواعد الإجراءات والاختيارات الواضحة والنتائج غير المبهمة - هي الخصائص عينها التي تجعلها غير ملائمة للنظرية الأدبية (14) . ويوضح إدواردز أن السبب في ذلك يرجع إلى مرونة النص الأدبي وصعوبة تطويعه لمعادلات رياضية . ويرى وليم ديريسيڤيتش William Deresiewicz أن تطبيق النظرية على الأعمال الأدبية يقلل من أهمية الأدب ، ويوحي بأن قيمة الأدب ترتبط بقابليته لتطبيق نظريات رياضية بعينها (n. pag) . ويمكن إضافة أن النظرية قد تقلص العمل الأدبي ، فضلاً عن أن الفن والأدب ليسا بحاجة إلى عامل الدقة الذي هو متطلب رئيسي في علوم الرياضيات . ومن ثم ، فإن ميكنة المشهد الأدبي وإثبات أنه يدل على صحة معادلة ما أو نظرية رياضية بعينها ، يخلعان عن الأدب بعض جماليته ، ويزيحان عنه بعض سمات التلقائية التي هي جزء أصيل من هُويّته . ويضيف وليم ديريسيڤيتش أن الأدب يرتبط بالتجربة الحياتية ، وأن تلك التجربة - التي لا نقرأ عنها فقط بل نعيشها أيضاً بوصفنا قراءً - لا يمكن وزنها أو قياسها على النحو الذي يحدث في حالة الصيغ والبراهين الرياضية (n. pag) .

تتمثل المشكلة الأكبر التي تواجه تطبيق نظرية الألعاب على الأدب في افتراض أن الشخصيات في كافة الأنماط الأدبية - نثراً أو شعراً أو مسرحاً - تتصرف دائماً بشكل عقلاني . فرغم نجاح النظرية في وضع تصور معين من خلال معادلات بعينها ، فهي تغفل الجانب العاطفي الذي يقف وراء اتخاذ قرار بعينه ، الأمر الذي يتعارض مع بعض النظريات الأدبية الأخرى التي تركز على دور العوامل العاطفية والإيديولوجية والسيكولوجية في الاختيارات المتعددة التي تقوم بها الشخصيات . فالألعاب ، بوجه عام ، تحكمها القواعد والقوانين ، وتتميز بالنهائية والمحدودية ، وهي الخواص التي تقف على النقيض من الخلق الأدبي الذي يتميز باللانهائية في التفسير والتشكيل والخلق . وهنا ، يجدر الاستشهاد ببيتر هاتشينسون Peter Hutchinson الذي يقول بأن من بين كل الألعاب المعروفة للإنسان ، يعد الأدب أقلها خضوعاً وانصياعاً للقواعد (5) . فحتى إذا نجحنا في تحليل قرارات الشخصيات وفق النظريات المتاحة ، فلا يعني ذلك أنه بإمكاننا التعميم على كل الشخصيات

تسرد لنا قصة أسرة تواجه الحياة بعد وفاة عائلها ، وتوضح الإستراتيجيات التي يتبعها كل فرد من أجل البقاء . يتمثل الصراع في الرواية في طرفين : الأسرة والفقر الذي يهددها بالفناء ، كما يتضح من المقولة الأشهر في الرواية : «لو كان الفقر رجلاً لقتلته» (ص ٧٥) . وبالنظر إلى الأخوة الأربعة ، تتمثل لنا إستراتيجية كل منهم في تعظيم فرص الفوز على الفقر ، وهو ما يتبدى من خلاله توازن ناش ؛ فالأخ الأكبر حسن يهديه عقله إلى التضحية بالتعليم والعمل والكدّ من أجل توفير لقمة العيش ومساعدة أخيه حسنين في استكمال تعليمه . كما يرى حسين أيضاً أن الإستراتيجية المثلى للبقاء هي الحصول على الكسب السريع ، فيلجأ إلى تجارة المخدرات . وهناك حسنين ، الأخ الأصغر ، الذي يمتلك طموحات جامحة في الانتقال من طبقته إلى طبقة أرستقراطية ، فيرى أن السبيل إلى ذلك هو الالتحاق بالكلية الحربية . وعندما يرى أن عواطفه تقف حائلاً دون تحقيق هدفه ، ينحي العاطفة جانباً ؛ فشأنه شأن حميدة ، يتخلص من خطيبته ، ابنة الجيران ، ويسعي – في محاولته لتعظيم فرص الفوز بحياة كريمة – إلى الزواج بفتاة من طبقة أرستقراطية . أما الأخت ، فتلجأ إلى العمل خيّاطة ، ثم تنحدر إلى هاوية البغاء . وتنتهي القصة بالقبض عليها في أحد بيوت الدعارة ، فيسارع حسين الضابط إلى إطلاق سراحها ، ويقودها إلى النيل لتنتحر غرقاً ، حتى يتخلص منها بوصفها تهديداً لنَهْجه في الترقي والصعود ، إلا أنه يخلص إلى أن العار صار جزءاً أصيلاً منه ، وينتهي به الأمر إلى الانتحار .

نظرية الألعاب والتحليل الأدبي : التحديات

بالنظر إلى الأمثلة السابقة ، نجد أن استعمال نظرية الألعاب في تفسير سلوك الشخصيات لا يقودنا ، حتماً ، إلى الاحتفاء بالقرارات المستندة إلى العقلانية ، وإنما يمنحنا منهجاً تفسيرياً قد نتفق معه أو نختلف . فتطبيق نظرية الألعاب على الإنسانيات بشكل عام ، وعلى الأعمال الأدبية بشكل خاص ، يعد بشيراً بسد الفجوة بين العلوم والإنسانيات ، تلك الفجوة التي استحوذت على فكر الكثير من المنظرين ، بدءاً من س . ب . سنو C. P. Snow في كتابه الشهير **الثقافتان** *The Two Cultures* . ورغم أن تطبيق النظرية على الأدب يعد خطوة إيجابية على طريق تداخل الأنظمة الذي يلقى الآن ترحيباً في الأوساط النقدية

بإستراتيجية أخرى أحنك ، استطاعت من خلالها زيادة فرص نجاحها في الهروب من الموت المحتوم بالحكي اللانهائي ؛ فقابلت إستراتيجية شهريار بالقتل اللانهائي - التي أراد بها تعظيم فرص الرجال في الانتقام من جنس النساء - بإستراتيجية لانهائية في الحكي استطاعت بها النجاة من الموت . فكما تقول فريال غزول في دراستها عن أهمية الأرقام في القصة الإطار، استطاعت لانهائية السرد أن تتغلب على لانهائية الموت ؛ حيث تؤكد الناقدة أن الأرقام تلعب دوراً في هذا التفسير ، فتشير - على سبيل المثال - إلى العنوان ألف ليلة وليلة ، الذي يتضح من خلاله كيف أن الرقم واحد بعد الألف يشير إلى إيقاف لانهائية الموت وإحلال الحياة محل الموت ؛ تلك الحقيقة التي تتأكد بمولد الأطفال الثلاثة لشهريار وشهرزاد (Ghazoul 37-41) .

وإذا اتبعنا مناهج الباحثين المشار إليهم سلفاً ، نجد أن النظرية قد تؤتي ثمارها في قراءة الصراع في أدب الواقعية أيضاً ، وعلى رأسه روايات نجيب محفوظ ، الذي أثرى الحركة الواقعية في الأدب العربي بأعمال عديدة . ومثلما الحال مع روايات جين أوستن وتفسير اتجاه بطلاتها من منظور تعظيم فرص المكسب في الزواج ، يمكن تطبيق ذلك على رواية زقاق المدق ، مثلاً ، فنجد أن البطلة حميدة ذات الجمال الأخاذ تستعمل عقلها لتصيّد أحسن الفرص في الحصول على زوج ينقذها من عالم الفقر . فهي تبدأ بعباس صاحب صالون الحلاقة الذي يضحي بعمله ويذهب للعمل مع الإنجليز حتى يتسنى له تحقيق أحلام حميدة في الفوز بالمال والخلاص من الفقر ، غير أن هذا التصرف لا يعول على العقل وإنما العاطفة . وفي الوقت ذاته ، تندفع حميدة وراء فكرة الثراء التي تسيطر على عقلها ، وتفكر في الارتباط بسليم - الأكثر ثراءً ووجاهة اجتماعية - عندما يعرض عليها ذلك ، فتسعى إلى اقتناص العرض لتعظيم فرصتها في الوصول السريع إلى الثراء . ولكنها سرعان ما تعدل عن تلك الإستراتيجية عندما يصاب سليم بأزمة قلبية ، إلى أن يقودها عقلها إلى إبراهيم فرج ، الذي يوهمها بأنه سيساعدها في تنفيذ أحلامها ، فتهرب معه وتحقق حلمها في الحياة الفارهة المليئة بالرفاهية ، وذلك من خلال عساكر العدو الذين يبتاعون شرفها ، فتستبدل بحياتها القذرة حياة جديدة أقذر . وكما هو الحال لدى شهريار الذي أباد النساء ، مستنداً إلى استنتاج عقلي وليس عاطفياً ، أبادت حميدة شرفها بمعادلة عقلية زائفة تربط الحياة الكريمة بالمال .

وبالمثل ، نجد رواية بداية ونهاية تقدم لنا شخصيات تتصارع مع الفقر لتعظيم فرصها في الترقي والهروب من الطبقة الدنيا التي تنتمي إليها . فالرواية

نظرية الألعاب والأدب العربي

ورغم أن نظرية الألعاب – حسب علمنا – لم تحظ بالتطبيق في مجال الأدب العربي ، فمن الممكن القول بأن مفاهيمها الرياضية المختلفة تصلح للتطبيق على أنظمة السرد في اللغة العربية . ومثلما بدأت النظرية في طرح ثمارها في روضة الأدب البوليسي المبني على التشويق والإثارة ، بما يؤكد أهمية إعمال العقل في الوصول إلى حل عقدة الحبكة الروائية ، فبإمكان الناقد إبراز دور الإستراتيجية والعقلانية في الروايات المبنية على التشويق . ولنأخذ مثلاً ألف ليلة وليلة ، أحد أبرز الأعمال الكلاسيكية الذي عُدّ بشيراً بمولد القصة القصيرة من حيث احتوائه على العديد من الحكايات داخل القصة الإطار . تدور هذه القصة حول الملك شهريار الذي قرر الانتقام من النساء قاطبة عند اكتشافه خيانة زوجته وزوجة أخيه . وبعد أن يترسخ داخله اقتناع بأن الخيانة جزء أصيل من طبيعة المرأة ، يقرر الزواج كل يوم من عذراء ، ثم يقتلها قبل بزوغ فجر اليوم التالي للعرس ، حتى لا تسنح لها فرصة خيانته ، إلى أن ينتهي به الأمر إلى الزواج بشهرزاد التي تعكف على حكاية قصص شائقة كل ليلة ، ولكن دون أن تنهيها ، الأمر الذي يثير فضول الملك ويؤجل قتلها ليلة تلو أخرى حتى أكملت معه ألف ليلة . والذي ينعم النظر في ثنايا القصة الإطار ، يرى إمكان قراءتها من زاوية نظرية اللعبة بما تطرحه من مفاهيم عن أهمية الإستراتيجيات والتفكير العقلاني .

فبادئ ذي بدء ، نجد أن قرار شهريار بقتل كل النساء لم يكن وليد عاطفة متهورة ، بل كان ثمرة استنتاج عقلاني توصل إليه من خلال الملاحظة . فبعد أن عاين خيانة زوجته وزوجة أخيه ، اتخذ قراراً عقلانياً بالسفر لتقصي حال النساء ، ولم يهرع – مثل أخيه – إلى قتل زوجته متأثراً بخيبته العاطفية . فقد رافق أخاه في رحلة ليتحرى عن كثب سلوك النساء ، حتى يتسنى له الحكم على ما إذا كانت هذه مشكلة خاصة بأهل بيته أم أنها مشكلة عامة . وبعد أن وقع فريسة لإحدى زوجات الجن القويات ، التي طالبته وأخاه بمضاجعتها ، انتهى إلى استنتاج عقلاني – وإن كان خاطئاً – مفاده أن الخيانة جزء من نسيج المرأة . وهكذا ، يتضح لنا أنه على النقيض من الكثير من القراءات التي تدعي أن قرار شهريار بقتل النساء هو محض جنون ، كان قراره مبنياً على فرضيات عقلانية توصل إليها من خلال الملاحظة والتفكير . ومن ناحية أخرى ، قابلت شهرزاد – آخر زوجاته المهددات بالذبح – إستراتيجيته

أوستن. ومن بين المفاهيم العديدة التي تقع ضمن منهجية نظرية الألعاب، قام تشو بتطبيق عناصر «الاختيار» و«التفضيلات» و«التفكير الإستراتيجي». فحاول تفسير مشاريع الزواج وترتيباتها، التي كانت محور اهتمام الأسر في القرن التاسع عشر، من منظور اللعبة ودور العقلانية في الإستراتيجيات المختلفة التي تنتهجها البطلات أو الأبطال لإتمام صفقة الزواج. ويرى تشو أن الفئات المهمشة، مثل النساء والأقليات السوداء، تتمتع بمهارات تفكير إستراتيجية أبرع من التي تملكها الفئات المهيمنة مثل البيض والذكور. وتفسر أورلي تشارلز وجهة نظر تشو هذه بأن الطبقات الأدنى في حاجة إلى تنمية مهارات إستراتيجية من أجل البقاء، وذلك من خلال تطوير بعض تقنيات التصرف (أو اللعب) التي من شأنها زيادة فرص نجاحها، أو بالأحرى بقائها، وتقليل الخسائر التي قد تلحق بها في إطار المعاملات الاجتماعية (Charles 612). وبهذا التحليل، يقلب تشو الموازين رأساً على عقب، فقد كانت نظرية الألعاب في الأصل تخدم أكبر قوتين عظميين في العالم إبان الحرب الباردة كما ذكرنا سلفا، ولكن تشو بأطروحته، التي لاقت الكثير من الجدل، يجعل النظرية موقعاً لهيمنة الطبقات الدنيا وانتصار إستراتيجياتها على إستراتيجيات الأطراف المهيمنة. يرى تشو أن أوستن تنسج في رواياتها كلها مجموعة عواطف متنافسة من شأنها أن تعكس الاختيارات المفضلة لدى الشخصيات، والعواطف متأرجحة عادة، الأمر الذي يجعل اختيارات الشخصيات في اللعبة الحياتية على قدر من الصعوبة. وقد ذهب تشو إلى أبعد من ذلك، فأوضح أن جين أوستن كانت على علم بمبادئ الألعاب، قبل ظهور النظرية إلى النور على يد نيومان، وذلك لإدراكها أن الناس تقوم باختياراتها بناءً على تفهمها التام للثمن الذي يدفعونه والربح الذي قد يعود عليهم (Chwe 5).

وفي كتابه **نظرية الألعاب المطبقة على شخصين**، يقول أناتول رابوبورت إن ما يجعل أي صراع قابلاً للتصنيف بوصفه لعبة أم لا – وفق نظرية الألعاب – ليس الجدية من عدمها، ولا اتجاهات المشاركين في اللعبة، ولا طبيعة الصراع نفسه وثماره، بل ما إذا كان ثمة اختيارات بعينها لأفعال بعينها وثمة نتائج معينة يمكن أن تخضع لتعريف واضح غيرِ مبهمٍ، وما إذا كانت نتائج الاختيارات الدارجة يمكن أن تصنف تصنيفا دقيقاً، وما إذا كان الأشخاص الذين يقومون بالاختيار لديهم تفضيلات واضحة للنتائج المرجوة، ومن ثم ينتهي إلى محدودية تطبيق النظرية في مجال الإنسانيات بوجه عام، والأدب على وجه الخصوص (Rapoport, *Two-Person* 17).

العصور الوسطى وعصر النهضة وأواخر القرن السابع عشر، موضحاً أن القاسم المشترك الذي يجمع الشخصيات في النصوص المختارة هو الرغبة في الفوز وتجنب الخسارة، الأمر الذي يجعل نظريات الألعاب الرياضية المختلفة حقلاً خصباً للغوص في أعماق تلك الشخصيات وتحليل الكيفية التي يتوصلون بها إلى اتخاذ القرار في غمار الصراعات المختلفة التي يخوضونها. ومن بين النصوص التي قام بالتطبيق عليها قصيدة **ترويلوس وكريسيد** Troilus and Criseyde لجيفري شويسر Geoffrey Chaucer و**ملكة الجن** The Faerie Queene لإدموند سبنسر Edmund Spencer. يفحص الناقد هنا مدى عقلانية الشخصيات في اختيار القرارات المثلى، ويتناول سبب الهزيمة التي تلحق بالشخصيات في صراعاتها الحياتية رغم وجود الاختيارات المثلى، وكيف أن الهزيمة التي قد تلحق ببعض الشخصيات تأتي من جراء سهولة التنبؤ بتفضيلاتهم، في ظل ظروف اجتماعية واقتصادية قد تفرض بعض ردود الأفعال والقرارات النمطية.

وقد أوضح ستيفن برامز أيضاً أن جميع فروع الأدب يمكن أن تخضع لتطبيق نظرية الألعاب، حيث يرى أن بإمكانها تزويد النظرية الأدبية بإطار قوي ومجموعة أدوات تنطوي على أهمية كبيرة (Brams 1). كما يرى أن النظرية لها دور بارز في كشف اختيارات الشخصيات ودوافعها، وتوفر إستراتيجيةٍ ممنهجة لتحليل الشخصيات المتماثلة في عدة روايات. ويذهب برامز أيضاً إلى أن نظرية اللعبة تدعم فهم المرء للعناصر الإستراتيجية للرواية، بل يقترح أن «التطبيق على النص الأدبي قد يفيد نظرية الألعاب ذاتها، ويدفع منظري الألعاب إلى توسيع آفاق النظرية أو تهذيبها، حتى تكون مرآة الموقف الإستراتيجي الذي تصفه» (5). كذلك قام تايلر ريب بتطبيق نظرية الألعاب على رواية مارك توين Mark Twain **مغامرات هاكلبيري فين** Adventures of Huckleberry Finn (١٨٨٤)، موضحاً كيف أن توين كان بارعاً في وصف الدوافع البشرية. استعان ريب بنظرية توازن ناش والإستراتيجيات التعاونية، فتوصل في نهاية الأمر إلى أن شخصيات رواية توين خاسرة بكل المقاييس (Reeb 110).

ومن أهم الدراسات التي قامت بتطبيق نظرية الألعاب على الأدب السردي دراسة مايكل سوك-يانغ تشو Michael Suk-Young Chwe، حيث ذهب إلى أن النظرية تمثل أرضاً خصبة لطرح نتائج نقدية عظيمة الفائدة إذا طبقت على روايات جين أوستن Jane Austen، إذ تكشف دوافع «السلوك الإنساني» في تلك الروايات. طبّق تشو النظرية على ست روايات لجين

توازنات ناش شيئاً مناسباً لهم ، فهذه التوازناتِ تتنبأ بسلوك الحيوانات على نحو جيد للغاية غالباً ، فهي تؤدي دوراً تنبؤياً في كل مرة تميل فيها إحدى عمليات التوافق إلى استبعاد الإستراتيجيات التي تحقق عوائد منخفضة» (Binmore 24). وقد أثبتت نظريات الألعاب المختلفة بمعادلاتها المختلفة - وعلى الأخص توازن ناش - نجاحها في تحليل الصراعات في الحروب والتسليح ، وكذا الاقتصاد الذي عوّل عليها في تحقيق أفضل المكاسب التجارية من خلال التنبؤ بالسلوك الإستراتيجي الذي قد تتبعه الشركات من أجل الهيمنة على السوق .

نظرية الألعاب وآفاق النقد الأدبي : الأدب الإنجليزي نموذجاً

بدأت نظرية الألعاب تشق طريقها ، مؤخراً ، نحو الإنسانيات بصفة عامة ، والأدب بصفة خاصة ، الأمر الذي أثار العديد من ردود الفعل بين مؤيد ومعارض . وقد أكد الكثير من النقاد ، مثل بينجامين بور Benjamin Poore ، إمكان تطبيق نظرية الألعاب على القصص السردية . فأجرى قراءة لنصوص شرلوك هولمز من زاوية نظرية الألعاب، وأوضح ما أطلق عليه لعب النص ، أو النظر إلى الأحداث المتشابكة في النص بوصفها أجزاء من لعبة تشترك فيها عدة شخصيات ، بهدف التفاعل المثمر في الأمور الحياتية ، من خلال التغلب على بعض المصاعب أو الفوز ببعض المكاسب . ويرى بور أن تطبيق بعض نظريات الألعاب على الأدب البوليسي بصفة عامة يعد مثمراً في فهم الإستراتيجيات التي تُبنى بها الحبكة وتتطور الشخصيات ، مشيراً إلى أن النظرية إذا طُبقت على أعمال شرلوك هولمز مثلاً ، فستساعد على «تجميع العديد من الجوانب الغريبة ، أو التي تبدو غير مترابطة في قصصه بوصفها ظاهرة ثقافية ترفيهية ومنتجاً أدبياً» (92). وتجدر بنا الإشارة هنا إلى الحقيقة التي يغفلها الكثيرون ، ألا وهي أن مبادئ نظرية الألعاب قد طُبقت على يد مورجنشتين قبل أن يتعاون مع فون نيومان ، عندما طرح كتيباً في عام ١٩٢٨ ، قدّم فيه قراءة جديدة للقصة البوليسية الأخيرة للكاتب آرثر كونان دويل Arthur Conan Doyle ، التي تحمل عنوان «المشكلة الأخيرة» "The Final Problem" ، فقام بتفسير سلوك الشخصيات من خلال المعادلات الصفرية (انظر Morgenstern). وقد أكد راسيل ج . بودي Russell J. Bodi فاعلية تطبيق نظرية الألعاب على الأدب بشتى فروعه ، شعراً كان أم مسرحاً أم نثراً ، فذهب إلى تطبيق النظرية على نصوص تنتمي إلى

تساعد اللاعب على اختيار خطوات اللعب في كل مرحلة. وقد جرى تقسيم الإستراتيجيات إلى: إستراتيجية مثالية optimal strategy، تحقق للاعب أكبر ربح ممكن في المنافسة مع غيره من اللاعبين، مع تقدير ذكاء اللاعب الآخر؛ وهناك أيضاً الإستراتيجية الصافية pure strategy، التي يمكن للاعب أن يختارها بمفردها أثناء اللعب. وقد أدى تقسيم الإستراتيجيات هذا إلى تقسيم الألعاب إلى: ألعاب متناهية finite games تحوي عدداً محدوداً من الإستراتيجيات؛ وألعاب لامتناهية infinite games تتميز بإستراتيجيات لامتناهية.

ومن المفاهيم الأساسية في نظرية الألعاب، التي ترتبط ارتباطاً وثيقاً بالإستراتيجيات، ما يعرف باسم توازن ناش Nash equilibrium، الذي قدمه جون ناش John Nash الفائز بجائزة نوبل عام ١٩٩٤ (انظر "Equilibrium"). والمقصود به عدد الإستراتيجيات التي توضع لتنظيم لعبة بعينها، والتي تمثل أفضل الردود المتبادلة مقارنةً بإستراتيجيات أخرى. ولكي نفهم دور الإستراتيجيات في توازن ناش، علينا شرح اللعبة الأشهر التي يرتبط اسمها عادة بها، ألا وهي لعبة مأزق السجين The Prisoner's Dilemma. تشير اللعبة إلى اثنين من اللصوص قُبض عليهما أثناء سرقة أحد المحلات، ونظراً إلى خطأ في إجراءات القبض عليهما يضطر رجال الشرطة إلى التفاوض مع المسجونين للحصول على اعترافات وإجراء المحاكمة. يُوضع كل مسجون في غرفة منفصلة عن الآخر لمدة ساعتين، ثم يخبر الضابط كل سجين على حدة بالاختيارات المتاحة وعواقب كل اختيار. فإن اختار أحدهما الاعتراف على الآخر في حين أنكر الآخر، يحصل الذي اعترف على صديقه على براءة، وأما الآخر فيحصل على أقصى عقوبة (الحكم بالمؤبد). وإذا أنكر الاثنان في الوقت نفسه، حصل كل منهما على أدنى عقوبة (سنة واحدة). أما إذا اعترف الاثنان في آن واحد، يحصل كل منهما على نصف العقوبة (عشر سنين). وبالتفكير الإستراتيجي الدقيق، يتضح أن أفضل الخيارات هو اعتراف كل منهما دون أي اتفاق سابق، وذلك نظراً إلى صعوبة التأكد من اعتراف الآخر أو إنكاره، الأمر الذي يسمح بالمغامرة والحصول على أقصى عقوبة إذا أنكر أحدهما واعترف عليه الآخر. ورغم أن الإنكار يبدو الخيار الأمثل في هذه المشكلة، فإن صعوبة التكهن بقرار الآخر يجعل من الاعتراف الحل الأمثل حتى يُتجنّب الحد الأقصى للعقوبة. وكما يقول كين بينمور: «ليس بالضرورة أن يكون اللاعبون عباقرة في الرياضيات حتى تكون

الأدنى» Maximum-Minimum Theorem ، التي تذهب إلى القول بأن هناك حلاً عقلانياً لكل الألعاب الصفرية (von Neuman and Morgenstern 33). وحسب تلك النظرية الرياضية، يحاول اللاعب تقليل الخسارة وزيادة المكسب من أجل المنفعة الشخصية؛ حيث يرى كين بنيمور Ken Binmore أن العلاقة بين اللاعبين تتسم بالعداوة الضارية، ولا توجد فرصة للتعاون (5). ويتطلب الفوز في هذه الألعاب الإلمام بتفضيلات الخصم وتوقع تحركاته ووضع إستراتيجية للتحركات المضادة، وخير مثال على هذه النظرية لعبة مطابقة العملات المعدنية Heads or Tails. وقد كانت الألعاب الصفرية فردية أساساً، مثل لعبة سوليتير Solitaire مثلاً، إلا أن نيومان ومورجنشتيرن أوضحا إمكان توسيع دائرة تطبيقها لتضم أكثر من لاعب. وسرعان ما تطورت نظرية الألعاب، واتسع نطاقها، لتقدم معادلات رياضية تتسم بالتطبيق على أكثر من لاعبيْن، ولتضم أيضاً لاعبين ذوي مصالح متداخلة، ومن ثم تتسم علاقتهم بالتعاون وليس التصارع. أما اللعبة غير الصفرية، فتفترض وجود مساحة واسعة للتنسيق والتعاون بين طرفي عملية الصراع، إذ قد يخسران معاً أو يكسبان معاً، ويكون هذا الوضع عادة في أوقات اعتيادية (وليس في وقت الحروب)، وإن كان هنالك تنافس وصراع بين الدول. وفي معظم الأحيان، يقع التنافس بين الدول والنظم تحت صنف الألعاب غير الصفرية.

وعقب الأبحاث التي عكف عليها الكثير من الرياضيين، تعددت الإستراتيجيات في نظرية الألعاب، الأمر الذي أدى إلى تشعّب الألعاب إلى ألعاب ساكنة، يتعين فيها - كما يرى محسن حسن المعموري - على اللاعبين اختيار إستراتيجيتهم في وقت متزامن دون معرفة ما يفعله المنافس (ص ١١٣)؛ وألعاب ديناميكية يتخذ فيها اللاعبون قراراتهم، الواحد تلو الآخر، الأمر الذي يضفي على اللعبة سمة التغير المستمر. كما يمكن أن تصنف إلى ألعاب بمعلومات كاملة، يكون فيها اللاعبون على دراية بكل نوايا الطرف الآخر في النتيجة التي يرغب فيها، وأخرى بمعلومات ناقصة يكون فيها أحد اللاعبين، على الأقل، على غير علم بنوايا منافسيه، وألعاب تعاونية يشترك فيها أكثر من فرد ضد فريق آخر يضم أيضاً أشخاصاً عدة (المعموري، ص ١١٣).

يتضح من التقسيم السابق أهمية الإستراتيجية في نظرية الألعاب. وتعرف الإستراتيجية بأنها جملة القواعد التي يعتمدها اللاعب في كل مرحلة من مراحل اللعب، وتتغير وفق تطور مسار عملية اللعب، وهي

معترك التطبيق في مناحي المعرفة المختلفة ، لم يُستقبل بحفاوة وترحيب مطلقين ، وإنما أثار جدلاً كثيراً بين مؤيد ومعارض ، بين من يجدها عظيمة النفع في توفير إستراتيجيات فضّ الصراعات ، وبين من يرى أنها يجب ألا تخرج عن إطار الرياضيات التطبيقية .

تنطوي نظرية الألعاب على وضع إطار تحليل نظري رياضي غير بحت لحالات تضارب المصالح ، بهدف الوصول إلى أفضل البدائل الممكنة لحل الصراعات . وهي تعتمد في الأصل على طرح حلول عقلانية ووضع إستراتيجيات من أجل التغلب على الخصم وتحقيق الهدف المنشود في ظل الظروف المعطاة ، بالاستناد إلى التوقع بوصفه منهجية أساسية . وحتى يتحقق النصر على الأطراف المعادية ، يتطلب الأمر الإلمام بعدة أمور ، منها : هُويّة الأطراف المشاركة في الصراع – أو اللعبة – واتجاهاتهم وتفضيلاتهم ، مع وجود إستراتيجيات منهجية يعمل من خلالها الأطراف للتوصل إلى حل المعضلة ، بالإضافة إلى الإلمام بكافة القرارات المتاحة وفاعليتها في الحصول على النتيجة النهائية ، حتى ذهب البعض إلى وصف النظرية بأنها «علم التفكير الإستراتيجي» . وبكلمات أخرى ، هي دراسة نماذج الرياضيات التطبيقية غير البحتة المستعملة في أساليب الصراع في شتى المجالات . إن العقلانية ، إذن ، هي كلمة السر في نظرية الألعاب ، إذ تحاول أن تمنطق تصرفات البشر من خلال مفاهيم عقلانية ومعادلات رياضية توضح الخيارات المتاحة أمام العقل الإنساني للتصرف في معضلات مختلفة ، يُنظر إليها بوصفها ألعاباً تخضع لقوانين معينة ، حتى وإن لم يكن هناك اتفاق بين الأطراف المشاركة في هذه اللعبة .

ولكي نفهم عمل نظرية الألعاب ، علينا إدراك أن التفاعلات البشرية إزاء نزاع أو مشكلة معينة قد تتصف إما بالتنافس أو التعاون ، فقد يتنافس شخص أو أكثر من أجل الفوز وتعظيم المنفعة الشخصية ؛ وقد يتعاون طرفان أو أكثر لتعظيم الربح أو تجنب الخسارة . ومن هنا ، ينبثق تقسيم الألعاب إلى صفرية zero-sum games ، وأخرى غير صفرية non-zero-sum games . تعد الألعاب الصفرية تمثيلاً رياضياً لموقف بعينه يكون فيه مكسب أحد المشاركين أو خسارته في اللعبة متوازناً تماماً مع مكسب الطرف الآخر أو خسارته ؛ بمعنى أنه كلما زاد مكسب الطرف الأول يقل مكسب الطرف الثاني ، وإذا حصد أحد الطرفين جميع النقاط فسيحصل الطرف الآخر على صفر . وتندرج تحت الألعاب الصفرية النظرية التي أطلق عليها فون نيومان ومورجنشتيرن «الأقصى –

رأى أنها قد تكون من أهم الإسهامات العلمية في القرن العشرين(1). ورغم أن نظرية الألعاب انبثقت من مجال الرياضيات التطبيقية، فقد آتت ثمارها - بادئ ذي بدء - في المجال العسكري، إذ عوّل عليها الطرف الأمريكي أثناء الحرب الباردة مع روسيا. ويتضح الدور المحوري الذي لعبته النظرية في سياسات أمريكا آنذاك من تكريم الرئيس الأمريكي آيزنهاور لفون نيومان ومنحه وسام الحرية لدراسته التي - حسب كلمة الرئيس - «تنطوي على أهمية قومية عظيمة أدت إلى تعاظم التقدم العلمي للبلاد في مجال التسليح» (Eisenhower n.pag).

وقد لاقت نظرية الألعاب ترحيباً واسعاً، إبان الحرب الباردة، من علماء الاجتماع والمخططين الإستراتيجيين والعسكريين، لكونها تسمح بمنْهجَة التنبؤ بسلوك الآخر، والتعامل معه تعاملاً إستراتيجياً، من أجل سحقه دون الوقوع فريسة عقدة الإحساس بالذنب الأخلاقي. ويرى ستيف هايمز Steve Heims أن الحكومة الأمريكية احتفت غاية الاحتفاء بالنظرية، لأنها قنّنت مبدأ التفكير بمبدأ المانوية Manichaeism - «نحن» و«هم» - كما دعمت الفكر الذي يتسم بالميكانيكية ويخلو من القدح الشخصي، تلك الأشياء التي كان من شأنها دعم سبل الخداع من أجل النصر، وهو ما كانت تهدف إليه أمريكا أثناء الحرب الباردة. ويضيف أن ظهور نظرية الألعاب كشف عن إمكان دراسة العلوم الاجتماعية من منظور رياضي، وبخاصة أن نظرية الألعاب أوضحت أن الصراع جزء أصيل من النسيج الاجتماعي في فترة ما بعد الحرب، وأن المنفعة الشخصية هي الهيكل الأساسي للمجتمع الحديث (293).

ورغم ما لاقته النظرية من ترحيب في الأوساط العسكرية، فهناك من رفض تطبيقها خارج نطاق الرياضيات؛ فمثلاً يرى أناتول رابوبورت أن نظرية الألعاب رغم كونها «فتحت آفاقاً جديدة للبحث العلمي، فقد تبنت دوراً مشؤوماً بتفسيرها وجهة نظر فرانسيس بيكون Francis Bacon بأن المعرفة قوة "بدائية وحيوانية"» (Rapoport, "The Use" 118)؛ فيوضح كيف أن صانعي القرار في البلاد صار شغلهم الشاغل هو الصراع على القوة، سواء في التجارة أو السياسة أو الشؤون العسكرية. وينتهي رابوبورت إلى أن القرارات المبنية على المنفعة الشخصية المحسوبة قد تؤدي إلى كارثة، ويؤكد أن القيمة الحقيقية لنظرية الألعاب تكمن في التنظير فقط، وليس التطبيق على أرض الواقع (118). وهكذا، يتضح كيف أن دخول نظرية الألعاب

نظرية الألعاب والتحليل الأدبي: الآفاق والتحديات

نجلاء سعد حسن

حظيت نظرية الألعاب Game Theory ، مؤخراً ، بكثير من الاهتمام في الأوساط النقدية الأدبية ، بعد أن أثبتت نجاحها في الاقتصاد والسياسة والدراسات البيولوجية ، وغيرها من مجالات المعرفة الإنسانية . فرغم اسمها الذي يوحي بحصر تطبيقها على الألعاب والمباريات فقط ، ورغم ارتباطها ببعض الألعاب الترفيهية كلعبة الداما Dama وألعاب إكس X Games والبوكر Poker ، فإن النظرية تحمل في طياتها إمكانات أعمق وأكثر ثراءً من المفهوم الضيق لمعنى اللعب ، لتضم كل المجالات الحياتية التي تحمل في ثناياها إمكان الصراع والتخاصم بين أطراف متضاربة المصالح . وهنا يكمن المعنى الحقيقي لكلمة «الألعاب» . فالهدف من النظرية إيجاد بدائل رياضية للتعامل مع الأطراف المتخاصمة ، والفائز في النهاية هو الذي يقدم أفضل الحلول للتعامل مع المعضلة التي يتصارع عليها الأطراف ، استناداً إلى التنبؤ بتحركات الخصم بوصفها إستراتيجية أساسية .

وقد ظهرت النظرية ، أول ما ظهرت ، في مجال الرياضيات والاقتصاد ، على يد عالم الرياضيات ألماني النشأة أوسكار مورجنشتيرن Oskar Morgenstern الذي قدّم النظرية في ١٩٤٤ في كتاب مشترك مع جون فون نيومان John von Neumann يحمل عنوان **نظرية الألعاب والسلوك الاقتصادي** *Theory of Games and Economic Behavior* (انظر von Neumann and Morgenstern) . وحسب ما يقول جيرمي كاجل Jeremy Cagle ، فقد عكف نيومان - منذ عام ١٩٢٠ - على دراسة ألعاب البوكر ، وغيرها من ألعاب التسلية ، كي يشتق منها بعض النظريات الرياضية التطبيقية (4) ، التي قد تسهم في حل بعض المعضلات الاجتماعية . وسرعان ما شقت النظرية طريقها إلى مجالات المعرفة المختلفة ، فتبوأت مكاناً جوهرياً في العلوم الاقتصادية والعسكرية ، حتى إن البعض من أمثال روبرت ليونارد Robert Leonard

---. «في ماهية الحقيقة». كتابات أساسية [الجزء الثاني]. ترجمة وتحرير إسماعيل المصدق. القاهرة: المجلس الأعلى للثقافة، ٢٠٠٣. ص ص ٣٩-٨٥.

«وقائع المؤتمر التاسع للأدباء العرب في تونس». الآداب ١٢ (أبريل ١٩٧٣): ص ص ١١-١٢ وص ص ٧٦-٨٧.

المراجع الأجنبية

Bakewell, Sarah. *At the Existentialist Café: Freedom, Being, and Apricot Cocktails*. London: Chatto & Windus, 2016.

"Bloomberg Billionaires Index." *Bloomberg*. October 21, 2019. <https://www.bloomberg.com/billionaires/>.

Case, James. "Digital Nervous Systems: Making Sense of Shared Information" [Book review]. *SIAM News* 32.10 (December 1999): <https://archive.siam.org/pdf/news/802.pdf>.

Dreyfus, Hubert L. *On the Internet*. London and NY: Routledge, 2009.

Forster, E. M. "The Machine Stops." <https://www.ele.uri.edu/faculty/vetter/Other-stuff/The-Machine-Stops.pdf>.

Gates, Bill and Collins Hemingway. *Business @ the Speed of Thought: Using a Digital Nervous System*. NY: Warner Books, 1999.

Raymond, Eric. *The Cathedral and the Bazaar: Musings on Linux and Open Source by an Accidental Revolutionary*. Beijing; Cambridge: O'Reilly Media, 1999.

Scarry, Elaine. *The Body in Pain: The Making and Unmaking of the World*. NY: Oxford UP, 1985.

--- . صقيع : تجربة جديدة من أدب الواقعية الرقمية . ٢٠٠٦ .
⟨ http://sanajleh-shades.com/other-accounts-of-the-author ⟩ .

--- . ظلال العاشق : التاريخ السري لكموش . ٢٠١٦ .
⟨ http://sanajleh-shades.com/other-accounts-of-the-author ⟩ .

--- . ظلال الواحد . ٢٠٠١ .
⟨ http://sanajleh-shades.com/other-accounts-of-the-author ⟩ .

سيل ، بيتر بي . **الكون الرقمي : الثورة العالمية في الاتصالات** . ترجمة ضياء ورّاد ، مراجعة نيفين عبد الرؤوف . وندسور ، المملكة المتحدة : مؤسسة هنداوي سي آي سي ، ٢٠١٧ .

شبلول ، أحمد فضل . **أدباء الإنترنت : أدباء المستقبل** . الإسكندرية : دار الوفاء ، ١٩٩٩ .

الشوك ، علي . «الأدب العربي والثورة التكنولوجية في النصف الثاني من القرن العشرين» . **الموقف الأدبي** مجلد ٢ ، العدد ١٢ (أبريل ١٩٧٣) : ص ص ١٠٣-١١٠ .

الشيخ ، محمد . **نقد الحداثة في فكر هيدجر** . بيروت : الشبكة العربية للأبحاث والنشر ، ٢٠٠٨ .

علي ، نبيل . **العرب وعصر المعلومات** . الكويت : المجلس الوطني للثقافة والفنون والآداب ، ١٩٩٤ .

فرجسن ، نيل . **الساحة والبرج : الشبكات والسلطة من الماسونيين الأحرار إلى فيسبوك** . ترجمة حسام نايل . بيروت ؛ القاهرة ؛ تونس : دار التنوير ، ٢٠١٩ .

الكعبي ، منجي . «الأدب العربي والثورة التكنولوجية المعاصرة في النصف الثاني من القرن العشرين» . **الموقف الأدبي** مجلد ٢ ، العدد ١٢ (أبريل ١٩٧٣) : ص ص ٧٣-٨٤ .

لسيج ، لورنس . **الكود المنظِّم للفضاء الإلكتروني : الإصدار ٢٫٠** . ترجمة محمد سعد طنطاوي ، مراجعة محمد فتحي خضر . القاهرة : مؤسسة هنداوي ، ٢٠١٤ .

هوسرل ، إدموند . **فكرة الفينومينولوجيا** . ترجمة فتحي إنقزو . بيروت : المنظمة العربية للترجمة ، ٢٠٠٧ .

هيدجر ، مارتن . «السؤال عن التقنية» . **كتابات أساسية [الجزء الثاني]** . ترجمة وتحرير إسماعيل المصدق . القاهرة : المجلس الأعلى للثقافة ، ٢٠٠٣ . ص ص ١٤٧-٢٠٤ .

المراجع العربية

اتحاد كتاب الإنترنت العرب. < https://www.arab-ewriters.com >.

أرندت، حنة. **أسس التوتاليتارية**. ترجمة أنطوان أبو زيد. بيروت: دار الساقي، ٢٠١٦.

---. **آيخمان في القدس: تقرير حول تفاهة الشر**. ترجمة نادرة السنوسي. الجزائر وبيروت: ابن النديم للنشر ودار الروافد الثقافية، ٢٠١٤.

أسليم، محمد. «عن مفهوم الكاتب الرقمي ونظرية الواقعية الرقمية». ميدل إيست أونلاين. ١٩ مارس، ٢٠٠٧. < shorturl.at/kKPQ1 >.

---. «قراءة في أعمال محمد سناجلة الرقمية». موقع محمد أسليم. أغسطس ٢٠١٢.
< http://www.aslim.ma/site/articles.php?action=view&id=107 >.

إدريس، سهيل. «شهريات». الآداب ١٢ (أبريل ١٩٧٣): ص ص ٢-٧.

إيزاك، جيفري. «نقاد الشمولية». **موسوعة كمبريدج للتاريخ، الفكر السياسي في القرن العشرين، المجلد الأول**. تحرير تيرنس بول وريتشارد بيلارمي. ترجمة مي مقلد، مراجعة طلعت الشايب. القاهرة: المركز القومي للترجمة، ٢٠٠٩. ص ص ٢٥٣-٢٨٠.

تروتسكي، ليون. «دروس من كومونة باريس». تعريب ناصر الحصري. الحوار المتمدن. ١٨ يوليو، ٢٠١٨. < https://bit.ly/35nleP9 >.

الخطيب، حسام. **الأدب والتكنولوجيا وجسر النص المُفرَّع**. رام الله: د.ن. [المؤلف؟]، ٢٠١٨.

سعد الله، أبو القاسم. «الأديب العربي والثورة التكنولوجية». **الموقف الأدبي** مجلد ٢، العدد ١٢ (أبريل ١٩٧٣): ص ص ٨٥-٩٤.

سليمان، حسين. «محمد سناجلة والكتابة الرقمية وتغييب مفهوم الأدب»، إيلاف. ٢٢ نوفمبر، ٢٠٠٦. < https://bit.ly/2pQOnlx >.

سليمان، نبيل. «"ظلال الواحد" للكاتب الأردني محمد سناجلة: الشكل الروائي مرتكزاً على أسرار شبكة الانترنت». الحياة. ٢٢ نوفمبر، ٢٠٠٢. < http://www.alhayat.com/article/1113783 >.

سناجلة، محمد. **رواية الواقعية الرقمية** [تنظير نقدي]. ٢٠٠٤.
< http://www.arab-ewriters.com/booksFiles/5.pdf >

---. **شات: رواية واقعية رقمية**. ٢٠٠٥.
< http://sanajleh-shades.com/other-accounts-of-the-author >

العاجل مثل هذا النظام. وبعد عامين، أصدر بالاشتراك مع كولينز هيمنجواي كتاباً بعنوان **الأعمال @ سرعة التفكير** *Business @ the Speed of Thought* يطوِّر فيه فكرته (Case n. pag).

5 كلمة cyborg اختصار لتعبير cybernetic organism الذي يعني «كائناً عضوياً سيبرانياً». ويعود أصل كلمة cybernetic إلى المصطلح الإغريقي kybernetes الذي يعني الطيار أو قائد الدفة أو الحاكم (سيل، ص ص ٢١-٢٢).

6 أحد مَن يثيرون هذه النقاشات أستاذ الفيزياء النظرية ميتشيو كاكو Michio Kaku في كتبه، بدءاً من تسعينيات القرن العشرين وأوائل القرن الحالي، مثل: رؤى مستقبلية، وفيزياء المستحيل؛ ومن خلال أحاديثه الإذاعية والتلفزيونية، وعلى يوتيوب.

7 يميز نبيل علي بين الـsoftware الذي يعني - توسعاً - الشق الذهني (ص ١١٥)، في مقابل الشق المادي hardware (ص ٦٦). فما يفصل بين الإنسان والآلة «مسار متصل من طبقات متدرجة تنقلنا - ونحن نتحرك من الإنسان صوب الآلة - إلى ما هو أكثر تجريداً، حتى تصل بنا إلى المآل الأخير لكل البرامج، ونقصد به ثنائية ''الصفر والواحد'' ذروة التجريد الحسابي والمنطقي» (ص ١١٦). فتستقر «الرموز في ذاكرة الكمبيوتر سلاسل من الأصفار والآحاد بعد أن تحولت هذه الرموز إلى أرقام عن طريق عملية الرَّقمنة، وتحولت الأرقام إلى مقابلها في النظام الثنائي الذي يمثل أقصى درجات التجريد الرياضي» (ص ٦١).

8 راجع مناقشة فرجسن لعدم انطباق قانون كُنْواي Conway بشأن هياكل النُّظم الكبيرة على الإنترنت، وتحديد برينتن Brinton وتشيانج Chiang لتبديل الرُّزَم packet switching والهرمية الموزّعة distributed hierarchy والتجزيء إلى وحدات modularization، بوصفها المفاهيم التي تجعل بنية الإنترنت تشاركية وليست سلطوية (فرجسن، ص ص ٣٥٨-٣٦٠).

9 يوجد خطأ طباعي في كتيب سناجلة التنظيري، إذ تتكرر الصفحات بدءاً من السطر الرابع من أعلى ص ٥٢ حتى السطر الثالث من أسفل ص ٦٤.

10 كومونة باريس: حكومة بلدية ثورية أدارت باريس في الفترة من ١٨ مارس حتى ٢٨ مايو، ١٨٧١ (انظر تروتسكي).

11 في مقال آخر، بعنوان «في ماهية الحقيقة»، يربط هيدجر ماهية الحقيقة بالانفتاح على الكينونة وحضور الكائن إلى النور وخروجه من تحجبه.

لذروة العدمية كما يتصورها هيدجر وشارحه العربي محمد الشيخ . وإني لأرجو أن تلفت هذه الدراسة الأولية النظر إلى ضرورة مناقشةٍ مسؤولة حول الأدب العربي الرقمي وفرضياته النظرية الكامنة ، بدلاً من تلقفه بوصفه موضة جديدة . قرأت مرةً : إن أخطر الخطر ألا يبدو الخطر خطراً ، وألا تعرف أنك في خطر .

الهوامش

* يتوجه الكاتب بالشكر والتقدير لمُحكمي ألف على انتقاداتهم الجوهرية لهذه المقالة في صورتها الأولى التي ترتب عليها إعادة هيكلتها وتركيزها .

1 ألقى هذه الكلمة الافتتاحية الرئيس التونسي بورقيبة الذي تولى الحكم عام ١٩٥٧ ولم يغادره إلا عام ١٩٨٧ .

2 تغلبت قضية حرية التعبير على مؤتمر تونس إلى درجة نشوب خلافات حادة بين رئيس اتحاد الأدباء العرب يوسف السباعي والأمين العام المساعد حينئذٍ سهيل إدريس ، انسحب على إثرها الوفد اللبناني عائداً إلى بلده ، بسببِ حديث إدريس عن أن السنوات العشرين المنقضية عانى فيها الأدباء من الاضطهاد وشتى ألوان الإرهاب والقمع في معظم البلاد العربية ؛ ومنها ما حدث قبيل انعقاد المؤتمر من إجراءات في مصر والبحرين والمغرب بحق أدباء وكتاب (انظر إدريس ؛ «وقائع» ، ص ص ٧٦-٧٧) .

3 ظهر مصطلح الهايبرتكست عام ١٩٦٥ على يد تد نيلسون Ted Nelson في أمريكا لوصف البنية غير السطرية non-linear للأفكار التي يعرضها الحاسوب ، والتي تخرج على الصيغة السطرية المعتمدة (الخطيب ، ص ١٧) . وفي عام ١٩٩٤ ، عرّفته موسوعة مايكروسوفت إنكارتا بأنه تسمية مجازية لطريقة تقديم المعلومات في الحاسوب ، يترابط فيها النص والصور والأصوات والأفعال ترابطاً شبكياً مركباً وغير تعاقبي ، بما يسمح للمستخدم بالتجول browsing بين موضوعات ذات علاقة دون التقيد بترتيب محدد . ويؤسس هذه الوصلات أو الروابط مؤلفُ وثيقة النص المفرّع أو المستخدِمُ (الخطيب ، ص ١١٨) .

4 في ربيع عام ١٩٩٧ ، انشغل جيتس بالبحث عن وصف مختصر لفكرة قيد التطوير في شركة مايكروسوفت ، فخطرت له عبارة «النظام العصبي الرقمي» digital nervous system ، وتوقّع أن كل شركة كبيرة سيكون لديها في القريب

خاتمة

يكمن الأصل المفسّر لهذه المآلات السياسية والاقتصادية والأنطولوجية في بنية الصُّنْع المادي ، التي تنطوي على موقعين لجسد الصانع هما الإسقاط والتبادل ، فتنجح البنية إذا تكامل الموقعان ؛ وتفشل إذا انفصلا ، فنكون عندئذٍ أمام تفكك بنية الصنع المادي (Scarry, 257) . وتخصص سكاري جزءاً مّن كتابها لهذه القضية من منظور ماركسي (ص ص ٢٤٣-٢٧٧) : «كل مرحلة جديدة تمكّن خط التبادل من الابتعاد أكثر فأكثر عن مصدره البشري ، تجعل المسافةَ المتنامية بين الشيء المصنوع وصانعه أكبر من أن تُجتاز في الواقع أو بفعل من أفعال الإدراك» (ص ٢٥٩) . وعندئذ ، يشير الشيء المصنوع إلى نفسه لا إلى صانعه ، بدءًا من أشياء مصنوعة أكثر تعيناً كالسلعة في صورها المتعاقبة ؛ مروراً بالأقل تعيناً كالدولة التي تشير إلى نفسها بدلاً من إشارتها إلى صانعيها ، وكبنية الإنترنت – بعالمها الافتراضي عالم الشاشة الزرقاء – التي تشير إلى نفسها بوصفها خالقاً يصنع إنساناً افتراضياً أكثر واقعية من الإنسان الحقيقي الواقعي الذي صنعها ، والذي هو على وشك الزوال بفضلها ؛ وانتهاءً بأشياء مصنوعة أكثر تجريداً وتسامياً وشمولاً كالنظام الرأسمالي الذي لن يعود يشير سوى إلى ذاته .

لقد حاولت في هذه المقالة استكشاف ملامح الجدل العربي حولَ الأدب والتكنولوجيا ، منذ بدايته للمرة الأولى في مؤتمر تونس ، مروراً بالخطيب وشبلول الذي تميز جدلهما بعلاقة واضحة مع التكنولوجيا الرقمية غلبت عليها الأداتية ، وتوقفت عند سناجلة وممارسته الإبداعية للأدب الرقمي ، وتنظيره لما يسمّى «الواقعية الرقمية» التي يعني بها زوال الإنسان والعالم الراهن كما نعرفه ، وحلول عالم الشاشة الزرقاء (الرقمي) محله . ولأن هذا الجدل لم يناقش الاحتمالين السياسي والأنطولوجي ، كلا ولا البعد الاقتصادي المتحقق فعلياً ، في الرّقمنة – حاولت استكشاف ما قد تؤول إليه التكنولوجيا الرقمية على المستوى السياسي بفضل قابلية بنية الإنترنت للتنظيم والسيطرة والتدخل الحكومي ؛ كما لامست بشكل سريع تحول الإنترنت فعلياً إلى فضاء للاحتكارات الأحادية والثنائية ولعبة المال الشرير . وأعقبت ذلك بمناقشة المآل الأنطولوجي المتوقع لما أسماه سناجلة «عالم الشاشة الزرقاء» ، فبيّنت أنه يمثل التجلي الأخير

عن أي تصور أخروي أو خلاصي : «والمتأمل في هذا الإنسان الجديد وفي كُنْهِ المستحدث ، وقد صار متعلقاً بالقوة ، لن يجده سوى صيرورة الإنسان إنساناً أعلى . . . وحده هذا الإنسان الأعلى من شأنه أن يطابق روح الاقتصاد الآلي المطلق . . . هذا الاقتصاد ضروري للإنسان الأعلى ، وذلك حتى يحقق له في الأرض التمكين المطلق» (الشيخ ، ص ص ٢٦٣-٢٧٤) . وأما كل ما عداه فصار موضوعاً يقبل التمثل والتصنيع والإنتاج .

وما من وجه قوة وعلو إلا واستدعى وجه ضعف وسقوط ، فلم يعد الإنسان يتحكم في التقنية وإنما صارت تتحكم فيه . وتلك هي النتيجة الحتمية لميتافيزيقا الذات الديكارتية التي تمثل التقنية الطور الأخير فيها . ثمة مصير مشترك بين الذات والطبيعة في هذه الميتافيزيقا ، «وليس هذا المصير المشترك سوى التقنية» (الشيخ ، ص ٥٦٣) ، وذلك أن التقنية في طورها الأحدث تتميز بهيمنة غير محدودة لا رادّ لها ولا يمكن مقاومتها (ص ٥٦٥) . فكان السقوط سقوطين : سقوط الإنسان وسقوط الكائن . إذ تدور الدائرة الآن على الإنسان حتى صار قابلاً بدوره للتصنيع والاستنساخ ، وحتى تحول

> إلى مجرد موظف في خدمة التقنية ، بل إلى قرد للتقنية . . . فكان أن فقد الإنسانُ بذلك كينونته ، وفقد الشيءُ ما هو به شيء . . . . والحال أن سقوط الإنسان والكائن ، إنما هما سقوطان متعالقان ؛ وذلك لأن التقنية الحديثة لم تعد تميز بين جوهر الإنسان وجوهر الأشياء ، بل صارت تهاجمهما معاً ، إذ صيّرت الجوهرين معاً مرصودين للاستعمال والاستهلاك . أكثر من هذا ، لئن صارت الأرض ومجالها مواد أولية ، فإن الإنسان نفسه صار مادة أولية مرهونة بأهداف تتجاوزه . (الشيخ ، ص ٥٧٤)

الحاصل أن تصور الإنسان في نظرية سناجلة عن «الواقعية الرقمية» يجعل الإنسان هدفاً مباشراً للرّقمنة ورهين أهداف تتجاوزه ، فيفقد بذلك كينونته ، بعد أن فقد العالمُ من قبل كائناته ؛ بل يختم سناجلة على العالم بختم العدمية الحقة حين يعمد إلى التبشير بعالم مصنوع بديل هو عالم الشاشة الزرقاء ، يغيب فيه الإنسان ، ويختفي الكائن ، وتحتجب الكينونة أشد الحجاب . وإن عالماً هذا حاله ليس بعالم .

الاستيقاف والاستحضار والرصيد، جميعها تبرز ماهية التكنولوجيا بوصفها كشفاً مستثيراً. بل إن «هذا الكشف المستثير لا يمكن له أن يحدث إلا بقدر ما يكون الإنسان بدوره مستثاراً لاستخراج الطاقات الطبيعية. لكن إذا كان الإنسان مستثاراً، مستحضَراً لأجل ذلك، أفلا ينتمي الإنسان أيضاً، وبكيفية أكثر أصلية من الطبيعة إلى الرصيد؟» (هيدجر، «السؤال»، ص ١٨١).

اللاعالم وخَتْم العدمية

تجد كيفية التقنية الحديثة في الكشف عن الطبيعة بوصفها خزّاناً ورصيداً أصلها في مسلك الإنسان مع نشأة علم الطبيعة بفرعيه في القرن السابع عشر: الفيزياء النظرية والفيزياء التجريبية. تقوم الفيزياء النظرية بصياغة النظريات وفق نماذج رياضياتية، وتختبر الفيزياء التجريبية هذه النظريات. وتمهد الفيزياء النظرية لماهية التقنية الحديثة وليس للتقنية. الفيزياء النظرية بنماذجها الرياضياتية هي التي تستوقف الطبيعة كي تعلن عن نفسها بوصفها حصيلة قوى قابلة سلفاً للحساب والعدّ، ثم لاحقاً تُستحضَر الفيزياءُ التجريبية للاستخبار عما إذا كانت الطبيعة المستوقفة ستعلن عن نفسها، وما الكيفية التي ستعلن بها عن نفسها. قَوام الفيزياء النظرية أن تعلن الطبيعة عن نفسها بوصفها القابلة للحساب والاستحضار كنظام من المعلومات (هيدجر، «السؤال»، ص ص ١٨٤-١٨٦). وكما يوضح محمد الشيخ، «وما اقتصر الأمر على الكائن الطبيعي وحده بل تعدّاه من الاختراع التقني إلى العمل الفني ومؤسسة الدولة والنظام البشري الشخصي والجماعي ... كلّ شيء صار يُدار ويُساس، وكل شيء صار يقدَّر ويحسب بالاعتبار العدّي الحسابي» (ص ٥٧٣).

في التقنية القديمة، كانت علاقة الإنسان بالطبيعة علاقة إقامة وتنصيب وتوطين وإبانة بلا إرغام أو استكراه. وأما في التقنية الحديثة، فتحولت علاقة الإنسان بالطبيعة إلى علاقة بعالم مُتَأَوَّل بوصفه تَمثلاً وإنتاجاً؛ بمعنى أنه لولا كوجيتو ديكارت الذي أسَّس الذات الإنسانية لما تحدَّد الكائن بوصفه موضوعاً، «ولَما تَركَ نفسَه يُتَمثّل أو يُنتَج موضوعياً، أي لما تركت الطبيعة نفسَها تُستكرَه وتُستغَل بعد أن بانت بأنها رصائد مرصودة، وقوى مخزّنة، وطاقات مودعة» (الشيخ، ص ص ٥٦٢-٥٦٣). وقد أتاح تصور الإنسان ذاتاً - في بدء الحداثة - أن يعلن مركزيته في العالم وأن يرسخ إرادته وقوته بمعزل

التي تعتمد الهندسة الوراثية بأحدث التقنيات العلمية للتدخل في تعديل صفات الكائنات الحية. لذا، يتميز الكشف في التكنولوجيا الحديثة بأنه استيقاف للكائن وقهره وإرغامه على الظهور بمظهر مفروض عليه. صار الإنسان في علاقته الحديثة بالكائنِ يقوم بدور الشرطي الذي يستوقف شخصاً مشدِّداً القبضة عليه تمهيداً لاعتقاله. التكنولوجيا الحديثة تعتقل الكائن فلا تَظهر الكينونة وتتوارى محتجبةً. والأصل في الإنسان جلاؤها وإتاحة انكشافها والإبانة عنها بطريقة الحدْب والرعاية والاهتمام التوقيري، فهو الكائن الوحيد على الأرض المؤهل لهذه المهمة. وحتى تتضح الفكرة أكثر، نقارن بين حالتين من تعاملِ الإنسان تكنولوجيا مع نهر طبيعي: التكنولوجيا القديمة التي تقيم جسراً خشبياً على النهر تريد الربط بين ضفتيه. ومع أن الجسر يستوقف النهر فهو يستوقفه استيقاف جلاء وظهور، بمعنى أن الجسر يمكن النهرَ من الانكشاف بالإشارة إلى كِينونته: كينونة النهر. أما التكنولوجيا الحديثة التي تنشئ مولِّداً كهربائياً على النهر فما فعلت سوى استيقاف النهر وإرغامه على إعطاء ضغطه المائي كي ينتج المولدُ التيارَ الكهربائي، فلا ينكشف النهر إلا بوصفه مزوِّدَ المولد الكهربائي بالضغط المائي، فتغدو هيئة ظهور النهر مُرْتهنة ومعتقَلة لحساب المولد الكهربائي (هيدجر، «السؤال»، ص ١٨٠؛ والهامش رقم ١٦، ص ٢٠٠). وكذلك الحال في تكنولوجيا التعدين وغيرها من تكنولوجيات الصناعة.

والأكثر من هذا أن نهج التكنولوجيا الحديثة في الكشف عن الكائن وإبانته يستهدف التوجيه والتأمين، بمعنى الاستخراج والتحويل والتوزيع (هيدجر، «السؤال»، ص ١٨٠). وبذلك تصبح الطبيعة رصيداً، ولا يعني الرصيد مخزوناً متوفراً من مادة أو سلعة، بل يعني – أنطولوجيا – كيفية كينونة الكائن في عصر السيطرة التكنولوجية:

الرصيد هو نوع اللاخفاء [الظهور] الذي يقوم فيه الكائن في مسلسل الإنتاج التقني الصناعي. في هذا المسلسل، يقوم الكائن رَهْن الإشارة من أجل استعماله في استحضار آخر، هذا الاستحضار لا يحافظ على الكائن، بل يبدِّده، يتلفه، أي يستهلكه. في عصر التقنية يصبح الكائن مادة للاستهلاك. (هيدجر، «السؤال»، ص ٢٠١)

الجارفة في خلوات نهاية الأسبوع تاركين كل ما يتعلق بالتكنولوجيا الرقمية، لاغتنام نزهة سيراً على الأقدام بين أحضان الطبيعة الريفية وبراح الوديان الفسيح، طمعاً في صفاء النفس ووهَج التواصل الحيّ المباشر بين بعضهم البعض (Bakewell 317). تعبّر ثنائية الرعب والرغبة هذه، عن ثنائية الوجود الزائف والوجود الأصيل، وهما تيمتان انشغلت بهما السينما العالمية انشغالاً وسواسياً مع أفول القرن العشرين وبزوغ فجر القرن الحالي، حتى يمكن القول بأن القلق الوجودي صار قرين القلق التكنولوجي (Bakewell 317-18). وحين سئل مارتن هيدجر في عام ١٩٦٦ - قبل هبوط أول مركبة فضائية أمريكية مأهولة على سطح القمر بثلاث سنوات - عن رأيه في احتمال ارتحال البشر إلى كواكب أخرى تاركين الأرض خلفهم، داخَله الرّوعُ والقلق الشديد، وردّ: «طبقاً لتجربتنا وتاريخنا البشري، وبقدر ما أفهم، أعرف أن كل ما هو جوهري وعظيم نشأ من حقيقة أن الإنسان لديه بيت وسكن، وأنه متجذّر في تراث» (كما ورد في 306-07 ,Bakewell). إن احتمال تَرْك الإنسان سطح الأرض للعَيْش في باطنها بفضل آلة كونية (فورستر)، أو احتمال العَيْش في عالم شاشة زرقاء بفضل التكنولوجيا الرقمية (سناجلة)، أو احتمال المغادرة إلى كواكب أخرى، ليثير سؤالاً جوهرياً حول مآل العالم. ويستدعي هذا السؤال بالضرورة أسئلة حول حقيقة الإنسان والكينونة في ظل التقنية أو التكنولوجيا.

يحدد هيدجر في مقاله «السؤال عن التقنية» ماهية التقنية بأنها كيفية في الكشف عن الكائن (ص ١٧٧). ويتضح ذلك حين نتأمل تكنولوجيا الزراعة القديمة، فالفلاح يحرِث الأرض ويبذر الحبوب، وما عليه بعدئذ سوى رعاية ازدهارها تاركاً قوى النمو الطبيعية الكامنة فيها تعمل عملها تلقائياً. بهذه الطريقة يدخل الفلاح القديم في علاقة انكشاف أصيل مع الكينونة، إذ يترك الكائنَ يكون وينكشف على ما هو عليه. وتمكين الكائنات من الانكشاف على ما هي عليه، هو مهمة الإنسان في انفتاحه على الكينونة، وهو أيضاً المحدد الأصيل لماهية الحقيقة.[١١] التكنولوجيا الحديثة كشف عن الكائن أيضاً، ولكن الكشف الذي يميزها ليس تَرْك الكائن يكون على ما هو عليه، أي ليس تمكينه من إبراز نفسه وإخراج نفسه على ما هي عليه، وإنما إرغامه وقهره والاستيلاء عليه، كما يجري في الزراعة الحديثة الميْكنة (هيدجر، «السؤال»، ص ١٧٩)، أو فيما يسمى الآن التكنولوجيا الحيوية الزراعية

موظفي فيسبوك السابقين على لون قمصانهم الرسمية: «القمصان البُنيّة صارت قمصاناً زرقاء، فكنا جميعاً جزءاً من كتيبة عاصفة الميديا الاجتماعيّ الجديدة» (فرجسن، ص ٤١٩)، في إشارة واضحة إلى التماهي مع زيّ جنود كتيبة العاصفة Sturmabteilung، أعضاء الجناح العسكري للحزب النازي.

حاولنا فيما سبق إيضاح أن المزاعم الليبرتارية الكامنة خلف نظرية سناجلة في «الواقعية الرقمية» تتغاضى عن - أو لا تدرك - التطورات التي أصابت بنية الإنترنت، وهي تطورات بدأت فعلياً منذ منتصف تسعينيات القرن العشرين فيما يجادل لسيج، وانعطفت انعطافات خطيرة على مستويين فيما نجادل: الأول سياسي، بفعل إمكان التدخلات الحكومية بما يجعل بنية الإنترنت مؤهلة لاحتمال تحول وشيك إلى توتاليتارية جديدة واسعة النطاق قد تشمل العالم بأسره؛ والثاني تجاري يتميز باحتكار شبْه أحادي أو ثنائي يسكن معه المحتكرون بُرجاً عالياً وأما بقية العالم فساحةٌ يرعى فيها رواد عالم الشاشة الزرقاء.

رابعاً، المآل الأنطولوجي لـ«نظرية الواقعية الرقمية»

استعرضنا سابقاً ثلاث محطات رئيسية للجدل العربي حول الأدب والتكنولوجيا: الأولى مؤتمر تونس عام ١٩٧٣، والثانية جدل حسام الخطيب وأحمد فضل شبلول في عامي ١٩٩٦ و١٩٩٧ على التوالي، والثالثة متمثلة في تصور سناجلة المثالي الليبرتاري لـ«الواقعية الرقمية» في مطلع القرن الحادي والعشرين. وقد غابت عن هذا الجدل - بمحطاته الثلاث - مناقشة الأبعاد السياسية والاحتكارية التي تنطوي عليها التكنولوجيا، لا سيما في مرحلتها الرقمية التي تنذر بتحويل وشيك لوجود الإنسان وعالمه كما عرفناه ونعرفه. سأحاول الآن استكشاف المآل الأنطولوجي في التكنولوجيا الرقمية التي يتطلع سناجلة إلى أفقها الوشيك بوصفه حياة بديلة في تصوره لـ«الواقعية الرقمية».

الإنسان والتكنولوجيا

يكشف سناجلة في كتيبه رواية الواقعية الرقمية عن حسٍّ تفاؤل عربي فَرِح بتحول العالم إلى شاشة زرقاء، وذلك مقابل رعب هائل عند الناس، وبخاصة في العالم المتقدم، من زحف التكنولوجيا الرقمية التي بدأت تحتل حياتهم الشخصية، وليس أدل على هذا الرعب من رغبتهم

بُرْج المال الشرير: FANG

جعلت الماهية التي يُفترض أن يكون عليها الإنترنت المستخدمين يعتقدون أنهم سيعيشون في كومونة رقمية أو افتراضية، ركيزتها العمل الطوعي التعاوني ومساواة الأنداد، فبرامج التشغيل سيعمل على تحسينها باطراد مبرمجون متطوعون بشكل تعاوني. عبّر عن هذه المثالية المتوقع استمرارها إريك ريموند Eric Raymond حين أصدر كتابه **الكاتدرائية والبازار** *The Cathedral and the Bazaar*، الذي يقارن فيه بين أنظمة التشغيل المغلقة التي لا تسمح لأحد بالتدخل فيها، والأنظمة الحرة مفتوحة المصدرِ التي تتيح التدخل من أجل التعديل والتطوير، وكانت مقارنته بينهما عنوانا على عالمين متناقضين متدابرين. ولكن تلاشت هذه الآمال العريضة مع صعود الاحتكارات الأحادية والثنائية التي مثلتها أولاً شركتا مايكروسوفت Microsoft وأبل Apple، ثم تلتها شركات أمازون Amazon وإي باي eBay وجوجل Google بأذرعها المتعددة الشبيهة بالأخطبوط. نجحت أبل مثلاً في «الجمع بين تصميم منتجات مغرية ونظام برمجيات مغلق ومحتوى رقمي حصري» (فرجسن، ص ٤١٢). وكلمة FANG هي كلمة السر المعبرة عن هيمنة الاحتكار على فضاء الإنترنت، وتعني ناباً ومخلباً وشوكة. تتألف الكلمة من الأحرف الأربعة الأولى لكلمات: Facebook، وAmazon، وNetflix، وGoogle (فرجسن، ص ٤١٨) لقد بدأ الاحتكار في تحويل الإنترنت إلى ساحة ذات بُرْج للمال الشرير غير مرئي، شبيه بالمخلب أو الناب أو الشوكة. والمحتكرون هم أغنى الرجال في العالم: بيل جيتس Bill Gates ١٠٧ مليار، كارلوس سليم Carlos Slim ٥٧٫٦ مليار، جيف بيزوس Jeff Bezos ١١٠ مليار، مارك زوكربيرج Mark Zuckerberg ٧١٫٦ مليار، لاري إليسون Larry Ellison ٥٩٫١ مليار (انظر "Bloomberg"). لم يَنتج ثراؤهم عن مشروعات تجارية أو صناعية، بل عن احتكار شبْه أحادي للبرمجيات والاتصالات والبيع بالتجزئة على الإنترنت والشبكات الاجتماعية والبرمجيات والبيانات. وهو احتكار يمنع قانون التنافس، فزوكربيرج مثلاً يملك تراكماً نقدياً هائلاً cash pile يجعله جاهزاً لشراء أي منافسٍ محتمل في مرحلة مبكرة (فرجسن، ص ص ٤١٧-٤١٨). يشكل هؤلاء بُرْجاً رفيعاً عالياً، ونحن نرعى أسفلهم في الساحة، دون قدرة منا على لمح بُرْجهم من النظرة الأولى.

في هذا السياق الاحتكاري الذي تجاوب معه نهج سياسي، لا سيما في إدارة فيسبوك، فجعله أشبه بالحكومة منه بشركة تقليدية، علّق أحد

حتى أصولها في الشبكة. فساد اعتقاد بأن الإنترنت هو فضاء التحرر واللاسيطرة. ولكن هذا الاعتقاد يعبّر عن الماهية التي يُفترض أن يكون عليها الإنترنت وليس عن ماهيته الفعلية، إذ لا تتوقف ماهية الإنترنت على معمار وحيد يحدد طبيعة الشبكة، بل ثمة معماريات ممكنة (لسيج، ص ٦٢). في جامعة شيكاجو، مثلاً، يمكنك توصيل الكمبيوتر بوصلة الإيثرنت ethernet، فتتصل بالإنترنت بلا عوائق ولا رسوم ولا رقيب. أما في جامعة هارڤارد فلن تستطيع الدخول إلى الشبكة إلا إذا كان الكمبيوتر مسجلاً، أي مرخصاً ومعتمداً ومتحققاً من هُوّيته، ويحدث ذلك بإضافة طبقة تحكّم إلى بروتوكولات الإنترنت يستحيل الاتصال إلا عبرها. بروتوكولات الإنترنت لا تفرض تحديد الهُوّية، لكن نقطة المرور المحلية هي التي تفرض ذلك. وكذلك الحال مع معلومات الموضع الجغرافي ومعلومات الاستخدام، بحيث يمكن تعقبها (لسيج، ص ص ٦٤-٦٧):

> ما الذي جعل هذا الأمر ممكناً؟ لم يكن ذلك من تخطيط وكالة الأمن القومي ولا إستراتيجية ابتدعتها مايكروسوفت. يعتبر ما حدث في حقيقة الأمر منتجاً ثانوياً لمعمار الإنترنت ومعمار شركات تقديم خدمات الإنترنت التي تتلقى رسوماً نظير الدخول إلى الشبكة. يجب أن تتعرف الشبكة على عنوان بروتوكول إنترنت، كما تشترط شركاتُ تقديم خدمات الإنترنت تقديمَ مستندات إثبات هُوّية قبل تخصيص عنوان بروتوكول إنترنت لأحد العملاء. وما دام هناك وجود لسجلات شركة تقديم خدمات الإنترنت، فمن الممكن تتبع أي تفاعلات على الشبكة. خلاصة الأمر، إذا أردت ألا يتم الكشف عن هُوّيّتك فاستخدم هاتفاً عاماً. (لسيج، ص٨٢)

إن الفرضيات الصريحة والضمنية في نظرية سناجلة - ومؤيّده أسليم - عن «الواقعية الرقمية»، بكل أصولها الليبرتارية هي في حقيقة أمرها حبر على ورق. وهي تعبّر إما عن خنوع مسلوب الإرادة والتفكير أمام التكنولوجيا الرقمية، أو تتعامى عن مآلها الممكن إلى فضاء هيمنة وسيطرة. بل الأكثر من هذا وذاك، تتعامى عن صيرورة التكنولوجيا الرقمية فعلياً إلى ساحة واسعة، يقوم في زاوية منها بُرْج للمال الشرير لا تلمحه العين من الوهلة الأولى.

اخترعوا شيئاً سيُحْكِم سيطرتَه عليهم في النهاية (Dreyfus 72-73) ؛ «هذا الظرف الحديث أعطاه نيتشه اسماً ، أسماه العدمية» (Dreyfus 72) .

عملت التوتاليتارية التقليدية – المدعومة بتكنولوجيا تقليدية – بأسلوب آلة عملاقة تُذكرنا بآلة إي . إم . فورستر E. M. Forster في قصته القصيرة «الآلة تتوقف» "The Machine Stops" المنشورة عام ١٩٠٩ ، آلة تستعبد الإنسان وتمسخه إلى مجرد ترس في نظامها الهائل ، كما أوضحت أرندت نفسها لاحقاً عند دراستها لحالة أدولف آيخمان الذي بدا مطيعاً ساذجاً وعاجزاً (آيخمان في القدس ، ص ٢٤) ، نتيجة قصوره العقلي والوجداني عن تحمل المسؤولية وعدم الاستجابة لنداء التفكير في ظل التوتاليتارية ، فجسّد قصورَ الوعي الأخلاقي في أشد حالاته تطرفاً : «فقر الخيال واللامبالاة خطير خطورة اقتراف إساءة عمْدية» (Bakewell 77) . مسلك آيخمان يماثل مسلك ڤاشتي Vashti في قصة فورستر . وقد نغامر متأملين تحليلات أرندت في كتابها بالقول إن التوتاليتارية التقليدية هي الاستجابة السياسية لمنطق العصر الآلي في ذروته ، بمعنى أن تكنولوجيا الآلة التي أفصح عنها حق الإفصاح شارلي شابلن بأعماله السينمائية – وما كان له أن يفصح هذا الإفصاح إلا نتيجة تعميم الآلية والمكننة تعميماً شاملاً له طبيعة الخطر – احتلت الإنسانَ دون أن يدري حتى أنتجت نظاماً سياسياً يعمل على مثال الآلة : التوتاليتارية . فهل يحق لنا الزعم بأننا في الكون الرقمي – البازغ فجره – أمام احتمال توتاليتارية متحولة من عبادة القائد إلى عبادة تكنولوجيا رقمية هائلة ، تنبأ بها فورستر وجسدها في قصته من خلال ڤاشتي والدة كونو Kuno المتمرد على عبادة الآلة؟ سؤال عسير ينطوي على أبعاد سياسية هائلة ، نكتفي بطرحه للتأمل ، ونحن نفكر في المآل السياسي لـ«الواقعية الرقمية» التي قدمها سناجلة عام ٢٠٠٤ ، ويتبناها أسليم ، بوصفها حياة افتراضية بديلة عن وَهَج الحياة الواقعية الحقيقية .

ثمة بُعد في التكنولوجيا الرقمية – وبنية الإنترنت مقصدنا هنا – يسمح بتحولها إلى فضاء للسيطرة والهيمنة ، سنحاول استكشافه . نشرت جريدة النيويوركر The New Yorker كاريكاتيراً لكلبين يجلسان أمام جهاز كمبيوتر ، يقول أحدهما للآخر : «على الإنترنت لا يعرف أحد أنك كلب» (لسيج ، ص ٦٧) . كان الكاريكاتير يعبّر عن اعتقاد منتشر بخصوص الإنترنت في بدايته : الجهالة ، بمعنى تجهيل عملية الاتصال بين المستخدمين عبر الشبكة دون معرفة هُويّتهم واستحالة تقصي تفاعلاتهم

مجتمع الإنسان العاقل. وستنشغل رواية الواقعية الرقمية بهذه التغيرات التي ستكون موضوعها الأساسي. (رواية **الواقعية الرقمية**، ص ٦٥)

ترجع غرابة هذا التعقيب إلى أن محتوى رواية **شات** الرئيسي يكشف عن بنية اجتماعية وسياسية جدِّ تقليدية تتناغم مع برمجية ماكروميديا فلاش المعزِّزة لسلطة الكاتب. فنحن أمام تنظيم اجتماعي وسياسي هَرَمي مكتمل الأركان، ولسنا حتى أمام نسخة رقمية لكومونة باريس الواقعية الحقيقية.[10] فهل يرجع قصور التجربة وتقليديتها إلى قصور وعي أطرافها الفاعلة، أم إلى قصورٍ ذاتي صميمي في بنية التكنولوجيا الرقمية نفسها يجعل منها امتداداً للأبنية الهَرَمية في أشد حالاتها هيمنة وسيطرة؟

توتاليتارية جديدة: أنت مُراقَب!

في عام ١٩٢٣، استُعملت كلمة «توتاليتارية» لوصف نظام حكم موسوليني الذي يفقد فيه الإنسان عقله وضميره حتى يجثو على ركبتيه تعبيراً عن إيمانه بأجهزة الدولة وزعيمها (إيزاك، ص ٢٥٦). واستَعملت الكلمة لاحقاً الفيلسوفة السياسية حنة أرندت لتصف ما أسمته «الأمة في الدرجة الصفر» (**أسس التوتاليتارية**، ص ٦)، حيث يسود التشظي والتفكك الاجتماعي والأخلاقي في الحياة الحديثة، فتغيب أخلاقيات الضمير وتحل القسوة واللامبالاة محل التشارك الوجداني وتتلاشى الرابطة الاجتماعية، ويختفي وَهَج التجربة الواقعية الحية، الأمر الذي يساعد على بذر أسس التوتاليتارية. لعبت الدورَ الأكبر في إحداث هذا الخنوع اللاإنساني تكنولوجيا إعلام الجماهير: الإذاعة ومكبرات الصوت والصحافة والمنشورات والسينما وموسيقى الحشود. هذه التكنولوجيا - التي صارت تقليدية الآن - هي التي صنعت الجماهير في المرحلة النازية، أو درجة صفر الأمة. وليس مصادفة - قبل أقل من قرن على بزوغ التوتاليتارية في أوروبا - أن ينظر كيركجارد Kierkegaard عام ١٨٤٦ إلى تكنولوجيا الطباعة وانتشار الصحف بوصفها تهديداً خطيراً لمستقبل أوربا، لأنها المسؤولة عن انتشار اللامبالاة وانعدام التفكير لدى الجماهير، فهي الشرير الحقيقي وراء هذا الجمهور/ الشبح، الذي سيصل بأوروبا إلى طريق مسدود، يذكرها دائماً بأن البشر

ملكة ووزيراً ، وتطور الأمر فانتخبوا مجلس وزراء وبرلماناً . وفجأةً ، قاد وزيره الأول محاولة انقلاب عليه : فبما أن الغرفة وطن الحب والحرية ، وبما أن الحرية شعارها ، فلماذا يكون نزار هو الملك ، بل لماذا تكون ملكة أصلاً؟ يجب أن يتحول النظام الملكي إلى جمهوري . اكتسبت الحركة الانقلابية تأييداً كبيراً ، ولكن تشكلت في مقابلها حركة معارضة للانقلاب من صبايا الغرفة اللواتي تمسكن بالنظام الملكي وبنزارَ ملكاً . في هذه الأثناء ، التزم الملك الصمت حتى اقترحت قائدة معارَضة الانقلاب إجراء استفتاء عام حلاً لهذا الموقف المتأزم . وجاءت النتيجة ضد حركة الانقلاب ، فاكتشف الملك نزار أن شعبيته أكبر مما كان يتوقع ، فأقال وزيره المنقلب وعيّن قائدة معارَضة الانقلاب في منصبه . ولكن المتمردين لم يسلموا بنتيجة الاستفتاء ، فخططوا لإثارة الفوضى في المملكة وغيروا هُويّاتهم الرقمية وشنوا هجوماً عنيفاً بالسباب والشتائم . التزم رؤوس النظام الملكي ومؤيدوهم الصمت أولاً ، ولمّا زاد الأمر عن حدّه ، قرروا الانسحاب ومغادرة الغرفة ، فلم يبق في مملكة الحب والحرية سوى المتمردين الأشرار ، فصارت الغرفة وطن البذاءة والمسالك اللاأخلاقية ، وقرر الملك قراره الأخير : «باسم دولة العشاق ووطن الحب والحرية ونظراً للتطورات اللاأخلاقية التي تتم في الغرفة فقد قررت مغادرة الغرفة إلى الأبد وإلغاء وطن الحب والحرية . التوقيع ملك مملكة العشاق نزار الأول» (رواية الواقعية الرقمية ، ص ٦٤) .

هذه التجربة ، على سذاجتها ، جعلها سناجلة لاحقاً محور روايته الرقمية شات ، ولعل السذاجة مصدرها أنها تكرّسِ لما يجري في العالم الحقيقي الواقعي فهي تمضي على مثاله حرفياً تقريباً ، بطريقة تتناقض مع هدف سناجلة من إيرادها في كتيبه ، حيث يقول :

ما أريد أن أقوله هو أن الزمن قد تغير والمكان قد تغير وبالتالي فإن الإنسان نفسه قد تغير تغيراً شمولياً بحيث إن الإنسان الرقمي يختلف كلية عن الإنسان العاقل سواء في اهتماماته أو مجتمعه أو آماله أو طريقة عيشه للحياة ذاتها ، فنزار كان يحب ويعشق ويمارس الحب والحياة وله كيانه الاجتماعي المتشابك وصداقاته وأعداؤه وطريقة حياة تختلف كلية عن محمد سناجلة الذي يعيش في

النموذج السطري (أو الخطي) ، إذ تتكون من ١٤ مشهداً متتابعاً - مع الحفاظ على وجود وصلات أو تفريعات داخل المشاهد - فلا يكون أمام القارئ خيار البدء من مواقع مختلفة ، وإنما ينقاد بسلطة الكاتب في تحديد مسار القراءة . كما يأتي محتواها كما لو كان تطبيقاً حرفياً لتصوره النظري عن الشخصية والموضوع في رواية «الواقعية الرقمية» (**رواية الواقعية الرقمية** ، ص ص ٣٦-٦٥) ؛ إذ تعالج الرواية لحظة تحول الإنسان الحقيقي الواقعي إلى إنسان رقمي افتراضي . تبدأ الرواية بـ«العدم الرملي» الذي يعيشه نزار في عالمه الحقيقي الواقعي ، فيجد القارئ نفسه مع نزارٍ أمام رعب الصحراء القاحلة ورمالها التي لا تنتهي ، مع مؤثرات صوتية تعزّز مشاعر الغربة والقلقِ . ثم حين يكتشف نزار الواقع الافتراضي على الإنترنت ، عبر منال مصادفة ، تبدأ حياته الحقيقية في الواقع الافتراضي ، فتنساب عندئذ خلفية بصرية مبهجة مع مشهدي التحولات ١ و٢ ، وبتوالي المشاهد تنساب موسيقى مريحة ، كما لو أن سناجلة يريد تأكيد أطروحته عن أن «الواقعية الرقمية» هي الواقع الأصيل وأن الواقع الحقيقي المعيش زائف . فُصل نزار من عمله ، في حياته الواقعية ، بسبب إدمانه الواقع الافتراضي ، وبدأ مع المشهد السابع - «وطن العشاق . . .» - في تأسيس مملكة الحب والحرية على الإنترنت (**شات** ، د . ص .) ؛ يقول في المشهد ١٢ المعنون بـ«وجود . . .» : «سأعيش في الأزرق السوبراني [sobranie] . . . تحيط بي ظلال العاشق والألياف الضوئية» (د . ص .) . ولكننا نكتشف أن رواية **شات** تستند إلى تجربة حقيقية عاشها سناجلة في حياته الواقعية ، أوردها من قبل في كتيبه التنظيري (**رواية الواقعية الرقمية** ، ص ص ٤٨-٦٤)[٩] ، لإيضاح طبيعة المجتمع الرقمي (الافتراضي) الآخذة في التشكل ، وإنسانه الرقمي (الافتراضي) البازغ فجره . وسنحاول استكشاف التضمينات السياسية المحتملة في هذه التجربة وفق ورودها في الكتيب .

اعتاد سناجلة في واقعِه الحقيقي المعيش الدخول إلى غرف الدردشة على الإنترنت ، وشكّل لنفسه صورة رقمية سمّاها نزار ، ثم اخترع نزار غرفة سمّاها love kingdom ، وكتب على بابها «وطن الحب والحرية» ، وجعل شعار الغرفة مقطوعة أدونيس الشعرية : «الحب نبيذ الكون/وهذا العالم دنّ/والأيام كؤوس» . صار الشعار سلاماً وطنياً لمملكة الحب والحرية التي ستغدو ملتقى كل الأحرار والعشاق في العالم . وبدأ الزوّار من العالم الافتراضي يتوافدون على الغرفة فاشتهرت . وبطبيعة الحال ، لكل مملكة ملك ، فكان نزار - المؤسس - هو الملك ، واتخذ لنفسه

دولة الخيال الرقمي : مثالية ليبرتارية

ينطوي تصور سناجلة لـ«الواقعية الرقمية» – الذي يحظى بدفاع أسليم – على مثالية ليبرتارية ، تتمثل في التحرر من الدولة بكل مؤسساتها ، ومن المجتمع بكل مؤسساته المتعارف عليها ؛ رغبة في نوع من الاجتماع البشري لا يسمح به الواقع الحقيقي المعيش ولا يتيحه سوى الواقع الافتراضي ، ورغبة في حرية مطلقة وإجماع بلا سلطة وإدارة جماعية طوعية (أناركية) . وهي المثالية الليبرتارية نفسها التي عبّر عنها جون بيري بارلو John Perry Barlow بردّه على قانون آداب الاتصالات الصادر عن الكونجرس الأمريكي عام ١٩٩٦ لتنظيم النشر على الإنترنت ، فجاء ردّه على هيئة «إعلان استقلال الفضاء الإلكتروني» ، وانتصر الأحرار الإلكترونيون على محاولة التدخل الحكومي (فرجسن ، ص ص ٣٦١-٣٦٢) . تكمن حوافز هذه المثالية الليبرتارية في أن بنية الشبكات الإلكترونية بنية لامركزية ، فبفضل الكود مفتوح المصدر ، تطور الإنترنت وفق هَرَمية موزّعة ذات نظام فائق التعقيد ، بما يجعلنا أمام تكنولوجيا ذات بناء لامركزي ، وهنا يكمن تعقيدها المفرط الحائل دون رسم خريطة له .[8]

ويعبّر سناجلة عن هذه المثالية الليبرتارية في روايته الرقمية الأولى **ظلال الواحد** ، سواء على مستوى البناء أو المحتوى ، فبنية العمل مفرّعة تحاكي بنية الإنترنت ذات الهرمية الموزّعة ، أو شجريّة البناء . وتسمح البرمجية المستخدمة في تكوين الرواية بتدخل القارئ ، بما يجعل السلطة موزّعة أيضاً بينه وبين الكاتب توزيعاً يحرج حقوق الملكية الفكرية (أسليم ، «قراءة» ، د . ص .) . ومن ناحية المحتوى ، نعثر في الوصلة رقم ٢ على بلاد يبلغها الراوي ، ونبلغها معه ، مكتوب على بوابتها «دولةِ الخيال الرقمي» فيقول الراوي لنفسه : «دولة من خيال تشبهني لأدخلها عَلي ألقى اليقين» (كما ورد في ن . سليمان ، د . ص .) .

يواصل سناجلة تفريع البناء بصورة أعقد في روايته الرقمية الثانية **شات : رواية واقعية رقمية** ، عبر مشاهد كتابية وسمعية وبصرية ، بما يستحيل معه إخراج العمل ورقياً ، ولكنه في المقابل يستخدم برنامج ماكروميديا فلاش في تكوين العمل ، بما لا يسمح بتدخل القارئ . هذا الاعتداد المفاجئ بسلطة الكاتب يُرجِّع صداه بقوة محتوى العمل ترجيعاً يتنافى مع المثالية الليبرتارية التي حددناها في نظريته عن «الواقعية الرقمية» . كما يأتي بناء الرواية وفق

إيضاح أسليم: الكاتب الرقمي و«الواقعية الرقمية»

أثار سناجلة بروايته الرقمية الأولى وتنظيره لـ«الواقعية الرقمية» موجة جدل توزّعت بين موقفي التأييد والرفض، فاحتفى مؤيدون برواية **ظلال الواحد** دون مناقشة أسس نظريته في «الواقعية الرقمية». وأما المعارضون فنوعان، الأول يمثله سعيد الوكيل الذي يرى أن **ظلال الواحد** لا ترقى إلى الرواية الرقمية كما ينبغي، وأن تنظير سناجلة لـ«الواقعية الرقمية» يأتي دون المستوى المطلوب (أسليم، «عن مفهوم»، د. ص.). وأما الثاني فيمثله حسين سليمان الذي يرفض هذا الجنس، جملةً وتفصيلاً، على أساس أن الأدب عماده الكلمة المكتوبة، وفي أضعف الأحوال الكلمة المسموعة (ح. سليمان، د. ص.). ومن ناحية أخرى، يتدخل محمد أسليم في الجدل الدائر لإزالة اللبس عن مفهومي الكاتب الرقمي و«نظرية الواقعية الرقمية». فيعرّف الكاتب الرقمي بأنه مَن يستعمل مجموعة برامج إلكترونية في إنتاج أدب رقمي يستحيل نشره ورقياً، ويكاد هذا الكاتب ألا يوجد، باستثناء سناجلة وقلة غيره لم تحقق تراكما مثل: أحمد خالد توفيق ومنعم الأزرق ومحمد أشويكة. وأما بشأن ما يسميه أسليم «نظرية الواقعية الرقمية»، فلا يُقصد بكلمة «نظرية» المعنى التقليدي المستعمل في نظرية الأدب، بل إطار عمل وتصور مشاريع وخطوط إبداع عامة أكثر منها قواعد مستخلصة من أعمال أدبية متراكمة، وبخاصة أن الأدب الرقمي لم يحقق بعد هذا التراكم. كما يرفع اللبس عن مصطلح «الواقعية الرقمية»، فهو لا يدل على مذهب أو اتجاه أدبي يتميز باستعمال الحاسوب والتداول على شبكة الإنترنت، وإنما المقصود به: «تأكيد أن الرقمية والعوالم الافتراضية هي بصدد الحلول حرفياً محل الواقع بكافة قطاعاته وأنشطته، بما يقتضي التعامل معها (أي الرقمية) باعتبارها واقعاً، أي أمراً ملموساً وموجوداً، يمكن أن يجلب الفرح للمرء، يسعده ويكافئه، مثلما يمكن أن يجلب له الشقاء والبؤس» (أسليم، «عن مفهوم»، د. ص.)، في تأكيد واضح على صيرورة العالم شاشة زرقاء.

ثالثاً، المآل السياسي لـ«نظرية الواقعية الرقمية»

سأحاول في هذا الجزء استكشاف المآل السياسي الذي يمكن أن تؤول إليه «الواقعية الرقمية»، عند سناجلة، على مستويين: الأول هو بنية بعض الأعمال الأدبية الرقمية ومحتواها؛ والثاني هو بنية الإنترنت.

هذا المقوِّم الموضوعي الخارجي هو حقيقة العالم وقد بات شاشة زرقاء، أو هو واقعية العالم الرقمية التي يجب على الأدب أن يتعامل معها. وثمة مقوِّم موضوعي داخلي يتعلق بحقيقة الأدب نفسه، وله شقان. يتعلق أولهما بفينومينولوجيا الأدب، بكل المعنى المعطى لكلمة فينومينولوجيا (انظر هوسرل). ونقطة الارتكاز الأولى في هذا الظهور هي الرقمنة - أو ثنائية الصفر والواحد بوصفها النموذج الرياضياتي في بناء الحاسب الآلي - التي دونها لن يظهر الأدب الرقمي، ولا الرواية الرقمية، كلا ولا الإنسان الافتراضي إطلاقاً.[7]

وتفرض فينومينولوجية رواية «الواقعية الرقمية» عليها الانبناءَ وفق الخيال المعرفي المستقبلي (وقد بات نموذجه رياضياتياً) وليس الخيال السلفي الارتدادي؛ أي أن تكون: مغامرة في الزمن الرقمي الافتراضي، وفي المكان الرقمي الافتراضي، وفي الواقع الرقمي الافتراضي (سناجلة، **رواية الواقعية الرقمية**، ص ٣١). وأداتا رواية «الواقعية الرقمية» البنائيتان الوحيدتان في ذلك: أولاً، تقنية التفريع وما تنطوي عليه من روابط وإحالات غير سطرية؛ وستكون لغتها - ثانياً - تصويرية مشهدية أو ترفيلية، عبر النص المُرفّل وفق ترجمة الخطيب لمصطلح hypermedia (ص ١١٨). ومن ثم، فأدوات هذه اللغة الأدبية الجديدة - أو بالأحرى تقنياتها التكوينية - هي الصوت والصورة والحركة واللون والموسيقى؛ بالإضافة إلى الكلمة التي لم تعد سوى جزء من هذا الكل التصويري المشهدي، والتي لا بد أن تتصف بحدود التوصيل الدنيا، كقلة الحروف وقصر العبارة التي لن تتعدى ثلاث أو أربع كلمات (سناجلة، **رواية الواقعية الرقمية**، ص ص ٩٥-٩٧)، فيما يشبه مبدأ منطقياً رياضياتياً للغة يغيب عنه الوَهَج. وتكفل هاتان الأداتان البنائيتان - التفريع والترفيل - قدرة دائمة على اتخاذ الرواية أشكالاً مختلفة، بسبب التطور الدائم في التقنيات الرقمية. فمن حيث الشكل، ستتميز رواية «الواقعية الرقمية» باللاتناهي الذي هو في أصله لاتناهي التكنولوجيا الرقمية ذات الأساس الرياضياتي. ويتعلق الشق الثاني في المقوِّم الموضوعي الداخلي بمحتوى الأدب، أو على وجه التحديد موضوع رواية «الواقعية الرقمية» وشخوصها. فموضوعها هو العالم كما تتمثله التكنولوجيا الرقمية أو مجتمعها الرقمي؛ وشخوصها الإنسان الافتراضي وليس الحقيقي، أو الإنسان الواقعي في لحظة تحوله إلى إنسان افتراضي.

القائمة. يقول: «وإذا كنا مرعوبين من هذا الإنسان القادم وقيمه، فلكم أن تتخيلوا رعب إنسان النياندرتال لو وُجِدَ الآن وعايش منظومة قيمنا» (ص ٤٦). ومن الممكن اعتبار هذا التَصور للعالم - بما فيه الإنسان والمجتمع والجغرافيا والحدود والدولة - تداعياً من تداعيات نزعة ما بعد الإنسانوية posthumanism أو transhumanism التي بدأت تدور نقاشات حولها مع أفول القرن العشرين ومطالع القرن الحالي بتأثير التطورات في مجال الفيزياء النظرية والتكنولوجيا الرقمية.[6]

مقوِّمات الأدب الرقمي في «الواقعية الرقمية»

يمثل العالَم، وقد أمسى شاشةً زرقاء، الأساسَ الداعي حتماً إلى أدب جديد هو أدب «الواقعية الرقمية». فهذا العالم الآخذ في التشكل يطرح على الأدب، وبخاصة الجنس الروائي، عدة تساؤلات من أهمها وأخطرها أثراً:

> هل تستطيع الرواية بشكلها الحالي أن تستوعب الثورة الرقمية المتسارعة في العالم، أم أنها يجب أن تتخلى عن مكانتها لصالح أشكال تعبيرية وإبداعية أخرى أكثر قدرة وجاذبية[؟] ... هل الروائي بشكله وأدواته الحالية قادر على المضي في مغامرة الرواية في ظل العصر الرقمي الآخذ بالتشكل؟... ما موضوع الرواية القادمة؟؟ ما لغتها[؟] ... وهل الكتاب - بشكله الورقي المعهود - قادر على استيعاب الرواية القادمة؟؟؟ أم أننا بحاجة إلى لغة أخرى وكتاب آخر؟؟؟ (سناجلة، رواية الواقعية الرقمية، ص ١٥)

وبالاستناد إلى إجاباته، يمكننا تقسيم مقوِّمات الأدب الرقمي إلى مقوِّم موضوعي خارجي يتمثل في الشاشة الزرقاء: هذا العالم الجديد الذي يُعرِّفه سناجلة بأنه «نوع من الوقائع أو الحقائق التي يجري صنعها وتكوينها عبر برامج وحاسبات... لتظهر وتتجسد بالشكل الذي تجري به على أرض الواقع فعلاً» (رواية الواقعية الرقمية، ص ١٣). وتشكل هذه الوقائع أو الحقائق في مجموعها اللامتناهي العالَم، وهو أيضاً لامتناهٍ، لأن الرَّقمنة digitization نفسها لامتناهية بسبب نموذجها الرياضياتي.

كلها. ستنهار الأسرة لانتفاء الحاجة إلى الزواج، وستزول الأوطان لزوال الجغرافيا ذاتها، وستزول الدول لانتفاء الحدود التي ستتلاشى تلقائياً. وهذه الانهيارات المتتابعة هي الأثر التلقائي لانتفاء أبعاد الزمان والمكان نتيجة انتشار التكنولوجيا الرقمية المعمَّمة (سناجلة، رواية الواقعية الرقمية، ص ص ٤٢-٤٤). سيبقى إنسان واحد فقط عند سناجلة:

لا كائناً كان إلاه، هو الواحد المعروف قبل الحد وقِبل الحروف، لا رادّ لمشيئته، ولا شيء أمام رغبته إذا أراد شيئاً فإنما يقول له كليك [click] فيكون، فأمره بين الكاف والكاف يكون... هو الروح الموجودة في كل مكان، ذاك الذي سيخترق الجدران ويعبر الأزمان ليأتي إليَّ وينقذني من عتمة القبر كما آمل ويعيد بعثي واستنساخي من جديد. (ص ٤٢)

ينطوي عالَم الشاشة الزرقاء هذا، على عدة مفاهيم. يتعلق أولها بالإنسان الافتراضي نفسه، فهذا الإنسان متوحد متفرد، يستغني بذاته عن الآخرين، وتنتفي عنه صفة الكائن الاجتماعي لانتفاء حاجاته وضروراته المرتبطة بغيره من البشر، فيعود إلى كينونته الفَردة التي هي طبيعته الجوهرية قبل نشأة الاجتماع البشري، و«كما قال المتصوفة قديماً الإنسان هو الكون الأصغر، فيه كل ما في الكون، هو نجم كائن قائم بذاته، وليس بحاجة للاجتماع ليتحقق، فحقيقته كينونته وكينونته تفرُّده» (سناجلة، رواية الواقعية الرقمية، ص ٤٧). وبغض النظر عن هذا السحب للتصور الصوفي من المستوى اللاهوتي إلى المستوى الاجتماعي، فهذا معناه انتفاء العلاقة بالآخر، أو على الأقل وَضْعها في حدودها الدنيا، عبر توسُّط الآلة الرقمية فقط دون وَهَج المباشرَة. ويتعلق ثانيها بالمجتمع، فالمجتمع، رغم انتفاء دواعيه التقليدية التي نعرفها، لن يتلاشى، وإنما سيوجد مجتمع لن يتعارف فيه بنو البشرِ بهُويّاتهم الحقيقية، بل سيكون لكل إنسان هُويّة افتراضية يشكلها طبقاً لرغباته (ص صٍ ٤٧-٤٨)؛ وذلك هو المجتمع الرقمي. بل يتكهن سناجلة، استناداً إلى تاريخ تطور الإنسان الطويل، بأن هذا الإنسان الافتراضي - الواحد بحضارته الرقمية الواحدة - سينسجم مع بيئته الجديدة انسجاماً كاملاً، كما ننسجم نحن مع بيئتنا وحضارتنا التقليدية

ما بعد الإنسان والمجتمع والدولة

في هذا العالم السحري الجديد - عالم الشاشة الزرقاء - لا بد أن يتغير شكلُ الحياة ويتغير الناس وتتغير العلاقات، ومن ثمّ المفاهيم والقيم، تغيراً كاملاً. فنحن نشهد الآن لحظة التحول من الإنسان العاقل الحقيقي الواقعي إلى الإنسان الرقمي الافتراضي الذي يحدده سناجلة بأنه:

> أشبه ما يكون بالبرنامج الإلكتروني ... سيأكل ويشرب ويحب ويضاجع بطريقة رقمية ... سيعيش في مجتمع رقمي بالكامل ... في مدينة مفترضة هائلة الضخامة، مدينة واحدة تشمل العالم كله، وهذه المدينة موجودة في الخيال فقط ... هذا الإنسان لن يضطر للذهاب إلى أي مكان، وذلك لأنه ببساطة موجود في كل مكان. (رواية **الواقعية الرقمية**، ص ص ٣٩-٤٠)

سيقضي هذا الإنسان الرقمي كل احتياجاته، وسيمارس كل أعماله وأفعاله من خلف شاشة زرقاء؛ بل يشطح سناجلة شطحاً بعيداً في بشارته بهذا الإنسان الافتراضي فيتوقع أن كمبيوتر العصر القادم سيكون داخل جسد الإنسان، عن طريق زرع رُقيقة داخل الدماغ البشري تتصل مباشرة بالإنترنت، ومعها قناع أو وَصْلة رُقيقات على منطقة عيني الإنسان وأذنيه تمكنه من الاتصال الفوري سمعياً وبصرياً في أي لحظة (ص ٤٠). وإذا كان ثمة من فعل يفعله هذا السايبورج cyborg،[٥] فلن يعدو ضغطة زرٍّ. فإذا استبدت به الرغبة الجنسية مثلاً، فما عليه سوى وضع المَجَسّات عَلى جسده والدخول إلى رابط الجنس، واختيار نموذج المرأة التي يشتهيها ليضاجعها بالطريقة التي يحبها (ص ٤٢). ولنا أن نتخيل بعد ذلك كيف سيلبي هذا الإنسان سائر احتياجاته ورغباته وأعماله الضرورية منها وغير الضروري.

وأما عن المجتمع القائم بمؤسساته الاجتماعية والسياسية والاقتصادية والدينية - بل حضارة البشر الراهنة بأكملها - فسيختفي مع التحول من الإنسان العاقل (الحقيقي الواقعي) إلى الإنسان الافتراضي (الخيالي الرقمي)، لأن منظومة القيم الأخلاقية والحضارية المتنوعة الكافلة لتلك المؤسسات، التي تدير مجتمعاتنا الحالية، ستختفي كما اختفى إنسان النياندرتال بمنظومته

فيرن Jules Verne ومَن على شاكلته (ص ص ١٧-٢٠)، وكل الإبداع العربي باستثناء ثلاثة مفسدين كبار - ورابعهم سناجلة! - هم: أبو تمام وابن عربي وأدونيس، الذين خرجوا على نظام اللغة المستقر وخيال الإبداع السلفي، فاتُّهموا جميعاً بالإفساد والزندقة والخروج على الملة نتيجة ثوراتهم اللغويَة النكراء (ص ص ٦٩-٩٢). وبعد كل هذه الإدانات الشاملة، يقدم سناجلة أساساً نظرياً شاملاً لما أسماه «رواية الواقعية الرقمية»، أو ما يمكننا وضعه بين مزدوجتين «نظرية الواقعية الرقمية». سأحاول الآن تحديد هذا الأساس الشامل واستكشاف ما ينطوي عليه من فرضيات عن الإنسان والمجتمع والعالم.

العالم شاشة زرقاء

في الكون الرقمي digital universe (انظر سيل) الذي نعيشه الآن، لم يعد العالم قرية صغيرة، بل أمسى أصغر من حجرة صغيرة في بيت؛ لقد صار العالم شاشة زرقاء (سناجلة، **رواية الواقعية الرقمية**، ص ١٢). وليست صيرورة العالم شاشة زرقاء محض استعارة عند سناجلة، بل ممارسة فعلية قائمة في جوانب حياتنا المعاصرة. فدون مغادرة أماكن جلوسنا خلف الشاشة الزرقاء، غدا بمستطاعنا التعلم في مدارس وجامعات لا وجود واقعياً لها سوى الوجود الافتراضي على الشبكة العنكبوتية، «بحيث أصبحنا نرى الآن خريجين يحملون الشهادات الجامعية من جامعات موجودة في الخيال فقط»؛ وكذلك في التسوق والتجارة، فـ«أصبح إنشاء الشركات وممارسة الأعمال لا يحتاج لأكثر من جهاز حاسوب واتصال بشبكة الإنترنت وعقلية متفتحة لتدخل بقوة إلى عالم تحقيق الأحلام» (ص ص ١٣-١٤).

ويتلقف سناجلة من أحد كتيبات بيل جيتس Bill Gates استعارته عن النظام العصبي الرقمي (**رواية الواقعية الرقمية**، ص ص ٢٧-٢٨). وبالاستناد إلى هذه الاستعارة الناشئة عن معالجة مشاكل محددة في تبادل المعلومات وإدارة الشركات والأعمال،[4] من الممكن استنباط سمة الكون الرقمي الجديد الرئيسية: كُنْ متصلاً وإلا ستصبح خارج الحياة. وهو ما عناه سناجلة حين تساءل: «ما الذي يعنيه هذا؟ ألا يعني أن العالم القديم انتهى؟ وأن عالماً جديداً مختلفاً تماماً آخذ في التشكل؟» (ص ٢٩).

ولكنه يحجِّم المرجعية التاريخية التي ميزت مؤتمر تونس، فيقصرها على المؤسسة الأدبية العربية فقط، بل ينشغل في جزء من كتابه بإثبات ريادته في الدعوة إلى ضرورة لحاق المؤسسة الأدبية بركب التكنولوجيا، فيعيد فيه نشر مقال له بعنوان «الطليعية أدب عصر الصاروخ» كان قد نشره من قبل في مجلة **المعرفة** العراقية عام ١٩٦٤ (الخطيب، ص ص ٢٨٦-٢٩٨).

ويتميز جدله أيضاً بأنه أقرب إلى التعامل الأداتي مع التكنولوجيا الرقمية منه إلى كونها حياة افتراضية بديلة عن الحياة الواقعية القائمة. ويماثله في ذلك كتاب شبلول **أدباء الإنترنت: أدباء المستقبل** الذي صدر في العام التالي مباشرة لصدور كتاب الخطيب. فنَهْجه تعريفي أداتي يسعى فيه إلى إغراء الأدباء والمثقفين باستخدام الكمبيوتر وشبكة الإنترنت، مستهدفاً عقد قران سعيد بين الأدب والتكنولوجيا (شبلول، ص ١١).

ثانياً، سناجلة وأسليم: «نظرية الواقعية الرقمية»

تحققت ظنون الخطيب بعد نصف عقد فقط، بفضل العولمة المتسارعة للتكنولوجيا الرقمية. ففي عام ٢٠٠١، أصدر محمد سناجلة أول رواية رقمية عربية بعنوان **ظلال الواحد** على موقعه في شبكة الإنترنت، اعتمد في بنائها تقنية النص المُفرَّع أو الهايبرتكست hypertext،[٣] فكان سناجلة أول أديب عربي يصمِّم الخيال الأدبي ويبنيه وفق تقنيات رقمية.

وفيما يقول سناجلة، تعرضت روايته لهجوم لم يفاجئه لسببين، أولهما رسوخ النسج على مثال سابق في العقلية العربية، فترفض المبتدَع بوصفه رجْساً يستوجب المحارَبة؛ وثانيهما أن كل بدعة تحتاج إلى اسم تُعرف به، وإلى الدفاع عنها، «وقد أطلقتُ على هذه البدعة الجديدة اسم رواية الواقعية الرِقمية» (**رواية الواقعية الرقمية**، ص ص ٨-٩). فأصدر كتيباً تنظيرياً إلكترونياً يحمل عنوان **رواية الواقعية الرقمية**، يتكون من أربعة فصول نشرها تباعاً على موقع **ميدل إيست أونلاين** في شهري مارس وأبريل من عام ٢٠٠٤، سعى فيه إلى إدانة العقلية العربية السلفية الناتجة عن استقرار اللغة العربية على أيدي اللغويين وأهل الكلام الذين قنّنوها وأعطوها شكلاً ثابتاً مستقراً بقي إلى الآن (ص ص ٧٣-٧٤)، وإلى إدانة الخيال السلفي الذي يقصد به كل الأدب العالمي باستثناء روايات الخيال العلمي للكاتب جول

الفلاسفة» ، بعد اتجاه التكنولوجيا اليوم إلى «ما يشبه وضع الهيمنة التامة على مرافق الحياة ومستوياتها» (ص ٩) .

ولا يفوت الخطيب بعد حملته على المؤسسة الأدبية العربية أن يحمل أيضاً على ممثلي الحرس القديم في الأدب المقارن ، قائلاً إن كتابه هذا يتصل أوثق اتصال بمشروعه في دراسات الأدب المقارن التي بدأها عام ١٩٩٢ ؛ ذلك أن نظرية الأدب المقارن وثبت وثبة نوعية مهمة في أواخر الثمانينيات ، فأخذت تطمح إلى اكتشاف شتى العلاقات بين الأدب وغيره من حقول معرفية وإبداعية أخرى ، بدءاً من العلوم الإنسانية حتى العلوم الطبيعية والتطبيقية . وعليه يقدم الخطيب دراسته للأدب والتكنولوجيا بوصفها مصدراً لاكتشاف الأبعاد المختلفة في بنية التفكير والتعبير عند الإنسان (ص ص ١٣-١٤) .

ويعتقد الخطيب أن القرن الحادي والعشرين لن يمثل انتقالاً من قرن إلى قرن ، بل من عالم إلى عالم آخر ، وأن خط التطور التكنولوجي سيقسم الحياة البشرية إلى مستويين : مستوى الأذكياء التكنولوجيين صانعي المصائر ، وعلى رأسها مصير العالم ؛ ومستوى سائر البشر المشغولين بالاستهلاك ، العاجزين عن تشكيل مصيرهم ناهيك عن مصير العالم من حولهم ؛ بل شرع أولئك الأذكياء التكنولوجيون يُجرون التجارب من أجل تغيير طبيعة الإنسان وتكوينه عن طريق التدخل في الجينات والموَرِّثات بطريقة بيولوجية طامحين إلى استصدار نسخ بيولوجية عن الإنسان (ص ص ٣١-٣٤) . ولأن مفهوم الحقيقة الإنسانية والطبيعية صارت تحدده تطورات العلم (ص ٨٣) ، وليس الفلسفة أو الأدب ، يشدد الخطيب على ضرورة أن تلحق بنية الخيال الأدبي ببنية الخيال التكنولوجي التي لا مبدأ لها سوى «اتبعوني والهثوا ، ليس إلا» (ص ٣٢) . وبدافع من حكمته وفطنته بقوانين التفاعل الحضاري ، يقول : «وما نظن إلا أن السنوات الأولى من القرن الحادي والعشرين ستشهد وصول الموجة الأولى إلى الوطن العربي ، وفقاً لقانون التأثر والتأثير الذي درجنا عليه ، وهو التلكؤ بفارق عقدين أو ثلاثة عقود من السنوات» (ص ١٢) . لكل هذه العوامل ، يأتي كتاب الخطيب على سبيل التعريف المبدئي الشامل بطريقة الكتابة الحاسوبية ، مع استجلاء علاقتها بدراسة الأدب وتدريسه ونقده والتنظير له وإنتاجه ، في إطار تصورات عامة حول تطورات العلاقة بين الثقافتين الأدبية والتكنولوجية (ص ١١) .

يتميز جدل الخطيب حول الأدب والتكنولوجيا بأنه أكثر تخصصاً ونوعية ، ويلامس تحولاً في بنية الأدب عبر تقنيتي التفريع والترفيل ،

جمود المؤسسة الأدبية مقابل التكنولوجي الحكيم

خفت الجدل حول الأدب العربي والتكنولوجيا بمرجعيته السياسية والاستعمارية بعد مؤتمر تونس، حتى أثاره عام ١٩٩٦ الناقد الفلسطيني حسام الخطيب في كتابه **الأدب والتكنولوجيا وجسر النص المُفرّع**. ولكن جدل الخطيب تميز بتغييب المرجعية السياسية والاستعمارية، وفي هذا يتقاطع الخطيب مع منظور بورقيبة في مؤتمر تونس، فيتجاهل الاحتلال الصهيوني للأراضي العربية، وآفة الحكم المطلق. ويكتفي بتشخيص مرض الثقافة العربية، الأصيل فيها، بأنه محافظة المؤسسة الأدبية العربية المتخلفة عن ركب التكنولوجيا. فداوَم طيلة عامين سابقين يلقي محاضرات عامة عن التحدي التكنولوجي الراهن المفروض على هذه المؤسسة، وتراوحت الاستجابات بين الإنكار الشديد والتشكك وعدم الاكتراث، ومقابل ذلك يحدد موقفه قائلاً:

> وقد صحّ لدى المؤلف أن التكنولوجيا سلاح ذو حدين، يمكن أن تفيد منه المؤسسة الأدبية ويمكن أن تتقوض على يديه. والأفضل دائماً هو البحث عن الجوانب الإيجابية وكيفية الإفادة السليمة منها، ومقابل ذلك فإن أسوأ ما يمكن أن تفعله المؤسسة الأدبية هو التجاهل والاستهزاء لأن هذا الموقف يؤدي إلى الإمعان في تهميش الأدب في عالم التكنولوجيا المقبل... [ف]محافظة المؤسسة الأدبية - ولا سيما في البلاد العربية - تؤدي يوميًا إلى ابتعاد الأدب عن خضم حركة المجتمع... بل أحيانا تجعل كل معاركه نوعاً من الديالكتيك المغلق أو سفاح المحارم. (ص ص ١٠-١١)

ولأن الأرض العربية جامدة مغلقة، وفق تصور الخطيب، يدور كتابه حول التحدي التكنولوجي الراهن الذي يفرض على الظاهرة الأدبية تغيراً تكوينياً في بنيتها، ألا وهو «العدول عن الكتابة السطرية، وتبنّي طريقة النص التكويني بمستوييه المفرّع hypertext والمرفّل hypermedia» (ص ١٠). ودافعه في هذا أن الواقع العالمي من حولنا يثبت تحقق مقولة راجت في القرن التاسع عشر: «التكنولوجيون هم الذين يغيرون العالم، لا

ما موقف الأدب من تبني الأنظمة العربية سياسةً علمية تكنولوجية تقلل من جدوى الأدب في المعركة الدائرة؟ ما موقف الأدب من مشكلة الغزو الثقافي للتقنيات الحديثة التي تمتلكها الدول الاستعمارية الكبرى؟ وعلى فرض تحقيق العرب مستوى تكنولوجياً متقدماً ، فسيواجه الأدب العربي الإشكالية نفسها التي واجهتها آداب الأمم الصناعية الكبرى بعد الحرب العالمية الثانية ، أي : المصارَعة في سبيل وجود الأدب وتأكيد وظيفته إلى جانب التكنولوجيا والآلة التي تسللت إلى كل شيء حتى الإنسان نفسه (ص ٧٥) . وفي معالجة الكعبي لهذه الإشكاليات ، يغلب عليه قدر من التفاؤل الموضوعي ، فيذكر الكمبيوتر الذي بدأ استعماله في الدراسات الأدبية واللغوية في بعض البلاد المتقدمة ، والذي سيُعمّم استخدامه في المستقبل ، حيث يجري العمل على تكوين قواميس لغوية ودوائر معارف إلكترونية (ص ٨٠) . وينتهي إلى أن موقف العرب ينبغي ألا يكون موقف الرافض للعلم والتكنولوجيا أو التصنيع الآلي (ص ٨٣) .

انطلق الجدل العربي في مؤتمر تونس من مرجعية تاريخية ، بدءاً من كلماته الافتتاحية وانتهاءً بأوراقه البحثية ، بل كواليسه أيضًا التي كشف عنها سهيل إدريس في مجلته **الآداب** . ويجمل أبو القاسم سعد الله مرجعية الجدل على النحو الآتي : محاولات ناجحة قريبة العهد للتخلص من الاستعمار الإنجليزي والفرنسي ؛ مجابهة محاولات بسط النفوذ الأجنبي ؛ تجارب جزئية فاشلة في الوحدة العربية ؛ هزائم متكررة على يد الصهاينة . هذه المرجعية التاريخية جعلت بعضَ العرب والأجانب يرون أن السبب الرئيسي للفشل العربي داخلياً وخارجياً هو تخلف العرب تكنولوجياً ، وضعف إيمانهم بالعلم ، وقصور الوعي العربي عن حركة التاريخ وتطوره (سعد الله ، ص ٨٦) . بل يذهب سعد الله إلى أن العرب ، إن ظلوا على ما هم عليه ، فلن يدخلوا عصر التكنولوجيا حتى في القرن الحادي والعشرين ؛ فثمة مشكلة اجتماعية ثقافية هي الأمية والجهل وانتشار الخرافة وسطوة التقاليد ؛ وثمة حكم مطلق يلاحق الأدباء والكتاب ويخشى من عمليات تحديث واسعة النطاق ؛ وثمة استعمار تقليدي لم يكد يرحل عن العرب حتى زرع قاعدة له في القلب العربي هي إسرائيل التي تلوح للعرب بحرب إلكترونية (ص ص ٨٧-٨٨) .

هكذا تحرك الجدل في مؤتمر تونس بتأثير مرجعية سياسية واستعمارية طاغية . وتَمثل الموقف العربي من التكنولوجيا في اعتبارها أداة تقدم ومجابَهة استعمارية .

بانقلابها النوعي الذي حقق تغييراً جذرياً في وظيفة الآلة» (الشوك ، ص ١٠٥) ، يتمثل في حلول الآلة محل الإنسان . بل ثمة أصوات غربية تقترح إعادة النظر في «الكتابة» نفسها ، على أساس أن الأدب المكتوب من نتاج الصناعة اليدوية ، فحدثت محاولات لجعل الكمبيوتر يؤلف الشعر ، بل هناك من يعتقد أن بوسع الكمبيوتر نظم الشعر وتأليف المسرحية على نحو أفضل من الإنسان بحلول نهاية القرن العشرين (الشوك ، ص ص ١٠٥- ١٠٦) . وفي هذا يقول علي الشوك :

ها نحن نواجه مرة أخرى الموقف الاغترابي من الآلة الذي يتأتّى من مزاحمتها الإنسان والتحكم بمصيره . ويبلغ هذا الموقف ذروته في الهلع من القوة التدميرية الهائلة للآلة المتمثل بالأسلحة الذرية والنووية . والحق أننا لو حاولنا أن نتقصى أسباب القلق والضياع والأفكار العبثية في الأدب العالمي الحديث لوجدنا أنها ترجع في جوهرها إلى الطبيعة اللاديمقراطية الطبقية ، وإلى الحالة الاغترابية التي تفترضها طبيعة العمل في هذه المجتمعات ، والفزع من الآلة وما تملكه من طاقة تدميرية هائلة . (ص ١٠٦)

ومن ناحية أخرى ، أثر السياق التاريخي بقوة في تناول موضوع الأدب والتكنولوجيا ، فهو سياق أزمة عربية مصيرية حادة في مواجهة الصهيونية وبقايا الاستعمار في ظل الثورة التكنولوجية المعاصرة . فشاعت دعوات تقلل من جدوى الأدب ، بل عدم صلاحيته وتعويقه جهود التنمية العلمية والتكنولوجية التي تطلعت إليها الأنظمة العربية وقتئذ ، والتي ستسعفها في معركتها مع الصهيونية والاستعمار ، وبخاصة أن التحدي الاستعماري يَمثل في الرهان على خضوع العرب مرة أخرى للهيمنة الاستعمارية «لعجزهم . . . عن تسيير المؤسسات الاقتصادية الكبرى الحيوية التي أقامها الاستعمار في بلادهم» (الكعبي ، ص ٧٤) لتخلفهم العلمي والتكنولوجي ؛ والمثال البارز هنا تسيير الملاحة في قناة السويس . وبعد نكسة ١٩٦٧ ، أخذ التكنوقراطيون والسياسيون يدينون الأدب لصالح العلم وتكنولوجيا التصنيع (الكعبي ، ص ٧٤) . وبتأثير هذا السياق التاريخي ، يحدد منجي الكعبي أزمة الأدب العربي في ثلاث إشكاليات :

هذه الأسئلة : «ماذا يكون مصير الأمة العربية عندئذٍ؟ وما سيبقى مما نعتز به من الحضارة العربية؟ وما تكون منزلةِ الثقافة العربية إذ ذاك من هذه الثقافات الغازية التي تكتسح العالم غرباً وشرقاً؟ وما حظ العربية في التعبير عن هذا العالم الجديد الذي يُزج بنا فيه ولا ينبغي أن نلجه القهقرى؟» (ص ١٢) . [1] وأما المستوى الثاني لعرض ثنائية التقدم والتخلف فحرّكته قضية الحرية التي اتخذت بُعْدين ، أولهما تحرير الأرض العربية المغتصبة من الكيان الصهيوني ، وثانيهما تعرية الأنظمة العربية الاستبدادية التي تكرّس التخلّف السياسي ، وتلاحق الكتّاب والأدباء بالمنع أو السجن ، فتضع حجاباً ثقيلاً على حرية التعبير [2]. وهو ما تجلى في ثلاث ورقات بحثية من الخمس ، تميزت بنبرة جدلية حادة ، تجسد نظرة العقلية النقدية والأدبية العربية إلى التكنولوجيا حينئذ .

لقد لعبت التكنولوجيا الجديدة - وقتئذ - دوراً جوهرياً في العالم الغربي ، بل ثمة من يعتقد في تفوقها على الإيديولوجيا . وأما في العالم العربي فلعب التخلف التكنولوجي الدور الأهم في هزيمة ١٩٦٧ ، حتى اعتقد البعض أن مشكلتنا في الأساس مشكلة إلكترونية ، وأننا

> لن نستعيد حقنا وماء وجهنا السليبين إلا عن طريق الجدارة التكنولوجية وحدها . . . فنحن نعيش في عصر لعل من حسناته أنه لا يرحم التخلف والتلكؤ . فإذا كانت أمة كالولايات المتحدة وهي في طليعة البلدان المتقدمة قد وجدت في القمر السوفييتي الأول تحدياً لمنعتها وكرامتها التكنولوجيتين فراحت تعيد النظر بمناهجها العلمية والتعليمية ، فما أحرانا نحن بأن نفعل شيئاً من هذا ، ما دمنا نواجه التحدي في عقر دارنا . (الشوك ، ص ص ١٠٣-١٠٤)

ولكن «شيئاً من هذا» لم يحدث . لذا يكاد الحديث عن أثر التكنولوجيا في الأدب العربي يكون من قبيل وضع العربة قبل الحصان ، بالنظر إلى حالة التردي العلمي والتعليمي والصناعي عند العرب ، وبخاصة أن الثورة العلمية الحديثة في الغرب تتجسد في الصناعة الإلكترونية والإنتاج الضخم بالجملة «الذي تنهض به وتسيره العقول الإلكترونية . أو بعبارة أخرى سنبقى بعيدين عن جوهر هذه الثورة العلمية الجديدة ما لم تشملنا

تحاول هذه المقالة أولاً تتبع الجدل العربي حول الأدب العربي والتكنولوجيا ، قبل محمد سناجلة ، الذي بدأ في تونس عام ١٩٧٣ ، ثم خفت حتى أثاره حسام الخطيب ، فخصّص كتاباً كاملاً بعنوان **الأدب والتكنولوجيا وجسر النص المفرّع** صدر عام ١٩٩٦، وفي العام التالي مباشرة أصدر أحمد فضل شبلول كتاباً بعنوان **أدباء الإنترنت : أدباء المستقبل** يسعى فيه إلى عقد زواج سعيد بين الأدب والتكنولوجيا الرقمية . وتسعى المقالة ثانياً إلى استكشاف فرضيات ما سُمِّي بـ«نظرية الواقعية الرقمية» عند سناجلة ، وما تنطوي عليه من تصور للإنسان والمجتمع والعالم ، لاقى عند بعض النقاد العرب تأييداً بل إيضاحاً دفاعياً . ثم أحاول ثالثاً ورابعاً تلمُّس المآل الذي من المحتمل أن يؤول إليه الإنسان والعالم سياسياً واقتصادياً وأنطولوجيا ، في ظل «نظرية الواقعية الرقمية» التي تريد تأسيس أدب عربي رقمي .

أولاً ، الجدل العربي حول الأدب والتكنولوجيا قبل سناجلة

في الفترة من ١٨ حتى ٢٥ مارس عام ١٩٧٣ ، انعقد في تونس المؤتمر التاسع للأدباء العرب ، وكان محوره الرئيسي الأول «الأدب العربي والثورة التكنولوجية في النصف الثاني من القرن العشرين» ، ونُشرت بحوثه في مجلة **الموقف الأدبي** ، أبريل ١٩٧٣ . وبالتزامن صدرت مجلة **الآداب** ، وبها تغطية لوقائع المؤتمر تضمنت نشر كلمات الوفود في حفله الافتتاحي (انظر «وقائع») .

يلفت النظر في الكلمات الافتتاحية عرض ثنائية تقدم العالم الغربي في مقابل تخلف العالم العربي بمستويين ، الأول تجريدي لا يضع في حسبانه حالة الأدب والأدباء في ظل الأنظمة السياسية العربية وقتئذ ، والاكتفاء بالإشارة إلى تعطل حركة «الاجتهاد» عند العرب في شتَّى المجالات وضرورة إقامة توازن جديد بين عناصر الثقافة يستهدف الإلمام بأهم مكتسبات العلم الحديث ، وبخاصة أن معظم مرافق حياة العرب ترتبط بما يأتي من الغرب من أدوات وآلات وخبرات ، «ذلك أن الذين يصنعون هذا العالم السحري الجديد كلهم من غير العرب» («وقائع» ، ص ص ١١-١٢) . وفي هذا العالم السحري الجديد الذي يفرضه الغرب على بقية العالم ، لا بد أن يلقي المثقفون والأدباء العرب على أنفسهم

الأدب العربي والتكنولوجيا الرقمية: محاولة استكشافية

حسام نايل

مقدمة

تسعى هذه المقالة إلى محاولة استكشاف أسس العلاقة بين الأدب العربي المعاصر والتكنولوجيا الرقمية، وفحص الفرضيات الداعية إلى ضرورة قيامها، وبخاصة بعد تحققها فعلياً حين أصدر الكاتب الأردني محمد سناجلة أول رواية عربية رقمية عام ٢٠٠١ بعنوان **ظلال الواحد** على موقعه الإلكتروني الشخصي، أدخل في تكوينها تقنيات رقمية يستحيل معها النشر الورقي، ثم أتبعها بكتيب تنظيري عام ٢٠٠٤ عنوانه **رواية الواقعية الرقمية**، يبشر فيه بميلاد أدب عربي جديد لعصر جديد هو عصر التكنولوجيا الرقمية، ويضع فيه أسس ما أسماه محمد أسليم «نظرية الواقعية الرقمية». وقد ترتب على كتيبه التنظيري إثارة جدل حول ما يُسمى «أدب عربي رقمي» يعتمد التقنيات الرقمية بوصفها مكوناً جوهرياً في الأدب. وينطوي تنظيره على مجموعة فرضيات حول الإنسان والمجتمع والعالم جديدة تماماً على السياقات العربية. ولم تكن دعوته بدعة عابرة أو هرطقة طائرة في الهواء، إذ ترتب عليها إنشاء مؤسسة فريدة من نوعها هي اتحاد كتاب الإنترنت العرب، الذي أسّسه سناجلة مع آخرين في مارس عام ٢٠٠٥، ولا يزال قائماً في الواقع الافتراضي (انظر اتحاد)، فاكتسبت دعوته سنداً قوياً. في هذه الأثناء وما بعدها، عُدّ سناجلة رائداً للأدب العربي الرقمي، وبخاصة بعد توالي أعماله الأدبية الرقمية، فصدرت تجربته الرقمية الثانية **شات: رواية واقعية رقمية**، عام ٢٠٠٥، والثالثة **صقيع: تجربة جديدة من أدب الواقعية الرقمية**، عام ٢٠٠٦، والرابعة **ظلال العاشق: التاريخ السري لكموش**، عام ٢٠١٦. وتَدافع نقاد الأدب يكتبون في تقنيات الأدب الرقمي ومؤهلات الكاتب الرقمي وأنسب البرامج الإلكترونية للكتابة الرقمية. ولم تكن دعوةُ سناجلة أول الأمر بل تتمّته، فثمة تاريخ عربي – وإن كان قصيراً – لجدل العلاقة بين الأدب العربي والتكنولوجيا.

---. "What I Learned under the Ground." Robery Kelly. April 20, 2019. <http://rk-ology.com/2019/04/>.

King, Andrew David. "Too Philosophical for a Poet": A Conversation with Charles Bernstein." *Boundary 2* 44.3 (August 1, 2017): 17-57.

Klippinger, David W. *The Mind's Landscape: William Bronk and Twentieth-Century American Poetry*. Newark: U of Delaware P, 2006.

Nemerov, Howard. *Reflexions on Poetry & Poetics*. New Brunswick, NJ: Rutgers UP, 1972.

Nietzsche, Friedrich. *Twilight of the Idols, or, How to Philosophize with the Hammer*. Trans. Richard Polt. Indianapolis: Hackett Publishing Company, 1997.

Olsen, Karen Yelena, ed. *On the Wing: American Poems of Air and Space Flight*. Iowa: Iowa UP, 2005.

Olson, Charles. *Collected Prose*. Berkeley: U of California P, 1997.

Perloff, Marjorie. "Spectral Telepathy: The Late Style of Susan Howe." *Transatlantica* 1 (2016): 1-15.

"Robert Kelly (Poet)." *Wikipedia*. March 13, 2019. <https://en.wikipedia.org/wiki/Robert_Kelly_(poet)>.

Robert Kelly: Work in Progress. <https://urlzs.com/kmm2p>.

Rothenberg, Jerome. "1960: A First Remembrance." *Jacket 2*. May 3, 2011. <https://jacket2.org/article/1960-first-remembrance>.

---. "Why Deep Image?" *Trobar* 3 (1961): 31-32.

Shucard, Alan. *American Poetry: The Puritans Through Walt Whitman*. Amherst: The U of Massachusetts P, 1988.

Siracusa, Joseph M. and Aiden Warren. *Presidential Doctrines: U.S. National Security from George Washington to Barack Obama*. NY: Rowman & Littlefield, 2016.

Sutro, Esther. *Nicolas Poussin*. London: Jonathan Cape and the Medici Society Ltd., 1923.

Trowbridge, John Townsend. "Reminiscences of Walt Whitman." *The Atlantic Monthly* 89.2 (February 1902): 163-75. <https://www.theatlantic.com/past/docs/unbound/poetry/whitman/walt.htm>.

Whitman, Walt. *Leaves of Grass: A Textual Variorum of the Printed Poems*. Vol. I. NY: New York UP, 1980.

---. *Poetry and Prose*. NY: The Library of America, 1982.

Williams, William Carlos. *In the American Grain*. NY: New Directions, 2009.

Zukofsky, Louis. *Prepositions: The Collected Critical Essays of Louis Zukofsky*. NY: Horizon P, 1968.

---. *Parsing*. NY: Asylum's P, 1976.

---. "Poetry and/or the Sacred." *Jacket* 14 (July 2001). <http://jacketmagazine.com/14/bernstein-sacred.html>.

---. *Recalculating*. Chicago: The U of Chicago P, 2013.

---. *Rough Trades*. LA: Sun & Moon P, 1991.

---. "TLS on Susan Howe and Rae Armantrout." *TLS*. September 23, 2011. *Jacket 2*. October 9, 2011. <https://urlzs.com/2xUX5>.

Bidart, Frank. *Star Dust*. NY: Straus and Giroux, 2005.

Bierds, Linda. *Roget's Illusion*. NY: G. P. Putnam's Sons, 2014.

Brigley, Zoë. "What is L=A=N=G=U=A=G=E Poetry?" *Zoë Brigley: Teaching Blog*. February 09, 2007. <https://blogs.warwick.ac.uk/zbrigley2/entry/what_is_language>.

Burton, Robert. *The Anatomy of Melancholy*. Philadelphia: Claxton & Company, 1883.

Clover, Joshua. *The Totality for Kids*. Berkeley and Los Angeles: U of California P, 2006.

Emerson, Ralph Waldo. *Emerson's Prose and Poetry*. Eds. Joel Porte and Saundra Morris. NY: W. W. Norton & Company, 2001.

Gray, Richard. *A History of American Literature*. Oxford: Blackwell, 2004.

Howe, Fanny. *Second Childhood*. Minneapolis: Graywolf P, 2014.

Howe, Susan. *Europe of Trusts*. NY: New directions, 1990.

---. *Pierce-Arrow*. NY: New Directions, 1999.

---. *The Quarry*. NY: New Directions, 2015.

---. *Singularities*. Hanover: UP of New England, 1990.

---. *That This*. NY: New Directions, 2010.

Joris, Pierre and Peter Cockelbergh, eds. *A Voice Full of Cities: The Collected Essays of Robert Kelly*. NY: Contra Mondum P, 2014.

Kelly, Robert. "aprA2003." *Robert Kelly Manuscripts*. *Bard Digital Commons*. April 2003. <https://urlzs.com/Xrmg5>.

---. "aprC2005." *Robert Kelly Manuscripts*. *Bard Digital Commons*. April 2005. <https://digitalcommons.bard.edu/rk_manuscripts/782/>.

---. "Ariadne." *Robert Kelly Manuscripts*. *Bard Digital Commons*. October 1991. <https://urlzs.com/Wh5wC>.

---. "junF1993." *Robert Kelly Manuscripts*. *Bard Digital Commons*. June 1993. <https://digitalcommons.bard.edu/rk_manuscripts/1270/>.

---. *Lapis*. Boston: Black Sparrow Books, 2005.

---. "May Day." *Robert Kelly Manuscripts*. *Bard Digital Commons*. June 2005. <https://digitalcommons.bard.edu/rk_manuscripts/442/>.

لكن كل هذه الافتراضات تصير بلا أهمية حين تتمرد الصور المركزية على بقية النص : صورة الحمار الوحشي في بيجامته الزاهية ، وهو يسير مُتَّئِدًا في سكينة هذا الصباح فوق العشب المخضلّ .

* * *

لكي تكتمل الدائرة ، يبدو أن لا مناص من العودة إلى عنوان المقالة : «إطلالة على الشعر الأمريكي "المعاصر": تأملات» ، وذلك للتأكيد ، أولاً ، على أن الأمر يتعلق هنا بمجرد إطلالة لا بدراسة مستفيضة ، لا لأن إنجاز مثل هذه الدراسة مستحيل ، بل لأن ذلك يتطلب وقتاً أطول ، ومجالاً أرحب من مجرد مقالة في مجلة دورية . فلا يمكن لأي إطلالة ، والإطلالة بطبيعتها نظرة وجيزة في زمنها ، وتتم عن بعد ، وعلى علوٍّ لا يسمح بالانغماس في المشهد ، أن تتعرف على جميع تشعباته وأن تحيط بكل جوانبه . ثانياً ، وُضعتْ صفةُ «معاصر» قصداً بين مزدوجين ، وذلك للتأكيد على الطابع الإشكالي لهذه الصفة ، وقد تمت مناقشة ذلك في سياقه . ثالثاً ، لا بد أيضاً من الإشارة ، دَرْءاً لأي التباس ، إلى العنوان الفرعي الذي ينص على أن هذا العرض مبني على تأملات شخصية في مجريات المشهد الشعري الراهن في الولايات المتحدة ، وذلك بالتركيز على عدد جدّ محدود من النصوص ، وهي بذلك لا يمكن أن تمثل المشهد في شموليته وضخامته وكل ما يكتنفه من تعقيدات مرتبطة بالتأريخ والتنظير والممارسة . رابعاً ، هذه التأملات لا تلزم إلا صاحبها . وأخيراً ، ليست هذه إلا محاولة لإشراك قارئ العربية في هذه الإطلالة على جزء من مشهد قد لا يكون مطلعاً على أغلب جوانبه .

* كل النصوص المقتبسة في هذه المقالة من ترجمة الكاتب .

المراجع

Ashbery, John. *Selected Poems*. NY: Viking Penguin, 1985.
Baraka, Amiri. "Somebody Blew Up America." <http://www.lem.seed.pr.gov.br/arquivos/File/livrosliteraturaingles/sbua2.pdf>.
Bernstein, Charles. *Log Rhythms*. NY: Granary Books, 1998.
---. *My Way: Speeches and Poems*. Chicago: U of Chicago P, 1999.
---. *Nude Formalism*. LA: Sun & Moon P, 1989.

فإن بوسع القارئ أن يتوقف عند البيت الثالث، وبوسعه كذلك أن يواصل ليتوقف عند البيت السادس فيتغير المعنى. وأيّاً كان اختيار القارئ، فإن الصورة المركزية تظل ثابتة: كلمةٌ غير منطوقة مكتوبةٌ على ردف القمر. ولعل هذا ما يفسر عجزَ السارد-الكاتب-الشاعر عن الهبوط من القمر. إذا كانت «نفسه» هي الكلمة المكتوبة، فإن هبوطه يعني أن يتركها هناك، أن يتخلى عن نفسه. فمن يُنزِّهُه عن العبث إن هو قرّر أن يفعل ذلك؟ ولأن «النفس» هي الكلمة المكتوبة، فلا بد أن تظل «ظهيرة اللغة»، كما يقول في قصيدة أخرى، «بعيدةً، بعيدة» (Kelly, "Ariadne" n. pag). وحين ينظر كيلي إلى فن الشعر، يتخذ، كما فعل قبله شعراء كثيرون، عبارة هوراس "ARS POETICA" عنواناً لقصيدته. ويكون تعريف فن الشعر صورة عميقة، بسيطة ومركبة: «سكينةُ الصباح/ونحو عمقها ينطقُ ناطقٌ»، نحو العمق، لا نحو السطح. صورة خبرية وفي الآن ذاته إنشائية. على خلفية سكينة الصباح، ينطق ناطق. الناطق نكرة: مجهول غير معروف. والمنطوق كذلك مجهول. قد يكون مقطعاً، أو كلمة، أو بيتاً، أو أنشودة. صوتٌ على خلفية صوت. ذلك فن الشعر. إخبار وفي الوقت ذاته إنشاء:

يُسمَّى هذا فن الشعر
بوالو وهوميروس يقفان قريباً
حمارٌ وحشي يسير على أجمة التلِّ فوق عشب مُخْضَلّ

المستبعَدُ يُخَلِّفُ طعمَ
زيفٍ في الفم خافتا
يُعلِّمَ المتكلمَ بعد ذلك
أن يقولَ قولاً أصدق.

(Kelly, "junF1993" n. pag)

لم يقل هنا «قول الصدق»، بل قال «قولاً أصدق»، مؤثراً بذلك النسبية على الإطلاق. لكن لماذا يقف بوالو بجانب هوميروس؟ ألأن بوالو كان قد ترجم هوراس ولونجينوس وتطاول فتجرأ على انتقاد بلاغة هوميروس؟ ألأن احتمال جمعِهما أمرٌ مستبعد؟ لا بأس، فالمتكلم يتعلم مما هو بعيد الاحتمال أيضاً، يتعلم من طعمه الزائف، أن يُؤثر النسبية على الإطلاق.

ويكون المحيطُ سماء .
أوروبا غيمةٌ نأتي منها
المرةَ تلو المرة .
وأمريكا في الأسفل هاهنا . (Kelly, *Lapis* 125)

هذا ما رأته العين . هذا ما تكلم عنه الخطيبُ المتكتم ، وبأمر من الاستنتاجات . ربابنةٌ يحاولون أن يحافظوا على توازن الطائرات على عُلوِّ آلاف الأقدام . لكن ، كيف غدوا فجأةً أحباراً؟ كيف صارت مكالماتُهم ترانيمَ ربانية؟ وهل تنجح صلواتهم في إنقاذ الهيكل المهلهل؟ وهل يظل الفضاءُ فضاء ، وتظل السماءُ محيطاً؟ وما بال القارة-الغيمة التي يواصل الأمريكان الهبوط منها نحو سفالة قارة دنيا؟ وإذا كانت الاستنتاجات قد أمرتْ الشاعرَ بأن يتكلم ، فأوْلى لها أن تأمر القارئ بأن يصمت . فليس مِن الهين على الشاعر أن يتكلم ، فلا بد للشاعر ، إذا تكلم ، أن يكون سارداً : أن يروي حكاية . وقبل ذلك ، لا بد أن يكتب . يكتبَ نفسَه ، لا أن يكتب عن نفسه . لا بد أن يصير كتابة . يقول كيلي في هذا المقطع :

لكي أتكلم
لكي أحكي

كتبتُ نفسي

على ردف القمر
وجدتُ كلمة
لم تُنطَق قط

أنا الآن عاجزٌ عن الاهتداء إلى طريق أهبط منه مرة أخرى .
(Kelly, "aprC2005" n. pag)

رغم نثريته الظاهرة ، فإن المقطع نُظِمَ بشكل مدروس تتيح التراكيبُ فيه أكثرَ من قراءة . المقطع سباعيُّ الأبيات ، وهو خالٍ تماماً من علامات الترقيم . الأبيات (الأعداد) فيه مرتبة على نحو : ٢ ، ١ ، ٣ ، ١ . وهكذا ،

المقدسة. قد يكون عُرْيُ الصوائت مُغوياً، ولكن وقار السواكن يعدل، بدون شك، كفتي الميزان. اللغة إذن لم تكن قط عفيفة، والكلمات فيها لم تَكنَّ قط عذارى. لكن لا يبدو أن أي شاعر قد تملكهن تماماً. فهن إنما يسمحنِ للشعراء المارقين بالمبيت. بالمبيت فقط. الكلمات/الفتيات يحفظن فعلا قداسة كؤوسهن، ويحفظن كلَّ تغير يلحق بهن. ومع ذلك، فإن النهر، كما جاء في قصيدة «تجربة»، «غيمةٌ لا يتذكرها أحد». هكذا، تظل الصورة العميقة في قصائد كيلي نِدّاً للغة الواصفة. ففي قصيدة «الخطيب المتكتم» "Secret Orator"، يصف السارد كيف مرّ ذات ليلة بالشاعر أودن، في جرينتش فليدج، وهو في أرذل العمر. كان يسرع الخطو، وكان، فيما يبدو، يعاني من متاعب الشيخوخة، لكن ذهنه الفتيّ كان ذا معرفة غزيرة؛ ذهنٌ يلهم السارد بأن يؤوِّل التجاعيد الشهيرة على وجه أودن بأنها تدوينات لحكم مأثورة، لعلها من تلك الحكم التي كان الشاعر نوڤاليس يرسلها إلى مواسم صيف لم تأتِ بعد. ولأن السارد نفسَه شاعر، فإنه يحشر نفسه مع أودن ونوڤاليس في زمرة الشعراء الضائعين، وسط قيم مطلقة جديدة، في أقاليم الشمال. وعنوان القصيدة مستوحى من كتاب روبرت برتون Burton الشهير **تشريح المناخوليا** *The Anatomy of Melancholy* حيث يصف برتون العين بأنها «خطيبٌ متكتم»، ويقول عنها إنها «القوّادةُ الرائدة، بوابةُ الهوى، فبالنظرات، والغمزِات، واللمحات، والبسمات الحميمة، وبالمحاورات العديدة كثيراً ما تُوفق العيونُ بين العشاق، ويَفهم بعضُها بعضا، قبل أن يتفوهوا بأي كلمة» (471). ورغم تَكَتُّم الخطيب، فإن الاستنتاجات تأمرُ الشاعرَ بأن يتكلم:

هناك حَبْرٌ
في كل قُمرة
ترنيمتُه

تُصلِّي لكي تتزن
الطائرةُ إذ تسندُ ركائزُ
الجناحين الهيكلَ المهلهلَ
لكي يظلَّ في الفضاء

فإنه، كالنهار، لا يحتاج إلى دليل. ولذلك، تكون مقاربته شبه دينية، مقاربة تُسلّم بالنعمة وتؤمن باللطف الإلهي. وفي إحدى مطولاته، «ما تعلمته وأنا تحت الأرض» - ويبدو أنها عن رحلة إلى العالم السفلي، مستلهمة من دانتي ومن أدب الرحلات إلى العالم الآخر عموماً - يصادف المتكلمُ صديقَه الشاعر فيليب سوبو Philippe Soupault، رفيق بروتون وأراجون ومترجم بليك إلى الفرنسية، وهو يقود بعض الحُجاج إلى صخرة كان القديس يوحنا في غابر العصور قد نقش عليها رسماً. كان القديس يحيى يأخذ الكتابة أو النقشَ بقوة، بجدية، وكان على الحجاج من المسيحيين الجدد، في ذلك العالم الغسقي، أن يتفكروا في نية القديس وهو يلوث بالنص، وبيديه المقدستين، صمتَ تلك الصخرة. وأياً كانت نية القديس، فلا شك في أنه كان يأخذ المكتوبَ بقوة. يتساءل المتكلم: هل كان ما كتبه أو نقشه القديسُ أصلاً نصاً؟ فيكون الجواب حاسماً: «لم يكن أحدٌ حجة ليعرف ما يجري في ذهنك وأنت تنظر» (Kelly, "What I Learned" n. pag).

وفي قصيدة «وجه الصيام» "Visage de carême" أيضاً، تسود اللغة الواصفة، رغم أن الموضوع يبدو ذا غنائية مرهفة:

لكن كيف استطعتُ أن أخمِّن
أن الكلمات فتيات؟

هل الصوائتُ العاريةُ وحدها
قادتْني إلى قلعتهن العفيفة

حيث يحفظن كأسَهنَّ المقدسة
ويحفظن كلَّ تغير جديد من تغيراتهن

وهل كنتُ أنا المارق المرئي الوحيد؟
لكنهن سمحن لي بالمبيت. (Kelly, "aprA2003" n. pag)

يوحي التساؤل الأخير هنا بأن المتكلم لم يكن المارق الوحيد الذي تمكن من التسلل إلى قلعة العفّة. ولعل في ذلك طعناً في عفة الكلمات/الفتيات، فقد تسلل إلى القلعة كثيرون قبله، ولا شك في أنهم شربوا جميعاً من الكأس

وأنها ماضية في سعيها الحثيث إلى صياغة صورة تُلامس نهايةَ الحلم-النحو-الكتاب، صورةِ تلامس فراغ صفحة غير مكتوبة . وفي النهاية ، حين يتم التعرف على مجاهل القصيدة ، تكون المعرفة مجرد استحضار بواسطة الذاكرة ، ويكون الفناء موضوع تلك المعرفة : الموتى ، وهلاك المعارف ، وهلاك المدن ، وأخيراً صفحات شبيهة بحقول ممتدة في العراء ، صفحات فارغة غير مكتوبة .

وفي مقابل هذه الصفحات الفارغة التي تنتهي إليها قصيدة «(صفحة من حلم :)» ، نجد هدية مهداةً إلى القارئ أو إلى الشاعر الحالم في قصيدة "Material Given in Dream, 2/3 April 2003" («مادة أهديت في حلم ، ٣/٢ أبريل ٢٠٠٣») . وليست الهدية هنا إلا تأملات حول الكتابة والكتاب ، يمكن أن تنسحب ، حسب ما تقدم ، على الحلم وعلى النحو :

الكتابةُ هي ما نفعله لنستحقَّ الكتاب . الكتابُ هبة .

Kitab

ونكدح ، إذ نكتبُ الكلمات ،
وحين يحالفنا الحظ ،
يكون ما كتبناه جزءاً من الكتاب .

ليس واضحاً أي علاقة تربط الحافزَ بالمهارة أو بالاجتهاد ، من جهة ، وبتحقق وجود الكتاب ، من جهة ثانية . فذلك الوجودُ لا يمكن التنبؤ به ، لكنه جليٌّ لا لبس فيه . يتصوره البعضُ كما يتصور المسيحيون النعمة .

(Kelly, "aprA2003" n. pag)

لنلاحظ أن الشاعر هنا يستعمل الكلمة العربية kitab (خذ الكتاب بقوة!) ولنلاحظ أن الهدية قُدِّمتْ في حلم ، ولذلك فإن الحالم ، حين يستيقظ ، لن يجد في يده غير الفراغ ، وسيدرك عندئذ أن العقرب وحدها هي التي تقدم الهدايا دون أن تتوقع مقابلاً . ولنلاحظ غيابَ الصور هنا وطغيانَ اللغة التقريرية الواصفة ، فهل يُستنتج من هذا أن الكتابةَ تَستنفد ذاتها حين تعكف على تأمل ذاتها؟ ليس بالضرورة . فمع أن وجود الكتاب يظل في ظهر الغيب ،

الرب المُتقِنة والعالمُ بعيد

ومن يستطيع أن يجزم
أنها بدتْ هكذا
تتواصلُ الكلماتُ لتصوغ هيئةً
أنيقةٍ دقيقةٍ تلامس الحلم ،
تلامس بياضَ الصفحة الأخيرة

ثم تواصلت الصفحة ، موضحةً ، بطريقة لا أمل لي في أن أوضحَ بمثلها ، تلك الأبياتَ القليلةَ التي رأيتُها فعلاً في الحلم ، ثم استطعتُ أن أحتفظ بها ... وسأتعرفُ فيما بعد على النبر البلفاستي في الكلمة الأخيرة من كل قصيدة ... تذكرتُ فتياتِ الوادي ، وتذكرتُ ماكنيس وكلّ الموتى ، تذكرتُ السككَ الحديديةَ الهالكة ، والمدنَ الهالكة ، والأصدقاءَ الهالكين ، والصفحاتِ العذراءَ أبداً ، تتهيأ لحياة جديدة ، وتذكرتُ حقولاً تبدو تماماً هكذا في العراء .

====================================

(*Robert Kelly: Work in Progress* n. pag)

يوحي العنوان بأن الأمر يتعلق بصفحة واحدة من حلم به صفحات كثيرة . في عمق الصورة إذن أنَّ الحلم كتاب ، وبما هو كذلك ، فإنه مكتوب . النحو حلم ، كتاب مكتوب ، لكنه مجهول البداية ومجهول النهاية . قد تتوالى الصفحات أمام الحالم-الناحي ، لكنه لا يدرك سوى الصفحة المعروضة أمامه . والواقع أن القصيدة نثيرة : صورة لنص منثور في قلبه أبيات منظومة . الشعر قلب النثر النابض : لا للحدود المفترضة . كانت بداية الجملة في صفحة سابقة ، والجملة وحدة نحوية مكتملة ، لكنها الآن أصبحت على الصفحة الحالية جزءاً ولم تعد مكتملة ، وهي بذلك خارج مجال نفوذ النحو ، أو مجال نفوذ الحلم . بداية الصفحة إذن ليست بداية ، ونهايتها مفتوحة على العراء . أما المقطع المنظوم في قلب الصفحة المنثورة فيُحذّر الشاعرَ-الناحي-الحالمَ ، يذكره بأنه الآن ، في غمرة الحلم ، مسلوب الإرادة : «أنتَ الآن في أيادي الربّ» . يُذكّره بأنه عاجز عن بلوغ أي يقين بخصوص البداية . لكنه يذكره أيضاً بأن الكلمات ، مع ذلك متواصلة ،

الوعي ويُنفَى إلى عالم الحلم. وسرعان ما ينشأ عن هذا الافتراض سؤال متعلق بالصمت: إن يكن النحو فعلاً حلماً، فهل الصمت إفاقة منه؟ في أفول الأوثان، يقول نيتشه عن عقلنة اللغة: «"المنطق" في اللغة - يا لها من أنثى عجوز محتالة! أخشى أننا لم نتخلص من الرب، لأننا لا نزال نؤمن بالنحو» (Nietzsche 21). المألوف، مرة أخرى، أن النحو مرتبط بالصوت. لكنه هنا مرتبط بالأحلام وبأضغاثها. فهل يَترتب أن الصمت يقظة من النحو/الحلم؟ أليس لليقظة ذاتها أحلامها الصامتة والصائتة؟ وماذا لو انعكست الآية فكان الصمت حلماً وكان النحو يقظة؟ إن يصح الافتراض في كل وجوهه، فإن المستقبل مجرد غد آخر مأهول بأجيال أخرى. فهل في ذلك إشارة إلى عود أبدي؟ ألن يكون ذلك مملاً وعقيماً؟ قد تكون الشهوات محببة، لكنها لا تقدم تفسيرات شاملة، لأن المنطق في اللغة مجرد عجوز محتالة. لكن القصيدة تنتهي إلى «صميم الجملة»، لتوحي بذلك بأن الحاجة إلى النحو أكثر من الحاجة إلى الشهوة: العاشق في حاجة إلى مصدر المعشوق، والمعشوق في حاجة إلى صفة العاشق. ولا حاجة بعد ذلك إلى أي حيل بلاغية. لكن العاشق صفة والمعشوق صفة، فأين العشق؟ الحاجة فقر وافتقار، فهل هذا هو صميم الجملة؟ الجملة. الصفة. المصدر. لا سبيل إلى الإفاقة من حلم النحو! وإذا كان من المستحيل أن تتم هزيمةُ الحلم-النحو، فما المانع من التحالف معه؟ يبدو أن هذا هو ما يقوم به الشاعر فعلاً في هذه القصيدة، إذ يحاول أن يستنقذ صفحةً منفلتةً من حلم منفلت، معتمداً على هُجْنة يمتزج فيها المنثور بالمنظوم، حيث يَدسُّ في طيات المنثور مقطعاً منظوماً يحرص مع ذلك على أن يرصَّه ببنط مختلف:

(صفحة من حلم:)

===================================

بدت الصفحةُ هكذا، أي أن الجملةَ كانت متواصلةً من صفحة سابقة، لكن، ما هي الصفحة السابقة من الحلم؟ فهل الجواب أوضح مما لو كنتُ قد سألتُ: ما هو الحلم الأسبق؟ لكنها بدتْ هكذا، كما تبدو الصفحة في كتاب...

أنت الآن في أيادي

كلّه ، بكل مكوناته الصورية ، هو البيت المقصود : هو بيت القصيد . لا عجب ، إذن ، في أن يستكين الشاعر إلى بلوغ بيت يظن أنه كان قد قصده ، فيقول في نبرة دفاعية متحفظة : «ما قصدتُ . . . أكثر مما كتبتُ» . الكتابة إذن قصد ، والقصد كتابة . فكل ما لم يُكتَب ليس مقصوداً . ولا شك في أن المعنى سيواصل ترنحَه أمام ظلال تطرحها الذواتُ الزائفة ، فتتسلل الشقشقة لتحوِّر الاستنتاجَ فيغدو : كل ما لم يُقصد ليس مكتوباً . نفي وإثبات . حتمية في المقصود ، وحتمية في المكتوب .

ولعل إزاحة الحدود بين التنظير والممارسة ، بين كتابة الشعر والتأمل النقدي في التجربة الشعرية ، ناجم عن العلاقة المتوترة بين المكتوب والمقصود . ويتجلى المزج الممنهج بين النظم والتأمل في هذا الانغماس - في اللغة الواصفة - الذي يفرض نفسَه سمةً بارزةً في قصائد كيلي :

إذا كان النحو حلماً ،
فهل الصمت يقظة؟
أذلك ما ينتظرنا
حين تعود الشمس ،
مجردُ غد آخر
مليء بناس آخرين؟
تعالي معي إلى ساعتي ،
أجل ، أحبُّ قبلاتك
لكن ، كلا ، إنها لَيست
تفسيرات شاملة .

أنا محتاج إلى أكثر من ذلك . محتاج إلى مصدرك ،
وأنت في حاجة إلى صفتي .
لا داعي إلى تشبيهات أخرى . فقد بلغنا معاً
صميم الجملة . (Kelly, "May Day" n. pag)

يوحي الافتراض الذي ينطلق منه المتأمل هنا بأن النحو حلم وليس علماً . والنحو ، حسب المألوف ، لغةٌ واصفةٌ ترصد حركية اللغة ، أو هو قواعد معيارية قائمة على الوجوب والجواز والامتناع . لكنه هنا يُقصَى من عالم

وما استطاع هوميروس أن يجدَ البيتَ/الخط
المقصودَ ولا الأعدادَ/الأبياتَ الهائلة المقصودة
التي ظلتْ كامنةً في أخاديد ذهنه
التي أحرقتْ فصار لونُها بنياً واستعادتْ
جاذبيتَها تحت ضباب أيار ، الرذاذُ المنعش
لم يستطع أن ينشد البيتَ المقصود ،
تَرنَّحَ المعنى تحت أشجار تفاح كئيبة
شُذبت في انتظار الربيع ، زهورُها كانت
واهنة الأريج ، بتلاتُها وردية الشحوب ،
حتى حسب العالمَ كلَّه من حوله البيتَ/الخطَّ
المقصود ،
قال : كتبتُ كل هذا
وما قصدتُ ، قال ، أكثر مما كتبت . (Kelly, "Ariadne" n. pag)

يظل البيت والخط يتنازعان في حقول الدلالة على مناطق النفوذ ، وفي البيت الثاني يلتحق بهما العدد والبيت ، ففي الكلمة الأصلية numbers تورية تحيل على الأعداد في الحساب ، وعلى الأبيات في النظم ، وبهذا يمكن أن يُختزَل الزوجان في البيتين (البيت/الخط ، والبيت/العدد) في ثالوث (الخط/ البيت/العدد) ليتأبَّدَ التنازع بين الكم المتصل والكم المنفصل ، وهو تنازع يفسح المجال لتوالي الصور العميقة/المعممة deep images . وهكذا ، يظل الكل (الخطوط ، والأبيات ، والأعداد) كامناً في الذهن ، أما الأبياتُ التي أفلتت وانتقلت مؤقتاً من الكمون إلى التجلي ، فقد سُفعتْ وفقدت رونقها . غير أنها ، وفي توالي الصور العميقة المعممة ، سرعان ما تستعيد نضارتَها بتوالي الفصول . ولا شك في أن الضباب والرذاذ يساعدان على الانتعاش ، لكن صور الشاعر عاجزةٌ عن إنشاد البيت المقصود . لم يعد البيت هنا مجرد بيت ، بل غدا ، على وجه التحديد ، «البيتَ المقصود» . فهل هناك بيت ، أو أبيات ، أو بيوت غيرُ مقصودة؟ لن يسع المعنى (القصد) هنا إلا أن يترنح تحت وطأة الصور المتوالية : وتَرنُّحُ المعنى ذاته هو أولى هذه الصور ، تليها صورة أشجار التفاح الكئيبة المشذبة المتطلعة إلى حلول موسم الربيع ، تليها الزهورُ واهنة الأريج ، ثم البتلات يمتزج فيها الوِردي بالشحوب . وأمام توالي هذه الصور يرتبك الشاعر فيحسب (حسابا ، وحسباناً) أن العالم

لن يعرفوا ، هؤلاء الشعراء القادمون ، وهم الغارقون في قصائدهم التافهة ،
رغبتَهم في أن يكونوا موجزين وجذابين ، ورغبتهم في آن يستغرقوا في النوم ،
أبداً لن يعرفوا . سيصوغون من الشظايا شظايا ، ويطرحون ظلال ذاتهم الزائفة،
ويجعلون الصدى صراخاً .
انظرْ إلى بيت من أبياتي وسترى دزينةً من قصائدهم القميئة منتظرة ، تتنفس هناك بهدوء ،
وتنتظر ، تنتظر أن يسرِّحها قلبُ الذهن أو قلب الجسد ، أو قلب الصدر ، أو قلب النفَس ،

رفقاً ، رفقاً ، ستجد في البيت من أبياتي دزينة ، وفي أعمالي الكاملة ،
ستجد أعداداً هائلةً لا حصر لها

تأملْ بيتاً/خطاً مثل هذا ────────────────────

(Kelly, "Ariadne" n. pag)

وليس يضاهي عنفَ إدانته لهؤلاء هنا ، ووصفهم بالتفاهة والزيف والتنطع والرداءة ، إلا الاعتداد المفرط بنفْسه وبشعره . ويُلاحَظ أن في تعبيره «يسرِّحها قلبُ الذهن أو قلب الجسد ، أو قلب الصدر ، أو قلب النفَس» أصداء من تنظيرات أولسن للنظم الإسقاطي ؛ أما دعوته إلى تأمل البيت/الخط فتقوم على ازدواج معنى كلمة line التي يمكن أن تحيل على الخط باعتباره مفهوماً هندسياً ، وعلى البيت باعتباره وحدة قياس في النظم . وهي هنا تحيل عليهما معاً . فهل البيت في النظم مجرد دالة خطية ، أو أنه مكون هندسي بالغ التعقيد يتلاعب في بناء القصيدة بالكم المتصل والكم المنفصل معاً؟ البيت والخط ، فيما يبدو ، وجهان للعملة ذاتها . وليس إدراك الطبيعة الملغزة لمفهوم البيت/الخط بالأمر الهين ، حتى على الشعراء الرواد المؤسسين مثل أولسن . فها هو كيلي يكتب :

غايته ، وللقلب أن يجد في البيت غايته ، وللذهن أن يقفز على كل شيء ويمضي مباشرة نحو البيت ، وللقلب أن ينقلب فيتراجع نحو المقطع ، لكن لا مفر لأي منهما من التوسل عبر السمع والنفس . ويتتبع أولسن منشأ السُّلالة في النظم فيؤكد :

إنما نشأ المقطع عن اقتران الذهن بالسمع . لكن المقطع ليس إلا المولود الأول من زنا المحارم المقترف في النظم (تلك الخطيئة المصرية ، دائماً تلد التوأم!) . والمولود الثاني هو البيت . وهما معاً ، المقطع والبيت ، ما يُنشئان القصيدة . معاً يُنشئان ذلك الكائن ، ذلك الـ ، ماذا عسانا أن نسميه ، ذلك «الذكاءَ الفرد» ، ذلك المتحكمَ في كل شيء . والبيت ينشأ (وأقسم على ذلك) عن النفَس ، عن تنفس الكاتب ، في اللحظة ذاتها التي يكتب فيها . . . فهو وحده ، أي الكاتب ، يستطيع أن يحدد البيت ، ويحدد مقاسَه ونهايته ، حيث يبلغ نفسُه نهايتَه . (242)

لكن بناء القصيدة لا يقوم بلبنة المقطع ولبنة البيت فحسب ، بل تتضافر في إقامته كافةُ العناصر . فالصورة والصوت والمعنى ، إضافة إلى المقطع والبيت ، تسهم جميعها في تحديد حركية القصيدة . ولذلك ينبغي اعتبار التوترات الفاعلة في القصيدة متأصلةً في كل هذه العناصر .

لنعد الآن من هذا الاستطراد عن النظم الإسقاطي إلى تيار الصورة العميقة لنستعرض تجربة روبرت كيلي أحد روادها الأفذاذ الذين أصَّلوه وأسهموا في تطويره ممارسةً وتنظيراً . وكيلي الآن في منتصف عقده الثامن ، وهو غزير الإنتاج ، نشر ما يربو على خمسين مجموعة شعرية . ويحدد الشعراءَ الذين أثروا في تجربته : كولردج ، بودلير ، باوند ، أبولونير ، فرجيل ، إسخيلوس ، دانتي ، تشوسر ، شكسبير ، درايدن ، لوركا ، رلكه ، هولدرلن ، ستيفنز ، شتاين ، دنكن ، أولسن ، وليامز ، بلاكبرن . وهو هنا إنما يذكر الشعراءَ الأموات ، فهم ، كما يقول : «دائماً مختلفون . إنهم يتغيرون على الدوام» ("Robert Kelly (Poet)" n. pag) . وليس يعادل تقديرَه هذا لشعراء من الماضي إلا استخفافه بشعراء المستقبل . يقول :

الإسقاطي ، وهو مفهوم يرتبط بالمنظور ، أي بالكيفية التي تُسقطُ فيها العينُ أو آلةُ التصوير مشهداً ثلاثي الأبعاد على صورة ثنائية الأبعاد . وفي مقاله الشهير الذي يحمل العنوان نفسه "Projective Verse" ، يضفي أولسن على النظم الإسقاطي صفات ثلاثاً : إذ يصفه بالمقذوف projectile ، والإيقاعي percussive ، والمستقبلي prospective ، ويضعه في مقابل النظم الذي تنتفي عنه صفة الإسقاط non-projective ، وهو ما اصطلح النقاد الفرنسيون على تسميته بالنظم «المنغلق» (239) . وينحاز أولسن إلى النظم الإسقاطي على حساب النظم التقليدي المنغلق الذي يرى أنه لا يزال ، رغم تجربة كل من باوند ووليامز ، سائداً في الشعر الأمريكي . وهكذا ، يوصي أولسن بأن يكون الشعر مسايراً العصر ، وأن يستوعب قوانين وإمكانات معينة للنفَس ، نفَس كاتب الشعر وكذلك سَمْعه ، كما يبشر بما يتيحه الانفتاح الذي يتصف به هذا النظم الإسقاطي الذي يدعو إليه من إمكانات لا تتيحها الأشكال المنغلقة (241) . فلو مارس الشاعر عمله في الفضاء المفتوح ، وهو ما يسميه أولسن «التأليف انطلاقاً من الحقل» composition by field ، بدلاً من البيت والمقطوعة والقالب الكلي ، أي ما يمثل الأساس في الأشكال الموروثة ، لكان أكثر وعياً بما يطلق عليه the kinetics of the thing ، أي حركية القصيدة (240) . فالقصيدة ، في عُرْفه ، طاقة تُنقَل ، عن طريق القصيدة نفسها ، من المصدر الذي استمدها منه الشاعر إلى القارئ . ويؤكد أولسن أن الشاعر ، لو اتخذ الفضاء المفتوح منطلقاً له ، لأدرك فوراً أهمية المبدأ الأساسي المتمثل في أن الشكل لا يمكن أن يكون إلا امتداداً للمضمون (240) . ثم ينتقل إلى توضيح الصيرورة التي يضفي فيها هذا المبدأ القالبَ الشكلي على الطاقة ، والتي تتلخص في أن المدركات الحسية ينبغي أن ترتبط وتتوالى دون انقطاع (240) . ولأن للنفَس والسمع أهمية خاصة في مفهوم النظم الإسقاطي ، لدى أولسن ، فإنه يقترح هذه الصيغة السداسية التي يتناظر فيها ، ويتآزر فيها ، كلّ من الذهن ، والسمع ، والإحساس ، والنفَس ، والمقطع ، والبيت :

الرأس ، عن طريق الأذن ، إلى المقطع
القلب ، عن طريق النفَس ، إلى البيت . (242)

ويبدو أن مركزية الأذن والنفَس في هذه الصيغة تكاد تهمش باقي الحدود ، لكن المركز لا يمكن أن يقصي المصدر أو الغاية . وللذهن أن يجد في المقطع

العميقة ، يعتبر روتنبرج القصيدة بنياناً طبيعياً ينشأ عن الرؤية الانفعالية ، ويدعو إلى محاولة رؤية العالم ، في كل تفاصيله الطبيعية والمعاصرة ، انطلاقاً من التسليم بانعدام الفروق بين الرائي والأشياء المرئية (Rothenberg, "Why Deep Image?" 31-32) . وبعد مضي نصف قرن على نشوء هذه الحركة ، يتذكر أن أهميتها تكمن في أنها قادت روادها إلى محاولة تأسيس نظرية شعرية قائمة على أسس عِرْقية ، أو ما يسميه ethnopoetics ، أي السعي إلى إنشاء نظرية جديدة/قديمة ترتبط بأعماق الثقافات واللغات الإنسانية وتترسخ فيها (Rothenberg, "1960?" n. pag) . ويرى كيلي أن هذا النمط من الشعر لا تسوده الصورة بالضرورة ، بل يشكلُ فيه إيقاعُ الصور الحركةَ السائدة في القصيدة . ويبدو أن كيلي قد استوحى هذا التوصيف من الشاعر السوريالي اليوناني نيكولاس كالاس Nicolas Calas ، الذي يَعتبر الإيقاعَ ناشئًا عن حركة الصور (Joris and Cockelbergh 9) . ويقترح كيلي هذا الأساس الإبستيمولوجي للعلاقة بين الشعر والصورة :

> تنشأ المدركاتُ عن الأحلام أو عن اليقظة ، عن اللاشعور أو عن شبكية العين اليقظة . والشعر ، مثل واقع الحلم ، منعطف يلتقي عنده ما قد تمّت معاناته بالتجربة ، وما لم تتم قط معاناته . إنه ، مثل واقع اليقظة ، تحققٌ لما تم تَصوره وما لم يتم تصوره . والمدركات تتجسد في اللغة لكي يتم التعبير عنها . الشعر لا يستطيع أن يعرض الإدراك في عريه . والصورة هي المُدرَك المكسو . (كما ورد في Joris and Cockelbergh 9)

وقد جرى استعمال الاسم في الإشارة إلى شعر كل من روتنبرج ، وكيلي ، ودايان واكوسكي Diane Wakoski ، وكليتون إشلمان Clayton Eshleman . وبعد ذلك ، تطور شعر الصورة العميقة كما مارسه الرواد ونظّروا له على يد الشاعر روبرت بلاي Robert Bly ، بحيث أصبح الأسلوب ميالا إلى أن يعتمد على المحسوس لا المجرد ، وإلى أن يتيح للصور أن تنتج التجربة ، ويتيح لهما معا أن يولدا المعنى .

ولا شك في أن حركة الصورة العميقة قد استلهمت تجربة مدرسة بلاك ماونتن ، عموماً ، وتجربة تشارلز أولسن ، على الخصوص ، في تنظيره للنظم الإسقاطي (Olson 239-49) . ويستند هذا النظم إلى مفهوم الفضاء

أربعاء من أربعاء يناير ، ١٨٩٤ ، ومن خلال تلك
الأصوات الاعتراضية ، قفزتْ إلى حتفها هيئةٌ ،
كونستانس وولسن – روائية ، صديقة حميمة
لـ هنري جيمس .
سقطتْ .
مكتئبةً محمومة ، مجنونة – ماتت من – الأنفلونزا – حبِّها له .
من عشقها الخائب لـ جيمس؟ ليس هناك من دليل .
سبع سنوات قبل تلك الليلة ، من منتصف نيسان إلى أواخر
أيار ، كانا يسكنان معاً بالمنزل نفسه في بلوسجواردو .
في فيلا ، ضخمة . ثم التقيا بعد ذلك ، سراً ، في جنيف .
سراً؟ ربما ، رغم أن التكتم كان هو الدافع آنئذ ، لا البذاءة . (40)

تقول الشاعرة إنها لا تمتح أبداً من سيرتها الذاتية ، لكنها تستلهم سِيَر الآخرين . ويصدق هذا ، فيما يبدو على القصائد المذكورة هنا ، ولكن العنصر الذاتي يظل ، وإن بشكل غير مباشر ، مُحدِّدِّاً أساسياً في صياغة هذه القصائد . فلولا الانشغالات الأكاديمية للشاعرة ، لكان مستبعداً أن تهتم بأي من فارادي ، أو روجيه ، أو داروين ، أو جيمس ، أو ڤرجينيا وولف ، أو أن تُلمّ بالمنجزات أو بالتفاصيل وتفاصيل التفاصيل الجديرة باهتمامات المؤرخ الأدبي المتمرس . ويتضح هذا على الخصوص في مثال جيمس ، حيث تقوم طريقة التناول على الاستفادة القصوى من تعدد الأصوات polyphony ، ومن المنهج الحواري dialogical ، وحيث يتم المزج بين النفحة الغنائية وتفاصيل السيرة الذاتية .

روبرت كيلي Robert Kelly

في بداية الستينيات ، ظهرت الحركة المعروفة باسم شعر الصورة العميقة Deep Image Poetry ، التي تزعمها كل من الشاعرين روبرت كيلي وجيروم روتنبرج Jerome Rothenberg . وقد استوحى روتنبرج هذا الاسم من التعبير الإسباني canto jondo (النشيد العميق) المقترن بشعر فريديريكو جارثيا لوركا . ويقول روتنبرج إن الاسم من ابتداعه هو ، وإنه استعمله في البدء لإخفاء طريقة في التفكير والكتابة تتميز بها السوريالية الفرنسية والدولية (Rothenberg, "1960" n. pag) . وفي مقالة عن مبررات الصورة

تُفضَّلُ مشاهدتُه في الضوء الموارب ، حين تقع
الأجزاءُ مائلةً فوق ظلالها ،
والأشعةُ والمقاطعُ المنكسرةُ
تُرسل خطوطاً منحرفةً مضيئة
تحمل انطباعاً بالاكتمال ، بانتفاء الانكسار . (10-11)

الكل إذن ، سواء في الطبيعة أو في اللغة ، ليس إلا وهماً منفلتاً لا سبيل إلى إدراكه ، ما دام التوسل إليه إنما يتم من خلال الأجزاء . النقص والانكسار حتميان ، لا مفرّ منهما . وإذ تتأمل الشاعرة إنجاز روجيه المعجمي ، تُعاين هذا الكوثر اللغوي الذي لا يتوقف :

في نسخته الأولى ، كان مكنز روجيه نصف ما هو
عليه في نسخته الأخيرة ، الكل أقرب إلى الحمق ،
الجزء أقرب إلى الحكمة ، والبداية أقرب إلى النهاية . (63)

وفي خضم هذا الكوثر ، تتسمع الشاعرة ثغاءَ آلاف المترادفات ، وأنين آلاف الأضداد ، وتتأمل المترادفات وهي تُمعن في الدوران لتغوص في أضدادها ، فتستنكر عبثَ محاولة العالم والمعجميِّ أن يدرك كُنْهَ المادة أو التناظر رغم أن الخطَّ يمتد أمامه من النجوم إلى المصباح ليتمثل ، في نهاية المطاف ، شيفرةً من غبار على شكل عُثَّة . فما دامت شرنقة اللغة ممعنة في تضخم أبدي ، فالكمال بعيد عن المنال بُعدَ الإله عن المجرة ، لكنه يظل من النقص قريباً ، قريباً . يواصل المعجمي محاولتَه العبثية فيرص قوائمَ الكلمات التي تبدو شبيهةً بأخاديد في الحقل يملأها المطر فيتشاكلان .
كان على الشاعرة أن تغوص في سيرة كل من فارادي وروجيه لكي تنشئ هذه القصائد . وهذا بالتحديد ما تفعله قبل أن تكتب القصيدة التي اختارت لها «سيرة» "Biography" عنواناً ، وتقول فيها :

يُميِّزُ المُنصتُ المتفانيّ في تلك الليلة صوتين سائدين :
من العوارض الخشبية فوق القنال ، شخيرَ الحمام ،
ومن المياه العكرة ، نقرات زوارق الجندول ،
الشبيهة بقشر الجوز الفارغ ، على الدرجات .

اختارت المرأةُ أن تعكس فقط ما كان يراه هو
وكان ذلك يفي بغرضه : كانت صورتُه مضمَّخة ،
ملمَّعة ، معروضة بزاوية ١٨٠ درجة . (Ashbery 188)

للفنان الذي يرسم صورته الذاتية أن يُعوِّل على المرآة ، لكنْ لا يمكن للرائي أو للمتأمل أنٍ يعول عليها . لا يمكن للمرآة إلا أن تكون جزءاً ، لأنها أبداً أصغر من أي كل يُفترض أن تعكسه . للمرأة الحرية في التلاعب بالأبعاد . لكن ما تفعله يظل مجرد تلاعب ، مجرد محاكاة . المرأة ، وإن بالتناسق ، مقيدة . أما الفكرة ، فإنها تبرز ، رغم الفقد المضاعَف ، طافية ، منسابةً ظافرة .

تسكب بيردز تأملاتها في قالب البانتوم pantoum الذي تعتبره اختياراً طبيعياً ، لأن بعض الأبيات فيه ، كما في المرآة ، يعكس بعضها بعضا . ويشبه هذا القالب ، الذي يُستعمَل في شعر الملايو ، قالبَ الڤيلانيل Villanelle في اعتماده على تواتر بعض أبيات القصيدة محورةً حسب ترتيب معين ، بحيث يكون البيت الثاني في المقطع هو البيت الأول في المقطع الموالي ، ويكون البيت الأخير في القصيدة تحويراً لمطلعها . والواقع أن التأملات هنا مستوحاة من تأملات مايكل فارادي Michael Faraday ، العالم البريطاني الشهير المعروف بإنجازاته المهمة في مجالي الكهرومغناطيسية والكيمياء الكهربائية ، حيث تستخدم بيردز شخصية فارادي قناعاً تنعكسُ فيه الانعكاسات ، ويتم من خلاله التأمل في التأملات . وكما تستحضر الشاعرة هنا قناع فارادي ، تستحضر قناع بيتر مارك روجيه Peter Mark Roget في ثلاث قصائد بعنوان «وهم روجيه» "Roget's Illusion" ، لتتناول الانشغالات الإپستمولوجية نفسها بالمعرفة ، والإدراك ، والحواس وحدودها . وروجيه (١٧٧٩-١٨٦٩) عالم وطبيب ومعجمي بريطاني اشتهر بـ مكنز روجيه *Roget's Thesaurus* المعروف الذي انكبَّ على تأليفه لفترة تزيد عن نصف قرن . تقول الشاعرة في المقطع الأخير من إحدى القصائد الثلاث :

كان قد كتب : الكُلَّ لا يُدرك .
لا سبيل إلى الإحاطة به ، بالقائمة كلها أو بالعجلة الدائرة .
يُفضَّل النظرُ إليه عبر الشرائح والفتحات ، عبر الأعمدة
والفجوات . الوهمُ الدائرُ حول ذاته .

العيش، وأنجليكانياً في الديانة (Bernstein, *My Way* 270-71). وهكذا، يظل برنشتاين متمادياً في رشق الأصنام بيذاءاته، ومتمادياً في جراءة تجاربه الصاخبة، إلى أن تُوِّج، أخيراً، وبعد ما يقرب من نصف قرن، بجائزة بولنجن Bollingen Prize عام ٢٠١٩، وهي جائزة معتبرة تمنح كل سنتين نالها شعراء كبار من أمثال باوند، وستيفنز، وأودن، وفروست، وكمنجز، وميريل، ومروين. ولكن الجوائز في سياق الشعر الأمريكي موضوع آخر صار مرتبطاً بمناورات سياسية واعتبارات شللية قد يُسلط عليها بعض الضوء «قانونُ جوري جريهام» The Jorie Graham Rule الذي لا يسمح بتضارب المصالح في تحكيم الجوائز.

ليندا بيردز Linda Bierds

كمثل فكرة تُفقَد أثناء التأمل مرتين
وتنساب طافية، مثل بجعة، بجانب زاوية سقوطها،
يتضاعف بُعدها عن قرينها كما المصباح عن مرآة
أبداً لن تسعَه، لن تسعَه أبداً كلَّه. (Bierds 51)

بهذا المقطع الرباعي تنهي ليندا بيردز قصيدتها "On Reflection"، «عن الانعكاس/عن التأمل» (51-50). للمرء أن يُعجب بصورة البجعة المنسابة على الماء رويداً، وله أن يتصور حِدَّة الأشجان المترتبة عن بُعد القرينة عن القرين، وله أن يغتمّ لأن الفقد والبعد يتضاعفان بوتيرة متواصلة. لكن، أيُّ فكرة هذه التي يتوقف وجودها على وجود قرين؟ هل كان للمصباح، سواء استوعبته المرآة أو لم تستوعبه، أن ينعكس (أن يقترن) بدون مرآة؟ وهل كانت المرآة تعكس بدون مصباح؟ ما كان ينبغي لهما. وما كان للفكرة إلا أن تغرق وتغرق في خضم التأمل. التأمل انعكاس، والانعكاس تأمل، وما بينهما أبعاد تتضاعف أو تتناصف. وليس للمرآة، عاكسةً أو متأملة، أن تكون بالكل محيطة. إنْ هي إلا حيلة لمحاكاة المرئي، ومدى المحاكاة محدود، كما أدرك أفلاطون منذ القدم. المرآة تضاعف المنعكسِ، لكن الفكرة تجعله ثلاثة أضعاف. ليس التأمل انعكاساً ولا الانعكاس تأملاً. لا يمكن أن يُعوَّل كلياً على وساطة المرآة، لأن المرآة بطبيعتها منحازة، كما يلمح إلى ذلك جون أشبري في قصيدته الشهيرة «بورتريه ذاتي في مرآة محدبة» "Self-Portrait in a Convex Mirror":

إن مهاجمة «النخبوية» بمثل هذا الصخب العنيف لن يقلل أبداً من قدرها، ولن يرتقي بالطليعية المزعومة ربع درجة. ولو واصل المرء قراءة هذه الشهادة الشعرية الفادحة، لوجد أن ذات الشاعر تزري بالشعر إذ تنعته بأقبح النعوت. وهكذا، يصير الشعر انحطاطاً، وإخفاقاً، وبذاءة، وفظاظة، وتهافتا، وتشظيا، وتناقضاً، ونشازاً، وتآمراً، وعقماً، وصبيانية، وتخنثاً، وهراء، وهُجْنة، وشروداً، وعصياناً، وصلعاً. كل هذا على سبيل المثال لا الحصر. وتبلغ هذه القصيدة ذروتها عند نهايتها، حيث يصدر الحكم بأن الشعر جدار فارغ مبنيٌّ من كل ما تنفر منه ذات الشاعر، مكتوب ببنط عريض وبمداد لا يكفّ عن التلاشي. ويبدو أن الشاعر هاورد نمروڤ Howard Nemerov كان محقاً حين نبّه، في المرحلة نفسها التي ابتدأت ترتفع فيها مثل هذه الأصوات الطليعية، إلى خطورة هذه التوجهات على الشعر وعلى الفن عامة:

> إذا بلغ الشعر مستوى الشطرنج حيث لا يقدر على التوليفات الأنيقة، العميقة، الحاسمة، إلا الجهابذة، ولا يقدّرها حقَّ قدرها إلا اللاعبون المتمرسون من ذوي الكفاءة، فإن ذلك سيبدو لكثير من الناس وضعا محزنا، وسيراه بعض الناس مجرد عاقبة لخطايا الشعراء، ولكنه لن يعني، إطلاقاً، أن الشعر، كما يزعمون، قد مات. بل العكس تماما هو الصحيح. حين يصبح الشعر مفرطاً في السهولة، ويكون سهلَ المنال أكثر مما ينبغي، يصير مختزلاً في بضع صيغ مشتقة، فيلبي حاجات الأذواق الوضيعة، والأذهان الخاملة؛ وحينئذ يكون الفن حقاً في خطر. (Nemerov 30)

لكن برنشتاين لا يفوِّت أي فرصة دون أن يندد بمثل هذه التوجهات «النخبوية». ففي معرض الحديث عن ألن جنزبرج بعد وفاته، يرى برنشتاين أنه يمثل الصورة المعكوسة لإليوت، إذ إنه رمز للثقافة الوضيعة في أحسن أحوالها، على حين يرمز إليوت إلى الثقافة الرفيعة في أسوأ أحوالها. فقد آل تطور إليوت الشعري إلى الانغلاق، والكبت، والسلطوية، ورهاب الأجانب. أما جنزبرج فقد كان ينزع إلى التفتح والانفتاح ومقاومة السلطوية. وهكذا، فإنه كان فوضوياً في السياسة، إباحيا في أسلوب العيش، وبوذياً في الديانة، على حين كان إليوت ملكياً في السياسة، ومستقيما في أسلوب

الخلفية سوداء ، والحروف بياض . كان يمكن أن تكون أمكر من القنفذ وأنحف من شهريار .

ويظل من الممكن أن تتصور دانتي أليجيري يحث على التخلي عن كل الآمال . ومع ذلك ، فإن إثبات الشخصية في الربع الأخير من قرن كانت السيطرةُ فيه للكبار ، قد يقتضي قدراً لا يُستهان به من التنطع والوَقاحة ، فالشعر ليس ، كما أريد له أن يكون ، «محواً للشخصية بل نزوة من نزوات الشخصية . لكن بالطبع ذوو النزوات وحدهم يعرفون ما معنى أن يرغب المرء في اتباعها» (Bernstein, Nude 4) . واضح أن هذا رد فعل ضد إليوت . فإذا كانت المعارضة المبنية أساساً على البارودِيا ، أي المحاكاة الساخرة ، سلاحاً متاحاً ، فماذا يمنع من استعماله في التهجم على كبيره الذي علمه السحر ، باوند ، وذلك بالتعريض بمبادئ النزعة الصورية Imagism التي لخصها فلينت Flint وروّج لها باوند : «لا تستعملْ إطلاقاً أيَّ كلمة تسهم في المعنى المباشر للشيء المرئي» (Bernstein, Nude 4) . وما المانع في أن يتبع المرءُ النزوةَ فيستعير من مجموعة أخرى للشاعر نفسه هذا التوصيف الدقيق الذي يبدو ملائماً لوصف فداحة التعري في بيانه الشكلاني الجسور ، حيث يرى أن التحليل الإعرابي للجمل «شيء آلي . لا يتطلب أي/تفكير . إنه استعراضٌ بكل تفاصيله» (Bernstein, Parsing 1) . وفي قصيدة أخرى بعنوان «التضامن هو الاسم الذي نطلقه على ما لا نستطيع أن نتمسك به» "Solidarity Is the Name We Give to What We Cannot Hold" ، يواصل الشاعر هذا الصراخ الموتور الذي يمكن أن يوصف بالستريبتيز التنظيري :

أنا واحد من الشعراء الشكلانيين العراة ، شاعرٌ يتميز
شعرُه بالتراكيب المتواثبة ، شاعرٌ متعدد الدروب ،
شاعرٌ مندهش ، شاعرٌ من شعراء التعبيرية الاجتماعية ،
شاعرٌ ذو نزعة باروكية ، شاعرٌ ذو ميول بنيانية ،
شاعرٌ إيديولوجي
. . .
أنا شاعرٌ يساري وأنا مستلق على أريكتي ،
وشاعرٌ وجودي وأنا في الشارع ،
أنا شاعر منتم وأنا وسط أصدقائي ،
وشاعر لا منتَمٍ وأنا في ميدان البلدة . (Bernstein, My Way 33)

كانت المرآة في الشقة تلمع، ولكنها لم تكن تعكس، لم تكن، على الأقل، تعكس الخواطر التي كانت تعبر ذهنه هو، أيّاً كانت هُويّته. كانت الرطوبة تغلف المكان مثل أولئك الحراس الخشبيين خارج قاعة السينما العتيقة، لكنها، فيما يبدو، لم تكن تلامس أي شيء، ولذلك تمادى في الاعتقاد بأن النور الذي كان قد انقطع يمكن إصلاحه بمعزوفة من معزوفات الفوغا. (Log Rhythms 8)

الكلام للشاعر والرسوم لزوجته الفنانة سوزان بي Susan Bee والوسيط مرآة. إصلاحُ البصر بالسماع! خدعةٌ من خدع الكون والفساد. لكن، لم لا، والمأسوف عليه، أورفيوس، كان يُحرِّك الحجرَ والشجر؟ على الغصون أوراق. والأوراق عيون. أيْ مصفوفة تُبيح حذف الأنف، وتبيح تربيع العينين، (٢ x عين)؟[2] لا بأس. فالغصون تتمرد فتصير خصلات سوداء تنتهك بياض الجبين. وعلى الشريط الأسود الذي يحاول أن يكبحها تمَّ تطريز هذا الشعار:

[لأنها كانت] أنحف من شهر أيار، فقد ضخَّتْ تلك الرافعةَ بعنف، كان المكان أضيق من أن يسع ذلك الذي لا يُسمى، أو يسعَ قنفذاً لا حدَّ لدهائه. (Log Rhythms 8)

حجران بعصفور واحد

الـ
خلاص
يأتي
و
الخ
لاص
يمضي
لكن
الز
وال
يظل
أبـ
داً
هنا
.

(Bernstein, *Recalculating* 30)

هكذا تتم محاكاة القياس المنسوب إلى فتجنشتاين Wittgenstein الذي تُعدّ الكلماتُ فيه نغمات تُعزف على مفاتيح سلم الخيال. (Brigley n. pag)، وفي ذلك مثلٌ على مركزيةٍ لغوية متطرفة قائمة على ألاعيب لفظية توحي بأن وراءها عمقاً ميتافزيقيا. وهذا الموقف ليس مستغرباً ممن ينهل من أوستين Austin وفتجنشتاين، على أن هذا الأخير كان يوصي بالصمت عما يستحيل الكلام عنه. ولعل الإنجاز المفترض هنا يكمن في أن العصفور الواحد يضرب، في الآن نفسه، حجرين؛ لكن انتفاء الروائع masterpieces يفرض نفسه، وهو هنا مفهوم، لأن «الزوال» (أي، النفي/الانتفاء) هو سيد الموقف. ولو تم التأمل في النص لتبين أن التقابل بين الخلاص redemption، باعتباره تبرئة ذمة، أي إنجازاً لوعدٍ أو سداداً لدين، والزوال transience، باعتباره نفياً وانتفاء ومحواً للدوام ماحقاً؛ فالحكمة هنا لن تكون أكثر من صياغة معادلة بسيطة يتنافى فيها المكونان: $1 + 1 - 1 = 0$، لكن، إذا كانت الكلمات لا تسعف، فما المانع من دعمها بالتشكيل؟ وهو ما يتم فعلاً في هذا المثال:

في معرض تعريفه الشعر الجيد: «إنه معلومات دقيقة عن الوجود الذي نشأت عنه» (Zukofsky 28).

تشارلز برنشتاين Charles Bernstein

«لم أكن أبداً من دعاة التنظير. إفراط في الكلام وقصور في الممارسة. الاحتماء بأروقة من نظريات كتبت بقصد الإلزام والإبهار والتعذيب، بل تعللنا بوعد السرعة في الوصول، والتعويض في التفسير، مهما بلغ زيف التفسير» (Bernstein, Rough 17). والكلام السابق للشاعر تشارلز برنشتاين، أحد رواد الحركة الشعرية الطليعية المعروفة بـ«شعر اللغة» Language Poetry التي ظهرت في أواخر الستينيات وبدايات السبعينيات من القرن العشرين. ويبدو أن الحركة استمدت اسمها من مجلة ا=ل=غ=ة L=A=N=G=U=A=G=E التي كان برنشتاين وبروس أندروز Bruce Andrews يشرفان على تحريرها. وكانت الحركة تضم شعراء آخرين من أمثال: مايكل پالمر، ولين هدجينيان Lyn Hejinian، ورون سيليمان Ron Silliman، وسوزان هاو، وغيرهم. ونصّبت الحركةُ نفسها عند ظهورها تياراً مناهضاً لما عدّته التيارَ السائد في الشعر الأمريكي في ذلك الوقت، وتقترن مواقفها بالميول اليسارية في السياسة، ومعاداة الثقافة السائدة. والواقع أن الشعراء الذين جرت العادة على تصنيفهم ضمن طائفة «ا=ل=غ=ة» ليسوا متجانسين. يقول برنشتاين: «إن ما يجمعنا هو النفور من سلسلة الحيل الشعرية المتعارف عليها أكثر من أي إملاءات أسلوبية من جانبنا... أنا وبروس ممن يتقنون الكولاج، أما القضايا المطروحة فقد كانت، إلى حد بعيد، مدبرة» (King 21-22). ولعل معاداة المؤسسة الشعرية، وهذا النفور من اتباع المكرس من مواضعاتها، هو ما جعل برنشتاين يبشر، في سياق آخر، بوجهة مختلفة: «في مواجهة الوظيفة الرهبانية للشعر أو الشاعر، أقترحُ ما هو هزليّ ومخيب للآمال، ما هو أخرقُ ومُندِّد: أقترح أن يكون مؤسساً أفقياً على ما هو اجتماعي، لا عمودياً على السماوات الزرقاء. وسيكون شعاري في إعادة صياغة كۿلكانتي: "المقدس يهلك إذا تم تصويرُه"» (Bernstein, "Poetry" n. pag). هكذا يعتقد الشاعر-المنظر أن بوسعه، بتسليط المدنس على المقدس، أن يقتنص حجرين بعصفور واحد، لكن التسليط لا يتأتى بغير سلطة، وهدم المؤسس، رغم الإنذار بدوام الزوال، إنما يقوم على استبدال مؤسَّس غيره به:

مأساة تريستان وإيزولده ، لا من منظور مواجه له ، بل من الخلف ، ومن منظور موارب . بحيث يتم التركيز لا على حبكة السرد أو شخصياته ، بل على أمور تَشكيلية مثل انكسارات الضوء ودرجات اللون :

الفراقُ يقتضي سعياً
آخر إلى جمعِ الشمل
أستعمل خيطاً أبيض
ونصفَ الورقة نفسها
وفي ضوء الشمس
أضعُ قطعة الزجاج في موضع
ينعكسِ فيه البحر
بنفسجياً وأزرقِ فيصوغ بيسر
من الأشعة المِطْواع
مولدَك أنت ويصوغ هيئتَك
من الضوء من ضوءٍ
الذاكرة حين ينسدلُ جفنان
وكذلك من ضوء الذهن
المنقول في إثارة الحلم

إن الدقةَ هي ما يجب أن
نتعامل معه بوسعنا أن
نُبعدَ الفضاء عن اللون . (S. Howe, *Pierce-Arrow* 136-37)

هل يكون إبعاد الفضاء عن اللون ، هنا ، ممكناً بفضل التحكم في الأشعة التي تم تطويعها ، وبالحفاظ على التوزان بين التأمل والتذكر ، بين الذهن والذاكرة ، وهما ، فيما يبدو ، المصدران الوحيدان للضوء هنا؟ يكاد الاعتماد على علم الظواهر يكون كليّاً في هذا السياق ، بحيث تتراجع إلى الخلفية عناصر الحبكة السردية ، مثل المولد والحلم والفراق واللقاء بعد الفراق ، وتكون الأهمية للأداة والوسيط (الخيط ، والورق ، والزجاج) ، لأن الدقة في التعامل مع الهيئة ، رصداً وتمثيلاً ، هي هنا أعز ما يُطلب . كأن الشاعرة هنا تستلهم فكرة لوي زوكوفسكي عن الدقة ، حيث يقول

«كنتُ أصادفه وسط أطلالٍ روما العتيقة وأحياناً في كامپانيا أو على ضفاف التيبر، ينجز رسوماً لكل شيء يستهويه. وأراه أحياناً عائداً إلى بيته حاملاً في منديله حجارة وطحالب وزهوراً مختلفة كان ينوي أن يرسمها بالضبط كما كانت في الطبيعة... سألتُه يوماً بأي وسيلة بلغ ذلك الكمال الرفيع الذي منحه مثل هذا المقام المتميز بين رسامي إيطاليا العظام. أجاب ببساطة: ما أهملت أي شيء». (Sutro 76).

بهذا يمكننا أن ندرك كيف صار النهار حرفاً مطبعياً/مطبوعاً تتغير فيه الأشكال المرئية. بهذا تغدو الحقيقة بأكملها عرضية، وبهذا تكتمل الدائرة.

وفي سياق آخر، تتضاعف المفارقات، فيتم تصورُ جماعات مجهولة طليقةً وفي الآن نفسه مقيدة، على الرغم من كونها مجهولة، وعلى الرغم من أن الحكم متفرع عن التصور. وهكذا، ينشأ ميثاق غليظ بين الصناعة والجنون: «بين المجنون والمصنوع ميثاق/جماعات مجهولة ملتزمة وطليقة» (S. Howe, *Singularities* 33). يبدو أن الشاعرة لا تهمل أي شيء. فلا عجب في أن يتفتتَ الإدراكُ تحت وطأة الحرف، ولا عجب في أن يصير الماضي حاضراً لمستقبل محايث. قد تجتمع أسراب وقد تعشش أسراب، لكن التذكر ما يبرح أن ينساب عبر قناة المعنى. بهذا تصير ذكرى العالم الشاسع موضوعاً للتأمل، وبهذا تجثم الهيمنة على العالم، فلا يبقى سوى خيار واحد: «الاصطدام بالتاريخ أو التواطؤ معه» كما تقول الشاعرة (*Singularities* 33). ولا نهاية لـ«سوء التقدير» حين يتعلق الأمر بالتاريخ، فحتى حين يدرك الوعي موضوعه، لا بد أن يتعثر علم الظواهر (*Singularities* 17).

ولعل هذا التعثر هو الذي يجعل مقاربةً سردية تقليدية مثل سردية تريستان وإيزولده تتم من منظور تشكيلي محض، كما هو الشأن في قصيدة "Rückenfigur". ويشير العنوان إلى تقنية في التأليف يمكن أن تستعمل في الرسم أو في الفنون البصرية عموماً، وتقوم هذه التقنية على النظر إلى الموضوع من الخلف، وأشهر مثال على ذلك لوحة **الشارد فوق بحر الضباب** *Wanderer above the Sea of Fog* لـكاسپار داڤيد فريدريش Caspar David Friedrich. وهكذا، يتم تناولُ الموضوع، أي

ميلٌ نحو الموسيقى تارة ، ونحو التشكيل تارة : تنويع «دنيوي» على معزوفة مفارقة ينشأ فيها التناغم عن عنف الارتطام ، وعن «شرود» قلم الرصاص ، وتسخيرٌ للضوء في تدبير الفضاء . وإذ يُبتر النص عند بزوغ النهار ، تلجأ الشاعرة إلى إضافة هذا إلى ذلك ، فتعرض فوراً هذه الملصَقة :

```
:en him carrying home in his handkerchief
ent stones and moss and flowers, which he
ided to paint from nature exactly as they were.
      I ask         ancient Rome and some
hed t' a or on the banks of the Tiber, making
      s of everything that struck his fancy.  I have
inguished rank among the greatest painters of
. He replied, simply: "Je n'ai rien négligé."
```

تعتمد الملصَقة هنا على القص واللصق والبتر والتكسير والسحق والإرباك والإلغاز والتظليل ، والتضليل ، وفي المرحلة النهائية ، على النسخ التصويري photocopy . وهذه محاولة لتعريبها ، حيث أستخدم علامة * للتعبير عن المفقود من النص :

**يتُه عائداً إلى بيته حاملاً في منديله حجارة وطحالب وزهوراً
**تَلفة كان *نوي أن يرسمها بالضبط كما كانت في الطبيعة .
روما الـ*تيقة وأحياناً في كامبانيا على ضفاف التيبر ، ينجز لكل
شيء يستهويه . **لتُه المقام الرفيع بين رسامي *** العظام .
أجاب ببساطة : ما أهملت أي شيء . (That This 86)

ولستُ أجد أبلغَ وصف لهذه الملصَقة من هذين البيتين المستعارين من القصيدة ذاتها : «النسخة الشبيهة بلغز شاذ/لغز فريد يواصل الانزلاق» (That This 81) . وفي عرض للمجموعة ، يصفُ تشارلز برنشتاين هذه الملصقة بأنها «كولاج تاريخي» (Bernstein, "TLS" n. pag) . ولإعادة الأمور إلى نصابها ، أورد هنا تعريباً للنص الأصلي الذي مارست عليه الشاعرة كل هذا العنف الشاعري :

يخبرنا بيللوري عن الانطباع الذي خلفه بوسان Poussin
لدى مرتادي الميدان . يقول المحامي بوناقنتيرا داراجون :

شكلاً لكن ذلك الشيء المعادي
للحرف المطبعي ذلك الذي لم يُظلَّل

على النحو الذي تتشكل به الموسيقى
من غيم ونار كانا فعلاً فيما مضى

ملموسين وهما الآن عرضيان مثل
نصف الحقيقة أو الحقيقة بأكملها . (S. Howe, *That This* 79-80)

فإن يكن التجريد نصف الحقيقة والتعيينُ نصفَها الآخر ، فإن الحقيقة بأكملها لا بد أن تُردَّ أسفل سافلين ، فتكون منطقةُ الصفر قرارَها . وفي مواجهة مثل هذه الحيرةِ ، في مواجهة مثل هذا التردد الإبستيمولوجي ، يصير التساؤل مشروعاً عندما تقترب القصيدة من نهايتها : «هل وُضع الذهنُ داخل ذهن آخر/بباطننا ، [داخل] ذهن مجهول لدينا [؟]» (*That This* 80) ؛ يبدو أن التجول في الحقول ووسط أشجار الحديقة في ضوء القمر قد أقنع الشاعرةَ بأن غرق الذهن في ظلمات ذهن باطني آخر كان ضرورياً لتقليص المسافات ، ولاستحضار أمور روحية ، وكان ضرورياً لكي يكون المتأمل المتوحد شاهداً على الشريعة المؤسِّسة ، ولكي يدلي بشهادته عن المذبح وعن الثلج وعن حركة التاريخ ووجهته ، «لأن النهار . . .» (*That This* 85) . هكذا يأتي التعليل مبتوراً ، لأن الجملة ، مثل شهرزاد ، تتوقف عند النهار .

في بداية قصيدتها «المعمار الصاخب» "Frolic Architecture" ، تستغرق الشاعرة في تأمل ذاتي متعثر عبر عتمات متوالدة : «لكي يكون هذا الكتاب تاريخاً/لظل هو ظلي/أنا [،] ظل باطنيٌّ كامن في ظل آخر غيره [،] ظل لظل آخر عليه أن يخدمه» (*That This* 39) . وذلك ، كما يبدو ، إشارة إلى مجموعة *That This* نفسها . فكما تتنوع هذه الظلال ، تتنوع أساليب المجموعة ، فهناك مقاطع نثرية ، ومقاطع غنائية ، هناك نفَس المراثي ، وهناك جولات تاريخية لاستكشاف الموروث الطهراني في منطقة نيو إنجلاند ، وذلك بالغوص في أرشيف عالم اللاهوت البروتستانتي جوناثان إدواردز Jonathan Edwards . ويتجاذب هذا التنوعَ في الأسلوب

أسرابٌ من كلمات تحلق
مجتمعة متوترة
كأنها أمْـــــــرٌّ

قُذفتْ به الغربان . (S. Howe, *Europe of Trusts* 32)

وما هذه الأسراب ، في سياق الاختلاقات المتوالدة ، إلا ثوان تحدّرت من دقائق عابرة ، كانت في الأصل ثقوباً في الغيوم . فهل تحلق أسراب الكلمات لتخرق الصمتَ الفيثاغوري أو لتكرسه؟ ففي مقابل هذا الصمت الحكيم الذي يُفترض أنه يحمي الحقيقة ، تنشأ الثرثرة ، وفي الثرثرة إهدارٌ للحكمة وانتهاكٌ للحقيقة ، فتكون الكلمةُ نواةً للثرثرة ، تتجمع جملةً أو تتجزأ حروفاً ، وتخرج – تخرق الصمتَ – فجأةً لتواصل سعيَها إلى الحقيقة ، لكن المآل حتماً هو الإخفاق ، وهكذا تسقط لتغرق في جدول حبر يكتب المتواليةَ اللامتناهية . وللمرء أن يتوهم أن غربان النهاية ، مثل الكلمات ، ليست إلا تجمعاً لغربان من فصيلة غراب پو . فكما تتجمع الكلمات جملاً يصيِّر غراب پو ، في سياق الاختلاقات المتناسلة ، جوقة ثرثارة ، تحاول عبثاً ، وبكل ما أوتيت من إيقاع وطباق وجناسٍ وألاعيب صوتية ، أن تغازل الحقيقة ، فتخرق بذلك الصمتَ وتنداح عنه صوتاً تنشأ عنه حكايات وأساطير متموجة . ليس في النص طبعاً ما يحيلُ مباشرة إلى غراب پو ، لكن السياق يشجع على أن تكون الثرثرة طليقةً تمضي في كل اتجاه .

ويظل رهان الشاعرة هو المحافظة على ما تسميه «التوازن بين الصمت ، والرؤية ، والكلام» (Howe, *The Quarry* 46) . ولكسب الرهان ، كان لا بد من استحضار «ذلك» بجانب «هذا» كما في عنوان مجموعتها *That This* ، ربما لتأكيد التناظر ، أو التنافي ، أو التكامل ، أو التوازن ، أو ربما للإشارة إلى «منطقة الصفر» "Zero Zone" . ولأن Z هو آخر حروف الأبجدية ، يتشكل النهار حرفاً مطبعياً سرعان ما يناهضه شكل غامض ، شكل اختلفت صياغته عن تشكل الموسيقى من تجريدٍ كان أساسُه ، فيما مضى ، ملموساً ثم فقد جوهرَه ، فصار الآن تجريداً عارياً من كل تَعيُّن :

النهارُ حرفٌ مطبعي حين تتغير
الأشياءُ المرئية ثم تتخذ

ويمكن القول إن تصنيف الشعر الأمريكي المعاصر حسب قوالب صارمة أمر عسير ، إن لم يكن مستحيلاً ، ذلك أن اتساع الرقعة الجغرافية وغزارة الإنتاج وتعدد الحساسيات الشعرية وتنوع الأسس النظرية ، أمور تجعل الدارس يحس أنه يسير باستمرار فوق رمال متحركة . فحتى التيارات الشعرية التي يرصدها المؤرخ الأدبي ، والتي يفترض أن تشكل بوصلة يهتدي بها الدارس ، تتداخل في كثير من الأحيان ، وتجعل عملية التصنيف تبدو صعبة ، بل ربما عقيمة . ومع ذلك ، فإن الغزارة والتنوع ، وغيرهما من العوامل الآنف ذكرها ، جعلت النقاد والمتتبعين يعنون في تصنيف الشعراء المعاصرين إلى قبائل وفئات عرقية متشرذمة ، فهؤلاء شعراء أفرو-أمريكيون ، وهؤلاء شعراء من أصول لاتينية ، وهؤلاء من أصول آسيوية ، وشاعرات النزعة النسوية . إن تعدد الروافد في المشهد الشعري المعاصر في الولايات المتحدة يجعل المشهد أعقد ، ولكنه يندرج في جدلية الوحدة والتنوع التي تعد عادة سمة للتجربة الأمريكية في عمومها . صار الكتاب الأمريكيون ، في الوقت الراهن ، مجرد كتاب في أمريكا ، كما يؤكد أحد النقاد : «وهذه فكرةٌ بسيطة ولكنها أساسية . القومية ، في مشهد الكتابة ، أقل الآن تحديداً وأقل تأثيراً مما كانت عليه من قبل ، وهي أكثر انفتاحاً على حكايات أخرى وعلى تواريخ أخرى . إن مشهد الكتابة حقاً عابر للقوميات» (Gray 564) .

نماذج تمثيلية

أتقدم هنا بعرض بعض النماذج من الشعر ، وهو عرض يُقدَّم هنا على سبيل التمثيل لا الحصر ، فهناك طبعاً عدد هائل من الشعراء في المشهد الأمريكي المعاصر ، وقد يفوق بعضهم الشعراء المدرجين في هذا السياق أهمية وإنجازاً ، ولكن المجال هنا لا يتسع إلا للتمثيل .

سوزان هاو Susan Howe

في نهاية قصيدة «الصمت الفيثاغوري» "Pythagorean Silence" لسوزان هاو - المحسوبة أحياناً على تيار «شعراء اللغة» - تجتمع الكلمات المتوترة وتحلق أسراباً فتبدو كتلةَ أمرٍ تُقذَفُ بها الغربان :

ويكشف هذا التيار أحياناً عن ميول طلائعية مضادة للثقافة السائدة ، تنزع إلى الخروج عن الأعراف الثقافية والاجتماعية ، وتدعو إلى هدم البنى القائمة قصد التخلص من تحكم المؤسسة وهيمنة الأجيال السابقة . ويتبنى بعض الشعراء المحسوبين على هذا التيار مواقف غوغائية أحياناً ، تنعكس في تدني مستوى التنظير والممارسة الشعرية لديهم ، بحيث يبتعد بعضهم عما يناهضونه من تمييز نخبوي مكرس ، ويقتربون مما يسمى الـ Kitsch ، أي الإنتاج البخس المتسم بالرداءة وسوء الذوق ، في استجابة لاهتمامات حشود العامة ، والنأي عن الذوق الرفيع . ويمكن التمثيل لشعراء هذا التيار بكل من جنزبرج Ginsberg ، وكورسو Corso ، وبوكوڤسكي Bukowski ، وغيرهم . وهكذا ، فإن الشعر أو الأنماط الشعرية لدى بعض شعراء تيار ما بعد الحداثة تُختزل فيما يمكن اعتباره خطابات سياسية ضيقة تفتقر إلى النضج ، توجهها اعتبارات ديماجوجية تدعي الدفاع عن الفئات المهمشة والحقوق المدنية . لكن تعميم هذا على كل الشعراء المحسوبين على هذا التيار مجانب للصواب ، فمنهم مَن كانت إسهاماته الشعرية والنقدية متميزة ومؤثرة ، كما هو حال شعراء مثل : زوكوفسكي Zukofsky ، وأوبن Oppen ، ورزنكوف Reznikoff ؛ وبعض الشعراء المنتمين إلى مدرسة بلاك ماونتن Black Mountain مثل : أولسن Olson ، وركسروث Rexroth ، وكريلي Creeley ، وبلاكبرن Blackburn . ويمكن أن يندرج في هذا التيار أيضاً شعراء من جماعة نهضة سان فرانسيسكو The San Francisco Renaissance مثل : دنكن Duncan ، وفرلينجتي Ferlinghetti ، ووليام إڤرسن William Everson ، وجاك سبايسر Jack Spicer . أما على الساحل الشرقي للولايات المتحدة ، فقد نشأت جماعة شعراء مدرسة نيويورك New York School Poets ، ومن أشهرهم : فرانك أوهارا Frank O'Hara ، وكنيث كوك Kenneth Koch ، وجون أشبري John Ashbery . وأخيراً ، لا بِد من ذكر الجماعة المعروفة بشعراء اللغة Language Poets باعتبارها رافداً مهماً من روافد تيار ما بعد الحداثة ؛ ويأتي بعض شعراء هذه المجموعة من خلفية فلسفية مرتبطة على الخصوص بفلاسفة ما بعد الحداثة في أوروبا ، ولهم نشاط صاخب على المستوى النظري ، ولكن المنجز الشعري لديهم يبدو متواضعاً ، ومن أشهرهم : تشارلز برنشتاين Charles Bernstein ، وكلارك كوليدج Clark Coolidge ، وروبرت جروني Robert Grenier ، وسوزان هاو Susan Howe ، ومايكل پالمر Michael Palmer .

هكذا ، وصف ريتشاردِ جراي وضع الكتاب الأمريكيين في تلك الحقبة . وهو وصف دقيق فعلاً . أما تيار الحداثة Modernism ، الذي كان وليد هذا التلاقح ، فيقترح جراي مقاربته من زوايا مختلفة (340) . أولها ذلك الإحساس المشترك السائد بين الحداثيين بالمنفى والاغتراب الثقافي ؛ وثانيها ميلهم في أشكالهم التعبيرية إلى الابتداع والإيحاء والتجريب والاستغناء عن الروابط ؛ وثالثها سمات أسلوبية محددة تتجلى في تعطيل التراكيب والأشكال التقليدية والمزج بين أساليب ومستويات في الكتابة جرت العادة على الفصل فيما بينها ، والمجازفة بإضفاء صفة التهافت أو التنافر على إنتاجهم ، في تحدٍّ واضح للتصورات المسبقة عن النظام والاستقرار والقيم (340) . وقد نشأت هذه السمات عن الإدراك التاريخي المشترك بين كتاب هذه الحقبة – أمريكيين كانوا أم غير أمريكيين – بأن الأمور تغيرت بشكل يعسر معه تناولها بالأساليب المألوفة . وقد كان هدف الحداثيين هو تغليب الشكل والبنية والرؤية الفنية على غيرها من العناصر ، قصد التمكن من الانتقال إلى وسائل جديدة وملائمة لإدراك الواقع الجديد والتعبير عنه .

تيار ما بعد الحداثة : يعد هذا التيار محاولة لتجاوز تيار الحداثة ، أو على الأقل محاولة الابتداء حيث انتهت الحداثة . فهناك مَن يرى أن تيار ما بعد الحداثة ليس إلا صيغة أشد راديكالية من صيغ الحداثة ، وهناك مَن يرى أن تيار الحداثة استنفد طاقته وانطفأت جذوته فأفل ليخلي المشهد لما بعده :

> كان تيار الحداثة يفقد بريقه متحولاً بذلك إلى تيار ما بعد الحداثة المتسم بمقاومته للغائية والانغلاق ، والتمييز بين الثقافة «الرفيعة» والثقافة «الوضيعة» ، ومناوأته للتفسيرات العظمى وأنماط السرد المتحكمة ، ونبذه الاعتقاد بوجود حقيقة واحدة مهمة ومتجانسة يمكن إدراكها في الفن . وهكذا ، صار دافع ما بعد الحداثة ، بتفضيله الأحكام المعلقة ، وإنكاره كل أشكال التراتبية ، وتشككه في الحلول والنهايات ، والاكتمال ، نتاجاً ميِّزاً لهذه الحقبة . وقد شجع هذا الدافع أنماط الكتابة المزدهرة على الهامش ، والرافضة للسلطوي في مقابل العشوائي ، التي تنطلق من كون العالم عشوائيا غير منتظم ، ومن أن الفن أيضاً كذلك . (Gray 558)

من الشعراء الأمريكيين طوال القرن العشرين ، بل يمكن القول إن تأثيره لا يزال ممتداً إلى الوقت الحاضر . ويمكن التمثيل لهذا التيار بشعراء من أمثال فروست Frost وساندبرج Sandburg ، وغيرهم كثير .

تيار الحداثة : هذا التيار ، على عكس التيار السابق ، منفتح على أوروبا وعلى العالم القديم عموماً ، ويتسم بميول كوزموبوليتانية والاعتماد في التنظير والممارسة على عبور الثقافات ، وهو تيار منحاز إلى القيم الكونية ، يستلهم تراث حضارات قديمة مثل حضارات بلاد الإغريق والفرس والهند والصين . كما يحاول التجديد من خلال تجاوز الأعراف والقوالب الشعرية المألوفة . ويمكن التمثيل لهذا التيار بشعراء مثل : إليوت Eliot ، وباوند ، ووليامز ، وهيلدا دوليتل Doolittle ، وستيڤنز Stevens . ويمكن القول إن هذا التيار كان الأهم في تاريخ الشعر الأمريكي ، بل امتد تأثيره خارج أمريكا بسبب تحقيقه إنجازات شعرية ملحوظة على مستوى التجريب جعلته يغير مسار الشعر ويخرج عن كل القوالب المألوفة ، وذلك من خلال النصوص الشعرية الرائعة مثل روائع إليوت (**الأرض الخراب** The Waste Land ، **الرباعيات** Four Quartets) وأناشيد باوند . ولا عجب في أن تكون هذه النصوص فاعلة ، لأنها لم تحصر نفسها في الاهتمامات الإقليمية الضيقة ، بل عانقت هموماً كونية تتجاوز الزمان والمكان ، واستندت إلى تراث متنوع مستمد من ثقافات مختلفة . وقد نشطت هجرة الكتاب الأمريكيين المغتربين إلى أوروبا ، على الخصوص بعد الحرب العالمية الأولى ، فكان لاحتكاكهم بزملائهم في القارة أثر كبير في مجرى تاريخ الآداب الغربية ، وكان التأثير متبادلاً بين الطرفين :

> ورغم أنهم ظلوا كتاباً أمريكيين ، فقد بدأوا يشاركون في تجارب النزعات الرمزية والسوريالية والدادائية ؛ أما الموارد اللغوية التي جلبوها معهم من العالم الجديد ، فقد تم تعزيزها وإغناؤها نتيجة لقائهم بالعالم القديم . وسواء غامروا بالرحيل إلى أوروبا والإقامة فيها لفترة محدودة ، أو أقاموا هناك معظم حياتهم ، أو ظلوا متشبثين بالإقامة داخل حدود الولايات المتحدة ، فإن الكثيرين منهم أصبحوا منخرطين في الحركات الأدبية والاتجاهات التي أنكرت المفاهيم التقليدية للتاريخ والجغرافيا . (Gray 340)

بالشعراء الأجانب ، وبمن يستورد بضاعتهم ، وبأولئك الذين لا يتمردون على الموروث . كل هؤلاء لا يمكن أن يهيئوا إلا تربة الأدب ، وذلك لا يكفي . وسيكون المستقبل ، في زعم ويتمان ، للشعراء الذين يعانقون أحلام أمريكا ، التي لا تحتاج إلى غيرها كي تبرر نفسها ، وهؤلاء الشعراء الذين استوعبوا أمريكا هم مَن ستبادلهم أمريكا الخلود .

وهكذا ، فإن مجموعة *أوراق العشب* تجسّد الشعرَ القومي المستقل عن كل تبعية للعالم القديم ، ذلك الشعر الذي سبق أن بشر به إمرسن ؛ فلا عجب إذن في أن يكون إمرسن من المتحمسين لشعر ويتمان ، وأن يكون من بين أول المهنئين . ولا عجب في أن يسجل ويتمان بأنه مدين لإمرسن الذي ساعده على أن يجد هُويّته : «كنتُ أجيش ، وأجيش ، وأجيش ؛ إمرسن أوصلني إلى درجة الغليان» (كما ورد في Trowbridge n. pag) .

الطريف أن شاعراً بقامة إدجار ألن پو Poe لم يكن ليروق لإمرسن أو ويتمان ، لأنه كان يغرد خارج سربهما ، ولأنه لم يكن يستوفي متطلباتهما السياسية والأخلاقية . ولهذا ، تراهما يقللان من شأنه ، فيسميه إمرسن «قارع أجراس» "jingle man" (كما ورد في Shucard 129) ، في إشارة ربما إلى استسهاله في النظم واعتماده التكرارِ في أوزانه ، وإسرافه في لزوم القوافي . أما ويتمان ، فرغم اعترافه بأن پو كان متحكماً في أدواته ، فقد صنفه ضمن «مصابيح الأدب الخيالي ، ساطعة وباهرة ، لكنها باردة لا دفء فيها» (Whitman, *Poetry* 873) . والطريف أيضاً أن پو قد ذاع صيته في القارة العجوز ، وخصوصاً في فرنسا ، حيث افتتن به كل من بودلير ومالارمه . وسيزعم وليام كارلوس وليامز ، فيما بعد ، أن الأدب الأمريكي مرتكز على پو : «عليه وحده ، وعلى أرضية صلبة» (Williams 224) .

التيارات الرئيسية

يمكن تصنيف التيارات المهمة في الشعر الأمريكي خلال القرن العشرين ، رغم ما قد يكون في مثل هذا التصنيف من إخلال وتبسيط ، على النحو الآتي :

التيار السائد : هو التيار الذي ظل ، بشكل أو آخر ، وفياً للنزعة القومية الإقليمية التي كان إمرسن قد دعا إليها ، وأسسِ لها كل من ويتمان وديكنسن Dickinson . ولقد ظل أثر هذا التيار فاعلاً في شعر كثير

في ذمة الماضي ، أما أمريكا اليوم فهي تَحققُ لما ينبغي أن يكون ، وهي الآن مرادفة لحاضر يقتحم المستقبل بكامل العنفوان (Whitman, *Leaves* 208) . وهكذا ، يتغنى ويتمان بعشيقته ، أمريكا ، وبتفوقها الأعظم ، ويتغنى بآلاف المدن وهي تزهر في تلك الجزر (211) . وفي مقطع آخر من أوراق العشب ، نجد الشعر متماهيًا مع الشعور القومي بهُوِيّة تتفوق على كل الهُوِيّات :

شعراء آسيا وأوروبا الخالدون أنجزوا عملهم وانتقلوا إلى أقاليم أخرى ،
وبقي هناك عمل لمّا يُنجز ، عمل يفوق كل ما كانوا قد أنجزوه
هذه الولايات هي القصيدة الأرحب ،
فليس فيها أمة واحدة وحسب ، بل هي تعج بأمة الأمم . (281)

وها هو ويتمان يبشر بنمط شعري قومي جديد ، نمط مستقل ومختلف تمامًا عما قبله ، نمط سيتفوق حتمًا على كل ما سبقه من موروث :

القوافي عابرة وأهلها عابرون ، القصائد المقطَّرة من قصائد غيرها عابرة ،
حشودُ المتأملين والمتأدبين عابرة ، وهي تخلف الرماد ،
المعجبون ، والمستوردون ، والأشخاص المطيعون ، لا ينتجون إلا تربة الأدب ،
أمريكا تبرّر نفسَها ، أنظروها ، لا قناع يمكن أن يخدعها أو يحجب أي شيء
عنها ، لديها ما يكفي من الرزانة ،
لا تتقدم لتستقبل إلّا أشباهها ،
إذا أقبل شعراؤها ، فإنها ستتقدم في الوقت المناسب لترحب بهم ، لا خوف من أن تخطئ ،
(بيّنةُ الشاعر ستظل مُرجأةً إلى أن يستوعبه وطنُه بمودة ، كما استوعب هو وطنَه) . (287)

واضح أن في البيت الأول غمزًا في النظم الملتزم بالقوافي ، وأن فيه أيضًا تفسيرًا لاختيار ويتمان للشعر المرسل . وفي المقطع أيضًا تعريض بالمعجبين

وإذا اتخذنا إمرسن Emerson مثلاً ، فإنه قد قام بهذه الرحلة ، وزار إنجلترا وفرنسا وإيطاليا وسويسرا ، وزار البندقية وروما وفلورنسا ، وقابل جون ستيوارت مل ، وانبهر بحدائق باريس ، وقابل ڤولتير ، وتعرف إلى أعلام الرومانسية الإنجليزية ، وردزورث وكولردج ، وصادق كارلايل . لكنه كان يدعو ، بعد عودته من الرحلة ، إلى الاستقلال الأدبي عن أوروبا . وكان هنري كيلي ، أحد مؤسسي الحزب الجمهوري ، قد أشار إلى أن الأمريكيين كانوا يغالون في التطلع إلى الخارج ، ومن ثم كان نداؤه عام ١٨٢٣ : «دعونا نصبح أمريكيين حقاً وصدقاً» (كما ورد في Siracusa and Warren 36) . ففي ظل التبعية الثقافية التي كانت لا تزال تربط أمريكا ببريطانيا ، وبأوروبا عموماً ، كان بعض الأمريكيين يحسون أن استقلالهم لم يكتمل بعد . فهذا إمرسن يحث ، في إحدى خطبه ، على السعي نحو إنشاء ثقافة قومية مستقلة : «لماذا لا يكون لنا شعر وفلسفة يقومان على الاستبصار لا على تقليد الموروث؟ . . . لنطالب بمنجزاتنا وبقوانيننا وبعباداتنا الخاصة بنا» (Emerson 27) . وفي خطاب آخر، يحث فيه المثقف الأمريكي على بلورة نفسه كياناً يتمتع بالاستقلال في التفكير ، نسمعه يبشر باقتراب نهاية التبعية الثقافية والفكرية ، حيث يقول : «إن يوم تبعيتنا ، أي تلمذتنا لزمن طويل على معارف بلاد أخرى ، يوشك أن ينتهي . فالملايين التي تندفع من حولنا نحو الحياة لا يمكن أن تقتات أبداً على البقايا الذابلة من محاصيل الأغراب» (كما ورد في Siracusa and Warren 56) . وفي مقاليه الشهيرين عن الطبيعة Nature وعن الاعتماد على الذات Self-Reliance ، لاحظ إمرسن أن الناس في العصور الحالية يتطلعون إلى الوراء ويجترون أحداث الماضي ، على حين كان الناس في عصور سابقة يرتبطون بالرب والطبيعة ارتباطاً مباشراً . ويتساءل لماذا لا نستعيد نحن هذه العلاقة الأصلية المباشرة بالكون ، هذه العلاقة القائمة على الاعتماد على الذات وعلى احترامها؟

أما ويتمان Whitman ، فقد تمكن ، بعفوية أسلوبه المطنب ، وبنظمه المرسَل ، وبنزعته الخطابية ومبالغاته ، أن يؤسس نمطاً شعرياً أمريكياً متميزاً عما سبقه . ومجموعته أوراق العشب Leaves of Grass زاخرة بالأمثلة على تمجيده العالم الجديد ، والهُويّة الأمريكية الناشئة ، والإيديولوجيا الديمقراطية والفردانية . وهو إذ يعبر عن تقبله الأم السابقة من أشوريين وصينيين وعبرانيين ، ويسجل تقديره واحترامه لكل الحضارات السابقة ، يؤكد أنه لم يكن ممكناً أن تكون إنجازاتها أبدع مما كانت ، وأنها الآن جميعاً

وتتواصل حدة اللهجة عند بركة ضد نظام يعتبره الشاعر ظالماً ، نظام تستحيل في ظله الرؤيا الإلهية ، فالكل قد رأى الشيطان في هذا الحدث الرهيب ، الكل رأه متجسداً في بومة :

مثل بومة تنفجر
في حياتك في دماغك في ذاتك
مثل بومة تعرف الشيطان
طوال الليلٍ ، طوال النهار ، إن كنت تسمع ، مثل بومة
تتفجّر نيراناً . ونسمع نحن الأسئلة تتعالى
لهباً رهيباً مثل مكاء كلب مسعور
مثل حامض تتقيأه نار الجحيم
مَنْ ومن ومن من من
هووووو و هوووووووووووووووووو . (Baraka n. pag)

هكذا تنتهي القصيدة بأن تتمدد كلمة who – مَن – لتصبح Whoooooooooooooo ، معبرة عن عواء هذا الكلب المسعور . والطريف أن الصيغة العربية هنا تشير إلى الضمير «هو» فتكون بذلك جواباً عن السؤال : مَنْ؟ أيْ ذلك المجهول الذي فجّر أمريكا .

كانت أوروبا بالنسبة إلى كتاب أمريكا عموماً ، وشعرائها خصوصاً ، هي تلك الـ«غيمة [التي] نأتي منها/المرة تلو المرة» ، حسب تعبير الشاعر روبرت كيلي Robert Kelly ، ويبدو أنها ستظل كذلك (Lapis 125) . رحلة الحج إلى القارة المنبع ، والعودة منها ، أو الإقامة الدائمة فيها ، كانت دائماً نمطاً مألوفاً متواتراً . ما على المرء إلا أن يتذكر حالات مشاهير الكتاب والشعراء والفنانين من أمثال إمرسن ، وملڤيل ، وهنري جيمس ، وجون هنري توتشمان ، وپاوند ، وإليوت ، وهمينجواي ، وجرترود شتاين ، وو . س . مروين ، وجون كايدج ، وجون أشبري ، وغيرهم . وهناك استثناءات نادرة لهذا التوجه الأوروبي ، مثل : إميلي دكنسن ووالت ويتمان . والجولة الأوروبية الكبرى The Grand Tour في أصلها رحلة ثقافية تعليمية ، وهو تقليد ابتدأ في بريطانيا في القرن السابع عشر ، وكان الهدف منه إتاحة الفرصة لأبناء الميسورين لزيارة الأماكن التي تمثل مهداً للتراث الفني والثقافي ، والتعرف عن كثب على مآثر الثقافة الكلاسيكية ، وعلى مآثر عصر النهضة التي تشكل منابع الحضارة الغربية .

واضح أن نبرة فرلينجتي مختلفة تماماً عن نبرة بيدارت، فهو هادئ، على عكس بيدارت الذي يبدو أنه أطلق العنان لانفعالاته. ولا تختلف النبرة وحدها هنا، بل تختلف النظرة إلى الموضوع أيضاً، فبيدارت منغمس تماماً في الحدث لأن الأمر بالنسبة إليه يتعلق بمرثاة أو مناحة، أما فرلينجتي فيستعير قناع المؤرخ ليتأمل الحدث بعمق وينفذ إلى ما أبعد من السطح. أما القصيدة التي أثارت الكثير من الجدل فهي قصيدة إمامو أميري بركة Imamu Amiri Baraka «مجهول فجّر أمريكا» "Somebody Blew Up America"، وهي قصيدة طويلة نسبياً، كان بركة يقرأها بمصاحبة عازف يعزف على الساكسفون. ويشبه بركة في هذه القصيدة بيدارت في العفوية والانفعال، ولكنه يشبه أيضاً فرلينجتي في نقده اللاذع للإمبريالية، على أن نبرة بركة هنا أعنف، وهو لم يكن أبداً يخفي نقمته على النظام الأمريكي، بسبب أصوله العرقية، وبسبب ما تعرض له من اضطهاد. وتقوم قصيدة بركة على التكرار في صيغة الاستفهام الإنكاري، فيتساءل مثلاً:

من يملك البنايات
من يملك الأموال
من يعتبرك غريباً
من الذي كان قد سجنك
من يملك الجرائد
. . .
من يملك النفط
من الذي لا يكدح
من يملك التربة
من الذي ليس زنجياً
من العظيم ولا أحد أعظم منه
. . .
من الذي اغتنى من الجزائر، ومن ليبيا، ومن هايتي وإيران، والعراق، والسعودية، والكويت، ومن لبنان ومن سوريا، ومصر، والأردن، ومن فلسطين. (Baraka n. pag)

Pearl Harbor، تُهاجَم أمريكا في عقر دارها. ارتفعت عندئذ أصوات تعلن، تبعاً لسنَّة أدورنو Adorno، أن كتابة الشعر غدت مستحيلة بعد الحادي عشر من الشهر التاسع. ولكن الشعراء كتبوا، وكتبوا الكثير، عن الكارثة. وكان تناول الموضوع لدى كل شاعر منهم مختلفاً. فهناك قصائد صدرت عن تأثر بالغ بفداحة المصاب، مثل قصيدة فرانك بيدارت Frank Bidart «اللعنة» "Curse" التي يصب فيها الشاعر نيران لعناته الغاضبة على منفذي الهجمات، ويحاول أن يتصور أبشع عقاب يمكن أن يحل بهم وهم بين ضحاياهم (Bidart 25). وكتب لورنس فرلينجتي Lawrence Ferlinghetti قصيدة «تاريخ الطائرة» "History of the Airplane" يتتبع فيها كيف غزت التكنولوجيا مملكة الطيور حيث كان السلام ملهماً للرواد الأوائل، ثم ظهرت الطائراتُ الحربية التي كان أصحابها يدّعون أنها «طيور السلام»:

ثم أقلعت القلعة الطائرة الشهيرة، مكتظةً بالبنادق
وبالتستوستيرون لتجعل العالم آمناً خدمة للسلام وللإمبريالية
لكن طيور السلام اختفت قبل هيروشيما كما اختفت بعدها.
(كما ورد في Olsen 168)

ويذكر الشاعر أن الاختراعات تواصلت، وأن المقاتلات بدأت تلقي بنعمها على العالم الثالث، وتَواصَل الطيران إلى أن بلغ الربابنة القرن الحادي والعشرين. ففي ذات يوم مشرق، رد العالم الثالث الضربة فارتطمت الطيورُ الهائلة بقلب أمريكا النابض، صارت أمريكا جزءاً من الأرض المحروقة:

وهبَّتْ عبر البلاد ريحٌ محملة بالرماد
ولبرهة طويلة من الأبدية
عمَّ اليأس وعمَّت الفوضى

وغمر الفضاءَ أحبابٌ مطمورون،
غمرته أصواتٌ وهمسات وصراخ،
غمرت الفضاءَ
في كل مكان. (169)

قصيدة أخرى في المجموعة نفسها ، «تجويف شجاع» "Valiant en abyme" ، بمشهد عمود النور الذي يظل مشرقاً في الشارع ، ظانّاً أنه هو الشمس ، وبإقرار الجمل الطيبة بأنها نسيتْ أين كانت قد ابتدأت (41) .

تلخص الشاعرة سوزان هاو Susan Howe المزاج السائد ، عند حلول الألفية الجديدة ، في هذه العبارات الانطباعية :

يُسمع في الليل كثيرٌ من الدق على الصخر لسبب يُعزى إلى الخطة الخماسية لتجهيز خدمة الإنترنت المجانية عبر الواي فاي ، لتكون متاحة في كل القطارات ، بما فيها القطارات البطيئة الرابطة بين الأقاليم . . . إنها الألفية الجديدة . ما بعد الحادي عشر من الشهر التاسع ، الأعلام المتلألئة النازفة ، مجزرة الحرب ، الحرب الشاملة على الإرهاب ، جوانتانامو ، البيانات الوصفية ، العلاقات الغرامية ، شق الصخور بالضغط المائي ، الأكياس البلاستيكية ، محطات الطاقة النووية ، تغير المناخ ، الاحتباس الحراري ، الثقوب السوداء ، الفناء المحتمل للجنس البشري . (كما ورد في Perloff 5)

ولعل هذا المزاج الذي يبعث على الإحباط هو الذي جعل الشاعر جوشوا كلوڤر يكتب بفرنسية ديموطيقية قصيدة بعنوان «ما الأمريكي في الشعر الأمريكي؟» "Qu'y-a-t-il d'américain dans la poésie américaine" يفتتحها بهذا الوصف : «هو في صميمه مجبول من الرمل ./وهذا من حسن الحظ ، وإلا فإنه كان سيكون حقاً صداعاً للرأس» (Clover 62) . ولعل الشاعر يقصد بهذا الوصف شعر جيله هو ، لا الشعر الأمريكي في عمومه .

ثمة أحداث تاريخية حددت مسارات تاريخ الولايات المتحدة الأمريكية وحددت بالتالي تاريخ آدابها . أول هذه الأحداث هو حرب الاستقلال عن الإمبراطورية (1775-1783) ، وثانيها الحرب الأهلية (1861-1865) ، وثالثها الحرب العالمية الأولى (1914-1918) ثم الثانية (1939-1945) ، وخامسها التورط في حرب ڤيتنام (1955-1975) ، وسادسها وأقربها إلينا هجمات الحادي عشر من الشهر التاسع (2001) . وما يهمنا في هذا السياق هو هذا الحدث الأخير ، نظراً لما له من تأثير مهم في المشهد الشعري المعاصر . كانت الصدمة قوية ، وكانت ردود الفعل عنيفة ؛ فلأول مرة ، بعد پرل هاربر

وستكتمل الدائرة . لكن لا يبدو أن الإنجاز كان هنا موفقاً تماماً رغم أن كل شيء يبدو على ما يرام . فرغم الشمس الشمس ، ورغم الاقتراب من الشمس ، ورغم أسماء الإشارة والظروف ، ورغم العرض الأليغوري ، ورغم أوهام السوق وأوهام الميدان ، ورغم النبوءات ، والتضحيات الرومانسية ، والحرص على الدقة في بناء الشكل ، والحرص على رصِّ الأبيات أشعةً ، ورغم توخي الدقة في تحديد المركز والمحيط والقطر والشعاع ، تُخفق العجلة ، تُخفق رغم انضباط أشعتها ، في التوهج ، وتظل الحلقة مفرغة . فمن الواضح أن هذه القصيدة مغرقة في الشكلانية : إنها القصيدة-الدائرة-الحلقة-العجلة ، كل بيت فيها شعاع ، وكل بداية نهاية : تظل الأشعة مظلمة لأن الشمس هنا شكلانية منطفئة . ولعل هذا ما يلمح إليه الشاعر في قصيدة نثرية بعنوان «العصور المظلمة» "The Dark Ages" ، حيث يقول :

البيت في الشعر شبيه بطريق ينيره مصباح ، طريق وجدتَ نفسك للتوِّ فيه . زنابقُ وثلةٌ من الأشرار تحت الأفاريز . يمكن أن نسمي نهايةَ البيت بالظلام ، ففي نهايته تنتهي الطريق ، وينطفئ المصباح ، وينسدُّ كل شيء . . . هبْ أنك كنت تنتظرني عند نهاية كل بيت ؛ أعني أنك قلت وردتَ في تلك الرسالة المرسَلة من العصور المظلمة . (Clover 33-34)

ولا يبدو أن هناك ما يدعو إلى رفض فرضية الانتظارِ هنا ، أو إلى رفض فرضية الرسالة المظلمة ، ما دام الجوّ السائد يوحي فعلاً بالعتمة . فالنجوم ، كما تقدم ، «مصابيح غريبة» ، والغيوم كتل سمينة ، والقمر لا يُدرَك إلا نصفه . وحتى حين تُفرَغ السماء من الغيوم ، لا يمكن أن يُتوقع إلا الفراغ . وهكذا تظل الكلمة ، ويظل الشعر ، كما يرد في قصيدة «تجويف» "En abyme" ، مجردَ ومضات نجوم تنوب عنا في التعبير : «نتصور النجومَ كلمات موجزة تومض في المساء ، وتقول شيئاً نود نحن أن نقوله»(Clover 35) . لكن الكلمات ذاتها سرعان ما تخبو وتغرق عند سواحل الظلام : «الكلمات تتدفق في اتجاه سواحل الغموض المظلمة» (35) . ولأن ارتطام الكلمات بالظلام وبالغموض أمر حتمي ، فإن الشاعر ، وقد صار أنضج ، ارتأى أن يتلاعب بعبارة هوميروس الشهيرة فيفرغ «المداد الداكن دكنة البحر في الجملة الداكنة دكنة الخمر» (35) . فلا عجب ، إذن ، في أن ينهي

وحين يتحقق التوازن المفترض ، وتنشأ الأحاسيس الجديدة ، ويتم إنشاء المقصلة أو النافذة الصغيرة ، يكتشف الشاعر/الناثر أن إلهاماً ما سينزل من السماء الصافية صفاء المقصلة ، وأن الطريق نحو تحقيق الآمال المفترضة لا يزال طويلاً :

. . . ولا يزال علينا أن نبتدع
شيئاً في صفاء المقصلة ،
أداةً تُعرف أيضاً بالنافذة الصغيرة . لكن ماذا نأمل
أن نرى هناك؟ الزواجَ بين الجميل والتافه؟
أنَّ السماء ، وقد أُفرِغَتْ أخيراً من الغيوم ،
لا بد أن تقول شيئاً جديداً؟ (Clover 10)

لكن المرجح أن السماء لن تلهم أي شيء ، وأنها لن تقول أي شيء جديد . المرجح أنها لن تلهم سوى مثل هذه البهلوانيات البصرية التي سبق أن مارسها كل من جيل أولسن وجيل برنشتاين :

اختار الشاعر Ça ira – أي «سيجوز هذا» ، أو أن التوفيق سيحالفه ، أو أن كل شيء سيكون في النهاية على ما يرام – عنواناً بالفرنسية لهذا العرض (Clover 30) . سيتم «الجواز» حتماً مهما تكن النقطة التي تبتدئ منها ،

ليجد الزهور تغمر اللونَ الفضي اللطيف ،
وتغطي الأصفرَ العزيز ، وتخفي الأزرقَ الحبيب . (Clover 30)

هكذا يفتتح الشاعر جوشوا كلوفر Joshua Clover قصيدة يعبر المتكلم في عنوانها عن أسفه لكونه كان قد أخفى اسم بلدته لمدة طويلة ، وفي العنوان من الغموض ما قد يوحي بأن اسم البلدة كان فعلاً «أسفاه» . افتتاحٌ منسوج على نمط سوريالي مألوف من حيث التناول والتصوير ، لكنه يفضي بسلاسة إلى هذا المشهد الذي يراوح بين الغزْل ونكث الغزل :

. . . امرأةٌ
كانت تصعد الدرج متجهةً نحو الخلف ، تاركةً المكتبة
للجرذان والقراء (تلك الفئران المتواضعة) ،
وكان كل شخص على التل ينتبه إلى صعودها الشبيه
بأحلام اليقظة يتذكر كم كان يستمتع بمشاهدة الأفلام إذ تُعرَض
معكوسة ، اللبنُ يندلق نحو الأعلى ليستقر في الكأس ذات
الحافة الزرقاء ، ويصب في النظام ، إنه الفعل الناقض
لما هو سامٍ . (Clover 9)

قد يبدو أن هذه الخوارق السوريالية تتحدى قوانين الفيزياء ، لكنها ، مع ذلك ، لا تخلو من وجاهة إپستيمولوجية . فمن يرقد في التصنيفات ويستيقظ في المفاهيم ، لا بد أن يحافظ على توازن ، قد يختل في أي لحظة ، بين التعاطي والإتيان بقصيدة النثر :

. . . نرقد في التصنيفات
ونستيقظ في المفاهيم لكن هل ينبغي
أن يُنفَق معظمُ النهار
في تتبع الملاحظات الشاردة ،
وفي تتبع قلوب الآخرين ،
وفي الحفاظ على توازن عرَضي
بين عقار الأوكسيكونتين و«النثر الشعري»
لكي تنشأ أحاسيس جديدة؟ (Clover 6)

سألتها : هل أناي متضخمة؟ تأرجحتْ من جانب إلى آخر
قائلةً : كلا . (F. Howe 29)

وفي قصيدة أخرى ، تتأمل عجوزٌ تقاوم البردَ القارس حجرَ الجمشت amethyst أمام المدفأة . يبدو أن الحجر كان قد جُلب من أرض الأسلاف ، من أكِل Achill ، إحدى الجزر الأيرلندية :

الحجر أرجواني شفاف .
يتلاعب ضوءُ المدفأة بلونه كما تتلاعب العيونُ بالدموع .
الطقس باردٌ حيث الشرقُ شمالٌ وحيث الأرضُ منبسطة ،
والمرءُ يشيخ . (F. Howe 54)

وينطوي الأصل اللغوي لكلمة الجمشت على الاعتقاد الخرافي بأن هذا الحجر يحمي من السُّكْر ، بل كان الرومان يعتقدون أنه يمنع التسمم . وإذ تستغرق العجوز في تأملات تتلاعب فيها بنزوات الأضواء والألوان ، تتوالى أمام ناظريها التمثلات . فهذا ، مثلاً ، راهب فوق صخرة من الصخور البحرية الهائلة على الساحل الجنوبي الغربي لأيرلندا ، منهمك في حكِّ عينيه المتجمدتين ، وفجأة تتراءى له اثنتا عشرة بجعة ومعها فتاة صغيرة وسط زبد البحر فوق حجر الجمشت الأرجواني . وذات صباح باكر ، تناثر على البركة رذاذ ثلج ، فبدا المشهد ، لعين البصيرة ، مثل حقل من نبات بخور مريم بأوراقه الأرجوانية الزاهية ، أو مثل مخيمات اللاجئين من سوريا . لكن العجوز لا تيأس ، فهي تدرك أن ستين عاماً ستمر قبل أن تتمكن الروح من عبور الجليد الفضي والوصول إلى حقول النعيم المحرَّمة . وهذا صوت آخر من جيل آخر يحاول أن يثبت تميزه بالجراءة وافتعال العنفوان :

كانت النجوم مصابيح غريبة ، وكان القمر نصف فرجة ،
وكانا يطوفان حتى دخلا إلى بهو المساء
حين أغمي على الغيوم السِّمان ،
وكان يبدو أنهما مرتبكان مثل مدعوٍّ وصل
متأخراً عن موعد العشاء ببضع دقائق

وهذا يعني أن ثمة قوتاً .
وعند المصب القريب
كانت قد انفصلتْ قارتان
وطار صائحاً
كروانٌ وحيد . (F. Howe 57)

كروانٌ وحيد . ينوح في شجن ، انفصال ، أو فراق ، أو تصدّع ، أو كسر مؤلم . صوت الشاعرة فاني هاو Fanny Howe في قصيدة يبدو أنها رسالة موجهة إلى هولدرلن ، حيث نصادف شاعراً يُلوِّن الزنجبيل شعرَه ، يهبط التل ، ويملأ قبعته بزهور البنفسج وبالأعشاب وبالماء ، ويتغنى بالحنين إلى نشوة الطرب ، ويتغنى بنسْوة المخيّم ، وبالظاعنة التي كانت تشبه عروسا من عرائس البحر تدير شؤون السفائن الغارقة . ولا يبقي في النهاية من أمل سوى التعاطف . وفي سياق آخر :

ماذا تعني لك السعادة ، أنت؟
قِطَعَ بلاطٍ سوداء ومنحدراً
من غيوم مضلعة .
قوسَ قزح رسمه طفلٌ
وتحته منزل .
ثياباً في آلة الغسيل
تصطفقُ طوال الليل . (F. Howe 64)

يبدو أن السؤال هنا ليس سوى ذريعة لتأكيد الجواب . ويتضمن السؤال مسألتين فلسفيتين ظلتا مطروحتين منذ الأزل : المعنى والسعادة . ولأن الجواب المباشر ظل مستعصياً ، فلا بأس من محاولة إعادة صياغته هنا بأسلوب تشكيلي يذكر بالغنائية البصرية لدى باول كلي Paul Klee ، والطفولة هنا ليست طفولة أولى بل هي «طفولة ثانية» "Second Childhood" ، قصيدة تتأمل فيها الشاعرةُ سبحتَها الخرافية :

لدي سبحة جنية تسمى «فضة» ترد على الأسئلة حين أعلقها في ضوء الشمس عند النافذة .

إطلالة على الشعر الأمريكي «المعاصر»: تأملات

حسن حلمي

مقدمة

الشعر؟ الشعر الأمريكي؟ الشعر الأمريكي المعاصر؟ المهمة صعبة فالشعراء بالمئات، وما يجعل المهمة أصعب أن كلمة «أمريكي» تنطوي على تنوع شاسع يستعصي على التصنيف. ولعل تشارلز أولسن Charles Olson كان على وعي بهذا حين حدد الكلمة في هذا التعريف الوارد في إحدى القصائد التي حذفها من ملحمته قصائد ماكسيموس: «الأمريكي مُركَّبٌ من أحداث تمثل في حد ذاتها هندسةً للطبيعة الفضائية» (كما ورد في Klippinger 134)*. ولعل هذا ما يعبر عنه تشارلز برنشتاين، بشكل مختلف، حين يجعل وجود أمريكا متوقفاً على استحالتها: «أمريكا مستحيلة، وهي، لذلك، أيضاً موجودة . . . ففي مقاومة مفهوم الهُويَّة الواحدة الموحدة تكمن استحالة أمريكا، واستحالة صياغة نظرية شعرية أمريكية» (Bernstein, My Way 113). أما كلمة «معاصر»، فواضح أنها كلمة زئبقية، منفلتة، إذ إن المعاصرة بطبيعتها نسبية، فما هو معاصر في لحظة زمنية قد يتوقف عن كونه معاصراً في اللحظة الموالية. وقد يتم استدعاء عصور غابرة لتعاصر أوضاعاً حاضرة. ولعل هذا سبب إدانة باوند Pound «متطلبات العصر». لا سبيل إلى إيقاف تيار الزمن أو إلى تجزئته. ولكن الشعر هناك. وأمريكا هناك. والمعاصرة، مفروضة أو مفترضة، هناك. فلنستمع، قبلِ الإبحار، إلى عينات من أصوات قد تمثل المشهد «المعاصر»، ولو تمثيلاً نسبيا:

لا يزال الزهرِ والعشبِ
ينموان طوعا وكان ليلكُ البحر
قد شقَّ المدرج.

Tomasello, M. *The Cultural Origins Of Human Cognition*. Cambridge: Harvard UP, 1999.

"Trends in International Mathematics and Science Study (TIMSS)." *National Center for Education Statistics (NCES)*. <https://nces.ed.gov/timss/>.

Vygotsky, L. S. *Mind in Society: The Development of Higher Psychological Processes*. Eds. M. Cole et al. Cambridge, MA: Harvard UP, 1978.

Wagner, D. *Literacy, Culture and Development: Becoming Literate in Morocco*. Cambridge: Cambridge UP, 1993.

Warren, B. et al. "Rethinking Diversity in Learning Science: The Logic of Everyday Sense-Making." *Journal of Research in Science Teaching* 38.5 (April 2001): 529-52.

Wells, G. *Dialogic Inquiry: Toward a Sociocultural Practice and Theory of Education*. Cambridge: Cambridge UP, 1999.

--- and R. M. Arauz. "Dialogue in the Classroom." *The Journal of the Learning Sciences* 15.3 (2006): 379-428.

Wilson, M. "Six Views of Embodied Cognition." *Psychonomic Bulletin and Review* 9.4 (2002): 625-36.

Teachers Need to Know." *Understanding Language: Language, Literacy And Learning in the Content Areas*. Eds. K. Hakuta and M. Santos. Stanford, CA: Stanford U, 2012. 32-43.

Rezat, Sebastian and Sara Rezat. "Subject-Specific Genres and Genre Awareness in Integrated Mathematics and Language Teaching." *EURASIA Journal of Mathematics Science and Technology Education* 13.7b (June 2017): 4189-210.

Ridge, N. et al. "Arab Migrant Teachers in the United Arab Emirates and Qatar: Challenges and Opportunities." *Arab Migrant Communities in the GCC*. Ed. Z. Babar. Oxford: Oxford UP, 2017. 39-64.

Rogoff, B. *The Cultural Nature of Human Development*. Oxford: Oxford UP, 2003.

Rymes, B. *Classroom Discourse Analysis: A Tool for Critical Reflection*. London: Routledge, 2015.

Saiegh-Haddad, E. and R. M. Joshi. *Handbook of Arabic Literacy: Insights and Perspectives*. Dordrecht: Springer, 2014.

Salloum, S. and S. BouJaoude. "Science Teaching and Learning in Multilingual Lebanese Middle School Classrooms." Biennial Meeting of the European Science Education Research Associate (ESERA), August 21-25, 2017, Dublin. Conference paper.

---. "The Use of Triadic Dialogue in the Science Classroom: A Teacher Negotiating Conceptual Learning and Teaching to the Test." *Research in Science Education* 49.3 (June 2019): 829-57.

Setati, M. et al. "Incomplete Journeys: Code-Switching and Other Language Practices in Mathematics, Science and English Language Classrooms in South Africa." *Language and Education* 16.2 (2002): 128-50.

Smit J. et al. "Using Genre Pedagogy to Promote Student Proficiency in the Language Required for Interpreting Line Graphs." *Mathematics Education Research Journal* 28.3 (September 2016): 457-78.

Snow, C. E. and P. Uccelli. "The Challenge of Academic Language." *The Cambridge Handbook of Literacy*. Eds. D. R. Olson and N. Torrance. Cambridge: Cambridge UP, 2009. 112-33.

Spolsky, B. *Educational Linguistics: An Introduction*. Rowley, MA: Newbury House, 1978.

Stetkevych, J. *The Modern Arabic Literary Language: Lexical and Stylistic Developments*. Chicago, IL: U of Chicago P, 1970.

Suleiman, Y. *The Arabic Language and National Identity*. Washington, DC: Georgetown UP, 2003.

Lave, J. *Cognition in Practice: Mind, Mathematics and Culture in Everyday Life*. Cambridge: Cambridge UP, 1988.

Lemke, J. L. "Articulating Communities: Socio-Cultural Perspectives on Science Education." *Journal of Research in Science Teaching* 38.3 (March 2001): 296–316.

---. *Talking Science: Language, Learning, and Values*. Norwood, NJ: Ablex Publishing, 1990.

Manches, A. and C. O'Malley. "The Effects of Physical Manipulatives on Children's Numerical Strategies." *Cognition and Instruction* 34.1 (February 2016): 27-50.

Martin, J. R. and R. Veel. *Reading Science: Critical and Functional Perspectives on Discourses of Science*. London: Routledge, 1998.

Mercer, N. *The Guided Construction of Knowledge: Talk amongst Teachers and Learners*. Clevedon: Multilingual Matters, 1995.

--- and L. Dawes. "The Value of Exploratory Talk." *Exploring Talk in School*. Eds. N. Mercer and S. Hodgkinson. London: Sage, 2008. 55-71.

Montgomery, S. L. *Science in Translation: Movements of Knowledge through Cultures and Time*. Chicago, IL: U of Chicago P, 2000.

Moschkovich, J. "Mathematics, the Common Core, and Language: Recommendations for Mathematics Instruction for ELLs Aligned with the Common Core." *Understanding Language: Language, Literacy And Learning in the Content Areas*. Eds. K. Hakuta and M. Santos. Stanford, CA: Stanford U, 2012. 17-31.

---. "Scaffolding Student Participation in Mathematical Practices." *ZDM* 47.7 (September 2015): 1067-78.

Nelson, K. *Language in Cognitive Development*. Cambridge: Cambridge UP, 1996.

Nemirovsky, R. et al. "When the Classroom Floor Becomes the Complex Plane: Addition and Multiplication as Ways of Bodily Navigation." *Journal of the Learning Sciences* 21.2 (2012): 287-323.

New London Group. "A Pedagogy of Multiliteracies: Designing Social Futures." *Multiliteracies: Literacy Learning and Design of Social Futures*. Eds. B. Cope and M. Kalantzis. London: Routledge. 2000. 9-37.

Pinker, S. *The Language Instinct*. NY: William Morrow, 1994.

Planas, N. and M. Setati-Phakeng. "On the Process of Gaining Language as a Resource in Mathematics Education." *ZDM Mathematics Education* 46.6 (November 2014): 883–983.

Quinn, H. et al. "Language Demands and Opportunities in Relation to Next Generation Science Standards for English Language Learners: What

Goodwin, C. and J. Heritage. "Conversation Analysis." *Annual Review of Anthropology* 19 (1990): 283-307.

Grøver, V., P. Uccelli, M. Rowe, and E. Lieven, eds. *Learning through Language: Towards an Educationally Informed Theory of Language Learning*. Cambridge: Cambridge UP, 2019.

Hall, R. and R. Nemirovsky. "Introduction to the Special Issue: Modalities of Body Engagement in Mathematical Activity and Learning." *Journal of the Learning Sciences* 21.2 (October 2012): 207-15.

Haeri, N. "Form and Ideology: Arabic Sociolinguistics and Beyond." *Annual Review of Anthropology* 29 (2000): 61-87.

Halliday, M. A. K. *An Introduction to Functional Grammar*. London: Arnold, 1994.

--- and J. R. Martin. *Writing Science: Literacy and Discursive Power*. Pittsburgh, PA: U of Pittsburgh P, 1993.

Heath, S. B. *Ways with Words: Language, Life and Work in Communities and Classrooms*. Cambridge: Cambridge UP, 1983.

Hoffman, C. "Luxembourg and the European Schools." *Beyond Bilingualism: Multilingualism and Multilingual Education*. Eds. J. Cenoz and F. Genesee. Clevedon: Multlingual Matters, 1998. 143-74.

Hornberger, N. H. "Educational Linguistics as a Field: A View from Penn's Program on the Occasion of its 25th Anniversary." *Working Papers in Educational Linguistics* 17.1-2 (Fall 2001): 1-26.

--- and F. M. Hult. "Educational Linguistics." *Encyclopedia of Language and Linguistics*. Ed. K. Brown. Oxford: Elsevier, 2006. 76-81.

Hult, F. M. "The History and Development of Educational Linguistics." *The Handbook of Educational Linguistics*. Eds. B. Spolsky and M. Hult. Oxford: Blackwell, 2010. 10-24.

Ioannidou, E. "Using 'Improper' Language in the Classroom: The Conflict between Language Use and Legitimate Varieties in Education: Evidence from a Greek Cypriot Cslassroom." *Language and Education* 23.3 (May 2009): 263-78.

Kress, G. and T. van Leeuwen. *Multimodal Discourse: The Modes and Media of Contemporary Communication*. London: Arnold, 2001.

Labov, W. *Sociolinguistic Patterns*. Philadelphia, PA: U of Pennsylvania P, 1972.

Lakoff, G. and M. Johnson. *Metaphors We Live By*. Chicago: U of Chicago P, 1980.

---. *Philosophy in the Flesh*. NY: Basic Books, 1999.

Lakoff, G. and R. E. Núñez. *Where Mathematics Comes from: How the Embodied Mind Brings Mathematics into Being*. NY: Basic Books, 2000.

Cenoz, J. and F. Genesee. *Beyond Bilingualism: Multilingualism and Multilingual Education*. Clevedon: Multlingual Matters. 1998.

Close, H. and R. Scherr. "Enacting Conceptual Metaphor through Blending: Learning Activities Embodying the Substance Metaphor for Energy." *International Journal of Science Education* 37.5-6 (March-April 2015): 839-66.

Cobb, P. et al., eds. *Communicating and Symbolizing in Mathematics, Perspectives on Discourse, Tools and Instructional Design*. Mahwah, NJ: Lawrence Erlbaum Associates, 2000.

Crozet, P. "L'arabe, langue scientifique: Un aperçu historique jusqu'au XIXe siècle." *Al-Logha* 4 (April 2003): 9-28.

Cummins, J. *Language, Power and Pedagogy: Bilingual Children in the Crossfire*. Toronto: Multilingual Matters, 2000.

Dagher, Z. and S. BouJaoude. "Science Education in Arab States: Bright Future or Status Quo?" *Studies in Science Education* 47.1 (March 2011): 73-101.

Ferguson, C. A. "Diglossia." *Word* 15.2 (1959): 325-40.

---. "Epilogue: Diglossia Revisited." *Southwest Journal of Linguistics* 10.1 (1991): 214-34.

Gee, J. P. *An Introduction to Discourse Analysis: Theory and Method*. London: Routledge, 2004.

---. "Language in the Science Classroom: Academic Social Languages as the Heart of School-Based Literacy." *Establishing Scientific Classroom Discourse Communities: Multiple Voices of Teaching and Learning*. Eds. R. K. Yerrick and W.-M. Roth. Mahwah, NJ: Erlbaum, 2005. 19-38.

---. *Situated Language and Learning: A Critique of Traditional Schooling*. London: Routledge, 2004.

Gerofsky, S. "Beyond the 'Qualitative/Quantitative' Split: Linguistics and Genre Studies as Research Methodologies in Education." *Education and Psychology: An Encyclopedia*. Eds. J. Kincheloe and R. Horn. Westport, CT: Greenwood Publishing, 2006. 497-503.

---. "Genre Analysis as a Way of Understanding Pedagogy in Mathematics Education." *For the Learning of Mathematics* 19.3 (November 1999): 36-46.

Glenberg, A. "Embodiment for Education." *Handbook of Cognitive Science: An Embodied Approach*. Eds. P. Calvo and T. Gomila. Oxford: Elsevier Science, 2008. 355-72.

Goldin-Meadow, S. "Talking and Thinking with our Hands." *Current Directions in Psychological Science* 15.1 (February 2006): 34-39.

--- and C. Morgan. "A Framework for the Study of Written and Spoken Discourse: School Mathematics in Palestine." *ZDM* 50.6 (November 2018): 1041-51.

--- and H. Straehler-Pohl. "Interrupting Passivity: Attempts to Interrogate Political Agency in Palestinian School Mathematics." *The Disorder of Mathematics Education*. Eds. H. Straehler-Pohl , N. Bohlmann and A. Pais. NY: Springer, 2017. 191-208.

Amin, T. G. "Conceptual Metaphor Meets Conceptual Change." *Human Development* 52.3 (May 2009): 165-97.

---. "Conceptual Metaphor and the Study of Conceptual Change: Research Synthesis and Future Directions." *International Journal of Science Education* 37.5-6 (March-April 2015): 966-91.

---. "The Language of Instruction and Science Education in the Arab Region: Toward a Situation Research Agenda." *The World of Science Education: Arab States*. Eds. S. BouJaoude and Z. Dagher. Vol. 3. Rotterdam: Sense Publishers, 2009. 61-82.

--- and D. Badreddine. "Teaching Science in Arabic: Diglossia and Discourse Patterns in the Elementray Classroom." *International Journal of Science Education*. June 28, 2019. <https://www.tandfonline.com/doi/full/10.1080/09500693.2019.1629039>.

--- et al. "Conceptual Metaphor and Embodied Cognition In Science Learning." *International Journal of Science Education* 37.5-6 (March-April 2015): 745-58.

Ammon, U. *The Dominance of English as a Language of Science: Effects on Other Languages and Language Communities*. Berlin: Mouton de Gruyter, 2001.

Bezemer, J. and C. Jewitt. "Multimodality: Key Issues." *Research Methods in Linguistics*. Ed. L. Litosseliti. London: Bloomsbury Publishing, 2018. 180-97.

Bezemer, J. and G. Kress. "Writing in Multimodal Texts: A Social Semiotic Account of Designs for Learning." *Written Communication* 25 (April 1, 2008): 166-95.

Brookes, D. T. and E. Etkina. "The Importance of Language in Students' Reasoning about Heat in Thermodynamic Processes." *International Journal of Science Education* 37.5-6 (March-April 2015): 759-79.

Brustad, K. "Diglossia as Ideology." *The Politics of Written Language in the Arab World: Writing Change*. Eds. J. Hoiglit and G. Mejdell. Leiden: Brill, 2017. 41–67.

خاتمة

كان الهدف من هذه المقالة إظهار مدى أهمية تخصصات مختلفة في العلوم الاجتماعية والإنسانية تندرج تحت عنوان «اللغويات التربوية» وتسهم في فهم المشاكل المختلفة المتعلقة باللغة وتعليم العلوم والرياضيات في العالم العربي. لقد قدمت خريطة عامة لهذه التخصصات، واستعرضت برامج بحثية جارية في سياقات مختلفة في العالم تحتوي على مفاهيم ومنهجيات بحثية ونتائج تشكل منطلقاً لبرنامج بحثي في العالم العربي. فهذه المقالة دعوة للباحثين من مختلف مجالات العلوم التربوية واللغويات والأنثروبولوجيا اللغوية وعلم النفس وغيرها للإسهام في هذا الجهد البحثي. مع التنبيه إلى أنه على الرغم من أن الإسهامات مطلوبة من تخصصات عديدة، فإننا نحتاج إلى إطار نظري يوضح إسهام كل تخصص في تكوين متماسك. وآمل أن تكون هذه المقالة نقطة انطلاق مفيدة لوضع الخطوط العريضة للهيكل النظري المطلوب.

المراجع العربية

بدوي، السعيد. **مستويات العربية المعاصرة في مصر**. القاهرة: دار المعارف، ١٩٧٣.

بوجودة، صوما وفؤاد صياح. «تعليم العلوم باللغة العربية: اتجاهات وحلول». **اللغة والتعليم**. تحرير قاسم شعبان. بيروت: الهيئة اللبنانية للعلوم التربوية، ٢٠٠٠. ص ص ١٤٥-١٧٠.

عبد العزيز، محمد حسن. «اللغة العلمية في العصر العباسي». **اللغة** ٤ (أبريل ٢٠٠٣): ص ص ٩-٢٨.

كروزيه، بسكال. «اللغة العربية، لغة علمية: موجز ناريخي حتى الفرن التاسع عشر». ترجمة أميرة مختار. **اللغة** ٤ (أبريل ٢٠٠٣): ص ص ٢٩-٤٥.

المراجع الأجنبية

Alexander, R. *Culture and Pedagogy*. Oxford: Blackwell, 2000.

Alshwaikh, J. "Investigating the Geometry Curriculum in Palestinian Textbooks: Towards Multimodal Analysis of Arabic Mathematics Discourse." *Research in Mathematics Education* 18.2 (July 2016): 165-81.

وبالتحصيل الأكاديمي عبر المواد المختلفة ، كما تتطلب إجراء أبحاث تقارن نماذج مختلفة لاستخدام اللغات عبر المراحل المدرسية (انظر Wagner) . فظاهرة ثنائية اللغة العربية تتطلب منا عدم التسرع في تعميم النتائج التي توصلت إليها الأبحاث التربوية في بيئات لغوية وثقافية مختلفة .

ويثير تعليم العلوم والرياضيات بلغة ليست لغة الطالب الأساسية أسئلة أخرى مهمة حول إستراتيجيات التدريس في الصف الدراسي والدور الذي يجب أن تلعبه اللغة الأساسية . فقد أجريت أبحاث كثيرة من المنظور الاجتماعي والثقافي للتعليم والتعلم لتحديد هذه الإستراتيجيات ، ناقشنا بعضها في الجزء الأول من هذه المقالة . ومن ناحية ، فإن النظر إلى التفكير العلمي والرياضي على أنهما استخدام متخصص للغة وغيرها من الأدوات الرمزية قد ساعد الباحثين على تحديد أهداف تربوية لغوية إلى جانب أهداف محتوى مواد العلوم والرياضيات . وقد أدى ذلك أيضاً إلى استقصاء الطرق الفعالة لدعم هذا الاستخدام المتخصص للغة في هذه المواد في سياقات متعددة اللغات تكون فيها لغة التدريس هي لغة أجنبية (انظر Setati et al) . ومن ناحية أخرى ، فإن النهج الاجتماعي والثقافي ينظر إلى التعلم على أنه المشاركة في نشاطات المادة لاكتساب مهارات التفكير العلمي والرياضي . ففي سياق تكون فيه لغة التدريس هي لغة أجنبية ، قد تتطلب هذه المشاركة استخدام الطلاب للغتهم الأساسية ، فهي موردهم اللغوي والذهني الأكثر تطوراً (انظر Planas and Setati-Phakeng) . وقد تناولت أبحاث كثيرة في بيئات متعددة اللغات حول العالم الخطاب الصّفي وكيف يعتمد الطلاب والمعلمون على لغتهم الأساسية بوصفها مورداً للمشاركة الفعالة ، وكيف يمكن توجيه الطلاب إلى استخدام هذه الموارد بشكل إستراتيجي (انظر ,Moschkovich "Scaffolding"; Setati et al.; Warren et al; Planas and Setati-Phakeng) . ورغم إجراء هذه الأبحاث في بيئات تربوية ، فإنها تستند إلى مفاهيم ومنهجيات بحثية من عدة فروع في اللغويات مثل تحليل الخطاب وتحليل المحادثة وتحليل الخطاب النقدي . وقد أجريت حديثاً بعض الأبحاث من هذا النوع في العالم العربي (انظر Amin and Badreddine; Salloum and BouJaoude)، ولكن هذه بداية متواضعة ، حيث نحتاج برنامجاً بحثياً واسع النطاق حتى نتمكن من صياغة توصيات تربوية تستند إلى معرفة علمية ذات صلة بسياقات متعددة اللغات في العالم العربي .

القراءة والكتابة وتعلم المواد من خلال اللغة العربية؟ وقد أوضح أمين وبدر الدين Amin and Badreddine مؤخراً في دراستهما عن أثر ثنائية اللغة العربية في الخطاب الصّفي عندما يتم تدريس العلوم باللغة العربية في لبنان أن هناك اختلافات في التفاعل بين المعلمة والتلاميذ ذات أهمية تربوية متعلقة بمدى وكيفية استخدام العامية اللبنانية مع اللغة العربية الفصحى، حيث تبيّن التنافس في هذه البيئة التربوية بين الأهداف اللغوية والأهداف المتعلقة بمحتوى المادة التي تدرس. وما زال هناك حاجة ماسة إلى المزيد من الأبحاث التي تتناول طبيعة الآثار التربوية لثنائية اللغة العربية (انظر Haeri).

يتضح مما سبق أنه عندما يتم تدريس العلوم والرياضيات باللغة العربية، فإننا نتعامل مع بيئة تربوية ذات لغتين (أو أكثر إذا كان هناك بالفعل مستويات أكثر؛ أو على الأقل، نوعان من لغة واحدة باختلافات كبيرة)، إحداهما لغة التعليم الرسمية ولكنها ليست لغة المتعلّم الأساسية. أما عندما يتم تدريس هذه المواد بلغة أجنبية، فيكون واضحاً أن لغة التدريس ليست هي اللغة الأساسية للطالب. وهناك أدبيات بحثية كثيرة حول فهم التحديات التي تنشأ في مثل هذه البيئات التربوية وكيف يمكن التغلب عليها (انظر Cenoz and Genesee). فقد تناولت بعض البحوث مسألة تصميم برامج التعليم الثنائي اللغة ودور لغة المتعلمين الأساسية عندما يكون الهدف هو تدريس العلوم والرياضيات بلغة أجنبية. وأحد الأسئلة الرئيسية المطروحة هو ما إذا كان من الأفضل البدء باستخدام اللغة الأجنبيّة من أول المرحلة الابتدائية أم تأخير استخدامها لعدة سنوات حتى يطور المتعلم مهاراته باللغة الأجنبية. ويكون الاختيار هنا بين إستراتيجيتين: الانغماس المبكر في لغة أجنبية أو تنمية المهارات الأكاديمية بلغة المتعلم الأساسية (أو اللغة الأولى). فمثلاً، في أمريكا الشمالية - أحد السياقات المدروسة جيداً - تشير الأبحاث إلى أن تأخير استخدام اللغة الأجنبية في تدريس مواد مثل العلوم والرياضيات لمدة تتراوح بين ٥ و٧ سنوات أمر مستحسن (انظر Cummins). ويعزز ذلك نتائج تشير إلى أن تطوير المهارات الأكاديمية باللغة الأساسية له نتائج إيجابية على المدى الطويل، بما في ذلك تأثير إيجابي في تعلم اللغة الأجنبية. وربما تكون هذه المقاربة اللغوية فعالة في المناهج الدراسية في العالم العربي أيضاً. ولكن سياسات تربوية لغوية بهذه الأهمية تتطلب إجراء أبحاث تتناول اكتساب اللغة الأساسية الشفوية، واكتساب مهارات القراءة والكتابة، وعلاقة كل منهما ببعضهما البعض

اللغة العربية تثير تساؤلات وقضايا من النوع نفسه في العالم العربي. لكن القضايا الاجتماعية والسياسية ذات طبيعة مختلفة، فهي تنطوي على التنافس (والعلاقة) بين الهُويّات المحلية من ناحية، والقومية العربية من ناحية أخرى، وترتبط بأسئلة حول استخدام اللغة في التعليم الرسمي. وقد طرحت هذه القضايا باهتمام شديد في النصف الأول من القرن العشرين (انظر Suleiman)، لكن التركيز قد تحول حديثاً إلى الاختيار بين اللغة العربية (بدون اهتمام بثنائيتها) ولغات أجنبية دولية، وبخاصة في تعليم العلوم والرياضيات.

وهناك أيضاً قضايا تربوية تتعلق بطبيعة هذه الثنائية في اللغة العربية. فإذا كانت العامية هي لغة الطفل العربي الأساسية، فهل يجب علينا التعامل مع اللغة العربية الفصحى الحديثة على أنها لغة أجنبية تتطلب اتباع طرق تعليم وفقاً لهذا التصنيف؟ تشير الأبحاث في مجال اللغويات النفسية Psycholinguistics إلى أن اللغة العربية لها الآثار المعرفية نفسها التي تحدثها الازدواجية اللغوية بشكل عام (انظر Saiegh-Haddad and Joshi). ومن ناحية أخرى، تشير البحوث التربوية إلى أن التحدث بلهجة عربية (مثل المغربية) يحضّ الأطفال على تعلم القراءة والكتابة باللغة العربية الفصحى أكثر من التحدث بلغة أخرى (مثل الأمازيغية) (انظر Wagner). علاوة على ذلك، فقد أشار بعض اللغويين الاجتماعيين إلى أن وصف التعايش بين الفصحى واللهجات العامية بـ«الثنائية» تبسيط لواقع أكثر تعقيداً، وقد يكون من الأوقع الاعترافَ بعدة مستويات، بما في ذلك المستوياتِ المتوسطة بين العامية والفصحى (انظر بدوي). لكن يجب الاعتراف أيضاً بأن ثنائية اللغة العربية «واقع نفسي»، بمعنى أن الشخص الذي يتعلم القراءة والكتابة باللغة العربية في حين يتقن عامية شفوية ينظر إلى العامية والفصحى على أنهما نوعان لغويان منفصلان. وهذا الواقع النفسي المعاصر قد يكون حديثاً نسبياً (انظر Brustad)، مما قد يزيد الأمر تعقيداً.

تثير هذه الاعتبارات في وصف واقع اللغة العربية وثنائيتها عدة تساؤلات: كيف تؤثر هذه الثنائية اللغوية (بوصفها واقعاً نفسياً)، والعلاقة الوثيقة بين الفصحى والاستخدامات الرسمية، في عملية التعلم باللغة العربية؟ وما معتقدات المعلمين حول ثنائية اللغة العربية ودور كل منهما في العملية التعليمية، وعلى وجه التحديد في الخطاب الصّفي؟ وما معتقدات الأطفال الصغار حول اللغة العربية وأنواعها؟ وهل تؤثر في اكتساب مهارات

التربوي للغة العربية ، وبخاصة عندما يكون الطلاب – وأحياناً المعلمون – لا يتقنون لغة أجنبية . وبالإضافة إلى هذا كله ، فهناك طلاب من مجتمعات الأقليات يلتحقون بالتعليم الرسمي في العالم العربي ممن تكون لغتهم الأم لغة غير العربية ، مثل الأرمنية والأمازيغية والكردية . وتثير هذه التعقيدات اللغوية أسئلة مهمة ، مثل : ما الدور الذي ينبغي (أو يمكن) أن تلعبه اللغات – أو أصناف اللغة المختلفة – في التعليم والتعلم؟ ما تحديات التعليم والتعلم عندما يتم استخدام لغة أجنبية لتعليم العلوم والرياضيات؟ ومن منظور تربوي ، هل ينبغي النظر إلى اللغة العربية الفصحى الحديثة على أنها لغة أجنبية؟ وعندما يتم استخدام أكثر من لغة في النظام المدرسي ، متى يجب أن يتم الانتقال من لغة إلى أخرى؟ وما الذي يحتاج المعلمون إلى معرفته لدعم التعلم في مثل هذه السياقات؟ هذه أسئلة مهمة ومتنوعة لن أقدم لها إجابات هنا ، ففهمنا لهذه السياقات والتحديات النابعة منها محدود للغاية . أما الهدف هنا فسيكون الإفادة من مقاربات بحثية في اللغويات التربوية تساعد على تحديد الدراسات التي تؤدي إلى إنتاج معرفيّ ذي صلة بالسياق العربي وتنوعه اللغوي الخاص .

دعونا نبدأ بظاهرة ثنائية اللغة العربية . يجب التوضيح أولاً أن ظاهرة الثنائية اللغوية ليست منحصرة في اللغة العربية . فقد وثّق اللغويون الاجتماعيون عدة بيئات لغوية تتعايش فيها لغة رسمية مستخدمة في القراءة والكتابة جنباً إلى جنب مع نوع لغوي مستخدم للتواصل في الحياة اليومية ؛ ورغم وجود اختلافات لغوية كثيرة ، يكون هذا النوع قريب الصلة باللغة الرسمية . من أمثلة ذلك التعايش بين اللغة العامية الإنجليزية الأمريكية الأفريقية إلى جانب الإنجليزية الرسمية المستخدمة في التعليم الرسمي في الولايات المتحدة (انظر Labov) ، وبين اللوكسمبرجية والألمانية في لوكسمبورج (انظر Hoffman) ، أو بين اللهجة القبرصية واللغة اليونانية في قبرص (انظر Ioannidou) . وقد ركز علماء اللغويات الاجتماعية والأنثروبولوجيا اللغوية على مسألة مهمة تظهر في كل هذه السياقات اللغوية ، ألا وهي العلاقة بين هذه الأنواع اللغوية والهُويّة . ففي كل هذه السياقات ، ترتبط اللغة الرسمية بالثقافة المهيمنة (انظر Hoffman; Ioannidou; Labov) ، حيث من الممكن أن يكون استخدام اللهجة الشفوية محاولة لتأكيد هُويّة المجتمع الناطق بها . وتتشابك الأسئلة التربوية حول اختيار وكيفية الإفادة من الأنواع اللغوية المختلفة في التعليم والتعلم مع قضايا اجتماعية وسياسية . فثنائية

في العالم العربي عادةً على التاريخ الاستعماري لمختلف دول المنطقة. وهكذا، تهيمن اللغة الإنجليزية بوصفها لغة أجنبية في مصر والأردن وليبيا وفلسطين وعمان وقطر والسودان والإمارات العربية المتحدة. وأما في الجزائر ولبنان وموريتانيا والمغرب وتونس، فالفرنسية هي اللغة الأجنبية الأكثر انتشاراً. مع العلم بأنه في الآونة الأخيرة، زاد استخدام اللغة الإنجليزية في بعض البلدان، وعلى حساب اللغة الفرنسية أحياناً. ويعد الاستعمار مصدر هذه الأنماط إلى حد كبير، إلا أن سليمان Suleiman يضيف أهمية (ونفوذ) الإنجليزية والفرنسية بوصفهما لغتين دوليتين تُجهزان الطلاب في جميع أنحاء العالم لسوق العمل العالمي (انظر Ammon).

وحتى لو نظرنا إلى اللغة العربية وحدها، فسنجد أننا نتعامل مع حالة تعدد لغوي. فاللغة العربية تعتبر من أفضل الأمثلة لظاهرة الثنائية اللغوية (انظر Ferguson). ويشير مصطلح الثنائية اللغوية إلى وجود نوعين من لغةٍ ما يستخدم كل منهما في سياقات حياتية مختلفة. فاللغة العربية الفصحى الحديثة تستخدم للقراءة والكتابة، في سياق التعليم الرسمي، وشفهياً في الخطب والمناسبات الرسمية؛ في حين يتم استخدام اللهجات المحلية (العاميات) للتواصل الشفهي في سياقات الحياة اليومية. ويجب أن نلاحظ هنا أن الفصحى ليست اللغة الأم لأي شخص، حيث يتم تعلمها من خلال التعليم الرسمي فقط. أما العامية، فهي اللغة التي يتعلمها الأطفال بشكل طبيعي عن طريق التفاعل والتواصل مع الآخرين في إطار حياتهم اليومية، معتمدين على القدرة البيولوجية لتعلم اللغة (انظر Pinker). لذلك، فالعامية (أو العاميات) التي يتعرض لها الطفل العربي هي التي تشكل مورده اللغوي الأساسي الذي يجلبه معه إلى المدرسة ليبدأ مشواره الأكاديمي.

يوضح هذا المسح اللغوي السريع أن تعليم الرياضيات والعلوم وغيرها من المواد وتعلمها في العالم العربي يتم في بيئات مختلفة متعددة اللغات. وحتى لو كانت لغة التدريس هي اللغة العربية الفصحى، فسيتعيّن على صانعي السياسات والمدرسين والمتعلمين اتخاذ قرار بشأن مدى وكيفية استخدام العامية (أو عدم استخدامها). وعلاوة على ذلك، ففي بعض البيئات التربوية (مثل دول الخليج، على سبيل المثال) يستخدم المعلمون والطلاب لهجات عربية مختلفة (انظر Ridge et al)؛ الأمر الذي يضيف مستوى آخر من التعقيد اللغوي. وعندما تستخدم لغة أجنبية - مثل اللغة الإنجليزية أو الفرنسية - بوصفها لغة تعليم، فعلينا طرح تساؤل حول الدور

لغوياً (انظر Goldin-Meadow) . وقد أظهرت بعض الدراسات أنه عندما يُطلب من الطلاب إنتاج إيماءات معينة (على سبيل المثال ، إيماءة على شكل V لتشجيع تجميع عدة عناصر لمعادلة رياضية) ، يقوم الطلاب بحل المسائل الرياضية بطريقة أفضل (انظر Goldin-Meadow) .

استعرضنا نوعين من الموارد اللغوية والذهنية في هذا الجزء من المقالة : أنماط استعمال اللغة قبل الالتحاق بالمدرسة ، والمعرفة النابعة من التفاعل الحسي الجسدي والكامنة في استعمال اللغة والرموز الأخرى . ولم تجرَ أبحاث لوصف وتحليل وتشخيص أهمية هذه الموارد في بيئاتٍ تربوية عربَية . وسدُّ هذه الفجوة مطلوب ، لأن هذه المقاربة البحثية قليلاً ما يصدر عنها توصيات تربوية عامة ، حيث تقدم نتائج ذات صلة شديدة الارتباط بالسياق المحدد الذي يجري فيه البحث .

مشكلة تعدد اللغات

يبيّن ما تم مناقشته حتى الآن عدة تحديات في محاولة فهم دور اللغة في تعليم وتعلم الرياضيات والعلوم ، ومن ثم ، تحديات تتعلق باللغة تواجه تحسين التعليم في هذه المواد . ولكن هناك جانباً آخر للتحديات اللغوية في تعليم العلوم والرياضيات ، هو التعدد اللغوي . ففي العالم العربي ، كما هو الحال في معظم أنحاء العالم (انظر New London Group) ، يتم التعليم الرسمي في سياقات متعددة اللغات (انظر Suleiman) . فبالإضافة إلى اللغة العربية ، يتم استخدام لغات أخرى (مثل الأرمنية والأمازيغية والكردية والآرامية الشرقية وعدد من اللغات في جنوب السودان) من قبل البعض في العالم العربي لأسباب تاريخية مختلفة . وبالإضافة إلى ذلك ، تُستعمل اللغة الفرنسية على نطاق واسع في الجزائر ولبنان والمغرب وتونس وموريتانيا بسبب الاستعمار الفرنسي . وعلاوة على ذلك ، يتم تعليم الطلاب لغة أجنبية (غالباً ما تكون اللغة الإنجليزية أو الفرنسية) بوصفها مادة في مناهج معظم البلاد العربية . ونزيد على ذلك ، أنه في بعض الأحيان (وهذه الظاهرة تزداد مع الوقت) تستخدم لغة أجنبية دولية بوصفها لغة تعليم لبعض المواد (عادة ما تكون العلوم والرياضيات) في العديد من المدارس الخاصة ، وحتى في بعض المدارس الرسمية (في لبنان ، على سبيل المثال) . وتعتمد اللغة الأجنبية المختارة في النظم التعليمية

وإخراجها) . وهذا يعني أن فهمنا وفكرنا المجرد يرتكزان إلى نظامنا الحسي الجسدي . ومن المثير للاهتمام أن هذه العلاقة الوثيقة بين المفاهيم المجردة ونظامنا الحسي الجسدي تظهر من خلال تحليل دقيق للاستعارات اللغوية التي تم وصفها على نطاق واسع في فرع اللغويات الإدراكية Cognitive Linguistics . فقد وثق الباحثون هذه الاستعارات في لغة الحياة اليومية ولغة العلوم (انظر Amin) والرياضيات (انظر Lakoff and Núñez) ، ومن ثم حددوا موارد معرفية نابعة من التفاعل الحسي الجسدي تساعد على فهم المفاهيم المجردة . وإذا جمعنا الفرضيتين ، نستطيع أن نلخص مقاربة الإدراك المجسد بالقول إنها توجّه الباحث إلى تحليل كيفية استخدام الأدوات المادية والرمزية ، وكذلك المعرفة الحسية الجسدية ، بوصفها موارد تُوظف في التفكير العلمي والرياضي .

ظهرت خلال العقد الماضي مجموعة كبيرة من الأبحاث تتناول تفاصيل التفاعل بين الأدوات المادية والرمزية والمعرفة الحسية الجسدية في بيئات تعليمية (انظر Amin et al.; Glenberg; Hall and Nemirovsky) . وقد توصلت هذه الأبحاث إلى عدة استنتاجات ذات أهمية تربوية . فعلى سبيل المثال ، إذا تعرض الأطفال لاستعارات كامنة في لغة الحياة اليومية أو في لغة العلوم والرياضيات ، فقد يساعدهم هذا على فهم بعض المفاهيم العلمية والرياضية ، ولكنها تعوق هذا الفهم أحياناً (فمثلاً ، غالباً ما تصف اللغة العلمية مفاهيم مجردة مثل الحرارة والطاقة مجازاً على أنها مواد ملموسة تنتقل من مكان إلى آخر) (انظر Amin, "Conceptual Metaphor Meets" and "Conceptual Metpahor and the Study"; Brookes and Etkina) .

ومن الممكن تصميم النشاطات التربوية في مادتي العلوم والرياضيات بما يتيح للمتعلمين فرصة استخدام أجسادهم بطريقة تنمي الموارد المعرفية الحسية الجسدية التي تساعد على فهم المفاهيم المجردة وتقلل الاعتماد على اللغة وغيرها من الأدوات الرمزية (انظر Close and Scherr; Manches and O'Malley; Nemirovsky et al) ؛ فقد صمم كلوس وشير بيئة تعليمية يسمونها «مسرح الطاقة» ، حيث يتولى المتعلمون دور وحدة من الطاقة ، فيستخدمون أجسادهم لتمثيل عمليات نقل الطاقة وتحولاتها ؛ وهناك أبحاث تم فيها تحليل إيماءات اليد التي يقوم بها المتعلمون أثناء الإجابة عن مسألة رياضية تكشف عن جوانب من تفكيرهم لا يمكننا اكتشافها عن طريق تحليل اللغة فقط - لأن بعض الإيماءات ترمز إلى مفاهيم غير مذكورة

ويساعد مفهوم النوع الأدبي على تفسير هذه الصلة . فإذا تخيلنا طفلاً مرّ بتجربة مناقشة قوائم الأشياء التي يمكن شراؤها من السوق ، والتي تم فرزها إلى «أشياء نحتاج إليها لتناول العشاء» أو «أشياء نحتاج إليها لتناول وجبة الإفطار» ، فهذا يُحضره لنشاط تصنيف النباتات والحيوانات في المدرسة . فالنوع الأدبي هنا ، وهو التصنيف ، مشترك بين استعمال اللغة في الحياة اليومية والمطلوب ممارسته في مادة العلوم . هذا يعني أن الأبحاث التي توثق أنواع الأنشطة التي يشارك فيها الأطفال في المنزل وفي مجتمعاتهم قبل الالتحاق بالمدرسة وأنماط استعمال اللغة في سياق هذه الأنشطة تساعدنا على تحديد أنواع الموارد اللغوية (ومن ثم الذهنية) التي سيجلبونها معهم إلى الفصل . ويوفر مجال الأنثروبولوجيا اللغوية بالأساس المفاهيم النظرية اللازمة والأدوات المنهجية لمثل هذا البرنامج الاستقصائي . وقد أجريت بعض الأبحاث من هذا النوع في أماكن مختلفة في العالم ، ولا سيما في الولايات المتحدة ، ووفرت معلومات كافية عن الموارد اللغوية لحديثي الالتحاق بالتعليم الرسمي تَمكّن على أساسها الباحثون التربويون من تفسير التفاوت بين طلاب ذوي خلفية اجتماعية-ثقافية مختلفة في التحصيل الأكاديمي بشكل عام (انظر Heath) ، وفي العلوم والرياضيات بشكل خاص (انظر Moschkovich, "Scaffolding"; Gee "Language" and *Situated*) . وتنبّه هائري Haeri إلى أنه لا يوجد برنامج بحثي من هذا النوع ، أي برنامج بحثي في الإثنوغرافيا اللغوية ، في السياق العربي . وتحتم أهمية القدرة على تحديد أسباب التفاوت بين الطلاب في التحصيل الأكاديمي الخوض في برنامج بحثي من هذا النوع ، وسدّ هذه الفجوة في اللغويات التربوية في العالم العربي .

وهناك نوع آخر من الموارد الذهنية ذو أهمية في التفكير العلمي والرياضي والتعلم في هذين المجالين . ففي العقود القليلة الماضية ، أطلق بعض الباحثين في العلوم المعرفية مقاربة الإدراك المجسد (انظر Lakoff and Johnson; Wilson) ، وقاموا بطرح فرضيتين رئيسيتين : الأولى ، مشتركة مع النهج الاجتماعي-الثقافي في علم النفس التنموي ، ومفادها أن التفكير المجرد يتم باستخدام أدوات مادية ورمزية . أي إن التفكير المجرد يتجسد في استخدام هذه الأدوات . والفرضية الثانية هي أن فهم المفاهيم المجردة يستند إلى المعرفة التي تنبثق من التفاعل الحسي والجسدي مع العالم من حولنا (مثل دفع الأشياء وسحبها ، ووضع الأشياء في حاويات

المطلوبة تدريجياً. لكن المشاركة الأولية تتطلب بعض الموارد اللغوية والذهنية. في هذا الجزء الثاني من المقالة، أناقش بعض الأبحاث والمقاربات المختلفة في اللغويات التربوية التي تصف طبيعة هذه الموارد وتحاول تفسير التفاوت بين المتعلمين في درجة استعدادهم للمشاركة في مهام التعلم المطلوبة منهم في إطار التعليم الرسمي. أركز هنا على مجالين من مجالات البحث بشكل خاص: أحدهما يستند إلى منظور الأنثروبولوجيا اللغوية (انظر Heath)، والآخر مستمد من منظور جديد في العلوم المعرفية cognitive sciences، هو مقاربة الإدراك المجسد embodied cognition (انظر Wilson).

وإذا كان المنظور المقدَّم هنا يشدد على أن التفكير الرياضي والعلمي يمكن وصفهما على أنهما استخدام متخصص للغة وعناصر النظم الرمزية الأخرى، فعلينا أن نسأل: ما الموارد الرمزية التي يمتلكها الأطفال عند التحاقهم بالتعليم الرسمي؟ من المؤكد أن المورد الأساسي هو لغة الطفل الأساسية، اللغة المحكية المتداولة في المجتمع الذي ولد فيه (وفي المجتمعات متعددة اللغات، يمكن أن يكون المورد الأساسي أكثر من لغة واحدة؛ وهي مسألة سنتناولها في الجزء التالي). ومن الممكن وصف المهارات اللغوية من حيث عدد المفردات المكتسبة وصحة الجمل المنطوقة نحوياً ودرجة تطورها؛ فالكفاءة في كلتا الحالتين تنبئ بنجاح وتحصيل أكاديمي، ولكن نطاق الكفاءة اللغوية المطلوب وصفها لتقييم استعداد الطفل للتعليم الرسمي أوسع من ذلك (انظر Gee, *Situated*).

يحدث النمو المعرفي المبكر عن طريق التفاعل بين الطفل والبيئة الطبيعية والاجتماعية. فنظريات علم النفس التنموي، وخصوصاً المقاربة الاجتماعية-الثقافية، تعطي الأولوية للبيئة الاجتماعية والنشاطات المختلفة التي يشترك فيها الطفل مع الآخرين، حيث تشكل هذه النشاطات سياق تعلم اللغة. وقد تطرق العديد من الباحثين إلى تشابك عملية تعلم اللغة والنمو المعرفي (انظر Tomasello; Nelson; Grøver et al.). ولقد وضحنا أن مهارات التفكير العلمي والرياضي يمكن فهمها على أنها مهارات توظيف عناصر اللغة والرموز الأخرى لتحقيق أهداف هذه المواد، وطبقنا مفهوم النوع الأدبي في هذا الصدد. ويمكننا تطبيق هذا المفهوم (وغيره) لوصف استخدام الناس للغة في حياتهم اليومية أيضاً. فقد توصلت بعض الأبحاث التربوية إلى أن نجاح الأطفال في التعليم الرسمي ذو صلة وثيقة بأنماط استخدام اللغة في المنزل ومدى تشابهها مع استخدامها في المدرسة (انظر Gee, *Situated*).

في المرحلة المتوسطة (الإعدادية) في لبنان ، حيث تدرس مادة العلوم باللغة الإنجليزية ، وإن كان الطلاب والمعلمون يستخدمن اللغة العربية إلى جانب لغة التعليم الأجنبية . وقد وثق هذا البحث أنماطاً مختلفة من التفاعل الصّفي في المدارس الرسمية والخاصة . وفي بحث ثان لسلوم وبوجودة Salloum and BouJaoude بعنوان "The Use of Triadic Dialogue" وصفا استعمالاً متميزاً للتخاطب الثلاثي من قبل المعلمة التي استطاعت الموازنة بين التدريس من أجل الفهم العميق وإعداد الطلاب لاختبار رسمي مهم . أما في مادة الرياضيات ، فقد وضع الشويخ ومورجان Alshwaikh and Morgan منهجية لدراسة النصوص المكتوبة والخطاب الشفهي في إطار تعليم الرياضيات في فلسطين . وقد وسّع الشويخ وسترالر-پول Alshwaikh and Straehler-Pohl النطاق البحثي ليشمل السياق الاجتماعي والسياسي لتعليم الرياضيات في فلسطين مع تناول علاقة هذا السياق بالتعليم داخل الصف المدرسي .

في الجزء الأول من هذه المقالة ، قدمت نظرية اجتماعية-ثقافية للتعليم والتعلم Sociocultural learning theory مع التركيز على دور اللغة في العملية التعليمية . ويمكننا اعتبار هذه النظرية أساس اللغويات التربوية ، وإن كنت قد وضّحت أيضاً دور منهجيات بحثية أخرى – مثل اللغويات الوظيفية ، والسيميوطيقية ، وتحليل الخطاب ، وتحليل المحادثة – التي نحتاجها لفهم دور اللغة في التعليم والتعلم . فقد ناقشت أبحاثاً استندت إلى هذه المنهجيات لتسليط الضوء على تحديات تعليم وتعلم العلوم والرياضيات . وقد تم إجراء عدد قليل فقط من هذه الأبحاث في العالم العربي . وهذه الأبحاث بداية واعدة ، ولكنها تحتاج إلى تطوير لتصبح برنامجاً بحثياً يشجع الآخرين على العمل من خلال المقاربة نفسها . فالأبحاث المستقلة لا تكفي ، لأن التوصيات والسياسات العملية يجب أن تستند إلى برنامج بحثي متماسك .

من أين تأتي مواردنا اللغوية والذهنية؟

هناك جوانب أخرى للبرنامج البحثي الذى تم عرضه حتى الآن . وكما أسلفت ، فالمقاربة الاجتماعية-الثقافية لدراسة التعليم والتعلم تنظر إلى التعلم باعتباره مشاركة في مهام أو ممارسات مادة ما . ومن خلال المشاركة المدعومة من قبل المعلم (أو متعلمين آخرين) ، يكتسب المتعلم المهارات

للنصوص العلمية والرياضية في السياق العربي. وهناك بعض الدراسات التاريخية التي تناولت تطور اللغة العربية بوصفها لغة تواصل علمي منذ القرن الثامن (انظر عبد العزيز وكروزيه وCrozet وMontgomery)، بل بوصفها محاولات لتحديث اللغة العربية كلغة تواصل علمي في القرنين التاسع عشر والعشرين (انظر Stetkevych; Suleiman). ولكن لا يوجد برنامج بحثي يصف الخصائص اللغوية والسيميوطيقية للنصوص العلمية والرياضية التي نطلب من الطالب العربي قراءتها والتعلم من خلالها، وإن كان الشويخ Alshwaikh قد بدأ في دراسة هذا الموضوع في تحليله لكتب الرياضيات المدرسية في فلسطين من منطلق سيميوطيقي. فهو يقوم بعرض إطار منهجي لتحليل الهياكل اللغوية والعلاقة بين اللغة والتمثيلات المرئية، ويستنتج دور المتعلم عند التفاعل مع النص. وتكمن أهمية هذه الأبحاث في كونها تساعد الباحث التربوي العربي على تشخيص التحديات التي قد يواجهها الطالب العربي وهو ينمي مهارته في استخدام هذه العناصر اللغوية والسيميوطيقية الأخرى.

وهناك برنامج بحثي ثانٍ يكمل الأول، وهو برنامج يوضح ويقيّم أنماط التفاعل الخطابي في فصول العلوم والرياضيات في العالم العربي. فثمة افتراض واسع الانتشار، يُشار إليه بطريقة عابرة، بأن التدريس في العالم العربي تلقيني بالأساس، ويعتمد على إلقاء المحاضرات من جانب المعلم بمشاركةٍ صغيرة من الطلاب. وعلى الرغم من أن هذا قد يكون صحيحاً، فثمة حاجة إلى برنامج بحثي تجريبي يعتمد منهجية تحليل الخطاب وتحليل المحادثة في إطار نظرة اجتماعية وثقافية للتعلم. ولتقييم هذا الافتراض بشكل نقدي، نحتاج إلى توثيق أنماط الخطاب الصّفي بتنوعها عبر البيئات التربوية المختلفة في دول العالم العربي، بخصوصياتها اللغوية والثقافية والسياسية.

وقد أجريت بالفعل بعض الأبحاث من هذا النوع، فقد تناول أمين وبدر الدين Amin and Badreddine أنماط الخطاب في فصلين من الصف الأول الابتدائي في لبنان، حيث يتم تدريس العلوم باللغة العربية. فقد قامت الدراسة بتسجيل دروس لمعلمتين ونسخ الخطاب الصّفي حرفياً. وقد بيّن تحليل هذا الخطاب الصّفي أن أنماطاً مختلفة من التفاعل الصّفي ترتبط بأنماط مختلفة من استخدام اللغة العربية الفصحى واللهجة العامية اللبنانية. وفي بحث آخر بعنوان "Science Teaching and Learning"، تناول سلوم وبوجودة Salloum and BouJaoude التفاعل الخطابي الصّفي

وهناك باحثون آخرون تناولوا جوانب الخطاب الصّفي في صفوف تُدرَّس فيها مواد العلوم والرياضيات على وجه التحديد (انظر ;.Cobb et al ;Lemke; Moschkovich, "Scaffolding"; Wells; Wells and Arauz). ففي صفوف العلوم يوضح لمكي Lemke ، على سبيل المثال ، أن المعلمين كثيراً ما يشيرون بطريقة ضمنية فقط إلى العلاقات بين المفاهيم التي يتم عرضها ، وهذا يصعب مهمة الفهم لدى الطلاب (انظر *Talking*) . أما ولز ، فيصف الاستخدامات المختلفة لما يسمى بالتخاطبِ الثلاثيِّ triadic dialogue ، وهو نمط مألوف يطرح فيه المعلم موضوعاً أو سؤالاً وينتظر ردًا من قبل الطلاب ، ثم يتابع من خلال التقييم والتوضيح أو تشجيع الطلاب على الاستطراد (انظر Wells; Wells and Arauz) . ويركز ولز على دور التخاطب الثلاثي في دعم التفكير العلمي الاستكشافي . وفي صفوف الرياضيات ، تصف موسكوفيتش Moschkovich الوسائل المختلفة التي يتبعها المعلم لدعم المتعلم للمشاركة في الخطاب الصّفي ، وعلى وجه التحديد استخدام الأسئلة لتوجيه الطلاب وهم يحاولون تفسير الرسوم البيانية .

تعلمنا أدبيات البحث العالمي هذه الكثير عن دور اللغة في تعليم وتعلم العلوم والرياضيات . فهناك بعض النتائج التي يمكن تطبيقها فوراً في صفوفنا المدرسية في العالم العربي . فنحن نستطيع أن ننصح معلماً في أي مكان في العالم بأن يخلق نمط خطاب صَفّي يعطي المتعلم فرصة ممارسة التفكير الرياضي أو العلمي من خلال استخدام اللغة – وغيرها من النظم الرمزية – المتخصصة في إطار تفاعلي ، حيث يعطي المعلم الدعم اللازم للطالب . ولكن الأهم من ذلك ، أن هذه الأبحاث العالمية تعطي الباحث العربي مقاربة لدراسة هذه القضايا لإنتاج معرفة ذات صلة بالسياق العربي بالإفادة من منهجيات اللغويات الوظيفية ، والسيميوطيقية ، وتحليل الخطاب ، وتحليل المحادثة ، ونظرية النمو المعرفي بمقاربتها الاجتماعية-الثقافية . تكمن أهمية هذا الإنتاج المعرفي المحلي في أنه يساعد على صياغة سياسات وتوصيات للممارسات التربوية ذات صلة بالواقع العربي . وأود أن أختتم هذا الجزء من المقالة بوصف موجز لبرنامجين بحثيين ، يعد الخوض فيهما ، من وجهة نظري ، ذا أهمية كبيرة .

تدعو الأبحاث التي تم استعراضها التربويين والباحثين العرب إلى النظر إلى التفكير العلمي والرياضي على أنه استخدام متخصص للغة والرموز الأخرى ، لذلك فهناك حاجة إلى وصف لغوي (وسيميوطيقي أوسع)

والتكرار، تقل حاجة المتعلم إلى دعم المعلم، وتنتقل مسؤولية إتمام النشاط بنجاح إلى المتعلم. وفي المواد التقنية، مثل العلوم والرياضيات، تتطلب النشاطات مهارات متخصصة في استعمال اللغة والنظم الرمزية الأخرى. ويساعد مفهوم النوع الأدبي المعلم (أو الباحث) على تحديد صفات المهارة المطلوبة (انظر Moschkovich, "Scaffolding"; Lemke, *Talking*).

إذن، فأهمية التفاعل التواصلي واضحة جداً، وهناك أبحاث كثيرة تصف الخطاب الصّفي وتقيمه، بما في ذلك التفاعل بين المعلم والطلاب وبين الطلاب أنفسهم. وقد وصف بعض هذه الأبحاث أنماط التفاعل الصّفي ذات الأهمية لكل المواد المدرسية بشكل عام. فقد وثق الباحثون مَن الذي يتحدث داخل الصف: المعلم أم الطلاب وأنماط التفاعل العامة: المحاضرة، التفاعل بين المعلم والطالب بوصفهما مجموعة صفية واحدة، والتفاعل بين الطلاب داخل مجموعات صغيرة، إلخ. (انظر Wells; Wells and Arauz). فعندما يتفاعل الطلاب في مجموعات، قد يأخذ هذا التفاعل شكل «النزاع» disputational talk حول آراء مختلفة، أو شكل «الخطاب التراكمي» cumulative talk حيث تقبل كل مداخلة دون انتقاد، ويضاف إليها، وقد يأخذ التفاعل شكلاً «استكشافياً» exploratory talk، بما في ذلك صفات التحليل النقدي الجماعي (انظر Mercer). وقد أجمعت بعض الأبحاث على أن التفاعل الاستكشافي هو الذي ينمي تفكير المتعلم بشكل أفضل (انظر Mercer and Dawes). كما أجريت أبحاث تقارن أنماط التفاعل التواصلي الصّفي، واكتشفت فروقات عبر الثقافات المختلفة حول العالم (في الولايات المتحدة، بريطانيا، فرنسا، الهند، وروسيا) ذات أهمية تربوية (انظر Alexander).

وقد أجريت هذه الأبحاث التي تناولت الخطاب الصّفي من منظور نظرية النمو الذهني ذات المقاربة الاجتماعية-الثقافية مع دعم من اللغويات. فالوصف والتحليل الدقيق للخطاب الصّفي يتطلب منهجية مناسبة مثل تحليل الخطاب Discourse Analysis (انظر Gee, *An Introduction*) أو تحليل المحادثة Conversation Analysis (انظر Goodwin and Heritage) اللذين يوفران للباحث المفاهيم ووسائل التحليل لوصف أدوار المتحدثين وتوظيفهم لعناصر لغوية مختلفة لأغراض معرفية واجتماعية، وأنماط التفاعل المختلفة. وتساعد هذه الأبحاث على تشخيص الخطاب الصّفي من حيث الجودة التربوية، وعلى توجيه المعلمين لخلق بيئة صَفّية أحسن (انظر Rymes).

مختلفة في العلوم والرياضيات (انظر Bezemer and Kress). و«النوع الأدبي» هو مجرد مفهوم واحد من نظرية مفصلة لوصف الاستخدام المتخصص للغة والأدوات الرمزية الأخرى في العلوم والرياضيات. وهناك أدبيات بحثية غنية في اللغويات الوظيفية والسيميوطيقية Semiotics (فرع يصف النظم الرمزية بأنواعها المختلفة ويحللها) تتعمق في دراسة الاستخدامات المختلفة للغة والنظم الرمزية الأخرى في المواد التقنية مثل العلوم والرياضيات (انظر Bezemer and Jewitt; Kress and van Leeuwen; Martin and Veel).

والاستخدام المتخصص للغة وغيرها من الأنظمة الرمزية يثير سؤالين لدى المهتمين بالأمور التربوية: ما مكونات النظم الرمزية التي تشكل تحديات للمتعلم؟، وكيف نصف عملية اكتساب مهارات توظيف عناصر اللغة والنظم الرمزية الأخرى المطلوبة لممارسة التفكير العلمي والرياضي؟ لقد تطرق بعض الباحثين للسؤال الأول. فحول مادة العلوم، يصف جي Gee في مقالة بعنوان "Language in the Science Classroom" خصائص اللغة العلمية (مثل استخدام الأسماء بدلاً من الأفعال للإشارة إلى العمليات الطبيعية) التي تخلق منظوراً مجرداً للظواهر والعمليات الطبيعية، وهو منظور يشكل صعوبة للمتعلم. وحول الرياضيات، يعرض جروفسكي وسميت وآخرون (انظر Gerofsky; Smit et al) الأنواع الأدبية وخصائصها التي يصعب تعلمها (مثل اللغة المستخدمة لفهم الرسوم البيانية وتحليلها). أما سنو وأوتشيلي Snow and Uccelli، فيصفان التحديات المتعلقة باكتساب المهارات اللغوية الأكاديمية بشكل عام. وجدير بالذكر أن عدداً من المحاولات العالمية لمراجعة المناهج المدرسية في مادتي العلوم والرياضيات حددت المهارات اللغوية المطلوب من الطالب اكتسابها في المادتين (انظر Moschkovich, "Mathematics"; Quinn et al)

أما السؤال الثاني، فهو كيف نصف عملية اكتساب مهارات توظيف عناصر اللغة والنظم الرمزية الأخرى المطلوبة لممارسة التفكير العلمي والرياضي؟ علمتنا نظرية التعلم والنمو الذهني الاجتماعية-الثقافية أن التعلم يحصل عن طريق الممارسة. فاكتساب أي مهارة يتطلب ممارسة النشاط الذي يعتمد على هذه المهارة لتحقيقه (انظر Lave; Rogoff). ومن ثم، فمَن يريد أن يساعد شخصاً آخر على اكتساب مهارة، مطلوب منه أن يصمم النشاط الذي يحتاج هذه المهارة ويقدم التوجيه (أو ما يسمى الدعم scaffolding) اللازم لكي يمارس المتعلم النشاط بنجاح. ومع الوقت

تفكير، وفهم دور التواصل في عملية التعلم. أناقش كلاً من هذه الأمور فيما يأتي، موضحاً الحاجة إلى تخصصات مختلفة في العلوم الاجتماعية والإنسانية، بهدف تحقيق فهم شمولي كاف يمكننا من تقديم توصيات عملية في قضايا متعلقة باللغة في تعليم العلوم والرياضيات.

من منظور نظرية ڤيجوتسكي، يمكن فهم التفكير على أنه استعمال متخصص للغة وغيرها من الأنظمة الرمزية لتحقيق أهداف معينة (انظر Vygotsky; Wells). في هذه المقالة، أركز على العلوم والرياضيات، متسائلاً: ما الأهداف التي نريد أن نحققها عندما نمارس التفكير في هذه الفروع المعرفية؟ وأفضل إجابة عن هذا السؤال تأتي من فرع من فروع اللغويات الحديثة، هو اللغويات الوظيفية (انظر Halliday). فهذه المقاربة لدراسة اللغة تصف وتحلل الكلمات والتركيبات النحوية أو هيكل نص أو خطاباً ممتداً من منظورٍ وظيفي لاختيار العناصر اللغوية. ففي العلوم، نستطيع أن نحدد أهدافاً علمية مثل وصف الأشياء وتصنيفها وتفسير الظواهر الطبيعية وعرض نتائج الأبحاث. ولكل هدف علمي عناصر لغوية مستعملة لتحقيقه (انظر Halliday and Martin). في اللغويات الوظيفية، يشير مصطلح «النوع الأدبي» genre إلى الاستخدام المتخصص للغة لتحقيق هدف معين. ورغم أن مصطلح النوع الأدبي يستخدم عادة لوصف وتحليل النصوص الأدبية، فنطاقه أوسع من ذلك. حيث يمكن استخدامه لوصف وتصنيف النصوص والخطاب الممتد في أي مجال. فمن الممكن النظر إلى التصنيف أو التفسير العلمي على أن كلاً منهما نص ذو خصائص لغوية معينة. ففي التصنيف، هناك العناصر اللغوية المستخدمة لإدراج أعضاء فئة معينة وعناصر لغوية أخرى لربط الفئات العامة بفئات أخرى أكثر تحديداً. أما في التفسير، فهناك عناصر لغوية مستخدمة لوصف الظواهر، وعناصر أخرى لوصف وربط العمليات الطبيعية المختلفة التي تسبب هذه الظاهرة. وينطبق هذا على مادة الرياضيات أيضاً، فلكل من البراهين الرياضية والإنشاءات الهندسية، على سبيل المثال، خصائص لغوية يمكننا وصفها (انظر Rezat and Rezat, "Genre" ,Gerofsky). لذلك، نجد أن تحقيق هذه الأهداف (أو ممارسة عمليات تفكير تؤدي إلى تحقيقها) يتطلب من المتعلم اكتساب مهارات لغوية معينة. ورغم التركيز هنا على اللغة، فالتعميم مطلوب للتأكيد على أن هناك نظماً رمزية أخرى – مثل الرسوم البيانية والتمثيلات الرياضية وغيرها – تستخدم لتحقيق أهداف

أخصص بقية هذه المقالة لمناقشة نظريات وأبحاث عبر تخصصات مختلفة في اللغويات التربوية ، ومصدر معظمها أدبيات البحث العالمي، الأمر الذي يساعد على فهم القضايا المتعلقة باللغة في تعليم وتعلم العلومِ والرياضيات ومعالجتها . ومن خلال هذه المناقشة ، أقترح برنامجاً بحثياً لفهم ومعالجة هذه القضايا في العالم العربي على وجه التحديد .

نظرة اجتماعية-ثقافية للغة في التعليم والتعلم

لا تشكل اللغة في المفهوم التقليدي للتعليم والتعلم إشكالية مطلوب فهمها . فمن منظور هذا المفهوم ، يتحمل المعلم مسؤولية توصيل المعرفة إلى المتعلم ، وتعتبر اللغة ، ببساطة ، أداة تواصل . وأكثر ما يمكن قوله عن اللغة في هذا المفهوم التقليدي هو أن بعض المعلمين يملكون مهارة «الشرح» أكثر من غيرهم . بمعنى آخر ، يعتمد تقييم المعلم على تحديد مدى قدرته على نقل المعرفة التي يحددها المنهج إلى الطلاب . وهذا المفهوم لدور اللغة في التعليم والتعلم قد عفا عليه الزمن . فمن منظور اللغويات التربوية ، يمكننا التعامل مع اللغة ودورها في التعليم والتعلم بوصفها إشكالية وطرح أسئلة واسعة النطاق ، ولكنها ذات أهمية عملية ، مثل : ما العلاقة بين المهارات اللغوية وتعلم المفاهيم ومهارات التفكير في مواد العلوم والرياضيات وغيرها؟ ما صفات الخطاب الصّفي التي تؤدي إلى التعلم المنشود؟ كيف يستطيع المعلم خلق البيئة التي تشجع ظهور نمط الخطاب المرغوب؟ ، وغيرها من الأسئلة المهمة التي تسهم مجموعة متنوعة من التخصصات المختلفة ضمن منهجية اللغويات التربوية في الإجابة عنها .

في قلب هذه المجموعة من التخصصات علم النفس التنموي Developmental Psychology وعلى وجه التحديد ، تبرز المقاربة الاجتماعية-الثقافية لدراسة النمو المعرفي للعالِم الروسي ليف ڤيجوتسكي Vygotsky . فمن خلال هذه المقاربة النظرية ، يمكننا تأطير دور اللغة في التعليم والتعلم بشكل أكثر فعالية . ومن مفاهيم هذه النظرية الأساسية ، أن اللغة هي أداة لتنظيم التفكير ، وأن تفكير المتعلم يتم دعمه في البدايةِ من قبل فرد آخر أكثر دراية ومهارة في سياق التواصل التفاعلي ، وتدريجياً يصبح تفكير المتعلم أكثر استقلالية مع تطور مهاراته اللغوية . تشجعنا هذه النظرة إلى دور اللغة في التعليم والتعلم على محاولة فهم اللغة بوصفها أداة

وبذلك ، فقد قصر مجال اللغويات التربوية المنبثق نطاق معالجته على القضايا المتعلقة باللغة والتعليم على وجه التحديد ، في حين وَسّع النطاق أيضاً بتبنيه لما سمي بـ«اللغويات التربوية» التي كان المقصود بها مقاربة بحثية تشمل فروع اللغويات المختلفة وغيرها من المجالات (غير اللغوية) التي تساعد على فهم القضايا المتعلقة باللغة والتعليم .

يُنظر الآن إلى اللغويات التربوية على أنها مقاربة بحثية متعددة الاختصاصات ذات توجه عملي problem-oriented (انظر ;Hornberger Hornberger and Hult; Hult) . وهي مقاربة تحاول الإجابة عن أسئلة عملية مرتبطة باللغة والتعليم ، مثل : ما أنماط الخطاب التفاعلي في الصف الدراسي التي تؤدي إلى تعلم أفضل؟ كيف يمكن تحسين طرق التدريس في سياق ذي تعدد لغوي؟ ما الأدوار الأنسب للغات المختلفة في المواد المدرسية وعبر مراحل التعليم في مجتمع متعدد اللغات؟ ما المطلوب من المعلمين فهمه عن اللغة لتحسين تدريس اللغة (سواء كانت اللغة الأم أم لغة أجنبية) ، وكذلك تدريس مواد مدرسية مثل العلوم والرياضيات وغيرها؟

تتخذ اللغويات ، بفروعها المختلفة ، مركزاً أساسياً في اللغويات التربوية ، ولكن هناك تخصصات أخرى تساعد على فهم ومعالجة القضايا المتعلقة باللغة والتعليم : فوصف وتحسين جودة الخطاب الصّفي يتطلب إثنوغرافيا لغوية Linguistic Ethnographies في الفصل المدرسي وفي المنزل ، ليتم وصف وتحليل تفاصيل استعمال اللغة من قبل المشاركين المختلفين لتحقيق أغراض مختلفة (فنعتمد لهذا على تخصص الأنثروبولوجيا اللغوية Linguistic Anthropology) ؛ وقد نحتاج إلى مسح معتقدات المعلمين والمتعلمين ومواقفهم تجاه اللغة والتعلم (فنعتمد على علم النفس التربوي Educational Psychology) ؛ وقد يتطلب الأمر أيضا فهم كفاءات المعلم وأساليب تطويره مهنياً (علم التربية Education) . أما في سياق متعدد اللغات ، فيتطلب تحديدُ أدوار اللغات المختلفة في المناهج المدرسية مراجعةَ مبادئ تصميم المناهج (علم التربية) ، بالإضافة إلى معرفة المعالم الأساسية لتعلم اللغة وآليات اكتسابها عند الأطفال متعددي اللغات (علم النفس التنموي) ، ويتطلب الأمر أيضاً وصفَ الخصائص اللغوية لمجالات المعرفة المختلفة مثل العلوم والرياضيات ، وغيرها (اللغويات الوظيفية Functional Linguistics) والمواقف المتضاربة تجاه اللغات المختلفة المتداولة في المجتمع (علم الاجتماع) .

للمشكلة ، يليها تقديم حلول لها ، لأن الأبحاث الأكاديمية المطلوبة من أجل ذلك لم تنفذ بعد . فبدلاً من ذلك ، سوف أقوم بعرض برنامج بحثي يرتكز على الأبحاث التي أجريت حول العالم ، مع مناقشة بعض الأبحاث التي أجريت في المنطقة العربية . وتستند هذه المقالة إلى دراسة سابقة لي حول هذا الموضوع بعنوان "The Language of Instruction" ، ركزت فيها على تدريس العلوم على وجه التحديد (انظر Amin) . وأود هنا أن أعمم المناقشة لتشمل مادة الرياضيات ، وأن أعرض برنامجاً بحثياً أكثر تماسكاً . أزعم هنا أن فهم الجوانب المختلفة لمشكلة اللغة في تعليم وتعلم العلوم والرياضيات في العالم العربي ، ومن ثم تحسين جودة التعليم في هذه المواد ، يتطلب برنامجاً بحثياً يتبع نهجاً متعدد التخصصات تحت عنوان «اللغويات التربوية» Educational Linguistics . هدفي هنا تقديم خريطة طريق توضح أنواع الأبحاث المطلوبة والتخصصات المختلفة في العلوم الاجتماعية والإنسانية التي سيتم النظر من خلال كل منها إلى مفهوم اللغة من منظور مختلف . وهذه الأبحاث مجتمعة تعطي رؤية متماسكة لمشكلة اللغة في تعليم العلوم والرياضيات . وعلى الرغم من أنني سأركز في هذه المقالة على العلوم والرياضيات ، فإن معظم النقاط العامة التي سأثيرها ستكون ذات صلة بالمواد الدراسية الأخرى ، مثل المواد الاجتماعية والإنسانيات .

ماذا تعني اللغويات التربوية؟

يصف هلت Hult تاريخ اللغويات التربوية وتطورها ، ويوضح أنها ظهرت باعتبارها مقاربة لدراسة اللغة والتعليم في سبعينيات القرن الماضي بوصفها رد فعل لفجوة ملحوظة في البحوث التي أجريت تحت عنوان «اللغويات التطبيقية» Applied Linguistics (انظر Spolsky) . وقد بدأ بعض الباحثين في هذا العقد توجيه النقد للغويات التطبيقية ، حيث رأى البعض أن نطاقها شديد الضيق من ناحية ، في حين رآه البعض الآخر شديد الاتساع من ناحية أخرى . كان نطاقها ضيقاً بمعنى أنها كانت مَعْنية بتطبيق نتائج اللغويات النظرية فقط ، ولكن نطاقها كان واسعاً جداً أيضاً حيث شمل هذا التطبيق مجموعة واسعة من المجالات مثل : الترجمة ، التخطيط اللغوي Language Planning ، البلاغة ، علم اللغويات الشرعي Forensic Linguistics ، بالإضافة إلى علم تعلم وتعليم اللغة ، وغيرها .

اللغويات التربوية ومشكلة اللغة في تعليم العلوم والرياضيات في العالم العربي

تامر أمين

مقدمة

يعتبر أداء الدول العربية في التقييمات الدولية التي تقارن تحصيل الطلاب في العلوم والرياضيات ضعيف جداً مقارنة بالدول الأخرى (انظر "Trends"). والتفسيرات المحتملة لذلك كثيرة، وتسهم جميعها بلا شك في فهم المشكلة بدرجات متفاوتة في مختلف البلدان العربية: فصول مكتظة وموارد محدودة، مناهج قديمة مكثفة المحتوى دون اهتمام جاد بالفهم والتفكير النقدي، كتب مدرسية مملة، ومعلمون يفتقرون إلى التدريب المناسب (انظر Dagher and BouJaoude). في هذه المقالة، أسلط الضوء على تفسير آخر ربما لم يُولَ اهتماماً كافياً: مشكلة اللغة (انظر، من بين الأبحاث القليلة التي أولته اهتماماً، بوجودة وصياح).

وهناك جوانب مختلفة لما أعنيه بـ«مشكلة اللغة». الجانب الواضح منها هو استعمال لغة أجنبية دولية - مثل اللغة الإنجليزية أو الفرنسية - بوصفها لغة تعليم رسمية في بعض البلدان (مثل لبنان الآن، والمغرب العربي سابقاً) التي تقدم تحديات للطلاب والمعلمين معاً بسبب ضعف الكفاءة في اللغة الأجنبية. كما أن هناك جانباً أقل وضوحاً يظهر عندما يتم تدريس العلوم والرياضيات باللغة العربية، ألا وهو ظاهرة ثنائية اللغة العربية diglossia بنوعيها: اللغة الفصحى، لغة القراءة والكتابة، والعامية المنطوقة، لغة الحياة اليومية. فهذه الظاهرة تعني أنه لا يمكن افتراض الكفاءة الكافية في الفصحى، لغة التعليم الرسمي. كما أن هناك جانباً ثالثاً أكثر عمقاً، وهو الدور الذي تلعبه اللغة (أياً كانت هذه اللغة) في التفكير العلمي والرياضي، والأدوار التي تلعبها في عمليات التعليم والتعلم.

أريد هنا مناقشة هذه الجوانب المختلفة لمشكلة اللغة في تعليم وتعلم العلوم والرياضيات في العالم العربي. لكن مقاربتي هنا لا تعد صياغة دقيقة

Ghosh, Amitav. "Petrofiction." *New Republic* 206.9 (March 1992): 29–34.

Hassan, Wael. "Postcolonial Theory and Modern Arabic Literature: Horizons of Application." *Journal of Arabic Literature* 33.1 (2002): 45-64.

Lazarus, Neil. *The Postcolonial Unconscious*. Cambridge: Cambridge UP, 2011.

Nixon, Rob. *Slow Violence and the Environmentlism of the Poor*. Cambridge, Mass.: Harvard UP, 2011.

Petrocultures. 2015. <https://petrocultures.com/>.

Potter, Lucy. "Postcolonial Resources, Pedagogical Resistance: An Energy-Driven Interview with Professor Jennifer Wenzel." *Journal of Postcolonial Writing* 53.3 (August 2017): 380-92.

Rancière, Jacques. *La politique de la littérature*. Paris : Galilée, 2007.

Saloul, Ihab. "'Performative Narrativity':Palestinian Identity and the Performance of Catastrophe." *Cultural Analysis* 7 (2008): 5-39.

Said, Edward. *Orientalism*. NY: Random House, 1994.

Singh, Jyotsna. Introduction. *The Postcolonial World*. Eds. Jyotsna G. Singh and David D. Kim. London: Routledge, 2016. 2-32.

Wenzel, Jennifer. "Decolonization." *A Companion to Critical and Cultural Theory*. Eds. Imre Szeman, Sarah Blacker, and Justin Sully. Hoboken, NJ : Wiley Blackwell, 2017. 449-64.

---. "How to Read for Oil." *Resilience: A Journal of the Environmental Humanities* 1.3 (Fall 2014): 156-61.

Williams, Patrick and Anna Ball. "Where is Palestine?" *Journal of Postcolonial Writing* 50.2 (2014): 127-33.

Zabus, Chantal, ed. *The Future of Postcolonial Studies*. NY: Routledge. 2015.

---. Introduction. *The Future of Postcolonial Studies*. Ed. Chantal Zabus. NY: Routledge. 2015. 1-16.

Yaeger, Patricia. "Editor's Column: The End of Postcolonial Theory? A Roundtable with Sunil Agnani, Fernando Coronil, Gaurav Desai, Mamadou Diouf, Simon Gikandi, Susie Tharu, and Jennifer Wenzel." *PMLA* 122.3 (May 2007): 633–51.

Young, Robert J. C. "Postcolonial Remains." *New Literary History* 43.1 (Winter 2012): 19-42.

المقريزي، تقي الدين أحمد بن علي. ضوء الساري في معرفة خبر تميم الداري. تحقيق وتعليق محمد أحمد عاشور. القاهرة: دار الاعتصام للطبع والنشر، ١٩٧٢.

منيف، عبد الرحمن. مدن الملح: التيه. بيروت: المؤسسة العربية للدراسات والنشر، ٢٠١٢.

ناجي، جمال. غريب النهر. بيروت: الدار العربية للعلوم، ٢٠١٢.

يانغ، روبرت. «بقاء أم بقايا ما بعد الكولونيالية؟» ترجمة حبيب الحاج سالم. مركز نماء للبحوث والدراسات. ⟨http://tiny.cc/4wdddz⟩.

المراجع الأجنبية

Ashcroft, Bill. "Future Thinking: Postcolonial Utopianism." *The Future of Postcolonial Studies*. Ed. Chantal Zabus. NY: Routledge, 2015. 235-53.

---. *Utopianism in Postcolonial Literatures*. London: Routledge, 2016.

---, Gareth Griffiths, and Helen Tiffin eds. *The Empire Writes Back: Theory and Practice in Post-colonial Literatures*. London and NY: Routledge, 1989.

Ball, Anna. *Palestinian Literature and Film in Postcolonial Feminist Perspective*. London and NY: Routledge, 2012.

Bhabha, Homi. "Foreword: Framing Fanon." Frantz Fanon. *The Wretched of the Earth*. Trans. Richard Philcox. NY: Grove P, 2004. vii-xli.

Bloch, Ernst. *L'Esprit de l'utopie*. Trad. Anne-Marie Lang et Catherine Picou-Audard. Paris : Gallimard, 1977.

Boehmer, Elleke. *Colonial and Postcolonial Literature: Migrant Metaphors*. London: Oxford UP, 2005.

Bernard, Anna. *Rhetorics of Belonging: Nation, Narration and Israel/Palestine*. Liverpool: Liverpool UP, 2013.

---, Ziad Elmarsafy, and Stuart Murray. Introduction. *What Postcolonial Theory Doesn't Say*. Eds. Anna Bernard, Ziad Elmarsafy, and Stuart Murray. NY and London: Routledge, 2016. 1-10.

---. *What Postcolonial Theory Doesn't Say*. NY; London: Routledge, 2016.

Böwering, Gerhard. "The Concept of Time in Islam." *Proceedings of the American Philosophical Society* 141.1 (March 1997): 55-66.

Brennan, Timothy. "Joining the Party." *Postcolonial Studies* 16.1 (March 2013): 68-78.

Farag, Joseph. *Politics and Palestinian Literature in Exile*. London: I. B. Tauris, 2016.

Foucault, Michel. "Des espaces autres." *Empan* 54.2 (août 2004) : 12-19.

المراجع العربية

أبو شهاب، رامي. **في الممر الأخير: سرديّة الشتات الفلسطيني من منظور ما بعد كولونيالي**. بيروت: المؤسسة العربية للدراسات والنشر، ٢٠١٧.

---. **الرسيس والمخاتلة: خطاب ما بعد الكولونيالية في النقد العربي المعاصر**. بيروت: المؤسسة العربية للدراسات والنشر، ٢٠١٣.

إبراهيم، عبد الله. **السردية العربية الحديثة**. بيروت: المؤسسة العربية للدراسات والنشر، ٢٠١٣.

أشكروفت، بيل، غاريث غريفيث، هيلين تيفن، محررون. **الرد بالكتابة: النظرية والتطبيق في آداب المستعمرات القديمة**. ترجمة شهرت العالم. بيروت: المنظمة العربية للترجمة، ٢٠٠٦.

برادة، محمد. **الرواية العربية ورهان التجديد**. دبي: دار الصدى، ٢٠١١.

الجهني، ليلى. **الفردوس اليباب**. الرياض: كتاب في جريدة، ٢ فبراير ٢٠٠٥.

الحارثي، جوخة. **سيدات القمر**. بيروت: دار الآداب للنشر، ٢٠١٠.

خال، عبده. **ترمي بشرر**. بيروت: دار الساقي للطباعة والنشر، ٢٠١٤.

دراج، فيصل. **الذاكرة القومية في الرواية العربية: من زمن النهوض إلى زمن السقوط**. بيروت: مركز دراسات الوحدة العربية، ٢٠٠٨.

---. «العودة المتخيلة: عودة الفلسطيني بين الوهم والمتخيّل». **مجلة الدراسات الفلسطينية** مجلد ٢٩، عدد ١١٦ (خريف ٢٠١٨): ص ص ١٤٩-١٥٣.

درويش، محمود. **حالة حصار**. بيروت: رياض الريس للكتب والنشر، ٢٠٠٢.

---. **ورد أقل**. بيروت: دار العودة، ١٩٩٦.

سعيد، إدوارد. **خيانة المثقفين: النصوص الأخيرة**. ترجمة أسعد الحسين. بغداد: دار نينوى للدراسات والنشر والتوزيع، ٢٠١١.

سلامة، محمد. «أدب العالم بين المركزية والتهميش: قراءة في الأدب العربي ما بعد الاستعمار». **ألف** ٣٤ (٢٠١٤): ص ص ٤٢-٦٦.

القصيبي، غازي. **أوبريت أرض الرسالات والبطولات**. مهرجان الجنادرية الثامن، الرياض، ١٩٩٣.

المدهون، ربعي. **السيدة من تل أبيب**. بيروت: المؤسسة العربية للدراسات والنشر، ٢٠١٠.

المغلوث، عبدالله. «حوار شامل مع الروائية السعودية ليلى الجُهني ٢ من ٣». **ناشري**. ٩ آذار/مارس، ٢٠٠٥. ⟨http://tiny.cc/jmgfcz⟩.

١٢ كتبت هذه القصيدة خلال الانتفاضة الثانية عام ٢٠٠٢ .

١٣ كتاب الإنطاء الشريف هو أول صك إقطاعي في الإسلام ، وفيه كتب الرسول محمد (ص) لتميم وأخيه أوس بن نعيم الداري . ولعَقبهما من بعدهما ، حَبْرى وبيت عينون . وهناك إجماع على أن كتاب الإنطاءَ حديث صحيح . انظر المقريزي ، ص ص ٩-١٢ .

١٤ كتب جيرهارد باورينج عن الاختلاف بين المنظور الإسلامي للزمن والمنظور الأوروبي التنويري له ، حيث اعتبر الأول ذا نظرة ذرية atomic للزمن آثرت في هذا المقال ترجمتها إلى سديمي تشبيهاً لها بذرات الغبار وتجمعات الغاز في الفضاء (انظر Böwering) .

١٥ الهيتروتوبيا مفهوم لدراسة المكان تكلم عنه ميشيل فوكو . ويقصد به الفضاءات المعزولة المحكومة بنقطة دخول ونقطة خروج ، تستطيع أن تجمع فيها شرائح متباينة من المجتمع تأتي لزيارة هذه الفضاءات لأغراض محددة ، مثل السفن والمقابر والمكتبات العامة وغير ذلك . يرى فوكو أن تنظيم هذه الفضاءات يعكس أنماطاً ثقافية قد تكون مخفية في غيرها (انظر Foucault) .

١٦ استقبال النظرية في النقد العربي يكاد يقتصر على هذا المنظور الشمولي (انظر أبو شهاب ، الرسيس ، ص ص ١٤٨-١٥٠) .

١٧ للاستزادة ، انظر موقع Petrocultures .

١٨ أول من أشار بتعجب إلى هذا الغياب المتواصل هو الكاتب الإنجليزي من أصول هندية أميتاب جوش في عرض نشره في عام ١٩٩٢ ، وفيه تساءل كيف تكون مدن الملح هي العمل الوحيد الذي تناول هذا الموضوع بالغ الأهمية في تاريخ البشرية (انظر Ghosh) .

١٩ مثل روايات **الآخرون** ، و**البحريات** لأميمة الخميس ، و**بنات الرياض** لرجاء الصانع ، و**هند والعسكر** لبدرية البشر .

٢٠ كانت الترجمة الثقافية موضوعاً مثيراً للجدل في الأوساط الأكاديمية في ثمانينيات القرن بعد نشر سلمان رشدي Rushdie لروايته **آيات شيطانية** The Satanic Verses .

٢١ في الفصول الأخيرة من **سيدات القمر** ، يذكر الراوي على لسان عبد الله ابن التاجر سليمان أن ظريفة غادرت عُمان إلى الكويت ، ثم عادت لتموت مبتورة القدمين في إحدى المستشفيات من دون أن يعلم أحد عن موتها أو مكان دفنها في إشارة صريحة إلى انقطاع العلاقة بين ماضي العوافي وحاضرها .

في الأكاديمية الغربية وانتهت عندما عيَّن كل قسمٍ مختصاً في هذه النظرية للتدريس فيه ، وبذلك تكون معركة النظرية أكاديمية صرفة (Yaeger 635) .

٢ يشهد على هذا القصور استقبال النظرية المتأخر في الأكاديمية الفرنسية وفي العالم العربي أيضاً .

٣ عنوان المقالة يخاتل القراء الذين يعتقدون بنهاية النظرية ليوهمهم بأن المقالة تتحدث عن الآثار الدارسة للنظرية ، وذلك بسبب الخلط بين الفعل بصيغة المضارع remains وبين الاسم بصيغة الجمع remains .

٤ دافعت آنا بيرنارد وزياد المرصفي وستيوارت موراي بشدة عن انغماس النظرية ما بعد الكولونيالية في التنظير في ثمانينات وتسعينيات القرن المنصرم ، واعتبروا ذلك مرحلة طبيعية في تطور أي منهج فكري (Bernard, Elmarsafy, and Murray, "Introduction" 4-9) .

٥ اعتبر لازوروس أن هذا الاتجاه يغذي التوجه الاستشراقي الكامن في الإبستيمولوجيا الغربية التي تميل إلى إحاطة الشرق بهالة من الغموض والسحر التي تستدعي تدخل الأكاديمي الغربي لتفكيك غموضها (Lazarus 16-17) .

٦ تمت ترجمة كتاب فانون إلى الإنجليزية عام ١٩٦٣ وصدرت الترجمة الثانية عام ٢٠٠٤ ، وكتب هومي بابا مقدمة لها .

٧ من المتمسكين بالمنهجية العلمانية إدوارد سعيد ، وقد نادى بضرورة علمنة النقد الأدبي في كتابه **العالم والنص والناقد** The World, the Text and the Critic ، في حين نادى أشكروفت وجريفيث وتريفين في The Empire Writes Back بإعادة النظر في العلمانية المتطرفة في منهجية ما بعد الكولونيالية .

٨ كتب محمد برادة باستفاضة عن تذويت الكتابة في الرواية العربية . انظر **الرواية العربية ورهان التجديد** .

٩ إيهاب سلول Saloul من مواليد مخيم جباليا للاجئين ومحاضر في الأدب المقارن في جامعة ماستريخت في هولندا .

١٠ وهذه الرغبة الصريحة في فصل الحلم بالعودة والأمل في السلام عن خطط السياسيين وفصائلهم هي أمر يؤكد عليه الكثير من الكتّاب ، ومنهم ربعي المدهون الذي يقول على لسان بطل روايته وليد دهمان عندما سُئل عن انتمائه السياسي : «أنا من مؤيدي السلام إلى أبعد الحدود ، وأكره العنف بكل أشكاله . . . هل يكفي ذلك؟» (ص ١١٤) .

١١ تكلم إرنست بلوخ Bloch عن هذا النوع من الأمل الطوباوي وربطه بفكرة المسيح المنقذ في العقيدة اليهودية والمسيحية .

على النحو الذي تميل إليه التيارات النقدية الغربية غالباً. كما أن دعم هذه الأعمال بتيار نقدي قوي الحجة يخرج الأدب العربي من النظرة الاستشراقية التي لا يزال - إلى حد ما - محصوراً بها في الجامعات العالمية والتي تضع جلّ اهتمامها في تدريس الأعمال الكلاسيكية مثل **ألف ليلة وليلة** و**المعلقات السبع**. وهذا الاتجاه يساعد أيضاً على تحييد الاستعمار وإبعاده عن المركز باعتباره المكوّن التاريخي الوحيد الذي تتمحور حوله هُويّات شعوب ما بعد الاستعمار، لكنه يُبقي الأسئلة عن تقاطعات الأدب والسياسة مطروحة وبقوة داخل أروقة النظرية.

وفي الختام، ستبقى ما بعد الكولونيالية أسلوباً في قراءة النصوص وليست نظريةً متكاملة في تفسير الحياة. وهي منهج انتقادي تحرري يضع بناء المستقبل نصب عينيه. وهذا يعني أن التحرر المنشود ليس بالضرورة تحرراً من الاستعمار، لكنه قد يكون تحرراً من المخيلة التي بنيناها على أنقاض حركات التحرر من الاستعمار الذي لا يزال يكبل مخيلتنا بقيوده ومفاهيمه الضيقه لمعنى المقاومة والأمة وتشكيل الهُويّة والمكان. كما أن تطور النظرية ونموها في عوالم اللغة الإنجليزية لا يعني أن تبقى مقيدة بحدود الدول الناطقة بالإنجليزية وإنتاجها الأدبي. فالبحث عن الحرية والعدالة مطلب إنساني لا يعرف قيود اللغات والجغرافيا. والعالم الآن لا يبحث عن حل لمشاكله بالتقنية الحديثة، إنما يرى الكثير أن التغيير السياسي والبيئي يبدأ بالعودة إلى ثقافة السكان المحليين، واستعادة خبراتهم في التعامل مع الطبيعة من حولهم، وإحياء قيمهم وعلاقتهم الحميمة مع الأرض التي جنّبت لقرون طويلة كوكبنا الويلات والكوارث التي جلبها الاستعمار بكافة أشكاله في عصرنا هذا. وفي هذا المنحى الجديد، ستعود ما بعد الكولونيالية إلى ما نادى به إدوارد سعيد من جدوى المقاومة الإبداعية المدعّمة بقيم إنسانية عالمية - وربما في بعض الأحيان ذات وازع ديني كما في الصمود الفلسطيني على خلاف ما نادى به سعيد - في مواجهة سيطرة الفكر الأحادي المهيمن ذي النزعة النيوليبرالية الذي اكتسح عالمنا اليوم بلا هوادة.

الهوامش

[1] ومن ذلك المقولة المعروفة لسيمون جيكاندي بأن ما بعد الكولونيالية بدأت بانضمام الطلاب من دول العالم الثالث إلى الدراسة في أقسام اللغة الإنجليزية

التصاقاً بالنظام الاقتصادي القديم، مثل متعب الهذال أو ظريفة محظيّة التاجر سليمان،[21] يعكس قلق الذات الجمعية الوليدة التي وجدت نفسها في خضم أمواج النظام العالمي الجديد بلا دليل ولا مرساة نجاة بعد أن صارت ترى العالم بعيون غير التي كان يرى بها أسلافها.

وإذا كان الأمل الطوباوي هو ما يغذي روح المقاومة في الأدب الفلسطيني، فإن التوجس من القادم الغريب الذي انبثق من باطن الأرض هو ما يُكبّل مخيلة الكتّاب في الخليج العربي ويمنعهم من رسم فضاءات أكثر تفاؤلاً واستبشاراً. ولو أمعنا النظر في توضع السرديات التي يقدمها الإنتاج الأدبي في فلسطين وفي منطقة الخليج، لوجدنا أنها – كما وصفها جاك رانسيير – تعمل على خلق فضاءات جمعية بالدرجة الأولى، لا غاية لها إلا نقض القيود التي تفرضها قوى العولمة والهيمنة الاقتصادية على المجتمعات المحلية في تلك المناطق. فهي نصوص سياسية تمارس سياسة الاعتراض، لكن ليس على طريقة الثورات والحروب، ولا على طريقة الأحزاب والخطابات السياسية، بل عن طريق خلق عوالم بديلة أو تعطيل سير العوالم القائمة واعتراض طريقها بمساءلتها وكشف عيوبها (Rancière 7). فالإنتاج الأدبي لأبناء الخليج العربي وفلسطين ليس أدباً ثورياً، ولا يسعى خلف إشعال الثورات، ولايعبأ بالسلطة ولا بالصراع عليها، لكنه مشغول برسالة أخلاقية وبقيم تحررية نبيلة تخاطب الجماعة. فهل ستأخذ ما بعد الكولونيالية منحىً أكثر براجماتية وتنزع عن الأدب رداء الشاعرية والأدبية وتدفع به إلى مصاف المعارف الإنسانية المتمركزة حول الغايات الأخلاقية السامية؟ فالأخلاقيات في الأدب لم تكن يوماً موضوعاً محبباً للنقاد، لكن التصدي للاحتلال ومقاومة ثقافة الاستهلاك وموجات العولمة العاتية قد تقلب الموازين.

الخاتمة

إن توظيف أدوات النقد ما بعد الكولونيالي في دراسة الأدب الفلسطيني والأدب في منطقة الخليج العربي يلقي الضوء على جوانب في الإنتاج الأدبي لهاتين المنطقتين نادراً ما تطرقت إليه الدراسات من قبل. فالبحث في سرديات الشتات والانزياح وأساطيرها يعيد توجيه دفة النقد الأدبي باتجاه الأساطير الجمعية وتشكلها وتمثلها على مستويات الفرد والجماعة بدلاً من التركيز على معاناة الفرد الذاتية وصراعاته الداخلية

في بريطانيا وبين نسوة العوافي اللواتي استحوذن على المشهد في **سيدات القمر**، وتركت لهن الكاتبة المجال لتدبير المكائد والدسائس لتكتفي هي بصوت الراوي العليم المشدوه بهذه العوالم الغامضة. فهذه العلاقة الملتبسة بين الكاتبة وشخوصها وعجزها عن حَمْل شخوص الحاضر على التفاعل مع شخوص الماضي – حتى اقتصر حضور لندن على بضعة مشاهد مقتضبة قرب النهاية ظهرت فيها بوصفها فتاة ناضجة مُعتدة بنفسها، لكنها مع ذلك لا تلتفت إلى التعليق على ماضي العوافي أو على نسائها – يُذكرنا بالمَخْرج الملتبس الذي وجده عبد الرحمن منيف لتقليص الفجوة بينه وبين شخوصه الذين لا يشابهونه في المستوى التعليمي أو الميول السياسية. ففي **مدن الملح** يتخلص منيف من متعب الهذال ويبعده عن الرواية ربما لأنه لا يحتمل كُلفة تمثيل شخصية من عالم بعيد عنه تماماً. وكذلك تفعل جوخة الحارثي فتُبعد الشخصية القريبة منها لندن عن مشهد الرواية حتى النهاية، لكي لا تفضح اغترابها وعزلتها عن عوالم العوافي. لكن النظرة الاستشراقية التي تكتنف النص تفضح هذا الاغتراب، وتُفصح عن الشرخ الذي يتجدد ويتسع بين الكاتبة وماضي العوافي قبل البترول.

والسؤال بعد كل هذا: لِمَ يبدو العالم الذي جلبه البترول بشعاً وموغلاً في الغرابة إلى هذه الدرجة؟ كيف تشترك هذه النصوص المتباينة في مواضيعها ومسرح أحداثها في تصوير الخراب الذي جلبه البترول، سواء للنظام البيئي كما وصفه خال أو لرمزية الوطن/الجسد كما فعلت الجُهني أو لرؤية الكاتب لعالمه وتاريخه كما فعلت الحارثي؟ كيف يعجز الكتّاب عن تخيل عالم بديل؟ ولمَ يبقون حبيسي هذا البرزخ الأبدي؟ لِمَ يغيب المستقبل أو حتى الإحساس بالتفاؤل والأمل عن هذه الروايات الثلاث؟ لماذا يستمر الكتّاب في استنساخ نموذج موران الذي اختطه عبد الرحمن منيف قبل ثلاثة عقود؟ هل النهاية الوشيكة والمرعبة لعصر الاعتماد على البترول بوصفه مصدراً للطاقة تُضيق الخناق أيضاً على خيال الكتّاب وعلى أقلامهم؟ إن استدامة فكرة الديستوبيا أو الأرض الخراب أو «بادية الظلمات» (عنوان الجزء الخامس من **مدن الملح**) وتكرار ظهورها في نصوص مختلفة وفي فترات زمنية متعاقبة يجعلنا نتساءل عما لو كانت الأرض اليباب، حيث المظهر الخلاب والوجه الفاتن الذي يخفي ثمرة متعفنة وفساداً ينخر كالدود، قد أضحت مجازاً/ثروةً متجددة لا تنضب، على عكس النفط الذي أتى بعوالمها، وعما لو كان اتفاق الكتّاب على تغييب الأصوات الأكثر

ثم تأكدت أنها أكلت حتى آخر لقمة في الصحن، وشربت الحليب المغلي بالحلبة حتى آخر قطرة. أعدت القهوة بالهال وطبق الفواكه والتمر، صفّت زجاجتي عطر وفنجاناً صغيراً من الزعفران في صينية مذهبة مع مجمر البخور، وضعت القهوة والأطباق وصينية العطور في الدهليز استعداداً لزيارات الجارات المرتقبة، استحمّت بالماء المخلوط بأعشابها الخاصّة - لم يلمس الصابون جسدها منذ خُلقت - ولبست أجمل ملابسها وتربّعت بجانب ابنتها الصامتة. (ص ١٦)

هذا الاستطراد في الوصف الحسي للمقتنيات والطقوس المحلية يكاد يكون هو العنصر الجمالي الطاغي على **سيدات القمر**. ويتكرر مثل هذا الوصف في كل مشهد يستقصي مرحلة مهمة من حياة أحد الشخوص، سواء كان مشهد زفاف أم خطوبة أم لقاء بين عاشقين. وهذا التركيز على الأشياء الحسية الساكنة كالمنازل والأثاث والأزياء أصاب الرواية كلها بالسكون، فأصبحت لغة السرد كما وصفها إدوارد سعيد - حين تحدث عن أعمال المستشرقين في القرنين الثامن والتاسع عشر - لغة ساكنة، لغة تخدم أغراض الباحثين، وتصلح لوصف المعروضات في المتحف، وتنفع للاستشهاد بها في الدراسات الأنثروبولوجية والتاريخية، لكنها تفتقد إلى نبض الحياة والتنوع والعُمق الذي يُحجم المستشرقون - وربما يعجزون - عن تصويره (Said 7). وهنا تظهر الحاجة إلى أدوات ما بعد الكولونيالية التي تفتش عن المحجوب والمسكوت عنه؛ فكيف تسللت هذه الغلالة الاستشراقية لتغطي ماضي العوافي كله؟ بل كيف اختفت العوافي بأسرها، بشوارعها وحاراتها وجوامعها وأسواقها، واقتصرت الرواية على الوصف الساكن للمقتنيات الماديّة؟

لكن ربما أرادت جوخة الحارثي أن تعطي قارئها تصوراً عن الستر الغليظ الذي يحول بينها وبين رؤية العوافي كما تراها سالمة وظريفة وميّا وغيرهن، فقدمت منذ الصفحات الأولى للرواية شخصية الابنة لندن التي غاب شخصها عن الرواية ولم تظهر إلا للحظات قصيرة قرب نهاية النص، لكن اسمها وغرابته كان حاضراً على ألسنة جميع أبناء العوافي منذ البداية. وبعيداً عن دلالة الاسم بذاته التي تشي بقلق العلاقة مع المستعمرِ البريطاني، فإن الحضور المتخفي لشخصية لندن يعكس شرخاً عميقاً وهوةً يصعب ردمها بين الكاتبة ما بعد الكولونيالية التي حصلت على تعليمها

يوماً بعد يوم بين حياة الكاتب ونتاجه الأدبي وبين البيئة المحلية التي يسعى إلى تمثيلها. وهذا يأخذنا مرة أخرى إلى سجال ما بعد الكولونيالية المحتدم حول أحقية التمثيل وإشكالية الترجمة الثقافية.[20] فجوخة الحارثي أكاديمية تحمل درجة الدكتوراه من جامعة إدنبره، تتشابه مع مثيلاتها من روائيات ما بعد الكولونيالية مثل أروانداتي روي Roy وجومبا لاهيري Lahiri في كونها من الجيل الأول من النساء في محيطها اللواتي ينلن تعليماً عالياً في المراكز الميتروبوليتانية في الغرب. في حين تتناول **سيدات القمر** العوالم الأنثوية لمجموعة من النسوة من طبقات اجتماعية مختلفة شهدن بأنفسهن تغيّر النظام الاقتصادي في سلطنة عمان من الاعتماد على تجارة الرقيق والبُنّ إلى نظام يعتمد على تصدير البترول ومشتقاته وما صاحب ذلك من نقلة في تعليم المرأة وتمكينها. فيغدو السؤال الأهم هنا هل الكاتبة الأكاديمية مؤهلة للحديث عن نساء بلدة العوافي جميعاً؟ أمهات وبنات وحفيدات؟ وهل تشاركهن اللغة والأدوات المعرفية؟ وهل يتقاسمن المنظور نفسه للعالم من حولهن؟

للوهلة الأولى تبدو الرواية ملتبسة؛ فالكاتبة عربية لكنها ترى بعيون غربية. فالتفاصيل الحسية والإغراق في وصف المقتنيات المادية، والاعتماد في دفع الأحداث لا على التسلسل والتشويق بل على الغموض والمكائد، وإلقاء بضعة خيوط عن الطقوس الروحانية لطرد أو تسخير الشياطين من أجل تضليل القارئ وإبعاده عن المكيدة الأساسية التي أنهت حياة أم عبد الله ابن التاجر سليمان، كل هذا جعل **سيدات القمر** تقع في فخ الاستشراق الجديد. فهي تقدم لنا العوافي كما يراها الغريب القادم من خلف البحار؛ غامضة وغارقة في عالم من مكائد النساء والرقيق، يلفها حجاب من سحر الشرق الذي تحاول الكاتبة رفعه بهدوء لتسمح لقارئها بأن يختلس النظر إلى تلك العوالم المجهولة كما فعل المستشرقون في القرنين الثامن والتاسع عشر. تقول الحارثي في وصفها لطقوس استقبال النفساء:

> كنست [سالمة] الحوض ونضحته بالماء، نفضت الغبار عن السجادة الفارسية الحمراء المطوية في المخزن وفرشتها في الدهليز، لمّعت الأواني الخزفية المصطفة في روازن الغرفة الوسطى، وفرشت على الأرض فراشاً جديداً لميا والمولودة، صنعت خبز الرقاق بنفسها للنفساء ومزجته بالسمن البلدي وعسل الجبل،

كتابتها سنة ١٩٩٦ (المغلوث، د.ص.). وهذا يرغمنا على تناولها في سياق مختلف بعيداً عن «الطفرة» في الإنتاج الروائي – النسائي بخاصة – التي شهدتها دول الخليج بعد الحادي عشر من سبتمبر، والتي جعلت من دراسة الذات الداخلية محوراً أساسياً تدور في فلكه [19]. فرواية **الفردوس اليباب** لا تحفل بذات الكاتبة ولا تأبه بها، بل هي رواية المكان والذات الجمعيّة بامتياز. فالكاتبة تؤسس بشكل واضح للربط بين حكايتها وبين تاريخ مدينة جدّة وتعتبر حكايتها مثل أسطورة حسن الكردي الذي رفع أسوار جدة على أجساد البسطاء من أبنائها. فالمدن لا تزدهر ولا ترتفع أسوارها إلا على رفات المستضعفين من أبنائها، **والفردوس اليباب** سحقت جسد البطلة صَبا لكي تكتب لنا الرواية، «فالكون بنفسه بدأ بآدم وحواء وشيطان وفردوس مفقود» (ص ٣٠). فالفردوس المفقود هي جدّة التي أجهضت فيها قصة الحب بين صَبا وعامر، وهي حكاية الذات الأنثى، وحكاية الشعب، وحكاية الأرض بعد أن هتك حماها الغريب وبدأ السوس ينخر لبَّها. وإذا كانت **ترمي بشرر** تتتبع السقوط بوصفه استعارة رئيسية، فإن **الفردوس اليباب** تتتبع التلوث وهو ينشب مخالبه ببطء في الجسد/الوطن الطاهر. فهما وجهان لعملة واحدة تمازجت وتماهت أوصالهما حتى إن خالدة صديقة صَبا أخذت تخاطب جثتها الهامدة بعد انتحارها قائلة: «أغمضي عينيك ودعي جدّة تخرج رويداً رويداً من خلاياك، وبمرور الوقت ستكتشفين أنك أنت مَن سيخرج من خلايا جدّة، وستكتشفين أيضاً أنك خرجت بعدد الصبغيات نفسه الذي لجدّة، وبترتيب الحامض النووي ذاته، وأنك لشدة تعلقك بها بدأت تصيرينها» (ص ٨٨). فالرواية هي من باب حديث الجسد المجروح للتنفيس عن كربه؛ وهي حكاية كل أمة/بلد صدقت الوعود المعسولة للقادم الغريب وسَعت مغمضة العينين نحو الخراب. وبما أنها رواية المكان بلا منازع، فهي مشغولة بمصير هذا المكان ومآله حتى بعد انتحار البطلة. لكن المستقبل الذي تَعِدُ به، قد فضحه عنوان الرواية سلفاً. فصَبا تكرر على مسامع صديقتها القول بأن «كل شيء انتهى وغار في الأعماق السحيقة حتى الفردوس المفقود، الفراديس في السماء وليست على الأرض، الفراديس للأنبياء وليست للخاطئين . . . الفراديس ستغدو يباباً يسلمنا للموت» (ص ٢٣).

وإذا كان خال والجهني يعبران عن اغتراب الذات الجمعيّة عن نظامها المعرفي بشكل مباشر، فإن جوخة الحارثي – الكاتبة العُمانية – في روايتها **سيدات القمر** تعطينا تصوراً مغايراً للهوة السحيقة التي تتعاظم

السكان المحليين ووضعهم خلف جُدُر عالية «لدواعٍ أمنية». وهذا التبديل في الأدوات، من وضع الخرائط إلى إقامة الأسوار، يعكس الارتباط الوثيق بين الإمبريالية - وصورها المستحدثة كالليبرالية الجديدة - وبين مصادرة المكان وإعادة تشكيله. فالجدران العازلة تعني نفياً للمكان والزمان وإلغاءً لهما من ذاكرة السكان الذين يؤمنون بأن كلّ «بعيد عن العين بعيد عن القلب». لذلك أطلقوا العنان لخيالاتهم لكي تستحضر ذلك الغائب المتخفي وتنسج الأساطير حول ما يجري خلف تلك الجدران. لكن أحداً لم يجرؤ على تسمية ذلك الدخيل بعينه، حيث اكتفى الجميع بلغة الاستعارة والمجاز ليعبروا بها عن عُنف إقصائهم.

والاستعارة التي يوظفها بطل فاضل طارق بطل رواية **ترمي بشرر** بشكل متكرر لوصف مراحل حياته هي السقوط. وكما يرى «فالسقوط حالة زمنية توصلك إلى القاع في سرعة متناهية، وبفعل التجاذب تكون مهيّأً لأن تسافرَ في لحظات السقوط المتعددة، وكل مرحلة تدنو بك من القاع تسجل حالة دنيا من حالات السقوط المتعددة، فالسقوط لا يحدث دفعة واحدة» (ص ٩٣). تسير الحبكة الرئيسية للرواية في خطين متوازيين، الأول خط مادي يرتفع إلى الأعلى مع ارتفاع جُدر القصر وأسهم سيّده في سوق المال، والآخر خط مجازي ينحدر بشدة ليتبع تساقط سكان الحارة واحداً بعد الآخر. فالرواية تقوم على توظيف الطباق بين الشخوص وبين الاستعارات. فكل ارتفاع يقابله سقوط، ومَن يقترب من القصر يصطلي بناره، ومن يبتعد عنه ينجو بنفسه من التهلكة. وهذا الطباق العجيب يعبّر عنه من أهل حارة النار بمقولتهم المُحيّرة التي تتكرر كثيراً في الرواية: «من هذا القصر ستخرج الحياة». فيغدو السؤال: بأي اتجاه ستخرج هذه الحياة؟ صعوداً أم هبوطاً؟

وإذا كانت **ترمي بشرر** صريحة ومباشرة في تصديها للعنف البطيء الذي بدأ يتسلل إلى مجتمعات الخليج العربي مع مشاريع الطفرة الاقتصادية، فإن **الفردوس اليباب** لكاتبتها ليلى الجهني استخدمت الاستعارة في تتبعها للخراب الذي بدأ ينخر كالسوس في أرض جدّة التي كانت تظنها أرض الفردوس الموعود. وهذه الرواية كانت ولا تزال موضعاً لكثير من التأويلات، ليس بسبب إغراقها في الترميز، ولكن بسبب البساطة المُفتعلة للحبكة. فهي تبدو للقارئ العجول كحكاية حب فاشلة انتهت بالخيانة والانتحار، لكن إحجامها عن رسم الشخوص بعمق يجعل منها حكايةً رمزية. وتجدر الإشارة إلى أن **الفردوس اليباب** صدرت عام ١٩٩٩ وتقول كاتبتها إنها فرغت من

الوحيد القادر على انتشالهم من سقوطهم، فأطلقوا عليه اسم «الجنّة» حرفياً وبلا مواربة. يستطرد الراوي في وصف بدايات القصر قائلاً:

جدر عالية تقف هناك
لم يعد من مدى سوى ظلال أحلامٍ يابسةٍ ضمرت جذورها في مخيلاتنا، غدت الأسوار سداً منيعاً تنقلب أبصارنا خاسئة لا تجتازها إلا بتخيل ما يمكن أن يحدث خلف تلك الأسوار الشاهقة.
في طور شبابنا الأول ونحن نحصي عدد الأنوار التي تضيء أسوار القصر، كنا نتصور أن حوريات يتساقطن من السماء ليحدث قدومهن كل هذه الجلبة المنبعثة من داخل القصر بنشوة.
هذه الخيالات المفرطة كان مبعثها تلك الجدر العالية التي كانت تقف سداً منيعاً أمام أبصارنا تاركة للخيال فسحة كبيرة لأن يحلق كيف شاء.
مع تشييد القصر جفّ البحر من أحداقنا كما لو كان تم تجفيفها بمئات الأطنان الإسمنتية فبقيت تنزّ لأعماقنا مكونة بركاً من الأسى والحزن. . . . .
غدا القصر عنواناً جديداً لحيّنا الذي تخلى عن اسمه جبرياً ورضي أن يستتر خلف شوارع متسعة، ومشجرة، ومضاءة.
من هذا القصر ستخرج الحياة.
جملة سرت في أوردة الزمن لتؤكد نبوءتها في كل حين (ص ص ٢٦-٢٧).

يختصر خالد عبده جماليات القصر الذي تم إنشاؤه على الأرض المغتصبة من حارة النار بالجُدر العالية والأسوار المنيعة التي أقيمت في وجه السكان المحليين، في إشارة صريحة إلى البنية الفكرية الجديدة التي أصبحت تقوم عليها الإمبريالية بصورتها المعاصرة. فالمستعمر القديم تخلى عن أدواته الأولى وشغفه بوضع الخرائط ورسم الحدود التي مكنته سابقاً من تمثيل فَهْمه لهُويّات الشعوب بشكل مادي على الأرض، ليتسلل مرة أخرى ويعبر عن هَوسه بإعادة خلق الشعوب وتشكيل ذواتها تبعاً لتصوراته هو عبر مشاريع التحديث والتطوير العقاري الذي لا يتأتّى إلا بعد استبعاد

بهوسها الشديد بمشاريع التطوير العقاري ومصادرة الأملاك العامة وتحويلها إلى ملكيات خاصة. فبطل الرواية الذي يروي لنا المراحل المتلاحقة لسقوطه الأخلاقي المريع يبدأ حكايته من حيث قام القصر المنيف على مشارف حارة «النار»/«الحفرة» ليكون سداً منيعاً بينها وبين البحر، ثم يخبرنا كيف وجد البحارة والصيادون وصانعو الشباك أنفسهم بلا مصدر رزق بعد أن استولى سيد القصر على كل متنفس لهم على شاطىء البحر. ولم يغن عنهم كل ما تراكم لديهم من معارف وخبرات ورثوها عن أجدادهم ولم تشفع لهم لدخول «جنّة» المشروع الجديد الذي صادر أراضيهم. وحتى محاولاتهم البائسة لمجاراة التطور والذهاب إلى مصر والسودان لتعلم حِرْفةٍ سياسة الخيول، بعد الشائعات التي سرَت بأن القصر سيكون مرتعاً لخيول نادرة، لم يكتب لها النجاح. وفي هذه اللحظة يبدأ مسلسل السقوط، فكل سور يرتفع بناؤه من القصر يقابله تردي أحد أبناء حارة الحفرة، إما بالموت أو بالانحطاط الأخلاقي. وكان مصير بطل الرواية هو السقوط في الرذيلة بعد أن جرّته خطيئةٌ ارتكبها أوّل شبابه مع إحدى فتيات الحارة لدخول القصر والانضمام إلى طاقمه ومن ثمّ الانزلاق في عوالم سفلية لم يستطع الخروج منها أبداً. ومع ذلك، يخاتل الراوي قارئه بالتركيز على نبوءة عمته خيرية التي كانت ترى في البطل بذرة خبيثة منذ طفولته، وقبل أي ظهور لمشروع القصر. إلا أن إمعان الراوي في استقصاء أخبار جميع أبناء حارة الحفرة الذين استماتوا من أجل دخول القصر، رغم المصائب واللعنات التي تحلّ بكل من يقترب منه، يؤكد الصوت الجمعيّ الذي يتحدث به الراوي طارق فاضل. فرواية ترمي بشرر ليست حكاية سقوط الفرد، بل هي الذات الجمعية التي سُحقت تحت عجلات التحديث والتطوير المتسارعة.

وهكذا، فإن السؤال الرئيسي الذي تتمحور حوله ترمي بشرر هو: مَن له الحق في تملّك القصر؟ هل هو سيد القصر أم أهل الحارة الذين صودرت أراضيهم؟ وهذه الثنائية المتنافرة التي جمعت بين سكان الحارة وسكان القصر أعطت سلطة المكان «الأليف الموحش» uncanny في عيون بطل الرواية وأصحابه. فالأرض التي كانت إلى وقت قريب أرضَهم، غدت ملكاً لغيرهم وهم الآن يدخلونها ليس بوصفهم أصحاب حق بل أجراء. لذلك لا يملك أهل الحارة أمام سطوة التحديث والتطوير القسري إلا النكوص إلى معتقداتهم الغيبية ليحتموا من هذا القادم الإسمنتي الغريب، وليسقطوا عليه مشاعر الرهبة والهيبة التي تعتريهم، فيصبح هو المقدس المهيب، وهو

سلّط على النصراني الّي لقى الزيت
علّ نبع الزيت يعمي عيونه
لولاه تحتاج المراجل شفاليت
تحتاج شي يقصر النذل دونه

فالشاعر هنا يربط بشكل مباشر بين عمليات التنقيب والاستخراج وبين انهيار المنظومة القيمية للبداوة وهو ما يعبر عنه بمسمى «المراجل»، ومن ثم لا يشتكي من اغتراب لذاته المنفردة في مجتمع جديد فقط، بل يتحدث عن انزياح لجماعات كاملة ليس من أراضيها بل من نظامها المعرفي والبيئي الذي تشكلت فيه قيمهم وذاكرتهم الجمعية خلال قرون طويلة. والقطيعة الزمنية التي يشتكي منها الشاعر هي من العلامات الفارقة لأي كتابة ما بعد كولونيالية تنظر إلى الماضي باعتباره زمناً ذهبياً يعجز الجميع عن الرجوع إليه بعد ظهور ذلك الدخيل الغريب الذي أحدث القطيعة الزمنية على غير ما يشتهيه أصحاب المكان الأصليون. لذلك، فإن تتبع الإنتاج الأدبي لأبناء الخليج العربي قد يساعد مَن يتبنى ما بعد الكولونيالية في إعادة تعريف معنى «الانزياح» الذي كان مرتبطاً بشكل مباشر وصريح بالاستعمار بمفهومه الكلاسيكي في القرن التاسع عشر، فاقتصرت دراسته على موجات الهجرة إلى العواصم الأوروبية أو اقتلاع سكان الكاريبي نتيجةً لتجارة الرّقيق، وغير ذلك من السرديات التي ظلت، لفترة طويلة، تغذي لوحدها مفهوم الانزياح في النظرية ما بعد الكولونيالية. فنحن الآن بصدد دراسة نوع مختلف من الانزياح تجد فيه الجماعات نفسها وعلى أرضها لكن أمام منظومة تراتبية جديدة تقوم على تهميش القيم والمعارف المحلية لترفع من شأن قيم ومعارف أخرى. وفي هذا السياق، تظهر الرواية بوصفها جنساً أدبياً يوظف المقاومة على مستويات عدة. فالرواية المكتوبة تقاوم ثقافة الصورة التي اجتاحت دول الخليج العربي وأصبحت – كما البترول الذي أدخلها على هذه المجتمعات التقليدية – تسلب الألباب بالوعود الموصولة بالنعيم والملذات الحسية والمتع الاستهلاكية. وأيضاً هي رواية مقاومة لأنها تستنطق أصوات المهمشين والمُغيبين في الرواية الرسمية لظهور البترول منذ أربعينيات القرن الماضي.

ومن أهم الروايات التي تبنت هذا المنظور لمفهوم الانزياح رواية *ترمي بشرر* للكاتب السعودي عبده خال، حيث تغوص بنا الرواية في عوالم ما يعرف في لغة الاقتصاد بالطفرة النفطية التي تتمثل في المخيال الاجتماعي

«الطّفرة» الذي أطلقه السكان لوصف هذه التغيرات وتمييزها عن غيرها من التجارب الجمعية التي مروا بها وما لبث أن استعارها منهم الاقتصاديون فيما بعد للحديث عن الفترة الزمنية نفسها. فالطفرة في اللغة العربية هي «الوثبة في ارتفاع» وهي تُعبّر عن انتقال عن المكان وتبديله، لكن البعد الزمني حاضرٌ أيضاً ويتجلّى في عنصري المفاجأة والسرعة اللذين تشير إليهما هذه الاستعارة بلا مواربة.

كان روب نيكسون من أوائل مَن حاولوا تتبع الكتابات الأدبية التي تناولت عملية التغيير والانزياح هذه في مجتمعات مختلفة وقدّم دراسة عميقة لها من منظور نقدي ثقافي في كتابه **العنف البطيء ونشطاء البيئة الفقراء** *Slow Violence and the Environmentlism of the Poor* الذي يقوم على تأصيل مفهوم «العنف البطيء»، ويعني به ذلك العنف الذي يتسلل ببطء إلى أجساد ضحاياه - الفقراء والمهمشين غالباً - بعيداً عن أضواء الكاميرات والشاشات الإخبارية. يرى نيكسون أن أحداث الحادي عشر من سبتمبر قد تكون مسؤولة إلى حد ما عن صرف أنظارنا لفترة طويلة عن هذا العنف البطيء الذي يتسلل من تحت أرجلنا. فسقوط البرجين، في مشهد سينمائي خطف أبصار العالم، جعل أنظارنا تبحث باستمرار عن عنف استعراضي يشابه ذلك المشهد بقوته ومؤثراته التصويرية فقط. أما الكوارث والتغييرات البيئية التي تتسرب ببطء إلى عالمنا إلى درجة نعجز أحياناً عن تتبع جذورها، فهي لن تحظى بالاهتمام نفسه لأنها من وجهة نظر سردية لا تقدم للكاتب والناقد رواية بحبكة مستقيمة يستطيع أن يلتقط خيوط بدايتها ويضع لها نهاية تراجيدية مُقنعة. وبذلك يكون العنف البطيء - كما يراه نيكسون - عنفاً يعبث بالملامح الجيولوجية للأرض المنتهكة وترتد آثاره على سكان هذه الأرض الذين يتجاوبون مع وَقْع الزمان الجديد بتشوهات جديدة لم يعرفها أسلافهم من قبل ويعبرون عنهَا بمجازات مختلفة (انظر Nixon).

ومن المفارقات أن الشعر الشعبي في الجزيرة العربية كان أسرع من الرواية في التقاط هذه العلاقة المجازية بين التشوهات الأخلاقية الجديدة التي عرفتها مجتمعاتِ الطفرة وبين النفط بوصفه دخيلاً على صحراء الجزيرة العربية ومتسبباً في تلوِّثها، حيث يقول الشاعر بندر بن سرور في قصيدته شائعة التداول شفهياً في دول الخليج العربي:

الدائم، ولأكثر من قرن، في سوق إنتاج النفط العالمي؟ [18] إذ كيف يكون البترول هو المجاز الأوحد الذي يختزل صورة دول الخليج في المخيلة العربية والغربية كما وصفها غازي القصيبي عندما قال: «نفط يقول الناس عن وطني» (انظر القصيبي)، ومع ذلك - باستثناء خماسية عبدالرحمن منيف - نكاد لا نرى له حضوراً في الإنتاج الأدبي لدول المنطقة؟ كيف نُعلل هذا التغييب القسري للسائل الأسود من ذاكرة الشعراء والكتاب؟ وبما أن ما بعد الكولونيالية تُعدُّ منهجاً في قراءة النصوص واستنطاق الأصوات المهمشة، وتسعى دائما إلى استظهار الكامن والمحجوب والمسكوت عنه، فإن ابتعاد النفط عن مخيلة الكتّاب ومجازاتهم وغيابه المتواصل يفضح قدراً من العنف والتهميش صَاحَبَ حضوره وعمليات استخراجه، فهو مُغيّب وليس بغائب وهو حاضر وموجود لكنّه مستور عن الأعين بحُجُب تخفف عن الكتاب والشعراء من ألم المواجهة واللقاء المباشر بينهم وبينه (Wenzel, "How to Read" 157).

وتزداد أهمية المجتمعات المحلية في الخليج العربي في هذا الحقل من الدراسات بسبب انتقالها المفاجئ والسريع من النظام الزراعي والرعوي إلى الاعتماد على الطاقة البترولية، متجاوزة الاعتماد على البخار أو الفحم كالمجتمعات الصناعية. وقد أجاد عبد الرحمن منيف في قراءة أثر هذه التغييرات في سلوك الناس في موران بقوله: «فالأبنية تقوم هنا وهناك وترتفع يوماً بعد آخر، الدكاكين تتراصّ وتتزاحم، الناس يتراكضون ويصرخون وينادون، وذاكرة الناس يعاد ترتيبها بصورة مستمرة، والقلق والهم يتزايدان لأن أحداً لا يعرف ماذا يخبئ الغد» (ص ٣٠٤). فظهور النفط تلازم مع إعادة ترتيب المكان، ومن ثمّ الذاكرة الجمعية ليس لسكان موران فقط بل للعقل العربي الجمعي أيضا. وهذه واحدة من أهم ركائز الدراسات ما بعد الكولونيالية التي ترى أن الانزياح أو الارتحال - سواء كان محلياً أم عالمياً - ترافقه حالة من فقدان الذاكرة الجمعية، لأن هذه الذاكرة لا تجسّد ذاتها إلا عبر المكان، فإذا انتُزعت منه قسراً فقدت قناتها الوحيدة في تمثيل حضورها (Ashcroft, *Utopianism* 65). فأهل موران في مدن الملح لم يرتحلوا فقط من مساكنهم، بل غيروا مفهوم الزمن، ووجدوا أنفسهم يقتحمون بغير إرادتهم عصر السرعة وليس بوسعهم سوى الركض والصراخ للحاق بما يمكن اللحاق به. من هنا، جاءت الاستعارات والمسمّيات الشعبية لهذه التغييرات ببعدين متوازيين، أحدهما مكاني والآخر زماني، مثل مصطلح

ما بعد الكولونيالية في دول الخليج العربي والمقاومة بالكتابة

يتبنى بعض المنشغلين بالنظرية ما بعد الكولونيالية منهجاً شمولياً يرى أن النظرية لا يجب أن تتجاوز الخطاب الاستعلائي الذي ينتجه الغرب عن نفسه وعن الآخر والخطاب التحرري الذي ينتجه المستعمَر لاستعادة حقه في تمثيل نفسه،[16] في حين يرى آخرون ومن بينهم بيل أشكروفت أن حيوية النظرية تنبع من ديمقراطيتها الجدلية التي تجعلها ميداناً مفتوحاً لا يستنكف عن استيعاب «الهوامش» المتباينة التي تريد اللحاق به يوماً بعد يوم (Ashcroft, "Future" 263). ومن هذه الهوامش التي نأمل أن يتسع صدر النظرية لاستيعابها هو ما بات يعرف في بعض الجامعات الأنجلوفونية باسم «دراسات الثقافة البترولية»،[17] وهي حقل ناشئ يُعنى برصد التحولات الاجتماعية والثقافية والفنية التي طرأت على بعض المجتمعات بعد لحظة اكتشاف البترول وبدء عمليات التنقيب على أراضيها. وخارطة هذه الدراسات تستحوذ عليها بشكل كبير كندا ونيجيريا واسكتلندا، ومعظمها يدور حول جماليات «الواقعية السحرية» وعلاقتها بدخول البترول إلى المخيلة الجمعية كحكاية أسطورية تَعد أبطالها بالثراء السريع دون عناء. ومن ذلك الدراسات التي قامت بها جنيفير وينزل Wenzel على الأدب النيجيري واستنتجت منها أن الأعمال الأدبية في نيجيريا توظف استعارات متماثلة للتعبير عن الوَقْع الساحر للحظة اللقاء بين السكان المحليين وبين البترول ومعدات استخراجه الحديثة. ورغم انشغالها بالأعمال النيجيرية فقط، فقد ذكرت في لقاء لها أنها لا تزال تتساءل عن سر الاختفاء الغامض لشخصية الشاعر غافل السويد وقبله متعب الهذال من مدن الملح بطريقة يحوطها الغموض الساحر (Potter 385)، وما الأبعاد الجمالية والفنية لإبعاد شخوص الشعراء النبطيين من الرواية بهذه الطريقة السحرية التي تخالف الأسلوب الواقعي للنص. وتضيف وينزل أن توظيف المخيلة المحلية في وصف المنتجات العصرية - كما فعل منيف عندما وصف حَيرة الأمير أمام «الطعام» الذي يجب أن يقدمه «للسيارة» (ص 439) - يثير الكثير من الأسئلة عن اللقاء بين المحلي والعالمي وعن المخيلة الجمعية للسكان المحليين وعن تصورهم للعلاقة بين الإنسان وبيئته المحيطة به.

لذلك، فإن السؤال الذي يتردد بكثرة بين المشتغلين بهذا المجال هو كيف تغيب المجتمعات الشرق أوسطية عن هذه البحوث رغم حضورها

على مقعدين متجاورين أعطى ربعي المدهون أرضاً واقعية ووقتاً مستقطعاً لبناء مدينته الفاضلة - مجازاً - التي يسودها العدل والسلام بين طرفي الصراع بشكل مقنع يقبله القارئ المعاصر ويعطيه الأمل في أن هذه المدينة الفاضلة المجازية قد ترى النور يوماً. فنحن لا نرى إلا «مسافران عاديان في فضاء عابر»، «يتراءى لهما ظل مأساتهما المشتركة التي لم تتوقف عن إنتاج نفسها عبر عشرات السنين» (ص ١١٤) ؛ لحظات وجيزة من السلام والعدالة لكنها محصورة بمقعدين متجاورين على ظهر طائرة، لتأتي بعدها لحظات الانتظار العصيب والمُهين على معبر بيت حانون لتمحو خطوط التعايش الباهتة التي تم رسمها في السماء. ومع تكاثر القصص وتوالدها داخل **السيدة من تل أبيب**، يسرد وليد دهمان حكاية مشابهة عن عجوزٍ فلسطينية جلست بجانب شاب إسرائيلي لطيف تمنت للحظات لو كان ابنا لها، لتفاجأ به بعد أيام أمام حاجز عسكري يصرخ بها لتعود إلى الوراء. وهكذا، تتكرر الحكايات داخل الرواية بالبنية السردية نفسها، فكل فرصة للتعايش وبَدْء الحوار مع الآخر يعقبها لقاء مؤلم ومُنهك على معبر أو نقطة تفتيش في إشارة صريحة إلى التمدد الخانق للاحتلال الذي يحاول خنق أحلام الفلسطينيين حتى في مهدها قبل أن ترى النور.

لكن ربعي المدهون يستمر في نسج خيوط الأمل عندما يضع القارئ وجهاً لوجه مع عادل البشيتي الذي كان يظنه مجرد شخصية وهمية تتداخل حكاياتها مع البطل الحقيقي وليد دهمان. ويزداد القارئ تشبثاً بالأمل الذي يرسمه المدهون بعد أن ينجح عادل البشيتي في العثور على الفتاة التي عاد إلى غزة ليبحث عنها بعد فراق دام عقوداً طويلة. فالعودة في مَجاز ربعي المدهون ممكنة، بل تحمل في داخلها وعوداً أخرى بحياة طيبة يسودها الحب والوفاء. وبعد هذا كله، تنتهي الرواية بمقتل الإسرائيلية دانا أهوفا وهيٍ تحمل في أحشائها طفلاً مجهول النسب لا تعرف أمه إن كان والده عربياً أم إسرائيلياً. فهو يكاد يختزل رمزية **السيدة من تل أبيب** بأسرها، فهي رواية المستقبل المجهول. وهذا الطفل هو وليد صراعات اليوم ونكبات الأمس التي تشابكت خيوطها، فلم يعد من الممكن الفصل بين الدماء التي اختلطت في أوردته. وهكذا فإن الصمود عند ربعي المدهون هو منطقة رمادية ضبابية، نرى فيها «ظلان لبيت واحد»، وتتعاقب على أرضها سيناريوهات الأمل والألم لكنها أرض لقاء ومواجهة عادلة لم تصطبغ بعد بدماء الشهداء ومزايدات السياسيين ومتاجراتهم.

يناضل لكي يبدو مختلفاً أيضاً عن اليوتوبيا بمفهومها الغربي التي تسعى إلى تخيل ورسم خطة لنظام سياسي أو اجتماعي مكتمل التفاصيل يحقق السلام والعدالة للجميع. فالصمود عند المدهون يعني الحضور المتواصل للأمل في النصر وتحقق السلام على شكل منفصل، بل ومتسام على الواقع الصعب. ففي رواية السيدة من تل أبيب يطرح الكاتب فكرة التعايش بين الفلسطينيين والإسرائيليين بوصفه مخرجاً وحيداً للصراع. لكنه يقدم الفكرة على شكل سرديّات طوباوية متلاحقة تعقبها في كل مرة صور واقعية مليئة بالخيبة والظلم. فتبدو الرواية كأحلام طفل غرير انكبّ على الورق يرسم عليه تخيلاته لعالم خالٍ من الصراعات لكنه، بين فينة وأخرى، يرفع رأسه ليصف لنا بدقة كلَّ ما يجري حوله من معارك وبرك دماء. يقول الكاتب على لسان وليد دهمان وهو يقلب في رأسه أحد سيناريوهات التعايش بعد أن جمعته الصدفة مع شابة إسرائيلية:

بل أتمنى أن يخرج الفلسطينيون والإسرائيليون من ساحة الحرب إلى العيش المشترك، ونتمشى أنا وهي معاً في أوتوستراد طويل لا عناء فيه ولا معابر. لا اغتيالات ولا انتحاريين. لا مجندين ولا مقاومين. لا صهيونية ولا حركة تحرر وطني فلسطينية. لا انتفاضة ولا مستوطنات. لا شارون ولا عرفات. لا أبو مازن ولا شاؤول موفاز. لا أباتشي ولا إف-١٦ ولا انتحاريين. بل مسافران عاديان في فضاء عابر. (ص ٩٦)

تختزل الجملة الأخيرة - «مسافران عاديان في فضاء عابر» - المشروع الروائي لربعي المدهون؛ فهو يحاول جاهداً أن يخلق هذا الفضاء العابر الذي سيحل معضلة المكان في مشروعه للتعايش. فالصراع ليس صراعاً على حدود مشتركة بين بلدين يتقاتلان، ولكنه صراع على أرض واحدة بين شعبين، أو كما عُبِّر عنه بالعنوان الداخلي لرواية شخصيته عادل البشيتي: «ظلان لبيت واحد». لذلك كان المكان الوحيد الذي يشعر فيه القارئ ببصيص من أملٍ في السيدة من تل أبيب هو ذلك المكان المعلق على ظهر طائرة متجهة صوب تل أبيب. فجاء الحل على طريقة «الهيتروتوبيا» التي وصفها ميشيل فوكو بعمق.[١٥] فالسلام على أرض فلسطين هو حلم طوباوي يُمعن في البعد يوماً بعد يوم، لكن لقاءً عابراً بين صحفي فلسطيني وممثلة إسرائيلية

نتيجةً للماضي ويتقدم بحركة مستمرة نحو المستقبل بخط مستقيم وأسباب يمكن استيعابها وحصرها (Böwering 56). لكن الصمود في **غريب النهر** يحمل تحدياً صارخاً لمفهوم الزمان في النظام المعرفي الاستعماري لأنه يقوم في الأساس على نظام معرفي مختلف تماماً في مفاهيمه الأساسية. فمفهوم الزمن في **غريب النهر** هو مفهوم مرتبط بالفكر الشعبي في المجتمعات العربية الذي يجرد الشخوص من فاعليتهم أمام الدَّهْر ويتمثل بصدق قول الشاعر: «ما بين غمضة عين وانتباهتها يغير الله من حال إلى حال». لذلك يبقى السؤال الأهم هو هل الشخوص في **غريب النهر** هم ضحايا للقوى الإمبريالية أم مشاركون في صناعة أقدارهم؟

ويستمر جمال ناجي في تغذية هذا المنظور الرومانسي للصمود الفلسطيني وبأن الفرج قادم لا محالة من دون أن يخبرنا كيف سيأتي أو متى، حتى يصل إلى نهاية النص، فيقدم لنا شخصية الابنة خلود التي يتجاوز عن وصف شكلها أو أبعاد شخصيتها لُيطنب في وصف شغفها بتاريخ قرية العباسية. ويتناول بصفة خاصة مهاراتها العجيبة في التفكير الإبداعي وقدراتها المذهلة على ابتكار حلول بسيطة لمشاكل قد تبدو عويصة لغيرها. فهي الوحيدة التي استطاعت أن تجد مخرجاً لتنفيذ الوصية بدفن جثة الغريب في أرض فلسطين من دون مشاكل. وكأن جمال ناجي بذلك يضع الابنة خلود في مقارنة فجّة مع الجيل الأول من المناضلات الفلسطينيات، وعلى الأخص الخالة «سَفَر» الحارسة الشخصية لياسر عرفات والمناضلة اليسارية المتمسكة بنموذج تشي جيفارا. وتنتهي الرواية بأن تستودع العائلة الابنة خلود خرائطَ قرية العباسية التي رسمها الضابط التركي، وكأن جمال ناجي يريد القول بأن مستقبل الصمود الفلسطيني في أيدٍ أمينة، شابة ذات فكر إبداعي قادر على خلق حلول جديدة لم يأتِ بها الجيل السابق من المناضلين الذين جربوا الكفاح المسلح واتفاقيات السلام. فالإبداع يتسامى على الواقع السياسي ويترفّع عنه ولا يتعاطى معه بشكل مباشر، لكنه في الوقت ذاته يعطينا الأمل في تغيير هذا الواقع بفضل قدرته على خلق عوالم وحلول أخرى لم نرها من قبلِ.

وإذا كانت **غريب النهر** تتناول الصمود بوصفه فهماً جديداً للصبر والانتظار وتتكئ على المعنى الديني/الشعبي لقيمة الفرج بعد الشدة والضيق في محاولة للرد على المشروع الاستعماري المهووس بالتطور والتقدم نحو مستقبلٍ يَفترض دائماً أنه أفضل، نجد ربعي المدهون يقدم لنا مشروعاً أدبياً أعمق وأنضج يتناول فيه الصمود الفلسطيني بوصفه بديلاً طوباوياً

أما أصل عمي اسمعين فيمتد إلى ماقبل «حكاية الإنطاء» التي يعتد بها ويحرص على الاستشهاد بها كلما سئل عن تاريخ حمولته ، وهي الحكاية التي ربطها بما نقله عن والده عبد الجبار أبو حلة ، عن جده اسماعيل ، عن جد أبيه ، فاروق الذي عمل كاتباً معاوناً لكاتب المراسلات الشريفة في محكمة القدس ، وقد حفظ حكاية الإنطاء تلك عن ظهر قلب بلغة عربية سليمة لا لحن فيها ، يحرص على أن يبدأها بنفسه كلما سردها على مسامع أبنائه فيقول : ولدتُ في قرية العباسية القريبة من يافا بعد سبعة أعوام من انتهاء الحرب العالمية الأولى ، لأبوين عربيين فلسطينيين هما عبد الجبار بن اسماعيل بن فاروق أبو حلة ، والسيدة عائشة بنت رشيد بن اسماعيل بن فاروق أبو حلة ، اللذان يتحدران من إحدى حمائل بني تميم من بني عبد الدار ، رهط الصحابي الجليل تميم الداري ، المتحدر من قبيلة عربية اسمها لخم ، أقامت في فلسطين قبل ألف وثمانمئة عام من ميلاد المسيح ، ثم انتشرت عائلاتها بعد الفتوحات الإسلامية في مناطق الخليل والساحل الفلسطيني ونابلس والسلط والكرك وغيرها . (ص ١٥)

ورغم أن جمال ناجي جعل حكاية نص الإنطاء هامشية في محور أحداث الرواية واكتفى بعد ذلك بثلاث أو أربع إشارات مقتضبة للنص ، فإن ظهورها في بداية الرواية ، وعمي اسمعين يحاول جاهداً أن يحدد للقارئ نقطة البداية لوعيه التاريخي ، يعطينا تصوراً واضحا للطريقة الرومانسية – وربما اللاهوتية – التي يرى بها الزمن ويفهم بها تتابع الأحداث من حوله . فالماضي حاضر أمامه في شكل سديم يتكاثف ثم يدور حول نفسه فلا يستطيع القارئ أن يميز أوله من آخره ، فهناك الحرب العالمية الأولى ، ثم بنو تميم من بني عبد الدار ، ثم قبيلة لخم ، ثم ميلاد المسيح ، ثم الفتوحات الإسلامية . وبهذا المنظور السديمي[١٤] للزمن تتطور أحداث الرواية بطريقة مشابهة . فنوائب الدهر تُقلّبُ حياة آل أبو حلة من حال إلى حال ، فلا يعرف القارئ إلى أين ستأخذه الأحداث ؛ هل عمي اسمعين يمضي نحو نكبة جديدة أم هو مقبل على يسر بعد عسر؟ وهذا المفهوم للزمن يخالف المفهوم الغربي الاستعماري القائم على فكرة التطور الذي يرى الحاضر

الذي يصل إلى غور الأردن وهو لا يملك في جيبه إلا بطاقة الإعاشة التي صرفتها له وكالة إغاثة اللاجئين الفلسطينيين، لكنه يتنازل عنها مقابل قطعة أرض بور يقوم هو وأبناؤه بزراعتها حتى صارت بيارة يباهي بثمارها سكان الغور كله، لتأتي بعد ذلك معركة الكرامة وأيلول الأسود ليجد القارئ أمامه جموعاً من آل أبو حلة ينحدرون من كل حدب وصوب باتجاه بيارة عمي اسمعين ليتركوه بعد ذلك وحيداً مهموماً لا ينقذه من رتابة الأيام إلا ظهور ابن أخيه شوكت التركي الذي يعيد تأطير الرواية ويفتتحها بحكاية مصطفى أبو حلة الذي نجا بأعجوبة من إحدى معارك الجيش العثماني في قضاء الشام لِيُمضي بقية حياته في إسطنبول بعيداً عن زخم النضال الفلسطيني في أوج اشتعاله. وتنتهي الرواية بمغامرة دفن الغريب مصطفى في الضفة الغربية لنهر الأردن ليؤكد بجثمانه انتماءه إلى الأرض التي خرج منها إبّان الحرب العالمية الأولى ولم يطأها بعد ذلك.

لكن الصمود في **غريب النهر** لا يظهر فقط في رمزية جثمان الغريب والإصرار على دفنه في الأرض المحتلة، بل يراوح الظهور بشكل متكرر في رمزين اثنين أحدهما يفتتح الرواية والآخر يختتمها؛ صك الإنطاء وشخصية الابنة خلود. فعمي اسمعين السبعيني المتمسك بمجموعة من المعتقدات الخرافية عن الموت والمستقبل ومصير أبناء العباسية لا يستطيع نقل هذه المعتقدات إلى أبنائه المتعلمين الذين انتشروا في أصقاع الأرض، لكنه يجد في «كتاب الإنطاء» ضالّته.[13] فهو نص مقدس ذو سلطة دينية قابلة للتوريث من جيل إلى جيل، أي للصمود والبقاء. فيقوم بكتابته بخط أنيق على لوح من الخشب ويضع له إطاراً مذهباً ويعلقه في صدر صالون الاستقبال في منزله. وبذلك يتحول كتاب الإنطاء من نص شفهي تناقلته الأجيال بطريقة حفظ الأسانيد - حدثني فلان عن فلان عن فلان - إلى نص مكتوب. والنصوص المكتوبة لها سلطة مقدسة في النظام المعرفي الاستعماري تختلف جذرياً عن الأقاصيص والمرويات الشفهية التي يهمشها النظام الاستعماري باعتبارها طوراً بدائياً للحضارة الإنسانية. كما أن صبغة النص الدينية ونسبته إلى الرسول محمد (ص) أضافت إلى الرواية بُعداً رومانسياً يأخذنا باتجاه الطوباوية الروحانية التي ترى في الأفكار الغيبية باعثاً على الأمل في التجديد وإعادة البناء وتُقصي العقلانية، في حين ترى في الانغماس في الواقع المادي سبباً في هلاك الحاضر وخرابه. وتبدأ حكاية نص الإنطاء على النحو الآتي:

بطولها مَعْنية بطرح تعريفات متعددة لهذه «البلاد على أُهبةِ الفجر»؛ فالقراء متحفزون ومتأهبون لصحبة درويش وهو يتنقل بين المعنى الجغرافي والتاريخي والعرقي والتراثي لهذه البلاد. فلكي يعمّ السلام، لا بد أن يتعلم كل من سيقيم فوق أرض فلسطين «نماذج من الشعر الجاهلي» (ص ١١)، ولا بد أن يتشاركوا في رواية «الألم» (ص ١٣). فحكاية غرف الغاز ستقابلها حكايات المخيمات، في ذلك الحين ربما «قد ينتهي الاحتلال ولا يتذكر الرضيع زمن الحصار» (ص ٢٤)، وهناك «سيكبر الطفل معافى، ويصبح شاباً» (ص ٢٥) قادراً على العيش بسلام على أرض وطن لم يُسمِّها درويش في القصيدة، لكنه رسمها بخياله كصورة طفل

سيلعب بطائرة من ورق
بألوانها الأربعة
أحمر، أسود، أبيض، أخضر
ثم يدخل في نجمة شاردة. (ص ٦٣)

فتداخل الرموز القومية في هذه الصورة يجعل حتى محمود درويش بكل فصاحته وبلاغته عاجزاً عن تسمية هذا الوطن الحلم/المستحيل الذي سيجمع على أرضه في المستقبل أعداء اليوم. ويصرُّ درويش على رسم هذا الحلم بصورة الطفل البريء تارةً أو بصورة العروس التي تبكي استشهاد حبيبها ليلة زفافهما تارةً أخرى لكي يحفظ لفكرته براءتها ومثاليتها ويتسامى بها عن المشاريع السياسية على أرض الواقع وما تلوثت به من مماطلة وغدر وخيانة لدم الشهداء.

ومن أهم الأعمال الروائية التي جعلت من الصمود الفلسطيني محوراً لها رواية **غريب النهر** لجمال ناجي، وتتميز عن غيرها من كتاباته بابتعادها عن مفهوم الكتابة الواقعية الذي عُرف عن ناجي واعتمادها على تعدد المرويّات داخل النص وتشابكها بطريقة الصُدف المفتعلة أحياناً. فيحارُ القارئ وهو يتابع كيف ينتقل الراوي العليم بكل شيء بين مروياته الممتدة من فترة ما قبل الحرب العالمية الأولى حتى يأخذه على حين غفلة إلى اتفاقية «وادي عربة»، فرواية **غريب النهر** تحكي مصير رهط من آل أبو حلة من قرية العباسية في قضاء يافا، وتأخذ القارئ فيما بعد إلى الأردن وتركيا ودول أمريكا اللاتينية. يتتبع الخيط الأول من الرواية حكاية عمي اسمعين

جنوب أفريقيا (سعيد، ص ٤٣). لكن محمود درويش نفسه ينبري مرة أخرى للإجابة عن هذا الإشكال بقوله «لو كان هذا المكان أقل ازدحاماً/ لكانت مدائحنا للتضاريس في شجر الحور أكثر» (**حالة حصار**، ص ٣٢)؛ فقدسية المكان وارتباطه بالموروث الديني للأديان التوحيدية الثلاثة يجعل الفكاك من المقدس والتأصيل لمقاومة إبداعية علمانية خارج عباءة الأديان الثلاثة أمراً صعباً إن لم يكن مستحيلاً.

كما يتجلى مفهوم الصمود في أبهى صوره في قصيدة محمود درويش الشهيرة «حالة حصار» التي يقول في مطلعها:

هنا، عند مُنْحَدَرات التلال، أمام الغروب
وفُوَّهَة الوقت،
قُرْبَ بساتينَ مقطوعة الظل،
نفعلُ ما يفعلُ السجناءُ،
وما يفعل العاطلون عن العمل:
نُرَبِّي الأمل.

بلادٌ على أُهْبَة الفجر.
صرنا أقلَّ ذكاءً،
لأنَّا نُحَمْلِقُ في ساعة النصر:
لا لَيْلَ في ليلنا المتلألئ بالمدفعيّة.
أعداؤنا يسهرون
وأعداؤنا يُشْعلون لنا النورَ
في حلكة الأقبية. (**حالة حصار**، ص ص ٩-١٠)

في «حالة حصار»، يوثق محمود درويش لمعنى الزمان والمكان الذي بدأ الفلسطينيون باستيعابه بعد خمسين عاماً من الصراع ضد الاحتلال.[١٢] فالاحتلال صار كالبطالة عن العمل وكالحكم بالسجن لا يعلم صاحبه متى يحين الإفراج، سرمديّة بطيئة خانقة ثقيلة الخطى لكنها ستنتهي يوماً ما. كل ما على الفلسطينيين عمله هو «أن يحملقوا في ساعة النصر» التي تلوح في آخر النفق. فالمكان صامد والزمان راسخ لا يتزحزح والمستقبل هو بيت القصيد الذي تُعقد عليه الآمال وتُكتب حوله الأشعار. فالقصيدة

تَضيقُ بنا الأرضُ تَحشُرنا في الممرِّ الأخيرِ ، فنَخْلعَ أعْضاءنا كي نمَرَّ
وتَعْصِرنا الأرضُ. يالَيْتنا قَمْحُها كي نَموتَ ونَحْيَا. وَيَا لَيْتَهَا أُمُّنَا لَتَرْحَمَنَا أُمُّنَا. لَيْتَنا صُوَرٌ للصُّخورِ التي سَوْفَ يَحْمِلُهَا حُلْمُنَا مَرَايَا. رَأَيْنَا وُجُوهَ الذين سَيَقْتُلهُمْ في الدِّفاعِ الأخيرِ عَنِ الرُّوحِ آخِرُنَا
بَكَيْنَا عَلَى عِيدِ أَطْفَالهم ورَأَيْنَا وُجُوهَ الذينَ سَيَرْمُونَ أَطْفَالَنَا مِنْ نَوَافِذِ هذا الفَضَاءِ الأخيرِ. مَرَايَا سَيَصْقِلُهَا نَجْمُنَا
إلى أَيْنَ نَذْهَبُ بَعْدَ الحُدُودِ الأخيرَةِ؟ أَيْنَ تَطيرُ العَصَافيرُ بَعْدَ السَّماءِ الأخيرةِ
أَيْنَ تَنَامُ النَّبَاتَاتُ بَعْدَ الهَوَاءِ الأخيرِ؟ سَنَكْتُبُ أسماءَنا بالبُخارِ المُلَوَّنِ بالقُرْمُزِيِّ سَنَقْطَعُ كَفَّ النَّشيدِ لِيُكْمِلَهُ لَحْمُنَا
هُنَا سَنَمْوتُ هُنَا في المَمَرِّ الأخيرِ هُنَا أَوْ هُنَا سَوْفَ يَغرِسُ زَيْتُونَه . . .
دَمُنَا . (وردٌ أقل ، ص ٣٥٦)

فالشاعر ، هنا ، يعلن الخروج من طور الضحية ويروي أفعال ذلك الطور بصيغة الماضي ، لكنه يستقبل القادم المجهول بالأمل وبالغرس والكتابة ، وهي أفعال توحي بتفاعل الذات مع محيطها السياسي والمادي ، ويؤكد على ذلك باستعمال صيغة المستقبل («سنكتب» ، «سنقطع» ، «سوف نغرس»). ومن المفارقات أن هذه القصيدة بوصفها الدقيق لحالة الانعتاق من دور الضحية وإعلان الالتزام بدور الحالم الفاعل كانت مصدر إلهام لكتابين نقديين تناولا بعمق حياة الذات الفلسطينية في الشتات وهما **بعد السماء الأخيرة** After the Last Sky لإدوارد سعيد Said و**في الممر الأخير** لرامي أبو شهاب. فالصمود هو حالة سكون وانتظار ، لكنه طاقة إبداع وقوة خلق. وهو وإن كان علمانياً في تجلياته وتطبيقاته وفي دعوته إلى المقاومة السلمية ، فهو يستمد رمزيته من الموروث الديني ويستند بشكل كبير إلى المفهوم الشعبي/الديني لمعنى الصبر وأن بعد العسر يسراً. وقد يبدو هذا المنحى بعيداً كل البعد عما طالب به إدوارد سعيد من تأصيل للمقاومة الفلسطينية بصورة علمانية إنسانوية بالدرجة الأولى تضمن لها القبول العالمي لدى جميع الثقافات مثل حركة مناهضة الفصل العنصري في

والصبر أو كما يسميه الفلسطينيون «الصمود» (Ashcroft, *Utopianism* 54). وهنا نستطيع القول بأن ما بعد الكولونيالية بدأت تدير ظهرها للماضي وتنشغل بأسئلة الحاضر والمستقبل، كما أنها يبدو تريد أن تتماهى مع الاهتمام المتزايد بدراسة المكان باعتباره الفضاء الأول الذي تتمثل فيه الهُويّة الثقافية بعيداً عن التركيز على الآخر والنظر إلى الهُويّة باعتبارها ناتجةً عن الاختلاف. ففكرة الصمود أمام آلة الاحتلال ومن خلفها تُجبر النقاد على إعادة النظر في معنى المقاومة بعيداً وبشكل كبير عن مفهوم المحاكاة والهجنة الثقافية، وغيرها من الممارسات الثقافية التي تعبر بها الشعوب المختلفة عن رفضها لهيمنة الاستعمار. فالصمود فعل غيبي قائم على الإيمان التام بأن العدل سيحل يوماً وأن الظلم سينجلي ولن تقوم له قائمة؛ لكن بلا تصور دقيق أو خطة واضحة المعالم لشكل هذه العدالة المنشودة وكيفية تحقيقها. بل هو نوع من الأمل الطوباوي مُبهم التفاصيل ومشوش الملامح، وهذا لا يضعف من قوة هذا الصمود لكن يضفي عليه بُعدا غيبياً يربطه بالعقيدة الدينية للفرد فيغدو الإيمان بالنصر مثل الإيمان بالله وملائكته وكتبه ورسله، إيماناً بعالم غيبي لا نرى ملامحه ونعجز عن تخيّل تفاصيله لكنه من حولنا ويحيط بنا.[11] وهذا في الحقيقة يُعيدنا إلى اللحظات الأولى لولادة المجتمعات الإنسانية، سواء بصورتها الحديثة المتمثلة في الدول أو بصورها الأقدم كالجماعات الدينية والإثنيّة. فهذه الجماعات بمختلف أشكالها قامت في بداياتها على رؤى طوباوية، أي على حلم أو وعد مقدس بحياة فاضلة يسود فيها العدل والسلام، يستوي في ذلك أشد الأنظمة الإمبريالية قسوة وفتكاً بالدماء مع أعتى الحركات التحررية المناهضة للاستعمار (Ashcroft, *Utopianism* 4). فالجميع يسعى خلف وعود مرسومة بمستقبل أفضل قد تأخذ شكل أفكار سياسية أو اقتصادية أو عقائد دينية، لكنها في جوهرها حلم طوباوي، حيث يلجأ الإنسان إلى خياله ليبحث عن العدالة والسلام والحب حين تضيق به السُبل ويجد نفسه محاصراً بواقع تَعِس لا يستطيع الفكاك منه. فالأحلام الموغلة في البعد عن الواقع المادي لا تأتي إلا من مخيلة أرهقها الخوف والألم حتى ضاقت بها الأرض بما رحُبت، فلجأت إلى عالم الخيال والكتابة لتخلق عالماً جديداً. وقد وصف محمود درويش هذه المحطة الأخيرة التي حُشرت فيها الذات الفلسطينية حشراً بعد عقود من حياة الشتات وبقيت عالقة فيها، فيقول:

يكون هذا الخط التبشيري مجرد امتداد للشِّعاراتية السياسية التي عُرفت عن السلطة الفلسطينية. لكنه يعود في مقالة نشرت له حديثاً في **مجلة الدراسات الفلسطينية** ليتناول بعمق أكثر فكرة العودة والانتصار ولو بعد حين، وبحث عن جذور هذا «الفكر التحريضي» كما أسماه عند جيل النكبة، مثل غسان كنفاني وجبرا إبراهيم جبرا، وصولاً إلى أعمال ظهرت حديثاً مثل رواية سليم البيك **تذكرتان إلى صفورية** (انظر «العودة»). وهذا التغيير في موقف فيصل دراج يعني أنه استطاع أن يجد الحد الفاصل بين الوضع السياسي والأدبِ، وبين الإدارة اليومية المضطربة والمشروع السياسي الواضح. فالأمل الذي تبشر به الرواية الفلسطينية قد كان مشروعاً سياسياً في الأصل، لكنه قائم وموجود الآن بمعزل عن سياسات الفصائل المتناحرة،[10] وهو صورة من صور المقاومة الإبداعية التي استطاعت بتمثلاتها الغيبية والرومانسية أن تتجاوز مصادرة الزمان والمكان على أرض الواقع.

ومحاولة دراج لتقصِّي البُعد التبشيري في الرواية باعتباره صورة من صور المقاومة سبقت واحداً من رواد ما بعد الكولونيالية الذي أخذ يبشر منذ فترة قصيرة فقط بقدرة الأدب الفلسطيني على إعادة طرح إشكاليات المقاومة وتعالق الفن بالسياسة وهو بيل أشكروفت، حيث تناول باستفاضة في كتابه **الطوباوية في الآداب ما بعد الكولونيالية** – *Utopianism in Postcolonial Literatures* – الذي صدر عام ٢٠١٦ بعض الأعمال الفنية الفلسطينية، وبخاصة التشكيلية، ليعرض للقارئ كيف تكون المقاومة بالفن عن طريق تحوير معنى الزمان والمكان. فوظيفة الأمل، وإن بدا طوباوياً بعيد المنال، هي بعث الروح في الحاضر المتردي عن طريق دفعه للسير قُدماً خلف هذا الأمل. ويرى أشكروفت أن هذه صفة إنسانية يشترك فيها البشر جميعاً لكنها في سياق مقاومة الاستعمار تأخذ صفة القداسة لارتباطها بجغرافية ما تحمل معنىً مقدساً للجماعة التي تريد التحرر. وبذلك يشترك الأمل الطوباوي في ما بعد الكولونيالية مع الفكر الطوباوي الأفلاطوني في السعي إلى تحقيق مشروع سياسي، لكنه يختلف عنه في القداسة التي يضفيها على مشروعه وبابتعاده عن وضع خطة مفصلة وإضحة المعالم، كما فعل أفلاطون في مدينته الفاضلة التي أصبحت وصفاً لكل مشروع حالم بالعدالة والسلام (18-3).

لذلك، فنحن نشهد احتفاءً بمفهوم جديد يبدو للبعض أنه تجلٍّ جديد للمقاومة لكن بصورة سلمية نابذة للعنف، وهو مفهوم الانتظار

بل سلسلةً من النكبات التي تتوالد ولا تتوقف عن التكرار - يُعدُّ طرحاً جديداً في دراسة تقاطعات الذاكرة والأزمة والفن . كما يجب أن لا نغفل محاولة الناقد رامي أبو شهاب في كتابه في **الممر الأخير** ، حيث دعا إلى تبنّي خطاب الشّتات في دراسة الأدب الفلسطيني عوضاً عن مفهوم المنفى لأن هذا الأخير يتمركز حول فردانية الكاتب ويعرض معاناته بمعزل عن السياق الجمعي للمأساة الفلسطينية . وما يجمع هذه الأعمال النقدية هو ظهورها المتأخر مقارنةً بالأبحاث التي قدمتها العلوم الإنسانية الأخرى حول الصراع الفلسطيني-الإسرائيلي منذ سبعينيات القرن العشرين .

ولو بحثنا أكثر عن مَن تناول الأدب الفلسطيني ممن يتبنون بعضاً من أدوات ما بعد الكولونيالية في العالم العربي لوجدنا بعضهم سبّاقين إلى استجلاء خصوصيات الرواية الفلسطينية . ومن أبرز مَن فعل ذلك الناقد فيصل دراج ، حيث تناول انشغال الرواية الفلسطينية بمفهوم المقاومة وتطوّر طرحها من طور بطولة الخير والانتصار الأكيد إلى طور الكفاح المسلح حتى الطور التبشيري الذي انتهت إليه بعد سلسلة من الخيبات والهزائم ، وكتب في وصفه قائلاً :

> إن السياسة الفلسطينية بدت ولفترة طويلة مجرد «عمومية شعاراتية» ، تنتقل من شعار إلى آخر ، ولا تبرر الانتقال أو تشرح أسبابه ، ولا تحدد بشكل دقيق معنى الشعار الذي تخلت عنه ، ولا معنى الشعار الذي أعقبه . حاولت الرواية الفلسطينية على مستوى المضمون أن تكون غالباً صوتاً تحريضياً ، موضوعه حلمٌ يتجدد يُدعى : فلسطين . وسواء ارتبطت بالسياسة الرسمية أم لم تكن مرتبطة بها ، فقد كان عليها أن تكون كتابة متفائلة تعد بالنصر ولو بعد حين . لم تميز هذه الرواية رغم الدور المنوط بها ، بين التفاؤل التاريخي الذي يطرح أسئلة كثيرة عن الحاضر والماضي وسبل النصر والهزيمة ، والتفاؤل الإعلامي الذي يذيب الأسئلة المعقدة في حكايات يومية سريعة الذبول . (الذاكرة ، ص ٧٣)

وهنا ، لا يُخفي فيصل دراج تعجبه من تشبث الرواية الفلسطينية بالأمل رغماً عن الواقع السياسي المتردي ، بل لا يخفي حتى مخاوفه من أن

ما بعد الكولونيالية واستشراف المستقبل في الأدب الفلسطيني

تبقى المفارقة الأقسى والأعنف في تاريخ ما بعد الكولونيالية هي في تناولها للأدب الفلسطيني ؛ فكيف تكون فلسطين حجر الزاوية في أعمال إدوارد سعيد، التي أسست للنظرية بشكل أكاديمي ، ولا يكون الأدب الفلسطيني أيضاً حجر الزاوية في الدراسات ما بعد الكولونيالية؟ قد يعود هذا التواطؤ على تغييب الأدب الفلسطيني إلى عوامل عدة ، منها أن فلسطين لم تعبر إلى المرحلة ما بعد الكولونيالية حتى الآن ، ومنها أن عدم ظهور فلسطين على الخارطة السياسية محا وجودها أيضاً من الدراسات ما بعد الكولونيالية وهي المولعة بالخرائط وتمثيلاتها في الواقع السياسي والمخيال الجمعي (Williams and Ball 129) ، لكن عدداً من الباحثين بدأوا في تحدي هذا الحظر المفروض على تناول الأدب الفلسطيني من منظور بعد كولونيالي ، وإن كانت جهودهم لا تزال فردية ومتفرقة (Williams and Ball 130) ، ومنها دراسة لمفهوم المقاومة والكفاح المسلح في القصة القصيرة الفلسطينية قام بها جوزف فرج Farag بعنوان **السياسة والأدب الفلسطيني في الشتات** *Politics and Palestinian Literature in Exile* عام ٢٠١٦ ، وقبلها دراسة عميقة للرواية والسينما الفلسطينية من منظور يجمع بين النقد النِسْوي وما بعد الكولونيالية قامت بها آنا بول Ball وظهرت عام ٢٠١٢ بعنوان **الأدب والسينما الفلسطينية من منظور نسوي ما بعد كونيالي** *Palestinian Literature and Film in Postcolonial Feminist Perspective*. وتكمن أهمية هذا العمل في بحثه عن تقاطعات الهيمنة الذكورية والاستعمارية مع مفاهيم الهُويّة الوطنية والحدود السياسية والشتات . وتلا هذا العمل كتاب آخر لآنا برنارد Bernard بعنوان **بلاغة الانتماء : الأمة والسرد وإسرائيل/فلسطين** *Rhetorics of Belonging: Nation, Narration and Israel/Palestine* ، وهو يتتبع بعمق كيف استطاع عدد من الكتّاب الفلسطينيين والإسرائيليين الدخول في منظومة الأدب العالمي من خلال توظيف السردية القومية وإعادة طرح الخلاف السياسي بوصفه مكوناً أساسياً للهُويّة الوطنية . وفي هذا الإطار ، لا ننسى أيضاً الدراسات التي قدّمها إيهاب سلول وإن كانت ضئيلة من حيث الكم (انظر ، على سبيل المثال ، Saloul)،[9] إلا أن سعيها إلى تقديم النكبة في الذاكرة الجمعية للفلسطينيين - ليس بوصفها حادثة منفردة

المُستعمِر (سلامة ، ص ٥١) ، لكن يبدو أن نيل لازوروس - المهموم بتصحيح مسار ما بعد الكولونيالية - يريد للنظرية أن تخوض في مناطق أعمق لم يتطرق إليها أحد من قبل ، حيث رصد في كتابه ثلاثة أنواع من النصوص الأدبية وشدّدَ على أن النظرية يجب أن تضمّ هذه النصوص إلى مناهجها ؛ وهي النصوص ذات الصبغة السياسية الصارخة والنصوص التي تعالج إشكاليات وتصورات القومية والهُويّة الوطنية بعد الاستقلال ، وأخيراً النصوص المكتوبة بلغات أخرى غير الإنجليزية (Lazarus 21) .

ومن المفارقة أن هذه الاتجاهات الثلاثة تشير إلى الإنتاج الأدبي للمناطق التي لم تحظ باهتمام شديد من جانب ما بعد الكولونيالية في العالم العربي ، وعلى وجه التحديد فلسطين ودول الخليج العربي . فالإنتاج الأدبي لهاتين المنطقتين من العالم العربي لا يزال مشغولاً بتشكل الهُويّة ورسم حدود الوطن الجديد في مخيلة أبنائه . ففي عصر العولمة والهُويّات العابرة للقارات ، يجد الكتّاب من فلسطين ودول الخليج العربي أنفسهم في وجه المدفع من أجل الإجابة عن الأسئلة التي لم يُحسن أسلافهم الإجابة عنها في الوقت الذي يناضلون فيه للخروج من الأطوار الهشّة لهُويّاتهم الوطنية الناشئة . فلا أحد يستطيع أن يعيد تعريف معنى المقاومة أو يقدم لها فَهْماً جديداً كما يفعل الفلسطينيون في الحكايات والأشعار التي يروونها عن سبعين عاماً من الاحتلال . في حين يقدم الكتّاب من دول الخليج العربي فَهْماً أعمق وتجربة مباشرة للخروج من النظام البيئي الذي عرفته المجتمعات المحلية منذ قرون طويلة إلى خضم النظام الاقتصادي الجديد . وما يجمع بين الأعمال الفلسطينية والخليجية أيضاً في هذه المقالة هو البُعد الجمعي للعمل الأدبي ، على عكس الاتجاه إلى تذويت الكتابة الذي طغى بشكل كبير على الرواية العربية المعاصرة ، والذي جعل الذاتية[8] هي سيدة الموقف ؛ حيث الكاتب منشغل بعرض الأصوات المتعددة والمتباينة داخل النص الواحد وكأن كل صوت يتصدى للقارئ باعتباره الأصوب والأبلغ . لكن الرواية ذات البُعد الجمْعي في فلسطين ودول الخليج العربي لا تزال مشغولة بالذات الجمعية ، فهي تتصدى بقوة وبتعسف لكل صوت يخالف الرؤية التي يريد الكاتب أن ينسبها إلى الجماعة ، فالسرد لا يلتصق بضمير المتكلم معبراً عن مخاوفه ورغباته ، بل هو اللسان الناطق للعقل الجمعي الذي يعبر عن تجربة الذات الجمعية في مواجهة الظرف المكاني والزماني المتغير .

٩) ، وتعددت الأعمال التي تبحث في تاريخ ظهور أول رواية عربية باعتبار أن الإجابة عن هذا السؤال ضرورية في تحديد هُويّة الرواية العربية : هل هي مستوردة أم وليدة ظروف اجتماعية وسياسية؟ وهذا الانصراف التام لإشكالية الرواية بوصفها جنساً أدبياً جديداً في العالم العربي زاد من عمق الفجوة بين النظرية وبين المجتمعات العربية التي تتخذ منها موضوعاً للدراسة ؛ سواء كان ذلك في الأكاديمية الأنجلوفونية حيث نشأت هذه الدراسات ، أو بين النقاد في العالم العربي . وهذا مثال حي للفجوة التي خلقتها بدايات النظرية بين التنظير المجرد والواقع الملموس ، فضلاً عن ما بعد الكولونيالية قد تفقد بعضاً من أهم منهجياتها وأدواتها النقدية عندما يتم استدعاؤها دون تمحيص للتطبيق على الأدب العربي . بل قد تضع أمام الناقد بعض العراقيل التي لم يعتد على التعامل معها ، ومن ذلك ما ذكره وائل حسن في مقالته الشهيرة «نظرية ما بعد الكولونيالية والأدب العربي الحديث» "Postcolonial Theory and Modern Arabic Literature" ، حيث استبعد بشكل قاطع قدرة ما بعد الكولونيالية على استيعاب الصراع الثقافي في العالم العربي الذي يتمحور معظمه – وفق ما يرى حسن إبّان نشر المقالة – حول الخلاف في تأويل النصوص الدينية ، وهو أمر يختلف بشكل جذري عن المنهجية التفكيكية وإعادة توزيع المركز والهامش وهي محور اهتمام النظرية (Hassan 56) . وفي الحقيقة ، فإن هذا التباين في الاهتمامات لا يعني قصوراً في الدراسات الكولونيالية فحسب ، بل يعني وجود فجوة كبيرة بين النظرية الأكاديمية المتمسكة بمنهجيتها العلمانية التنويرية[7] وبين ثقافات عالم ما بعد الاستعمار التي تتخذ منها موضوعاً للدراسة والتي لا يزال المقدس يحتل مكانة خاصة في تكوينها الجمعي .

كذلك ، وبسبب ارتباط مفهوم الكولونيالية بالاستعمار البريطاني والفرنسي في المنطقة ، فإن تطبيقات ما بعد الكولونيالية اقتصرت على الإنتاج الأدبي لدول المغرب العربي ومصر والسودان ولبنان باعتبار أنها دول عَبَرَت مراحل مقاومة الاستعمار والاستقلال ، ومن ثم تكوّن الهُويّة «ما بعد» الكولونيالية بمفهومها وتسلسلها الكلاسيكي المعروف . وبالتالي ، فإن دخول أدب هذه الدول إلى منظومة النصوص الأولية لما بعد الكولونيالية كان سلساً وبلا ممانعة أكاديمية ، حتى إن رواية موسم **الهجرة إلى الشمال** للطيب صالح تمكنت من الدخول إلى المناهج في العديد من الجامعات حول العالم ، ويتم تدريسها باعتبارها تجربة أصيلة في كتابة التابع ومواجهة

وهذا المنحى قد يبدو على الأقل عودة إلى الجذور العربية للدراسات ما بعد الكولونيالية ، فمن المعلوم أن هذه الدراسات نهضت على أكتاف المفكر إدوارد سعيد حين كان يحمل وزر المنفى ووجع وطنه الأم فلسطين . ويضاف إلى ذلك الإسهامات الأولى لمنظري ما بعد الكولونيالية - مثل فانون وألبير ميمي Memmi - اللذين سبرا أغوار الاستعمار من خلال اتصالهما بالمستعمر الفرنسي في الجزائر . كما ليس بوسعنا أن نُغفل سعي ما بعد الكولونيالية الدائم إلى تجاوز حدود النُظم والمنهجيات العلمية ؛ فالذي يجمع مَن ذكرنا من رواد النظرية ليس جذورهم في الثقافة العربية فقط ، بل نهلهم أيضاً من مشارب علمية وأكاديمية متباينة ، مثل الطب النفسي والفلسفة الاجتماعية والعلوم السياسية وغيرها ، الأمر الذي يجعل البحث عن التقاطعات مع العلوم الإنسانية الأخرى عودة إلى جذور النظرية التقاطعية مع علوم الجغرافيا والبيئة والتاريخ والسياسة والأدب .

لذلك ، يرى الكثير بأن ما بعد الكولونيالية بصورتها الحالية أصبحت أكثر تعددية وانفتاحاً ، وتوضعُها داخل التيارات الثقافية والسياسية أصبح يشار إليه بالبنان بسبب فاعليته وتجدده المستمر (Singh 5) ، لكنها لا تزال متمسكة بمنهجيتها التي تضع عدسة التاريخ أمام كل محاولة لقراءة النص لاستنطاق تقاطعات القوة وشبكات الهيمنة المتخفية خلف السرديات والشخوص . فالغاية والهدف الأسمى لدى هذه النظرية باق لم يتغير ، فهي مشروع نظري ومنهجي يسعى إلى تقويض الخطابات المهيمنة بكافة صورها ، وإلى فتح المجال أمام المجتمعات المهمشة على اختلاف ثقافاتها وأعراقها لكي تحكي مروياتها وتضع سردياتها المحلية جنباً إلى جنب مع السرديات المتمركزة مِن زمن . وهذه الأجندة الصريحة في توجهاتها التحررية قادرة على مدِّ النظرية بأسباب البقاء والاستمرار حتى بعد تحييد الاستعمار والنظر إليه بوصفه تاريخاً انتهى على أرض الواقع ، لكن لا يزال يلقي بظلاله القاتمة على عالمنا اليوم .

الأدب العربي وما بعد الاستعمار

انشغل معظم مَن يتبنى ما بعد الكولونيالية ، أو على الأقل بعض أدواتها التحليلية في العالم العربي ، بلحظة اللقاء مع الآخر الأوروبي وبظهور الرواية بوصفها جنساً أدبياً لم يعرفه العرب قبل هذا اللقاء (إبراهيم ، ص

في مفهوم السيادة في مرحلة ما بعد الاستعمار، وحق الدفاع عن الأرض بغاباتها وأدغالها وأنهارها وجبالها كان الفتيل الذي أطلق شرارة المقاومة والمناداة بالتحرر. لكن انشغال النظرية بفكرة محاورة المركز الميتروبوليتاني والرد بالكتابة على المشروع الاستعماري حَرَف بوصلتها عن محورية الفكرة الأصيلة التي ترى أن الاستعمار بكافة صوره الحديثة والقديمة ما هو في جوهره إلا حرب تُشن على الأرض بمكوناتها البشرية والجيولوجية، وهذا بلا شك يعني عودة إلى دراسة وتحليل جذور الهيمنة الاستعمارية ومفاهيم السيطرة بكافة أشكالها.

تغيير المسار والبحث عن التقاطعات

وهكذا، ظهر الاتفاق الراهن بين المشتغلين بالنظرية حالياً على ضرورة الحفاظ على منهجيتين متوازيتين، إحداهما تنشغل بتجارب الأم والشعوب ولقائها مع الحداثة والعولمة، والأخرى تنصرف إلى الأرشيف الكولونيالي وسردياته التي تحكي - وتتتبع - عنف اللقاء بالآخر المستعمِر. هذا الاتفاق يمكن استجلاؤه بوضوح من موقف الدراسات الكولونيالية من بعض الأعمال المؤسسة للنظرية مثل كتاب **معذبو الأرض** *The Wretched of the Earth* لفرانز فانون Fanon الذي يعد من أوائل مَن اختط مسار التحليل النفسي لسيكولوجية المُستعمِر والمُسْتعمَر. ففي مقدمته للترجمة الثانية لكتاب فانون اعترف هومي بابا صراحةً بأن صوت فانون القادم من ستينيات القرن المنصرم، وهو ينادي بالتوزيع العادل لثروات الشعوب، يبدو كمَن أصاب عين الحقيقة في وسط المعارك الثقافية الدائرة اليوم في الأوساط الأكاديمية التي تقتصر على مفاهيم الهُويّة وحق الاعتراف بالتمثيل وإشكاليات اللغة (Bhabha xviii). وهذا الاعتراف من هومي بابا نفسه - وهو واحد من أهم مَن أسبغ على ما بعد الكولونيالية طابعها ما بعد البنيوي - يُعدُّ حرْفاً عنيفاً لبوصلة النظرية باتجاه جذورها في النقد المادي والماركسي، وكأن هومي بابا يرجونا أن نعيد قراءة فانون كما لو كنا لم نفعل ذلك من قبل. وهذا يدل على أن الفترة الزمنية التي تفصلنا عن مرحلة الاستقلال في تاريخ العالم ما بعد الكولونيالي وما أعقبها من خيبة أمل في بعض الدول والأنظمة التي قامت على أنقاض الاستعمار أعطت المنشغلين بالنظرية فهماً أعمق للعلاقة بين البُعد التنظيري والحقائق المادية على أرض الواقع (Wenzel, "Decolonization" 459-62).

ومنذ عام ٢٠١٢ ، بدأت الأعمال التي تتحدث عن تغيير خارطة الدراسات ما بعد الكولونيالية تتوالى ، ومن أبرزها كتاب **مستقبل الدراسات ما بعد الكولونيالية** – *The Future of Postcolonial Studies* – تحرير شانتال زابوس Zabus – الذي أسهم فيه كوكبة من رواد النظرية أجمعوا بدورهم على تجاوز الخريطة الكلاسيكية للنظرية التي تقتصر على أستراليا وكندا وجزر الكاريبي والهند ليتخطوها باتجاه مناطق لم تتطرق إليها النظرية من قَبْل مثل الصين والقرن الأفريقي وجزر الموريشوس ودول البلقان والشرق الأوسط . تتحدث شانتال زابوس في الكتاب عن خمسة اتجاهات تقاطعية يجب أن تنتهجها الدراسات الكولونيالية في المستقبل القريب ، ويحظى الأدب العربي بنصيب الأسد منها ، وبخاصة ما يتعلق بصعود تيارات الإسلام السياسي وتغيير النظام الاقتصادي في المنطقة من نظام زراعي ورعوي بالدرجة الأولى إلى نظام يعتمد على الموارد الطبيعية كالبترول والغاز أو على تحويلات أبنائه المهاجرين في الخارج (Zabus, "Introduction" 12) . وبعد عام واحد من صدور هذا الكتاب ، قام المرصفي وبيرنارد وموراي بتحرير مجموعة من المقالات لعدد من أبرز المتخصصين في النظرية ونشرها في كتاب بعنوان **ما لا تقوله النظرية ما بعد الكولونيالية** *What Postcolonial Theory Doesn't Say* . وكما يشي عنوان الكتاب ، فهو معنيٌّ بتتبع نواحي القصور والأسئلة التي كانت النظرية تغض الطرف عنها لسبب أو لآخر ، وينادي بأن تكون هذه المحاور المسكوت عنها مُنطلقاً لإعادة توجيه دفة النظرية باتجاه القضايا المادية التي تزداد إلحاحاً بالنسبة إلى جميع المشتغلين بالنظرية يوماً بعد يوم . وهذا النفور المتأخر من الإغراق في التنظير والجدل حول المفاهيم الأساسية التي تقوم عليها النظرية قد يكون هو المحرك الأساسي لهذه الرغبة الشديدة في تغيير مسار الدراسات ما بعد الكولونيالية ،⁴ وبخاصة بعد الانتقاد الحاد الذي وجّهه نيل لازوروس في كتابه **اللاوعي ما بعد الكولونيالي** *The Postcolonial Unconscious* عام ٢٠١١ ، والذي اعتبر الابتعاد عن معالجة الفروقات الاقتصادية ووقائع الحياة اليومية في دول ما بعد الاستعمار فشلاً ذريعاً للنظرية يتوجب عليها إصلاحه بدون تأخير (Lazarus 16-17) .⁵ ويتضح هذا الخلل أكثر في الإغفال المتواصل على مدى عقدين من البحث الأكاديمي لبُعدين مهمين هما مفهوم الطبيعة ومفهوم المقاومة (Potter 383) ، رغم أن هذين المفهومين بالذات كانا المحركين الأساسيين لسعي الشعوب إلى محاربة الاستعمار . فحق استغلال الموارد الطبيعية كان يشكل ركناً أساسيا

يزداد عنفواناً كلما ابتعد عن مركزيته (Young 3). فقد عُرفت الدراسات الكولونيالية بحذقها في تقصي الإيديولوجيات المختبئة خَلف النصوص وبتوجسها الدائم من خطابات الهيمنة حتى بين ثنايا إنتاجها المعرفي، الأمر الذي أعطاها زخماً خاصاً بين النظريات الأخرى؛ فعينها الناقدة تكون في أشرس حالاتها عندما تتناول نصوص مَن يتبنون منهجها، كما أنها لا تستنكف عن تبني وجهات نظر منتقديها وتضمينها في تيارها النقدي مثلما فعلت مع كبير منتقديها إعجاز أحمد (Boehemer 12)، وهذا يجعل ما بعد الكولونيالية قادرة على البقاء وعلى الاستمرار في العطاء والمقاومة مع غيرها من نظريات عالمية الأدب، حتى وإن كان هذا البقاء خارج الأكاديمية الأنجلوفونية التي بدأت تُشيح النظر عنها.

وإذا كانت نظرية الأدب العالمي قد بدت بديلاً شرعياً يستطيع تلافي بعض نواحي القصور التي عجزت ما بعد الكولونيالية عن تجاوزها والرد عليها، إلا أن إغفال الأدب العالمي لمفهوم المقاومة وتَبعاته السياسية والقومية هو ما أعاد ما بعد الكولونيالية إلى الظهور مرة أخرى، ليس برفقة حركات التحرير كما فعلت في ستينيات القرن الماضي، لكن هذه المرة برفقة حركات المقاومة التي تجاوزت حدود الدول السياسية وأعادت تعريف معنى المساندة والتعاطف بين الشعوب مثل حركة «حياة السود مهمة» Black Lives Matter وثورات الربيع العربي. فما بعد الكولونيالية تفوقت على غيرها بإيمانها التام والتزامها بقدرة الأدب والفنون على المقاومة وعلى طرح بدائل ممكنة مُتخيلة لعالم أفضل تتحقق فيه العدالة والمساواة والحرية. وهنا أصبح الحديث عن إعادة التوجيه وتحرير النظرية من الإغراق في التجريد والتنظير موضوعاً متداولاً بكثرة بين رواد هذه النظرية في السنوات الأخيرة؛ حيث بدأ الحديث عن ضرورة تحرير النظرية من قيود ما بعد البنيوية والانصراف عن إشكاليات اللغة والهُويّة والهجرة والخطاب الاستعماري، والانشغال بالمواضيع المادية الملحة مثل خطاب المقاومة السياسية والإبداعية والنشاط السياسي وحركات مناصرة البيئة (Brennan 69). كذلك فتح المجال للتفاعل والتداخل مع النظريات الأخرى مثل الدراسات الدينية والنقد البيئي والنقد الماركسي ونظريات الصدمة وغيرها. وهناك مَن ينادي بخوض غمار مناطق جغرافية لم تتناولها النظرية من قبل، من أجل التماهي مع الاتجاه الأخلاقي المتزايد في الدراسات الإنسانية الذي بات يدعو إلى التركيز على حقوق الإنسان في وجه قوى الاستعمار الجديدة (Zabus, "Introduction" 11).

جانبي المحيط الأطلسي . ولوهلة ، قد يبدو للباحث أن هذه الدراسات لم تعد تحظى بالاحترام والتقدير الذي كانت تحظى به في تسعينيات القرن الماضي (Bernard, Elmarsafy, and Murray, "Introduction" 2) ، حتى كادت الأصوات تتفق على إعلان نهايتها وانتفاء الحاجة إليها . ومن ذلك ما قامت به جمعية اللغات الحديثة MLA حين نشرت ما اتفق عليه مجموعة من المختصين في هذا المجال حول نظرتهم لمستقبل هذه النظرية في مؤتمر عُقد في عام ٢٠٠٧ بعنوان «نهاية نظرية ما بعد الكولونيالية» "The End of Postcolonial Theory" من أن النظرية استنفدت أدواتها النقدية ولم تعد قادرة على مواجهة الإمبريالية والليبرالية الجديدة بصورها المستحدثة . وتعددت بعد ذلك الأصوات التي تنتقد النظرية من الداخل من بينِ كبار نقادها ، كالقول بأن البنية التحتية التي قامت عليها النظرية أساساً – بوصفها رداً على سعيٍ النظام الإمبريالي إلى جَعْل أقسام اللغة الإنجليزية في الجامعات انعكاساً له في مركزيته الأوروبية وتهميشه أصوات التابعين – جَعَلَت النظرية محصورة بإطارها الأكاديمي وبأدواتها النقدية الأنجلوفونية ،[1] ومن ثم عاجزةً عن احتواء تيارات نقدية أو أعمال أدبية من خارج العالم الناطق باللغة الإنجليزية .[2] وهذه الانتقادات بالذات تلقاها دعاة الأدب العالمي بصدر رحب ليجعلوا منها مرتكزاً لدعوتهم إلى عالمية الأدب التي حاولوا من خلالها تلافي بعض نواحي القصور في ما بعد الكولونيالية بسبب اتساع المجال النقدي لنظرية الأدب العالمي ، وعدم ارتباطها بشروط تاريخية كالاستعمار ، ولقدرتها على التفاعل مع التغيرات السياسية في عالمنا اليوم . فالأزمات المالية وصعود التيارات الشعبوية وتسلمها مقاليد الحكم في الولايات المتحدة وإيطاليا والبرازيل ، مثلاً ، لا يبدو موضوعاً قد تتطرق له ما بعد الكولونيالية بسبب انشغالها التام بحركات التحرر والمقاومة منذ ستينيات القرن الماضي على عكس الدعوة إلى عالمية الأدب .

ورداً على هذا التشاؤم المتزايد حول نهاية النظرية ما بعد الكولونيالية ، نشر روبرت يانغ ورقة بحثية بعنوان "Postcolonial Remains" ترجمت إلى العربية بعنوان «بقاء أم بقايا ما بعد الكولونيالية؟» (انظر يانغ)،[3] استبعد فيها بشدة كل صوت ينادي بدق المسمار الأخير في نعش النظرية ، ودعا إلى النظر في آثارها وتشعباتها الأكاديمية التي تتضاعف بلا توقف في مختلف العلوم الإنسانية ، فليس من المعقول أن يتوقف هذا الزخم الذي

الدراسات ما بعد الكولونيالية والأدب العربي:
بحث عن الجذور أم تغيير للمسار؟

سامية الحديثي

لطالما ارتبطت الدراسات ما بعد الكولونيالية باللغتين الإنجليزية والفرنسية دون غيرهما من اللغات. فعلى مدى ثلاثة عقود ظلت حبيسة أقسام اللغة الإنجليزية في الأكاديمية الغربية؛ فلا نكاد نسمع لها صوتاً خارجها، رغم تأثيرها الذي لا ينكره باحث جاد في بقية العلوم الإنسانية الأخرى. وقد يكون ذلك بسبب ارتباطها الوثيق بدراسة النصوص الأدبية وبمفهوم إعادة كتابة التابع بوصفه رداً على تهميشه الطويل أو ما يعرف بالإنجليزية بـ writing back، الأمر الذي جعلها محصورة في كتابات الشتات والمهجر والثقافات الهجينة باعتبارها النتيجة المباشرة والمحسوسة للاستعمار الأوروبي في القرنين الثامن والتاسع عشر. لكن انكبابَ ما بعد الكولونيالية على دراسة كتابات المهاجرين والأقليات يُغفل جانباً مهماً، هو أن معظم الشعوب التي تعيش في عالم ما بعد الاستعمار اليوم تنتج أعمالاً أدبية بلغات محلية لم يَعبُر أصحابها المحيطات ولم يتغرّبوا في العواصم العالمية؛ ومن ثم لم يجد إنتاجهم الأدبي الاهتمام الذي يستحقه من الدراسة والنقد إلا فيما ندر. وقد تخسر النظرية بتجاهل هذا الإنتاج رافداً مهماً في دراسة تلك الشعوب وفَهْم مراحل تشكل وعيها بالذات وبالآخر.

أين تقع الدراسات ما بعد الكولونيالية في عالمنا اليوم؟

مضى على صدور كتاب *The Empire Writes Back* – الذي قام بتحريره بيل أشكروفت Ashcroft وآخرون والذي ترجم إلى العربية بعنوان الرد بالكتابة، والذي يكاد يتفق معظم النقاد على أنه العمل الذي دشّن النظرية ما بعد الكولونيالية في الأكاديمية الغربية، (Zabus, "Introduction" 5) – أكثر من تسعة وعشرين عاماً خاضت خلالها ما بعد الكولونيالية معارك لا تحصى داخل المؤسسات الأكاديمية على

Shumaker, Wayne. *English Autobiography: Its Emergence, Materials and Form*. Berkeley: U of California P, 1954.

Smith, Sidonie and Julia Watson. Introduction. *Getting a Life: Everyday Uses of Autobiography*. Minneapolis and London: U of Minnesota P, 1996. 1-24.

---. *Life Writing in the Long Run: A Smith and Watson Autobiography Studies Reader*. Michigan: Michigan Publishing Services, 2016.

---. *Reading Autobiography: A Guide for Interpreting Life Narratives*. Minneapolis and London: Minnesota UP, 2010.

---, eds. *Women, Autobiography, Theory: A Reader*. Wisconsin and London: U of Wisconsin P, 1998.

Spengemann, William. *The Forms of Autobiography: Episodes in the History of a Literary Genre*. New Haven: Yale UP, 1980.

Stanley, Liz. *The Auto/Biographical I: The Theory and Practice of Feminist Auto-Biography*. Manchester and NY: Manchester UP, 1992.

Stanton, Domna. "Autogynography: Is the Subject Different?" *The Female Autograph: Theory and Practice of Autobiography from the Tenth to the Twentieth Century*. Chicago and London: Chicago UP, 1987. 3-20.

Swindells, Julia. *The Uses of Autobiography*. London: Taylor and Francis, 1995.

Wagner-Egelhaaf, Martina. "Introduction: Autobiography/Autofiction Across Disciplines." *Handbook of Autobiography/Autofiction*. Boston and Berlin: De Gruyter, 2019. 1-7.

Gilmore, Leigh. *Autobiographics: A Feminist Theory of Women's Self-Representation*. Ithaca and London: Cornell UP, 1994.

---. "The Mark of Autobiography: Postmodernism, Autobiography, and Genre." *Autobiography & Postmodernism*. Eds. Kathleen Ashley, Leigh Gilmore, and Gerald Peters. Amherst: U of Massachusetts P, 1994. 3-18.

Golley, Nawar Al-Hassan. *Arab Women's Lives Retold: Exploring Identity through Writing*. Cairo: The American U in Cairo P, 2007.

---. *Reading Arab Women's Autobiographies: Shahrazad Tells Her Story*. Austin: U of Texas P, 2003.

Goodwin, James. *Autobiography: The Self-Made Text*. NY: Twayne Publishers, 1993.

Gratton, Johnnie. "Autofiction." *Encyclopedia of Life Writing: Autobiographical and Biographical Forms*. Ed. Margaretta Jolly. London: Routledge, 2001. 86-87.

Jelinek, Esstelle C. *The Tradition of Women's Autobiography: From Antiquity to the Present*. Boston: Twayne Publishers, 1986.

---. *Women's Autobiography: Essays in Criticism*. Bloomington: Indiana UP, 1980.

Jolly, Margaretta. *Encyclopedia of Life Writing: Autobiographical and Biographical Forms*. London: Fitzroy Dearborn, 2001.

Kaplan, Caren. "Resisting Autobiography: Out-Law Genres and Transnational Feminist Subjects." *Women, Autobiography, Theory: A Reader*. Eds. Sidonie Smith and Julia Watson. Wisconsin and London: U of Wisconsin P, 1998. 208-16.

Lejeune, Philippe. *On Autobiography*. Trans. Katherine Leary. Minneapolis: U of Minnesota P, 1989.

Misch, Georg. *A History of Autobiography in Antiquity*. Cambridge: Harvard UP, 1951.

Moore-Gilbert, Bart. *Postcolonial Life-Writing*. London and NY: Routledge, 2009.

Olney, James. *Metaphors of the Self: The Meaning of Autobiography*. NY: Princeton UP, 1972.

Pascal, Roy. *Design and Truth in Autobiography*. London: Routledge and Paul, 1960.

Reynolds, Dwight F. *Interpreting the Self: Autobiography in the Arabic Literary Tradition*. Berkeley: U of California P, 2001.

Rosenthal, Franz. *Die arabische Autobiographie*. Volume 1 of *Studia Arabica*. Roma: Pontificium Institutum Biblicum, 1937.

بوث، ماريلين. شهيرات النساء: أدب التراجم وسياسات النوع في مصر. ترجمة سحر توفيق. القاهرة: المركز القومي للترجمة، ٢٠٠٨.

حافظ، صبري. «رقش الذات لا كتابتها: تحولات الإستراتيجيات النصية في السيرة الذاتية». ألف ٢٢ (٢٠٠٢): ص ص ٧-٣٣.

دومة، خيري. «رواية السيرة الذاتية الجديدة: قراءة في بعض "روايات الكاتبات" في مصر التسعينيات». مجلة كلية الآداب - جامعة القاهرة مجلد ٦٣، العدد ١ (يناير ٢٠٠٣): ص ص ٩-٦٢.

رووكي، تيتز. في طفولتي: دراسة في السيرة الذاتية العربية. ترجمة طلعت الشايب. القاهرة: المركز القومي للترجمة، ٢٠٠٩.

عاشور، رضوى. أثقل من رضوى: مقاطع من سيرة ذاتية. القاهرة: دار الشروق، ٢٠١٣.

---. الحداثة الممكنة: الشدياق والساق على الساق، الرواية الأولى في الأدب العربي الحديث. القاهرة: دار الشروق، ٢٠١٢.

عبد الدايم، يحيى إبراهيم. الترجمة الذاتية في الأدب العربي الحديث. القاهرة: مكتبة النهضة المصرية، ١٩٧٥.

القاهرة ١٦٢ (مايو ١٩٩٦). عدد خاص بعنوان «السيرة الذاتية: المستقبل .. سيرة الماضي».

كمال، هالة. «كتابة الذات والوطن في مذكرات رضوى عاشور». المنديل المعقود: دراسات في أعمال رضوى عاشور. تحرير وتقديم فاتن مرسي. القاهرة: دار الشروق، ٢٠١٦. ص ص ٥٨-٨٧.

المراجع الأجنبية

Abdel Nasser, Tahia. *Literary Autobiography and Arab National Struggles*. Edinburgh: Edinburgh UP, 2017.

Anderson, Linda. *Autobiography*. London and NY: Routledge, 2011.

Brodzki, Bella and Celeste Schenck. Introduction. *Life/Lines: Theorizing Women's Autobiography*. Ithaca and London: Cornell UP, 1988. 1-15.

Derrida, Jacques. "The Law of Genre." Trans. Avital Ronell. *Critical Inquiry* 7.1 (Autumn 1980): 55-81.

Dix, Hywel. "Introduction: Autofiction in English: the Story so Far." *Autofiction in English*. London: Palgrave Macmillan, 2018. 1-23.

⁷ يضم الكتاب ملحقاً يشتمل على ستين نوعاً من أنواع «سردية الحياة» بين سردية وفعل وسيرة وكتابة وقصة وحكاية ورواية وبورتريه، على سبيل المثال لا الحصر.

⁸ تعددت الصيغ المقترحة لترجمة مصطلح autofiction بين التخييل الذاتي وتخييل الذات وخيال الذات، ولكنني أميل إلى طرح واستعمال مصطلح رواية الذات، حيث إن صيغة التخييل توحي بالجانب التقني للكتابة، ومن ثم تبدو لي صيغة ترسخ هذا الاتجاه في الكتابة بوصفه تقنية فنية دون أية إحالة إلى مسألة النوع الأدبي. أما مصطلح رواية الذات، فيشير قضية النوع الأدبي، وبخاصة فيما يتصل بالمساحة التي يحتلها بين الفن الروائي والكتابة الذاتية، وذلك دون استبعاد السمات التقنية، بما يعضد رحابة مصطلح رواية الذات للتعبير عن مصطلح autofiction بوصفه تعبيراً عن مفهوم أدبي متطور يسع قضية النوع الأدبي وتقنية الكتابة.

⁹ لا يزال التعريف السائد لمصطلح «رواية الذات» هو التعريف المستند إلى معناه في النقد الفرنسي، حيث نجد على سبيل المثال أن التعريف الموجود للمصطلح في موسوعة كتابة الحياة الصادرة في لندن عام ٢٠٠١ هو التعريف القائم على نصوص فرنسية، ولا يتطرق إلى معناه في النقد الأنجلوفوني، ما يشير إلى عدم استقرار المصطلح بعد في الثقافة واللغة الإنجليزية، واعتماده على التراث الأدبي الفرنسي (انظر Gratton).

¹⁰ على سبيل المثال، يُعقد مؤتمر دولي بعنوان «رواية الذات - النظرية والممارسات والثقافات - رؤية مقارنة» Autofiction – Theory, Practices, Cultures – A Comparative Perspective في جامعة أوكسفورد في الفترة ١٩-٢٠ أكتوبر ٢٠١٩، لطرح أهم القضايا المتعلقة بمصطلح «رواية الذات» في إطار النظرية والكتابة عبر الثقافات.

¹¹ للمزيد حول السيرة الذاتية في كتابات رضوى عاشور، انظر كمال.

المراجع العربية

ألف ٢٢ (٢٠٠٢). عدد بعنوان «لغة الذات: السير الذاتية والشهادات».

باحثات ١١ (٢٠٠٥-٢٠٠٦). عدد بعنوان «حفريات وتحريات: حيوات نساء عربيات».

بدر، عبد المحسن طه. تطور الرواية العربية الحديثة في مصر (١٨٧٠-١٩٣٨). القاهرة: دار المعارف، ١٩٦٣.

الهوامش

1 لم تلق دراسات السيرة الذاتية وكتابة الذات اهتماماً نقدياً كبيراً في النقد العربي المعاصر، حيث نجد أبحاثاً معدودة في هذا المجال في العالم العربي، لعل أبرزها ما ورد في الآتي: عدد خاص من مجلة **القاهرة** المصرية صدر بعنوان «السيرة الذاتية: المستقبل .. سيرة الماضي» في عام ١٩٩٦ (انظر **القاهرة**)، وعدد من مجلة **ألف** بالجامعة الأمريكية بالقاهرة صدر بعنوان «لغة الذات: السير الذاتية والشهادات» في عام ٢٠٠٢ (انظر **ألف**)، وعدد من كتاب **باحثات** الدوري صدر بعنوان «حفريات وتحريات: حيوات نساء عربيات» في بيروت عام ٢٠٠٦ (انظر **باحثات**).

2 قدم فرانتز روزنتال Rosenthal أول دراسة للسيرة الذاتية العربية، وذلك في دراسة مقارنة لنصوص عربية صدرت باللغة الألمانية عام ١٩٣٧ عن السيرة الذاتية العربية.

3 يقدم كتاب ماريلين بوث **شهيرات النساء: أدب التراجم وسياسات النوع في مصر**، الصادر باللغة الإنجليزية والمترجم إلى اللغة العربية، دراسة مهمة لتراجم النساء في العصر الحديث بين الكتب والصحافة، مع إفراد فصل كامل تتناول فيه كتاب زينب فواز.

4 يرجع مفهوم «قانون النوع» إلى مقالة ديريدا بالعنوان نفسه التي صدرت عام ١٩٨٠، وفيها يتناول كيف أن النص يُدرج تحت خانة النوع أو الجنس الأدبي، إلا أن النص بدوره يعدّل من مفهوم النوع الأدبي الذي يُدرج فيه. وبالتالي، يرى أن النص يشارك في نوع أدبي أو في أنواع أدبية متعددة، إلا أن هذه المشاركة لا ترقى إلى حد الانتماء. ولهذا، فهو يطلق على «قانون النوع» مبدأ السيولة، فهو ليس قانوناً خالصاً لأنه متغير مع كل ريادة في حقله (انظر Derrida).

5 للمزيد عن النقد النِّسْوي لمفهوم السيرة الذاتية عند لوجين، انظر Stanton.

6 منها على سبيل المثال: مركز البحث في تاريخ الحياة وكتابة الحياة Centre for Life History and Life Writing Research الذي تأسس عام ١٩٩٩ في جامعة ساسكس في بريطانيا، ومركز البحث في كتابة الحياة Centre for Life-Writing Research الذي تأسس عام ٢٠٠٧ في كلية كنجز في جامعة لندن، ومركز أوكسفورد لكتابة الحياة Oxford Centre for Life-Writing الذي تأسس عام ٢٠١١ في جامعة أكسفورد.

مع النظرية النقدية والعلوم الاجتماعية ، مع عدم إغفال إرهاصات قد لا تبدو بعد واضحة جلية ومحددة على الساحة النقدية .

وقد انطلقت هذه المقالة من فرضية مفادها أن السيرة الذاتية بوصفها نوعاً أدبياً وأسلوباً بلاغياً نشأت في مساحة بينية ، وفي كثير من الأحيان هامشية ، فيما بين الكتابة الأدبية والتاريخية ، وظلت تتنقل بين هذين المجالين قرباً وبعداً على مدار عقود طويلة ، وعبر الثقافات المختلفة ، وإن ظلت في مجملها محصورة في إطار العلوم الإنسانية . إلا أن العقود القليلة الأخيرة ، بما شهدته من تحطيم لحدود الحقول المعرفية ، انعكست بدورها على السيرة الذاتية ، لا من حيث الشكل فحسب ، ولا من حيث المضمون فقط ، ولا بمجرد تجاوز قضايا النوع الأدبي والانتقال إلى قضايا الخطاب الثقافي ، وغيرها من سمات وخصائص السيرة الذاتية ، وإنما أحدثت طفرات في دراسات السيرة الذاتية ، حيث تحول النص في حد ذاته إلى ساحة للتفاوض حول الهُويّة والتجربة والبنية ، بل حول فعل الكتابة في حد ذاته . وفيما يتصل بالسيرة الذاتية العربية ، سلطت هذه الدراسة الضوء على نموذج فريد يشير إلى السيرة الذاتية بوصفها نصّاً هجيناً يجمع بين الإبداع والتنظير ، وبين الكتابة والنقد ، وبين السيرة والمذكرات والدراسة النقدية والمقال ، ممثلاً في لمحة من لمحات كتابة الذات عند رضوى عاشور التي تجمع بين الكتابة الذاتية والنقدية ، وتستعين بتقنيات أسلوبية تمتد إلى جذور الأدب العربي بقدر ما تعي تطورات فعل الكتابة والنظرية الأدبية في الفكر الغربي .

وإنني إذ آملٍ في أن تكون هذه المقالة قد قدمت السيرة الذاتية بوصفها مجالاً معرفياً حيوياً ممتداً عبر التاريخ والجغرافيا ، فإنني أود التصريح في الختام بأن من أهدافها المستترة هو طرح الاتجاهات الجديدة في السيرة الذاتية النِّسْوية وما بعد الكولونيالية ، ومفاهيمها الأوسع ممثلةً في كتابة الحياة ورواية الذات ، بحيث تدفعنا المعرفة بهذه الاتجاهات إلى الاشتباك الفكري الثقافي معها لإنتاج نظرية عربية للسيرة الذاتية ، والإسهام في صياغة التيارات الجديدة والناشئة عالمياً ، وبخاصة في ظل المزيد من تجاوز وتحطيم الحدود المتوقع في ظل الثورة الإلكترونية . وإذا كانت هذه المقالة قد سعت إلى ملء فجوات معرفية ، فقد كشفت عن فجوات أكثر لا تزال تنتظر ، وبخاصة في إطار واقع نراه جلياً في الأدب العربي المعاصر ، حيث تظل كتابة السيرة الذاتية بوصفها فعلاً إبداعياً تسبق الجهود النقدية في مجال دراسات السيرة الذاتية العربية بسنوات ضوئية .

والأحرى مدى ابتعادها – عن الأطر النظرية التقليدية ، إلا أننا نجدها في حديثها عن توظيف اليوميات في سيرتها الذاتية تنطلق من واقع الممارسة ، وكيف فرضت اليوميات نفسها على السيرة الذاتية . ثم يعود صوت المؤلفة التي تتحدث من واقع تجربتها ليتوارى خلف صوت الباحثة الناقدة والمنظِّرة التي التقطت أشكال الكتابة الجديدة في عصر الثورة الإلكترونية لتضعها في إطار نظري مستقبلي حول ما شهدته الكتابة الذاتية من تطورات (وبخاصة في ظل ثورة يناير ٢٠١١ في مصر) ، وما يستدعيه ذلك من اهتمام نقدي يضيف أبعاداً جديدة ، شكلاً ومضموناً ، إلى نظرية السيرة الذاتية ، وممارساتها على أرض الواقع المادي والافتراضي ، وتياراتها الناشئة واتجاهاتها الجديدة .

الخاتمة

لقد سعت هذه المقالة إلى تقديم خريطة معرفية للسيرة الذاتية المقارنة في الأدبين العربي والإنجليزي . وقد تتبعت نشأة هذا النوع الأدبي في الأدب الغربي والأوروبي ، مع تسليط الضوء على تاريخ السيرة الذاتية وتطورها ، عبر إشارات إلى أبرز الأعمال الأدبية والنقدية التي تناولتها . كما تطرقت المقالة إلى قضايا منهجية ، تنطلق من مسألة المصطلح وصياغاته وتطوره وتنوعه تبعاً لسياقه الزمني والمكاني ، وسلطت الضوء على أهم المفاهيم المكوّنة لنظرية السيرة الذاتية المستقرة منذ عدة عقود رغم هشاشة بداياتها . كذلك ، تلمست هذه المقالة أوضح الاتجاهات الجديدة ، ومنها ما تبلور على مدى السنوات القليلة الماضية ، ومنها ما هو قيد التكوين . وقد استعانت المقالة في ذلك بمصادر نقدية راسخة ، كما حرصت على عرض أهم التيارات والكتب التي عملت على بلورة نظرية السيرة الذاتية ، بقدر ما أسهمت في زعزعتها ، ومن ثم إجبارها على التطور لا الركود . كما حاولت المقالة تحديد مدى الجهد البحثي والنقدي العربي في الاشتباك مع نظرية السيرة الذاتية الغربية ، وسعت إلى تقديم الإسهامات اليسيرة في هذا المجال ، سواء تلك الصادرة من داخل مدرسة النقد العربية أو في إطار الدراسات الأدبية والعربية في الغرب الأنجلوفوني . أما الجانب الأصعب فقد كان في التدقيق في اختيار وعرض أبرز الاتجاهات الجديدة ، بما يعكس نتاج تقاطعات النظرية الأدبية

متسلسل زمنياً أو يخلط بين الأزمنة. وأعي أنهما، أعني السيرة والمذكرات، على تشابههما، يختلفان في أن المتوقع غالباً من الشكل الأول هو حكاية العمر بمختلف مراحلها، أما المذكرات فغالباً ما تركز على مرحلة بعينها أو تجربة بالذات من تجارب حياة ممتدة. ولكن ما جدّ عليّ دون سابق نيّة أو إعداد، هو النقل المباشر لحدث يومي أسجل بعض تفاصيله ومشاعري تجاهه، وهو ما يدخلنا في نوع ثالث من الكتابة أقرب لليوميات . . . لا استرجاع هنا، بل مواكبة آنية. (ص ٢٧١)

وتشير هذه الفقرة إلى وعي عاشور بعدم التزامها بحدود النوع الأدبي وقيوده، فحتى وهي تكتب سيرتها الذاتية تدرك تنقلها بين سمات السيرة الذاتية والمذكرات في التعريف النقدي الراسخ لهما بوصفهما نوعين أدبيين. وهي من ثم تؤكد عدم انزعاجها بكسر تلك الحدود المتعارف عليها فيما يتعلق بمسألة النوع الأدبي، ولكنها تشركنا أيضاً في توظيفها لليوميات في سيرتها الذاتية، التي يأتي وصفها لاستعمالها في الكتابة دليلاً آخر على رحابة مساحة الخيال في كتابة السيرة الذاتية عند عاشور.

أما الجانب الأهم في هذا التحليل الذاتي للكتابة الذاتية فيتمثل فيما أوردته عاشور من ملاحظات نقدية حول التطورات القائمة بالفعل على مستوى الكتابة الذاتية في ظل الثورة الإلكترونية، حيث تقول:

هنا لا بد من التنويه أن هذا التعريف المستقر لليوميات لم يعد مستقراً، إذ فكّكته أشكال الكتابة على الشبكة الإلكترونية، البرقي منها والمستفيض، بين «تغريدة» و«حالة» و«مذكرة» و«مدوّنة» و«تعليق»، وغيرها من أنواع التفاعل. باختصار، تناسخت اليوميات في عصر الثورة الإلكترونية من تعبير مغلق على الذات لا يسعى إلى إشراك الغير فيه، إلى شكل من أشكال التواصل الاجتماعي الفوري واسع المدى. (ص ٢٧٢)

مرة أخرى، تجمع عاشور هنا بين الكاتبة والناقدة. وهي إن كانت فيما سبق تنطلق من البدايات النظرية لتفنّدها وتكشف عن مدى مطابقتها -

والتضمين والإسقاط والتصدير والمواراة، أم أن الخيال هو المسئول؟ هل هو الخيال أم العقل المنظم؟» (ص، ٢٥٣)، لتخلص من خلالها إلى دور المؤلفة في «فعل الكتابة»، انطلاقاً منٍ «معارف وخبرات وقناعات ومشاعر وذائقة ووعي وانتباه، تتكثف جميعاً وتتلخص في نظرة، هي نظرتي أنا إلى الدنيا ونفسي» (ص ٢٥٣).

وأودّ هنا أن أتوقف عند عدة نقاط تكشف عن إسهامٍ عاشور في التنظير للسيرة الذاتية عبر كتاباتها لسيرتها الذاتية. أولاً، لقد أفردت الكاتبة مساحات في سيرتها الذاتية لتأمل عملية الكتابة نفسها والتنظير لكتابة الذات. ثانياً، هي تستعين بأشكال السيرة الذاتية التقليدية في التراث العربي، حيث تتنقل بين السرد الذاتي والمقالة ذات الطابع العلمي النقدي، كما تلجأ من آن لآخر إلى صيغة المخاطب («عزيزي القارئ» و«عزيزتي القارئة»)، وهيٍ من سمات الكتابة العربية التقليدية المستندة إلى الثقافة الشفاهية. ثالثا، تكشف عاشور عن فهم دقيق للسيرة الذاتية بوصفها نظرية نقدية، حيث تطرح تساؤلات هي في قلب النظرية حول الكتابة، والخيال، والبنية، والأسلوب، ومحاكاة السيرة للواقع، والإشكاليات المتصلة بدور الذاكرة والنسيان. وأخيراً، نراها تبرهن على سلطة كاتب أو كاتبة السيرة الذاتية («المؤلفة») في التحكم في النص والكشف عن نظرة شخصية للمجالين العام والخاص، وتنتهي إلى أن كتابة «نص سيرة صريح»، من ثم، لا يختلف كثيراً عن غيره من النصوص، ومنها النص الروائي.

ولا تتوقف عاشور عند تأمل الفروق بين الكتابة الذاتية والروائية، كما فعلت في الفصل الحادي والعشرين، وإنما تستكمل رؤيتها النقدية بفصل لاحق، هو الفصل الثالثِ والعشرون، الذي تفرده للحديث عن السيرة الذاتية بوصفها نوعاً أدبياً، وذلك كما يشي عنوان الفصل «بين السيرة واليوميات»، حيث تسعى إلى تحديد موقع كتابها هذا ضمن أنواع الكتابة الذاتية، مستهلةَ الفصل بقولها:

> أعي منذ بدأت كتابة هذا النص أنني أجمع فيه بين السيرة الذاتية والمذكرات، وهما نوعان مختلفان من الكتابة، وإن اشتركا في التأريخ للذات وتقديم التجربة الشخصية وتصنيفها وتأملها والتعليق عليها، باسترجاع مراحل العمر بشكل

أو ربما تختلف كثيراً . . . لا أحتاج في حالة كتاب السيرة الصريح الذي أكتبه سوى النظر حولي ووارئي وفي داخلي لأرى وأتذكر . كأنني أنقل نقلاً ، فالأحداث مكتوبة سلفاً ، وكذلك الشخصيات والأماكن والأزمنة . . . ربما أضيف تعليقاً أو خاطرة أو بعض تأملات هنا أو هناك . تظل المهمة رغم ذلك ، أبسط ، ويبدو الخيال بلا وظيفة أو دور ؛ ينفرد العقل بمهامّ حكي ما سبق أن خبرته ورأيته وسمعته وأحسست به . كأنه آلة تلقمها الذاكرة ما تلقمها ، فتنتج الكلام . (ص ٢٥٢)

تكشف عاشور هنا عن وعي كبير بالفرق بين الكتابة الروائية والذاتية ، وتستند في ذلك إلى تجربتها الشخصية بوصفها كاتبة وناقدة توضح عملية الكتابة وبناء النص استناداً إلى الذاكرة ، وبأقل قدر من توظيف الخيال لعدم الجنوح بعيداً عن السيرة واقتراباً من الرواية . وهذه الكتابة الذاتية بمنظورها التقليدي القائم على نقل الواقع هي ما تسميه «كتاب السيرة الصريح» . ولكن الناقدة والكاتبة ما تلبث أن تتوقف أمام تلك المقولات النظرية الراسخة بشأن كتابة السيرة الذاتية ، وإذ بها تفنّد كل ما سبق لها قوله ، وذلك في الفقرة الآتية :

ولكن ما أقوله ليس صحيحاً في جملته . وإن لم يخل تماماً من الصحة ، فهو لا ينطبق إلا على جزء منه . وإلا كيف أفسر التفاوت بين فصول كتاب تكتب بيسر ، وهي دائماً الأقوى ، وفصول تتعثر كتابتها وتستدعي المراجعة مرة واثنتين وثلاثاً؟ . . . ثم من قال إن الأحداث والشخصيات مكتوبة سلفاً؟ لا يعني حضورها في أرض الواقع ، أنها مكتوبة ، إذ يتعين عليك لكتابتها قراءتها وصياغتها واكتشاف علاقات تربطها في سياق متماسك له معنى . (ص ص ٢٥٢-٢٥٣)

وهكذا ، تستدرك الكاتبة فتتحدث من واقع تجربتها الشخصية في بناء السيرة الذاتية ، في عملية تتضمن القراءة والصياغة فالكتابة . وتلحق ذلك بتأملاتها حول دور الذاكرة في السرد الذاتي في سلسلة من الأسئلة : «والذاكرة؟ . . . هل هي المسئولة عن تنظيم هذه المادة وهيكلتها

و«الذاكرة» و«التمثيل» ، بما يندرج تحتها من مفاهيم ثقافية واجتماعية ونفسية وسياسية ، وما أدى إليه ذلك من تراجع الالتفات إلى العناصر النصية والأدبية ، فيبدو أن مفهوم «رواية الذات» يعيد بؤرة التركيز على عناصر النص نفسه ، لا الواقع القائم خارج النص ، الذي يشكك الفكر ما بعد الحداثي ومناهجه وتداعياته في وجوده الموضوعي المستقر .

هذا ، ولا يزال السؤال الذي تطرحه الإسهامات النقدية القليلة الحالية فيما يتعلق ببلورة مصطلح «رواية الذات» قائماً : هل يمكن اعتبار «رواية الذات» نوعاً أدبياً genre جديداً ، له شكله الفني ، ويعبر عن تجارب معاصرة ، أم أنها أقرب إلى تقنية وأداة أسلوبية technique ترتبط بالنص لا الواقع ؟ أم هي تجمع بين هذا وذاك؟ ومن ثم ، هل يمكن لمفهوم «رواية الذات» أن يتبلور في نظرية نقدية جديدة تجمع بين الدراسة التاريخية والأدبية والاجتماعية والسياسية ، تتضمن أنواعاً فرعية تحتل «رواية السيرة الذاتية» ومرادفاتها في الثقافة العربية ، كالسيرة الذاتية الروائية أو الأدبية ، جانباً منها؟ إنها أسئلة تفتح مجالات للبحث وتنبئ بظهور اتجاهات جديدة عابرة لحدود الإنسانيات ومتقاطعة مع العلوم الاجتماعية في السنوات القادمة .[10]

السيرة الذاتية النقدية والجمع بين التنظير والإبداع

من الاستعمالات المبهرة للسيرة الذاتية العربية ما قامت به رضوى عاشور في سيرتها الذاتية أثقل من رضوى من رضوى (٢٠١٣) ، رابطةً بين تجربة الذات والوطن على مستوى المحتوى ،[11] على حين أضافت إلى شكل السيرة الذاتية وبنيتها جوانب تجعلها امتداداً لتراث السيرة الذاتية في الأدب العربي ، وإنْ كانت تعكس في الوقت نفسه معرفتها بتطورات السيرة الذاتية نظريةً وممارسةً . تقوم رضوى عاشور بسرد لقطات وتجارب من حياتها ، لنجدها تتوقف في الفصل الحادي والعشرين عند تذكر أحداث الثورة وما بعدها ، لتكسر السرد الذاتي ويخفت صوت رضوى المواطنة المصرية والأستاذة الجامعية والمرأة المريضة ، ليحل محلها صوت الناقدة المنظِّرة للكتابة ، وهو ما يتضح من عنوان الفصل «مقال قصير عن الكتابة» ، الذي تخاطب فيه قراءها عن فعل الكتابة كما تعايشه قائلة :

ولأن هذا الكتاب ليس رواية بل سيرة ذاتية ، تتطابق فيها المؤلفة والراوية والمروي عنها ، تختلف المسألة بعض الشيء ،

التاريخية والتجارب الشخصية بوصفها حقيقة (Dix 5-6). وهكذا، يمكن القول إن البحث من منطلق «رواية الذات» لا يهتم بنقاط التلاقي بين الرواية والسيرة الذاتية على مستوى النوع الأدبي كما هو الحال في الممارسات التحليلية لأعمال «رواية السيرة الذاتية»، وإنما يتجاوز ذلك إلى التركيز على الأدوات السردية والأسلوبية ممثلة في الضمائر المستعملة في السرد بين المتكلم والمخاطب والغائب، والصوت المهيمن على النص، والتناقضات التي يكشف عنها دور الذاكرة في النص، ذلك إلى جانب عناصر أشمل مثل التناص intertextuality وعتبات النص paratexts ورواية الرواية metafiction، على سبيل المثال لا الحصر. وفي كتاب صدر مؤخراً بعنوان **كتاب السيرة الذاتية/رواية الذات** Handbook of Autobiography/Fiction، من تحرير مارتينا فاجنر-إيجيلهاف Wagner-Egelhaaf، تشير الكاتبة إلى أن قراءة «السيرة الذاتية» فيما بعد الحداثة تعي دور السرد والخيال في صياغة الذات، بينما ترى أنها تختلف في أن عملية الكتابة نفسها في «رواية الذات» هي عملية واعية، بل مقصودة، في التلاعب بالكتابة وإضفاء العناصر الروائية على السيرة الذاتية (Wagner-Egelhaaf 2).

ويمكن تلمس فارق منهجي آخر بين مفهومي «رواية السيرة الذاتية» و«رواية الذات» نتيجة الحقل المعرفي الذي تبلور كل منهما في إطاره. فقد نشأ الاهتمام بتعريف «رواية السيرة الذاتية» من داخل الدراسات الأدبية، التي حرصت على التعامل مع هذا النوع الأدبي بوصفه في الأساس عملاً روائياً يتقاطع مع حياة مؤلفه، من جانب، ومع نوع من الكتابة الأدبية الراسخة هي السيرة الذاتية، من جانب آخر. ومن ثم، فإن المقاربة القائمة من منظور «رواية السيرة الذاتية» هي مقاربة مستقرة داخل الدراسات الأدبية وفن الرواية على وجه التحديد، ومن هنا، ينصب اهتمامها على البحث عن تقنيات الكتابة الذاتية وملامحها ومرجعياتها داخل النص، في إطار عام يستند إلى نظرية النوع الأدبي. على حين نرى أن نشأة مفهوم «رواية الذات»، وبخاصة في السنوات القليلة الماضية، ينطلق أساساً من مساحات الكتابة الذاتية واتجاهاتها الجديدة، ممثلة في كتابة الحياة وسردية الحياة، التي لا تستند إلى النظرية الأدبية بقدر ما تحتل مساحة بينية تتداخل فيها المناهج التحليلية والنقدية من الإنسانيات والعلوم الاجتماعية. ونظراً لانطلاق مفهوم «رواية الذات» من تلك المساحة التي شهدت تركيزاً كبيراً في العقدين الأخيرين على بلورة مفاهيم «الذات» و«الحياة» و«التجربة»

رواية الذات

يرجع مصطلح «رواية الذات» autofiction[8] إلى الكاتب الفرنسي سيرج دوبروفسكي Doubrovsky الذي استعمله في عام ١٩٧٧ في مقدمة روايته Fils التي تعني ابن أو أبناء أو خيوط لتمييز روايته عن غيرها من النصوص الروائية ونصوص السيرة الذاتية. وقد صاحب ذلك على مدار السنوات اهتمام نقدي بهذا النوع من الكتابة، فصار مصطلح «رواية الذات» في النقد الفرانكوفوني يشير إلى ما هو معروف في النقد الأنجلوفوني والعربي بـ«رواية السيرة الذاتية» autobiographical novel، أيْ الرواية التي تتضمن عناصر من حياة مؤلفها أو مؤلفتها. هذا، وقد شهدت السنوات الأخيرة، وفي ظل نشأة وتطور مفاهيم مثل كتابة الحياة وسردية الحياة، عودة الاهتمام النقدي بالمساحات التي تتقاطع عندها الأنواع الأدبية، وفي حالتنا هذه تتقاطع كتابة الذات مع فن الرواية. ومن هنا، نجد على سبيل المثال سميث وواتسون تفرقان بين «رواية السيرة الذاتية» و«رواية الذات» من منطلق اهتمام الأولى بالمرجعية الواقعية للشخصيات والأحداث المروية، بينما يحمل مفهوم «رواية الذات» تأثيرات كتابات رولان بارت الذاتية والنقدية منذ السبعينيات في فرنسا،[9] كما تؤكدان أنه بينما تستند «رواية السيرة الذاتية» إلى مفاهيم متعلقة بالنوع الأدبي وتقنيات الكتابة الروائية، فإن «رواية الذات» هي أقرب إلى أسلوب وتقنيات في الكتابة لا تعمل على تجانس الذات مع الرواية بقدر ما تكشف عن التلاعب والتناقض بين العناصر الذاتية والروائية على مستوى النص ذاته دون الرجوع إلى الواقع (Smith and Watson, *Reading* 259-60).

لقد ظل مصطلح «رواية الذات» مستعملاً في الدراسات الفرانكوفونية، ولم يتم الالتفات إليه بوصفه مفهوماً مغايراً لمفهوم «رواية السيرة الذاتية» في سياق الدراسات الأدبية الأنجلوفونية إلا في السنوات القليلة الماضية، وذلك بصدور أول كتاب عن **رواية الذات بالإنجليزية** *Autofiction in English* من تحرير هايويل ديكس Dix، ويضم العديد من الدراسات التي تفتح حالياً النقاش النقدي والتنظيري حول مفهوم «رواية الذات»، والتي تزعزع على سبيل المثال مفهوم «ميثاق السيرة الذاتية» الذي طرحه لوجين منذ عقود، وتطرح مفهوماً بديلاً هو «ميثاق رواية الذات» autofictional pact الذي صكه جاك لوكارم Lecarme مشككاً في إمكان التطابق بين المؤلف والراوي والشخصية المحورية في السيرة الذاتية، وكذلك القدرة على تدوين الأحداث

مختلف الأنواع والمجالات والتخصصات والثقافات . هذا ، وقد زاد من انتشار مفهوم «كتابة الحياة» خلال السنوات القليلة الماضية أن سعت بعض الجامعات الكبرى إلى تأسيس مراكز علمية لكتابة الحياة تضمن أرشيفات للنصوص ومشروعات بحثية .[6] وتتسم أهمية هذا المصطلح في اتساعه ليشمل كافة أشكال وأنواع كتابة الذات وكتابة الحياة . كما أنه يسمح مجالاً عابراً للتخصصات والأفرع المعرفية المختلفة ، تتقاطع عنده الإنسانيات مع العلوم الاجتماعية ، بل والعلوم الطبيعية والفنون ، التي نجدها مثلاً في أعمال السيرة الذاتية الموسيقية أو سيرة الحياة الطبية أو التاريخ الشفاهي أو رواية الذات ، وغيرها على سبيل المثال لا الحصر .

هذا ، ولا يزال الجهد النقدي والنظري المصاحب لنشأة هذا الاتجاه الجديد في طور التكوين ، ولعل آخره كتاب سميث وواتسون **كتابة الحياة على المدى البعيد** *Life Writing in the Long Run* (٢٠١٦) الذي يتضمن إسهاماتهما في بلورة مفهوم «كتابة الحياة» بما يشتمل عليه من أشكال تقليدية كالسيرة الذاتية والمذكرات واليوميات ، مروراً بكتابة الحياة المتأثرة بالتطورات التكنولوجية والفنية مثل المذكرات المرسومة وسيرة الحياة والسيرة الذاتية الإلكترونية ، وانتهاءً بأشكال أخرى كالمانيفستو والشهادة والمقالة الذاتية والشهادة الحية في سياقات حقوق الإنسان . ويأتي هذا الكتاب تتويجاً للجهود النظرية التي طرحتها سميث وواتسون سابقاً عبر مفهوم «سردية الحياة» في كتابهما **قراءة السيرة الذاتية : دليل إلى تأويل سرديات الحياة** *Reading Autobiography: A Guide for Interpreting Life Narratives* (٢٠١٠) ، حيث يفردان الفصل الأول من الكتاب لتعريف المصطلح والتفرقة بين كتابة الحياة وسيرة الحياة ، وبين كتابة الحياة والرواية ، وبين كتابة الحياة والتاريخ (5-15) . ومن الملاحظ حرص المؤلفتين على تعريف المصطلح الناشئ في علاقته بالمصطلحات والأنواع الأدبية الراسخة ، وعلى رأسها مفهوم «السيرة الذاتية» الذي يوردانه في عنوان الكتاب الفرعي . ورغم استعمالهما مصطلحي «كتابة الحياة» و«سردية الحياة» بما يبدو أحياناً كمترادفين ، فيبدو أن «كتابة الحياة» تشير إلى النص ، بينما تحمل «سردية الحياة» بعداً نظرياً أكبر يتجاوز فعل الكتابة وينقل النص من حدود الكتابة والنوع الأدبي إلى حيز الخطاب وإشكالياته وتقاطعاته .[7]

الذاتية العربية المكتوبة في عصر ما بعد الاستعمار تظل تستحضر التجربة الاستعمارية، ومراحل التحرر الوطني بوصفها تجربة دفينة ومؤثرة. أما الفصل الأخير الذي يقدم لمحة من السيرة الذاتية في القرن الحادي والعشرين، فيركز على العلاقة بين كتابة السيرة الذاتية واللحظة الثورية.

وفي إطار هذا الاتجاه الجديد في دراسات السيرة الذاتية نجد بارت مور-جيلبرت Moore-Gilbert في كتابة الحياة ما بعد الكولونيالية *Postcolonial Life-Writing* (٢٠٠٩) يعقد مقارنات بين الكتابة الذاتية في سياق ما بعد الكولونيالية وما يقابلها في الثقافة الغربية، فيقدم دراسة رائدة في السيرة الذاتية ما بعد الكولونيالية منطلقاً من نظرية السيرة الذاتية الغربية التي يقسمها إلى ثلاث مراحل في القرن العشرين، بدءاً بميش، ومروراً بباسكال وانتهاءً بلوجين، وهي المراحل التي غاب عنها الاهتمام بالسيرة الذاتية خارج دائرة أوروبا (Moore-Gilbert xi-xiii). أما بداية الخروج من تلك الدائرة الضيقة، فيعزوها الكاتب إلى الجهد النقدي الذي اضطلعت به النِّسْويات منذ ثمانينيات القرن العشرين من ناحية في قراءة السيرة الذاتية من منظور نِسْوي، وكذلك نشأة وتطور دراسات ما بعد الكولونيالية في الفترة ذاتها. ولعل من أهم إسهامات هذا الكتاب هو ما يتضمنه من إشارات إلى أهم السير الذاتية التي خرجت من بلدان خضعت للاستعمار، وذلك في مرحلة ما قبل الاستقلال وما بعده. هذا، ويتناول الكتاب عدداً من الكتابات الذاتية أو «كتابات الحياة» life-writing بالتركيز على قضيتين محوريتين، هما الذات والهُويّة وتمثيلهما الثقافي، وقضية النوع والسرد وكتابة الذات. وهكذا، ينجح الكاتب هنا في إخراج «السيرة الذاتية» من حدود ذلك النوع الأدبي، ليطرح مفهوم «كتابة الحياة» بديلاً لمفهوم «السيرة الذاتية» وأفرعها الضيقة، بما يتوافق مع الاتجاهات الأخرى الجديدة في نظرية السيرة الذاتية، ما بعد الحداثية والنِّسْوية وعبر القومية.

كتابة الحياة وسرديات الحياة

ظهر مصطلح «كتابة الحياة» و«سردية الحياة» life-narrative في بداية الألفية مع نشر مارجريتا جولي Jolly موسوعة كتابة الحياة *Encyclopedia of Life Writing: Autobiographical and Biographical Forms* (٢٠٠١)، التي تشتمل على كافة أشكال وأنواع التعبير عن الحياة من سيرة ذاتية ومذكرات ويوميات ورسائل وروايات سيرة ذاتية وروايات الرسائل عبر

عربيات من أجيال متباينة ومجالات مختلفة ، مثل هدى شعراوي وفدوى طوقان ونوال السعداوي ، طارحةً أسئلة حول قضايا الشكل والمحتوى والبنية والنوع الأدبي في علاقتها بالجندر ، كما تطرح تساؤلات بشأن مدى ملاءمة مناهج التحليل الغربية في تناول النصوص العربية . أما كتابها اللاحق ، **إعادة حكي حيوات النساء العربيات** Arab Women's Lives Retold ، الذي قامت بتحريره في ٢٠٠٧ ، فتتناول فيه جوانب عديدة من كتابة السيرة الذاتية النسائية العربية ، بدءاً من مشروعها لسد الفجوة القائمة في دراسة السيرة الذاتية النسائية العربية ، حيث تحرص على أن يضم الكتاب دراسات تجمع بين كاتبات من مختلف البلدان العربية من المقيمات في العالم العربي وفي المهجر ، مروراً بقضايا مثل الهُجْنة الثقافية والكتابة الذاتية النسائية عبر القوميةِ ومسألة الهُويّة الفردية والجماعية ، انتهاءً بالقضية السياسية والنِّسْوية ممثلةً في المقولة الراسخة في الفكر النِّسْوي بأن المسألة الشخصية هي قضية سياسية .

السيرة الذاتية ما بعد الكولونيالية

وهنالك اتجاه آخر متنامٍ في دراسات السيرة الذاتية عند تقاطعها مع نظرية ما بعد الكولونيالية ، ولعل من أهمها في السياق العربي كتاب **تحية عبد الناصر** Abdel Nasser الصادر مؤخراً **السيرة الذاتية الأدبية والكفاح الوطني العربي** Literary Autobiography and Arab National Struggles (٢٠١٧) ، الذي يتناول السيرة الذاتية العربية في القرن العشرين ، ليستكمل ما بدأه رينولدز في كتابه عن السيرة الذاتية العربية ما قبل الحداثة . هذا ، وتضع الكاتبة كتابة السيرة الذاتية العربية في سياق الحداثة والتحرر من الاستعمار ، باتباع منهج مقارن بين النصوص المختلفة ، لتبدأ بسيرة طه حسين **الأيام** في مقارنة مع كتاب صنع الله إبراهيم **تلصص** ، ثم تنتقل إلى مذكرات كل من لطيفة الزيات وآسيا جبار باعتبار سيرتيهما أقرب إلى المذكرات ، كما تفرد فصلاً للكتابة الذاتية الفلسطينية ممثلة في محمود درويش ومريد البرغوثي ، ومنها إلى سيرتين مكتوبتين باللغة الإنجليزية من منظور المهجر ، وهما سيرة إدوارد سعيد ونجلاء سعيد ، ثم هيفاء زنكنة وعالية ممدوح ، انتهاءً بفصل عن كتابي رضوى عاشور ومنى برنس باعتبارهما نصين من «مذكرات التحرير» . هذا ، وتخلص عبد الناصر إلى أن تجربة الاستعمار والاحتلال والإمبريالية هي تجربة عميقة في وعي كُتّاب وكاتبات السيرة الذاتية المعاصرة ، إلى الدرجة التي جعلت العديد من كتابات السيرة

الذات في السيرة الذاتية والإشارة إلى عملية القراءة والتأويل في الوقت ذاته، كما يشكك في وجود هُويّة متكاملة واحدة، بل يراها متعددة ومتغيرة تبعاً لسياقاتها وخطاباتها (Gilmore, Autobiographics 185). ومن هنا، لا تكتفي جيلمور بالهُويّة النِّسْوية في السيرة الذاتية، بل تتعداها لتتبع تقاطعاتها مع اللون والعِرْق والطبقة والجنسانية.

ولعل من أهم ملامِح ذلك التيار في نظرية السيرة الذاتية هو تمرده على قضية النوع الأدبي وما يطلق عليه «قانون الأب»، ممثلاً في مفهوم «ميثاق السيرة الذاتية» لدى لوجين ومفهوم «قانون النوع» the law of the genre عند جاك ديريدا Derrida،[4] حيث توضح ستانتون، على سبيل المثال، أن ما طرحه لوجين يزعم وجود اتفاق بين الكاتب والقارئ على وجود حقيقة موضوعية ثابتة يتم نقلها في السيرة الذاتية بصدق كامل، مع وجود فاصل تام بين الحقيقة والخيال.[5] كما يرفض التوجه النِّسْوي في دراسات السيرة الذاتية استبعاد أنواع كالرسائل واليوميات من مجال السير الذاتية المعتمدة والمعترف بها، وهو استبعاد يكتسب لدى النِّسْويات بعداً إضافياً بسبب ارتباط الرسائل واليوميات في الثقافة الغربية بالنساء والفئات المهمشة، بينما استحوذ الرجال على التعبير عن الذات عبر السير الذاتية والمذكرات. ومن جانبها، حملت كارين كابلان Kaplan نظرية السيرة الذاتية عبر الحدود الجغرافية بالتفاتها إلى الجوانب النِّسْوية عبر القومية transnational feminism في الكتابة الذاتية لتطرح مفهوم «الأنواع الخارجة على القانون» out-law genres، في إشارة إلى مفهوم ديريدا بشأن «قانون النوع»، مؤكدة أن تلك الأنواع الخارجة على القانون تقع في الهامش الثقافي وتعبّر عن جهود للتفاوض بين الهُويّة الذاتية والعالم، وبين التاريخ الشخصي والاجتماعي، ومن ثم ترى في تلك الأنواع المغايرة تعبيراً عن المقاومة والنضال من أجل البقاء الثقافي لا مجرد تعبير جمالي عن تجربة ذاتية (Kaplan 130)، مستشهدةً في ذلك بأنواع أدبية مثل أدب السجون، وغيرها من الكتابات الذاتية الناجمة عن صراعات سياسية بين الغرب الإمبريالي وحركات التحرر والنضال الوطني، حيث تنخرط الكاتبة في عملية تفاوض سياسي بناءً على موقعها من هذا الصراع في لحظة الكتابة.

هذا، وقد مضت نوار الحسن غولي Golley على نهج أقرب إلى النِّسْوية عبر القومية، مع تركيزها على السير الذاتية لنساء عربيات في كتابها الأول *قراءة السير الذاتية للنساء العربيات Reading Arab Women's Autobiographies* (٢٠٠٣)، الذي تناولت فيه الكتابات الذاتية لكاتبات

النسائية *Life/Lines: Theorizing Women's Autobiography* (١٩٨٨) ، الذي أشارت المحررتان في مقدمته إلى أهمية البناء على الجهد النظري الذي أسسته كل من جيلينك وستانتون . وهكذا ، طرح هذا الكتاب عدة دراسات تجمع بين المنظور الأدبي والنِّسْوي في قراءة السير الذاتية النسائية ، وفتح مجالات جديدة مثل قضايا موقع الذات الأنثوية في النص بالتركيز على عناصر كالصوت والنوع والهُويّة بتقاطعاتها مع الهُويّات المهمشة مثل نساء أمريكا اللاتينية ، بما أضافه ذلك إلى أنواع السيرة الذاتية من نوع جديد هو الشهادة testimonio بوصفها من الأشكال الشائعة في التعبير عن التجربة الذاتية في ثقافة أمريكا اللاتينية . كما ضم الكتاب دراسات أخرى خرجت بنظرية السيرة الذاتية من حدودها الغربية البيضاء لتتطرق إلى كتابات النساء السود في أمريكا وسيَر نسْويات شرقيات مثل مذكرات هدى شعراوي . كذلك ، تجاوز هذا الاتجاه الجديد حدود النوع الأدبي ، حيث التفتت بعض الدراسات إلى الشعر النسائي الذاتي والسيرة الذاتية النسائية عبر الرسائل ، بل والسيرة الذاتية النسائية السينمائية . ولعل العمل الأشمل في ذلك هو الكتاب الموسوعي **النساء والسيرة الذاتية والنظرية** *Women, Autobiography, Theory* (١٩٩٨) ، وهو كتاب آخر من تحرير سميث وواتسون يتضمن أبواباً عن التجربة والفاعلية ، والذات ، والأنواع ، والتاريخ ، والصوت والذاكرة ، والجنسانية والجسد ، والسياسة والتربية والتعليم .

تتضمن دراسات السيرة الذاتية النسائية مداخل عديدة ، منها التاريخية والنقدية ، ومنها ما ينطلق من الدراسات النسائية *Women's Studies* ، ومنها ما يستعين بأدوات دراسات الجندر *Gender Studies* ، ولكن يمكن كذلك تتبع مسار آخر ، هو المسار الملتزم بالنظرية النِّسْوية وتناول النص النِّسْوي ، حيث نجد على سبيل المثال أن ستانلي تهتم بالسير الذاتية النِّسْوية وتسعى إلى صياغة منهجية نسْوية لدراسة السير الذاتية ، وهو ما أوضحته في كتابها ، حيث ترى أن السِيَر الذاتية النِّسْوية (أيْ التي تكتبها نساء نِسْويات) هي نصوص تعمل على مزج الأنواع الأدبية بوعي وثقة ، فيتجاور في أعمالهن الواقع مع الخيال ، والذات مع الآخر ، والسيرة الذاتية وسيرة الحياة والأفراد والجماعات ، وذلك بشكل عمدي مقصود ، بحيث لا تتجاور تلك العناصر فحسب ، بل تتداخل (Stanley 247) . كذلك ، طرحت لي جِيلمور مصطلح علم السيرة الذاتية *Autobiographics* بوصفه مفهوماً نقدياً نِسْوياً يجمع بين الكاتبة والقارئة ، حيث يقوم بتوصيف تمثيل

صراعها مع المجتمع كما هو الحال في السيرة الذاتية التقليدية ، وإنما باعتبار النص مساحة للفاعلية والتفاوض والمقاومة . فكاتب أو كاتبة السيرة الذاتية يمارسان سلطة فاعلة في تمثيل ذاتيهما في ممارسة واعية تتضمن عمليات الفرز والاختيار والصياغة والبناء ، ومن هنا ، لا تقتصر دراسة السيرة الذاتية - في ظل ما بعد الحداثة - على تتبع التجربة المرويّة ، وإنما تلتفت بالقدر نفسه من الأهمية ، إن لم يكن بدرجة أكبر ، إلى لحظات الصمت والمسكوت عنه في السيرة الذاتية . كذلك ، يتضح لدينا منحى متزايد في دراسات السيرة الذاتية في التركيز على قراءة السير المتنوعة قراءة متوازية ، لا بهدف خلق سردية تاريخية لتطور هذا النوع الأدبي ، وإنما على اعتبار أن كتابة السيرة الذاتية هي عملية إنتاج معرفي ، وأن التجربة الشخصية هي مصدر للمعرفة التي لا تتوقف عند السرد وإنما تتجاوزها لتصبح نواة لمقاومة الصور النمطية وأداة للتمكين والتغيير والتأريخ .

اتجاهات جديدة في كتابة الذات

السيرة الذاتية والنظرية النِّسْوية

تعدّ دراسات السيرة الذاتية النسائية Women's Autobiography Studies من أهم الاتجاهات الجديدة في دراسات السيرة الذاتية ، وتعود إرهاصاتها إلى ثمانينيات القرن العشرين عند تقاطع نظرية السيرة الذاتية Autobiography Theory مع النظرية النِّسْوية Feminist Theory ، وترجع بداياتها النقدية إلى أعمال جيلينك ، وعلى وجه التحديد كتابها الرائد **تراث السيرة الذاتية النسائية** The Tradition of Women's Autobiography (١٩٨٦) ، وكتاب آخر يضم مجموعة من الدراسات المتخصصة من تحريرها بعنوان **السيرة الذاتية النسائية : مقالات نقدية** Women's Autobiography: Essays in Criticism (١٩٨٠) طُرحَ فيه مفهوم الجندر بوصفه أداة تحليلية للسيرة الذاتية ، واستند المنهج التحليليّ فيه إلى مفهوم اختلاف تجارب النساء ومن ثم التعبير عنها شكلاً ومضموناً . وفي عام ١٩٨٤ ، جاءت دومنا ستانتون Stanton بمفهوم كتابة الذات الأنثوية في كتابها الذي حمل العنوان نفسه The Female Autograph (١٩٨٤) ، وذلك سعياً منها إلى خلخلة التركيز على الحياة لصالح كتابة الذات . وقد تبع ذلك كتاب من تحرير بيللا برودسكي Brodzki وسيليست شينك Schenck بعنوان **خطوط/الحياة : التنظير للسيرة الذاتية**

والرواية ، باعتبارها من مزايا ذلك النوع الأدبي لا من عيوبه ، في ضوء تشكيك ما بعد الحداثة في وجود حقيقة موضوعية ثابتة وذات مكتملة وسردية كاملة في ظل خطابات تمثيل الذات self-representation التي ترى في كتابة الذات عملية تمثيل ثقافي . كما أسهمت ما بعد الحداثة في نقل مركز الاهتمام من النص وجمالياته إلى كاتب أو كاتبة النص وما يتمتع به كلاهما من سلطة في إنتاج المعنى وتوليد المعرفة (Gilmore, "The Mark" 7) . ولم يقتصر الأمر على مراجعة التعريفات والحدود والتصنيفات المتعلقة بمسألة السيرة الذاتية وأفرعها ونقاط تلاقيها مع الأنواع الأخرى ، بل تجاوز الأمر ذلك إلى مراجعة مفاهيم محورية راسخة في السيرة الذاتية التقليدية مثل مفهوم الحقيقة ، والصوت ، والذات ، والآخر ، والهُويّة .

ومن جانب آخر ، برز داخل دراسات السيرة الذاتية تيار يلتفت إلى وظيفة السيرة الذاتية ، واضعًا في الحسبان الوساطة التي تتم خلال كتابة السيرة الذاتية بين الذات والمؤلف أو المؤلفة، من ناحية ، وبين السياق الفكري وعلاقة فعل السيرة الذاتية بالمجتمع ، من ناحية أخرى . ومن هذا المنطلق ، توضح لنا جوليا سويندلز Swindells في مقدمة كتاب **استخدامات السيرة الذاتية** *The Uses of Autobiography* (١٩٩٥) أن فعل كتابة السيرة الذاتية يحمل بين طياته سلطة كاتبه أو كاتبته التي تعبر عن الذات وتدعي امتلاك الوعي بالذات والمجتمع . ومن هنا ، يتعين على دراسات السيرة الذاتية تقصي التناقضات الكامنة بين الذات والمجتمع والتوترات القائمة في النص بين الوعي الفردي والمحيط الاجتماعي والثقافي والسياسي والصراع بين الفرد والمجتمع (Swindells 2) . كذلك ، نجد تصاعداً في الرؤية التي تنظر إلى الذات في السيرة الذاتية بوصفها جزءاً فاعلاً في صياغة الخطاب لا موضوعا للخطاب . ومن جانبهما ، تقدم المنظرتان الأبرز في العقدين الأخيرين للسيرة الذاتية ، سيدوني سميث Smith وجوليا واتسون Watson ، تعريفاً محدداً لمفهوم ما بعد الحداثة في علاقته بالسيرة الذاتية ، وذلك استناداً إلى ارتباط اللحظة التاريخية بما بعد الحداثة ، وانطلاقاً من عولمة الرأسمالية والتحول الذي تشهده حدود المكان والزمان بفعل شبكات الاتصالات الإلكترونية ، وما ترتب على هذا وذاك من زعزعة فكرة وجود هُويّة موحّدة وذات ثابتة مستقرة يتم التعبير عنها بشكل منتظم ومحكم (Smith and Watson, Introduction 3) .

ولعل من أهم ملامح السيرة الذاتية المعاصرة ونظريتها الالتفات إلى خطاب الذات، لا بوصفه إعلاناً عن إسهام أو إنجاز وانتصار الذات في

سردية نثرية استرجاعية مكتوبة بواسطة شخص واقعي بشأن وجوده، حيث يكون التركيز على حياته الفردية، ويحكي قصة شخصيته على وجه التحديد (Lejeune 4). ومن ثم، تختلف «السيرة الذاتية»، بهذا المعنى، عن المذكرات وسيرة الحياة والرواية الشخصية والقصيدة الذاتية واليوميات والبورتريه الذاتي والمقالة الذاتية، وذلك بناء على عدد من العناصر المحددة، هي: شكل اللغة (سرد نثري)، والموضوع (الحياة الفردية وقصة الشخصية)، موقع المؤلف (المؤلف والراوي متطابقان في الاسم)، موقع الراوي (الراوي والشخصية المحورية متطابقان، والمنظور الاسترجاعي بالنظر إلى الماضي من موقع الحاضر) (Lejeune 4). وهكذا، تختلف المذكرات memoirs عن السيرة الذاتية autobiography، لأنها لا تركز على تجربة الفرد بقدر تركيزها على السياق السياسي والاجتماعي والثقافي، وكذلك تختلف سيرة الحياة biography لعدم تطابق الراوي والذات، كذلك لا يتطابق الراوي والذات/البطل في الرواية الشخصية personal novel، ولا تنتمي القصيدة الذاتية autobiographical poem إلى النثر، بينما تختلف اليوميات journal/diary عن السيرة الذاتية من حيث لحظة الكتابة وغياب الرؤية الاسترجاعية للأحداث، وكذلك ليس البورتريه الذاتي self-portrait نثرياً، في حين لا تقدم المقالة رؤية استرجاعية. أما العامل الآخر الذي يراه لوجين الأكثر شيوعاً في السيرة الذاتية – وما يطلق عليه «ميثاق السيرة الذاتية» autobiographical pact – فهو استعمال صيغة ضمير المتكلم «أنا» الذي يعبر عن كل من المؤلف والراوي والشخصية المحورية في النص (Lejeune 13).

هذا، وقد شهدت تسعينيات القرن العشرين نقلة في دراسات السيرة الذاتية، وبخاصة مع التطورات التي نجمت عن انتشار نظريات ما بعد الحداثة، وما نجم عنها من مراجعات لمفهوم الذات وسياسات الهُويّة وتحليل الخطاب. ومن هنا، ظهرت دراسات تتناول السيرة الذاتية، لا من منطلق التجربة المروية أو الشكل الأدبي، وإنما من منظور سياسات الهُويّة، وتمثيل الذات باعتبار نص السيرة الذاتية موقعاً يتم فيه صياغة الهُويّات الثقافية (Gilmore, "The Mark" 4). ومن جانب آخر، أسهمت ما بعد الحداثة في زعزعة الحدود الفاصلة بين الأنواع الأدبية، ومن ثم مراجعة تراث السيرة الذاتية الغربية ومكانتها في الدراسات الأدبية، مع التأكيد المتزايد على موقع السيرة الذاتية بين التاريخ والخيال، وبين الموضوعية والذاتية، وبين السيرة

الذاتية ، ٢) صياغة الحياة في شكل ونسق محكم يصنع حياة متكاملة ، ٣) تقسيم حياة الفرد إلى مراحل مع الربط بين تلك المراحل وما بها من تجارب ، ٤) خلق علاقة بين الذات والعالم ، بما يتطلبه ذلك من التزام الذات بموقف محدد يعبر عن لحظة الكتابة ، يُتأمَّل ويُؤوَّل من خلالها الماضي ، وهو موقف تكتسبه الذات من واقع ما حققته وأنجزته عبر حياتها ، ٥) تقديم رؤية للذات قائمة على بنية قوية موحدة ومحكمة ، ٦) تعتمد صياغة حياة الذات على عناصر الاختيار والحذف ، حيث يختار كاتب السيرة الذاتية الوقائع والأحداث التي يرويها وأدوات التعبير وأسلوب الكتابة المستعمل في السرد (Pascal 9-10). وقد عبّر باسكال ، وهو من رواد التنظير للسيرة الذاتية ، عن موقف تجاه هذا النوع الأدبي ينطلق من إطار الدراسات الأدبية ، ويعتبر الرواية هي الإطار الأدبي الذي يحدد معايير السيرة الذاتية ، وهو ما يتضح في النقاط السابقة التي تعلي من قيمة بنية النص وأسلوب الكتابة برؤية واضحة وموحدة أقرب إلى السرد الروائي منها إلى الكتابة التاريخية . بل نجده يقلل من قيمة «الحقيقة» في السيرة الذاتية ، فيرى الأولوية في بنية النص ووحدة التجربة واتساق الشخصية ، لا في مدى مصداقية الأحداث بوصفها مرآة للواقع . وهو موقف يتفق مع رؤية ناقد آخر من رواد دراسات السيرة الذاتية ، هو جيمس أولني Olney ، في كتابه **مجاز الذات : معنى السيرة الذاتية** *Metaphors of the Self: The Meaning of Autobiography* (١٩٧٢) ، حيث يرى أن أفضل تناول للسيرة الذاتية هو التعامل معها بوصفها تعبيراً عن رغبة الإنسان في وضع بنية وفرض نظام ، بدلاً من التركيز على جوانبها الشكلية أو التاريخية (Olney 3) ، وهو ما يكشف عن مقاربة للسيرة الذاتية من منطلق العمل الأدبي . ومن جانبه ، سعى ويليام سبينجمان Spengemann في كتابه **أشكال السيرة الذاتية** *Forms of Autobiography* إلى تأكيد عمليات التذكر والتأمل والتخيل في السيرة الذاتية ، وما تتضمنه من جماليات أسلوبية ولغة رمزية (120ff) .

أما التعريف الراسخ للسيرة الذاتية في النظرية الأدبية الغربية فهو ذلك الذي قدمه فيليب لوجين في كتابه **عن السيرة الذاتية** *On Autobiography* الصادر بالفرنسية في عام ١٩٧٥ ، ثم مترجماً إلى الإنجليزية في ١٩٨٩ ، الذي يعد المرجع الأصلي لنظرية السيرة الذاتية وتطورها عبر العقود القليلة الأخيرة . قام لوجين بتقديم تعريف واضح للسيرة الذاتية على أنها

لا الكتابة التاريخية. هذا، وقد شهدت نظرية السيرة الذاتية تطورات كبيرة منذ تسعينيات القرن العشرين عند تقاطعها بالنظرية الأدبية وأثر المدارس الفكرية مثل ما بعد البنيوية والتفكيكية والنِّسْوية في مفهوم السيرة الذاتية، إذ صارت نظرية السيرة الذاتية تعترف بهشاشة الحدود الفاصلة بين هذين النوعين في سياق التقاطعات بين الرواية والتاريخ، وبين الواقع والخيال. وهذا ما تؤكده التيارات الجديدة المتأثرة بالنظرية التفكيكية في نظرية السيرة الذاتية منذ تسعينيات القرن العشرين، ومنها، على سبيل المثال، الرؤية التي تقدمها ليز ستانلي Stanley في كتابها المهم **الأنا في سيرة الحياة/الذاتية** *The Auto/Biographical I* (١٩٩٢)، حيث ترى أن سيرة الحياة والسيرة الذاتية إنما هما نوعان متداخلان، يقدمان مراجعة للماضي أو جزء منه باستعمال الذاكرة وممارسة الاختيار، بما يجعل السيرة الذاتية وسيرة الحياة مزيجاً من الواقع والخيال (Stanley 92).

نظرية السيرة الذاتية

تعود بدايات التنظير للسيرة الذاتية إلى مطلع القرن العشرين، مع صدور كتاب جورج ميش Misch **تاريخ السيرة الذاتية في العصور القديمة** *History of Autobiography in Antiquity* الذي صدر في جزأين باللغة الألمانية في عام ١٩٠٧، ثم تمت ترجمته إلى اللغة الإنجليزية في عدة طبعات منذ عام ١٩٥٠. وهو عمل لا يقتصر على التأريخ للسيرة الذاتية في العصور القديمة، وإنما يتطرق إلى تأثير تلك النصوص المبكرة في تطور السيرة الذاتية في العصور اللاحقة. ولكن السيرة الذاتية لم تنل اهتماماً نقدياً يذكر حتى ثلاثينيات القرن العشرين، مع ما شهدته تلك الفترة، بين الحربين العالميتين وفي أعقاب الحرب العالمية الثانية على وجه التحديد، من طفرة في الكتابات الذاتية وما صاحبها من اهتمام نقدي على الساحة الأوروبية، مع ما شاب مفهوم السيرة الذاتية حينذاك من خلط بينها وبين المذكرات وسيرة الحياة وغيرهما من أشكال الكتابة الذاتية والتاريخية. وبحلول خمسينيات القرن العشرين وستينياته، ظهرت كتابات نقدية تسعى إلى تحديد موقع السيرة الذاتية من الدراسات الأدبية والتاريخية، وبلورة تعريف لهذا النوع الأدبي، وهي جهود اتسمت في مجملها بتأكيد السمات الأدبية في السيرة الذاتية.

ومن جانبه، قدم باسكال توصيفاً للسيرة الذاتية يقوم على الآتي:
١) إعادة صياغة الحياة أو مرحلة من مراحلها مع التركيز على التجربة

ذكريات لما عايشه أو شاهده صاحبها من أحداث عامة كبرى ، حيث لا تكون حياة الفرد في المذكرات هي العنصر الأساسي ، وإنما تأتي حياة الفرد ضمن سياق سياسي تاريخي ثقافي يكون هو الأهم في النص (Goodwin 4-6) . وهكذا ، يرجع جودوين جذور «السيرة الذاتية» الأوروبية إلى ثلاثة أنواع نثرية من الكتابة الذاتية ، هي : الدفاع apology والاعترافات confessions والمذكرات memoir . وتعتمد تلك الكتابة على الكشف عن الذات ، سواء بالدفاع عنها في وجه الاتهامات ، أو الكشف عن خبايا النفس طلباً للمغفرة أو الخلاص ، أو تصوير الذات في سياق سياسي اجتماعي تاريخي واسع . وكلها ، على تنوعها ، نصوص مكتوبة تنطلق تاريخياً من مساحات فلسفية وروحانية وثقافية ، يجمعها التمركز حول التعبير عن الذات والحياة .

ولكن جودوين يميز تلك الأنواع عن «اليوميات» diaries و«الرسائل» letters التي تختلف عن غيرها في البعد الزمني ، حيث يتم كتابة السيرة الذاتية أو المذكرات في لحظة زمنية لاحقة للأحداث المروية ، على حين تتسم اليوميات والرسائل بالآنية وقرب الذات من التجربة وسردها (Goodwin 10-11) . ويتفق معه باسكال الذي يؤكد وجود تقاليد خاصة بكتابة السيرة الذاتية التي تميزها عن غيرها من أنواع الكتابة ، بل يتخذ موقفاً صارماً في تقييمه للكتابة الذاتية ، حيث يعد السيرة الذاتية والمذكرات والذكريات «سيرة ذاتية حقّة» true autobiography مستبعداً اليوميات والرسائل ، نظراً لما تحمله السيرة الذاتية والمذكرات والذكريات reminiscences من رؤية ناضجة وبنية محكمة ونظرة تأملية وتأويلية للأحداث ، لا مجرد سرد آني لها ، كما هو الحال في اليوميات والرسائل (Pascal 3-5) . ولكنه مع ذلك يفرق أيضاً بين السيرة الذاتية واليوميات ، حيث يكون التركيز في السيرة الذاتية على الفرد والذات ، بينما لا يقل الاهتمام في الذكريات بالآخرين ، جنباً إلى جنب الذات (Pascal 5) .

هذا ، ويفرق باسكال كذلك بين سيرة الحياة biography والسيرة الذاتية autobiography ، حيث يرى أن سيرة الحياة تستند إلى الوقائع وتسردها ، بينما تعتمد السيرة الذاتية على الذاكرة التي قد تكون متحايلة أو خادعة (Pascal 18-19) . وكان أول من فرّق بين السيرة الذاتية وسيرة الحياة ، ومن ثم التاريخ ، هو وين شوميكر Shumaker في كتابه **السيرة الذاتية الإنجليزية** *English Autobiography* (١٩٥٤) ، من منطلق الحدود الفاصلة بين الأنواع ، على اعتبار أن السيرة الذاتية نوع من الكتابة الأدبية

الكتابة الذاتية والتاريخية والروائية في نص واحد محكم له قواعده المغايرة لما سبقه في الأدب العربي، مثلاً في «الترجمة الذاتية» و«السيرة الذاتية» كما ورد أعلاه. ولكن تجدر الإشارة هنا إلى أن الدراسات الأدبية العربية لم تلتفت كثيراً إلى تناول تلك الأنواع الجديدة تناولاً نقدياً جاداً، وبخاصة فيما يتصل بالسيرة الذاتية بوصفها ممارسة أدبية عربية معاصرة، رغم كثرة نصوصها عبر أجيال من كتّاب وكاتبات القرن العشرين ومطلع القرن الحادي العشرين. ولعل من أبرزها الدراسة الفريدة التي قام بها خيري دومة في قراءته لروايات كاتبات ما صار يعرف حالياً بجيل التسعينيات (تسعينيات القرن العشرين)، منطلقاً من كون النصوص أعمالاً روائية تحمل تجارب ذاتية، فتندرج من ثم تحت مسمى «رواية السيرة الذاتية» التي تضفي على السيرة الذاتية بنيتها، قائلاً: «لكي تصبح السيرة الذاتية شكلاً متماسكاً لا بد من صبها في القالب الروائي الأساسي» (دومة، ص ١٤)، وهي رؤية نقدية تنطلق من داخل نظرية الرواية وتحدد موقع الكتابة النثرية بقدر قربها من بنية الرواية. وهو موقع يختلف عن التوجه الآخر الذي ينظر إلى السيرة الذاتية من منظور ثقافي لا روائي، وينطلق من داخل نظرية السيرة الذاتية الغربية وتطوراتها وتعدّد مساراتها في العقود القليلة الأخيرة وخروجها من إطار الدراسات التاريخية والأدبية، والإنسانيات بشكل عام، لتتقاطع وتتلاقى مع مجالات معرفية جديدة في العلوم الاجتماعية.

وعلى صعيد آخر، نجد أن جيمس جودوين Goodwin في دراسته التاريخية للكتابة الذاتية يوضح أن الملامح الأساسية للسيرة الذاتية (الأوروبية) تقع في المصطلح ذاته، الذي يمكن ترجمته حرفياً بوصفه الحياة الذاتية المكتوبة autobiography، حيث يتكون المصطلح من ثلاثة جذور، هي: الذات auto والحياة bio والكتابة graphy؛ إذ يعتمد في تعريفه على أصل المصطلح، ويخلص إلى أن مصطلح «أوتوبيوجرافي» يقوم على علاقة حيوية تبادلية بين تلك العناصر الثلاثة (Goodwin 3)، رابطاً بين هذا النوع الأدبي وجذوره النثرية الممثلة في **دفاع سقراط** *Apology* في القرن الرابع قبل الميلاد، وعلى وجه التحديد في كتابة الاعترافات والمذكرات لاحقاً، وعلى رأسها **اعترافات القديس أوغسطين (ق ٤-٥) وحياة القديسة تريزا الأفيلية** *The Life of Saint Teresa of Avila by Herself* (ق ١٦)، بينما تحمل **سيرة بينفينوتو تشيلليني الذاتية** *The Autobiography Of Benvenuto Cellini* سمات «المذكرات» memoir بوصفها نوعاً من الكتابة الذاتية التي تقدم

فروع الكتابة التاريخية (Reynolds 39)، وهو نوع تقليدي في الأدب العربي الرسمي، بل الشعبي، كثيراً ما كان يجمع في السرد بين ضمير المتكلم وضمير الغائب. هذا، وقد تطورت السيرة في القرن العشرين، وبخاصة في ظل التقاطعات الثقافية بين الشرق والغرب وتجربة الحداثة وتطور الوعي بالذات والروح الفردية، لتتبلور في نوع أدبي جديد هو «السيرة الذاتية» المعبّرة عن سيرة حياة الذات بصوت/قلم الذات ومن منظور الذات.

هذا، وتختلف «السيرة» عن «الطبقات» التي اتخذت شكل كتب أقرب إلى القواميس التي تضم العديد من سِيَر الحياة الموجزة، والتي يتم تصنيفها بناءً على «طبقة»، أي فئة، أو أصحاب مهنة في المجتمع (Reynolds 40)، ولعل من أشهرها كتاب **الطبقات الكبير** لصاحبه ابن سعد (ق ٨-٩)، و**طبقات الأعيان** (ق ١٨) لصاحبه ابن عجيبة، وكتاب زينب فواز **الدر المنثور في طبقات ربات الخدور** (ق ١٩).[3] وكل سيرة حياة موجزة ترد في الطبقات تسمى «ترجمة»، وهي كلمة مشتقة من اللغة الآرامية targum، وتعني معلومة عن سيرة شخص، كما صارت تحمل في اللغة العربية معنى النقل أو التأويل في علاقته بالحديث عن شخص، حيث يوضح رينولدز مفهوم «الترجمة» بكونه معلومة عن حياةٍ شخص، وهي صورة غير مطابقة وغيرِ كاملة لحياة ما، ولكنها تقدم تعريفاً بالشخص وإسهاماته وإنجازاته، رجلاً كان أم امرأة (Reynolds 42). هذا، ولم تكن الحدود قديماً جلية بين الكتابة عن شخص وبين الكتابة عن الذات، حيث إن بنية الترجمة في حد ذاتها بوصفها نصّاً كانت تجمع بين حياة الشخص كما يسردها غيره وبين مقاطع من كتابات الشخص نفسه، ومن ثم يخبرنا رينولدز بأن «الترجمة» كانت تشتمل على قصة حياة الفرد وإنتاجه الأدبي، ومن ثم كانت المقاطع الذاتية والغيرية تجتمع في نص واحد وتتنقل عبر كتب التراجم والطبقات غير قاصرة على نوع واحد من السرد والقص (Reynolds 43).

وهكذا، فإن الكتابة عن حياة الذات، فيما يعرف حالياً بمفهوم السيرة الذاتية، إنما خرجت في الأدب العربي من رحم تراث الطبقات والتراجم التي كانت بدورها نوعاً من الكتابة التاريخية. هذا، وقد شهدت «الترجمة» و«السيرة» تطوراً كبيراً في القرن العشرين، ربما يرجع إلى خروجها من حدود سياقها التاريخي وتراثها الأدبي، ونتيجة لتأثر الكتاب المحدثين والمعاصرين بالكتابة الذاتية الأوروبية، مما أدى إلى بلورة فروع تجمع بين

وافياً كاملاً ، عن تاريخه الشخصي ، على نحو موجز ، حافل بالتجارب والخبرات المنوّعة الخصبة ، وهذا الأسلوب يقوم على جمال العرض ، وحسن التقسيم ، وعذوبة العبارة ، وحلاوة النص الأدبي ، وبث الحياة والحركة في تصوير الوقائع والشخصيات ، وفيما يتمثله من حواره مستعينا بعناصر ضئيلة من الخيال لربط أجزاء عمله ، حتى تبدو ترجمته الذاتية في صورة متماسكة محكمة ، على ألا يسترسل مع التخيل والتصور حتى لا ينأى عن الترجمة الذاتية ، وبخاصة إذا كان يكتب ترجمته في قالب روائي . (ص ١٠)

ولعل هذا التعريف يضع الترجمة الذاتية الفنية في مساحة أقرب إلى السيرة الذاتية الروائية أو رواية السيرة الذاتية ، وهما تعريفان يستعملان مترادفين لذلك النوع الأدبي الذي تتقاطع فيه التجربة الذاتية مع فنيات الكتابة الروائية في العصر الحديث ، التي لا تقتصر على «المحتوى» والمضمون الذي ينقل «التجارب والخبرات» و«التاريخ الشخصي» ، وإنما تتجاوز ذلك إلى مساحات الشكل الأدبي مثلاً في جماليات الكتابة الأدبية ، من بنية نصية وأسلوب جميل وحبكة محكمة ، في سرد يجمع بين الواقع والخيال ، أيْ بين الكتابة التاريخية والروائية .

وِمن هنا ، يتضح جانب مهم من «السيرة الذاتية» بوصفها مصطلحاً ومفهوما نقديا يحمل سمات هجينة ، إذ يشير إلى نوع من الكتابة التي تنجم عن تلاقي الكتابة التاريخية بالكتابة الروائية ، سواء في الشرق أو الغرب ، مع تنوع أصولها في الثقافتين العربية والإنجليزية وتطورها من أنواع أدبية سابقة سائدة ، تمتد إلى ما قبل العصر الحديث ، وما قبل بدء التنظير للسيرة الذاتية في القرن العشرين . ومن هنا ، تنبع أهمية ما قام به رينولدز من شرح دقيق لأنواع الكتابة في الأدب العربي في العصر ما قبل الحديث ، التي سبقت بلورة السيرة الذاتية أو الترجمة الذاتية بوصفهما مصطلحين مستقرين في النقد الأدبي المعاصر . ففي الفصل الثاني من كتابه ، يوضح بدايات الكتابة الذاتية العربية ممثلة في أدب «السيرة» ، و«الطبقات» ، و«التراجم» ، حيث يعرف «السيرة» بأنها كلمة مشتقة من السير أو الرحلة ، بمعنى كونها كتابة عن حياة شخص ، وكان المصطلح يشير في العصور القديمة والوسطى إلى الكتابة الأدبية التي تسهب في الحديث عن حياة شخص بوصفها فرعا من

وذلك على خلاف كلمة «الترجمة» المشتقة من اللغة الآرامية ، التي صارت تستعملُ للإشارة إلى «التاريخ الموجز للفرد» ، وإن كان المصطلحان يستعملان كثيراً بوصفهما مترادفين (عبد الدايم ، ص ٣١) . ولا يتطرق عبد الدايم بالتفصيل إلى المصطلحات المتصلة بكتابة الذات والحياة في الأدب العربي ما قبل الحديث ، وإنما يتناول بقدر من التدقيق مفهوم الترجمة الذاتية بمعنى تاريخ الفرد كما يرويه بذاته ، وهو يفرق في ذلك بين «الترجمة الذاتية» بفروعها و«الترجمة الذاتية الفنية» :

يمكن القول بأن الترجمة الذاتية الفنية ليست هي تلك التي يكتبها صاحبها على شكل «مذكرات» يعنى فيها بتصوير الأحداث التاريخية ، أكثر من عنايته بتصوير واقعه الذاتي ، وليست هي التي تكتب على صورة «ذكريات» يعنى فيها صاحبها بتصوير البيئة والمجتمع والمشاهدات أكثر من عنايته بتصوير ذاته ، وليست هي المكتوبة على شكل «يوميات» تدور فيها الأحداث على نحو متقطع غير رتيب ، وليست في آخر الأمر «اعترافات» يخرج فيها صاحبها على منهج الاعتراف الصحيح ، وليست هي الرواية الفنية التي تعتمد في أحداثها ومواقفها على الحياة الخاصة لكاتبها ، فكل هذه الأشكال فيها ملامح من الترجمة الذاتية ، وليست هي ، لأنها تفتقر إلى كثير من الأسس التي تعتمد عليها الترجمة الذاتية الفنية . (ص ٣)

وهكذا ، يوضح عبد الدايم الفروق الراسخة في نظرية السيرة الذاتية التي تميز بين السيرة الذاتية وبين فروعها المختلفة التي حرصت نظرية السيرة الذاتية على تحليلها وتحديد ملامح كل منها ، وإن كان لا يسعى هنا إلى التعريف بتلك الفروع بقدر ما يفرق بين السيرة الذاتية والسيرة الذاتية الأدبية ، أيْ الترجمة الذاتية والترجمة الذاتية الفنية ، التي يحدد سماتها على النحو الآتي :

والترجمة الذاتية الفنية هي التي يصوغها صاحبها في صورة مترابطة ، على أساس من الوحدة والاتساق في البناء والروح . . . وفي أسلوب أدبي قادر على أن ينقل لنا محتوى

بوصفه «أول نص في أدبنا الحديث يمكن اعتباره سيرة ذاتية رائدة» (ص ١٨)، حيث تعبر شخصية البطل «الفارياق» عن فارس الشدياق على مستوى الاسم والتجارب والرحلات التي يتضمنها الكتاب. ولكن لا يمكن الجزم تماماً بانتماء هذا الكتاب إلى السيرة الذاتية على مستوى النوع الأدبي، بل يظل يحتل حيزاً خلافياً إذا وضعنا في الحسبان تأكيد رضوى عاشور في كتابها **الحداثة الممكنة** (٢٠١٢) على كون **الساق على الساق** هو أول رواية عربية، وإن كان بطلها «الفارياق» هو نفسه «شخصية أتوبيوجرافية اختار لها منشئها اسماً منحوتاً من المقطع الأول من اسمه، فارس، والمقطع الأخير من اسم عائلته، الشدياق» (ص ١٧). وهكذا، فإن تباين الآراء النقدية الرصينة بشأن موقع عمل مثل **الساق على الساق** إنما يؤكد على مرونة الحدود النظرية الفاصلة بين الأنواع الأدبية بشكل عام وبين السيرة الذاتية والرواية، بل بينها وبين المقامة وأدب الرحلات وغيرها من أشكال الكتابة الأدبية.

مفاهيم نظرية ونقدية مقارنة

قضية المصطلح

يتطرق عبد الدايم إلى تطور المصطلح الذي يشير إلى كتابة الذات أو الحياة موضحاً الخلط السائد بين مصطلحي «السيرة» و«الترجمة» قائلاً:

> وإذا نحن تتبعنا تطور الترجمة الذاتية في الأدب العربي في العصور القديمة والوسطى، لنتبين تطور هذا الاصطلاح، وجدنا أن لفظتي «ترجمة» و«سيرة» كانتا تدوران حول معنى «تاريخ الحياة»، وقد اتخذ التأريخ للفرد صوراً مختلفة لدى العرب، وكانت «السيرة» أولى هذه الصور، وقصد بها حياة الرسول الكريم ومغازيه . . . ثم تعددت أنواع التأريخ للأفراد بعد ذلك، فكان «الجرح والتعديل» و«الطبقات» ثم «التراجم» في العصور المتأخرة التي تلت عصر الرواية والتدوين. (ص٣٠)

ومن هنا، يتضح أصل مفهوم «السيرة» من حيث إشارتها إلى التأريخ لحياة الرسول، حيث جرى تعميمها لاحقاً لتدل على «التاريخ المسهب للفرد»،

ومن الجدير بالذكر أن تحليل عبد الدايم لا يقتصر كسابقيه على التركيز على مضمون التجربة تبعاً للتصنيف الوارد أعلاه، وإنما يحرص في كتابه على طرح قضية الشكل والمصطلح فيتناولها من منظور يجمع بين المعرفة بنظرية السيرة الذاتية الغربية، جنباً إلى جنب تأصيل المصطلح في إطار الثقافة العربية وتاريخ الأدب العربي. كما أنه لا يكتفي، على سبيل المثال، بتناول التجربة التي يعبر عنها كتاب طه حسين **الأيام**، بل نجده يتوقف عند هذا العمل ليتناوله من منظور النوع الأدبي، ليخلص إلى أنها ليست بالرواية الفنية الصرفة ولا بالترجمة الذاتية الكاملة، إذ لا تندرج تماماً تحت مفهوم الرواية الواقعية، ولا تخضع لتعريف السيرة الذاتية، وإنما هي «ترجمة ذاتية روائية» (عبد الدايم، ص ٤٥٩)، وهو المفهوم الذي يقابل ما صار يعرف حالياً في النظرية الغربية للسيرة الذاتية بمصطلح رواية السيرة الذاتية autobiographical novel أو رواية الذات autofiction. وهكذا، تحتل قضية المصطلح موقعاً محورياً في تناول عبد الدايم لتاريخ السيرة الذاتية العربية، مفضلاً مصطلح «الترجمة الذاتية» على غيره من المصطلحات النابعة من التراث الأدبي العربي أو تلك الواردة من الثقافة الأوروبية، وكاشفاً عن فهم عميق للمصطلحات والمفاهيم المتعلقة بالكتابة الذاتية.

ولا تفوتني هنا الإشارة إلى دراسة صبري حافظ «رقش الذات لا كتابتها: تحولات الإستراتيجيات النصية في السيرة الذاتية» (٢٠٠٢)، التي يعرِّف فيها السيرة الذاتية من منطلق مفهوم لوجين، ثم يتناول أهم ملامح «الذات الكاتبة» والهُويّة المتغيرة في إطار الكتابة الذاتية في الأدب العربي منذ نهاية القرن التاسع عشر، ليخلص إلى «سيولة الذات وحركيتها وتناقضها مع ذاتها باستمرار» (ص ١٧). وفي استعراضه لما أسماه «خيوط النشأة والرحلة واللغة» (ص ص ٢٢-٢٦)، يحدد المساحات الأساسية لتطور السيرة الذاتية العربية الحديثة والمعاصرة. ففي خيط النشأة، يروي كتّاب السيرة نشأتهم الاجتماعية في إطار ناقد لمجتمعهم، وتصبح السيرة الذاتية تعبيراً عن «انتصار الفردي على الجمعي» (ص ٢٣)، وفي خيط الرحلة تتجسد الكتابة عن التنقل على مستوى المكان والزمان «بحيث يصعب الفصل بين الرحلة والذات المرتحلة» (ص ٢٤)، بينما يختص الخيط الثالث باللغة، بحيث يتم استعمال اللغة أداةً تقوم «برقش الذات في النص» (ص ٢٥).

هذا، ويرى حافظ أن جذور السيرة الذاتية العربية الحديثة ترجع إلى كتاب فارس الشدياق الساق على الساق فيما هو الفارياق (١٨٥٥)،

الذاتية لتصبح عملاً روائياً متكاملاً» (بدر، ص ٢٩٧). ومن الملاحظ أيضاً أن تحليل بدر لتلك النصوص لم يلتفت إلى قضية المصطلح أو النوع الأدبي في حد ذاته بقدر تحليله لمضمونها بوصفه تعبيراً عن الغربة والذاتية والتعالي. فلم يلتفت إلى خصوصية «رواية الترجمة الذاتية» بوصفها نوعاً أدبياً بقدر ما انصب اهتمامه على طبيعة التجربة التي تعبر عنها الرواية، انطلاقاً من موقعها ومضمونها الروائي، لا من تقاطعاتها مع السيرة الذاتية بوصفها نوعاً أدبياً. ومن هنا، جاء تقييمه لتلك الأعمال بوصفها أعمالاً روائية غير متكاملة، بسبب انغماسها في التعبير عن تجارب شخصية.

ولعل الدراسة الأهم في تاريخ السيرة الذاتية العربية، التي يتضح أن رينولدز قد استند إليها في كتابه، هي كتاب يحيى إبراهيم عبد الدايم **الترجمة الذاتية في الأدب العربي الحديث** (١٩٧٥)، حيث يستعمل مصطلح «الترجمة الذاتية» للإشارة إلى مفهوم «السيرة الذاتية» كما نعرفه اليوم (وسيتم التطرق إلى مسألة المصطلح في الجزء التالي من هذه المقالة). ونجده يذكر في مقدمة كتابه «قلة الدراسات الجادة التي عالجت الأعمال الأدبية التي تدخل في هذا الجنس» (عبد الدايم، ص ب)، ويقصد هنا «الترجمة الذاتية»، مؤكداً أنه حتى تلك الدراسات التي التفتت إلى «الترجمة الذاتية»، أيْ السيرة الذاتية، «لا تمنحنا مفهوماً فنياً للترجمة الذاتية»، وإنما تهتم بتاريخ وتطور السيرة الذاتية في الأدب العربي (ص ص د-هـ). وفي الفصل الثاني من كتابه، يتناول يحيى عبد الدايم تطور «الترجمة الذاتية» بوصفها امتداداً للسير والتراجم عبر العصور القديمة والوسطى، بينما يخص المؤلف هنا كتابه بالعصر الحديث، فيضع تصنيفاً لفروع الترجمة الذاتية تشتمل على أربعة أنواع: ١- الترجمة الذاتية في الإطار الفكري، وهي تتسم بالحرص على استعمال العناصر الفنية في الكتابة، مثلما فعل عبد القادر المازني وأحمد أمين وعباس محمود العقاد. ٢- الترجمة الذاتية الآتية في الإطار السياسي، ومن أهم كتابها أحمد لطفي السيد ومحمد فريد وعبد العزيز فهمي وعبد الرحمن الرافعي. ٣- الترجمة الذاتية الروائية ممثلة في كتاب **تخليص الإبريز في تلخيص باريز** لرفاعة الطهطاوي، وحديث عيسى بن هشام لإبراهيم المويلحي، و**ليالي سطيح** لحافظ إبراهيم وكتاب **الأيام** لطه حسين. ٤- الترجمة الذاتية المصوِّرة للعالم الخاص، ومن أبرزها مذكرات جورجي زيدان، ومذكرات يوسف وهبي، ومذكرات فاطمة رشدي، ومذكرات فاطمة اليوسف، ومذكرات طالب بعثة بقلم لويس عوض (عبد الدايم، ص ص ٨٤-١٠٤).

للأحداث بقدر ما تحرص على الكشف عن خبرات وممارسات متعددة لصاحبها أو صاحبتها، وهو ما انعكس على تقسيم السيرة الذاتية إلى أجزاء معنية بجوانب من الشخصية كالأسرة والتعليم والأعمال والإنجازات (Reynolds 246). وإذا كان خطاب السيرة الذاتية في الثقافة الغربية يقترب من مساحات السرد الروائي، فإن السيرة الذاتية في الثقافة العربية تنتمي بدرجة أكبر إلى الكتابة التاريخية. ومن هنا، لعب كتاب **الأيام** بقلم طه حسين دوراً كبيراً في الانتقال بالسيرة الذاتية العربية من مساحات الكتابة التاريخية إلى الكتابة الروائية، سواء في بنية النص ذاته أو في صوت الراوي الذي كان يتبادل الأدوار بين المؤلف والبطل والراوي، في كسر لقاعدة من أهم قواعد السيرة الذاتية التي أرساها أحد مؤسسي نظرية السيرة الذاتية، فيليب لوجين Lejeune في طرحه مفهوم «ميثاق السيرة الذاتية» (الذي سيتم التوقف عنده لاحقاً عند تناول نظرية السيرة الذاتية).

وإذا كان رينولدز قد أشار إلى كتاب طه حسين **الأيام** بوصفه علامة مميزة في تطور السيرة الذاتية العربية وتحولاتها في القرن العشرين، فقد سبقه عبد المحسن طه بدر في ذلك، إذ أفرد الفصل الثالث من كتابه **تطور الرواية العربية الحديثة في مصر (١٨٧٠-١٩٣٨)** الصادر في القاهرة عام ١٩٦٣ للحديث عمّا أسماها «رواية الترجمة الذاتية» بوصفها من فروع «الرواية الفنية»، فتناول بالتحليل عدداً من «روايات الترجمة الذاتية» التي تتضمن كلاً من روايتي **الأيام** و**أديب** لطه حسين، ورواية **زينب** لمحمد حسين هيكل، ورواية **إبراهيم الكاتب** لعبد القادر المازني، ورواية **سارة** لمحمود عباس العقاد، وروايات **عودة الروح** و**عصفور من الشرق** و**يوميات نائب في الأرياف** لتوفيق الحكيم، وهي الأعمال التي يراها عبد المحسن طه بدر نتاجاً لاحتكاك مؤلفيها بالثقافة الغربية، لا من حيث التأثر بالأنواع الأدبية الشبيهة، بل من حيث تمثيل ظاهرتين، هما شعور هؤلاء الكتّاب بالغربة عن مجتمعهم و«عجزهم عن الانتماء إلى هذا الواقع» (بدر، ص ٢٨٩) وما صاحبه من «الإحساس المفرط بالذات» (بدر، ص ٢٩٢)، الأمر الذي أدى إلى «أن رواياتهم التي تركوها كانت تتصل اتصالاً مباشراً بحياتهم ومشاكلهم الذاتية، بحيث أصبحت هذه الروايات مرتبطة بفن الترجمة الذاتية» (بدر، ص ٢٩٧). ومن الجدير بالذكر هنا أن بدر يرى في «رواية الترجمة الذاتية» نوعاً أدبياً يفتقد إلى الفنية الروائية، ومرحلة لا بدّ لكاتبها من أن يتجاوزها، تتبعها محاولات وخطوات «للتخلص من آثار الترجمة

١٨) ، وانتهاءً بسيرة علي مبارك (ق ١٩) . كما يتضمن الكتاب إشارات إلى السير الذاتية لكل من أبي حامد الغزالي (ق ١١-١٢) وابن خلدون (ق ١٤-١٥) ، ويذكر نماذج لاحقة من كُتّاب السيرة الذاتية في بدايات القرن العشرين وأبرزهم طه حسين وجورجي زيدان .

هذا ، ويتناول رينولدز في فصول كتابه ، بقدر من التفصيل والتحليل ، سيرة كل من ابن بلقين وابن حجر والسيوطي بوصفها نماذج لكتابات أدبية تقوم على تصوير الذات ، ما بين تركيز على الحياة الشخصية لدى ابن بلقين (بدايات ق ١١) ، والذات في سياق تاريخي عند ابن حجر العسقلاني (ق ١٥) ، والأسلوب الفني لدى السيوطي (نهايات ق ١٥) . ويؤكد رينولدز أن نشأة السيرة الذاتية العربية في القرن التاسع الميلادي ترجع إلى أدب التراجم الذي كان ينتمي إلى الكتابة التاريخية (Reynolds 47) ، بينما شهدت نهايات القرن الحادي عشر وبدايات القرن الثاني عشر ازدهاراً في الكتابة الذاتية وحرصاً على توثيق التاريخ الشخصي (Reynolds 52) ، وهي الكتابة التي اتخذت أشكالا متنوعة بين سير سياسية وأدبية وروحانية (Reynolds 65) ، في حين انتشرت في القرنين الرابع عشر والخامس عشر السير الذاتية العربية انتشاراً كبيراً في العالم العربي والناطق بالعربية (Reynolds 55) ، واتسمت بوعي كُتّابها بالغاية من الكتابة والإفصاح عن الدافع إلى كتابة سيرهم والدفاع عن أنفسهم من اتهامات بالزهو أو الزيف (Reynolds 66) ، كما تشهد نهايات القرن الخامس عشر على وجود وعي لدى الكُتّاب العرب بتراث السيرة الذاتية العربي (Reynolds 64) ، بما يوحي بأن تاريخ كتابة السيرة الذاتية العربية يحمل بين طياته خطاباً نقدياً واعياً بهذا النوع الأدبي (Reynolds 72) .

وفي ختام دراسته ، يعقد رينولدز مقارنة بين السيرة الذاتية العربية والأوروبية ، يوضح فيها أن تراث السيرة الذاتية الأوروبية ، وإن انطلق من الكتابات الفكرية والدينية ، فقد تطور في اتجاه متأثر بالرواية بوصفها نوعاً أدبياً راسخاً في القرن التاسع عشر ، وأدى التلاقي بين السيرة الذاتية والرواية إلى نشأة نوع أدبي فرعي ، هو رواية النشأة والتطور Bildungsroman ، التي تسرد سيرة الذات في بناء روائي يجمع بين الواقع والخيال ، ويستعين بالتطور الزمني للأحداث بوصفه الأساس في تصوير حياة الفرد أدبياً . أما فيما يتعلق بالسيرة الذاتية العربية ، فقد ارتبطت بداياتها بأدب التراجم والسير ، فتأثرت من ثم بشكل تلك التراجم التي لا تلتزم ببنية التتابع الزمني

معدودة، أبرزها دراسة دوايت رينولدز Reynolds تأويل الذات: السيرة الذاتية في التراث الأدبي العربي Interpreting the Self: Autobiography in the Arabic Literary Tradition، التي تركز على العصور ما قبل الحديثة، والتي سبقتها دراسة أخرى وإن ركزت على تجارب الطفولة في السيرة الذاتية العربية، هي كتاب تيتز رووكي بعنوان في طفولتي: دراسة في السيرة الذاتية العربية (١٩٩٧)، وقد صدرت منه ترجمة إلى اللغة العربية (٢٠٠٩). هذا، ولا يستند كتاب رووكي إلى تاريخ السيرة الذاتية العربية في سياقها وامتدادها التاريخي، بل يتناول تجارب الطفولة من منظور النظريات الغربية حول السيرة الذاتية بوصفها نوعاً أدبياً، وأهم الموضوعات التي تطرقت لها السِيَر المتضمنة في الدراسة. ولذا، تظل دراسة رينولدز هي الأهم، حيث تؤرخ للسيرة الذاتية العربية في سياقها التاريخي والاجتماعي، دون فرض الأطر النظرية الغربية عليها، بل التحرر منها وعدم تقييم السيرة الذاتية العربية من منطلقاتها. ومن هنا، يستهل رينولدز كتابه بتأكيد أن تاريخ كتابات السيرة الذاتية العربية يعود إلى أكثر من ألف عام، ويحدد نشأتها خلال القرن التاسع الميلادي منبثقة من رحم أدب التراجم والسير، مفنّداً من ثم المقولات الراسخة في النقد الغربي بشأن نشأة السيرة الذاتية في أوروبا (كما ادّعى جورج جوسدورف Gusdorf، على سبيل المثال)، بل ارتباطها بالثقافة الغربية المسيحية (كما أشار باسكال، على سبيل المثال)، ليحطم من ثم ما يعدّه أكذوبة أصل السيرة الذاتية بوصفها نوعاً أدبياً أوروبياً انتشر لاحقاً شرقاً وغرباً (Reynolds 17-18).

وحين يتناول رينولدز تاريخ السيرة الذاتية العربية، يشير إلى ما هو مكتوب باللغة العربية منذ القرن التاسع حتى القرن التاسع عشر الميلادي. ولا يكتفي بتحليل تلك النصوص لتسليط الضوء على جوانب السيرة الذاتية فيها، وإنما يحرص أيضاً على تجاوز حدود النوع الأدبي التي صاغها مؤرّخو السيرة الذاتية الغربية في سياقها الأوروبي.[2] كما يفرد باباً كاملاً في كتابه لنصوص سيرة ذاتية عربية مترجمة إلى اللغة الإنجليزية، تتضمن كلاً من: حنين بن إسحق (ق ٩)، الترمذي (نهايات ق ٩ وبدايات ق ١٠)، المؤيد الشيرازي (بدايات ق ١١)، عماد الدين الكاتب الأصفهاني (نهايات ق ١٢)، عبد اللطيف البغدادي وابن العديم وأبو شامة (ق ١٢)، ابن السمناني (ق ١٤)، عبد الله الترجمان (ق ١٥)، جلال الدين السيوطي (نهايات ق ١٥)، العيدروس (ق ١٧)، يوسف البحراني (ق

الذي لا يقتصر على التعبير عن تجربة صاحبته الروحانية ، وإنما يتضمن الكثير من خبراتها الحياتية . كما أنه يختلف عن كتاب القديسة جوليانا في كونه لا يبدأ بلحظة متصلة برؤية دينية ، وإنما ينطلق من تجربة زواجها وحياتها المرفهة الباذخة ، ثم تنتقل إلى الحديث عن لحظة الوعي الروحاني التي أصابتها وهي في نهاية الثلاثين من عمرها لتهجر أسرتها وزوجها وتعيش حياة التدين والكفاف . كما تتحدث عن زياراتها الدينية إلى القدس وروما ورحلاتها إلى إسبانيا وألمانيا ، وتصف كثيراً من الشخصيات التي قابلتها والمواقف التي تعرضت لها ، كما تسرد رؤاها الروحانية وحواراتها المتخيلة مع المسيح (Jelinek, *The Tradition* 15-17) . ومن الملاحظ أن أهمية هذا الكتاب لا تقتصر على كونه يقدم رواية امرأة ويعبر عن تجربة امرأة ، ولا في قيمته بوصفه نصاً دينياً يكشف عن لحظة تحول وتمسك وتفان في الفكر والحسّ والفعل الإيماني ، وإنما تسلط جيلينك الضوء هنا على ملامحه بوصفه نصاً أدبياً من حيث بنيته غير الخطية وأسلوبه التحليلي وتركيزه على التجربة الذاتية ومشاعرها وأحداثها الدقيقة (Jelinek, *The Tradition* 17-18) . ولعله من اللافت هنا أن جيلينك لا تعقد مقارنة بين **كتاب مارجيري كيمب واعترافات القديس أوغسطين** ، رغم أن العملين يركزان على الوعي الروحاني وهجر ملذات الحياة في سبيل الحياة الإيمانية ، بينما تحرص على عقد مقارنة بين **كتاب مارجيري كيمب وكتاب القديسة جوليانا رؤى الحب الإلهي** ، فيما يبدو اختياراً واعياً لترسيخ فكرة التيار التاريخي في كتابات السيرة الذاتية النسائية وبداياتها ذات الطابع الروحاني . وهو المنحى الذي تنتهجه جيلينك عبر صفحات كتابها حين تتتبع كتابات النساء الذاتية عبر القرون ، مروراً بالقرن السابع عشر فالثامن عشر فالتاسع عشر ، في كل من بريطانيا والولايات المتحدة الأمريكية . كما أنها لا تكتفي بالتتبع الزماني ، ولكنها تقدم تصنيفاً لمراحل تطور تلك الكتابة ، بين كتابات نفسية ومهنية وتقليدية وإصلاحية ومتمردة ، وتنتهي إلى التركيز على السير الذاتية الأدبية والنِّسْوية (أيْ المعبّرة عن تجارب النضال النِّسْوي من أجل حقوق النساء) في القرن العشرين .

السيرة الذاتية في الثقافة العربية

وإذا كان الاهتمام بتاريخ السيرة الذاتية الغربية قد بدأ منذ بدايات القرن العشرين ، فلم تلقَ السيرة الذاتية العربية اهتماماً نقدياً إلا في أعمال

لتركز على شكل النص وما يقدمه من نموذج لتأريخ الذات واكتشاف النفس (Anderson 17) . وترفض أندرسون النظر إلى **اعترافات القديس أوغسطين** بوصفها نقطة تحول توقفت عندها السيرة الذاتية لقرون عديدة ، بل تعدّها نصاً ينتمي إلى مسار تاريخي في الكتابة الذاتية ، فلا يمثل قطيعة مع ما سبقه من نصوص في العصور القديمة ، ولا هو متفرد في العصور الوسطى .

السيرة الذاتية النسائية

نشأ التأريخ لكتابات السيرة الذاتية في الغرب في بدايات القرن العشرين ، عند تقاطع الدراسات التاريخية والدراسات الأدبية . ومع تطور الدراسات النسائية والنظرية النِّسوية وتقاطعاتها مع الدراسات الأدبية والتاريخية منذ سبعينيات القرن العشرين ، ظهر اتجاه جديد يؤسس لوجود تيار للكتابة الذاتية النسائية مصاحب لمفاهيم الأدب النسائي وتاريخ النساء . وتعدّ إستيل جيلينك Jelinek من الأصوات المبكرة التي طرحت مسألة وجود تاريخ للسيرة الذاتية النسائية أسّست له في كتابها الرائد **تراث السيرة الذاتية النسائية منذ العصور القديمة حتى اليوم** *The Tradition of Women's Autobiography: From Antiquity to the Present* ، الذي تعيد فيه سرد تاريخ تطور السيرة الذاتية ، مع تسليط الضوء على إسهامات النساء في الكتابة الذاتية عبر التاريخ بما يشكل تاريخاً للسيرة الذاتية النسائية . وهي إذ تنطلق في كتابها من العصور القديمة ، بدءاً من مصر القديمة ، نجدها تسلط الضوء على إحدى أميرات الأسرة الخامسة (حوالي ٢٤٥٠-٢٣٠٠ ق .م .) التي تركت شذرات من صلواتها على جدران مدفنها (Jelinek, The Tradition 11) . وقد تكررت الأصوات النسائية الذاتية في العصرين اليوناني والروماني وبدايات انتشار المسيحية في أوروبا ، وذلك في مساحات التعبير الشعري والروحاني ، وبخاصة كتاب القديسة جوليانا Dame Juliana of Norwich التي عاشت في النصف الثاني من القرن الرابع عشر وتركت كتاباً بعنوان **رؤى الحب الإلهي** *Revelations of Divine Love* يركز على آلام المسيح ، وإن تضمن إشارات ذاتية عن نشأة الكاتبة وتجربتها الروحانية التي روتها بصوتها وأملتها على كاتبها وإن لم تكن قد كتبتها بنفسها لكونها أميّة (Jelinek, The Tradition 14-15) .

ولكن الصوت النسائي الذاتي الأبرز في العصور الوسطى يتضح في كتاب مارجيري كيمب *The Book of Margery Kempe* (١٤٣٦-١٤٣٨)

بينما تؤسس نظرية السيرة الذاتية الغربية نشأة هذا النوع من الكتابة بكتابٍ **اعترافات القديس أوغسطين** (الصادر حوالي ٣٩٨-٤٠٠ م) بوصفه نموذجاً مبكراً للسيرة الذاتية الممتدة إلى العصر الحديث (-Pascal 22-23; Anderson 17 18). إلا أن السيرة الذاتية الحديثة هي نتاج تاريخ طويل من الكتابات الذاتية في الشرق والغرب اتخذت أشكالاً متنوعة عبر الزمان والمكان منذ العصور القديمة، وتناولتها أعمال رائدة في تأريخ السيرة الذاتية. ويوضح روي باسكال Pascal في كتابه المبكر عن السيرة الذاتية وعنوانه **الصنعة والحقيقة في السيرة الذاتية** Design and Truth in Autobiography أن ما يميز **اعترافات القديس أوغسطين**، بوصفها نصاً، كونها تمثل نقطة تحول وعملاً مؤسِّساً لاتجاه جديد في الكتابة الذاتية المتسمة بالآتي: التأثر بالثقافة المسيحية المستندة إلى قيمة الاعتراف، وتقديم الفرد في علاقته بحركة الزمن والتاريخ، جنباً إلى جنب مع الوعي بالنفس البشرية التي تربط بين دواخل الذات والحياة الخارجية، والتأسيس للكتابة الذاتية الأدبية التي تعرض صورة مجازية للذات وهي تدخل حجرة الذاكرة فتلتقط أجزاء الشخصية وتجمعها في سردية كاملة تكشف عن تطور حياة الفرد الروحية، كما يتم تصوير الأحداث بالاستعانة بأدوات الكتابة الأدبية وتفاصيل الزمان والمكان والشخصيات الواقعية والرمزية، وكذلك سيادة صوت المؤلف الراوي البطل العارف بالأحداث وما يصاحبها من أفكار ومشاعر شخصية (Pascal 22-23). وقد ظلت **اعترافات القديس أوغسطين** هي السيرة الذاتية المتكاملة الوحيدة السائدة عبر العصور الوسطى في أوروبا، التي شهدت كتابات ذاتية روحانية عديدة وإن لم تنجح في الجمع بين الأحداث الخارجية وآثارها على الشخصية الدفينة (Pascal 24).

ومن جانبها، تؤكد ليندا أندرسون Anderson على مكانة **اعترافات القديس أوغسطين** بوصفها أصل السيرة الذاتية الغربية الحديثة التي تمثل نقطة بداية تاريخية للسيرة الذاتية من ناحية، ولما صارت تمثله من نموذج يحاكيه الآخرون في نصوص لاحقة (Anderson 17). ولكن أندرسون ترى في ذلك إجحافاً لكثير من الكتابات الذاتية، حيث أدت **اعترافات القديس أوغسطين** إلى تثبيت شكل السيرة الذاتية بوصفها نوعاً أدبياً، خارج أي سياق تاريخي، استناداً إلى ذلك النموذج (Anderson 18). أما أهمية **اعترافات القديس أوغسطين** الكبرى فلا تقترن لدى أندرسون بتجربة الصراع الإنساني مع شروره الدفينة، ولا بالتجربة الروحية والتحول إلى العقيدة المسيحية ومن ثم الاعتراف بخطايا الماضي، وإنما تتجاوز المحتوى

تحليلياً بينياً خلال العقدين الأخيرين ، مع تسليط الضوء على المسارات التي اتخذتها داخل العلوم الإنسانية وعبرها ، وخروجها من حدود علاقة الفرد بالواقع إلى قضايا الذات والتاريخ والمجتمع والسرد . ومن هنا ، تنقسم المقالة إلى ثلاثة محاور أساسية ، تشتمل كل منها على جوانب متعلقة بكتابة الذات من منظور مقارن ، وهي على النحو الآتي . أولا ، «كتابة الذات ونشأة السيرة الذاتية» ، حيث أتتبع تاريخ السيرة الذاتية الغربية ومكانة **اعترافات القديس أوغسطين** The Confessions of Saint Augustine باعتباره نصاً مؤسساً لكتابة السيرة الذاتية الغربية ، ثم ألحقه بقراءة لمفهوم السيرة الذاتية النسائية التي نشأت بوصفها اتجاهاً يسلط الضوء على دور النساء في تاريخ السيرة الذاتية . وأخيراً ، أتناول ضمن هذا المحور تاريخ السيرة الذاتية وموقعها في الأدب العربي . ثانيا ، «مفاهيم نظرية ونقدية مقارنة» ، وأستهل هذا المحور بتناول قضية المصطلح لأعرض مصطلح السيرة الذاتية بوصفه مفهوماً محدداً في النظرية الأدبية ، وكذلك في تقاطعاته مع مصطلحات أخرى تتصل بكتابة الذات والحياة . وحين أتناول قضية المصطلح ، فإني أنظر إليها في إطار نظرية السيرة الذاتية الغربية ، وكذلك في إطار الدراسات العربية . ثم أنطلق إلى عرض نظرية السيرة الذاتية وأهم قضاياها وتياراتها وإسهاماتها في العلوم الإنسانية والاجتماعية على مدار العقود الماضية . ثالثا ، «اتجاهات جديدة في كتابة الذات» ، حيث أركز هنا على أهم الاتجاهات المتبلورة والآخذة في التشكل منذ تسعينيات القرن العشرين ، ومنها السيرة الذاتية والنظرية النسْوية ، والسيرة الذاتية ما بعد الكولونيالية ، وكتابة الحياة وسردية الحياة ، ورواية الذات ، وأنهي هذا المحور بسيرة رضوى عاشور الذاتية التي تجمع في حد ذاتها بين كتابة الذات والرؤية النقدية للسيرة الذاتية بوصفها نوعاً أدبياً . وفي خاتمة المقالة ، أتطرق إلى أهمية الاتجاهات الجديدة في كتابة الذات ، وأدعو إلى أن تواكب الحركة النقدية العربية تدفق الكتابة الإبداعية .

كتابة الذات ونشأة السيرة الذاتية

سردية البدايات : «اعترافات القديس أوغسطين»

ربما ترجع أولى كتابات السيرة الذاتية إلى الرسائل المحفورة في المعابد والجدران المصرية القديمة (Jelinek, *The Tradition* 11) ، كما أن التراث العربي حافل بكتابات ذاتية تعود إلى القرن التاسع الميلادي وتمتد إلى الحاضر ،

من «السيرة الذاتية» إلى «كتابة الحياة»: مسارات وتقاطعات عبر العلوم الإنسانية والاجتماعية

هالة كمال

تتناول هذه المقالة كتابة الذات بوصفها مفهوماً انطلق مع صياغة مصطلح «السيرة الذاتية» الذي نشأ في العلوم الإنسانية وتبلور في نظرية معرفية، هي «نظرية السيرة الذاتية» Autobiography Theory، الآخذة في التطور منذ بدايات القرن العشرين على هامش الدراسات التاريخية والأدبية. وتنطلق المقالة من قناعة بأن الموقع الهامشي والبيني لكتابة الذات أتاح لهذا النوع الأدبي مساحات للتطور داخل الإنسانيات وعبرها. ومن هنا، تسعى هذه المقالة إلى تقصي مسارات السيرة الذاتية بوصفها نوعاً أدبياً مستقراً، وإن ظل واقعاً على هامش الدراسات الإنسانية والاجتماعية، رغم - وربما بفعل - تقاطعاته مع الكتابة التاريخية كأدب التراجم، ومع الإبداع الأدبي كفن الرواية. هذا، وتوضح هذه المقالة السيرة الذاتية بوصفها نوعاً أدبياً يحتل مساحة بينية داخل العلوم الإنسانية، وما شهدته من تطورات في مساراتها، محافظةً على سماتها البينية مع عبور الحدود بين الإنسانيات والعلوم الاجتماعية. وقد أدى ذلك إلى نشأة مفاهيم جديدة مثل «كتابة الحياة» Life-Writing بوصفها مساحة بينية أشمل، تتجاوز نقاط التلاقي داخل الدراسات الإنسانية بين الرواية والسيرة والتاريخ، لتنقل دراسات السيرة الذاتية إلى مجال أرحب يتجاوز حدود النص إلى مجال الخطاب الثقافي، ويتماس مع العلوم الاجتماعية وسياسات الهُويّة والتجربة والذاكرة والمعرفة والفاعلية، على سبيل المثال لا الحصر، وما صاحب ذلك من ظهور تيارات واتجاهات جديدة تتجاوز حدود الأنواع الأدبية التقليدية وتزعزع منهجياتها المستقرة وتطرح أشكالاً جديدة من التعبير عن الذات.

وتهدف المقالة إلى ملء فجوة في دراسات السيرة الذاتية المقارنة في الثقافتين الأنجلوفونية والعربية، بتسليط الضوء على البدايات والمسارات من منظور مقارن.[1] ومن هنا، تتناول المقالة بدايات السيرة الذاتية autobiography، نظرية وممارسةً، ثم تركز على المسارات التي اتخذتها بوصفها نوعاً أدبياً ومنهجاً

Mehrez, Samia. "Translating Gender." *Journal of Middle East Women's Studies* 3.1 (Winter 2007): 106-27.

Moghadam, Valentine M. "Islamic Feminism And Its Discontents: Toward A Resolution of the Debate." *Signs: Journal of Women in Culture and Society* 27.4 (2002): 1135-71.

Mohanty, Chandra Talpade. "Under Western Eyes: Feminist Scholarship and Colonial Discourses." *Boundary 2* 12/13 (Spring-Autumn 1984): 333–58.

El Nossery, Nevine. "Women, Art, and Revolution in the Streets of Egypt." *Women's Movements in Post-"Arab Spring" North Africa*. Ed. Fatima Sadiqi. London: Palgrave Macmillan, 2016. 143-57.

Olimat, Muhamad S. *Arab Spring and Arab Women: Challenges and Opportunities*. London: Routledge, 2013.

"On 'Why Do They Hate Us?' and Its Critics. *The Arabist*. April 29, 2012. <https://urlzs.com/qw5oy>.

Revisiting Archive in the Aftermath of Revolution, Haus der Kulturen der Welt, Berlin (Lecture Hall), October 26-28, 2018. <https://urlzs.com/8k7R3>.

Roy, Arundhati. *The God of Small Things*. NY: Random House, 1997.

Sadiqi, Fatima, ed. *Women's Movements in Post-"Arab Spring" North Africa*. London: Palgrave Macmillan, 2016.

Said, Edward. *Orientalism*. NY: Pantheon Books, 1978.

---. *The World, the Text, and the Critic*. London: Faber and Faber, 1983.

El Said, Maha, Lena Meari, and Nicola Pratt, eds. *Rethinking Gender in Revolutions and Resistance: Lessons from the Arab World*. London: Zed Books, 2015.

Shalaby, Marwa and Valentine M. Moghadam, eds. *Empowering Women after the Arab Spring*. NY: Palgrave Macmillan: 2016.

Shamsie, Kamila. *Broken Verses*. NY: Mariner Books, 2005.

Spivak, G. C. "Can the Subaltern Speak?" *Marxism and the Interpretation of Culture*. Eds. Cary Nelson and Lawrence Grossberg. Baskingstoke: Macmillan Education, 1988. 271-313.

Tadros, M. *Resistance, Revolt, and Gender Justice in Egypt*. Syracuse: Syracuse UP, 2016.

Tucker, Judith. *Women in Nineteenth-Century Egypt*. Cambridge and NY: Cambridge UP, 2002.

Wadud, Amina. *Qur'an and Woman: Rereading the Sacred Text from a Woman's Perspective*. NY: Oxford UP, 1999.

Zeidan, Joseph T. *Arab Women Novelists: The Formative Years and Beyond*. Albany, NY: State U of Albany P, 1995.

hooks, bell. "Essentialism and Experience." *American Literary History* 3.1 (Spring 1991): 172–83.

---. *Feminist Theory: From Margin to Centre*. Boston: South End P, 1984.

Jayawardina, Kumari. *Feminism and Nationalism in the Third World*. London: Zed Books, 1986.

Kahf, Mohja. *E-mails from Scheherazad*. Gainesville: UP Florida, 2003.

---. *The Girl in the Tangerine Scarf*. NY: Carroll & Graf: 2006.

Kamal, Hala. "A Feminist Autobiography: *Teta, Mother and Me, An Arab Woman's Memoir*" [Review]. *Al- Ra'ida, Arab Diaspora Women* 27.116-17 (Winter/Spring 2007): 82-84.

---. " In Search of Fatima: A Palestinian Story." *Al- Ra'ida* 126-127 (Summer/Fall 2009): 94-97.

---. "Translating Women and Gender: The Experience of Translating the *Encyclopedia of Women and Islamic Cultures* into Arabic." *Women's Studies Quarterly* 36.3&4 (Fall and Winter 2008): 254-68.

---. "'Women's Writing on Women's Writing': Mayy Ziyada's Literary Biographies as Egyptian Feminist History." *Women's Writing* 25.2 (2018): 268-87.

Kandiyoti, Deniz. "Disentangling Religion and Politics: Whither Gender Equality?" *IDS Bulletin* 42.1 (January 2011): 10-14.

---. "Disquiet and Despair: The Gender Sub-Texts of the 'Arab Spring.'" *Open Democracy*. June 26, 2012. <https://www.opendemocracy.net/en/5050/disquiet-and-despair-gender-sub-texts-of-arab-spring/>.

---. *Gendering the Middle East: Emerging Perspectives*. NY: Syracuse UP, 1996.

---. "Guest Editor's Introduction: The Awkward Relationship: Gender and Nationalism." *Nations and Nationalism* 6.4 (2000): 491-94.

---. "Promise and Peril: Women and the 'Arab Spring.'" *Open Democracy*. March 8, 2011. <https://urlzs.com/aVGrA>.

---. "The Triple Whammy: Towards the Eclipse of Women's rights." *Open Democracy*. January 19, 2015. <https://urlzs.com/ig6yH>.

Khalil, Andrea, ed. *Gender, Women and the Arab Spring*. London and NY: Routledge, 2014.

Kristeva, Julia. "Women's Time." Trans. Alice Jardine and Harry Blake. *Signs* 7.1 (Autumn 1981): 13–35.

de Lauretis, Teresa. *Alice Doesn't: Feminism, Semiotics, Cinema*. Bloomington, IN: Indiana University Press, 1984.

Majaj, Lisa Suhair et al. *Intersections: Gender, Nation and Community in Arab Women's Novels*. Syracuse, NY: Syracuse UP, 2002.

Makdisi, Jean Said. *Beirut Fragments: A War Memoir*. NY: Persea Books, 1990.

--- and Nicola Pratt. *What kind of Liberation? Women and the Occupation in Iraq*. Berkeley: U of California P, 2009.

Alif: Journal of Comparative Poetics 19 (1999). Special issue on "Gender and Knowledge: Contribution of Gender Perspectives to Intellectual Formations."

Alif: Journal of Comparative Poetics 22 (2002). Special issue on "The Language of the Self: Autobiographies and Testimonies."

Arendt, Hannah. *The Human Condition*. Chicago: Chicago UP, 1958.

Ashour, Radwa, et al. "Arab Women Writers." Trans. Mandy McClure. *Southwest Review* 94.1 (2009): 9–18.

Butler, Judith. *Bodies that Matter: On the Discursive Limits of "Sex."* NY: Routledge, 1993.

---. *Gender Trouble: Feminism and the Subversion of Identity*. NY: Routledge, 1990.

Conrad, Joseph. *Heart of Darkness*. Eds. O. Knowles and A. Simmons. Cambridge: Cambridge UP, 2018.

Elsadda, Hoda. "Egypt: The Battle over Hope and Morale." *Open Democracy*. November 2, 2011. <https://www.opendemocracy.net/en/5050/egypt-battle-over-hope-and-morale/>.

---. *Gender, Nation and the Arabic Novel: Egypt 1892-2008*. Syracuse and Edinburgh: Syracuse UP and Edinburgh UP, 2012.

---. "Travelling Critique: Anti-imperialism, Gender and Rights Discourses." *Feminist Dissent* 3 (2018): 88-113.

---. "A War against Women: The CSW Declaration and the Muslim Brotherhood Riposte." *Open Democracy*. April 3, 2013. <https://www.opendemocracy.net/en/5050/war-against-women-csw-declaration-and-muslim-brotherhood-riposte/>.

Eltahawy, Mona. "Why Do You Hate Us?" *Foreign Policy*. April 23, 2012. <http://foreignpolicy.com/2012/04/23/why-do-they-hate-us/>.

El-Gawhary, Karim and Heba Ra'uf Ezzat. "An Interview with Heba Ra'uf Ezzat." *Middle East Report* 191 (November-December 1994): 26–27.

Ghoussoub, Mai. *Imagined Masculinities: Male Identity and Culture in the Modern Middle East*. Beirut: Saqi, 2000.

Habermas, Jürgen. "Modernity - An Incomplete Project." *The Anti-Aesthetic: Essays on Postmodern Culture*. Ed. Hal Foster. NY: The New P, 1998.

Hall, Stuart. "Cultural Identity and Diaspora." *Colonial Discourse and Post-Colonial Theory: A Reader*. Eds. Patrick Williams and Laura Chrisman. London: Harvester Wheatsheaf, 1994. 227-37.

«معهد دراسات المرأة» . **فيسبوك** . ‹ https://urlzs.com/LzUyH › .

المقدسي ، جين سعيد ، نهى بيومي ورفيف صيداوي ، تحرير . **النسوية العربية : رؤية نقدية** . بيروت : مركز دراسات الوحدة العربية ، ٢٠١٢ .

المقطري ، بشرى . **ماذا تركت وراءك؟ أصوات من بلاد الحرب المنسية** . بيروت : رياض الريس للكتب والنشر ، ٢٠١٨ .

«من نحن» ، **تجمع الباحثات اللبنانيات** . ٢٠١٥ . ‹ https://urlzs.com/yLs1N › .

«من نحن» . **المرأة والذاكرة** . ‹ https://urlzs.com/DacPa › .

«من نحن» . **مؤسسة المرأة الجديدة** . ‹ https://urlzs.com/BsxjK › .

يزبك ، سمر . **تسع عشرة امرأة : سوريات يروين** . ميلانو : منشورات المتوسط ، ٢٠١٨ .

المراجع الأجنبية

Abou-Bakr, Omaima. 'The interpretive Legacy of *Qiwamah* as an Exegetical Construct." *Men in Charge? Rethinking Authority in Muslim Legal Tradition*. Eds. Ziba Mir-Hosseini, Mulki Al-Sharmani, and Jana Rumminger. Oxford: One World, 2015. 44–64.

---. 'Turning the Tables: Perspectives on the Construction of 'Muslim manhood.'" *Hawwa: Journal of Women of the Middle East and the Islamic World* 11 (2013): 89–107.

Abouelnaga, Shereen. *Women in Revolutionary Egypt: Gender and the New Geographies of Identity*. Cairo: AUC P, 2016.

Aboulela, Leila. *Minaret*. NY: Black Cat, Grove/Atlantic, 2005.

Abu-Lughod, Lila. *Do Muslim Women Need Saving?* Cambridge, Mass.: Harvard UP, 2013.

---, ed. *Remaking Women: Feminism and Modernity in the Middle East*. Princeton, NJ: Princeton UP, 1998.

Ahmed, Leila. *A Border Passage: From Cairo to America – A Woman's Journey*. NY: Farrar Straus & Giroux, 1999.

---. *Women and Gender in Islam: Historical Roots of a Modern Debate*. New Haven and London: Yale UP: 1992.

Ahmed, Sara. *The Cultural Politics of Emotion*. London and NY: Routledge, 2004.

Al-Ali, Nadje. *Iraqi Women: Untold Stories From 1948 to the Present*. London; NY: Zed Books, 2007.

الطريقي، أنس. «تقديم ملف النسوية الإسلامية». مؤمنون بلا حدود. ١٣ يونيو، ٢٠١٦. ص ص ٣-٥.

عابدين، سارة ومروة أبو ضيف. وبيننا حديقة. القاهرة: دار روافد، ٢٠١٧.

عاشور، رضوى. أثقل من رضوى. القاهرة: دار الشروق، ٢٠١٣.

«عن الجمعية». جمعية دراسات المرأة والحضارة. ٢٠١٠.
⟨ http://www.aswic.net/about.aspx ⟩.

«عن كحل». كحل: مجلة لأبحاث الجسد والجندر.
⟨ https://kohljournal.press/ar/about ⟩.

فصول: مجلة النقد الأدبي عدد ٣، مجلد ٢٦ (ربيع ٢٠١٨). عدد بعنوان «الدراسات النسوية».

«قالت الراوية». المرأة والذاكرة. ⟨ goo.gl/Wfvqu3 ⟩.

القلماوي، سهير. «المرأة في ألف ليلة وليلة». ألف ليلة وليلة. القاهرة: دار المعارف، ١٩٥٩. ص ص ٢٩٧-٣١٩.

كمال، دنيا. سيجارة سابعة. القاهرة: دار ميريت، ٢٠١٢.

كمال، هالة. «قالت الراوية: تقديم». قالت الراوية: حكايات من وجهة نظر المرأة من وحي نصوص شعبية عربية. تحرير هالة كمال. القاهرة: مؤسسة المرأة والذاكرة، ١٩٩٩. ص ص ٧-٧٤.

---. «مقدمة». مدخل إلى البحث النسوي ممارسة وتطبيقاً. تحرير شارلين ناجي هيسي-بايبر وباتريشا لينا ليفي. ترجمة هالة كمال. القاهرة: المركز القومي للترجمة، ٢٠١٥.

---. «مقدمة: النقد الأدبي النسوي والترجمة النسوية». النقد الأدبي النسوي. تحرير وترجمة هالة كمال. القاهرة: مؤسسة المرأة والذاكرة، ٢٠١٥. ص ص ٩-٥٥.

المرابط، أسماء. القرآن والنساء. المغرب: الرابطة المحمدية للعلماء، ٢٠١٠.

مرسال، إيمان. كيف تلتئم: عن الأمومة وأشباحها. القاهرة: كيف ت، ٢٠١٧.

المرنيسي، فاطمة. الحريم السياسي: النبي والنساء. دمشق: دار الحصاد، ١٩٩٣.

---. الخوف من الحداثة: الإسلام والديمقراطية. دمشق: دار الجندي، ١٩٩٥.

---. نساء على أجنحة الحلم. بيروت: المركز الثقافي العربي، ١٩٩٨.

---. هل أنتم محصنون ضد النساء؟ ترجمة نهلة بيضون. بيروت: المركز الثقافي العربي، ٢٠٠٤.

مستغانمي، أحلام. ذاكرة الجسد. بيروت: دار الآداب، ١٩٩٣.

بدر، عبد المحسن طه. **تطور الرواية العربية الحديثة**. القاهرة: دار المعارف، ١٩٦٣.

البصري، عائشة. **الحياة من دوني**. القاهرة: مكتبة الدار العربية للكتاب، ٢٠١٨.

بن سلامة، رجاء. **نقد الثوابت: آراء في العنف والتمييز والمصادرة**. بيروت: دار الطليعة ورابطة العقلانيين العرب، ٢٠٠٥.

بنمسعود، رشيدة. **المرأة والكتابة: سؤال الخصوصية/ بلاغة الاختلاف**. الدار البيضاء: أفريقيا الشرق، ١٩٩٤.

التلمساني، مي. **دنيا زاد**. القاهرة: دار شرقيات، ١٩٩٧.

خليفة، إجلال. **الحركة النسائية الحديثة**. القاهرة: المجلس الأعلى للثقافة، ٢٠١٧.

خليل، هالة، إخراج. **نوارة**. شركة ريد ستار، ٢٠١٥.

ذاكرة للمستقبل: موسوعة الكاتبة العربية. تحرير أمينة رشيد وآخرين. ثلاثة مجلدات. القاهرة: المجلس الأعلى للثقافة ومؤسسة نور، ٢٠٠٣.

الراضوي، نائلة السليني. **تاريخية التفسير القرآني**. بيروت: المركز الثقافي العربي، ٢٠٠٢.

الرايس، حياة. **جسد المرأة من سلطة الإنس إلى سلطة الجان**. القاهرة: دار سينا للنشر، ١٩٩٥.

رمضان، سمية. **أوراق النرجس**. القاهرة: دار شرقيات، ٢٠٠١.

الزيات، لطيفة. **الباب المفتوح**. القاهرة: الهيئة المصرية العامة للكتاب، ١٩٨٩.

---. **حملة تفتيش في أوراق شخصية**. القاهرة: دار الهلال، ١٩٩٢.

---. «شهادة مبدعة». **أدب ونقد** ١٣٥ (نوفمبر ١٩٩٦): ص ص ١٧-٢١.

---. **من صور المرأة في القصص والروايات العربية**. القاهرة: دار الثقافة الجديدة، ١٩٨٩.

السعداوي، نوال. **أوراقي... حياتي**. بيروت: دار الآداب، ٢٠٠٠.

---. **مذكرات طبيبة**. القاهرة: دار المعارف، ١٩٨٥.

سليمان، منيرة. «تأملات في ما لم تقله شهرزاد: من الإبداع إلى الأداء». **ألف** ٣٩ (٢٠١٩): ص ص ١٥٢-١٧٢.

صالح، الطيب. **موسم الهجرة إلى الشمال**. بيروت: دار العودة، ١٩٨٧.

الصدة، هدى، تحرير وتقديم. **الفتاة لصاحبتها هند نوفل ١٨٩٢**. القاهرة: مؤسسة المرأة والذاكرة، ٢٠٠٧.

--- وعماد أبو غازي. **مسيرة المرأة المصرية: علامات ومواقف**. القاهرة: المجلس القومي للمرأة، ٢٠٠١.

الطحاوي، ميرال. **الخباء**. القاهرة: دار شرقيات، ١٩٩٦.

⁹ ضم هذا الكتاب تسعة وثلاثين بحثاً ، كانت جميعها قد قدمت خلال مؤتمر عقد في الجامعة الأمريكية في بيروت عام ٢٠٠٩ . نظم المؤتمر تجمع الباحثات اللبنانيات بالتعاون مع ملتقى المرأة والذاكرة في القاهرة ، ومعهد الدراسات النسائية في جامعة بيرزيت في فلسطين المحتلة ، وبرنامج أنيس المقدسي للآداب في الجامعة الأمريكية في بيروت .

¹⁰ على سبيل المثال ، قام المجلس العربي للعلوم الاجتماعية بتنظيم ورشة عمل تدريبية باللغة العربية بعنوان «منهجيات البحث في التاريخ الشفوي من منظور الجندر» ، من ١٧ إلى ١٩ يونيو ٢٠١٩ في بيروت ، لبنان .

المراجع العربية

أبو بكر ، أميمة . «التراث التفسيري لمفهوم القوامة بوصفه صياغة تأويلية» . **القوامة في التراث الإسلامي : قراءات بديلة** . تحرير زيبا مير حسيني ، ملكي الشرماني ، جانا رامينجر . ترجمة رندة أبوبكر . القاهرة : بروموشن تيم ، ٢٠١٦ .

أبو زيد ، ليلى . **رجوع إلى الطفولة** . الرباط : المدارس ، ١٩٩٣ .

--- . **عام الفيل** . بيروت : المركز الثقافي العربي ، ٢٠١١ .

أبو زيد ، نصر حامد . **دوائر الخوف : قراءة في خطاب المرأة** . بيروت والدار البيضاء : المركز الثقافي العربي ، ٢٠٠٤ .

--- . **المرأة في خطاب الأزمة** . القاهرة : دار نصوص ، ١٩٩٤ .

أبو النجا ، شيرين . **عاطفة الاختلاف : قراءة في كتابات نسوية** . القاهرة : الهيئة المصرية العامة للكتاب، ١٩٩٨ .

أحمد ، ليلى . **المرأة والجنوسة في الإسلام : الجذور التاريخية لقضية جدلية حديثة** . ترجمة منى إبراهيم وهالة كمال . القاهرة : المجلس الأعلى للثقافة ، ١٩٩٩ .

«أدب الاعترافات حرام» . أخبار الأدب . ٢٧ يوليو ، ١٩٩٧ . ص ٣ .

ألف : **مجلة البلاغة المقارنة** ١٩ (١٩٩٩) . عدد بعنوان «الجنوسة والمعرفة : صياغة المعارف بين التأنيث والتذكير» .

ألف : **مجلة البلاغة المقارنة** ٢٢ (٢٠٠٢) . عدد بعنوان «لغة الذات : السير الذاتية والشهادات» .

أمين ، نورا . **قميص وردي فارغ** . القاهرة : دار شرقيات ، ١٩٩٧ .

العربي ، فقد عانت النسويات كثيراً من نظرة الاستخفاف الأكاديمية والمجتمعية . لكن مع الدأب والمثابرة في الإنتاج المعرفي والبحثي والعمل العام ، قامت مجلة فصولٍ ، المعروفة بصرامتها الأكاديمية ، بتخصيص عدد كامل للنسوية ، مثلاً (٢٠١٨) . وبعد أن كانت النساء يُوصمن بتغليب العاطفة والمشاعر ، تحولت العاطفة إلى أحد العوامل التحليلية ، كما أكدت سارة أحمد S. Ahmed في كتابها **السياسات الثقافية للعاطفة** *The Cultural Politics of Emotion* (٢٠٠٤) .

الهوامش

[1] في المجمل ، تنطلق المقالة دائماً من مصر ، مع محاولة التأشير على كافة الجهود اللافتة للنظر في بلدان أخرى .

[2] الاسم الحقيقي للكاتبة المصرية أليفة رفعت (١٩٣٠-١٩٩٦) هو فاطمة رفعت .

[3] في عام ١٩٩٣ ، تأسست جمعية نور - دار المرأة العربية للنشر في القاهرة وبيروت ، لتوفير منبر لطرح قضايا نسوية عربية ، وذلك من خلال أبحاث وورش عمل ، وكذلك عبر إصدار نشرة **نور** المتخصصة في التعريف بأحدث الإصدارات النسوية وتقديم مراجعات لكتب .

[4] كان هذا التشظي والتقوقع على الذات إحدى سمات كتابة جيل التسعينيات .

[5] وهو ما أدى إلى تعميق الخلط بين البحثي والتنموي ، فكل ما كان يتناول النساء كان يندرج تحت مظلة «دراسات المرأة» .

[6] في وقت مبكر للغاية ، وعلى وجه التحديد عام ١٩٧٣ ، تأسس معهد الدراسات النسائية في العالم العربي التابع للجامعة اللبنانية الأمريكية بهدف إنجاز بحوث أكاديمية عن النساء في العالم العربي . ويسعى المعهد إلى تحقيق مجموعة من الأهداف ، من بينها تعزيز مكانة النساء في العالم العربي عبر إعداد برامج تنموية وتعليمية ، ودعم تغيير السياسات المتعلقة بحقوق المرأة في المنطقة ، والانخراط في البحوث الأكاديمية التي تتناول موضوع النساء في العالم العربي ، وإدخال الدراسات النسائية في مقررات الجامعة اللبنانية .

[7] لفهم فلسفة المشروع والمسار الذي تبناه ، انظر ، «قالت الراوية» ؛ كمال ، «قالت الراوية» ؛ سليمان .

[8] يبدو هذا المصطلح - المنحدر من دراسات ما بعد الاستعمار - وكأنه يحل مؤخراً محل مصطلح «العالم الثالث» .

كان للثورات العربية تأثير كبير في الرؤية البحثية الغربية التي لم تكن تجد غضاضة في احتكار الحديث عن الآخر ونيابةً عنه. ومن ثم، فإن الغرب الذي دأب على قراءة المجتمعات العربية، وقراءة حياة النساء بوصفهن مؤشراً ثقافياً دالاً، لم يعد في استطاعته أن يستمر في ذلك بعد أن شهد الإرادة والصوت متجسدين في مواقع الثورة. بمعنى آخر، توقف الغرب بشكل كبير عن الكتابة عن المجتمع العربي، وبدأ يكتب معه. إلى حد كبيرٍ، لم يعد العالم العربي يمثل مادة خاماً للبحث، ولكنه أصبح مشاركاً في إنتاج المعرفة، وبخاصة بعد صعود دراسات الثقافة الدارجة. في كل كتابٍ محرر في الغرب عن «نساء العالم العربي/ الإسلامي» نجد أصواتاً بحثية من المنطقة تسهم في تشكيل الرؤية (انظرٍ مثلاً Olimat; Khalil; Shalaby and Moghadam). وكأن هناك توجهاً جديداً فرضه الشرط الموضوعي على الرؤية البحثية التي ترغب في حيازة قيمة نفعية. لا بد أيضاً أن نأخذ في الاعتبار انتعاش دينامية العلاقة بين المحلي والعولمي، أو الخصوصية الثقافية والعالمية التي تنطلق معرفياً وإمبريقياً من مفهوم ارتحال النظرية، وهذا التفاعل هو ما تحول إلى أحد موضوعات البحث أيضاً، كما ترى الصدة Elsadda في مقالتها بعنوان «النقد المرتحل» "Travelling Critique".

حاولت هذه المقالة - بقدر المستطاع - التغلب على التحديات الكامنة أمام تقديم توصيف معرفي دقيق لوضع دراسات الجندر والنسوية في مجال العلوم الإنسانية في العالم العربي. إلا أنها تحديات صعبة، ولا يمكن تجاوزها إلا إذا أخذنا في الاعتبار عدة عوامل. فأولاً، هناك قدرة البحث النسوي على التجاوب مع السيولة الشديدة للمشهد السياسي والمجتمعي في المنطقة، ومن ثم فهو يُطور من آلياته ومنهجياته وموضوعاته بشكلٍ مستمر لتزدهر مثلاً الدراسات التي تتناول ذاتية اللاجئات. وثانياً، أصبحت دراسات الجندر واضحة تماماً في كل مناهج العلوم الإنسانية في العالم العربي، بالإضافة إلى توالي ظهور برامج مخصصة لها. أما أخيراً، وهو ما يتوجب أن نمنحه أهمية كبيرة، فإن ما وقع في العالم العربي من تغييرات جذرية قد ساعد البحث النسوي على التقريب بين النظرية والواقع، مما ساعد على زيادة الإنتاج البحثي، وازدياد التشبيك بين المؤسسات بشكل ملحوظ. في النهاية، لا بد أن نتذكر كم كانت الرحلة صعبة وغير ممهدة إطلاقاً أمام الفكر النسوي في العالم

العربي الإسلامي» ، والثاني في عام ٢٠١٩ بعنوان «سوسيولوجيا الجسد» . أما على المستوى النظري ، فقد بدأت الأبحاث النسوية تتعامل مع الجسد الأنثوي بوصفه أحد العوامل التي تُشكل الذاتية ، ومن هنا كانت نظرية الأدائية لجوديث باتلر مفيدة بوصفها مدخلاً .

إلا أن شهادات النساء لم تكتف بالجسد الذي تحول إلى طرف رئيسي في علاقات القوى ، بل امتدتَ لتكشف عن أهوال الاعتقال والحروب . فأصدرت مثلا الكاتبة السورية سمر يزبك كتاباً يضم شهادات نساء كُنَّ يناضلن ضد النظام وعنوانه **تسع عشرة امرأة : سوريات يروين** (٢٠١٨) ، وأصدرت المناضلة اليمنية بشرى المقطري كتاباً مماثلاً عنوانه **ماذا تركت وراءك؟ أصوات من بلاد الحرب المنسية** (٢٠١٨) . انتشرت شهادات النساء في أماكن النزاع المسلح ، وبدأت مصطلحات جديدة تدخل في نطاق البحث النسوي مثل «عبور الحدود» و«رحلة اللجوء» . وفي عام ٢٠١٨ ، حصلت رواية **الحياة من دوني** للكاتبة المغربية عائشة البصري على جائزة أفضل كتاب عربي في مجال الرواية في معرض كتاب الشارقة ، وهي رواية تضم شهادات نساء اغتصبن في الحروب من أماكن متفرقة في العالم . وتحول تأثير الحروب في النساء (وفي أجسادهن ، وبخاصة بعد ما ارتكبته داعش من انتهاكات) إلى سياق يهتم به البحث النسوي من ناحية تأثيره في الذاتية والفاعلية .

أكدت هذه الشهادات وجود أصوات منسية ومهمشة تماماً . ولا يمكن إعادة هذه الأصوات إلى الحياة بدون التعمق في مسألة قراءة الأرشيف ، وهكذا ظهر مؤخراً توجه تقنين مناهج البحث النسوي في الأرشيف . تصاعد توثيق حاضر الثورات العربية ، وبعد خفوتها عاد الاهتمام بالماضي ، ليمثل البحث في الأرشيف فعلاً من أفعال المقاومة ضد الإقصاء والتهميش اللذين تمارسهما السلطات الحاكمة من ناحية والسلطة البحثية من ناحية أخرى . وقد تنبه الباحثون لذلك ، فعقد بيت ثقافات العالم في برلين ندوة على مدار يومين في عام ٢٠١٨ بعنوان «إعادة قراءة الأرشيف إثر الثورات» . ويلفت النظر في برنامج الندوة البحث الذي قدمته الباحثة اللبنانية لمياء مغنية حول إعادة قراءة وثائق مستشفى الاضطرابات النفسية والعصبية في لبنان (انظر *Revisiting*) . وفي هذا السياق ، يمثل عمل مؤسسة المرأة والذاكرة الذي ينطلق من إعادة البحث في الأرشيف فعلاً مقاوماً . كما أصبحت المنهجيات النسوية لقراءة الأرشيف أحد المواضيع الرئيسية التي تدور حولها ورش العمل .[١٠]

مع الواقع المادي . كما عمد البحث النسوي إلى تقديم قراءة ثقافية لمدلول الجسد ، مع إعادة الاستعانة بنظريات ما بعد البنيوية ، وبخاصة ما قدمه ميشيل فوكو Foucault . كما أدت الثورات إلى تسليط الضوء على أهمية نظرية التقاطع التي تأخذ في الاعتبار الجندر مقترناً بعوامل أخرى كالطبقة والقومية والدين واللون .

لم يعد النص والنقد منفصلين ، وكأن الحراك الثوري قد أسهم في تقليص الفجوة بين الأكاديمي والناشط ، بين النظرية والممارسة . إلا أن كل ذلك لم يمنع مجموعة من الباحثات النسويات أن يعدن تقييم الأمر كله ، من أجل مواكبة المتغيرات على الساحة العربية ، فصدر كتاب **النسوية العربية : رؤية نقدية** عام ٢٠١٢ ، وهو من تحرير جين سعيد المقدسي ونهى بيومي ورفيف صيداوي .[9] يضم الكتاب أربعة فصول ، هي : «تنوع المقاربات والمفاهيم في الخطاب النسوي» ، «معضلة التسوية في سياق الحروب والنزاعات» ، «مقاربات ورؤى حول "النسوية الإسلامية"» ، «النسوية في سياق معولم» . دفع الحراك الثوري الباحثين والباحثات إلى تبنّي مناهج الدراسات البينية والنقد الثقافي ، وتولدت رؤى بحثية جديدة دفعت بالخطاب النسوي إلى الوقوف على قدم المساواة مع الواقع الاجتماعي والسياسي . بيد أن تدفق الحديث حول توظيف السلطة للجسد وتدفق شهادات النساء شجع منتديات بحثية على الظهور . فعلى سبيل المثال ، تأسست **كحل : مجلة لأبحاث الجسد والجندر** في عام ٢٠١٤ في بيروت ، وهي مجلة نصف سنوية نِسْوية تقدمية عن النوع الاجتماعي والجنسانية في مناطق الشرق الأوسط وجنوب شرق آسيا وشمال أفريقيا . واللافت للنظر أنها أول منتدى يطرح المنهجيات الكويرية . وبالإضافة إلى هدف المجلة في إنتاج معرفة عن الجسد لا تندرج تحت الخطاب الاستشراقي ، «تأمل هذه المجلة أن تغيّر من الهيمنة المسيطرة على التكوين المعرفي ، وأن تضمن لمناطقنا ومجتمعاتنا دوراً محورياً في إعادة تحديد التقاطعات والتحديات الخاصة بها فيما يتعلق بالأبحاث النسوية والجنسانية» («عن **كحل**» ، د . ص .) . تكتسب المجلة أهميتها أيضاً من كونها مصدراً مفتوحاً يتيح كل مواده باللغة العربية . على صعيد آخر ، تلاحق المؤسسات الأكاديمية مسألة دراسة الجسد أيضاً . فعلى سبيل المثال ، أقامت كلية العلوم الاجتماعية بجامعة عبد الحميد بن باديس ، بمستغانم في الجزائر ، مؤتمرين عن الجسد : الأول في عام ٢٠١٢ بعنوان «إشكالية الجسد في الخطاب

مع ازدهار الدراسات البينية والثقافية لتصبح هي المنهج البحثي الرئيسي السائد ، وبتغير شكل المنطقة ، احتلت مسألة الصوت الفردي أهمية في مقابل خطاب الدولة القمعي الشمولي ، وظهرت صفحات ومنتديات ومجموعات مغلقة ومفتوحة على مواقع التواصل الاجتماعي ، وكلها تنتمي إلى جيل صاعد يتبنى خطابا ومفردات مختلفة تماماً ، حيث تُطرح أسئلة عن مسلمات لتكون الإجابة خلخلة لتعريفات المتن السائد . ومن هنا ، أصبحت دراسة الخطاب النسوي - بكل أشكاله التعبيرية - على مواقع التواصل الاجتماعي أحد الموضوعات البحثية الرئيسية .

ولإزاحة الحضور النسائي الكثيف في الفضاء العام ، عمدت السلطة الأبوية إلى توظيف أقدم حيلة دأبت على استخدامها ، وهي هتك الجسد الأنثوي . دأبت علاقات القوى التي تبدأ من أصغر وحدة (العائلة) ، حتى أكبر وحدة (مؤسسات الدولة) على جعل الميزان مائلاً لصالح الرجل ، فتحول الشعور بالتفوق والقوة إلى مرادف للجنس البيولوجي (ذكر = قوة ، امرأة = ضعف) . بدا من الطبيعي لهذا الذكر المتفوق (منحة من المجتمع) أن يعمد إلى التحرش بجسد المرأة ، وبدا له أيضاً أنها توافق على ذلك الفعل في أفضل الأحوال ، أو أنها لن تتمكن من الإتيان برد فعل في أسوئها . وهكذا ، ظل الصمت سائداً من ناحية النساء ، والإنكار هو المسيطر على خطاب المجتمع (أو تكذيب المرأة إذا أعلنت) . لكن الأمور لا تبقى على حالها ، فقد تصاعدت قوة الخطاب النسوي العابر للحدود مع ظهور مصطلح «الجنوب العالمي» "The Global South"،[8] بالإضافة إلى الحراك الثوري الذي أسهم في تشكيل جيل جديد - من النساء والرجال - يحمل وعياً مغايراً ، بل رافضاً ، لوعي أسلافه ، جيل تركزت معركته على كسر حاجز الصمت ، فتغيرت المنظومة الخطابية بأكملها ، وهو أكثر ما يُغضب السلطة الأبوية ، التي لم تتمكن من مواجهة التيار الجارف الذي أعلن بكل وضوح : «أنا أيضاً» "Me too" ، وتدفقت شهادات النساء عن التحرش ، وظهر البحث النسوي الذي يتناول العنف الجنسي ضد النساء (انظر Tadros) . لم يقتصر الأمر على شهادات النساء ، بل ظهر أيضاً في فن الكاريكاتير الذي تحول إلى سلاح بعد عام ٢٠١١ . تعود شهادات الناجيات من العنف إلى احتلال المشهد ، وتتحول إلى نصوص يعكف الباحثون/الباحثات على قراءتها منهجياً ، لتظهر مثلا دراسات الجسد الذي يحل محل النص الأدبي في كونه مؤشراً على تصارع المحمول الثقافي

تستحق التأويل ، بل يؤهله ليكون أداة تحليلية قادرة على تأويل جزء مهم من الموقف السياسي الاجتماعي ، سواء كان قصيدة تخلخل السلطة الأبوية التي تُعيد النساء إنتاجها (كما في كتابة سارة عابدين) ، وتصطدم بالخطاب السلطوي عبر طرح أسئلة جديدة (كما تفعل هدى عمران) ، أو رواية تنطلق من رؤية الذات للمجتمع (كما في سيجارة سابعة لدنيا كمال) ، أو فيلماً يمنح صوتاً لكل من لا صوت له كفيلم نوارة الذي كتبته وأخرجته هالة خليل ، أو صورة تكشف وتقاوم . يحمل النص الجديد أيضا قسوة السؤال ونبرة الاتهام عبر خطاب جذري ، لمِ يُعلن بقوة عن نفسه إثر الثورة مباشرة ، إلا أن تجلياته بدأت في الظهور بداية من عام ٢٠١٢ ، لتؤكد حدوث تغير في الطريقة التي تُشكل بها الذات رؤيتها للعالم والطريقة التي تقارب بها النساء الفضاء العام . ومن ثم ، ظهر التغيير في التوجهات البحثية .

لا بد من التأكيد على أهمية الشعر النسائي الذي كُتب إثر الثورات العربية . فقد كان الجنس الأدبي الأسبق في التعبير عن رؤى مختلفة عن السائد ، وتلاه المسرح . إن أهمية تسليط الضوء على الخطاب الشعري الجديد لدى الشاعرات الشابات ، يكمن في الكلمة الأساسية الدالة ، وهي «الصوت» . هذا وقد كانت ثنائية الصمت والصوت دوماً مسألة إشكالية في النظرية النسوية ، فبينما رأت بعضهن أن الصمت أداة للمقاومة ، ترى أخريات أن الصوت هو الوسيط الذي يجب أن تستحوذ عليه النساء . ولكن الأمر كله يدور حول اللغة ، وهي لعبة لا يسهل الفوز فيها ، فطبقاً لتيريسا دي لوريتيس : «اللغة ، التي لا نملك عليها سيادة ، لأنها بالفعل مزدحمة بنوايا الآخرين ، هي في النهاية أكثر من كونها لعبة» (de Lauretis 2) . وقولها هذا بمثابة صدى لغيرها من الناقدات النسويات اللاتي يركنّ إلى كيفية قيام اللغة السائدة بتقييد الصراع النصي ، بينما تقدم في الوقت ذاته وسيلة لإحداث القطيعة والتقويض . ومن هنا ، جاءت أهمية ما تفعله هؤلاء الشاعرات الشابات في اللغة السائدة . فنراهن يستحوذن عليها بما يحقق مصالحهن ، كما يحطمن روابطها الاجتماعية والجمالية لإنتاج قصيدة شعرية تقف وحدها وحدةً متمردة . ويتسم شعر هؤلاء الشابات بالنقد اللاذع لكل سرديات المجتمع القائمة ، كالأمومة مثلاً التي قامت سارة عابدين ومروة أبو ضيف بتفكيكها تماماً في ديوانهما المشترك وبيننا حديقة (٢٠١٧) ، حيث قامتا بالبناء على ما قدمته إيمان مرسال في كتيبها كيف تلتئم : عن الأمومة وأشباحها (٢٠١٧) .

تؤكد هذه الروح التقدمية لدى الجيل الطليعي العلاقة الجدلية بين المحلية والعالمية ، فالإنتاج الفني الطليعي يُحدث صدمة مجتمعية تجاه تفكيك الفرضيات المحلية الثابتة ، وفي الوقت ذاته ، يظل دائماً محلقاً بعيداً عن السقوط في قبضة العولمي . صاغ الجيل الصاعد خطاباً يرتكز على مناهضة المحلي والعولمي ، ومن هنا أصبح وجوده خطراً يهدد وجود البنى القديمة : لاحظ مثلا ردود الفعل تجاه مقال منى الطحاوي Eltahawy المكتوب في ٢٠١٢ بالإنجليزية بعنوان «لماذا يكرهوننا؟» (انظر "On Why") . علينا أن نحاول قراءة كيف نجحت النساء - بوصفهن جزءا من المواطنين المنخرطين سياسياً - في التعامل مع مفهوم الهُويّة وتأكيد تعدد مواقع الذات مع تجاوزهن مفهوم الجسد الضيق ، لا عبر الفن وحده وإنما من خلال علاقة جديدة قائمة بين الفن والسياسة تعتبر من أهم إنجازات الثورات (فيما عرف باسم أرتيڤيزم Artivism) . المجمل هو أن الثورات العربية منحت النساء قنوات جديدة وإبداعية لإثبات الفاعلية والتعددية الصوتية (انظر Abouelnaga) .

وضمن هذا الخطاب الصاعد الجديد ، ثارت النساء على الصورة الحداثية التي فُرضت عليهن شكلاً . فالخطاب الوطني القوي للدولة الأبوية قام بدعم - ونشر - صورة ثابتة للجندر ترى النساء مؤشرات ثقافية للهُويّة الوطنية . وفي معرض تناولها للعلاقة غير المستقرة بين الجندر والوطنية ، تقول كانديوتي إن أحد وسائل إنعاش شعبية الخطاب الوطني تأتي عبر «تخصيص موقع ملتبس للنساء عن طريق تعريفهن باعتبارهن مواطنات شريكات في الوطن والمسؤولات عن الحفاظ على القيم الوطنية . إن هذا الالتباس هو في العادة مكمن عدم قدرة النساء على بلوغ مكانة المواطنين كاملي الحقوق» (Kandiyoti, "Guest" 491) . أدت تلك الصورة الثابتة للنساء إلى تهميش قطاع كبير منهن ، ومن هنا كان صعود الطليعة يعني صعود النساء ، وما يقود إليه من تشكيل مواقع جديدة للذات تتضح ، بشكل جمالي ، في المساحات البديلة المتصارع عليها . في هذا السياق ، تصاعدت قوة الدراسات الثقافية ، حيث تم التعامل مع طرق التعبير الفنية الجديدة بوصفها نصوصاً قابلة للتحليل ، وعاد اسم حنا أرندت للظهور ، وبخاصة فيما يتعلق بمفهوم «مساحة للظهور» (Arendt 199) . وأصبح من الطبيعي قبول تسجيل رسائل ماجستير ودكتوراه عن هذا النص الجديد في أقسام اللغات .

إن تشكل هذا النص الجديد وانطلاقه من داخل مواقع مختلفة فُرض عليها التهميش لفترات طويلة لهو أمر يمنح النص سلطة معرفية وجمالية

زيدان Zeidan (١٩٩٥). شكلت هذه الموسوعة أرضاً صلبة تمكن البحث النسوي من إعادة قراءة المنجز الثقافي، وتسمح بالتعامل مع الكتابات النسوية الحديثة بوصفها امتداداً لتاريخ طويل كان في طي النسيان.

في عام ٢٠١١، فقدت الكثير من الأنظمة شرعيتها، وما عاد هناك مبرر للفاعلية النسوية أن تحتمي بعباءة أي طرف. ولأن غضب الجماهير - نساءً ورجالاً - ضد الأنظمة بدأ من الشارع (المجال العام) الذي كان مستلباً لعقودٍ طويلة، فقد شكّلت طرائق التعبير الثورية عن الذات الفردية والجماعية فتحاً لمجال الدراسات الثقافية النسوية، كما سمحت الثورات بإعادة قراءة للحركات النسوية ذاتها (انظر Sadiqi) وقراءة إنجازاتها في ميادين التحرير العربية، بالإضافة إلى هزيمتها على مستوى الجندر (انظر El Said, Meari, and Pratt).

أياً كانت نتائج الثورات العربية، فقد وُلد بالتأكيد نص جمالي جديد من قلب الحراك الثوري على الأرض، وهو ما أتاح فرصة لقراءة التغيرات التي ظهرت في عملية بناء الجندر وفَهْمه مثل: فن الشارع، الجرافيتي، غناء الراب، الكوميكس، الكاريكاتير، مع كل أشكال التعبير التي ظهرت على وسائل التواصل الاجتماعي (انظر El Nossery). وكان لهذا النص (ولا يزال) تجليات عديدة، حيث تم فيه، وعبره، توثيق المطالب والاحتجاجات وأرشفتها (حتى وإن تم محوها أو تدميرها لاحقاً). يتميز هذا النص الجديد ببعده عن الأحادية وإقراره بتعددية الهُويّات الجندرية. فبالإضافة إلى ما عكسه من مواقف سياسية مختلفة للنساء، تضمّن النص الجديد رؤى متعددة عن الجندر، تكاد أحياناً تكون محل خلاف. أفسحت ثورة ٢٥ يناير المجال أمام انطلاق الاختلافات التي سبق كبتها وقمعها في إطار إعلاء التجانس والاحتفاء المستمر به. وقد أظهر انطلاق الثورة وجود تعددية حقيقية على عدة مستويات: إيديولوجية وثقافية ودينية وتعليمية وطبقية وجندرية، وهي تعددية أتاحت نشأة النص الجديد، وكذلك نشأة جيل جديد يقارب وعيه مفهوم الطليعة.

وفي تناقض مثير للدهشة، نجد أن ما يضفي على الطليعة سلطة هو عدم سعيها إلى السلطة كما أوضح هابرماس من قبل (Habermas 3)، بل إنها تسعى إلى العدالة الاجتماعية على اختلاف تجليّاتها، وكأن النسوية عادت إلى التعريف الأصلي: حركة سياسية تطالب بالمساواة والعدالة.

يلمس الباحث في أدبنا الحديث ظاهرة تبعث على الدهشة ، وهي التناقض الواضح بين مكانة الرواية التي تتقدم لتحتل مكانها على قمة الفنون الأدبية في هذا الأدب وبين ندرة الأبحاث والدراسات التي كُتبت عنها سواء من الناحية التاريخية أو النقدية ، وحين كنتُ أفكر في موضوع أتقدم به لنيل الدكتوراه لم يكن حصاد بيئتنا من مصر في الأبحاث في هذا الموضوع يتجاوز الرسالة التي تقدم بها محمود حامد شوكت لنيل درجة الدكتوراه من قسم اللغة العربية بكلية الآداب جامعة القاهرة . (ص ٥)

تبدو المقدمة من أهم أجزاء الكتاب ، لأن بدر يحدد فيها الفترة الزمنية ، ويؤكد أن دراسة الإنتاج الذي ظهر في القرن التاسع عشر كان أمراً لا بد منه ، كما أنه يحدد المفهوم الذي ينظر به إلى الرواية . فبالنسبة له ، الرواية الحديثة هي الرواية الفنية ، وما عدا ذلك يدخل في إطار الرواية التعليمية أو رواية التسلية والترفيه . وعليه ، فقد صنف رواية **حسن العواقب** (١٨٩٩) للكاتبة زينب فواز ، ورواية **قلب الرجل** (١٩٠٤) للكاتبة لبيبة هاشم في روايات التسلية والترفيه . وبهذا تم إغلاق الباب أمام إعادة النظر في التاريخ الأدبي .
من هنا ، تنبع أهمية موسوعة **ذاكرة للمستقبل** التي صدرت عن المجلس الأعلى للثقافة عام ٢٠٠٣ في ثلاثة مجلدات . تؤكد هيئة التحرير في مقدمة المجلد الأول أن الغرض من هذه الموسوعة هو

رصد ظاهرة وتقديمها للقراء العرب بما يتيح لهم معرفة أفضل بذلك الحضور الثقافي المؤثر في مجتمعاتنا العربية . . . المؤكد ، ومهما كان تقييمنا لمجمل إنجازات الكاتبة العربية الحديثة ، أن في نصها – أقصد مجموع النصوص التي أنتجتها – إضافة ما : وجهة نظر مختلفة ، أو نبرة صوت مغايرة ، أو حساسية تخصها وتميزها ، تشكلت عبر قرون من الصمت والقهر المفروضين عليها في عالم طال به العهد محكوماً بالأبوية . (ص ١١)

تشكل هذه الموسوعة إضافة للمكتبة العربية ، إذ سبقتها عدة موسوعات عن الكاتبات العربيات ، لكنها باللغة الإنجليزية وأشهرها موسوعة جوزيف

في مسار تراكمي. فمن وجهة نظر التاريخ الرسمي، كانت حكاية النساء تدور دوماً حول الحقوق العالمية الأساسية الحديثة: الحق في الانتخاب، الحق في العمل، الحق في التعليم، الحق في الصحة، أي الحقوق المتعلقة بالمجال العام. لكن سرديات النساء كانت تؤكد دوماً أن الخاص هو العام، وعليه توجهت الجهود النسوية إلى هدم الفصل الحاد بين المجالين.

إلا أن حكاية النساء، كأية حكاية أخرى، تتضمن بالتأكيد أشكالاً من التعددية، بل والتناقض أحياناً. في حين أن المرأة التي تحتفي أجهزة الدولة بصورتها تعكس تصوراً واحداً، فهي المرأة التي تحقق إرادتها وفاعليتها عبر رجل وسيط، هي امرأة مضحية بنفسها، إما في سبيل ابنها أو زوجها أو وطنها. فعلى سبيل المثال، يتم دائماً تقديم هدى شعراوي، وهي من زعيمات الحركة النسوية في مصر في بدايات القرن العشرين، بوصفها المرأة التي تحدت الضباط الإنجليز عندما كانت مصر تحت الاحتلال البريطاني، دون الإشارة إلى السلطة التي اكتسبتها من كونها ابنة الطبقة الأرستقراطية. بينما كانت المروية الرسمية - صيغة الدولة الرسمية - تبدأ دوماً بدور النساء في ثورة ١٩١٩، نجد المؤرخين والباحثين، نساءً ورجالاً، يرجعون إلى أبعد من ذلك لتسليط الضوء على تأثير الحملة الفرنسية التي بدأت عام ١٧٩٨ في سياسات الهُويّة الجندرية في مصر (انظر Zeidan; Ashour et al)، أي بينما كانت الدولة تركز دائماً على شخصيات نسائية فردية من التاريخ الحديث، وعلى رأسهن هدى شعراوي، نجد ميلاً من الباحثات إلى إعادة قراءة التاريخ لإدراج عاملي الاستعمار والطبقة (وهما العاملان اللذان تسعى المروية الرسمية إلى محوهما والتعتيم عليهما بوصفهما من عوامل تحليل وقراءة وصياغة السياسات الجندرية).

وبالمثل، وبنبرة يقينية، عمد النقاد في مجال الأدب إلى اعتماد رواية زينب لمحمد حسين هيكل بوصفها الرواية العربية الأولى. تظهر هنا إشكالية المنظور الذي كُتب به التاريخ الأدبي لنشأة الرواية وتطور النثر، وما إذا كان هذا التاريخ يعكس وثائق القرن التاسع عشر. تُشكل مسألة ظهور وغياب عنصر الجندر في كتابة التاريخ الأدبي مجالاً لا يزال مفتوحاً للإسهامات المعرفية. فمثلاً، يعتمد كل نقاد الأدب على كتاب **تطور الرواية العربية الحديثة** لعبد المحسن طه بدر الذي صدر عام ١٩٦٣، وتنبع أهميته مما يقوله المؤلف نفسه في المقدمة:

الرسمية. بدأت مجموعة من الباحثين والباحثات عملية التنقيب في الأرشيف ليتم إعادة طباعة العديد من الكتابات المنسية والمهملة التي سبقت كتاب قاسم أمين تحرير المرأة. وبهذه المناسبة، صدرت العديد من الترجمات عن المجلس الأعلى للثقافة بالقاهرة، ومنها كتاب ليلى أحمد المرأة والجنوسة في الإسلام الذي قامت منى إبراهيم وهالة كمال بترجمته. وبمجرد صدور الكتاب، تزعمت جريدة الشعب حملة ضده، كما اتهمت وزارة الثقافة بإهدار المال العام على كتب تسيء إلى الإسلام، ووصل الأمر إلى إصدار الأزهر توصية بمصادرة الكتاب. كما شهد المؤتمر ذاته هجوماً شديداً من الإسلاميين، فقد كانت تلك الفترة تشهد ذروة صعود الخطاب الإسلامي.

لم تكن مسألة إعادة قراءة التاريخ الإسلامي كما فعلت المرنيسي (٢٠٠٤)، ورجاء بن سلامة (٢٠٠٥)، أو إعادة كتابة الموروث الشعبي (مشروع «قالت الراوية» في مؤسسة المرأة والذاكرة، مثلاً)[7]، أو إعادة قراءة فاعلية النساء على مدار التاريخ بالأمر السهل، فقد جاء رد فعل دوائر المثقفين والسلطة إما معادياً أو لامبالياً. فبينما اعتاد المثقفون على تسفيه المقاربات النسوية والتقليل من شأنها، وكان جل اهتمامهم هو العمل على نقد تطبيقي لهذه الرواية أو تلك، لم تكن نسوية الدولة على استعداد لتقبل أي إحياء للذاكرة أو إعادة صياغة للذاكرة الجماعية خارج حيز السلطة. هذا وقد قامت الدولة، بالطبع، بالاستحواذ جزئياً على الذاكرة المضادة، فبما أن نسوية الدولة قامت بتعزيز الصلة بين قضية المرأة والقضية الوطنية، وهو ما يخدم توطيد أركان السلطة، كان هدفها استعمال الذاكرة المستعادة أيضاً لخدمة أغراضها. فمن خلال إنكار التعددية، والتعامل مع النساء بوصفهن حاملات الهُويّة الثقافية للوطن، قدمت الدولة نفسها بوصفها المصدر الأساسي المدوّن للتاريخ الرسمي («الصحيح») الذي لا يجب أن تشوبه مرويات أخرى، ومنها بالطبع تاريخ النساء.

عمدت الدولة إلى ترسيخ الذاكرة الممنهجة عبر المقررات المدرسية التي ترتكز على تقسيم المراحل السياسية والعصور التاريخية بشكل خطي، بوصفها مدخلاً رسمياً لقراءة التاريخ. وفي هذا الإطار، تبدو المروية عن النساء من وجهة نظر التاريخ الرسمي دوماً مبهرة، بسبب الوحدة المتماسكة والبنية الخطية المتبعة في المقاربة، فقد تعاملت الكتب المدرسية والخطاب الإعلامي مع تاريخ النساء على أنه يمضي من نقطة إلى الأخرى

معلن، وهو ما أوضحته الباحثة التركية دنيز كانديوتي Kandiyoti في مقال لها بعنوان «الضربة الثلاثية» "The Triple Whammy".

بتغير شكل المنطقة، بات واضحاً أن الاختيار المتاح هو منح النساء مساحة لأصواتهن. فإذا كانت الخطابات التنموية التي توظفها نسوية الدولة تربط بين التهميش والفقر، فقد أصبح عامل الجندر نفسه بمثابة المهمش كلياً. من هنا مثلاً، بدأت تظهر أهمية شهادات الكاتبات التي تشير إلى الأصوات المهمشة. واحتل الصوت المحلي دوراً كبيراً في تشكيل رؤى الأبحاث، فتم تسليط الضوء على السيرة الذاتية بوصفها أحد الأجناس الأدبية. وقد قامت مجلة ألف بإصدار العدد رقم ٢٢ في عام ٢٠٠٢ بعنوان «لغة الذات: السير الذاتية والشهادات». كذلك أصبحت السير الذاتية والمذكرات النسائية ضمن المصادر الأولية لعديد من الرسائل العلمية. وانكبّ طلاب الدراسات العليا على تحليل مذكرات نوال السعداوي (١٩٨٥، ٢٠٠٠)؛ جين سعيد المقدسي Makdisi (١٩٩٠)؛ لطيفة الزيات (١٩٩٢)؛ ليلى أحمد L. Ahmed (١٩٩٩)؛ ليلى أبو زيد (١٩٩٣)؛ فاطمة المرنيسي (١٩٩٨) ورضوى عاشور (٢٠١٣)، على سبيل المثال وليس الحصر، من منظور جندري. لكن بمرور الوقت، أصبحت السيرة الذاتية مقرراً مستقلاً بذاته في مرحلة الدكتوراه، كما هو الحال في قسم اللغة الإنجليزية بجامعة القاهرة على سبيل المثال. واقترنت دراسة الصوت النسائي، في هذه السير، بمصطلح الفاعلية الذي أصبح مسيطراً في الدراسات النسوية لكونه يسهم في ضبط علاقات القوى وشكل تقسيم الأدوار بين الجنسين. وقد برز بقوة اسم الباحثة هالة كمال Kamal التي تبحرت في دراسة السيرة الذاتية النسوية في دراسات مثل "A Feminist Autobiography" و"In Search of Fatima" و"Women's Writing on Women's Writing".

وقبل بداية الألفية بعام واحد، وعلى وجه التحديد في عام ١٩٩٩، عقد المجلس الأعلى للثقافة مؤتمر «مائة عام على تحرير المرأة» احتفالاً بمئوية كتاب قاسم أمين، وظهرت توجهات تاريخية نسْوية تسعى إلى إعادة قراءة التاريخ (على غرار المؤرخين الجدد)، وانتعشت عملية البحث في الأرشيف، فظهرت كتابات عائشة التيمورية وزينب فواز وغيرهما، ليتم دحض مقولة أن رواية زينب لمحمد حسين هيكل هي أول رواية عربية. ولا تزال إعادة قراءة الوثائق تكشف الكثير من المغالطات التي قدمتها السردية التاريخية

أما في مجال الدراسات الأدبية ، فقد انصب اهتمام الباحثات أيضاً على تقاطعات الجندر والأمة في الروايات النسوية العربية (انظر Majaj et al) .

أما الفجيعة الثانية التي شكلت توجه الألفية الثالثة ، فكانت اشتداد وطأة الحصار الأمريكي على العراق والإعلان عن حرب وشيكة ، وهو ما حدث بالفعل ، فسقطت بغداد يوم ٩ أبريل في عام ٢٠٠٣ . أدى حصار العراق إلى تنبيه المجتمع المدني ودوائر البحث الأكاديمي إلى ضرورة تغيير وجْهة البوصلة المعرفية . فقد كانت هذه الدوائر على وعيٍ بما يحدث للعراقَ (بقيادة قوى كبرى) ، بدون المقدرة على تغيير الأمر دولياً . ومن ثم كان أحد أشكال المقاومة منح الأصوات المهمشة مساحة من أجل محاولة توازن علاقات القوى . وعاد البحث الميداني ليتبوأ أهمية في العلوم الإنسانية ، أي إن الحرب فرضت على النظري أن يأخذ في الاعتبار المادي والحياتي . وقد كرست نادية العلي – النسْوية العراقية الألمانية – جزءاً كبيراً من أعمالها للعراق ، سواء كان ذلك الإنتاج في شكل كتب (انظر Al-Ali; Al-Ali and Pratt) أو مقالات علمية . بشكل عام ، تصاعدت قوة المصطلحات الخاصة بالتهميش والأصوات المنسية . إلا أن توظيف الغرب عموماً ، وأمريكا بشكل خاص ، لخطاب ضرورة إنقاذ النساء في العراق من صدام حسين ، وفيما بعد – وبشكل أوضح – في أفغانستان (أي من حزب طالبان) ، من أجل إضفاء شرعية على الحرب ، قد دفع بالنسويات إلى التنبه لخطورة توظيف المصطلح الشهير الذي يعود إلى الأزمنة الكولونيالية ، ألا وهو «إنقاذ المرأة المسلمة» . وقد أوضحت ليلى أبو لغد في كتابها الصادر عام ٢٠١٣ **هل تحتاج المسلمات إلى إنقاذ؟** (انظر Abu-Lughod, *Do Muslim*) أن هذه الحجة قد تم توظيفها في كل أشكال التدخل الأجنبي في بلدان العالم الثالث ، وذلك بمباركة من النسويات الغربيات . على الجانب الآخر ، تؤكد هدى الصدة Elsadda في مقالتها بعنوان «حرب ضد النساء» "A War against Women" توظيف الاستعمار منذ أزمنة بعيدة للنساء من أجل إضفاء شرعية على الحروب ، إلا أن الأنظمة القمعية (في ثوب إسلامي) ترفع أيضاً شعار الحفاظ على القيم وأن «نساؤنا مختلفات» من أجل إضفاء شرعية على انتهاك الحقوق . ومع ازدياد وتيرة الحروب في المنطقة العربية وتحوُّل النساء (وأجسادهن) إلى عنصر استقطاب تمارسه كل الأطراف المتنازعة (فيما عدا النساء أنفسهن) ، بدا واضحاً أن الحركة النسوية وإنتاجها المعرفي واقعين تحت حصار غير

هكذا، عادت فكرة «تحسين صورة الإسلام»، وبالمقابل ظهرت صورة المرأة المسلمة، فبدأت الكاتبات والمفكرات الأمريكيات ذوات الأصول العربية، أو العربيات المقيمات هناك، في تكريس جهودهن من أجل «تحسين» الصورة، وظهر مثلاً اسم الشاعرة والروائية والكاتبة ذات الأصل السوري مهجة قحف (انظر Kahf)، وتحولت هُويّة العرب الأمريكيين إلى موضوع بحثي رئيسي. وعاد مفهوم الهُجْنة الذي ظهر في مجال دراسات ما بعد الاستعمار إلى الظهور في مجال دراسات الهُويّة النِّسْوية. ومن هنا، بدا التباعد واضحاً بين أولويات المقيمات في الغرب وأمريكا، وأولويات المقيمات في العالم العربي. فعلى سبيل المثال، تحول الحجاب إلى دال ومدلول وعلامة إيديولوجية تحظى باهتمام النسويات اللواتي يكتبن بالإنجليزية، وهو ما فعلته ليلى أبو العلا Aboulela في روايتها المنارة *Minaret* الصادرة عام ٢٠٠٥، في حين أن الأمر لا يحتل الأهمية نفسها في العالم العربي (أي إن ارتداءه أو خلعه لا يشكل هاجساً بحثياً).

احتلت دراسات/سياسات الهُويّة مساحة كبيرة في الفكر النسويِّ العربي. وعلى غرار ما فعله السود في أمريكا، قامت النِّسْويات العربيات بانتهاج رؤية مغايرة للفكر النسوي الغربي من أجل إعادة الاعتبار لهُويّة متغيرة في عالم سياسي يتسم بالسيولة الشديدة. وبدأت دراسات سياسات الهُويّة توظف فكر إدوارد سعيد، وبخاصة في مسألة ارتحال النظرية (انظر Said, *The World*)؛ ورؤى ستيوارت هال الخاصة بهُويّة السود (انظر Hall)؛ وبيل هوكس (انظر hooks)، على سبيل المثال وليس الحصر. كما ظهر الاهتمام بعلاقة الجندر بالدولة والتحديث، ومن هنا ظهر مصطلح «الذات المجندرة» بفعل التشريعات ومفهوم المواطنة والممارسات اليومية (انظر Abu-Lughod, *Remaking*; Kandiyoti, *Gendering*; Ghossoub). ولا يمكن كذلك إهمال صعود اسم المنظرة النسوية جوديث باتلر في العالم العربي التي قامت - على غرار منهج فوكو - بتفكيك ثنائية الجنس والجندر، وأكدت أن الهُويّة الجندرية تعتمد على نظرية الأداء. وقد أفادت هذه النظرية الإنتاج المعرفي النسوي العربي، حيث أسهمت في الكشف عن الضوابط المؤسسية التي تحكم أداء الجندر، وهي كلها ضوابط ترتكز على علاقات قوى سائدة ومهيمنة، مما يجعل إمكانية التحرر مرتبطة بتفكيك البنى الخطابية القديمة (انظر Butler). وبدا واضحاً، مؤخراً، أن الكثير من الرسائل العلمية تتخذ من نظرية الأداء منهجاً لقراءة الأعمال الأدبية.

بينهما في عام ٢٠٠٥ في نيويورك، وقد أثار ذلك ردود أفعال كثيرة. وهناك أيضاً ليلى أحمد L. Ahmed، المصرية الأمريكية التي عُرفت بكتاب **المرأة والجنوسة في الإسلام** Women and Gender in Islam (١٩٩٢)، كذلك هناك التونسية نائلة السليني الراضوي التي أثار كتابها **تاريخية التفسير القرآني** (٢٠٠٢) ضجة كبيرة. وقد عملت عالمة الاجتماع المغربية المعروفة فاطمة المرنيسي على تفنيد حديث «لم يفلح قوم ولَّوا أمرهم امرأة» في كتابها **الحريم السياسي: النبي والنساء** (١٩٩٣). وفي المغرب هناك أيضاً أسماء المرابط صاحبة كتاب **القرآن والنساء: قراءة للتحرر** (٢٠١٠). ومن مصر لمع مبكراً اسم هبة رؤوف عزت التي نادت عام ١٩٩٤ بإطلاق حركة نسائية إسلامية (انظر El-Gawhary and Ezzat)، وكذلك اسم أميمة أبو بكر وبخاصة عملها عن تاريخية مفهوم القوامة (انظر أبو بكر وAbou-Bakr). وما يميز أبو بكر هو توظيفها لمنهجيات النقد الأدبي وأدواته في إعادة قراءة النصوص الإسلامية. وهو نهج المفكر المصري الراحل نصر حامد أبو زيد، حيث قدم كتابين عن المرأة اعتمد فيهما منهجية التأويل للنص بما يجعله قابلاً للتطبيق في الواقع الراهن، وهما: **المرأة في خطاب الأزمة** (١٩٩٤) و**دوائر الخوف: قراءة في خطاب المرأة** (٢٠٠٤). وفي عام ١٩٩٩، أسست منى أبو الفضل جمعية دراسات المرأة والحضارة في مصر، وأعلنت أنها تسعى «لتأسيس منظور إسلامي للمعرفة النسوية، وتهتم في هذا السياق بالمراجعة الفكرية ذات التوجه الأكاديمي للإنتاج الفكري والعلمي الخاص بالمرأة، سواء ما يتعلق بالكتابات النسوية الغربية أو الكتابات العربية المعاصرة أو الكتابات الإسلامية التراثية» («عن الجمعية»، د. ص.).

مع مطلع الألفية الثالثة، كان شكل الخريطة السياسية والمعرفية قد تغير تماماً. فمع انهيار البرجين في نيويورك في الحادي عشر من سبتمبر عام ٢٠٠١، بدا الاستقطاب مسيطراً على الإعلام والخطاب المجتمعي. تلخص الكاتبة الباكستانية كاميلة شمسي Shamsie ما حدث في روايتها **آيات محطمة** Broken Verses التي صدرت بالإنجليزية عام ٢٠٠٥ في حوار قصير:

ثم ماذا؟
ثم سقط البرجان.
ومن ثم لم تعد فرداً بل ديناً بأكمله. (45)

عن قضايا إنسانية قديمة ومستمرة» (**النقد الأدبي النسوي**، ص ٤٩) . وتدريجياً ، تم تسييد استعمال مصطلح الجندر كما هو بدون أي ترجمة . إلا أن انتعاش دراسات الترجمة (وهي مختلفة عن فعل الترجمة) ، قد حدا بالترجمات النسوية إلى الحصول على مساحة واضحة . ومن هنا ، ظهر مصطلح «الترجمة النسوية» ، الذي صاغته هالة كمال في مقدمتها لترجمتها لكتاب **مدخل إلى البحث النسوي : ممارسة وتطبيقاً** (ص ص ٧- ١٦) ، وأعادت تناول شروط الترجمة النسوية في مقدمتها لترجمتها لكتاب **النقد الأدبي النسوي** (ص ٣٩) .

مع منتصف التسعينيات ، بدا واضحاً أن مفهوم الجندر قد وجد لنفسه مكاناً راسخاً في العالم العربي . ولأنه مفهوم مرتحل ومرن ولديه القدرة على الاستجابة لمعطيات المجتمع ، فقد ظهر توجه النسوية الإسلامية ، أي إعادة قراءة - وتأويل - أوضاع النساء والتأويلات الفقهية الخاصة بهن ، من منظور إسلامي . والجدير بالذكر أن مصطلح النسوية الإسلامية قد ظهر للمرة الأولى في إيران ، من خلال مجلة **زنان** النسائية التي كانت تصدر في طهران ، وأسستها شهلا شركت عام ١٩٩٢ (Moghadam 1143) . بدا المفهوم ملائماً لكلِ النسويات اللواتي أردن إنتاج معرفة جديدة من داخل الإطار الإسلامي ، إيماناً منهن بأنه لا يجوز أن يبقى المجال الديني تحت الوصاية الأبوية الذكورية التي لا تأخذ فاعلية النساء بعين الاعتبار ، بل تسعى إلى مأسسة دونية النساء . وفي المقدمة التي كتبها أنس الطريقي لملف «النسوية الإسلامية» في مجلة **مؤمنون بلا حدود** ، يعرف النسوية الإسلامية بأنها تمثل

> فرعاً من النسوية الكونية ذات الولادة الغربية في ستينيات القرن العشرين . ويحمل لها النعت إسلامية علامة تميزها ، تكمن مقارنة بالنسوية المسيحية الغربية في كونها تعتبر الدين الإسلامي أحد أهم مصادر تلك الهيمنة الذكورية اللامشروعة ، فتعمل على كسرها من داخل الإسلام نفسه بتعريضه لتأويلية جديدة في مصادره الكبرى أو الفرعية . (ص ٣)

برز مبكراً اسم الباحثة الباكستانية الأمريكية رفعت حسن ، ثم اسم الأفرو-أمريكية أمينة ودود Wadud التي اشتهرت بكتابها **القرآن والمرأة** *Qur'an and Woman* (١٩٩٩) ، ثم قامت بإمامة الصلاة لرجال ونساء دون فصل

النمطية للنساء في الثقافة السائدة بتأسيس مؤسسة المرأة والذاكرة، انطلاقاً من فكرة أن «أهم المعوقات التي تواجه المرأة العربية حالياً غياب مصادر المعرفة الثقافية البديلة بشأن أدوار النساء في التاريخ وفي الحياة المعاصرة» («من نحن»، ا**لمرأة والذاكرة**، د.ص.). وفي عام ١٩٩٤، تأسس معهد دراسات المرأة بجامعة بيرزيت (الذي أسسته أيلين كتاب بالمشاركة مع أخريات) تحت مسمى برنامج دراسات المرأة، ثم تحول إلى معهد عام ١٩٩٨ (انظر «معهد دراسات المرأة»). وفي عام ١٩٩٥، تأسس تجمع باحثات لبنانيات بوصفه «منتدى للحوار وللتبادل الحرّ للأفكار والخبرات. ويوفّر التجمّع لعضواته، المعنيّات بإنتاج الدراسات والأبحاث، فسحة تشجّع عضوات التجمّع فيها على التعبير عن أفكارهن، وعلى الالتقاء التفاعلي مع بعضهن ومع آخرين مهتمين، وعلى تشبيك يطلق قدراتهن» («من نحن»، **تجمع الباحثات اللبنانيات**، د.ص.). كان عقد التسعينيات فترة غنية أتاحت للحركة النسوية أن تبلور خطابها في العالم العربي، كما بدا واضحاً أن تبادل الخبرات هو حجر الأساس في تشكيل خطاب معرفي لا تنقصه الشرعية التي كانت محل تشكيك دائم.[٦]

في عام ١٩٩٩، صدر العدد رقم ١٩ من مجلة ألف التي تصدر عن الجامعة الأمريكية بالقاهرة، وكان عنوانه هو «الجنوسة والمعرفة: صياغة المعارف بين التأنيث والتذكير»، وهو ما يعني أن هيئة التحرير قد اختارت ترجمة كلمة الجندر إلى «الجنوسة». وتتساءل محرز: «لماذا اخترنا الصيغة المتمادية في الجوهرية لترجمة "جندر" في الوقت الذي نمتلك لغة - ومع اعتبار أن اللغة هي عملية بناء المعنى - قادرة إلى أبعد درجة على التجديد الخلّاق، كما تبين من مثال "الجنوسة" المستحدثة، التي صاغتها محررات مجلة **ألف** ولكن لم يستخدمها أحد» (Mehrez 112). وبالفعل، لم يلق المصطلح قبولاً، وظل استعمال مصطلحي «النوع الاجتماعي» و«الجندر» هو السائد. وفي عام ٢٠٠٨، كتبت هالة كمال مقالاً عن خبرتها بوصفها منسقة مشروع ترجمة **موسوعة النساء في الثقافات الإسلامية** إلى العربية، وارتأت ضرورة توحيد المصطلحات، وعلى رأسها الجندر (Kamal, "Translating" 259). وفي عام ٢٠١٥، أعلنت كمال أنها لا تجد غضاضة «في استخدام مصطلح أعجمي تبلور في ظل النظرية النسوية، مثلما لا نجد غضاضة في استخدام مصطلحات أعجمية أخرى كمصطلح الديمقراطية أو الليبرالية أو الراديكالية والتي تبلورت في ظل النظرية السياسية، وإن كانت قد صيغت كمصطلحات حديثة معبرة

«جندر» كما هي، لكنها كانت مثار استهجان (وكان الشائع هو الإشارة إلى المجال بأكمله بمصطلح «دراسات المرأة»)،[5] بما أن منهج البنيوية - على سبيل المثال - كان هو المنهج النقدي السائد في التسعينيات، وهو بدوره قد تبلور في مكان آخر. وعندما أقول إشكالية، لا بد أن أؤكد أنني لا أراها هكذا، فأنا مع ارتحال النظرية كما فصلها إدوارد سعيد. فالنظرية ترتحل من مكان إلى آخر، لتعيد تشكيل نفسها طبقاً للمكان الذي حلت به، كما استفاض إدوارد سعيد في شرح هذه المسألة في فصل بعنوان "Travelling Theory" في كتابه **العالم والنص والناقد** *The World, the Text, the Critic*. فعلى سبيل المثال، ظهرت آثار الارتحال النظري مبكراً في الخطاب النسوي المصري، إذ سافر الوفد النسائي المصري لحضور مؤتمر المرأة الدولي في روما عام 1923، وفي عام 1927 قامت رئيسة الوفد - هدى شعراوي - بتأسيس الاتحاد النسائي المصري. وفي هذا الارتحال يكتسب الخطاب طبقات دلالية جديدة، ويترك بعضاً من نفسه في المكان الآخر، فتكون ذروة هذا الارتحال خطاباً عابراً للقوميات والأوطان، وهو خطاب ظهر في أواخر القرن العشرين، وأصبح لا بديل عنه في القرن الحادي والعشرين.

ورغم أن النقاش في هذا السياق يركز على الإنتاج البحثي والأكاديمي، فتجب الإشارة إلى ازدهار العمل التنموي فيما يتعلق بقضايا النساء منذ بداية فترة التسعينيات (ومن قبلها بالطبع). حتى أنه يمكن القول إن المنظمات النسوية غير الحكومية شكلت جزءاً كبيراً من المجتمع المدني الذي كان يتصدى لقضايا شائكة، ويعي أهمية الدخول في تحالفات، معتمداً على آلية التشبيك من أجل إنجاز خطوات طبيعية في المسألة النسوية، مستعيناً في ذلك بالاتفاقيات الدولية التي صدّقت عليها الدول العربية، وبخاصة اتفاقية إلغاء أشكال التمييز كافة ضد المرأة (سيداو) وآليات الأمم المتحدة. لم يكن غريباً من ثم ظهور التجمعات البحثية النسوية في تلك الفترة أيضاً، حيث أصبح هناك توجه إلى إنتاج معرفة نسوية بديلة نابعة من الحراك الديناميكي المحلي. فتأسست مؤسسة المرأة الجديدة بالقاهرة في عام 1991، وارتكزت رؤيتها على أن «النضال من أجل تحرير النساء جزء من نضال أوسع من أجل الديمقراطية، والعدالة الاجتماعية، أو العرقي أو الديني أو أي شكل من أشكال العلاقات القمعي» («من نحن»، مؤسسة المرأة الجديدة، د. ص.). وفي عام 1992، قامت مجموعة من الباحثين والباحثات المهتمات بتغيير الصورة

المقولة الماركسية «لن تتحرر المرأة إلا بتحرر المجتمع». وفي المقابل، كان الجيل الجديد يرى أن هناك خصوصية متميزة لقضية المرأة في المجتمعات العربية لا يُمكن إغفالها، وبخاصة مع سقوط السرديات الكبرى المتمثلة في حرب الخليج الثانية (على غرار ما نادى به ليوتار Lyotard منظر ما بعد الحداثة).

عادت النبرة الاعتذارية إلى الصعود في مواجهة أسئلة من قبيل: هل هناك أدب نسائي وآخر رجولي؟ كان يلازمنا بعض الارتباك في الندوات التي كانت تنتهي بنقاش يحمل أحياناً نبرة تهكّمية؛ فمن الذي يذكّرنا بالإسلام إلى الذي يؤكد أنه يحترم زوجته، انتهاءً بالمتحذلق الذي يؤكد أن الأدب هو الأدب. وعندما نشرت لطيفة الزيات شهادتها بوصفها مبدعة في مجلة **أدب ونقد**، بدا أن الأدب النسوي قد ربح جولة في مواجهة المعارضة الشديدة. فقد قالت: «أعمالي الإبداعية تحمل بصمتي كامرأة، كهذا النتاج التاريخي الاجتماعي لمجتمع معين في فترة من فترات تطوره، وتحمل بصمتي كهذه المرأة الفريدة التي هي أنا» («شهادة مبدعة»، ص ١٨). ثم دخلنا في التحليلات النقدية التي ارتأت أن كل كتابات النساء ليست إلا سيراً ذاتية، وانتشر هذا الأمر في دوائر المثقفين من أجل إنكار موهبة الخيال وقدرة الكاتبات على التخييل. وفي عام ١٩٩٧، وعلى وجه التحديد في شهر يوليو، نُشر خبر في جريدة **أخبار الأدب** تحت عنوان «أدب الاعترافات حرام»، وجاء فيه: «أكد الدكتور نصر فريد واصل مفتي الديار المصرية أنه لا يجوز للمرأة أن تؤلف كتاباً تعترف فيه بما أمر الله بستره، وهو ما يطلق عليه ''أدب الاعترافات''» (ص ٣). إلا أن وطأة النقد خفتت كثيراً مع نهاية عقد التسعينيات، وبخاصة بعد أن حصلت رواية **ذاكرة الجسد** (١٩٩٣) للكاتبة الجزائرية أحلام مستغانمي عام ١٩٩٨ على جائزة نجيب محفوظ للأدب التي تنظمها الجامعة الأمريكية في القاهرة. وفي عام ٢٠٠١، تم تصنيفها بوصفها واحدة من بين أفضل مائة رواية عربية (انظر **أخبار الأدب**). كان جزءا من اللغط الحادث في تلك الفترة هو رفض الساحة النقدية لأي كتابة عن الجسد، حتى حين أصبح يُشار إلى الكتابات النسوية بأنها «كتابة الجسد». ولذلك، جاء كتاب **جسد المرأة من سلطة الإنس إلى سلطة الجان** للباحثة والكاتبة التونسية حياة الرايس، في عام ١٩٩٥، كسراً لدائرة اتهامات لا طائل من ورائها سوى إعادة إنتاج أفكار أبوية ترى جسد النساء عورة.

كانت الإشكالية الأخرى هي ترجمة المصطلحات الخاصة بدراسات الجندر إلى اللغة العربية. كنت لا أرى غضاضة إطلاقاً في استعمال كلمة

أهم العوامل التحليلية المقترنة بالجندر، من أجل أن يتجنب تهمة «النسوية البيضاء» وإعادة إنتاج الفكر الإمبريالي.

وفي السنوات الأخيرة من التسعينيات، بدا أن هناك تغيراً جذرياً في شكل الساحة الأدبية، وظهر مصطلح الكتابة النسوية. ليس المقصود هو تحديد نقطة زمنية لبداية الكتابة النسوية، فهذا خطأ منهجي. لكن، بدلاً من ذلك، يمكن الإشارة إلى توقيت ظهور مصطلح الكتابة النسوية والنقد النسوي في المجال العام: الصحافة الثقافية، الحوارات مع الكاتبات، هجوم النقاد. بدأ الأمر بمؤتمر المرأة العربية الذي نظمته دار نور للنشر[3] عام ١٩٩٥، وهو عام فارق، لأنه العام الذي انعقد فيه مؤتمر المرأة العالمي في بكين، وأصدر فيه جوزيف زيدان Zeidan كتابه **الروائيات العربيات** Arab Women Novelists مع التركيز على ما أسماه «السنوات التأسيسية» (١٩٩٥). وفي النصف الثاني من عقد التسعينيات، ظهرت كتابات ميرال الطحاوي (**الخباء**، ١٩٩٦)، مي التلمساني (**دنيا زاد**، ١٩٩٧)، نورا أمين (**قميص وردي فارغ**، ١٩٩٧)، وسمية رمضان (**أوراق النرجس**، ٢٠٠١). طرح إدوار الخراط مصطلح «كتابة البنات» في ندوة بعنوان «كاتبات من مصر» أقيمت بمكتبة القاهرة في سبتمبر ١٩٩٥، وفعلت بركسام رمضان الشيء نفسه في سلسلة حوارات بصحيفة **الأخبار** أسمتها «موسم كتابة البنات». وظهر مصطلح «الكتابة النسوية». بعض الكاتبات تقبلن المصطلح وبعضهن رفضن الانصياع له، وهو أمر له دلالة. فقد ارتأت بعضهن - ليس فقط من مصر ولكن بعضاً من العالم العربي أيضاً - أن المصطلح به عزل أو تحقير أو تهميش. ومن هنا، لم يتمكن المصطلح من الحصول بسهولة على مساحة في الخطاب النقدي (انظر بنمسعود). كان الهجوم الذي لاقته هذه الكتابات شديداً، بدعوى التشظي الواضح في الخطاب السردي والتركيز على الذات في مقابل الجماعة، ولم يكن السجال سهلاً؛ فقد كان الأمر المبطن المسكوت عنه هو صراع بين خطابين، أو بالأحرى رؤى إبستيمولوجية متناقضة بين جيلين،[4] ناهيك عن تركز السلطة النقدية في يد جيل أكبر كان لديه القدرة على تفنيد هذه الكتابات والنقد المصاحب لها (انظر أبو النجا). ولا تزال كتابات هذا الجيل تحظى باهتمام نقدي (انظر Elsadda, Gender). كان هناك رفض لرؤى إبداعية جديدة تشتبك مع المجال الخاص الذي لامسته بمهارة لطيفة الزيات في **الباب المفتوح**، لكنها أغلقت الباب عبر تصوير الانخراط في النضال الوطني بوصفه حلاً أمثل لمشكلات الطبقة البورجوازية، وهو ما يعضد من

إلى تحليل الشكل الذي رسم به الكاتب العربي الشخصيات النسائية في أعماله . ورغم افتقار هذا الشكل من التحليل إلى العمق النقدي الذي يتطلبه النص الأدبي - فالمسألة تقتصر على دراسة رسم الشخصيات - فقد ظل سائداً تقريباً طوال فترة التسعينيات من القرن الماضي . في الوقت ذاته ، لا يمكن أن نتجاهل أهمية الدراسة التي قدمتها الراحلة لطيفة الزيات عام ١٩٨٩ بعنوان **من صور المرأة في القصص والروايات العربية** ، وكذلك الفصل الذي قدمته سهير القلماوي في رسالة الدكتوراه عن صورة المرأة في ألف ليلة وليلة (١٩٤٣) . بشكل عام ، بدت مسألة قراءة الصورة وقد انتشرت وانسحبت على الأفلام السينمائية والمسلسلات التلفزيونية ، ليبدو وكأننا بصدد ما يشبه واقعية اشتراكية نسوية .

ومع اقتراب الألفية ، كانت نظرية ما بعد الاستعمار قد انتعشت تأثراً بكتاب **الاستشراق** (١٩٧٨) لإدوارد سعيد (انظر Said, *Orientalism*) ، ومقال «**زمن النساء**» (١٩٧٩) لجوليا كريستيفا (انظر Kristeva) ، ومقال «**تحت عيون غربية**» (١٩٨٤) للناقدة تشاندرا موهانتي (انظر Mohanty) ، ومقال «**هل يمكن أن يتكلم التابع؟**» (١٩٨٨) للناقدة الهندية جاياتري سبيفاك (انظر Spivak) . إلا أن الملحوظ أن انتعاش هذه الدراسات قد ظهر بشكل أقوى في أقسام اللغات ، وتصاعدت وتيرة النقد التطبيقي لأعمال أدبية من الهند وأفريقيا والعالم العربي . كان ذاك زمن دراسة رواية الهندية أرونداتي روي **إله الأشياء الصغيرة** (١٩٩٧ ، انظر Roy) ، و**قلب الظلام** (١٩٠٢) للبولندي جوزيف كونراد (انظر Conrad) ، وموسم **الهجرة إلى الشمال** (١٩٦٦) للسوداني الطيب صالح و**الباب المفتوح** (١٩٦٠) للمصرية لطيفة الزيات و**عام الفيل** (١٩٨٠) للمغربية ليلى أبوزيد . وهكذا ، عادت النسوية الأكاديمية تلتحف بغطاء سياسي جديد ، فالأعمال التي تُطبق عليها تلك النظرية تمنح النساء صوتاً في فترات ما بعد الاستعمار ، وتسلط الضوء على التمييز ضدهن في فترات الاستقلال الوطني . وتدريجيا ، دخلت مفاهيم دراسات ما بعد الاستعمار النسوي إلى حقل الدراسات الأدبية ، وبدا في وقت ما أن مفهوم «**الهُجْنة**» هو الحل السحري لكافة المشاكل التي يخلفها الاستعمار ، وأهمها الصراع بين التقليد والحداثة . من هنا ، كانت الهُوّة قد اتسعت بين النظرية الأدبية والواقع الذي يموج بمشكلات لم تتطرق إليها النظرية بعد ، وأهمها ما اصطرح على تسميته «**تأنيث الفقر**» . كان على النقد النسوي آنذاك أن يضع في الحسبان عامل الطبقة بوصفه أحد

فعل الشارع تجاه المسيرة النسائية في ميدان التحرير في القاهرة يوم 8 مارس من عام 2011، أي بعد رحيل مبارك بفترة وجيزة (Elsadda, "Egypt" n. pag).

ومع مجيء الثمانينيات من القرن العشرين، اجتاحت النيوليبرالية العالم؛ وهو ما دفع بالمعارضة الإسلامية إلى الظهور. وهو ما جعل الدولة بدورها تعمد إلى منافسة هذا التيار على أرضية حقوق النساء (Kandiyoti, "Disentangling" 11). وبالطبع، تتحول حقوق النساء إلى أكبر وسيلة مقايضة بين الطرفين. وفيما بين نسوية الدولة والخطاب الإسلامي (الرافض للفكر النسوي من منطلق أن الإسلام منح المرأة كافة حقوقها)، تحولت المسألة النسوية إلى مؤشر دال على الهُويّة. فمَن يملك تحديد هُويّة النساء (وكأن هناك هُويّة واحدة) يحكم المشهد الاجتماعي الذي يؤثر بدوره في السياسي. وفيما بين نقطتين ثوريتين (1919 و2011)، ظل السؤال النسوي مكوناً أساسياً في الخطاب السياسي العام، بوصفه أرضية يُمكن مقايضتها بحقوق بديلة. هكذا، ظلت الأنظمة تسعى إلى المزاوجة بين مكتسبات الحداثة العالمية، فتقوم بالتوقيع، مثلاً، على اتفاقية إلغاء أشكال التمييز كافةً ضد النساء، والمعروفة باسم سيداو، وفي الوقت ذاته تتحفظ على أهم بنود فيها، بحجة أنها تناهض الشريعة الإسلامية، مما يحوّل هذه الاتفاقيات إلى حبر على ورق، لا فائدة منها سوى استعراض الحداثة أمام المجتمع الدولي (انظر المرنيسي، الخوف).

المدهش أنه رغم التباين السياسي الواضح بين بداية القرن العشرينٍ ونهايته، ظلت النبرة الاعتذارية تلازم الخطاب النسوي، وكان عليه دائماً أن يثبت أن المناداة بحقوق النساء لا تخالف الشريعة الإسلامية، وذلك من أجل دحض الفكرة القائلة بأن الفكر النسوي ليس إلا منظومة غربية تهدف إلى تفكيك الأسرة وهدم الثوابت. وقد ظهر ذلك بوضوح إثر انعقاد مؤتمر السكان في مصر عام 1994، والمؤتمر الدولي الرابع للنساء تحت رعاية الأمم المتحدة في بكين عام 1995 الذي طرح أصواتاً جديدة تقدم خطاباً متميزاً فيما يتعلق بمسائل الجندر. ويبدو أن هذا الخطاب الجديد كان مهدداً للكثيرين، حتى أن المؤتمر شهد تحالفاً بين الأزهر والفاتيكان. ولم يظهر تأثير وثيقة مؤتمر بكين في مصر إلا من خلال إشكالية وصول النساء إلى مراكز صُنْع القرار ومصطلح «صورة المرأة»، وأصبحت تلك «الصورة» في الفن والأدب والإعلام هي الشغل الشاغل لمعظم المؤسسات.

على المستوى الأكاديمي، أطل الفكر النسوي في الجامعات المصرية من خلال تيمة صورة المرأة في دراسة الأدب. وسعت تلك الدراسات

شرعية تبرر وجوده بوصفه مكوناً أصيلاً وليس مستورداً من الغرب. وبتغير اللحظة السياسية، تتغير معايير الشرعية، وبتغير الأطراف الفاعلة في السلطة، تتغير المسافة - بعداً أو قرباً - من الخطاب النسوي. وبالنظر إلى هذه المؤشرات التي تُشكل الشرعية، يُمكن فَهْم نضال الخطاب النسوي من أجل التواجد في قلب المنظومة السائدة على مستوى الخطاب والممارسة، وليس مجرد تواجد نسائي خالص يدعم الأجندة الوطنية.

أصبح ظهور النساء في الفضاء العام مرتبطاً بمشاركتهن في النضال الوطني ضد الاستعمار والإمبريالية والاحتلال. ظل هذا هو المسوِّغ الأوحد للحركة النسوية، بمعنى أنها امتداد للأجندة الوطنية. وبشكل مفارق، كان كتاب الباحثة السيريلانكية كوماري جاياواردينا Jayawardina الذي صدر عام ١٩٨٦ بعنوان **النسوية والقومية في العالم الثالث** *Feminism and Nationalism in the Third World* هو أحد الكتب التي أسست مفهوم نِسْوية العالم الثالث، إذ تناولت جذور الحركة النسوية في عدة بلدان منها مصر وتركيا. وكانت تسعى إلى تأكيد أن النسوية ليست إيديولوجية غربية دخيلة، بل هي جزء رئيسي من حركة تحرر البلدان. فخروج النساء في النضال الوطني يمنحهن حق المطالبة بالحقوق. هنا، ربما لا بد من تذكر «مؤتمر المرأة الأفريقي الأسيوي» الذي عُقد في القاهرة في يناير ١٩٦١، بحضور وفود من ٣٦ دولة وأسس للفكرة نفسها (خليفة، ص ص ٢٨٣-٣٠٢). وبمراجعة جدول أعمال المؤتمر - وعلى رأسها دور المرأة في النضال وحفظ السلام - وتوصيات المؤتمر، ندرك أن هذا الخطاب المعتمد على الحقوق العامة (المساواة في الميدان الاقتصادي، الحقوق السياسية والقانونية، الاستقلال الوطني) هو الذي ظل مسيطراً على الساحة ومُشكلاً أركان الخطاب النسوي المقبول لدى الجماهير. تشرح الباحثة التركية دينيز كانديوتي Kandiyoti أن هذا القبول الشعبوي قد دفع الحكام (مثل ناصر وبورقيبة) إلى المناداة بهذه الحقوق بوصفها جزءاً من الخطاب الإصلاحي والتنموي الذي يهدف إلى «الصالح العام» (Kandiyoti, "Disquiet" n. pag). إلا أن تضمين الأنظمة الحاكمة لحقوق النساء (التعليم، العمل، الحقوق السياسية، الرفاه) قد أفرز تدريجياً «نِسْوية الدولة» التي استلبت الخطاب النسوي، ودفعت بالمؤسسات التنموية غير الحكومية إلى الظهور لتكون مجرد «ملحقات مساعدة وديعة» لهذا الخطاب (Kandiyoti, "Promise" n. pag). ارتبطت النسوية بمصطلح «السيدة الأولى»، ففقدت شرعيتها مرة أخرى، وهو ما ظهر بوضوح في رد

الصوت النسوي الأدبي والصحفي . بثقة ، يجوز القول إنه في البدء كانت الكلمة ، وهو ما تذكرنا به مقدمة موسوعة ذاكرة للمستقبل : «بدأت هذه الجهود في العقدين الأخيرين من القرن التاسع عشر في سوريا ولبنان ومصر ، وتواصلت حتى الحرب العالمية الأولى ، وبدت مدهشة في قوتها ، فالبدايات غالباً ما تكون واهنة وعلى استحياء ، ولكننا نتوقف عند بدايات واضحة وعفيّة وكثيفة» (مجلد ١ ، ص ١٢) . ظهر بوضوح صوت عائشة تيمور (١٨٤٠- ١٩٠٢) في مصر ووردة اليازجي (١٨٣٨-١٩٢٤) في لبنان . ثم صدرت أول مجلة نسائية في العالم العربي عام ١٨٩٢ ، هي **الفتاة** لصاحبتها هند نوفل . وفي افتتاحية العدد الأول ، تشرح نوفل للقراء أن المجلة «لم تنشأ إلا لتكون مرآة تجلو محاسن الحسناء وتظهر جمال الغيداء ، وتزين صفحاتها بما يصل إليها من درر أقلام الفاضلات ونفائس لأفكار الأديبات في المواضيع العلمية والفصول التاريخية والمناظرات الأدبية والشذرات الفكاهية» (كما ورد في الصدة ، ص ٢١) . ثم توالت الكتابات ، ومنها ، على سبيل المثال وليس الحصر : **الدر المنثور في طبقات ربات الخدور** لزينب فواز عام ١٨٩٤ ، حيث عملت على تأريخ أسماء النساء المنسيات في التاريخ ، وربما كانت أول مَن يعيد قراءة التاريخ من وجهة نظر امرأة ، ثم ظهر صالون الأميرة نازلي فاضل عام ١٨٩٧ ، وإن اقتصر على النخبة المثقفة ، وصولاً إلى كتاب قاسم أمين **تحرير المرأة** الذي صدر عام ١٨٩٩ ، وكان زلزالاً فكرياً .

اللافت للنظر أن مسألة الكتابة كانت من أول الحقوق التي طالبت بها النساء العربيات ، حتى أنه في عام ١٩٠٨ خاضت فاطمة راشد معركةً سفور الأسماء ، أي تشجيع النساء على الإمضاء بأسمائهن الحقيقية بدلاً من الأسماء المستعارة (الصدة وأبو غازي ، ص ٣٠) . ولا يُمكن أن ننسى أن العصر الحديث قد دفع امرأة إلى تبني اسم مغاير للحقيقة من أجل عدم إحراج العائلة .[٢] وتبع ذلك افتتاح الجامعة المصرية في العام نفسه ، ثم تسلمت نبوية موسى وظيفتها بوصفها معلمة لغة عربية في عام ١٩٠٩ . استمرت النسوية تحاول أن تبلور مساحة وجود عن طريق الكلمة والصوت ، حتى اندلعت ثورة ١٩١٩ ، فألقت النساء أنفسهن في الشوارع أمام بنادق الإنجليز (خليفة ، ص ٢٢٠) . وبدا أن الحدود بين المجالين ، الخاص والعام ، على وشك أن تُمحى . لكن في اللحظة ذاتها حدث شيء آخر : فقد اكتسب اقتحام النساء للفضاء العام شرعية من كونهن يدافعن عن استقلال مصر في وجه المستعمِر ، ومنذ ذاك اليوم كان على الفكر النسوي أن يكتسب

بالجديد؟ ومن ناحية أخرىٍ. ومن القديم الذي تأسس عليه هذا الجديد؟ ولذلك ، ستكون هناك دائماً إشارات إلى سياقات مختلفة سواء زمنية أو تاريخية أو سياسية ، من أجل فهم منبع الجدة . يكمن التحدي الثالث في استحالة الإلمام بالمصادر كافة ورصدها ، فالإَنتاج المعرفي النسوي في المنطقة العربية قد تزايد بشكل ملحوظٍ ، وعليه ستحاول المقالة رصد المصادر التأسيسية ، وهو ما لا يعني مطلقاً عدم أهمية ما لم يرد ذكره . أما التحدي الأخير ، فهو محاولة فضّ الخلط الدائم الذي يقع في مجال الدراسات النسوية بين البحثي والتنموي . لا تسعى المقالة إلى رصد الجهود المحترمة التي قامت بها النساء في مجال التنمية البشرية (جمعيات ، منظمات غير حكومية ، مشاريع اقتصادية ، رفع الوعي ، دراسات عن العاملات ، إلخ .) ، بل تسعى إلى محاولة الإمساك بالمحطات الفكرية التي كانت نتاجاً لحراك لافت في المجال العام وفي سياقات اجتماعية وسياسية محددة .[1] ولا بد من الإشارة ، أيضاً ، إلى أن المقالة قد تبدو في الظاهر أنها تتتبع المسار الخطي للنسوية في العالم العربي ، لكن الحقيقة أن كل مؤشرٍ إنتاج معرفي يتقاطع ، ويشتبك ، مع ما قبله وما بعده ، ويطور ذاته أيضاً .

منذ الربع الأخير من القرن العشرين ، تبلور الخطاب النسوي وتغلغل - شكلياً - في مفاصل أجهزة الدولة والبرلمان والإعلام والدين ، بل أصبح يحتل مساحة واضحة في خطابات التطرف الديني . وهو ما أدى إلى تحويل النسوية بوصفها جسد النساء وخطابهن - من حيث هو دلالةٍ ماديةٍ - إلى مساحة استقطاب وصراع . لكن بالرغم من كل ما قد يبدو حراكاً ديناميكياً في خطاب المجال العامِ ، تبقى كل هذه الضجة مفتعلة ، وإن كانت ذات أهدافٍ سياسية دائماً ، غير مرتكزة إلى أي رؤية منهجية . تتناول هذه المقالة تطور الخطاب النسوي العربي على مستوى التنظير والممارسة ، مع التركيز على تأثره بالشرط السياسي والاجتماعي الذي يعيد تشكيل موقع الصوت النسوي في الفضاء العام وقدرته علىٍ خلخلة منظومة علاقات القوى . ومن أجل فهم هذا التطور ، لا بد من فهْم المحطات الرئيسية التي شكلت الخطاب النسوي في اشتباكه مع المنظومة الخطابية السائدة ، والتي تعتمد على التحالف الوثيقٍ بين الأبوية والرأسمالية .

لا مفر من البدء دائماً بالقرن التاسع عشر ، حيث كان الحراك النسائي المجتمعي ظاهراً ،ليس فقط في الطبقات العليا المتعلمة ، بل أيضاً في الطبقات الأدنى منها (انظر Tucker) . إلا أن ذاك القرن يكتسب أهميته من ظهور

النسوية العربية: مواقف وممارسات

شيرين أبو النجا

لا يمكن اعتبار النِّسْوية في كليتها أحد التوجهات الجديدة في العلوم الإنسانية، إلا إذا كنا نقصد أنها ظهرت مع الحداثة التي لا تزال مجتمعاتنا العربية تحاول الإمساك بجوهرها، والتي كلما ذكرها كاتب فإنه يفتح قوسين ويكتب: حقوق الإنسان، الديمقراطية، حقوق النساء. في الوقت ذاته، لا بد من الإشارة إلى أن النسوية ليست خطاباً واحداً مصمتاً، بل هي متعددة ومتغيرة ومرنة في التكيف مع الشروط المادية والتاريخية والجيو-سياسية المحيطة بها. وهي بذلك تتشابه مع مفهوم الهُويّة من حيث كونه غير ثابت ومرناً ومتغيراً.

تهدف هذه المقالة إلى تناول التوجهات البحثية والرؤى المعرفية الجديدة التي انتهجتها النسوية في مجال العلوم الإنسانية في العالم العربي، وهو تناول يحاول تتبع الأفكار الرئيسية التي وجهت المسار الفكري النسوي بشكل أدى إلى تراكم خبرة معرفية، من ناحية، كما كشف عن مناطق معتمة جديرة بالبحث، من ناحية أخرى. ومن ثم، لا تسعى المقالة إلى جمع معلومات أو رصد أحداث مطلقاً؛ إذ لم تعد هذه مهمة منطقية في زمن مواقع البحث الإلكترونية. وفي محاولة فهم مسار الفكر النِّسْوي، يواجه هذا المسعى عدة تحديات. يكمن التحدي الأول في المصطلح ذاته - النسوية - إذ يبدو وكأن هناك تعريفاً واحداً وشكلاً محدداً له. لا بد من التأكيد أن الفكر النسوي في العالم العربي يتسم بالتعددية، لأنه يستجيب للسياق الذي يفرزه أو يناهضه أو يشجعه، ويتفاعل معه. لا أحاول الإقرار بمسألة الخصوصية الثقافية، لأنها تفتح احتمالات كثيرة، منها رفض الفكر النسوي برمته. من وجهة نظري، تتفاعل النسوية، بشكل مباشر، مع السياق السياسي والمجتمعي والمنظومة الحقوقية. ومن هنا، تختلف الممارسات النسوية من بلد عربي لآخر، طبقاً للأولويات ومنظومة علاقات القوى. أما التحدي الثاني، فهو متعلق بتحديد الإطار الزمني، فما المقصود

Deleuze. *Logique du sens*. Paris : Minuit, 1969.

Derrida, J. "De l'économie restreinte à l'économie générale." *L'Ecriture et la différence*. Paris : Seuil, 1967. 369-408.

---. "La Différance." *Marges de la philosophie*. Paris : Minuit, 1972. 1-29.

Entretiens sur les notions de genèse et de structure. Sous la direction de Maurice de Gandillac, Lucien Goldmann, Jean Piaget. Paris : Mouton, 1965.

Foucault, M. *L'Archéologie du savoir*. Paris : Gallimard, 1969.

Heidegger, M. *Chemins qui ne mènent nulle part*. Trad. Wolfgang Brokmeier. Paris : Gallimard, 1962.

---. *L'Être et le temps*. Trad. Alphonse de Waelhens. Paris : Gallimard, 1964.

---. "Lettre sur l'humanisme." *Questions III et IV*. Trad. Jean Beaufret et al. Paris : Gallimard, 1966. 65-127.

---. "Logos." *Essais et conférences*. Trad. André Préau. Préface de Jean Beaufret. Paris : Gallimard, 1980. 249-78.

---. *Nietzsche II*. Trad. P. Klossowski. Paris : Gallimard, 1971.

---. *Q'appelle-t-on penser ?* Trad. Gérard Granel et Aloys Becker. Paris : PUF, 1959.

Lukács, J. *Histoire et conscience de classe*. Trad. K. Axelos et J. Bois. Paris : Minuit, 1956.

Marx, K. et F. Engels. *L'Idéologie allemande*. Trad. Henri Auger et al. Paris : Les Éditions Sociales, 1968.

³ انظر مقدمة كتاب فوكو التي أعاد فيها نشر حواره مع «حلقة الإبستيمولوجيين» (Foucault 9-28).

⁴ انظر أعمال الندوة التي أقيمت تحت عنوان «التكوين والبنية» (١٩٥٩)، ونشرت (١٩٦٥) بعنوان *Entretiens sur les notions de genèse et de structure*.

⁵ يقول ألتوسير:

الحقيقة أن الإيديولوجية لا شأن كبيراً لها بـ«الوعي». هذا إذا افترضنا أن لهذا اللفظ معنى واحداً... صحيح أن الإيديولوجية منظومة من التمثلات، بيد أن هذه التمثلات لا صلة لها بـ«الوعي». إنها في أغلب الأحيان صور، وأحياناً تصورات، لكنها لا تفرض ذاتها على معظم الناس إلا بوصفها بنيات دون أن تمر بـ«وعيهم». إنها موضوعات ثقافية تدرك وتقبل وتعاني وتعاش. فتفعل فعلها في البشر عبر مسلسل يفلت من أيديهم. إن الناس يحيون إيديولوجيتهم مثلما كان معتنق الديكارتية يرى، أو يرى، القمر على بعد مئتي قدم منه، ليس بوصفه شكلاً من أشكال الوعي، وإنما موضوع من موضوعات عالمهم، بل بوصفه عالمهم ذاته. (Althusser 239-40)

المراجع

L'Abécédaire de Gilles Deleuze. Pierre-André Boutang, 1988-1989.

Althusser, L. *Positions*. Paris : Les Éditions sociales, 1976.

---. *Pour Marx*. Paris : Maspero, 1965.

Automates, réseaux, interfaces : Sur l'œuvre de Gérard Chazal. Coordonné par Jean-Claude Beaune, François Dagognet et Daniel Parrochia. Lyon : Université Jean Moulin-Lyon 3, 2007.

Barthes, R. *Le Grain de la voix*. Paris : Seuil, 1981.

Beaufret, J. "Préface." Martin Heidegger. *Essais et conférences*. Trad. André Préau. Paris : Gallimard, 1980. i-xv.

---. "Préface." Martin Heidegger. *Le Principe de raison*. Trad. André Préau. Paris : Gallimard, 1962.

---. *Dialogue avec Heidegger*. Tome III. Paris : Minuit, 1974.

Blanchot, M. "Le Rire des Dieux." *N.R.F.* 151 (Juillet 1965) : 91-105.

Cassin, Barbara. "Grecs et Romains, les paradigmes de l'Antiquité chez Arendt et Heidegger." *Politique et pensée* [Colloque Hannah Arendt]. Paris : Payot, 1989. 17-42.

وبعد . .

لم يسمح لنا الفكر الفلسفي المعاصر بأن نعرضه وفق خانات تصنفه مذاهب وتيارات ، وقد استعضنا عن ذلك بالوقوف عند ما يمكن أن نعده مفهومات-مفاتيح ، حصرناها أساساً في مفهومات البنية والسلب والتناقض والاختلاف والتاريخ والتراث والإيديولوجية. ولم يكن هدفنا في هذه المقالة الوجيزة فحص هذه المفهومات كما تطورت في الفلسفة المعاصرة ، ولا تدقيق مسارها عند كل واحد من الفلاسفة الذين ذكرناهم ، كما أننا لا ندعي أننا حددناها تحديداً نهائياً . ولم يكن هدفنا إلا الوقوف عند أشكال الخلخلة التي ما فتئت تتعرض لها، والمقاومات التي ما فتئت تبديها عند كبار الفلاسفة المعاصرين .

لا يخفى أن المنهج الذي اتبعناه هنا لا يروم أساساً الاستيفاء والضمّ الكلي ومتابعة أشكال التطور ، ومحاولة خلق عائلات فكرية ، وإنما السعي إلى القبض على الشيء ذاته le même الذي يقال اليوم في الفلسفة بأنحاء متباينة . ولا شك في أن القارئ قد تبيّن أن المدار الذي تدور حوله هذه الفلسفة هو في الأساس إعادة النظر في فلسفات الوعي ، ومراجعة مفهوم الزمان ، مع ما يتولد عن تلك المراجعة من إعادة النظر في مفهومات الأصل والاستمرار الزمني . هذا ما كان ميشيل فوكو قد بلوره في مقدمته لحفرياته في المعرفة حينما كتب : «أن نجعل من التحليل التاريخي خطاباً للمتصل ، ومن الوعي البشري ذاتاً فاعلة هي مصدر كل صيرورة وممارسة : هذان وجهان للمنظومة الفكرية نفسها. في هذه المنظومة يُنظر إلى الزمان بوصفه توليداً لكليات موحِّدة ، وإلى الثورات بوصفها وعياً بالذات» (Foucault 22) .

الهوامش

[1] برنامج وثائقي من إنتاج بيير أندريه بوتانج Boutang ، سُجِّل بين عامي ١٩٨٨ و١٩٨٩ ، وهو عبارة عن سلسلة محاورات مع كلير بارنيه Parnet .

[2] الإشارة هنا إلى سعي جيل دولوز إلى أن يذهب بمفهوم الشبكة إلى مداه الأبعد محاولاً تحريره من المفهومات العضوية للانتظام والغائية ، ومن أجل ذلك يوظف مفهوم الجذمور Rhizome ، ذلك النبات الأخرق الذي لا بداية له ولا نهاية ، ولا أصل ولا غاية ، والذي ينمو من الوسط .

تربط الناس فيما بينهم . الإيديولوجية علاقة بالعلائق ، إنها ليست علاقة بسيطة ، وإنما علاقة مركبة ، علاقة بعلاقة ، علاقة من الدرجة الثانية على حد تعبير ألتوسير نفسه (Althusser, *Pour Marx* 240) [5].

فحتى إن قرّبنا الإيديولوجية من مفهوم اللاشعور ، فهي لن تكون لاشعورَ ذات سيكولوجية . ليس اللاشعور منطقة معتمة تسكن أدمغتنا . اللاشعور هنا هو الفجوة أو الانفلات écart الذي توجد فيه التشكيلة الاجتماعية بالنسبة إلى ذاتها . اللاشعور هو هروب التشكيلة الاجتماعية عن ذاتها . ذلك أن العلائق الاجتماعية لا تعاش في مباشَرتها ، وإنما تعاش مبتعدة عن ذاتها . بلغة نيتشه إنها تعاش ملونة مؤولة مغلفة ، أي أنها لا تُعطى في تلقائيتها . هذا الابتعاد أو الانفلات ، الذي لا يتوقف كثيراً على ما لدى الأعضاء الفاعلين في المجتمع من وعي به ، هو ما يمكن أن نطلق عليه الوهم الإيديولوجي . وهو وَهم لا يفترض بالضرورة ، وكما اعتقد فوكو ، حقيقة تقابله ، ولا ذاتاً تحمله ، ولا مادة توجد «تحته» ، لأنه ليس إلا التشكيلة الاجتماعية في انفصالها عن ذاتها ، فكأن له وجوداً موضوعياً ، إنه «موضوعات» .

ثم إن الآلية الإيديولوجية لا تقف عند الدفاع عن مصالح ، ولا تقتصر على القلب والتغليف ، وإنما تخلق الوحدة وتتصيد الاختلاف لتقهر . لا يمكننا أن ندرك الآلية الإيديولوجية إن نحن بقينا تحت قهر «نظرية المصالح» . لذا ، يقول ألتوسير إن لهذه الآلية دوراً مهماً من حيثُ إنها تشد أواصر المجتمع وتغلف تناقضاته ، فتجعل التناقض انسجاماً ، والاختلاف تطابقاً ، والتعدد وحدةً .

على هذا النحو ، تعد الآلية الإيديولوجية آلية فعّالة . إنها ليست مرآة عاكسة منفعلة تعكس الواقع الاجتماعي وما يتفاعل فيه ، وإنما هي عامل محدّد ، وفعالية نشطة ، ومقاومة مستميتة . للإيديولوجية قدرة جبّارة على التلوُّن والتقنّع ، وقدرة خارقة على التلوين والتقنيع وخلق الأوهام ، وهي لا تكتفي بتشويه الأفكار وقلب الحقائق . ووظيفتها ليست وظيفة إبستيمولوجية ما دامت آلية لخلق التطابق وقهر الاختلافات .

لو استعملنا الإيديولوجية بهذا المعنى ، فربما تعذر الحديث عن موتها ، ما دامت آلية أساسية لخلق ما يعمل بوصفه واقعاً ، أو لخلق ما يعمل بوصفه مجتمعاً متراصَّ البناء . وربما لن نجد ، حينذاك ، حرجاً في استعمالها بوصفها مفهوماً ، ليس لتحليل الواقع وتأويله ، بل ربما حتى للإسهام في تغييره .

* * *

الأقل إعادة تأويله، والانفتاح على ما عرفه المفهوم عند بعض الماركسيين المجريين، ولوكاش على الخصوص (انظر Lukács)، ثم عند جرامشي Gramsci، ولا سيما عند ألتوسير.

من أجل ذلك كان لازماً أن يظهر فلاسفة ماركسيون متفتحون على مستجدات الفكر المعاصر، وخصوصاً ما سُمّي بـ«فلسفات التوجس» philosophies du soupçon، لا لتنقيح المفهوم وإنقاذه، وإنما لإخراجه من الإشكالية الماركسية التقليدية التي لم تستطع أن تتحرر من فلسفة الكوجيتو، ولا أن تفكك ثنائيات الميتافيزيقا، وعلى الخصوص الثنائي بنية فوقية/بنية تحتية، وكذا الثنائي نظرية/تطبيق، ولم تتمكن على الخصوص من فصل المفهوم عن «نظرية المصالح».

لا نعتقد أن بإمكان المرء أن يتحدث اليوم عن الإيديولوجية من غير أن يضع في الحسبان تحولات الفكر الفلسفي المعاصر، ولا سيما الإسهامات الأساسية للتقويض الهايدجري لمفهومات البراكسيس واللوجوس والتقنية، وكذا لما تعرّضت له فلسفات الشعور على يد أصحاب التحليل النفسي، ولما أصاب مفهوم الحقيقة على يد نيتشه.

هنا، تبدو القيمة الكبرى للإسهام الألتوسيري في هذا المضمار. فقد أوضح لوي ألتوسير أن الإيديولوجية ظلت، حتى عند ماركس نفسه، مرتبطة بنظرية عن الوعي، ومشدودة أساساً إلى نظرية المصالح، وإلى مفهوم معين عن الحقيقة. هذا ما يُمْكننا أن نجمله بقولنا إنها ظلت مرتبطة بميتافيزيقا الذاتية، وبإبستيمولوجيا لا تَحيد كثيراً عن العقلانية التقليدية، بل تستمد منها أسسها. فهي إذن إبستيمولوجيا ترتكز على الكوجيتو، وتعتمد المباشرة في إدراك المعاني، وتجعل من الذات المفكرة سند الوجود. يكفي الرجوع في هذا الصدد إلى الكتاب المهم الذي جمع فيه ألتوسير مجموعة من المقالات تحت عنوان **دفاعاً عن ماركس** Pour Marx، حيث أوضح، منذ منتصف ستينيات القرن الماضي، أن التمثلات الإيديولوجية لا علاقة لها بالوعي، وأنها «موضوعات ثقافية تُدرك وتُقبل وتُعانَى وتعاش، فتفعل فعلها في البشر عبر مسلسل يفلت من أيديهم» (239). استعمال كلمة موضوع هنا هو محاولة من ألتوسير أن يبيّن أن الإيديولوجية لا تسكن الأدمغة، وإنما هي، على حد تعبيره، مستوى من مستويات التشكيلة الاجتماعية، إنها حالةٌ في «الأجهزة الإيديولوجية للدولة» (Althusser, Positions 2). فالوهم الإيديولوجي ليس كامناً في التمثلات، وإنما في العلاقة التي تربط تلك التمثلات بالعلائق التي

لوقت غير قصير ، ظل المفهوم رهين تأويل معين كان يتخذ مرجعية له بالأساس ما جاء في مخطوط **الإيديولوجية الألمانية** :

إن إنتاج الأفكار والتمثّلات والوعي يكون ، قبل كل شيء ، وبصفة مباشرة ، وثيق الصلة بالنشاط المادي للبشر وبتبادلهم المادي . إنه لغة الحياة الفعلية . فتمثّلات الناس وتبادلهم الفكري ، يظهر ، هنا أيضاً ، بوصفه تجلياً مباشراً لسلوكهم المادي ، فإذا كان التعبير الواعي للأفراد عن العلائق الفعلية تعبيراً خادعاً ، وإذا كان هؤلاء يقلبون الواقع رأساً على عقب في تصوراتهم ، فما ذلك إلا نتيجة فعاليتهم المادية المحدودة وما يترتب عنها من علائق . (Marx et Engels 51)

وقلّما كان شُرّاح مفهوم الإيديولوجية يولون اهتماماً للكتابات اللاحقة لهذا المخطوط الذي خُطّ كما نعلم سنة ١٨٤٥ ، وظل عرضة للإهمال . تلك الكتابات ظهرت في الأدبيات الماركسية ذاتها ، أو في غيرها ، فأعادت النظر في مفهوم الوعي الانعكاسي ، واعترفت للأفكار بدورها في التاريخ وأعادت للبنية الفوقية أهميتها وفعاليتها ، بل أعادت النظر في تحديد مفهوم الإيديولوجية ذاته .

إلا أن الذين أولوا عنايتهم لهذه الكتابات ، ودعوا إلى تجاوز التحديد الذي جاء في مخطوط **الإيديولوجية الألمانية** والتفتح على ما لحقه ، اقتصروا على ما جاء في رسائل ماركس وإنجلز من إعادة اعتبار للعوامل الإيديولوجية ودورها في التاريخ الإنساني ، حيث أسند مؤسِّسا المادية التاريخية للأشكال الحقوقيّة والنظريات السياسية والفلسفية والعقائد الدينية دوراً معيّناً وإن لم يكن الدور الحاسم . فما يُسمّى بالعقيدة الإيديولوجية يعمل عمله في البناء التحتي ولا يقتصر على عكس ما يتم فيه .

لا يخفى أن هذا لم يعمل في النهاية على إعادة النظر الجذرية في المفهوم . صحيح أنه أدخل عليه بعض التنقيح ، إلا أن الأهم هو أنه لم يعمل على إعادة النظر في الأسس الفلسفية التي يقوم عليها ، والتي تتمركز أساساً حول ما تعطيه الفلسفة التقليدية من دور أساسي للذات المفكرة . كان لازماً ، والحالة هذه ، ليس الاكتفاء بتنقيح المفهوم أو العمل على توسيعه ، وإنما تجاوز الموقف الماركسي التقليدي في كليته ، أو على

بعضها بعضاً. لكن هذه النفوس تظل مكبوتة مقموعة تحت ضغط الشكل الذي يفرض به التراث سيادته. ذلك أن هذا الشكل، بعيداً عن أن يسمح بإدراك ما ينقله، فإنه يسهم غالباً، على العكس من ذلك، في تغليفه، قامعاً محتواه ليجعل منه مجرد بداهات، أي حواجز تخفي ذاتها بظهورها.

كان محللو الإيديولوجيات يعتبرون هذا التغليف من عمل الآلية الإيديولوجية التي تخلق الأوهام وتحنّط الفكر وتكلّس الهُويّات، غير أن أغلب المفكرين المعاصرين أصبحوا يبدون كثيراً من التحفظ في استعمال هذا المفهوم. إلى حدّ أن بإمكاننا أن نجزم أن مفهوم الإيديولوجية هذا ربما كان هو الضحية الكبرى التي أعقبت حركات الخلخلة المعاصرة التي قوّضت فلسفات الكوجيتو، وخلخلت مفهوم التاريخ. فهل لا يزال لهذا المفهوم ما يبرر استعماله في الفكر المعاصر؟

في مفهوم الإيديولوجية

أصبح كثير من المفكرين المعاصرين يستشعرون، لا أقول نوعاً من الحرج، وإنما على الأقل نوعاً من التردّد في استعمال مفهوم الإيديولوجية. وربما لا يعود ذلك أساساً إلى ما نسمعه، هنا وهناك، عن عصرنا من أنه عصر «موت الإيديولوجيات»، وإنما إلى عدم الدقة الذي يكتنف الاستعمال الحالي للمفهوم. ذلك أن هذا المفهوم الذي ما انفكّ يشوبه الغموض منذ ميلاده، يظهر أنه قد فقد كل قيمة من جرّاء الانتقادات التي تعرّض لها من طرف مفكرين لهم مكانتهم المرموقة في الفكر المعاصر. وعلى كل حال، فمعظم هؤلاء يُبدي نفوراً من استعماله، حتى وإن كان يستعيض عنه بمفهومات غير بعيدة عنه أشد البعد. هذا ما يمكننا أن نقوله عن مفهوم اللامفكر فيه عند هايدجر، أو مفهوم اللاشعور عند فرويد، أو مفهوم الوثن عند نيتشه.

قد يقال إن هذه الانتقادات المتلاحقة علامة على ديناميكية وحيوية وقدرة متواصلة على المقاومة، وإن المفهوم، إن كان قد ضعف تداوله، فإن معانيه ما انفكت حاضرة في الفكر المعاصر، ولا تزال مهيمنة على المواقف الفكرية والتحليلات السياسية. لذا فربما وجب، قبل البتّ في مشروعية استعماله، حصر معانيه ومتابعة تكوّنها، وليس من سبيل إلى ذلك، على ما يبدو، إلا بالعودة إلى نشأته وملاحقة تطوره.

غالباً ما يسهم ، على العكس من ذلك ، في تغليفه وحجبه ، وهو يحط من محتواه ، ويجعل منه مجرد بداهات ، فيحول دون بلوغ المنابع الأصلية التي نهلت منها المقولات والمفهومات التقليدية في جزء منها على الأقل» (Heidegger, L'Être 28) .

عندما بلغ هايدجر سن الثمانين كتبت حنة أَرنْدت : «أحدهم . . . إذ انفصم الحبل الذي يشده إلى التراث ، اكتشف المَاضي من جديد . . . فاستعاد الفكر حيويته ، وتمكن من استنطاق الذخائر الثقافية للماضي ، تلك الذخائر التي كنا نعتقد أنها ماتت ، وها هي الآن تقدم لنا أشياء تخالف أشد المخالفة ما كنا نعتقده» (cité par Cassin 21) . فوحده الفكر القادر على خلق الانفصال هو الذي يستطيع أن يعيد الوصل ويتمكن من استعادة الذخائر التي حجبها الماضي : «يقتضي الحوار مع التراث إذن أن يُحَرَّر الفكر الذي نُقل إلينا فيتمكن من العودة إلى ما اختزن فيه وادُّخر ، إلى هذا الذي لم ينفك عن الوجود ، هذا الذي يهيمن على التراث منذ بداياته ، وكان دوماً أسبق منه متقدماً عليه ، دون أن يفكر فيه بوضوح ، ودون أن ينظر إليه بوصفه أصلاً» (Heidegger, Nietzsche II 283-84) .

ليس استذكار التراث ، إذن ، استرجاعاً لمبدأ تفسيري نعلّل به تسلسل الوقائع التاريخية . ولا يتم النظر إلى التراث هنا من خلال فلسفة في التاريخ ترد التاريخ إلى كلية ميتافيزيقية . إن الاسترجاع هنا استرجاع لهُويَّاتنا من حيث إن ذلك التراث تراثنا المنسي . غير أن النسيان لا يعني الغياب . إنه ليس قوة سلبية . النسيان قدرة إيجابية تغلق ، من حين إلى آخر ، أبواب الوعي ونوافذه فتحول دون تدفق الماضي وسعيه إلى أن يحضر ويتجمد ويتطابق . ليس العود إلى التراث ، إذن ، رجوعاً إلى ماض تأريخي ، فالتراث يعنينا ويهم حاضرنا فيما ينطوي عليه من غموضٍ وما يقوى عليه من طاقة مستقبلية . لكن ذلك لا يعني مطلقاً أن الأمر يتعلق «ببعث نفس خالدة» تحيا عبر السنين ، وإنما ، على العكس من ذلك ، «بإبراز نفوس فانية» طالها النسيان وهمشها التاريخ .

إن البحث عن الأصل لا يؤسّسٍ ، إنّه يربك ما ندركه ثابتاً ، ويحرّك ما نفترضه ساكناً ، ويُجزّئ ما نراه موحّداً ، ويفكّك ما نعتبره متطابقاً . تقصّي الأصول ، والحالة هذه ، هو التقويض الدائم لهُويّاتنا . ذلك أن الهُويّة التي نسعى إلى الحفاظ عليها وإخفائها تحت قناع ليست هي ذاتها إلا محاكاة ساخرة : فالتعدّد يقطنها ، ونفوس عدّة تتنازع داخلها ، والمنظومات تتعارض فيها ويقهر

ينكشف الفجر في حقيقته التي كانت محجوبة» (-Beauffret, "Préface" [Es
sais] xiii) . ليس المغيب هنا مكاناً تغيب عنده الإشراقة ، وهو ليس ثقافة بعينها . فالغرب L'occident ليس وطناً ولا عرْقاً ولا أمة ولا قومية ولا بلداً ، إنه لحظة انكشاف فجر لم يكفَّ عن الإشراق . فإذا كان العالم الإغريقي مهدَ الفكر وفجره ، فربما لا يستمد ذلك الفجر عمقه إلا إذا نُظر إليه من خلال المغيب . فليست العودة إلى الإغريق بقصد إبراز المعجزة الإغريقية ، ولا لمعرفتهم معرفةٍ أكثر إتقاناً . حيث يرى هايدجر إننا لا نبحث في الفكر الإغريقي حباً في الإغريق ، وطلباً للمعرفة ، وسعياً وراءه . لا نبحث فيهم من أجل حوار أدق ، وإنما في ما يمكن أن يرقى ، من خلال هذا الحوار ، إلى مستوى القول . ذلك هو الشيء ذاته الذي يهم الإغريق ، ويهمنا بكيفيات مختلفة ، ذاك هو ما ينقل الفجر نحو قدر مغيبه . وفقاً لهذا فحسب ، يصبح الإغريق إغريقاً بالمعنى التاريخي الأصيل : «فليس الإغريق في استعمالاتنا اللغوية خاصيةً عرْقية ، ولا موطناً ولا ثقافة أو حضارة ، الإغريقي فجر قدر انكشف على ضوئه الوجود بوصفه موجوداً» (Heidegger, Chemins 274) .

ليست علاقتنا بالأصول إذن علاقة تأريخية ، إننا لا نعثر فيها على مبدأ تفسيري نعلل به تسلسل الوقائع فيما بعد . إن استرجاع الأصول معناه أن نجد أنفسنا في وحدة القدر الذي هو قدرنا ، والذي صدر عنه كلام ما انفكّ يعود نحونا في الوضوح-الغامض للتراث ، «وحينئذ ، لن يكون التراث وراءنا إلا ظاهرياً ، من حيث هو ماضٍ تأريخي يمكن لعلم التاريخ أن يعرضه علينا ، إنه ليس وراءنا بقدر ما هوَ يعنينا ويهم حاضرنا فيما ينطوي عليه من غموض ، وفيما يقوى عليه من طاقة مستقبلية» (Beauffret, "Préface" [Principe] 31-32) . لذا ، يقول هايدجر عن اليونان «فجر الفكر الأوروبي» : «في الوجود التاريخي الأصيل لا نكون لا على مسافة بعيدة ، ولا على مسافة قريبة من اليونان . إننا نكون بالنسبة إليهم في التيه والضلال» (Heidegger, Chemins 406) .

هذا التيه يجعل التراث عند هايدجر يتصف بخاصية مزدوجة : فبينما يشكل التراث عند هيجل ذخيرة العقل الواعي بذاته ، ولحظاتٍ لنمو الفكر ، فإنه ، في نظر هايدجر ، ينبوع وحاجز . فالتراث الذي لا يمكن للفكر أن يتجاوزه إلا بمحاورته ، والذي هو الكفيل بأن يمهّد لما لم يفكر فيه ، يشكل في الوقت ذاته حاجزاً دون ذلك . يقول هايدجر : «إن التراث الذي يفرض سيادته ، بعيداً عن أن يسمح بإدراك ما ينقله ، فإنه

نيتشه فيما بعد بـ«حمى التاريخ» التي طبعت القرن التاسع عشر الألماني، وطرحت مسألة العودة إلى الأصول طرحاً فلسفياً، فأعادت النظر في مفهوم التراث ذاته. ولعل الفيلسوف المعاصر الذي بلور هذه المسألة على الوجه الأكمل هو مارتن هايدجر. فماذا يعني التراث لديه؟

مسألة التراث

يشير هايدجر إلى أن القديم لا يفتأ يلاحق الإنسان. تفيد هذه الملاحظة مفهوماً معيناً عن التاريخ لا ينحل إلى مجرد حركة صيرورة تقدمية يتجاوز فيها اللاحق السابق، وإنما يغدو، على العكس من ذلك، حركة حاضر يمتد بعيداً نحو الماضي، ولا يكون تذكراً له فحسب، وإنما تنبؤاً واستقبالاً. لا تتحدد حركة التاريخ عند هايدجر بوصفها شيئًا تمّ وحصَل مثلما هو الأمر عند هيجل، فالتاريخ لا يتم بوصفه حصولاً، والحصول لا يقتصر على انسياب الزمن. إن التاريخ ليس تعاقباً لعصور، وإنما هو اقتراب للشيء ذاته. بيد أن هذا الاقتراب لا يعني إرجاع التاريخ إلى حاضر دائم، إنه، على العكس من ذلك، ابتعاد عن الأصول. التاريخ حركة «تفلت من يديها لحظة البداية وتضيّعها» (Heidegger, Q'appelle-t-on penser ? 117). ذلك أن الحاضر لا يحضر، كما سبق أن قلنا، أما الماضي فهو لا يحضر ولا يمضي. إن الحاضر دوماً حاضر «مرجّأ»، وهو في تباعد دائم عن نفسه. إنه تائه ضال.

النتيجة الأولى التي تتمخض عن هذا المفهوم عن التاريخ هي أن التراث ليس مفهوما زمانياً. فهو لا يتطابق ونمط الزمان الماضي. وهو ليس «شيئاً مضى، ليس موضوعاً من موضوعات الوعي التاريخي». إنه لا يوجد وراءنا، وإنما «يجيء صوبنا لأننا معرّضون له ولأنه قدرنا» (Heidegger, Q'appelle-t-on penser ? 117). وبالمثل، لا يعني مفهوم القدر هنا خلوداً سرمدياً أو جبرية كونية، وإنما يردنا إلى الأصل التاريخي، لا بوصفه بداية زمنية و«أصلاً أول» فالأصل، هنا، ليس لحظة متميزة من لحظات التاريخ. الأصل ليس مبدأ تفسيرياً، إنه ليس مبدأ ولا بداية زمنية، بل إن البداية، على العكس من ذلك، هي الغلاف الذي يحجب الأصل ويخفيه.

إن الأصل لا ينفكّ يبتدئ، إنه الفجر الذي لا ينفجر بغتةً، والذي لا يفصح عن مكنونه إلا مساء الفكر. فالفجر، كما كتب جان بوفريه، «يظل معتماً بالنسبة إلى ذاته من حيث هو إشراقة أولى، ويأتي الأفول والمغيب كي

لتوجيه العقل ، ولا بتبيّن حدود الصلاحية ، وإنما سيغدو مقاومة ، ومقاومة تكافئ في عنادها لا صلابة الأخطاء ، ولا قوة الأوهام ومكرها ، وإنما ما يدعوه دولوز البلاهات والتّرّهات les bêtises .

بإمكاننا أن نتفهم ، والحالة هذه ، دعوة مَن يدعون إلى نبذ الفلسفة ، ولكن ليس بوصفها مقاومة تتعقب البلاهة وترصد «حماقات» مجتمع الفرجة ، وإنما بوصفها أنساقاً تسعى إلى أن تسن للعلوم قواعد لعبتها ، وتملي على الفرد قواعد سلوكه .

مهمة أخرى لا يمكن للفلسفة أن تجد بديلاً يقوم عوضها في القيام بها هي عملية الدفن ذاتها . ذلك ما كان هايدجر قد أكد عليه منذ بدايات القرن الماضي ، عندما أشار إلى أن تجاوز الفلسفة لا يمكن أن يتم إلا بإحياء ماضيها ، وبدفنها من جديد . ففي كلمة dépassement هناك الماضي passé . من هنا ، اتخذت كلمة نهاية عند هايدجر وهو يعلن «نهاية الفلسفة لبداية الفكر» معنى غنياً ، فهي نهاية حُبْلى بالأصول والأسس . إنها عودة ورجوع . ذلك أن الأصل لا يكفّ عن الابتداء . والنهاية هي تحرير للفكر وعودة إلى ما اختزن فيه وادّخر ، عودة إلى هذا الذي لم ينفك عن الابتداء ، هذا الذي يهيمن على التراث الفلسفي منذ بداياته . «مصيبة» الفلسفة عند هايدجر ، أو «لعنتها» على الأصح ، هي كونها عائقَ ذاتها ، فكأن حياتها رهينة بموتها والعكس . ذلك أن تاريخ الفلسفة ، الذي لا يمكن للفكر أن يتجاوزه إلا بمحاورته ، والذي هو الكفيل وحده بأن يمهّد لما لم يفكر فيه ، يشكل في الوقت ذاته حاجزاً دون ذلك .

ها نحن نلمس حيوية الفلسفة و«حياتها» ، حتى عند محاولة الحديث عن موتها ونهايتها . ذلك أننا سرعان ما نجد أنفسنا مضطرين ، حتى عند لحظات الاحتضار الأخيرة ، إلى طرح مفهومات الموت والنهاية موضع سؤال ، والتمييز بين البدايات والأصول ، وبين التأريخي l'historique والتاريخي الأصيل l'historial . في أيّ سياق يا ترى يمكن أن تعالَج هذه الأمور المعقدة إن لم يكن في سياق الفلسفة ذاته؟

هذا التمييز بين التأريخي والتاريخي الأصيل جعل الفكر المعاصر يعيد النظر في تاريخه ، بل وفي مسألة التاريخ ذاتها . وكلنا يذكر ما خطّه ماركس وإنجلز في مخطوط الإيديولوجية الألمانية *L'Idéologie allemande* من أن لا علم إلا التاريخ . ولم يكن ذلك في الحقيقة إلا بلورة لما سيدعوه

غير أن ما يبدو هو أن الفلسفة طال احتضارها. فهي ما فتئت تتلقى خبر إعلان موتها وهذا منذ «اكتمالها» على يد هيجل. صحيح أن إعلان الموت جاء من منابر متنوعة، وصدر عن أصوات متعددة وبأسماء متنوعة: إما باسم المعرفة العلمية التي عُلّقت عليها كبير الآمال، أو باسم التاريخ، معرفةً وواقعاً، أو باسم البراكسيس Praxis، على أساس أن الفلاسفة لم يعملوا إلا على تأويل العالم دون تغييره.

ورغم ذلك، فإعلان الموت يتخذ اليوم نبرة خاصة، وهو يأتي من جهة يبدو أن لها اليوم سلطة عليا، وأنها هي التي تبتّ في الأمور وترعى الحقيقة وتصنع الرأي. الخصم الأكبر للفلسفة اليوم ليس ما كان يوسم بالخطأ عندما كان يوكل إليها ما سُمي زمناً طويلاً بحثاً عن الحقيقة، ولا هو حتى ما يسمى إيديولوجية على أساس أن مهمة الفلسفة، كما كان يقال، هي فضح الأوهام. خصم الفلسفة اليوم هو البلاهات والترّهات التي يصنعها مجتمع الفرجة، ويحاول الإعلام بما يمتلكه من قوة جبارة أن يرسخها وينشرها ويكرّسها.

وربما كان هذا الأمر في حاجة إلى قليل من التوضيح. وما دمنا قد تحدثنا في البداية عن دولوز وموقفه من «موت الفلسفة»، فلنتوقف قليلاً عند ما يقوله عن دور الفلسفة والخصوم الذين واجهتهم عبر تاريخها. فقد سبق له - إرساءً للنهج الذي يمكن للفكر، أو لنقل على الأصح الذي يتبقى للفكر نهجه في عالمنا المعاصر - أن ميّز بين أشكال متعددة من اللافكر، وبالتالي من المقاومات التي يمكن للفكر أن يتخذها، وللأدوار التي يتبقى للفلسفة أن تلعبها. ففي وقت اتخذ اللافكر مسمى «الخطأ»، وكانت مهمة الفكر هي الحيلولة دون الوقوع في الأخطاء. من أجل ذلك، كان الهوس الأساسي للفكر هوساً معرفياً إبستيمولوجياً، وكان على الفكر أن يستخلص القواعد التي تمكّنه كما يرى أبو الفلسفة الحديثة ديكارت: «أن يمتنع من أن يحسب صواباً ما ليس كذلك».

عندما انتبه الفكر أن هذا التحصين المنهجي لن يمكّنه من تفادي الأوهام التي تعمل خُفْية، والتي تتمتع بقدرة على التستر والمقاومة، تسلّح بالنقد لفضح هذه الأوهام، وتحديد شروط الصلاحية، أو كما قيل تحديد «مجال الاستخدام المشروع للعقل».

وابتداء من القرن التاسع عشر، لن يكتفي الفكر لا بوضع قواعد

21) . ينعت هؤلاء الميتافيزيقا بأنها فلسفة الحضور ، وهم إذ يسعون إلى تجاوزها ، يعيدون النظر في مفهوم الحاضر ، أي في مفهوم الزمان الذي كرّسته الميتافيزيقا التي فهمت الوجود «بدلالة نمط معين للزمان هو نمط الحاضر» (Heidegger, L'Être 42) ، على حد تعبير هايدجر . ذلك أن المفهوم العادي والفلسفي التقليدي ، من أرسطو حتى هيجل ، لا يدرك الزمان إلا انطلاقاً من الحضور . وكل ما ستقوم به الفلسفة في شكلها الحديث ، ابتداء من ديكارت Descartes حتى هيجل ، هو أنها ستحوّل الحضور إلى مثول أمام الذات الفاعلة sujet . إنها ستحوّل المثول إلى موضوع يوضع أمام ذات فاعلة ، موضوع سيكون خاضعاً للسيطرة التقنية لهذه الذات . فحتى الجدل الهيجلي إذن ، سيجعل التاريخ حركة لحاضر دائم . وحتى عندما يتحدث هيجل عن التجاوز ، فهو لا يحيد عن مفهوم الحضور الذي يظل يطبع جميع أنماط الزمان عنده .

تجاوز الميتافيزيقا معناه ، إذن ، نحت مفهومٍ مخالف للزمان . لا عجب ، إذن ، أن يتخذ الكتاب الأساس لهايدجر عنواناً له **الكينونة والزمان** L'Être et le temps . وحينئذ ، سيتحقق حصول التاريخ بوصفه قدراً لحقيقة الوجود الذي يبلغ قدره من حيث إنه «يعطي نفسه ويحجبها في آن» (Heidegger, Lettre 109) . على هذا النحو ، فإن الحاضر لا يحضر ، وهو في انفصال وتباعد دائمين عن نفسه . من هنا ، يرفض هؤلاء مفهوم التجاوز الهيجلي ، ويستبعدون كل تاريخ منسجم وزمان متصل يتوخّى متابعة خطوط التطور ، وتعيين الغايات وبناء الهُويّات ، ويبدي نفوراً حاداً من التفكير في الاختلاف وتقويض الصورة المطمئنة للهُويّة المتطابقة مع نفسها .

هذا التجاوز للفلسفة اتخذ عند هؤلاء أسماء متنوعة ، فمنهم مَن تحدث عن تقويض الميتافيزيقا ، ومنهم مَن تحدث عن تفكيك ثنائياتها ، ومنهم مَن اكتفى بالحديث عن الخروج منها . بل إن منهم مَن ذهب حتى إلى إعلان موتها على غرار الميتات التي ألحقت بالإيديولوجيا والسينما والأدب والمؤلف والناقد ، فبأي معنى يُتحدَّث في هذا السياق عن تجاوز الفلسفة بل «موتها»؟

موت الفلسفة

سُئل جيل دولوز مرة عن موقفه ما يُقال عن موت الفلسفة ، فردّ بأن ليس هناك موت وإنما محاولات اغتيال . تُحشَر عبارة «موت الفلسفة» عادة ضمن «موكب» من العبارات المماثلة ، التي تنذر بميتات لا حصر لها .

هي بالضبط حركة توليد الفوارق والاختلافات، إنها انتقال ملتو ملتبس من مخالف لآخر، انتقال من طرف التعارض إلى الطرف الآخر» (Derrida, "La Différance" 13). الهُويّة إذن حركة انتقال، ليس نحو آخر خارج عنها، وإنما بين «أركانها» ومقوِّماتها.

هذا التفكير البَيْنيّ يدفع هؤلاء إلى إعادة النظر في الثنائيات التي كرّستها الميتافيزيقا، لا ليُعْلوا من طرف على حساب الآخر، كأن يعيدوا المجد للجسد على حساب الروح، أو للمظهر على حساب العمق، أو للمبنى على حساب المعنى، ولا ليَروا في ذلك قضاء على التقابل، وإنما علامة على ضرورة، بحيث يظهر كل طرف من طرفي الثنائيات على أنه الآخر ذاته. هنا يدخل الزمان في تحديد الكائن، لا لضمّه وحصره، وإنما لجعله مُعلَّقاً en suspens في حركة إرجاء دائم. ذلك أن الاختلاف لا يشير إلى الفروق وحدها، وإنما إلى الإرجاء والبَوْن والبينونة. الاختلاف مباينة بجميع معاني اللفظ. لإبراز هذا المعنى المزدوج للكلمة، يضطر جاك دريدا إلى ابتداع كتابة مغايرة لكلمة différence، فيكتبها بحرف a. يقول دريدا:

> المباينة la différance إذن هي حركة توليد الفوارق. إنها ما يجعل حركة الدلالة غير ممكنة، اللهم إلا إذا كان كل عنصر حاضر متعلقاً بشيء آخر غيره، محتفظاً بأثر العنصر السابق، فاتحاً صدره لأثر علاقته بالعنصر الآتي. فإذا أقحمنا الاختلاف بهذا المعنى داخل الهُويّة، تكون هناك مسافة تفصل الحاضر عما ليس هو لكي يكون هو ذاته.
> (Derrida, "La Différance" 13)

وهكذا، «يدخل الزمان في تحديد الكائن لا لحصره وضمّه، وإنما لجعله معلَّقاً في حركة إرجاء دائم، بحيث "يدّخر" نفسه، ولكن، لا كما هو الأمر في الجدل الهيجلي حيث فُهم الادّخار داخل اقتصاد ضيق» (Derrida, "De l'économie" 405)، وإنما «يدخرها، بمعنى أنه يحفظها ويرجئها إلى حين» (Derrida, "La Différance" 21).

يُنقل التصدع إذن إلى مفهوم الزمان ذاته، ذلك أننا عندما نقحم الاختلاف «داخل» الهُويّة «تصبح هناك مسافة تفصل الحاضر عما ليس هو لكي يكون هو ذاته»، على حدّ تعبير دريدا (Derrida, "La Différance").

سجنه داخل «منطق» التعارض. فالوحدة التي يعرضها أمامنا الاختلاف بوصفه حركة لامتناهية للجمع والتفريق ليست هي وحدة الأضداد. السلب لا يواجه بين الكائن ونقيضه، وإنما ينخر الكائن ذاته. السلب هو الحركة اللامتناهية التي تبعد الذات لا عن نقيضها فحسب، بل عن نفسها أولاً وقبل كل شيء. الإبعاد والتقريب يتم هنا «داخل» الكائن إن صحّ الحديث عن داخل، لا بين الكائن ونقيضه. الاختلاف قائم في الهُوِيّة. لهذا السبب يؤكد دولوز: «يتعلق الأمر ببعد إيجابي بين المتخالفين: إنه البعد الذي ينقل أحدهما نحو الآخر من حيث هما مختلفان» (Deleuze 237). الانتقال إذن من الجدل نحو الاختلاف هو انتقال من مفهوم عن الكائن وعن الزمان وعن الهُوِيّة نحو مفاهيم «مخالفة». إنه الانتقال نحو توحيد لا يصالح بين الأضداد، وإنما يعرضها أمامنا متباينة مجتمعة في الحضور ذاته، ونحو وحدة لا تتوخّى لحظة التركيب، وهُوِيّة لا تؤول إلى التطابق. إنه تجاوز للميتافيزيقا ولـ«منطقها».

لعل أهم ما في هذا التحديد لمفهوم الاختلاف هنا، ليس لحظة الإبعاد بين الطرفين، إذ إن ذلك يبدو من بَدَهِيّات الاختلاف، المهم هنا هو كَوْن الاختلاف إذ يُبعد بين الطرفين يقرِب بينهما. هذا التقريب غالباً ما يُهمَل في تحديد الاختلاف. وحتى إن أخذ بعين الاعتبار، فإنه يُرَدُّ إلى مجرد لحظة التركيب الجدلية. وما يميز «الاختلاف» بالضبط عن الجدل، هو كَوْن هذا التقريب ليس هو التركيب الجدلي، ليس هو المصالحة بين الأضداد.

لن يعود الاختلاف مجرد تعارض بين نقيضين، بل إنه يغدو ابتعاداً يقارب بين الأطراف المختلفة (لا نقول يركّب أو يوحّد بينها). وإن أردنا الكلام عن وحدة هنا، فإنها الوحدة بوصفها حركة لامتناهية للضمّ والتفريق. في هذا المعنى يقول هايدجر شارحاً ما يعنيه هيراقليط باللوغوس: «هذا التوحيد الذي ينطوي عليه فعل ليجيين Leguein لا يعني أننا نقتصر على جمع الأضداد والمصالحة بينها. الكلَ الموحّد يعرض أمامنا أشياء يتنوع وجودها وقد اجتمعت في الحضور ذاته» (Heidegger, "Logos" 276-77). هي إذن وحدة لا تُصالح بين الأضداد ولا تركّب فيما بينها، وهو اختلاف لا يرتد إلى تناقض، وهي هُوِيّة لا تؤول إلى تطابق، هُوِيّة هي عبارة عن حركة انتقال، هُوِيّة يشرخها الزمان، هُوِيّة ما تنفك تعود. هُوِيّة عبارة عن تكرار.

وإن كان مفكرو الاختلاف يحتفظون لمفهوم الهُوِيّة بمكان، فلأنه يغدو عندهم هُوِيّة الاختلاف. في هذا المعنى يقول جاك دريدا: «الهُوِيّة

قد يقال إن إثبات الاختلافات والتناقضات وعمل السلب لم يكن لينتظر مجيء هؤلاء ، فهذه المفهومات مفهومات مُغْرِقة في القدم ، وإن كان الفكر الجدلي قد طوّرها وجعلها وراء حياة الفكر ، وهذا منذ القرن التاسع عشر . وقبل أن نعرض لما يأخذه هؤلاء على هذا الفكر الجدلي ، لنتوقف عند ما يَعنونه بـ«الاختلاف» . فما المقصود بالاختلاف في هذا السياق؟ يجيبنا الفيلسوف الفرنسي جان بوفريه Beaufret قائلاً :

لنتأمل كلمة différence ، هذا نقل فرنسي يكاد يكون حرفياً للكلمة الإغريقية ديافورا . فُورا آتيةٌ من الفعل فيري feri الذي يعني في الإغريقية ، ثم في اللاتينية : حَمَل ونَقل . . . . الاختلاف ينقل إذن ، فماذا ينقل؟ إنه ينقل ما يسبقِ في الكلمة ديافورا فورا ، أي السابقة ديا التي تعني ابتعاداً وفجوة . . . . الاختلاف ينقل طبيعتين لا تتميزان في البداية ، مبعداً إحداهما عن الأخرى . إلا أن هذا الابتعاد ليس انفصاماً . إنه ، على العكس من ذلك ، يقرّب بين الطرفين اللذين يُبْعِد بينهما . (Dialogue 188)

ولكن أليس هذا التقريب هو بالضبط ما يسميه الفكر الجدلي مصالحة الأضداد وتركيباً؟ يجيبنا هايدجر :

إننا لا نقتصر على جمع الأضداد وضمّها والمصالحة بينها . الكل الموحَّد يعرض أمامنا أشياء يتنوع وجودها ويتباين وقد اجتمعت في الحضور ذاته ، مثل الليل والنهار ، الشتاء والصيف ، السِّلم والحرب ، اليقظة والنوم ، ديونيزوس وهاديس ، إن هذا الذي ينقل (الشيء نحو ضده) ، عبر المسافة البعيدة التي تفصل الحاضر عن الماضي ، إن هذا الديافيرومنون Diaferomenon ، هو ما يعرضه اللوجوس في حركة انتقاله . وفعل اللوجوس ينحصر في عملية النقل هذه . (Heidegger, "Logos" 267-68)

ما يعيب الجدلَ بالضبط هو خضوعُه لقانون السلب . يريد الاختلاف تحرير السلب من هيمنة الكل ، وعدم توقيف عمله بفعل أيِّ تركيب ، أو

الفلسفية بامتياز ، وأغلبهم مَارَسَ الفلسفة داخل أسوار الجامعة . ويكفي أن نذكر أسماء هايدجر ودريدا ودولوز كي نقتنع بذلك . غير أن اهتمامهم هذا يتوخَّى بالضبط الانفصال عن الفلسفة ، أو الميتافيزيقا كما يحلو لهم أن يقولوا . يتسلَّحون من أجل هذه الغاية بما يسمِّيه بعضهم تقويضا ، أو ما يدعوه الآخر تفكيكاً ، أو «خروجاً» . الكلمة التي يؤثرها أغلبهم هي كلمة «تجاوز» dépassement ، تجاوز الميتافيزيقا ، تاريخاً ومنطقاً ، قاصدين بالميتافيزيقا ، على غرار هايدجر ، لا فرعاً من فروع الفلسفة ، ولا فناً من فنون الدراسة ، وإنما تاريخ الكائن ، أو بنية الوجود .

نستطيع أن نقول إن حوار هؤلاء يتوجه أساساً صوب هيجل Hegel ، أو لنقل صوب الفكر الجدلي بصفة عامة بما فيه «التيار» الماركسي . إلا أن ذلك الحوار سرعان ما يمتد ، عبر هيجل ، إلى تاريخ الفلسفة بمجمله ، وسيقول بعضهم تاريخ الكينونة ، ليكشف عن بنيته الأنطو-ثيو-لوجية كما يقول أتباع هايدجر ، أو بنيته الأفلاطونية ، كما يقول أتباع نيتشه Nietzsche ، إن صح الحديث هنا عن أتباع .

يعيب هؤلاء على الفكر الجدلي وامتداداته كَونه ظل يوظف مفهوماً فقيراً عن الاختلاف ، وكَونه ، من ثمَّ ، بقي عاجزاً عن أن ينحت مفهوماً عن الهُويَّة l'identité يبعدها عن التطابق . ذلك أنهم يميزون الذاتي le même عن المتطابق l'identique . كما يعتبرون أن الذات مشروخة مجروحة منخورة ، وهي في تباعد ملازم عن نفسها ، لذا فهم لا يحتاجون إلى تعارض «خارجي» كي يقيموا الاختلاف ، ما داموا ينظرون إلى الآخر على أنه بُعْدُ الذات عن نفسها . فليس السلب عندهم هو ذاك الذي يَفد من خارج الذات ليتعارض معها ، وإنما ما ينخرها من «داخل» . السلب هو حركة تباعد الذات عن نفسها . وفي هذا الإطار ، يعتبر ميشيل فوكو علامة التساوي التي يضعها منطق الميتافيزيقا ليعبِّر عن تطابق الهُويَّة مع نفسها ، إشارةً إلى القنطرة التي تصدّع الذات وتجعلها في هروب عن نفسها . فبينما يثبت التناقض العلاقة أ = لاأ التي تمثل طرفين يتحركان نحو التطابق ويسعيان إليه ، فإن الذاتية أ = أ تجعل كل طرف يفقد بفضل الآخر كيانه الذاتي . على هذا النحو ، يعيب هؤلاء على التناقض الجدلي كَونه لا يذهب بالاختلاف إلى أبعد مدى ، إذ سرعان ما يردّه نحو التطابق . فليس التناقض عند الجدليين اختلافاً أكبر في نظرهم إلا نسبةً إلى التطابق وبدلالته .

يحل محله ويوسّع حمولته من غير أن يفقد تلك القدرة على الخلخلة وفكّ البناءات : ذاك هو مفهوم الاختلاف . ولا ينبغي أن ننسى أن «مفهوم» الاختلاف هذا كان قد استعاد حياته مواكبة لمفهوم البنية ذاته ، وذلك منذ البداية وعند «مؤسِّس» البنيوية في مجال اللسانيات فرديناند دو سوسور de Saussure . وكلنا يذكر تلك العبارة التي كنا نجدها عند أصحاب اللسانيات أو السيميولوجيا أو الأنثروبولوجيا أو الإبستيمولوجيا على السواء ، والتي تؤكد أن «البنيوية تبدأ عندما نؤكد أن مجموعات متباينة يمكن أن تتقارب فيما بينها ، لا برغم اختلافاتها ، بل بفضل تلك الاختلافات» .

لعل هذا هو ما جعلنا نجد أنفسنا ، بعد «ضجة» البنية ، أمام المفكرين أنفسهم ولكن تحت اسم آخر هذه المرة هو «مفكرو الاختلاف» . حاول هؤلاء ، كلٌ في مجاله - سواء مع بارت في ميدان السيميولوجيا الأدبية ، أو مع ليڤي-ستروس في مجال الأنثروبولوجيا ، أو مع ألتوسير وجماعته في ميدان الأبحاث الماركسية ، أو مع ميشيل فوكو في مجال تاريخ المعرفة ، أو مع دريدا Derrida ودولوز في ميدان تاريخ الفلسفة - أن يفتحوا الفكر على مزيد من «قوة الخلخلة» .

فكر الاختلاف

لا نقول «فلسفة الاختلاف» ، فالأمر لا يتعلق لا بالفلسفة بالمعنى المعهود للكلمة ، ولا حتى بمذهب أو تيار فلسفي . نحن أمام فكر ربما يتعذر ضمّه تحت اسم بعينه ، فكر غير متجانس . كان دريدا قد تحدث عن جيله من الفلاسفة فأشار إلى أن الاختلافات فيما بينهم كانت على أشدها ، وأن لا انسجام كان يربط بعضهم ببعض . وإن كان ولا بد من ضمّ أصحاب «فكر الاختلاف» pensée de la différence تحت اسم واحد ، فهم يؤثرون ، كما سبق أن أشرنا ، لفظ شبكة ، هم يشعرون أنهم ينخرطون في شبكات مقاومة ، وأغلبهم يستعملون اللفظ عندما يتحدثون عن «حركتهم» . كل هذا ليبرزوا أن هدفهم الأساس هو أن ينفصلوا عن الفلسفة ، عن تاريخ الفلسفة ويتجاوزونه ، أو كما يقول بعضهم «يخرجون منه» . لا يعني ذلك أنهم يناصبون العداء لكل تأريخ فلسفي على غرار بعض الوضعيين . ربما كان عكس ذلك هو الصحيح . إذ يمكن أن نؤكد أنهم من أكثر المفكرين اهتماماً بتاريخ الفلسفة ، فهم فقهاء النصوص

قلنا ، بل امتدت لتطول ميادين الدراسات الإبستيمولوجية والأنثروبولوجية والتاريخية ، هو إعادة النظر في مجالات بحث متنوعة وخلخلة ركائزها الفلسفية ودعاماتها الإبستيمولوجية . معنى ذلك أن البنيوية في نظره لم تكنْ مجرد منهج جديد يعيد النظر في مناهج تلك الدراسات ، وإنما كانت تحوّلًا إستراتيجيًا في تناول الموضوع الإنساني ، حتى لا نقول إنها كانت «موقفًا» فلسفيًا مغايرًا . وقد تجلت تلك المغايرة فيما تميَّز به ذلك الموقف من قوة خلخلة اتخذت أسماء متنوعة كالحفر والتقويض والتفكيك ، عملت أساسًا على إعادة النظر في المفهوم الذي كرّسته أكثر الفلسفات ثوريةً عن «النقد» .

ما أثار اهتمام بارت ، إذن ، هو الجرأة النقدية التي تمخضت عن ظهور هذه الحركة ، التي لم تعمل فحسب على زرع نفَس جديد في ما كان يسمى تاريخًا للأدب ، أو ما كان يسمى «نقدًا» أدبيًا ، وإنما أعادت النظر في مفهوم الكتابة ذاته ، وما يصحبه من مفهومات كالنص والمؤلف والقارئ والعتبات ، ومكّنت أكثر الفلسفات إيمانًا بالسلب والجدل والتناقض من أن تعيد النظر في «ثوابتها» . ولعل أهم تلك الثوابت هو مفهوم الجدل نفسه ، وما يحيط به من مفهومات كالسلب والتناقض والاختلاف . ويكفي أن نتذكر هنا أسماء لوي ألتوسير Althusser ولوسيان جولدمان Goldmann وموريس جودوليه Godelier ونيكوس پولانتزاس Poulantzas ولوسيان سوباج Sebag ، كي نستعيد الجدالات الثرية التي لم تقتصر خلال الستينيات من القرن الماضي على مفهومات النص والمؤلف والقارئ والبنية السطحية والعميقة ، والمعنى الأوّلي والثانوي ، وإنما امتدت إلى مفهومات المنظومة والتناقض والنشأة والتكوّن . لقد عمل كل هؤلاء المفكرين ، عبر زوايا مختلفة ، على «نزع» السيادة عن التصور الدياكروني diarchronique تخفيفًا لما أحيط بمفهوم الزمان التاريخي من تقديس ، كما حاولوا فضح الأشكال المقنّعة التي كانت تتخذها فلسفات الكوجيتو Cogito لتحتمي بالكتابة الأدبية والاستمرار الزمني . ويكفي أن نتذكر في هذا الصدد الجدال الذي دار بين ليڤي-ستروس Lévi-Strauss وسارتر Sartre حول مسألة التاريخ ، وذاك الذي جرى بين فوكو وجماعة الإبستيمولوجيين[3] حول مسألة القطائع التاريخية ruptures ، أو ذاك الذي طبع الستينيات من القرن الماضي بصفة أعمّ حول الأسئلة التي أثيرت بصدد الثنائي : التكوين/البنية genèse/structure .[4]

على ضوء ذلك ، سرعان ما تبيَّن البنيويون قصورَ مفهوم البنية ذاته بل «فقره» الأنطولوجي . ولعل ذلك هو ما دعاهم إلى اللجوء إلى مفهوم

كيف نرسم صورة عن الفكر والحالة هذه؟ لعل الحلّ المناسب هو أن نُقيم في هذا الشتات فنحاول كشف الفروق وتعيين الاختلافات. وربما كان الوقوف عند ما يدعى اليوم «فكر الاختلاف» أنجع وسيلة للتمكن من تلك الإقامة بهدف رسم الفروق التي تميز الدلالات التي يعطيها الفكر اليوم للمفهومات الأساسية التي اشتغل بها حتى الآن، كمفهوم الهُويّة ومفهوم الذاتية ومفهوم التراث ومفهوم الجدل ومفهوم السلب ومفهوم الإيديولوجية. فربما كانت أنجع طريقة لولوج الفكر الفلسفي المعاصر هي الوقوف عند مختلف التحولات التي عرفتها هذه المفهومات. قد يرد البعض بأننا لسنا في حاجة إلى أن نغرق في هذا الشتات بين المفهومات، فيكفي أن نقتصر على مفهوم أساس ربما يكون هو مفتاح الولوج إلى الحداثة الفلسفية. في هذا الإطار، يرى البعض أن الفكر المعاصر يقدم لنا نفسه اليوم «موحّداً» تحت ما أطلق عليه «نزعة بنيوية»، وأن مفهوم البنية تمكّن من أن يضم حوله لسانيين وأنثروبولوجيين وعلماء اجتماع، بل فلاسفة بمَن فيهم بعض الماركسيين. وقبل أن نبيّن أن مفهوم البنية هذا، سرعان ما أخلى المكان لـ«مفهوم» الاختلاف، فلنحاول أن نقف عنده عسى أن نتبين تحولاته وربما حدوده كذلك.

من البنيوية إلى «فكر الاختلاف»

كان رولان بارت Barthes قد نبّه عند نهاية الستينيات من القرن الماضي، والبنيوية لا تزال في أبهى عهود ازدهارها، إلى أن هذه الحركة لا تقتصر على التأكيد بأن العالم والثقافات والنصوص بنيات، وأن قضية البنيوية، رغم ما قد يتبادر إلى الذهن أول مرة، ليست هي البنية وما تثيره من إشكالات، إذ «لا يكفينا الحديث عن بنيات النصوص لكي نكون بنيويين... وإلا فستكون البنيوية عريقة في القدم: فكوْن العالم بنية، وكوْن الأشياء والحضارات بنيات، هذا أمر عرفناه منذ زمن بعيد، أما الجديد فهو التمكن من الخلخلة (99).

قد يبدو غريباً للوهلة الأولى أن يصرف أحدُ أعمدة «الحركة» البنيوية ذهنَنا عن مفهوم البنية في تحديده للبنيوية، وألا ينظر إلى البنيوية في مكوّناتها مفضلاً الاهتمام بمفعولها. إلا أن هدفه، على ما يبدو، هو أن يثير انتباهنا إلى أن ما ميّز تلك الحركة، التي لم تقتصر على مجال الأدب والفلسفة كما

وقْع على المعارف وبنائها ، وعلى العلائق الاجتماعية ، بل البشرية بصفة عامة ، وهذا حتى قبل ظهور الإنترنت .

قام مفهوم الشبكة ليحل محل مفهوم التشجير والربط العمودي . الشجرة جهاز يُغرس في الفكر كي ينبت في استقامة ، ويُثمر أفكاراً تُنعت بالصائبة . تنبت الشجرة انطلاقاً من بذرة . إنها تتجذر في أصل ، وتعلو صَوبِ اتجاه عمودي واحد . وسرعان ما تغدو آلة للتفرّعات الثنائية . الشجرة تجذر وتفرّعات . لا عجب أن يتحدث القدماء عن «الشجرة المنطقية» و«شجرة المعرفة» و«شجرة الأنساب» . فمقابل «الشجرة المنطقية» ، ستسعى الشبكات إلى أن تنسج علائق أفقية تربط بين المتصل والمنفصل ، بهدف إدراك معقولية الأشياء وطبيعة الكائن . إلا أنها لن تحيد ، رغم ذلك ، عن الهوس التقليدي للبحث عن الانتظامات والغائيات .[2]

ما يميّز الشبكة عن التيار والمذهب والمدرسة ، إذن ، هو ما يفصل الخطوط المتقاطعة عن الدوائر المنغلقة . الشبكة هي تلك «الروح» التي تسود فضاء فكرياً يغتني بإسهامات عدد من المفكرين الذين يعملون جميعُهم ، كما عبّر عن ذلك هايدجر ، على «قول الشيء نفسه» le même الذي ليس تطابقاً l'identique . «الشيء نفسه» لا يعني بطبيعة الحال إجماعاً يوحّد مفكرين ، وإنما «مداراً» يستقطبهم ، و«رهاناً فكرياً» يشغلهم . لا يعني ذلك أنّ هؤلاء المفكرين متطابقون في أقوالهم ، بل إنّ اختلافهم يكون خدمةً لـ«الشيء نفسه» . فنحن هنا أمام «تركيبات جغرافية» ، وليس إزاء «نشأة تاريخية» .

لن يعود ميدان الفكر ، كما شاء له الهيجليون ومَن دار في فلكهم ، نفياً وإيجاباً ، قائماً على أساس مشترك . ولن يُنتظر من المفكرين أن يطرحوا الأسئلة ذاتها ، ويوظفوا التصورات عينها . لن يكون هناك ما من شأنه أن يجمع المفكرين ويضمّهم داخل عائلة واحدة وتاريخ وتاريخ موحّد ، لا المذهب ولا التيار ولا «النظرة إلى العالم» . كل ما سيتبقّى هو حركات متفردة وخطوط متقاطعة . حينئذ ، سيغدو عمل الفكر أساساً ليس بناء المذاهب ولا رصد التيارات ولا تكوين «النظرات إلى العالم» ، وإنما فك الوحدات الموهومة بحثاً عمّا هو متفرد . إبراز التفردات singularités هو وقوف عند الحدث داخل الفكر ، بل لعله السبيل إلى إبراز الفكر بوصفه حدثاً . لن نكون حينئذ ، وكما أثبت فوكو Foucault ، لا أمام وحدات ، ولا إزاء كليات ، وإنما أمام صيرورات مبعثرة لامتناهية تظل تعمل خُفْية فيما وراء ما قد نتوهم أنه «انتماءات» فكرية .

والوحدة . نحن اليوم أمام سعي وراء توليد الفوارق وتفكيك الهُويّات والانحياز إلى الهوامش ، باللجوء إلى مفهومات الاختلاف والتعارض البنيوي والتعدد والمنظورية perspectivisme ، والوقوف عند الحدود والنهايات .

لا عجب أن يطبع ما سُمّي عصر «أفول الإيديولوجية» نفورٌ من الضمّ والتوحيد ما نفتأ نلمسه عند كبار المفكرين المعاصرين الذين لم يعودوا يرضون أن يُدمَجوا في «عائلات فكرية» ، ولا أن يُقحَموا ضمن مذاهب ومدارس ، ويُحشَروا ضمن تيارات وعقائد ، وهم يقبلون بالكاد أن «ينخرطوا» في شبكات فكر . قبل أن نحاول نسج خيوط هذه الشبكات ، لنتساءل أولاً ما الذي يميز الشبكة عن التيار والمذهب؟

في مفهوم الشبكة

سُئل جيل دولوز في الأبجدية L'Abécédaire[1] عما إذا كان فكره يشكل مدرسة ، أو على الأقل ، ما إذا كان يلتئم هو مع آخرين في مدرسة واحدة؟ فأجاب أنه ، بالكاد ، يمكن أن يُعَدَّ منخرطاً في شبكة réseau . الشبكة لا تتحدد بلونها ومضمونها وطبيعتها ، بقدر ما تتعين بعلاقتها . إنها تتحدد إستراتيجيا وإجرائيا ، فهي مثل دروب هايدجر Heidegger التي ترتسم في الغابات بفعل السير ومن جرّائه ، وليست هي ما يهديه ويخطط له ، ويخط مساراته .

الأصل اللاتيني للكلمة الفرنسية réseau هو retis الذي يدل على الخيط . تحيل الشبكة إذن ، حتى في غير اللغة العربية ، إلى الخيوط والنسيج . الشبكة تشابُك خيوط . وقد ارتبطت الشبكة دائما بالحِرَف والتقنية ، إلا أنها اقتصرت حتى نهاية القرن الثامن عشر على حرفة النسيج . وظّفت الكلمةُ منذ أفلاطون شتى أنواع التوظيف ، وهكذا نُظر إلى الجسم وإلى الدماغ ، بل إلى الجسم الاجتماعي ، على أنه شبكة أو سلسلة من الشبكات . غير أن القرن الذي سيعرف ازدهاراً كبيراً للمفهوم ، كما أثبت داجونييه Dagognet (انظر Automates) ، هو القرن الثامن عشر الأوروبي ، حيث غدت الشبكة مفتاحاً لتفسير كل ما هو طبيعي . ومع الثورة الصناعية ستقام شبكات صناعية مقابل الشبكات الطبيعية ، وهنا سيغدو المهندس هو مخطط الشبكات وواضعها . ستظهر ، بشكل متواقت ، شبكة السكك الحديدية وشبكة التلغراف ، ثم بعد ذلك الشبكات الكهربائية إلى أن نصل إلى شبكة الإنترنت . لا ينبغي أن ننسى ما كان لذلك من

المسارات الحديثة في الدراسات الفلسفية

عبد السلام بنعبد العالي

إن فكرة العود الأبدي عند نيتشه هي أقوى إثباتات الفكر المعاصر. لماذا؟ لأنها تضع محل الوحدة اللامتناهية التعدد اللامتناهي، ومحل الزمان الخطي، زمان الخلاص والتقدم، زمانَ المكان الدائري . . . ولأنها تضع موضع سؤال تطابق الكائن وخاصيةَ وحدة ما هو الآن وهنا. وتبعاً لذلك، لأنها تضع موضعِ سؤال وحدةِ الأنا l'égo، وبالتالي وحدة النفس. فضلاً عن كل هذا، فإن هذه الفكرة تضعنا في عالم تكف فيه الصورة عن أن تكون ثانوية بالنسبة للنموذج، عالم يكون فيه للخدعة نصيب من الحقيقة، عالم لا أصل له، وإنما ومضات لا تنتهي يحتجب فيها في إشراقة اللف والعودة غيابُ الأصل.

-- بلانشو Blanchot

لن يتعلق الأمر برسم التيارات الكبرى التي تتوزع حسبها اليوم الدراسات الفلسفية، لا لأن عملاً مثل هذا لا يمكن أن ينجز في مقالة مختصرة فحسب، وإنما لأن الفلسفة اليوم لا تميل إلى تصنيف نفسها ضمن تيارات محصورة محدودة العدد، ولا تتوزع وفق مذاهب متمايزة، بقدر ما تنحل إلى شبكات فكرية تضمّ مفكرين يقولون الشيء ذاته le même بأنحاء مختلفة.

مقابل «فكر» يترعرع في أحضان عائلات (مقدسة أكانت أم لا) يرتاح لها، نجد أنفسنا اليوم إزاء فكر يتيم. أو لنقل، بتعبير دولوز Deleuze، مقابل «فكر» معمّر يستقر في موقع بعينه، نحن أمام فكر رحّال لا موقع له. فمقابل الجيولوجيين المولعين بالحفر في الجذور، نلفى الجغرافيين الماسحين للأراضي. مقابل همّ بناء الوحدات وخلق التطابق ورسم التيارات والنظرات إلى العالم، وذلك بتوظيف مفاهيم الانسجام والكلية والاستمرارية

اتجاهات جديدة في العلوم الإنسانية :
خريطة معرفية

يُكرَّس هذا العدد من ألف لرصد الجهود المبذولة من أجل إعادة تعريف الإنسانيات، وتبديل مسارها، في ضوء حقائق الواقع الكونية من الناحيتين المؤسسية والفكرية. ويمكن تفسير تعبير «الخريطة المعرفية» الوارد في العنوان بطرق مختلفة. فالفهم الحرفي المباشر، بمعنى تبديل التوجه الجغرافي، يشير إلى الجهود التي تبذل من أجل إعادة تعريف العلاقة بين عالمي الشمال والجنوب، أو بين التراثين الفكريين الغربي واللاغربي. كما يمكن أن يشير إلى إعادة رسم خريطة العلوم الأكاديمية الحديثة ممثلةً في الدراسات البينية والتعددية في مجال الإنسانيات، وأيضاً عن طريق اجتذاب الإنسانيات إلى آفاق جديدة في حقلي العلوم البحتة والعلوم الاجتماعية. إن رسم خريطة ما يعني البحث عن مؤشرات إلى التحولاتِ في أجناس أدبية مثل الرواية والشعر والترجمة الذاتية أو الغيرية، فكثيراً ما نقع على إرهاصات الجديد في المسارات الأدبية والفنية قبل تبلورها في الحقل الأكاديمي. وفي هذا العدد تسهم الحقول المعرفية المختلفة والأجناس الأدبية المتعددة في صياغة الاتجاهات الجديدة في الدراسات الكلاسيكية، والنظرية الأدبية، واللغويات، ودراسات الترجمة، إلخ.. عبر رصدها في بحوث ودراسات. ولا بدّ من التنويه إلى أن العلوم الإنسانية ليست بجزيرة منفصلة؛ فهي تتأثر بما حولها من حقول معرفية مثل الرياضيات، والطب، والتقنية الرقمية، ودراسات الإعاقة، وأسئلة الجنوسة، كما توضح مقالات هذا العدد.

ألف مجلة بينية محكَّمة تصدر سنوياً في الربيع وتتضمن مقالات نقدية بالعربية والإنجليزية والفرنسية. ترحب ألف بالمقالات غير المنشورة من قبل في مجالات الإنسانيات المتعددة، ومنها – على سبيل المثال لا الحصر – الأدب والدراسات الثقافية.

وستدور محاور الأعداد القادمة حول :
ألف ٤١ : الأدب والتاريخ ومناهج التأريخ
ألف ٤٢ : الأدب في مواجهة الفناء
ألف ٤٣ : علاقات الأخوية/الأختية في الأدب والفن

بناءً على تكريس صعود النيو-ليبرالية السياسي لنوعية من العقلية التجارية المهيمنة على السياسة العامة والمجال العام نفسه، فقدت الجامعات الكثير من استقلاليتها و«الحرية الأكاديمية» التي كانت ملازمة لها. فما كان يوماً مكاناً يمكن الزملاء من تبادل معارفهم مع بعضهم البعض ونقل ما عرفوه إلى جيل الشباب بروح الترابط، صار مكاناً لممارسة الأعمال التجارية. ونتيجة لذلك، أصبحت الإنسانيات، أو العلوم الإنسانية، من الأنواع المهددة بالانقراض... المطلوب هنا هو عملية تهجين متعددة الأبعاد، مشروع ضخم للتعلم الاجتماعي-الثقافي. نحن في العلوم الاجتماعية والإنسانية نحتاج إلى توحيدِ قوانا مع العلماء والمهندسين لتطوير برامج تعليمية وبحثية تمكّن مواطنينا من الاستفادة بشكل أكبر من إنجازاتنا الفنية واكتشافاتنا العلمية، عوضاً عن مجرد منحهم المزيد من الأدوات ليلعبوا بها على حساب قدرة المعمورة على الحفاظ على الحياة، كما أصبحنا نرى الآن.

أندرو جاميسون، «من أجل تعزيز الخيال الهجين»، مجلة *N.T.M*. عدد ١٦ (٢٠٠٨): ص ص ١١٩ و١٢٢.

القسم الإنجليزي

الافتتاحية ٨

ديفيد كونستان : معالم التنوع في الكلاسيكيات ٩

كلير جاليان : المنعطف المقوِّض للاستعمار في الإنسانيات ٢٨

أنطونيو باتشيفيكو : المنحى الثقافي في دراسة الأدب العربي ٥٩

يوسف اليعقوبي : إعادة توجيه نظرية ما بعد الكولونيالية : الفكر العربي-الإسلامي والمنهج التفكيكي وإمكان التعددية النقدية .. ٨٥

ليڤاي تومسون : إعادة توجيه الحداثة : مسارات التبادل بين الشعر العربي والفارسي ١١٥

براين جيمس باير : من الترجمة الثقافية إلى استحالة الترجمة : تنظير الترجمة خارج مجال دراسات الترجمة ١٣٩

نادية حشيش : نحو شمولية الإنسانيات الطبية ١٦٤

ياسمين سويد : نحو آفاق جديدة في أدب الإعاقة : السايبورج وإعادة تعريف الإعاقة في أدب الشباب ١٨٦

الملخصـات الإنجليزية للمقالات ... ٢١٢

تعريف بكتّاب العدد بالإنجليزية ٢١٩

المحتويات

القسم العربي

الافتتاحية .... ٨.

عبد السلام بنعبد العالي : المسارات الحديثة في الدراسات الفلسفية ... ٩.

شيرين أبو النجا : النسوية العربية : مواقف وممارسات .... ٣٢.

هالة كمال : من «السيرة الذاتية» إلى «كتابة الحياة» : مسارات وتقاطعات عبر العلوم الإنسانية والاجتماعية .... ٦٥.

سامية الحديثي : الدراسات ما بعد الكولونيالية والأدب العربي : بحثٌ عن الجذور أم تغيير للمسار؟ .... ١٠٤.

تامر أمين : اللغويات التربوية ومشكلة اللغة في تعليم العلوم والرياضيات في العالم العربي .... ١٤٢.

حسن حلمي : إطلالة على الشعر الأمريكي «المعاصر» : تأملات .. ١٦٨.

حسام نايل : الأدب العربي والتكنولوجيا الرقمية : محاولة استكشافية .... ٢١٥.

نجلاء سعد حسن : نظرية الألعاب والتحليل الأدبي : الآفاق والتحديات .... ٢٤٧.

الملخصات العربية للمقالات .... ٢٦٦.

تعريف بكتّاب العدد بالعربية .... ٢٧٣.

ألف ٢٦ : شهوة الترحال : أدب الرحلة في مصر والشرق الأوسط
ألف ٢٧ : الطفولة : بين الإبداع والتلقي
ألف ٢٨ : الاقتباس الفني : مقارباتٍ تطبيقية ومفاهيم نظرية
ألف ٢٩ : الجامعة وهمومها : محلياً وعالمياً
ألف ٣٠ : الفجيعة والذاكرة
ألف ٣١ : أمريكا الأخرى
ألف ٣٢ : التخييلي والوثائقي : دراسات ثقافية في الأدب والتاريخ والفنون
ألف ٣٣ : الصحراء : الجغرافيا الإنسانية والاقتصاد الرمزي
ألف ٣٤ : أدب العالم : رؤى ومناظرات
ألف ٣٥ : نماذج معرفية جديدة لدراسة آداب الشرق الأوسط
ألف ٣٦ : الصداقة : تمثلات وتنويعات ثقافية
ألف ٣٧ : الأدب والصحافة
ألف ٣٨ : الترجمة وإنتاج المعرفة
ألف ٣٩ : الدراما العابرة للقوميات : المسرح والأداء

سعر العدد :

في جمهورية مصر العربية : ٦٠ جنيهاً مصرياً
في البلاد الأخرى : الأفراد : ٦٠ دولاراً أمريكياً
المؤسسات : ١٢٠ دولاراً أمريكياً

النسخة الإلكترونية : الأعداد ١-٣٩ متوفرة على http://www.jstor.org

المراسلة والاشتراك على العنوان الآتي :

مجلة ألف
قسم الأدب الإنجليزي والمقارن
الجامعة الأمريكية بالقاهرة
ص . ب . ٢٥١١
القاهرة ١١٥١١
جمهورية مصر العربية

هاتف : ٢٧٩٧٥١٠٧-٠٢-٢
البريد الإلكتروني : alifecl@aucegypt.edu
الموقع الإلكتروني : https://huss.aucegypt.edu/alif

صورة الغلاف : أياد في صندوق لهدى لطفي ، وسائط مختلطة على خشب ، ٤٠ x ٤٠ سم ، ٢٠١٨ . إهداء من الفنانة .

© حقوق النشر محفوظة لقسم الأدب الإنجليزي والمقارن بالجامعة الأمريكية بالقاهرة ، ٢٠٢٠ . توزيع قسم النشر بالجامعة الأمريكية بالقاهرة .
رقم الإيداع بدار الكتب : ٢٠/٦١٨٨
الرقم الدولي الموحد للدوريات : ٨٦٧٣-١١١٠
الرقم الدولي الموحد للكتب : ٩٧٨١٦١٧٩٧٩٦٦٨

أعداد ألف السابقة ناقشت المحاور الآتية (متوفرة بالسعر المذكور) :
ألف ١ : الفلسفة والأسلوبية
ألف ٢ : النقد والطليعة الأدبية
ألف ٣ : الذات والآخر : مواجهة
ألف ٤ : التناص : تفاعلية النصوص
ألف ٥ : البعد الصوفي في الأدب
ألف ٦ : جماليات المكان
ألف ٧ : العالم الثالث : الأدب والوعي
ألف ٨ : الهرمنيوطيقا والتأويل
ألف ٩ : إشكاليات الزمان
ألف ١٠ : الماركسية والخطاب النقدي
ألف ١١ : التجريب الشعري في مصر منذ السبعينيات
ألف ١٢ : المجاز والتمثيل في العصور الوسطى
ألف ١٣ : حقوق الإنسان والشعوب في الأدب والعلوم الإنسانية
ألف ١٤ : الجنون والحضارة
ألف ١٥ : السينمائية العربية : نحو الجديد والبديل
ألف ١٦ : ابن رشد والتراث العقلاني في الشرق والغرب
ألف ١٧ : الأدب والأنثروبولوجيا في أفريقيا
ألف ١٨ : خطاب ما بعد الكولونيالية في جنوب آسيا
ألف ١٩ : الجنوسة والمعرفة : صياغة المعارف بين التأنيث والتذكير
ألف ٢٠ : النص الإبداعي ذو الهوية المزدوجة
ألف ٢١ : الظاهرة الشعرية
ألف ٢٢ : لغة الذات : السير الذاتية والشهادات
ألف ٢٣ : الأدب والمقدس
ألف ٢٤ : حفريات الأدب : اقتفاء أثر القديم في الجديد
ألف ٢٥ : إدوارد سعيد والتقويض النقدي للاستعمار

رئاسة التحرير : فريال جبوري غزول، وليد الحمامصي
نائب رئاسة التحرير : محمد بريري
مدير التحرير : رامي أمين
معاونو التحرير : منة طاهر ، حسام نايل ، بشرى هاشم

هيئة التحرير (بالترتيب الأبجدي للاسم الأخير) :

أميمة أبو بكر (جامعة القاهرة)
سعد البازعي (جامعة الملك سعود)
محمد برادة (جامعة محمد الخامس)
ريشار جاكمون (جامعة إكس-مارسيليا)
صبري حافظ (كلية الدراسات الشرقية والأفريقية ، جامعة لندن)
أسعد خير الله (الجامعة الأمريكية في بيروت)
سيزا قاسم دراز (الجامعة الأمريكية بالقاهرة وجامعة القاهرة)
أيرا دووركن (جامعة تكساس)
أندرو روبين (جامعة تكساس)
دوريس شكري (الجامعة الأمريكية بالقاهرة)
رندة صبري (جامعة القاهرة)
جابر عصفور (جامعة القاهرة)
زياد المرصفي (كينجز كوليدج لندن)
هدى وصفي (جامعة عين شمس)

أسهم في إخراج هذا العدد :

رندة أبو بكر ، روجر آلن ، دعاء إمبابي ، تشارلز بتروورث ، أماني بدوي ، محمد أمين براهيمي ، نبيل بولُص ، مايكل بيرد ، منى بيكر ، جيهان البيومي ، مي التلمساني ، هالة حليم ، أحمد خان ، سليمان بشير ديان ، قمران راستجار ، كريستوفر راندل ، كاثلين ساڤيل ، بشير السباعي ، سوزان ستيڤنز ، مها السعيد ، جون سوانسون ، دانييل سيلدن ، سيد ضيف الله ، زينب طه ، نعيمة عبد الجواد ، حسن عبد الرحمن ، تحية عبد الناصر ، ڤنسنت كراپانزانو ، موللي كورتني ، إليوت كولا ، كريستينا لي ، مارجريت ليتفين ، ميجان ماكدونالد ، ليلى المالح ، خزيمة المتنبر ، غسان مراد ، خالد المطاوع ، أنور مغيث ، جريتشين مكالو ، حسناء رضا مكداشي ، ستيڤن نيميس ، علي هادي ، سعيد الوكيل ، مايكل وود .

مجلة البلاغة المقارنة
العدد الأربعون، ٢٠٢٠

اتجاهات جديدة في العلوم الإنسانية:
خريطة معرفية